CONCORDANT
DISCORD

CONCORDANT DISCORD

THE INTERDEPENDENCE
OF FAITHS
BEING THE GIFFORD LECTURES
ON NATURAL RELIGION
DELIVERED AT ST. ANDREWS
IN 1967–1969

BY

R. C. ZAEHNER

OXFORD
AT THE CLARENDON PRESS
1970

Oxford University Press, Ely House, London W. 1

GLASGOW NEW YORK TORONTO MELBOURNE WELLINGTON
CAPE TOWN SALISBURY IBADAN NAIROBI DAR ES SALAAM LUSAKA ADDIS ABABA
BOMBAY CALCUTTA MADRAS KARACHI LAHORE DACCA
KUALA LUMPUR SINGAPORE HONG KONG TOKYO

PRINTED IN GREAT BRITAIN
AT THE UNIVERSITY PRESS, OXFORD
BY VIVIAN RIDLER
PRINTER TO THE UNIVERSITY

POUR MANON

A la très chère, à la très-belle
Qui remplit mon cœur de clarté,
A l'ange, à l'idole immortelle,
Salut en l'immortalité!

Never on earth can a man bring back one close to
him once he has departed this life so that he can
see him. Yet whatever he may long for among the
living and the dead, or whatever else he may long
for and cannot obtain, all that will he find if he
will but go to that city of Brahman within the
heart.

PREFACE

LITTLE need be said by way of introduction to this series of Gifford Lectures since all that is necessary will be found in the first chapters of this book. This work in fact combines on a much larger scale the themes of two earlier books, *Mysticism Sacred and Profane* and *The Convergent Spirit*. In the first of these an attempt was made to show that mysticism is a far more varied phenomenon than is generally supposed, while in the second it was argued that the mystical and therefore 'solitary' religions on the one hand and the 'solidary' religions which see salvation in collective rather than individual terms on the other meet or rather could meet in Catholic Christianity.

The Gifford Lectures are normally spread over two years. There is, then, a natural break between the first series of lectures (Chapters I–X in this book) and the second one (Chapters XI–XX). Apart from the first two chapters, which serve as an introduction, the first series sets the problem of the varieties of mystical experience and an attempt is made to find a solution largely from the Indian sources. In the second half of the book a consideration of the Taoist classics forms the link between the 'solitary' mysticism of India and the 'solidary' vision of Neo-Confucianism. This leads on to a consideration of Zen and through Zen to the medieval Christian mystics. The rest of the book is devoted to a re-appraisal of Christian doctrine in the light of the religions already studied and of the thought of some 'fringe' Catholics of the recent past from Rousseau to Bernanos and Teilhard de Chardin. The 'golden thread' that binds the book together is St. François de Sales.

In the tedious business of correcting proofs I am indebted not only to the extremely efficient and vigilant readers of the Clarendon Press but also to Mr. Julian Baldick who was good enough to go through the numerous quotations with me thereby alleviating what is normally the most irksome of tasks. To all these I am sincerely grateful.

In addition, I am most grateful to Éditions du Seuil for their kind permission to include extracts from the works of Teilhard de Chardin in a translation of my own which differs somewhat from the English versions published by Messrs. Collins, and also to Messrs. Collins for concurring in this permission. I would also thank Messrs. Routledge & Kegan Paul for permission to quote from the works of C. G. Jung and Librairie Plon for permission to quote from the novels of Georges Bernanos.

R. C. Z.

All Souls College, Oxford
June 1970

CONTENTS

I

CONCORDANT DISCORD

Introduce unity into diversity, and you create order; order yields harmony, proportion; harmony, where you have perfect integrity, begets beauty. There is beauty in an army when it has order in the ranks, when all the divisions combine to form a single armed force. There is beauty in music when voices, which are true, clear, distinct, blend to produce perfect consonance, perfect harmony, to achieve unity in diversity or diversity in unity—a good description might be discordant concord; better still, concordant discord.

EVER since I had the honour of being invited to give the Gifford Lectures here at St. Andrews, I had no doubt of what the theme of these lectures would be. The theme was to be, precisely, 'unity in diversity' or 'diversity in unity'. For this, it seemed to me, was a theme that was eminently consonant both with the views of Lord Gifford, the founder of these lectures, and with the intentions of the late H. N. Spalding, the founder of the Professorship of Eastern Religions and Ethics at the University of Oxford which I now hold. The exact title, however, eluded me until I stumbled on the words with which I have opened this series of the Gifford Lectures. They are the first words of the first chapter of the first book of the *Traité de l'amour de Dieu* of St. François de Sales; and it seemed to me that this wise, civilized, and urbane French saint had in some measure anticipated the theme of my lectures and had found the ideal phrase to express what I hoped I should be saying. This was scarcely surprising, for, after all, 'there is nothing new under the Sun', as Ecclesiastes the Preacher had long ago remarked. All that we normally do is to reword and rearrange the ideas of others in our own discordant concord or concordant discord. It is good to realize that we can rarely hope to do more than this.

François de Sales was, of course, writing in a different context and for a different public. In his day, the early seventeenth century, there had as yet been no 'encounter' of religions—to use the current catchword. 'Encounter' in the true sense of the word there had of course been with Islam—the encounter of the Crusades and their aftermath, a war of two religions which had sprung from the same Judaic root, waged on both sides for the greater glory of God and with a singleness of purpose which in this more materialistic age of bourgeois relativism seems to be not only perverted, misguided, and wrong, but also frankly incomprehensible

B

except on its lowest level of predatory greed. This was an 'encounter' all right, not a 'dialogue', to use that other cliché so much beloved in ecumenical circles. Islam was known as a dangerous enemy with religious values of its own, the nature of which was only vaguely known, though it was of course assumed that these values were not Christian values, and scarcely anyone bothered to find out what common ground there was between the two religions. 'Encounter' was quite enough. The two religions fought each other: they did not think it necessary to find out about each other. They saw only the diversity, never suspecting that there might also be a unity: they accepted the discord without worrying their heads as to whether or not this might perhaps conceal a deeper concord.

Of the religions of further Asia—of India and China—Europe knew almost nothing. When St. François de Sales was writing, the first contact with the spiritual values of the East had only just been made—by the Jesuit missions to Asia inaugurated by Francis Xavier. He and his successors adopted a quite new missionary technique—they sought to win the hearts of these Asians to Christ by studying the religions by which they lived, and to bring them to what they considered to be the crowning truth of Christianity through the very religions that they professed. They were the precursors of the modern ecumenical movement in its widest sense—a movement which, though starting within Christianity, at present shows signs of reaching out towards some universal form of religion which, though in the foreseeable future it cannot be more than a 'discordant concord' or rather a 'concordant discord', is nevertheless beginning to make the ideas of Lord Gifford and H. N. Spalding seem curiously topical, for since Teilhard de Chardin 'convergence' has been very much in the air.

The Gifford Lectureship, you will remember, was endowed for the purpose of 'promoting, advancing, teaching, and diffusing the study of Natural theology' in the widest sense of that term, in other words, 'the knowledge of God, the Infinite, the All, the First and Only Cause, the One and Sole Substance, the Sole Being, the Sole Reality, and the Sole Existence, the knowledge of His Nature and Attributes, the knowledge of the Relations which men and the whole universe bear to Him, the knowledge of the Foundation of Ethics or Morals, and of all Obligations and Duties thence arising'.

To this Lord Gifford added a rider on how he personally would have wished this literally immense—this immeasurable—subject to be treated:

I wish [he said] the lecturers to treat their subject as a strictly natural science, the greatest of all possible sciences, indeed, in one sense, the only science, that of Infinite Being, without reference to or reliance upon any supposed special exceptional or so-called miraculous revelation. I wish it considered as astronomy or chemistry is.

What Lord Gifford was asking for, then, was what the Germans have taught us to call *Religionswissenschaft*, of which, in its English translation as 'science of religion' at least, I have always been intensely suspicious, because 'science' in English, as Lord Gifford himself saw, means the 'natural sciences'; and the natural sciences, whether it be astronomy or chemistry or anything else, are concerned with 'nature', that is, with extended matter, with the whole phenomenal world which, as science is making increasingly clear, depends for its existence on mathematical law. Religion, however—and I do not at present propose to waste your time by seeking an acceptable definition of that word—religion, as Lord Gifford again emphasized, is concerned with Infinite Being: it is concerned, in fact, with what by definition cannot be measured or defined. There can, then, be no science of religion in a sense that there is a science of astronomy or chemistry, because what is infinite must necessarily surpass the human understanding. If we could understand God, he would thereby cease to be God. The most we can hope to do is to catch a glimpse of 'a form of [him], what of [him] is you, what of him is in natural phenomena',[1] as a Hindu sacred text puts it. And since the Infinite Being cannot be comprehended by a finite intelligence, the student of religion must of necessity take into account, so far as he is able, 'supposed special exceptional or so-called miraculous revelations'; for these 'revelations', whether we choose to consider them as miraculous or not, are the only pointers we have to that Infinite Being which we can never know. Lord Gifford's wish, then, is by its very grandeur impossible of fulfilment, and I see no other way of fulfilling it, even partially, except by bringing together the traces of himself that this Infinite Being appears to have left scattered over the face of the globe, to reconstruct an image of him; and though this image will, in the very nature of the case, be little more than a caricature, it may yet throw some light on what the pseudo-Dionysius called the 'divine darkness'. And this I am surely entitled to do, for Lord Gifford then went on to say:

I have intentionally indicated, in describing the subject of these lectures, the general aspect which personally I would expect the lectures to bear, but the lecturers shall be under no restraint whatever in their treatment of their theme; for example they may freely discuss . . . all questions about man's conceptions of God or the Infinite, their origin, nature and truth, whether he can have any such conceptions, whether God is under any and what limitations, and so on, and I am persuaded that nothing but good can result from free discussion.

[1] *Kena* Upanishad 2:1.

Such, then, were the terms laid down by the founder of these justly famous lectures. The lecturer is, in fact, given *carte blanche* to express whatever view he likes, but he is at the same time discouraged from serving up the stale remains of the standard Christian orthodoxies to which Lord Gifford seems to be referring when he speaks of 'so-called miraculous revelation', and from any discourse that denies Infinite Being in any shape or form. To neither of these temptations am I likely to succumb.

Lastly Lord Gifford laid down that 'the lectures shall be public and popular, that is, open not only to students of the Universities, but to the whole community without matriculation, as I think that the subject should be studied and known by all, whether receiving education or not'. For the lecturer the essential word here is surely 'popular'. And what a relief that is! For nowadays teachers in what used to be called 'arts' subjects are so bemused by the exacting demands of so-called 'scientific' scholarship, the whole wearisome business of a perpetual return to original sources (whether you know the language they are written in or not), of keeping up with the newest writing in one's own 'field', as they call it, however trivial, abstruse, abstrusely trivial or trivially abstruse this may be, of wading through commentaries, of commenting on commentaries and so laboriously on, that they seldom if ever have the time or even the inclination to think. All this the Gifford Lecturer is mercifully spared: for these lectures are or should be 'popular', and a popular lecture is one addressed to the 'people', not to the scribes. For once the wretched don can at least try to shake off the tyranny of his books and exclaim with the poet Mallarmé:

> La chair est triste, hélas! et j'ai lu tous les livres.
> Fuir! là-bas fuir! Je sens que des oiseaux sont ivres
> D'être parmi l'écume inconnue et les cieux! [7]

This is a liberating experience: but it does not mean that I shall in any way neglect my sources, if only because they are rather more interesting than anything I have to say, or that I propose to equate what the French call *vulgarisation* with what the British mean by the same word. All I hope to be able to do (and from experience I well know that in all probability I shall fail) is to present my material in as simple a way as the obscurity of the subject permits, so that the 'people' as well as the scribes will be able to understand something. To this end I shall, so far as in me lies, try my hardest to avoid the pestiferous academic jargon which does so much to confuse and bemuse the popular mind—that poison which is becoming the bread of life on which the academic body feeds. As far as I am concerned there is only one cardinal academic virtue, and that is clarity.

So much, then, for what Lord Gifford expected from the lectures he so generously founded.

H. N. Spalding too, in founding the Chair of Eastern Religions and Ethics at the University of Oxford which I now hold, had views similar to those of Lord Gifford in mind, for he too looked forward to a new harmony of religions, a new Renaissance, as he put it, but this time with God at its centre, in which the newly discovered riches of the Eastern religions would serve as a leaven to raise the unbelieving lump that Western civilization was fast becoming. In founding the Chair he defined the functions of the Professorship in the following terms:

The purpose of the Professorship shall be to build up in the University of Oxford a permanent interest in the great religions and ethical systems . . . of the East, . . . to set forth their development and spiritual meaning, and to interpret them by comparison and contrast with each other and with the religions and ethics of the West . . ., with the aim of bringing together the world's great religions in closer understanding, harmony, and friendship. . . .

At that time it seemed to me that the terms of reference within which the Professor was to work were so wide that it was quite impossible for any one man to cope with them, 'for each of the great world religions, treated as an historical study alone, would fully occupy the lifetime of any one man, however long-lived'.[1] Moreover, every teacher of the comparative study of religions is bound to be accused of being at many points superficial and to that extent a charlatan. The 'field' or, as I should prefer to call it, the 'parish' of most scholars is strictly limited (and the more they limit it, the happier they seem to be: they are less easily found out). The student of comparative religion, at least as H. N. Spalding conceived of him, has the world as his parish; and, in so far as this is true, he will be a thoroughly mediocre parish priest, since he is bound to know some of his parishioners better than others and will know best of all those whom he loves best, for, as the mystics of all religions and ages teach us, you cannot love what you do not know. Like the biblical God his operations will be operations of grace, that is to say, he will have his favourites, unless he is content to be, in the words of the late Aneurin Bevan, a 'desiccated calculating machine'.

When I delivered my inaugural lecture in 1953 the magnitude of the task appalled me. I felt rather as Pascal must have felt when confronted with the silent immensities of space: 'Le silence éternel de ces espaces infinis m'effraie.' So too I was awed by the infinite spaces of man's thought about his origins, his middle course, and his final end.

[1] See below, p. 430.

It is true that today I know a little more than I did then; but this has in no way diminished my sense of awe. Quite the contrary: for the more a man comes to know about the religions of mankind, the more he despairs of ever knowing enough, from ever grasping enough to see in them some coherent design. It is perhaps not irrelevant to recall that my election to the Spalding Chair of Eastern Religions and Ethics occurred after my absence from academic life for some ten years. During that time I had been in various forms of Government service abroad in which truth is seen as the last of the virtues and to lie comes to be a second nature. It was, then, with relief that I returned to academic life because, it seemed to me, if ever there was a profession concerned with a single-minded search for truth, it was the profession of the scholar.

Until my election to the Spalding Chair I had been a highly specialized scholar in the Zoroastrian religion in its last phases before it succumbed to the onslaught of Islam. My interest, it is true, had always been religious, but my training had been linguistic, and in linguistic studies accuracy and a rigorous regard for the facts are the indispensable means for arriving at any new linguistic fact—I mean, for instance, the meaning of a word which had hitherto been unknown. This is, in many ways, an admirable training, for it teaches you a respect for truth even in its minimal manifestations; and if one learns to respect truth in what is small, then one will not despair of finding truth in what is great, not even perhaps in what is very great, great beyond measure, the Infinite Being whose 'truth' Lord Gifford invited his lecturers to consider.

I must confess that when I applied for the Spalding Professorship, which I never really expected to get—so minimal were my qualifications— I had omitted to read the founder's preamble. It was, then, with something of a shock that I read that the 'aim' of the Professorship was 'to bring together the world's great religions in closer understanding, harmony, and friendship'. This aim seemed absurdly starry-eyed at the time: it seems much less so now for reasons that I shall shortly explain. And yet it did seem to me—freshly returned as I was from a career of professional lying —that to tie a Chair even to so noble an object as understanding, harmony, and friendship between the great religions was to set bounds to the objective pursuit of truth. In Jansenistic protest against this I said: 'Nor do I think that it can be a legitimate function of a university professor to attempt to induce harmony among elements as disparate as the great religions of mankind appear to be, if, as seems inevitable, the resultant harmony is only to be apparent, verbal, and therefore fictitious. Such a procedure may well be commendable in a statesman. In a profession that concerns itself with the pursuit of truth it is damnable.'[1]

These words created an unfortunate impression at the time, and were I to rewrite them today I might properly omit the words 'as seems inevitable' and for the too striking 'damnable' substitute the more prudent 'to be deplored'. For the rest, I stand by the position I then held; for the kind of 'harmony' which early practitioners of the art of comparing and contrasting religions had sought to elicit *has*, in fact, too often been 'apparent, verbal, and therefore fictitious'. In the case of my predecessor in the Spalding Chair, later President of India, Sir Sarvepalli Radhakrishnan, one could not help feeling that this so desirable 'harmony' was produced by positing that his own form of Vedāntin monism—the theory that Reality is one and that all multiplicity is therefore to some extent illusory, being no more than an appearance—was the ultimate Truth, and that all the religions were thus simply empirical paths leading towards this same Truth. Such a position can, of course, be substantiated by carefully selected quotations from other religious systems and the philosophies allied to them, but such support (if you can call it support) will then be 'apparent, verbal, and therefore fictitious', for it leaves wholly out of account the core and centre of the non-Indian religions from the scriptures of which these quotations are violently wrenched. This method I still find 'damnable'—to be rejected, that is, since, in the long run, it leads not to understanding, harmony, and friendship, but to misunderstanding, discord, and a friendship which, however sincere it may appear to be, is ultimately valueless because it is based on a fundamental misunderstanding: it is based on a lie.

Hence the title I have chosen for these lectures. We must force nothing: we must not try to achieve a 'harmony' of religions at all costs when all we can yet see is a 'concordant discord'; and I would have you note that St. François de Sales speaks first of a 'discordant concord', but then thinks better of it and corrects to 'concordant discord'. At this early stage of contact with the non-Christian religions, this surely is the most that we can hope for.

Both Lord Gifford and H. N. Spalding were universalists. While neither, I think, would have gone as far as Rāmakrishna, the nineteenth-century Hindu revivalist, in asserting that all religions are essentially the same, and though neither probably saw syncretism as a viable solution to the discordant coexistence of religions, both were impatient of religious orthodoxies and the rigid dogmatic attitudes they breed. In 1952 the election of a Roman Catholic, and a convert at that, to the Spalding Chair

---

[1] Below, p. 429.

seemed to many both a reactionary step and one scarcely in accordance with the founder's intentions, particularly as at that time my purely academic qualifications scarcely fitted Mr. Spalding's known requirements. For, after all, what did I know? At that stage I had not even published a book. True, my first book, the only one I have written which can rank as 'pure' scholarship, as its title, *Zurvan, a Zoroastrian Dilemma*, would lead one to suspect, had already been accepted for publication, but my reputation, such as it was, rested on articles on Zoroastrianism, mainly philological, that I had written before the war. With Zoroastrianism, then, I was very familiar and my Iranian background had also made me reasonably familiar with Islam. This, however, was not at all what Mr. Spalding had been looking for. His principal interest, as he made clear in the preamble to the statute that inaugurated the new Chair, was in the religions of India—in Hinduism and Buddhism. In the first of these fields I had no competence except that I had a nodding acquaintance with the principal Hindu sacred books, while in the second I had no competence whatever. Despite all this I found myself elected; and like Adam, after he had eaten of the tree of the knowledge of good and evil, I found myself naked and ashamed.

It would have been easy, I suppose, to have plodded along in the old Zoroastrian–Islamic rut without paying more than a nodding attention to the great religions of India. It would have been easy; but it would have been dishonest. And one thing at least Zoroastrianism had taught me, and that was that the Lie is the very principle and fountain-head of evil. Hence I proceeded to delve deep into the Hindu classics and discovered a whole new world of what Lord Gifford would have understood as 'natural religion' which, like the indwelling God himself, seemed, in the words of C. G. Jung, to have 'no knowable boundaries and to encompass me on all sides, fathomless as the abysms of the earth and vast as the sky'.[1]

In my inaugural lecture and in the earlier part of a later book, *At Sundry Times*, I had stressed the discord rather than the concord of religions. This was in principle right; for it is the duty of the scholar, even on the popular level, first to analyse the differences and only then to look for a possible synthesis which might make some sense of the heterogeneous elements analysed. Even with the little knowledge I had then it seemed clear to me, as I stated in my inaugural lecture, that 'it is . . . only too true that the basic principles of Eastern and Western, which in practice means Indian and Semitic, thought are, I will not say irreconcilably opposed; they are simply not starting from the same premises. The only common ground is that the function of religion is to provide release: there is no agreement

[1] C. G. Jung, *Answer to Job*, E.T., London, Routledge & Kegan Paul, 1954, p. 180.

at all as to what it is that man must be released from. The great religions
are talking at cross purposes.'[1]

The variety of religions is indeed a scandal and an offence; and it would
be foolish to seek an easy way out without doing violence to any of them.
How, then, is one to approach this problem?

Science is all the rage these days, and so it should be since it is the only
sphere of human activity perhaps where truly original work can still be
done—original work which has transformed this planet of ours in a century
and which, being itself like the 'matter' it investigates morally neutral, is
pregnant with immensities of good and evil. It has become fashionable for
workers in the arts faculties to describe themselves as 'scientists'—social
scientists, scientists of religion, and so on. This, as far as I can see, means
no more than that they try to be accurate and objective. In religion I very
much doubt whether it is possible to be either; for if it is true that it is the
Infinite which is the subject of these studies, what can this have to do with
the various objects of scientific inquiry which, of their very nature, are
concerned with the finite and definable? Again 'objectivity' sounds all very
fine in theory, and it is possible to write books on religion with what
appears to be a rigorous impartiality. That the result is almost certain to
be dull is beside the point, for it is generally assumed that dons (with some
illustrious and some notorious exceptions) are by the very nature of their
calling dull. What is not beside the point is that complete objectivity is
never attainable in practice except in minute points of scholarship. You
can be objective, say, about the interpretation of one verse of the Bible,
but is it possible to be totally objective about the interpretation of the
Bible as a whole? For once you deal with a sacred text or with a given
religion, you are bound to interpret it, and any interpretation is bound to
be influenced, either for or against, by previous interpretations as well as
by one's own theological bias or, what is worse, by a general distaste for all
things not empirically verifiable.

What I mean can be illustrated by my own case as well as by any other.
Of the books I have written some are intended to be objective: others,
quite frankly, are not. The three books I have written on Zoroastrianism
were intended to be objective if only because there are now only about one
hundred thousand Zoroastrians surviving, and a description of their faith
as it existed up to the time of the Muslim conquest in the seventh century
A.D. is unlikely to arouse any fury of theological passion today: yet in order
to write even a descriptive book, you have to select what *you* consider to
be most important; and once you do this you have already ceased to be

[1] Below, p. 439.

objective. If this is true of Zoroastrianism, then how much more true must it be of Hinduism? How can you do impartial justice to so complex a religious phenomenon with its millennial history and its millions of present-day adherents in the compass of one volume in the 'Home University Library'? You cannot. In my own volume I sought to bring into relief what seemed to me to be the most significant development in Hinduism, namely, its movement towards monotheism, towards the belief in one supreme and personal God, from a pantheism in which no clear distinction is drawn between God, the One, and the All, or between God, man, and the universe. I am convinced that this is in fact the major trend in the historical development in Hinduism because the evidence seems to me to point that way. Who is to say, however, that I wrote as I did and selected as I did not so much because the weight of the evidence imposed itself objectively on my mind as because my theistic and Christian subjective mind seized on the evidence so presented and imposed its own image upon it? The objection is valid, but at least I can say this much in reply. Any man with any convictions at all is liable to be influenced by them even when he tries to adopt an entirely objective approach; but let him recognize this from the outset and guard against it. If he does this, he will be less liable to deceive himself and others. The greatest sinners in this respect are perhaps the Indian philosophical commentators on the great Hindu scriptures themselves, for, almost without exception, they seek not so much to bring out the meaning of the text itself as to impose their own private opinion on to it. This is, of course, equally true of the patristic commentaries on the books of the Old Testament. The commentators, however, both of the Old Testament and of the Hindu sacred books *are* justified in what they do, for 'objectivity' in the interpretation of scripture is quite a modern idea. What the ancient commentators were setting out to do was to describe what a given sacred text meant to *them*; and since they were philosophers they expected their sources to be consistent. Sacred books, however, rarely show any obvious consistency: they refuse to be pigeon-holed. Any system that claims to derive from them, therefore, must distort them at some point. The function of the modern commentator who does aim at objectivity, then, should be to accept the inconsistencies as they stand, to see them in historical perspective, and to try to follow any trend of ideological development they may or may not display.

So much for the 'objective' or descriptive method. Another method which I have tried to follow in a series of books from *Mysticism Sacred and Profane* to *The Catholic Church and the World Religions* has been to study the non-Christian religions from the only point of view that can be central to me, that is, the point of view of Catholic Christianity, at least as I understand it. This was the method of the Jesuit missionaries of the seventeenth century. What they did, and what I have increasingly tried to do, was to study the main texts of the non-Christian religions in their historical development, to study them, so far as is possible, from inside, and having so studied them to try to correlate them with aspects of Catholic Christianity which are of importance to me. This is the precise opposite of what I believe is called 'crisis' theology, which would set up over against the non-Christian religions an arbitrary biblical Absolute, or what Paul Tillich once called the 'Protestant principle', which he fantastically claimed was 'the ultimate criterion of all religious and all spiritual experiences', for Protestantism, he would have us believe, 'as a principle is eternal and a permanent criterion of everything temporal'.[1] I confess that I have never been clear as to what Tillich understood by this 'eternal Protestant principle', unless he meant himself. With *this* type of theology and with the still fashionable 'religionless Christianity' and 'death of God' theology, so much of which has been fathered off on to poor Dietrich Bonhoeffer, I have little sympathy, perhaps because I just do not understand it and therefore have no wish to refute it. I prefer rather to align myself again with St. François de Sales who said with his usual good sense: 'I cannot criticize authors, nor authorize criticism, of a doctrine that I do not understand.'[2]

I ought perhaps to go further and confess that I think that I am allergic to theology in general and to German theology in particular. Perhaps I would not go all the way with Charles Péguy when he writes: 'The Germans delight in confusion. They even congratulate themselves on it—luckily for them. They even take pride in it: this is what they call profundity (or depth).'[3] Not all the way perhaps, but a good part of it.

Since my first book on 'comparative religion', *Mysticism Sacred and Profane*, was published, there has happened what surely must be the greatest single religious event since the Reformation—not so much an event as a person—the person of Pope John XXIII and the event of the *aggiornamento* that he set in motion. It was the personality of Pope John, the sheer, obvious goodness of the man that changed the whole mind and heart of Catholic Christianity overnight. Post-Reformation Catholicism— owing to the secession of the northern provinces of the Church—had

---

[1] Paul Tillich, *The Protestant Era* (abridged ed.), Chicago, Phoenix Books, 1957, p. viii.

[2] E.T., *The Love of God: a Treatise*, p. xxxiii.

[3] *Œuvres en prose 1909-1914*, ed. Pléiade, p. 1351: 'L'Allemand se plaît dans la confusion. Il s'en félicite même et heureusement pour lui. Il en fait même son orgueil et c'est ce qu'il nomme profondeur.'

really ceased to be Catholic at all. Its claim to universality, already weakened by the Eastern schism, now made little if any sense. The counter-reformation was rather a protest against the protest of Protestantism: it was deliberately exclusive, and to exclude is surely the reverse of the 'Catholic principle', the principle whose instinct must always be to include and absorb whatever is not directly opposed to the teaching of Christ as interpreted by the Catholic tradition. The Catholic principle can be summed up in Christ's words: 'Anyone who is not against you is for you.'[1] The opposite principle, the 'Protestant principle' if you like, is equally proclaimed by Christ: 'He who is not with me is against me; and he who does not gather with me scatters.'[2] These apparent contradictions are typical of all religious traditions; and they should not surprise us, for all revelations in the end remain mysteries, and the Hindu scriptures are singularly wise when they say: 'The gods seem to love the obscure and hate the obvious.'[3]

The changes for which Pope John and the Council he inaugurated were responsible are too well known for me to summarize them. Not only has the Roman Catholic Church entered into fruitful conversation with the non-Catholic churches, it has also taken cognizance of the non-Christian religions and has conceded that they too are repositories of truth in one or more of its manifold aspects. This is not entirely new, since for some time now Roman Catholic theologians have been seeking to reconcile Indian philosophy with Thomism, the traditional philosophy of the Catholic Church. Yet this does not seem to be a very fruitful approach, for however important philosophy may be as an 'explanation' of a given religion—and it is undoubtedly very important in Hinduism—it can never coincide with the religion itself. All too often its clarifications rob that religion of the essential mystery at its heart: by explaining overmuch and by explaining away they eviscerate the very thing they are supposed to be investigating.

If we are to 'revive the religious sciences', as Al-Ghazālī claimed to have done for Islam in the eleventh century, we must go beyond philosophy to those texts which the great religions themselves hold most sacred; for it is through these writings that 'all nations' must obviously 'seek the deity and, by feeling their way towards him, succeed in finding him'.[4]

That God had revealed himself outside Jewry St. Paul seems to have taken for granted. Vatican II follows him in this; but it needed a John XXIII to reaffirm what the early Church had always understood, namely, that all truth, wherever we find it, must proceed from God.

---

[1] Luke 9:50.   [2] Luke 11:23; Matthew 12:30.
[3] *Brihadāranyaka* Upanishad 4:2:2.   [4] Acts 17:27.

This had been almost entirely forgotten in the intervening centuries, and in the West even Augustine is not guiltless in this respect. The Council's approach, inspired as it was by Pope John, then, reversed a centuries-old trend in the history of Christian missionary activity. It laid down categorically that 'the Catholic Church rejects nothing which is true and holy in these religions. She looks with sincere respect upon those ways of conduct and of life, those rules and teachings which, though differing in many particulars from what she holds and sets forth, nevertheless often reflect a ray of that Truth which enlightens all men.'[1]

Had they lived I think that Lord Gifford and H. N. Spalding would have been astonished at this bewildering volte-face in a Church that, since the Council of Trent, had become notorious for its dogmatic narrowness and its dogged refusal to move with the times. Suddenly, as if by the touch of a magic wand, the Roman Church, in which many sincere men could only see the Anti-Christ and the Whore of Babylon, transformed itself into something that was at least recognizable as an authentic member of the Church of Christ. The Roman Church was seen to be not the Catholic Church indeed, since so many sincere Christians remained outside it, but to be once again the Catholic Church in potency; for it would be foolish to suppose that there will ever be a Catholic Church in act until the end of time, if then.

Nor did the Council merely declare that the Catholic Church rejected nothing 'which is true and holy in other religions'. It also had a word or two to say about each of the major non-Christian religions and the contribution that, in its opinion, each made to the symphony of faiths to which all were invited to join their voices.

'In Hinduism', it declared, 'men contemplate the divine mystery and express it through an unspent fruitfulness of myths and through searching philosophical inquiry. They seek release from the anguish of our condition through ascetical practices or deep meditation or a loving, trusting, flight towards God.'

All this is true enough, but it is not a little strange that the Council should omit to tell us that the 'unspent fruitfulness of [the Hindu] myths' contained at its very centre the belief in an incarnate God. Surely this is, for a Christian, a matter of the deepest significance, for where else in the history of religion do we find a belief in God made man except in Christianity itself? To the Jews the very idea was intolerable, and Jesus' claim to be the Son of God was, for the Jews of his time, utter blasphemy, and

[1] *The Documents of Vatican II*, E.T., London–Dublin, Geoffrey Chapman, 1966, p. 662.

Caiaphas only symbolized the general feeling by rending his clothes. No Hindu of the time of Christ would have dreamt of doing so, and the difficulty with which Christian missionaries have all along been faced has been not so much that their assertion that Jesus of Nazareth was the Son of God, was considered blasphemous or even incredible as that they should be so naïve as to suppose that he was the *only* incarnation of God. To the Hindus this looked rather like a narrow provincialism. Yet in their acceptance of the possibility of divine incarnation they stood and stand much nearer to Christianity than the Old Testament ever did or than Islam was to do.

Similarly of the Buddhists the Council speaks with approval. 'Buddhism', it declares, 'in its multiple forms acknowledges the radical insufficiency of this shifting world. It teaches a path by which men, in a devout and confident spirit, can either reach a state of absolute freedom or attain supreme enlightenment by their own efforts or by higher assistance.'

'Release from the anguish of our condition': 'a state of absolute freedom, supreme enlightenment'. The words reflect Hindu and Buddhist attitudes clearly and accurately enough; and they are noble ideals. But are they in any way compatible with the ideals of traditional Christianity? For, according to the Christian myth, God did not assume our human condition in order to win release from the anguish of it: that would make nonsense of Gethsemane and the Cross itself. Rather 'he consented to partake of our humanity in order that we might share in his divinity', as the Roman Catholic Church itself declares in its daily liturgy. Yet the Council apparently sees no irreconcilable contradiction here. How this can possibly be we shall have to investigate in future lectures.

For Christianity's traditional rival and enemy too, Islam, the Council has only words of peace and conciliation:

Upon the Moslems, too, the Church looks with esteem. They adore one God, living and enduring, merciful and all-powerful, Maker of heaven and earth and Speaker to men. They strive to submit whole-heartedly even to His inscrutable decrees, just as did Abraham with whom the Islamic faith is pleased to associate itself. Though they do not acknowledge Jesus as God, they revere Him as a prophet. They also honour Mary, His virgin mother; at times they call on her, too, with devotion. In addition they await the day of judgement when God will give each man his due after raising him up. Consequently, they prize the moral life, and give worship to God especially through prayer, alms-giving, and fasting.

The age of anathemas indeed seems to have passed away. No approach to the non-Christian religions could be more conciliatory than this. But the statements of the Council do not really point the way to an eventual harmony of religions. While not denying the deep differences that separate the great religions from one another, they gloss them over and, in doing so, they suggest that such harmony is attainable. I very much fear that along these lines 'the resultant harmony [will be] only apparent, verbal, and therefore fictitious'. For while I am very willing to concede that, if the central doctrine of Christianity is that God becomes man in order that man may become God, then Hinduism can be seen as very much more of a *praeparatio evangelica* than can the Old Testament for which such an idea is blasphemous. The same, however, cannot be said for either Buddhism or Islam; for Buddhism, in its earliest form, does not admit of a personal God and condemns material Nature out of hand because, being transient, it can only be a source of sorrow. Since this is so, there can be no redemption for it: it can only be transcended. That there is truth in this basic Buddhist assumption I have no doubt, but it is a truth that is very different from the basic assumptions of Christianity as usually understood. So too with Islam: the Council is very careful to list all those matters on which Islam and Christianity agree. In its widely eirenic spirit it prefers to slur over Islam's emphatic rejection of the central Christian doctrine of the atonement and its rooted dislike of the doctrine of the Holy Trinity. Here again there is no harmony, only a not very 'concordant discord' in which the discord is between what each religion has come to believe to be the very core of its teaching. There is discord between Jesus Christ, the Son of God, and Muhammad, the Apostle of God (since Christians have never acknowledged the prophethood of Muhammad), between the Holy Trinity and the emphatic Koranic statement: 'God is one, God is eternal: he did not beget nor was he begotten, and there is not one equivalent to him.'[1] And yet in the most important matter of all there is harmony, and this is expressed in the first affirmation of the Muslim's basic credo: 'I bear witness that there is no god but God.' The relationship between Christianity and Islam has indeed always been one of 'concordant discord' in which discord has usually prevailed.

How, then, is even a 'discordant concord' to be extracted from the confusing pattern the world religions present? Not, I am reluctantly convinced, by any purely theological or philosophical approach. Dr. Trevor Ling has recently had some hard things to say about Christian theology and I find it difficult to disagree with him:

In modern times [he writes][2] it is theology which once again has been threatening

---

[1] Koran, 112.
[2] Trevor Ling, *Buddha, Marx, and God*, London, Macmillan, 1966, p. 197.

to dominate Christianity. Theology, that is, as the study of other men's study of those documents which in the first place were thrown up in the enthusiasm of spiritual experience; theology as an undertaking which is at several removes from and well insulated against the reality of which the scriptures speak; theology as an intellectual activity, characterized by reading and expounding and arguing and counter-arguing, so that for much of Christianity the authority has become the professor's gown in the pulpit or the 'open book' before the congregation, rather than any living encounter with reality.

This is in no sense an exaggeration. Christianity has from the beginning been plagued with theology: it has been plagued with the rational spirit of the Greeks prying into what theology itself calls the mysteries of faith, busily defining the indefinable. God knows that the Christian religion needs re-presenting to a world for which its traditional doctrines no longer have any meaning whatsoever. Let us not deceive ourselves. For the common man, in the Protestant countries at least, the Christian religion has no longer any meaning or relevance to life as it is lived today. It is a game played by theologians for theologians: the world shrugs its shoulders and passes by on the other side. Catholicism was first attacked by Luther: Christianity as a whole then became the butt of the self-satisfied rationalism of the Enlightenment. Ridicule gave way to violence, and the French Revolution, in the name of reason and humanity, delivered a direct and savage onslaught on the Church, and this was in no wise abated under the Directoire which continued to persecute the Church in the name and the interests of a triumphant bourgeoisie; for this was the prelude to the drama of bourgeois society in which we are still actors. There is only this one difference: the Directoire had the honesty to worship mammon in spirit and in truth. We still prefer to pay lip-service to God.

Basically standards have not changed, and our society is quite as secular as that of the Directoire; but whereas people no longer try to set up new religions in competition with Christianity as was fashionable in nineteenth-century France, and whereas Protestant Christianity in traditionally Protestant countries is in manifest decline, never has there been such a spate of theological thinking, such an output of 'study of other men's study of those documents which in the first place were thrown up in the enthusiasm of spiritual experience'.

In all my writing on comparative religion my aim has been increasingly to show that there *is* a coherent pattern in religious history. For me the centre of coherence can only be Christ. It could scarcely be otherwise since I have freely accepted the 'bondage' of the Catholic Church, and I would scarcely have done this if I had not thought that in that very

bondage there was also 'release' and that this was in fact the true religion—
for me. This does not mean that I am particularly anxious to go around
converting people, because I am not at all convinced that Catholic Christianity need be the true religion for everyone else; and I am perfectly
aware that many—particularly among the young—are far more interested
in Zen Buddhism than they are in Christianity. Good luck to them, if they
are at all serious in their exotic aspirations. For, surely, there are two
Christianities—the Christianity of the letter which kills and the Christianity of the spirit which enhances or should enhance life. The letter, that
is, not so much literalism but the taking for granted of an inherited
religion, 'entire generations of catechism, of habit, of catechistic habit',
as Péguy puts it[1]—this letter kills; and theology too, particularly modern
theology with its ridiculous labels—crisis theology, dialectical theology,
religionless Christianity, death of God theology, krisis, kairos, and heaven
knows what else—with its fraudulent introduction of obsolete words
mascarading as something new in order to convince the simple-minded
that these words clothe a new idea—*kerygma* for preaching, 'hermeneutics'
for exegesis—theology has become the passionate pastime of the few, a
ponderous game that leaves the many absolutely cold. Small wonder, then,
that Mr. Alan Watts, with whom I am rarely in agreement, should write
in a book he has significantly entitled *Beyond Theology*: 'Christianity
therefore impresses the modern Westerner as the most impossibly complicated amalgamation of odd ideas, and though it is his spiritual birth-
right and the faith of his fathers, it is very much easier to make him
understand Buddhism or Vedanta.'[2] Mr. Watts is speaking of the de-
Christianized majority, and I agree with him in this, except that I would
add that the corollary is also true. It is quite as difficult to help a neo-
orthodox Protestant to understand Buddhism or Vedāntism, because he
is so used to seeing God as totally other, as wholly transcendent, that he
has never stopped to consider the kingdom of God within him. His Hindu
counterpart thinks of little else.

I might have chosen as the sub-title of these lectures, 'A Symphony of
Faiths'. For you may remember that, in the introduction to the last movement of his great Choral Symphony, Beethoven introduces the themes of
the three previous movements only to reject them summarily with some
very caustic comments from the cellos. In much the same way I have
rejected as irrelevant to my theme almost everything that would find a
natural place in a theological seminary, that is, Christian theology and

---

[1] Charles Péguy, op cit., p. 451.
[2] Alan Watts, *Beyond Theology*, London, Hodder & Stoughton, 1964, p. 85.

modern theology in particular. There is, after all, as St. François de Sales said, no point in criticizing a doctrine you do not understand, much less one that, so far as you understand it, you find antipathetic.

> La chair est triste, hélas! et j'ai lu tous les livres.
> Sad, sad is the flesh, and I have read all those books.

Well, not all of them, but quite enough to make me realize that of all that I have read only an infinitesimal part of them has profited me at all. Moreover, as a don, as a scribe, it is difficult not to lose that spontaneity and openness one should bring to all one's reading as one should to friendship. It is only when one is ill, perhaps, and thereby delivered from the slavery to the letter and the book, the slavery from which no don can escape, that one becomes a reader, one of those 'pure readers', of whom Péguy speaks, 'who read for the sake of reading, not to educate themselves, not to work; pure readers . . . who not only can read but want to read, who solely and simply read, . . . who read a work solely and simply for the sake of reading it and taking it in, to feed and nourish themselves on it as on a precious foodstuff, in order to promote growth in themselves, to promote their inner, organic dignity, not at all to use it as something *to work with*, to promote one's social status in a secular society'[1]. These are wise words, and when I first read them, I did not take them sufficiently to heart for the good and sufficient reason, I am afraid, that I am paid to do just what Péguy considered to be a desecration of 'pure' reading: I am paid first to educate myself and secondly *pour travailler avec*—to use what I have read as something to work with. The joy has turned into tedium, and it is the tedium that one is likely to transmit.

It is true that my election to the Spalding Chair has meant a partial emancipation from the tyranny of the book since in a 'parish' that comprises the whole world the number of books one *can* read is strictly limited. But even so vast a parish remains a parish, and the intellectual sheep demand to be fed, as they have every right to do, since it is they who in the last analysis pay the parish priest. Once again this means to read *pour travailler avec*, and this too often kills all interest both in the teacher and in the taught. To be invited to give these Gifford Lectures, then, brought me an immense feeling of relief, for I can, like the cellos in Beethoven's Ninth Symphony, dismiss all that I neither like nor understand and concentrate on what, for me if for no one else, constitutes the 'concordant discord' which the orchestra of religions is trying to bring to our ears.

How, then, is our symphony to be composed? Many elements will have

---

[1] Charles Péguy, op. cit., p. 105.

been excluded, first and of necessity those of which I am ignorant, for as St. François again says:[1] 'Penser savoir ce qu'on ne sait pas, c'est une sottise expresse', (To think one knows what one does not know is wilful stupidity); and secondly those for which I have neither sympathy nor understanding. For what, then, do I have sympathy, you may well ask. Quite simply, for the 'great religions' both of East and West, expressed not as H. N. Spalding would have it 'in philosophic, poetic, devotional, or other literature, in art, in history, and in social life and structure', but in those texts that each religion holds most sacred and in the impact that these have caused. It is in these, and not among the philosophers and theologians that depend on and distort them, that you will find harmonies far more profound and discords far more telling than you are likely to meet with in the philosophic systems so confidently built upon them. The trouble with our own scriptures is, of course, that we are far too familiar with them, and familiarity breeds not so much contempt as lassitude. So, in my own case, I am far more at home with the Hindu scriptures than I am with the Old Testament, and this is true to a lesser extent in the case of the Taoist and Confucian classics and to a lesser extent still with the Buddhist scriptures. It seems to me that the Indian religions in particular have something to teach us and that this 'something' can help us to deepen our own religion and open up insights that were only dimly perceived before. The study of these 'exotic' religions can help us to see our own religion in a new way, and can shake us out of the 'habit' of religion, for once anything becomes a habit, it dies on you and becomes a fossil.

Indian religion is mystical through and through, and a consideration of mysticism will necessarily take up a large part of these lectures. It may be true that all religions tend to converge towards the same point; but it is none the less true that they start from very different points. 'The great religions', when we start to study them, do indeed appear to be 'talking at cross purposes'; and no study of them can be fruitful unless these basic differences are freely admitted. These differences are at their most uncompromising between the Hebraic and Islamic prophetic religions on the one hand and the mystical traditions on the other; but there are striking differences too between the mystical traditions themselves. No responsible person can ignore these differences: he can minimize them as Hindu writers frequently do; or he can seek to correlate them in a more or less orderly pattern, and this is what I have tried to do in some of my more recent books. I do not pretend that this is necessarily the right way to deal with the problem. For me it is the only way, for this is the way I have come

[1] *Introduction à la vie dévote*, III, 5.

to see things. Like Teilhard de Chardin I see my own religion, Catholic Christianity, in terms of creative evolution, but an evolution in which each of the world religions has or will have its distinctive and individual part to play. I know only too well that 'there is nothing new under the sun', and that much that I shall have to say will have been conditioned by some modern fringe French Catholics like Péguy, Bernanos, and Teilhard de Chardin. For these three Christianity, whether Catholic or Protestant, had got into a legalistic and theological rut; the spontaneity had gone out of it; it had become as dry as the valley of dry bones of Ezekiel. Teilhard succeeded in breathing a little life into it; but despite Teilhard's dismissal of Eastern mysticism as *périmé*—out of date like last year's *guide Michelin*—I venture to think that there is much in Eastern religion that is still valid, and it is my hope to show in these lectures that not only is this so, but that Christianity has much to learn from them, much indeed it *must* learn from them if it is ever to become not in name only but in truth the Catholic Church whose very name, as Augustine saw, implies that it was designed by its founder to become the religion of the whole human race. How this can be we cannot as yet see even 'in a glass darkly'. The obstacles, largely of our own making, are Himalayan; but this need not discourage us overmuch. After all the Prince of Peace promised us first not peace but the sword.[1]

[1] Matthew 10: 34.

II

JUSTICE AND GRACE

'MAY they all be one. Father, may they be one in us, as you are in me and I am in you.'[1] How often has this been quoted, and not least by the protagonists of Indian religion, for whom unity tends to be everything. For Catholics too unity has been the guide-line of their spirituality as it had been of their ecclesiastical policy. The unity achieved in mystical prayer, however, is something very different from a unity of ecclesiastical organization that is not freely accepted. In both cases the concept of unity should be the same—a 'recollection' or gathering together in the one case of all the faculties of the soul into its 'apex' which some mystics claim to be inseparable from God, and, in the other, of all men who are willing to accept the fellowship of the one Church. The mystical prayer of the early Church has much in common with the mystical insights of the Hindus, and most educated Hindus would agree that any approach to unity between the great religions must be conducted on a mystical or contemplative plane. How far this is practicable we shall be examining in the sequel. There have, however, been scandals or stumbling-blocks which have stood between them and Christianity: first the dogmatic formulations of the Christian faith, secondly the Church's infamous record in the matter of persecution, and thirdly, in more modern times, the easy assumption of superiority on the part of the missionaries and the claims of a monopoly of truth that they have staked on behalf of their beliefs. Scandals there had to be, and the history of the Church is surely one long scandal.

It is true that the Church has spent much effort in defining the great mysteries of the Incarnation and the Holy Trinity. In the process it has caused much rancour and dissension, and since these truths in any case pass all rational comprehension, non-Christians and post-Christians may be forgiven for wondering what it is all about and for losing patience at what seems to be an exercise, both futile and impious, in trying to pin down and pigeon-hole the infinite and its inscrutable relationship to the finite.

Scandals, indeed, there had to be: and Jesus himself foresaw them. 'Do not suppose that I have come to bring peace in the earth', he had said in words at which Origen alone was perhaps brave enough not to

John 17: 21.

blanch. 'It is not peace that I have come to bring but the sword.' And the sword of the Catholic Church has been a scandal which has left ineffaceable scars not only on the bodies of others but even more so on its own. And the paradox is—and what in religion is *not* paradox—that it was the great Augustine who, as Bishop of Hippo, first sanctioned the active persecution and cowardly hounding down of heretics. This surely was in the character of the man, for this convert from Manichaean dualism to Neoplatonic monism saw not only the Neoplatonic One as indwelling and informing his own soul; he also saw the whole Neoplatonic hierarchy of being reflected in the structure of the Catholic Church. Christ had prayed: '*May* they all be one.' Augustine, in his enthusiasm and pride, thought it his duty to see to it that they *were* one. The inner unity he had found in himself he longed to see mirrored and perfected in the One Catholic and Apostolic Church. The end was right and good, even in accordance with what seems to be a common tendency of Nature itself which appears to grope uncertainly forward from the chaos of multiplicity to ever higher forms of organic unity, but the means were surely against Nature, against God, and against Christ. Augustine destroyed the bodies of individual Christians in order that Christ's body, the Church, might be *seen* to be One. How did this doctor who wrote so eloquently on the Holy Trinity not understand that since even in God unity, singleness, and simplicity must at the same time make room for diversity, so too in the Church there must be many mansions?

Ironically enough it was Augustine himself, the apostle of unity through persecution, who sowed the seeds of the Reformation which shattered the enforced unity he had been at such pains to establish. The predestinarian doctrines of the enemy of Pelagius had been much modified by saner spirits in the Middle Ages, and it was precisely the Augustinian denial of the freedom of the human will to co-operate with divine grace in any significant way that the Reformers were to seize upon to use as the sword with which they were to cleave open the unity of the Catholic Church. How true did Christ's saying, then, prove to be: 'It is not peace that I have come to bring but the sword.' The greatest disaster that has befallen Christendom was, perhaps, the conversion of Constantine and the consequent involvement of Caesar in the affairs of God and of God's Church in the affairs of Caesar. Second to this was the transformation of the Church from the status of a Church persecuted for Christ's sake into a Church persecuting in the name of Christ; and for this the great Augustine must bear a heavy burden of blame.

On many occasions Professor Arnold Toynbee has contrasted the exclusivity of the Jewish religion, based as it is on the Jewish belief that the Jews are the chosen people, with the large tolerance of the Buddhists and Hindus. This plague of exclusiveness, he claims, was inherited by both the Christians and the Muslims: hence their lamentable record. It was, perhaps, inevitable that this should be so, for of its very nature the prophetic spirit is the reverse of tolerant, and the God whose mouthpiece it claims to be is, as we all know, a jealous God whether he calls himself Yahweh or Allah.

In a former book I divided the religions of the world roughly into two groups—the prophetic and the mystical. The prophet, be he true or false, brings or thinks he brings a message from a highly personal God which he is unable to control. It comes in spite of himself because he is what used to be called 'possessed'. Mystics too may be 'possessed', but their 'possession' is, as we shall see, of a different order. The editors of the Jerusalem Bible define prophecy far better than I can, for the prophets are the wild men of my universal parish, the deeply discordant element that, from Moses to Barth, has scarcely for a moment ceased to disrupt the concord that more gentle and civilized men have striven to create and maintain. 'The genuine prophet', the editors of the Jerusalem Bible write, 'is fully aware that he is a mouthpiece, no more; his words though his own are not his own. He has no doubt that the word of God has come to him and that he must pass it on to others. The source of this conviction is a mysterious, we may call it mystical [I will return to this] experience of a direct contact with God . . . the prophet, like the mystic, is raised to a "supranormal" psychological state by this divine intervention. . . . There are two aspects to the message, threat and consolation. Jeremiah was sent "to tear up and to knock down, to build up and to plant". And indeed the message often makes bitter hearing, a tissue of menaces and reproaches, so much so that severity comes to be a sign that the prophet is genuine. . . . This is because the true prophet is haunted by the idea of sin, the obstacle to the will of God. The prospects of salvation are, however, never forgotten. . . . In God's dealing with his people, pardon and punishment are complementary.'[1] The God who inspires these prophets is, in the words of Radhakrishnan, 'not only irrational but cruel, vindictive, and uncivilized'.[2] Well, it would be surprising if the *mysterium tremendum*, the 'tremendous mystery' of which Rudolf Otto wrote, were not all these things. This is the God of the Old Testament, and this is the God of the Koran; and because both these

[1] *The Jerusalem Bible*, London, Darton, Longman & Todd, 1966, pp. 1116–17.
[2] S. Radhakrishnan, *Religion in a Changing World*, London, George Allen & Unwin, 1967, p. 43.

deities, or, if you will, both these aspects of deity are apparently incompatible with the Hindu idea of the hidden depths of what they call Brahman, Islam and Hinduism have never found living together easy, so much so indeed that in the end a separate state, Pakistan, had to be carved out of India, so 'jealous' did the Islamic God appear to be.

Both Judaism and Islam are religions of prophecy and law. God chooses prophets through whom he reveals himself, and through whom he reveals a detailed system of law. Christianity, as we all know, claims to be the fulfilment of Judaism, and it therefore sees itself as the 'new Israel', the legitimate continuation of the Old Testament community. Jesus Christ, however, or at least his immediate followers made claims that ranked him very much higher than the prophets. For Christians Jesus is God made man, and this makes it impossible to treat Christianity simply as a prophetic religion. From the very beginning a mystical element is present, and it is this, if anything, that entitles Christianity to speak of itself as unique. It cannot be broadly classified as either prophetic or mystical: it falls somewhere between the two. This we shall have to be considering later.

Judaism is distinguished by the fact that its sacred book is, in theory at least, a history book: it is a *progressive* revelation made by a highly personal God *in time*, and this revelation comes through a whole series of prophets in the course of history. Other religions are based on a structure of myth— myth being of its nature something that is independent of time. It is a symbol of something that is thought to be eternal: it is something that is ever renewed and re-enacted in ritual. The purpose of myth and ritual is to bring man into direct contact with the eternal processes of renewal both in the cosmos and in himself. And it was this that the Hebrew prophets were reacting against. Their God, whatever his origins may have been, reveals himself with ever increasing insistence as *not* being the God of Nature: hence the claim of the Jews to be the chosen people. And from the point of view of the history of religions this is not an idle claim. Hence it has always annoyed syncretistic liberals because, of all the religions of the world, Judaism, like Islam, has obstinately refused to compromise its identity. It has consciously separated itself from the Gentiles on the grounds that it alone has received the true revelation from the One True God. It alone has been granted prophets, sent not only to proclaim the One True God who, so far from being identical with Nature, utterly transcends it, but also to denounce all the other 'gods', the Baalim, as being false. Yahweh *is* a jealous God, and this exclusivity *has* characterized not only Judaism but also Christianity and Islam, its daughter faiths, ever since. Professor Toynbee is perfectly right about this, and from his point of view of pantheistic humanism the whole Jewish phenomenon must appear deplorable.

Judaism does not deny that there is no prophecy outside Israel (Balaam, for instance, was not a Jew), but in point of fact, with two exceptions, prophecy is confined almost entirely to Israel, for to treat the Chinese sages as prophets (as Professor H. H. Rowley did in his *Prophecy and Religion in Ancient China and Israel*)[1] is to strain the meaning of the word 'prophet' unbearably. The two exceptions are, of course, Muhammad, the Prophet of Islam, and Zoroaster, the prophet of ancient Iran.

Zoroaster is a unique phenomenon, for in Israel prophecy was, from the time of Moses, inseparably linked with the official religion. In the case of Zoroaster this was not so. So far as we can see, Zoroaster must have grown up in a 'pagan' atmosphere in eastern Iran (in all probability in ancient Chorasmia), a long, long way from Israel and the whole Semitic world. And yet, if the editors of the Jerusalem Bible are right in their definition of prophecy, then Zoroaster must qualify. True, we have no certain knowledge of the kind of religious atmosphere into which Zoroaster was born, but it seems clear that despite persecution he denounced the *daiva*s, the traditional gods, and proclaimed the exclusive majesty of one supreme God, Ahura Mazdāh, the 'Wise Lord'. Like the Hebrew prophets, Zoroaster both hears and sees God and transmits his message. This is not myth but direct experience of what the prophet considers to be transcendent reality, a holy God speaking to him and through him. The message again is substantially the same as that of the Hebrew prophets: God is holy and righteous, he rewards and punishes good and evil deeds. All this is experienced directly: 'Then, Mazdāh, did I realize that thou wast holy when I *saw* thee in the beginning, at the birth of existence, when thou didst ordain a [just] requital for deeds and words, an evil lot for evil [done] and a good one for a good [deed]: by thy virtue [shall all this come to pass] at the last turning-point of creation.'[2] Or again: 'Now have I *seen* him with my eyes, knowing him in Truth to be the Wise Lord of the Good Mind and of [good] deeds and words.'[3] The prophet not only sees him but hears him, imploring him to speak to him 'with the tongue of his mouth'.[4] This is a personal experience of a personal God, and the prophet is the recipient of a message from God. As with the Hebrew prophets so with Zoroaster, the message he receives from God has two

[1] H. H. Rowley, *Prophecy and Religion in Ancient China and Israel*, London, Athlone Press, 1956.
[2] Yasna 43: 5.   [3] Ibid. 45: 8.   [4] Ibid. 31: 3.

aspects, 'threat and consolation', rewards for the faithful, punishment for those who refuse to receive the new monotheistic message. As with the Hebrew prophets so too the *Gāthā*s or 'Songs' of Zoroaster mingle events in the life of the prophet himself with the message he has to deliver. Despite previous uncertainty about his date Zoroaster's mission seems now to be firmly set within a given historical context—the period immediately preceding the rise of the Achaemenian Empire. This is no timeless revelation of eternal truth of a kind we will meet with in the Hindu scriptures, but a revelation to a chosen individual at a particular time and in a particular historical situation. This, indeed, is a unique phenomenon in the history of the Indo-European peoples; and it is all the more strange in that this isolated prophet from the central Asian steppes was to influence and complement the main stream of prophetic religion, Israel itself, through the bringing together under the house of Achaemenes of the Semites of western Asia and the Indo-European tribes of central Asia. If we accept the traditional date of Zoroaster, then the period of his prophetic activity will coincide with the Babylonian captivity of Israel and will immediately precede the foundation of the Achaemenian Empire by Cyrus the Great in 550 B.C. Of the personal religion of Cyrus we know nothing, but we do know that his predecessors in the house of Achaemenes were worshippers of Ahura Mazdāh, and that although they sometimes speak of him as the 'greatest of the gods', he was very much *their* god who bestows the kingdom on them. Neither in their inscriptions nor in the inscriptions of the great Darius, whose religion shows distinct Zoroastrian elements, is any God other than Ahura Mazdāh mentioned by name. This is, of course, no proof that the early Achaemenids were monotheist, but they do seem to have worshipped their own God, Ahura Mazdāh, who was also the God of Zoroaster, to the exclusion of others, though this did not prevent them from acknowledging for political reasons the deities of the conquered Babylonians.

Be this as it may, the founding of the Persian Empire under Cyrus and the conquest of Babylon in 539 brought the Jews liberation from the Babylonian captivity and resulted in their return to the land of Israel. Contact between the early Zoroastrian community and the Jewish exiles there must certainly have been, and it is therefore likely that Judaism assimilated certain Zoroastrian ideas which had not previously been part of their tradition—most obviously the elevation of Satan from the rank of a mere accuser to that of God's spiritual adversary and man's implacable enemy, the concepts of heaven and hell as places of reward and punishment after death, and the idea of the last judgement. To the Jews Cyrus appeared as an almost Messianic figure, the Lord's 'shepherd'[1] and his 'anointed'[2] whom God 'calls by his name'[3] although 'he does not know him'. He is the liberator of the chosen people from the slavery and exile of Babylon, the prototype of the Messiah.

Through the Persian conquest, then, Zoroastrian ideas seem to have entered into Judaism, and through Judaism into Christianity and Islam— the existence of heaven and hell as places of reward and punishment, the existence of a positive power of evil which, though always subservient to God, is none the less exceedingly real and exceedingly powerful, and a final reckoning on the last day.

Again the two religions agreed on their interpretation of time. It was not, as it was for the Indians and for all whose religion is based on what seems to be the regular cycle of death and rebirth in Nature, an endless cyclical motion, forever returning to where it started, only to repeat the process ever again. Rather it has a beginning and an end: it is a progression in a straight line from an original catastrophe (much more marked in the Hebrew tradition than in the Zoroastrian) to the final establishment of a Messianic kingdom which will put an end to sin and suffering. This is, of course, a gross simplification, but the essential point remains. Both religions see creation as moving towards a definitive end, and this end is the transformation of existence. This transformation is not a final separation of spirit from matter, since 'salvation' is a 'making whole', not a separation, but the resurrection of the whole man, his body quite as much as his soul. That this was the authentic Jewish view is, of course, well known. For the Zoroastrians too 'salvation' must include the body as well as the soul, for death is not natural to the human race. In Zoroastrianism it is not so much man who sins as a higher power which is the very principle of death; for against the Holy Spirit of God, sometimes described as his 'son', there stands the Evil Spirit who is his twin. This spirit, one is given to understand, is not evil in himself but evil by choice, and it is by a free choice too between one or other of these spiritual alternatives that man is saved or damned. In a justly celebrated passage this momentous choice which takes place 'in the beginning' is vividly described:

In the beginning those two Spirits who are the well-endowed (?) twins were known as the one good and the other evil, in thought, word, and deed. Between them the wise chose rightly, not so the fools. And when these Spirits met they established in the beginning life and death that in the end the followers of the Lie should meet with the worst existence, but the followers of Truth with the Best Mind. Of these two Spirits he who was of the Lie chose to do the worst

[1] Isaiah 44: 28.   [2] Ibid. 45: 1.   [3] Ibid. 45: 4.

things; but the Most Holy Spirit, clothed in rugged heaven, [chose] Truth as did [all] who sought with zeal to do the pleasure of the Wise Lord by [doing] good works.[1]

Death, then, enters the world through a wrong choice of the powers of evil, and final salvation is seen as the destruction of the powers of death themselves and the rehabilitation of the whole man in body and in soul.

Zoroaster, perhaps the most surprising figure in the history of religions, was a prophet in a distant land which, so far as we know, had known no prophets before him and was to know none after him. Through the spread of the Persian Empire his ideas were to come into contact with the great Jewish prophetic tradition itself: into this his followers were to inject some of his characteristic ideas. Some twelve hundred years later another prophet was to arise who was to change the face of much of the civilized world. This was, of course, Muhammad, the Prophet of Islam.

Islam is, perhaps, only a problem for Christians. In terms of purely prophetic religion it presents no problem, not even to the Jews. For the Jews indeed prophecy came to end with the closing of the canon of the Old Testament. This, however, means no more than that the Jews regard their own revelation as having been completed at that point: what follows is rather a matter of classification and learned commentary. That God should have, in his inscrutable wisdom, sent a prophet among their Arab kinsmen would not necessarily appear strange to them, particularly as the God who speaks to Muhammad speaks in tones as cogent and peremptory as any that he had used to their own prophets. For the Jews it would not seem extraordinary that the Arabs should in their turn be favoured with a revelation similar to what they had themselves received from Moses, since the law proclaimed in the Koran might quite easily be regarded by them as a modification of their own Mosaic law, redefined to suit a different people in different conditions at a different historical moment. Moreover, what Dr. Ling calls the 'first-order' theology of the Koran is more or less identical with that of the Old Testament. In both 'revelations' the essential dogma that God is One, and that any association of other gods with him is an abomination, is tirelessly affirmed. Absolute obedience to this God is demanded in both. Dire threats are uttered against the disobedient and fair promises are made to those who are obedient and do good works. Islam too lays tremendous emphasis on an awful day of judgement, the horrors of hell fire, and the joys of paradise. God is certainly terrible as he is in the Old Testament, but he is also, and more essentially, 'the Merciful, the Compassionate'. No one can, I think, read the two books concur-

[1] Yasna 30: 3–5.

rently without coming to the conclusion that it is the same God speaking in both: the accents of prophecy are unmistakable. Quite as much as the Hebrew prophets Muhammad is fully aware that he is a mouthpiece, no more (he habitually calls himself a 'warner'); but in the case of Muhammad even the words are not his own, they are God's, and in most of the Koran God speaks in the first person and addresses Muhammad in the second. The revelations are not normally introduced as in the Old Testament with the words 'Thus saith the Lord', but with a direct command, 'Say', and the revelation of what the Prophet is to say follows. The revelation is more direct, and unlike the Hebraic revelation which extended over hundreds of years, it is all revealed to Muhammad in some twenty years between A.D. 610, when, according to tradition, he was some forty years old, and A.D. 632, shortly before his death. Islam, then, claims to be the prophetic religion *par excellence*, and if one admits the validity of prophecy at all, it is difficult to resist or disprove the claim. Moreover, the Koran relentlessly insists that it merely confirms what has been sent down before: it claims to confirm both the Torah and the Gospel. In its 'first-order' theology this is in the main true—at least in so far as the Torah is concerned. The Koran, however, draws heavily on both the Old and New Testaments and their apocrypha; and there are frequently discrepancies between the older revelations and the new. This, of course, is also true of any single sacred book, and particularly of a prophetic one. The language of prophecy is the language of men possessed by God, if you like, but possessed none the less, and it is not impossible that the human element may distort the message in the process. This is not a matter I can argue now since we shall have to study the great religions in considerable detail before we can begin to suggest any conclusions even tentatively. At this stage we can do no more than note that though the Torah and the Koran largely agree on essentials, they differ quite considerably on matters of detail. From the Jewish point of view this can only mean that the Koran simply got details of the Jewish tradition wrong, and this in turn must mean that though the Koran may be a revelation of sorts, it is a revelation in which the human element, always subject to error, is very much in evidence. From the Muslim point of view, on the other hand, as the Koran itself says, it can only mean that when there are discrepancies, these must be due to the fact that the Jews are either concealing something that had been revealed to them or that they have consciously or unconsciously tampered with the sacred text. Here we must let matters stand for the moment.

I have purposely not discussed the standing of Christianity in the over-all picture of the prophetic Semitic tradition because Christianity is not

by any means exclusively a prophetic religion. For both the Jews and the
Muslims the figure of Christ as depicted in the New Testament must be a
scandal, since for both the idea of an incarnate 'Son of God' is blasphemous. Caiaphas rent his robes; Muhammad, on his side, defended Jesus,
the Messiah, from ever having made so monstrous a claim, and in the
Koran it is Jesus himself who repudiates all such claims with horror.
Whether there is any way of reconciling the Jesus of the Koran with the
Jesus of the Gospel I have already discussed in a previous book.[1] My
arguments were ingenious: I no longer quite believe them.

To the modern secular mind there is something oddly barbaric about the
Old Testament and the Koran: we are no longer impressed by a God who
stands in unrelenting judgement on an erring world. Radhakrishnan, then,
is not untypical when he denounces the God of prophecy as being 'not
only irrational but cruel, vindictive and uncivilized'. It is rather theologians like Barth and Tillich who strike an anachronistic note with their
wearisome emphasis on judgement. This may have meant something when
we were still living in the aftermath of the Second World War and under
the threat of a third. In the present climate of uneasy coexistence, with
tensions somewhat relaxed, this ancient God is losing all credibility except
perhaps for a 'remnant' of neo-fundamentalists. The loss of Christian
faith has brought no one back to either Judaism or Islam, but it has led
many people to search for a different kind of God altogether—the kind
of God they think we may find in India. The interest raised by Dr. John
A. T. Robinson's book *Honest to God* proves this clearly enough. As Jung
has said: 'If I accept the fact that a god is absolute and beyond all human
experience, he leaves me cold. I do not affect him, nor does he affect me.
But if I know, on the other hand, that God is a mighty activity in my soul,
at once I must concern myself with him; he can then become even unpleasantly important, and in practical ways too.'[2] Hence the current
interest in Zen—and drugs.

Radhakrishnan's strictures on the prophetic religions are natural
enough. The Old Testament and the Koran, for all the majesty of their
language, make dreadful reading today, and it has always seemed to me
that, in confining the former to the Latin tongue, the medieval Church
acted with uncommon wisdom. There seems little point in denying it: the
Old Testament read in its literal sense is a literally dread-full book; and
the attitude of the second-century heretic, Marcion, has always seemed

---

[1] R. C. Zaehner, *At Sundry Times*, London, Faber & Faber, 1958, pp. 195–217.
[2] Richard Wilhelm and C. G. Jung, *The Secret of the Golden Flower*, E.T., London,
Kegan Paul, Trench, Trubner & Co., 1938, p. 129.

natural to me, for he could not see how the bloodthirsty and sometimes almost paranoiac deity of the Old Testament could also be the loving Father preached by Jesus Christ. Origen was fully aware of the force of these arguments: how could a just God, let alone a loving one, visit the sins of the fathers on their children, and how could he boast of creating misfortune? This and hundreds of other passages drawn from the Old Testament could only lead the simple Christian to believe about God what he would hardly believe of the most cruel and unjust of men. Hence the necessity for allegorical interpretation. This, however, can be overdone, and the fathers certainly did so. Thus secular man today is either disgusted with the barbarities of the Old Testament, or more likely he has never read them. As to the fathers, if *per impossible* he should read them, he would no doubt 'dislike' them as much as Gandhi 'disliked' the Book of Numbers.[1] The same is true of the Koran, for the God of the two books is recognizably the same. The blustering and the hectoring, the threats and often the sheer cruelty cannot impress once the sense of reverence has gone: and the sense of reverence *has* gone, and it would be surprising indeed if there was a return to this antique and seemingly irrelevant God. This does not mean that the Church was wrong to keep the Old Testament as part of its canon, if only as a relic, for the mission of Christ is scarcely comprehensible except against an Old Testament background. It does mean, however, that the Church has not only a right but a duty to interpret it in the light of the revelation in Christ. If this necessarily allegorical interpretation no longer carries conviction, then should not the whole venerable but embarrassing document be respectfully swept under the carpet until such time as the theologians have succeeded in drawing new meanings out of it relevant to man as he is today?

Ever since the Enlightenment Christianity has appeared a little old-fashioned; for the Enlightenment was interested rather in reason and justice than in grace, and 'grace' is the hall-mark of Christianity. The Protestants, so far from playing down this Pauline conception, elevated it into the one self-sufficing principle: *sola fides, sola gratia*: 'faith only, grace only'. Grace is a beautiful word in English: we associate it with 'gracious, graceful, gratitude', and so on. Less readily do we associate it with 'gratuitous', and yet theologically this is far nearer its real meaning. 'Gratuitous' means 'freely bestowed', and what in common English seems to be most freely bestowed is an insult, a 'gratuitous insult'. Stripped of its traditional associations 'grace' means 'favour', almost 'favouritism', as Michelet was not slow to point out. It was by grace, by favouritism that

[1] M. K. Gandhi, *An Autobiography*, Pt. I, ch. xx.

the Jewish race was chosen out from all the races of the world, by grace
and not by merit than some are saved and not damned, and that the
saints of the Church attain sanctity. Grace and the divine right of kings
went closely together, royal favour reflecting divine grace, and this surely
was one of the reasons why the French Revolution swung so violently
against the Christian religion, for in the alliance between the altar and the
throne it saw the spiritual and temporal facets of the doctrine of grace—
the latter depending for its sanction on the former. This case was forcefully put by Michelet in the introduction to his *History of the French
Revolution.* Fascinated by the 'concordant discord' that might have
existed between Christianity and the Revolution, he saw that the French
Revolution was at the same time the heir and the adversary of Christianity
—heir because it welcomed the idea of fraternity, adversary in almost
everything else. Christianity was essentially an arbitrary religion (and how
many times have Christians made the same charge against Islam!): the
French monarchy was likewise an arbitrary form of government. Neither
was sincerely interested in justice. 'Only faith can save, not any works of
justice.' This is Michelet's accusation against Christianity. 'No justice
outside faith. Whoever does not believe is unjust. Without faith is justice
any use? None.'[1] Faith again is a pure gift of grace gratuitously given
without cause or motive. So too the gratuitous self-immolation of Christ,
the 'prodigious sacrifice' as Michelet himself calls it, which is supposedly
the source of all grace, does not really take away the sins of the world: the
divine mercy does not efface the arbitrary 'justice' of God. No, 'judgement
reappears more hard than ever, a judgement without justice, or at least a
judgement the justice of which will be forever hidden from our sight. The
elect of God, God's favourite, receives from him not only faith but the
gift of doing just works, the gift of salvation.' Justice ceases to be an active
virtue, ceases to be a passion in the heart of man and becomes something
wholly 'passive, transmitted as a gift by God to the chosen of his heart'.
Man is not capable of improving himself; he is not even capable of promoting justice on his own initiative, 'for if grace . . . were not gratuitously
given as its very name implies, if it had to be earned by works of justice, it
would be justice: it would no longer be grace. Such, says the Council [of
Trent], has been the unwavering belief of the Church. And so indeed it
had to be, for this is the basis of Christianity. Outside these limits there is
philosophy, there is no longer religion. Religion means the religion of grace,
of salvation gratuitous and arbitrary, granted at God's good pleasure.'[2]

---

[1] Michelet, *Histoire de la Révolution française*, ed. Pléiade, vol. i, p. 26.
[2] Ibid., pp. 27–9.

What Michelet says is scarcely an exaggeration, and his identification of religion with grace, with favouritism, applies as much to Judaism and Islam as it does to Christianity. All attempts, he says, to produce a reasonable dogma must be set aside—and the Revolution was forever seeking just that—for there can be no compromise between the arbitrary concept of grace freely given and freely withheld and justice as it is understood by men. For Michelet, as for the Revolution whose passionate historian he was, the Christian religion was the ideological justification of absolute monarchy. As interpreted by himself and the whole revolutionary generation he represented, this was simply taken for granted. True, the theology he attacks is rather that of the reformers than that of the Council of Trent; for on the Catholic side it has usually been maintained, with little plausibility, that man must co-operate with grace in order to win salvation, but this of course assumes grace, the divine gift gratuitously and arbitrarily given, without which there can be no co-operation. These were fine distinctions that Michelet cheerfully brushed aside since the core of the matter remains: in Christianity as in Islam man, when left to his own devices, is incapable of saving himself.

The French Revolution inaugurated our secular age against the Church which it identified with the *ancien régime*—an identification which Pope Pius VI never attempted to deny. For this total misunderstanding of the new forces that were opening up a new era, the significance of which he could not see, he ended his days as a prisoner of the Directoire in Valence. Yet the revolutionaries did not aspire, as the Russians were later to do, to abolish religion as such, for they still thought that man needed a religion if only to let off emotional steam; but the new religion, if there was to be one, would have to be in accordance with the principles of the Revolution. The virtual suppression of the Roman Catholic Church in France, however, left a vacuum which the revolutionaries could find no means of filling. They were not even against organized religion (for this is a contemporary phenomenon), but they were quite unable to create a religious organization that had any degree of credibility. Robespierre's bizarre attempt to institute a cult of the Supreme Being (with which modern humanists and indifferentists should surely sympathize) was a notorious failure, for the Supreme Being represented only a 'political neutrality between the Revolution and Christianity, between Justice and Grace'; it was 'utter sterility, aridity, the void'.[1] Both under the Directoire and throughout the nineteenth century the search for a more reasonable cult continued, the first in the field being Theophilanthropy, founded by one

---

[1] Ibid., vol. ii, p. 813.

Haüy and secretly financed by La Revellière-Lépeaux, himself one of the directors and, oddly enough for the times in which he lived, an honest man.[1] The fall of Robespierre and the establishment of the Directoire marked the beginning of what Balzac was to call the triumph of 'medio-cracy' in France, the bourgeois era which is still very much with us, and the ideas of the estimable La Revellière-Lépeaux seem to foreshadow much that goes by the name of religion today:

> I can only descry two ideas [he writes] which are essentially religious; the existence of God and that of the soul. From these two dogmas a third emerges, that of a future life. I cannot, then, accept any religion as true and useful except that which is usually called 'natural religion' because only natural religion agrees with reason, and only natural religion can supply a solid basis for public and private morals. Also I cannot help inclining towards whatever cult deviates least from natural religion which consists in the love of God and of man—in what was later to be called Theophilanthropy.[2]

These words might be said to be the charter of what today would be called indifferentism; and this is surely what religion means to the great majority of decent, unthinking men today. Few of us are practising Christians any more, many are agnostics, some atheists, but there is still perhaps a majority which likes to associate the name of religion with the three crucial stages of life, birth, marriage, and death, and this majority cannot in any real sense be considered Christian, it is rather Theophilan-thropist. Not for these the 'unconditional seriousness' which Tillich demands from the religiously committed.[3] A vague belief in God and the soul, in 'natural religion', in an after-life and love, is quite enough. The French Revolution made a direct attack on the institutional Church and the religion of prophecy and grace which it enshrined: its successors were in search of something more in accord with the spirit of the bourgeois age, something comfortable, reasonable, and undemanding which would lend an air of decency and respectability to a civilization in pursuit of material wealth.

The nineteenth century continued the revolutionary reaction against what Michelet calls the religion of grace and favour. This was the age of religious liberalism, of Auguste Comte's positivist religion, the Saint Simoniens, as well as of Marx. The tendency all the time was not so much to destroy religion (the Roman Catholic Church, it was thought, could be relied on to destroy itself by its own blunders and its apparent identification

---

[1] *Mémoires de Larevellière-Lépeaux . . . publiés par son fils*, Paris, Plon, 1895, vol. ii, p. 166.

[2] Ibid., p. 161.   [3] Paul Tillich, *The Protestant Era*, p. xi.

with a system of government that had gone for ever), it was rather to set up religions that did not clash with the new perspectives which the natural sciences were opening up, and which should be based on reason. Man was in search of a true 'natural religion' in which neither dogma nor miracle should play any part. 'To obey reason', Cousin had said, 'is the very essence of duty, a duty higher than all others, being the basis of all without itself being based on anything except the essential link between liberty and reason. It could be said that there is only one duty—to remain reasonable.'[1]

In the nineteenth century liberal opinion in Europe thought that Christianity had had its day. This seemed as self-evident to Marx as it had seemed to Comte. The theory of evolution had made the God of Christianity both implausible and irrelevant: the 'tissue of threats and reproaches' had been torn to shreds and Yahweh was left without an audience. The faith of the purveyors of religion in the nineteenth century was a faith in reason, science, and evolution, a faith in ineluctable progress. The older Protestant churches seemed to have become mere adjuncts of the Protestant monarchies, while the Catholic Church seemed to be digging its own grave by setting its face against all reasonable concessions to science and, without learning anything from the past, by supporting an outmoded political order which had long since served its purpose. There seemed to be nothing to stand in the way of the onward march of rational and scientific man.

This spirit of free inquiry welcomed the discovery of the Eastern religions which were then becoming increasingly well known. The first of these to impinge on the European consciousness was Confucianism, many of the sacred books of which had been translated by the Jesuit missionaries in the seventeenth century. The reasonableness of the Confucian doctrines was immediately hailed by such distinguished leaders of the Enlightenment as Leibniz, Spinoza, Voltaire, and Malebranche,[2] and when the sacred books of the Hindus and Buddhists were in their turn translated into the main European languages their reception was no less enthusiastic. Here at last, it seemed, were religions which were in accord with human reason, for they seemed to have much more in common with philosophy than with 'religion' as it had hitherto been understood in Europe. Here were religions which knew nothing of a 'jealous' God or of the harsh spirit of intolerance which had plagued Europe since Augustine first turned his fury against the Donatists and Pelagians. Neither Hinduism

---

[1] Quoted in D. G. Charlton, *Secular Religions in France 1815–1870*, Oxford University Press, 1963, p. 102.

[2] See Raymond Dawson, *The Chinese Chameleon*, Oxford University Press, 1967, p. 54.

nor Buddhism was an intolerant creed since prophecy played no part in their more gentle view of life. To many it seemed that these religions might in some measure fill the vacuum that a discredited Christianity seemed to be on the point of leaving. The nineteenth century too saw the birth of the comparative study of religions, and this in turn dealt a further blow to Christianity, for it showed that eastern Asia and particularly India possessed religions whose spiritual treasures were at least as rich as those of Christianity, and that Christianity, so far from being unique, was simply one among many religions to be studied on the same level and by the same standards as they.

It cannot, however, be said that these religions made any great impact outside the intelligentsia. This was because until the outbreak of the First World War belief in progress was still fairly universal. It took the two world wars to shatter this illusion and thereby create a religious vacuum that has yet to be filled. This has in its turn created a far wider interest in Eastern religion (which, in practice, means Indian religion and its offshoots) than has ever existed before. The nineteenth-century attempts to construct new 'rational' religions out of nothing had failed as they were bound to do: they had scarcely survived birth. On the other hand, the whole doctrinal structure of Christianity had not only come to be questioned but had been seen to be irrelevant to a society which had become increasingly master of its surroundings. Might not the answer, then, lie in those primeval religions of India which seemed to care little if at all for faith in a personal God, but which promised a way of release from all the nagging worries of human life? Moreover, these religions did not ask you to worship God 'in fear and trembling'—never a particularly pleasing prospect to 'natural' man—rather they asked you to retreat into yourself in order that you might find the 'kingdom of God within you'. Western man had grown tired of a religion which, though in its essence half-prophetic and half-mystical, had almost entirely lost touch with the mystical element; and it was this that he was groping for though he might not know it, and this the Indian religions could offer him in full measure.

For Indian religion is mystical through and through, and in Chinese religion too there is a quiet current of nature mysticism, the essence of which, in both its Taoist and its Confucian manifestations, is harmony—'perfect harmony' which, as St. François de Sales says, means to achieve 'unity in diversity or diversity in unity'. This is the keynote of Chinese religion. How do matters stand in India, and why is there so keen an interest in Indian religion today?

This interest in Indian religion is in fact an interest in only two aspects of it—the monistic Vedānta on the Hindu side, Zen on the Buddhist. Both have one thing in common, the theory or dogma of *karma*, a word which originally meant no more than 'action' but which came to mean that whatever one does automatically and irrevocably recoils on oneself. 'As a man acts, as he behaves, so does he become. Whoso does good, becomes good: whoso does evil, becomes evil. By good works a man becomes holy, by evil works he becomes evil.'[1] This is the law of Nature as it applies to human beings: it is *dharma*, the cosmic law in which all beings cohere— *dharma*, a word of protean significance, for it can also mean 'religion', 'way of life', 'righteousness', 'justice', and 'law', all of which are aspects of the one cosmic law. It is the word that both the Hindus and Buddhists use to designate their own 'religions' or 'ways of life'. To follow this *dharma*, they maintain, is merely to recognize things as they really are and to behave accordingly. *Dharma* is, then, both *justesse* and *justice*, both correct seeing and just dealing. Man, then, is responsible for his own destiny irrespective of the grace or favour of any god. This is the law of Nature. But what of Nature itself? For the Hindus and the early Buddhists there is no salvation in this world. Salvation is rather salvation *from* this world into a realm that is beyond time and space. Thus, though the material universe may be controlled by just laws, no amount of just dealing will bring a man salvation, for salvation means not 'life everlasting' as Christians are apt to phrase it, but a state of being that does not last at all because in it time is transcended. It was, then, not for nothing that Aldous Huxley called the first novel he wrote after his conversion to Vedānta *Time must have a Stop*, for he rightly saw that beneath all the extravagant mythology and con- flicting metaphysics the core of Indian religion was the conviction based on actual experience that man at his deepest level is beyond space and time, beyond causation and all earthly flux, beyond all action and volition, and therefore beyond good and evil, detached from all material things, from pleasure as from pain, sufficient unto himself, possessing nothing because he needs nothing, autarchic, free, and invulnerable. This is the true nature of the soul of man and there can be no salvation for him until he realizes this his true immortal state. The attraction of this kind of religion to secular man is that it demands no assent to dogmas of any kind; for it teaches that this state of timeless bliss is or can be a matter of experience here and now if only one knows how to set about it.

Now, if it is indeed possible to reach this state where, as Tennyson said, 'death is an almost laughable impossibility', then surely the effort is worth

[1] *Brihadāranyaka* Upanishad 4: 4: 5.

making. Aldous Huxley who, in this way, is typical of post-Christian man, certainly thought so and therefore immersed himself in the writings of the Vedānta and Zen Buddhism. He meditated much but never succeeded in achieving this state which the Buddhists call enlightenment until he took mescalin. Under the influence of the drug he thought that he at last understood what the mystics of all religions had been talking about:

> *Istigkeit*—[he wrote] wasn't that the word Meister Eckhart liked to use? 'Is-ness.' The Being of Platonic philosophy—except that Plato seems to have made the enormous, the grotesque mistake of separating Being from becoming, and identifying it with the mathematical abstraction of the Idea. . . . The Beatific Vision, *Sat Chit Ananda*, Being-Awareness-Bliss—for the first time I understood, not on the verbal level, not by inchoate hints or at a distance, but precisely and completely what those prodigious syllables referred to.[1]

Here, then, resurrected from ancient India via Japan was a religion that could satisfy such men in this secular society of ours as still thirsted for the infinite and refused to be content with anything less. Huxley had had a vision of what he thought was an aspect of Absolute Truth, and this Truth had for centuries been enshrined in the scriptures of the Hindus and Buddhists. This was the true *philosophia perennis* whose roots were in India but whose branches spread throughout the entire world—among the Taoists in China, with Plato and the Platonists in the ancient Mediterranean world, among the Sūfīs in Islam who, having seen this truth, rejected the whole Islamic law as a feeble approximation to it, and finally in Christianity—in the fourth Gospel and St. Paul and in the whole line of Christian mystics which for Huxley reached its zenith in Meister Eckhart.

At the time when Huxley wrote *The Doors of Perception* this seemed little more than a pipe-dream. Only after years of searching and fierce austerities had the Buddha achieved enlightenment. Now it turns out that this same enlightenment which, so far as it can be described at all, is to see the ineffable One in the many, the eternal Now in the fleeting flux of Time, unity in diversity, a discordant concord and a concordant discord, can burst upon you under the influence of LSD. This is mysticism, and this is the Truth, unvarying in all men, present in all men, the Truth to catch a glimpse of which Yogins in India and Zen Buddhists in China and Japan, the contemplative orders in Christendom, and the Sūfīs in Islam had spent years in unremitting spiritual exercise and contemplative prayer. This is the Truth that a man can only realize after he has undergone countless incarnations in this transient and miserable world, and only then if his dispositions are right and if he strives for it unremittingly. This

[1] Aldous Huxley, *The Doors of Perception*, London, Chatto & Windus, 1954, pp. 12–13.

Truth, this ineffable discordant concord, can now, it appears, be experienced, if only for a few hours, by taking mescalin or LSD. The Theophilanthropists and their successors who had tried to found rational religions which might take the place of a discredited Christianity had been wasting their time. There was after all no need for God, soul, after-life, or love: for the Truth is that All is One and One is All, now, everywhere, and for ever. This, we are told, is what mysticism is about, mysticism which, according to one authority, is a 'constant and unvarying phenomenon of the universal yearning of the human spirit for personal communion with God'.[1] Personal communion with God? But what if there is neither person nor God, as the Buddhists maintain? Should we not rather say 'to be at one with the All', or as another writer on this perplexing subject has put it, 'to pass from our normal state of self-consciousness into cosmic consciousness'?

[1] A. J. Arberry, *Sufism*, London, George Allen & Unwin, 1950, p. 11.

III

COSMIC CONSCIOUSNESS

'COSMIC consciousness.' The phrase was first given currency in a book of that title by Richard Maurice Bucke in 1901. 'A classic in its field', the blurb of the twenty-third and latest printing informs us, 'this exceptional book has had a large continuous sale for over half a century'. The soul, the Bhagavad-Gītā informs us, is single as is the Godhead; and what is single and simple invariably attracts. Dr. Bucke's book is nothing if not simple and single-minded. His subject is mysticism, which, in all its manifestations, he identifies with what he calls 'cosmic consciousness'. The meaning of these words we shall be considering during this lecture.

Bucke was a Canadian 'of good sturdy English stock on both sides, whose father was a graduate of Trinity College, Cambridge, and a clergyman'. He was, we are told, a 'matter-of-fact scientist' and had been 'superintendent of . . . the Provincial Asylum for the insane at Hamilton, Ontario, and in 1877 of the London (Ont.) Hospital'. He ended his career as the President of the American Medico-Psychological Association. He was, then, eminently 'scientific' and respectable. This was only one side of his brain, however, for in 1867 he fell under the spell of Walt Whitman, the effect of whose verses on him had been 'extraordinary, instantaneous and permanent. They opened a new door in his mind.' Then in the spring of 1872 he had a strange experience of 'illumination', the effects of which proved ineffaceable although the experience never returned. This is how he describes it:

It was in the early spring, at the beginning of his thirty-sixth year. He and two friends had spent the evening reading Wordsworth, Shelley, Keats, Browning, and especially Whitman. They parted at midnight, and he had a long drive in a hansom (it was in an English city). His mind, deeply under the influence of the ideas, images and emotions called up by the reading and talk of the evening, was calm and peaceful. He was in a state of quiet, almost passive enjoyment. All at once, without warning of any kind, he found himself wrapped around as it were by a flame-colored cloud. For an instant he thought of fire, some sudden conflagration in the great city; the next, he knew that the light was within himself. Directly afterwards came upon him a sense of exultation, of immense joyousness accompanied or immediately followed by an intellectual illumination quite impossible to describe. Into his brain streamed one momentary lightning-flash of the Brahmic Splendor which has ever since lightened his life; upon his heart fell one drop of Brahmic Bliss, leaving thenceforward for always an after-taste of heaven. Among other things he did not come to believe, he saw and knew that the Cosmos is not dead matter but a living Presence, that the soul of man is immortal, that the universe is so built and ordered that without any peradventure all things work together for the good of each and all, that the foundation principle of the world is what we call love and that the happiness of every one is in the long run absolutely certain. He claims that he learnt more within the few seconds during which the illumination lasted than in previous months or even years of study, and that he learned much that no study could ever have taught.[1]

This illumination was the genesis of Dr. Bucke's book. The experience he analyses as cosmic consciousness is the common experience of what are usually called nature mystics. As so often, it lasted only for a few moments, and it does, then, seem rather extraordinary that he should have based his whole view of life on an experience of such short duration. This, however, does indicate the overwhelming impression the experience brought with it, and mystics of all schools at least agree on this. William James, too, in his justly celebrated Gifford Lectures of 1901–2 entitled *The Varieties of Religious Experience*, bears eloquent testimony to this, and that despite the fact that his own experience was induced by drugs. Today, of course, this would cause no surprise. On the contrary, should one be foolhardy enough to deny the identity of drug-induced ecstasies with the more controlled raptures of the orthodox mystical traditions which appear in all the great religions, one is likely to be treated as stuffy, reactionary, and, if one also adheres to a religion of one's own, as blinkered and blinded by precon-ceived ideas and irrational dogmas. In James's day, however, to suggest that a mystical experience might be induced by drugs was novel, daring, almost shocking. But as in the case of Aldous Huxley and mescalin, James was convinced that under nitrous oxide he had discovered aspects of reality more real than anything we normally experience, real almost to the exclusion of ordinary experience, almost to the point of denying any validity to that experience:

One conclusion [he wrote] was forced upon my mind at that time, and my impression of its truth has ever since remained unshaken. It is that our normal waking consciousness, rational consciousness as we call it, is but one special type of consciousness, whilst all about it, parted from it by the filmiest of screens, there lie potential forms of consciousness entirely different. We may go through life without suspecting their existence; but apply the requisite stimulus, and at

---

[1] R. M. Bucke, *Cosmic Consciousness*, New York, E. P. Dutton, 1966 (23rd ed.), pp. 9–10.

a touch they are there in all their completeness, definite types of mentality which probably somewhere have their field of application and adaptation. No account of the universe in its totality can be final which leaves these other forms of consciousness quite disregarded. . . . Looking back at my own experiences, they all converge towards a kind of insight to which I cannot help ascribing some metaphysical significance. The keynote of it is invariably a reconciliation. It is as if the opposites of the world, whose contradictoriness and conflict make all our difficulties and troubles, were melted into unity.[1]

We know rather more about the effect of drugs today. We know, for instance, that though the reaction James describes is reasonably common and in accord with the general testimony of the nature mystics, horrific and 'diabolical' reactions are also well attested, as James was clear-headed enough himself to realize.[2] If psychedelic drugs attest the existence of a timeless heaven, they none the less point to the existence of a timeless hell. Bucke's luminous certainty that 'the happiness of everyone is in the long run absolutely certain' appears to be but one side of the picture. These states, whether induced by drugs, or arising out of what appears to be pure chance, or bestowed by what is believed to be divine grace, may reveal either pure concord, or discordant concord, or concordant discord, or even discord pure and simple. It may be true that 'the Kingdom of God is within us', yet few of us are ever conscious of it. Many indeed find it easier to believe that beside the kingdom of God, the mystic harmony, there is also within us the sombre kingdom of Satan, the kingdom of discord, anxiety, un-ease.

Bucke's book must be regarded as a pioneer work, and yet it is not wholly outdated. Its assumptions are evolutionary, and his main thesis is that as man has risen in the evolutionary scale, he has passed through four stages:

These four stages are, first, the perceptual mind—the mind made up of percepts or sense impressions; second, the mind made up of these and recepts—the so called receptual mind, or in other words the mind of simple consciousness; third, we have the mind made up of percepts, recepts, and concepts, called sometimes the conceptual mind or otherwise the self conscious mind—the mind of self consciousness; and fourth, and last, we have the intuitional mind—the mind whose highest element is not a recept or a concept but an intuition. This is the mind in which sensation, simple consciousness and self consciousness are supplemented and crowned with cosmic consciousness.[3]

And cosmic consciousness

shows the cosmos to consist not of dead matter governed by unconscious, rigid, and unintending law; it shows it on the contrary as entirely immaterial,

---

[1] William James, *The Varieties of Religious Experience*, London, Longmans, Green & Co., 1919 reprint, p. 388.

[2] Ibid., p. 426.   [3] R. M. Bucke, op. cit., p. 16.

entirely spiritual and entirely alive; it shows that death is an absurdity, that everyone and everything has eternal life; it shows that the universe is God and that God is the universe, and that no evil ever did or ever will enter into it; a great deal of this is, of course, from the point of view of self consciousness, absurd; it is nevertheless undoubtedly true.[1]

This is pantheism with a vengeance—a large body of doctrine, one would have thought, to draw out of a few moments' experience, however ineffable. Now, it is an irritating habit among mystics of all religions and of none that they tend to speak of the infinite 'knowledge' their experience is alleged to produce, whereas, in point of fact, the mystic knows neither more nor less than he knew before. This, however, is not what is meant: what the mystic means is that he sees with the spirit's eye depths of reality that were not accessible to him before. And so Bucke rightly adds:

All this does not mean that when a man has cosmic consciousness he knows everything about the universe. We all know that when at three years of age we acquired self consciousness we did not at once know all about ourselves; we know, on the contrary, that after a great many thousands of years of experience of himself man still to-day knows comparatively little about himself considered even as a self conscious personality. So neither does a man know all about the cosmos merely because he becomes conscious of it. It has taken the race several hundred thousand years to learn a smattering of the science of humanity since its acquisition of self consciousness, so it may take it millions of years to acquire a smattering of the science of God after its acquisition of cosmic consciousness.[2]

With Bucke we enter into the world of evolutionary time: we are already in the world of Teilhard de Chardin, of mysticism made meaningful. But we are still in the sphere of 'natural religion', for Bucke, who in this respect is both modern and Giffordian, will have no truck with the supernatural; for 'cosmic consciousness', he says, 'must not be looked upon as being in any sense supernatural or supranormal—as anything more or less than a natural growth'.[3]

Every writer on mysticism points out, sometimes as if it were for the first time, that though there is considerable variation in the manner in which mystical experience is interpreted, this does not mean that the core of the experience is not for that reason identical. All the mystics agree that what they experience cannot be expressed in words; and if it is expressed in words, then the sharpest paradoxes cannot be avoided. The 'opposites' are not so much abolished as transcended. You cannot say of the cosmic being to which cosmic consciousness gives access, 'It is at rest', without adding also, 'It moves': you cannot say that it is One without adding that

[1] Ibid., pp. 17–18. [2] Ibid., p. 18. [3] Ibid., p. 12.

it is also All. This will strike us in the early Hindu texts, in the classics of both the Taoists and the Confucians in China, and in many latter-day mystics who have broken loose from all religious adherence. There are, of course, divergences from this norm as we shall presently see; for if this can be considered the *philosophia perennis*, it too, like the Christian Church, is bedevilled with heresies. Bucke himself, it seems to me, represents one of these. The content of his 'vision' after all seems to have been rather meagre, and the 'intellectual illumination' he derives from it must there-fore be suspect as an interpretation of the experience. For what did he in fact experience? A light within himself, exultation and joy, 'an intellectual illumination quite impossible to describe' (he promptly proceeds to describe it), a 'lightning-flash' and a 'drop' of 'Brahmic Bliss'. The latter phrase he seems to have derived from Emerson, since there is no evidence at all that he had any deep acquaintance with the Hindu scriptures from which the term derives. So much for the actual experience as he has put it into words. The 'intellectual illumination quite impossible to describe', however, he then proceeds to describe in some detail. The cosmos, he says, is not dead matter but a living presence, the soul is immortal, all things work together for the good of each other, the principle of the world is love, and the happiness of all is in the long run certain. The cosmos, moreover, is entirely immaterial, entirely spiritual, and entirely alive.

We all know that our views on matter have been radically changed during the last century: matter is no longer something stable and palpable but has become indistinguishable from energy. Thus to declare that the cosmos is immaterial is to deny all reality, all vitality to the very stuff of the universe. This is not a mistake that the Indians, much less the Chinese, made in their classic formulations of the cosmos and cosmic consciousness. For them, as we shall see in more detail in subsequent lectures, matter and spirit are rather two sides of one reality, yet it has been a major trend in the mysticism of all religions to reject matter outright and to adhere to spirit only. The reasons for this are plain enough, for the early Buddhists were perfectly right in pointing out and stressing *ad nauseam* that the natural world of matter is transient, and what is transient has no self, no permanent substratum, and that what is thus insubstantial is in the long run un-ease, dis-ease, dis-quiet, and sorrow. Cosmic consciousness, however, takes us out beyond the material world into a state in which Bucke says 'death is an absurdity'. Proust too had said: 'It is understandable that the word death can have no meaning for the man [who has had such an experience]: situated, as he is, outside time, what could he fear for the future?'[1] Such a

---

[1] Marcel Proust, *A la recherche du temps perdu*, ed. Pléiade, vol. iii, p. 873.

state in which time, and therefore death, are transcended is what the Buddhists mean by Nirvāna.

Bucke was a clergyman's son who, however, never believed in his father's religion. He was also a medical man with a firm belief in evolution. In an earlier book, *The Convergent Spirit*, I tried to interpret the Genesis account of the Fall in terms of evolutionary theory so far as I understand it. I tried to show that in these terms the Fall can best be seen as a *felix culpa*, a 'happy fault', as it is called in the liturgy of the Easter Vigil in the Roman Catholic Church, the evolutionary necessity of emerging into self-consciousness out of group consciousness. Whether or not the root sin of mankind, which is self-centredness, could have been avoided, once man had learnt to say 'I', I do not know, since I find it impossible even to imagine man's situation in those twilight days before history began. That self-consciousness did in fact lead to disastrous results human history and the very pathos of our human condition are there to prove. Bucke too sees human evolution as a rise, not a fall, from simple consciousness through self-consciousness to cosmic consciousness. His handling of the theme is strictly in accordance with natural religion and is in some ways still characteristic of modern humanism:

There is a tradition, probably very old [he writes], to the effect that the first man was innocent and happy until he ate of the fruit of the tree of the knowledge of good and evil. That having eaten thereof he became aware that he was naked and was ashamed. Further, that then sin was born into the world, the miserable sense whereof replaced man's former feeling of innocency. That then and not till then man began to labor and to cover his body. Stranger than all (so it seems to us), the story runs, that along with this change or immediately following upon it there came into man's mind the remarkable conviction which has never since left it but which has been kept alive by his own inherent vitality and by the teaching of all true seers, prophets and poets that this accursed thing which has bitten man's heel (laming him, hindering his progress and especially making this halting and painful) should eventually be crushed and subjugated by man himself—by the rising up within him of a Saviour—the Christ.

Man's progenitor was a creature (an animal) walking erect but with simple consciousness merely. He was (as are to-day the animals) incapable of sin ... and equally incapable of shame (at least in the human sense). He had no feeling or knowledge of good and evil. He as yet knew nothing of what we call work and had never labored. From this state he fell (or rose) into self consciousness, his eyes were opened, he knew that he was naked, he felt shame, acquired the sense of sin ..., and learned to do certain things in order to encompass certain ends—that is, he learned to labor.

For weary eons this condition lasted—the sense of sin still haunts his pathway ... he is still ashamed. Where is the deliverer, the Saviour? Who or what?

The Saviour of man is Cosmic Consciousness—in Paul's language—the Christ. The cosmic sense (in whatever mind it appears) crushes the serpent's head— destroys sin, shame, the sense of good and evil as contrasted one with the other, and will annihilate labor, though not human activity.[1]

Now, it is the custom of nature mystics to assume that their own experience, even though it last only for a few moments, must be normative of all such experiences. Bucke goes further and produces a theory of human evolution based on his own intuitional experience on the one hand and his reading of the evolutionary process on the other. In his little prose poem which I have just cited one thing seems to stand out. There is a certain perfection about what he calls the state of simple consciousness and there is a similar though larger perfection about the state of cosmic conscious- ness. In the first state 'man was innocent and happy, . . . incapable of sin or of the feeling of sin and equally incapable of shame. He had no feeling or knowledge of good and evil. He as yet knew nothing of what we call work [in Sanskrit work is called *karma*] and had never labored.' Such was his state before he had risen to self-consciousness and such will be his state when he rises yet further to cosmic consciousness; for cosmic con- sciousness, surprisingly identified with the Christ according to St. Paul, arises to 'destroy sin, shame, the sense of good and evil as contrasted one with the other', and in the end it 'will annihilate labor, though not human activity'. This is indeed a 'memorable fancy', as Blake would say: for it could surely be plausibly maintained that cosmic consciousness is no more than a return to 'simple consciousness', a regress into what Jung calls the collective unconscious rather than a progression forward to something higher and more perfect. For the Old Testament is not alone in postulat- ing a golden age of original innocence in an idealized past: this is even more characteristic of Taoism, and the great Taoist sage, Chuang Tzǔ, sees man's rise into self-consciousness and civilization not as a rise at all, but as a fall from an idyllic past where death was indeed an absurdity because one must needs be self-conscious to be conscious of death at all. So too cosmic consciousness not only brings us the experience of im- mortality but also destroys the sense of sin, shame, and the knowledge of good and evil. Surely this is not progress but regress: it is not an evolution of man to a status of a demigod but rather a devolution to that of a brute.

The great weakness of Bucke's case is that he confuses an experience which he was privileged to receive, and which is probably as old as time and as widely extended as space, with the evolutionary progress of man. Bucke himself realizes this, for he admits that 'given a world peopled with

[1] R. M. Bucke, op. cit., pp. 6–7.

men having Cosmic Consciousness, they would vary both in the way of greater and less intellectual ability, and greater and less moral and spiritual elevation, and also in the way of variety of character, more than would the inhabitants of a planet on the plane of Self Consciousness'.[1] He further weakens his case by maintaining against all the evidence that cosmic consciousness, understood in its widest sense, is a relatively recent phenomenon, and that it necessarily brings with it a corresponding moral elevation, and this despite the fact that, according to him, 'the race whose evolution is most rapid will be the most subject to breakdown', and that 'those functions in any given race whose evolutions are the most rapid will be most subject to breakdown, . . . commonly called insanity'.[2]

Bucke, I repeat, was a pioneer: and he was a rash one. His claim that cosmic consciousness destroys sin, shame, and the sense of good and evil, though it can be substantiated in some cases, is scarcely compatible with his counter-claim that it brings about moral elevation. His further claim that it will 'annihilate labor, though not human activity' is at the best a dream, for there is no evidence at all that it can or will do any such thing. There seems to be no doubt today that it is technology that will annihilate labour, while it is drugs rather than the onward march of evolution which will be called in to promote that cosmic consciousness which is to fill the gap left by the annihilation of labour. For the enemy of tomorrow, if it is not to be total war, is likely to be total boredom. Cosmic consciousness can no doubt destroy the boredom; and, if we are to believe James and Huxley and many others, drugs can unleash cosmic consciousness, though at present a beatific reaction cannot be assured.

All this makes Bucke's vision seem a little dated. And yet there is nothing new about cosmic consciousness: it is as old as the hills and has from the beginning been the very stuff of Hinduism in India and of Taoism in China.

Bucke admits that his hypothesis 'requires that cases of cosmic consciousness should become more numerous from age to age, and not only so but that they should become more perfect, more pronounced. What [he goes on to ask] are the facts?' His answer leaves one speechless. 'Putting aside minor cases', he says, 'such as must have appeared and been forgotten by hundreds in the last few millenniums . . . at least thirteen are so great that they can never fade from human memory—namely: Gautama (that is, the Buddha), Jesus, Paul, Plotinus, Mohammed, Dante, Las Casas, John Yepes [alias St. John of the Cross], Francis Bacon [alias Shakespeare], Jacob Behmen, William Blake, Balzac, Walt Whitman.'[3]

[1] Ibid., p. 66.   [2] Ibid., p. 59.   [3] Ibid., p. 67.

Making all allowances for the fact that, in the nature of the case, a Canadian doctor writing in 1901 could scarcely be expected to have had any deep knowledge of the great world literatures, let alone of the Oriental ones, his list of the thirteen paragons 'so great that they can never fade from human memory' is so bizarre as almost to defy comment. It is of little consequence that he advances the absurd theory that since among his thirteen, only five fall within the first eighteen hundred years of his history of cosmic consciousness, which he dates from Gautama the Buddha, while eight fall within the subsequent six hundred years, this must mean that man is now evolving to a wider diffusion of cosmic consciousness. This is of little consequence, because the thirteen could well be expanded into a hundred of which at least half would precede Dante, and his whole theory would thereby automatically collapse. What is significant, however, is that he should cite these thirteen names as being 'so great that they can never be forgotten', because they, of all others, had reached heights of cosmic consciousness unattained by any others. For what have these people in common? For Bucke, of course, it was cosmic consciousness, and let us repeat his own account of the matter:

This consciousness shows the cosmos to consist not of dead matter governed by unconscious, rigid and unintending law; it shows it on the contrary as entirely immaterial, entirely spiritual and entirely alive; it shows that death is an absurdity, that everyone and everything has eternal life; it shows that the universe is God and that God is the universe, and that no evil ever did or ever will enter into it.

No sane man, surely, can read such a message into the teachings of the great religious teachers Bucke chooses to include in his motley rout. That there are 'mystical' elements in Jesus and Paul few would deny, but how can it honestly or sanely be said of either that they taught or thought that God and the universe were identical? After all, they were both rooted in the Jewish tradition and even Bucke can find little of cosmic consciousness there. The case of Muhammad is even more grotesque. The Koran, however allegorically you may choose to interpret it, does *not* teach that the cosmos is entirely immaterial, that God and the universe are identical, or that no evil did or ever will enter into it. It teaches omnipotence, judgement, compassion, vengeance—and these exercised by a God who utterly transcends the universe which he simply commands into existence saying, ' "Be", and it is'. For the moment we will say nothing of Plotinus, Dante, John of the Cross, Jakob Boehme, or Blake, all of whom are generally regarded as being mystics of some sort. The inclusion in the list of Bartolomé Las Casas, an obscure Spanish priest who accompanied the

Spanish Conquistadors to Cuba, and whose writings do not appear even to have been published, passes all comprehension, as for that matter does that of Shakespeare. But for Dr. Bucke all things are possible: for cosmic consciousness is a protean creature and assumes many names, 'but', he says, 'they have not been understood and recognized'.[1] Hence for more than three hundred years people have been foolish enough learnedly and pedantically to discuss the identity of the enigmatic Mr. W. H. This, however, can never be known, because for those who have eyes to see he is not a human being at all but simply a symbol for cosmic consciousness!

You may think that I have been wasting your time on the case of Dr. Bucke. My only justifications can be that his book has been continuously in print since 1901, that there exists a society devoted to his thought, that these are popular lectures, and, last but certainly not least, that he represents an attitude towards mysticism that is both commonly held and in his case so uncritically extreme as to demolish his own premises by the very absurdity of his conclusions. His self-assurance is amazing, but this is typical of many who claim to have had mystical experiences of the type he describes: they have seen with the eyes of certainty and they *know*. Bucke himself, in his less enthusiastic moments, knew this. After all, he had spent a lifetime in studying mental and nervous diseases and had himself concluded that mental breakdown attacked first the highest and most newly developed faculty, that is, in this case cosmic consciousness.[2] This is not, of course, to suggest that Bucke was mad (he quite plainly was nothing of the kind), but it is to suggest that his shattering experience had warped his rational judgement in the matter of the experience itself. This is borne out by his own judgement of the case. 'The greatest of these men', he writes, 'are in a sense in the position, though on a higher plane, of children who have just become self conscious. These men have just reached a new phase of consciousness—have not yet had time or opportunity to exploit or master this. True, they have reached a higher mental level; but on that level there can and will be comparative wisdom and comparative foolishness, just as there is on the level of simple or of self consciousness.'[3] This seems to me to be a thoroughly rational and cool-headed appraisal of a variety of phenomena that are usually classed as mystical experience; and as Al-Ghazālī, the great Muslim mystical theologian, says in a similar context: 'Reason is God's scale on earth.'[4] According to the same authority,

[1] R. M. Bucke, op. cit., p. 62.
[2] Ibid., pp. 55–9.
[3] Ibid., p. 79.
[4] From the *Mishkāt al-Anwār*; see R. C. Zaehner, *Mysticism Sacred and Profane*, Oxford, 1957, p. 158.

however, what Bucke calls cosmic consciousness and he 'prophecy' or the 'prophetic spirit' is beyond the reach of reason, and reason is all too prone to reject it.[1] So too Bucke, when writing as a doctor, can write very shrewdly about mystical experience. When, however, he speaks under the influence of cosmic consciousness or what Al-Ghazālī would call the 'prophetic spirit', he becomes absurd because his experience, since it was of extremely brief duration and never repeated, gave birth to what he himself called 'comparative foolishness'.

Of the thirteen paragons of cosmic consciousness we now have three outstanding—Gautama the Buddha, Balzac, and Walt Whitman, and even these seem a strangely assorted company. Let us take Balzac first.

It seems strange that the illustrious author of the *Comédie humaine* should figure in such untidy company as one of the thirteen giants of cosmic consciousness. Yet in his case it is not at all absurd, for Balzac not only created the most convincing portrait of an epoch that has ever flowed from the pen of genius, he also wrote a series of studies of a very different nature, the *Études philosophiques*. Among these there are three, *Les Proscrits*, *Louis Lambert*, and *Séraphîta*, which together form what he calls his *roman mystique*, his 'mystical novel'. These, together with that most evocative of short stories, *Jésus-Christ en Flandres*, stand out from the rest of his prodigious output by the total difference of theme. Here Balzac is speaking not of the *grandeurs et misères*, the greatness and misery of human beings as they are (and no one has ever understood human nature in all its degradation and sublimity as well as he), he is speaking of human beings as they should be or perhaps as they really are in eternity. *Les Proscrits*, *Séraphîta*, and *Jésus-Christ en Flandres* are allegories enacted in remote times: they have a timeless quality about them and are in no way connected with the grand design of the *Comédie* itself. *Louis Lambert*, however, it is generally agreed, represents the young Balzac himself, or rather that part of him which was anchored in another world. Here we have the story of Balzac as he might have been, had he allowed cosmic consciousness to get the better of him instead of himself canalizing and utilizing it to produce perhaps the most grandiose literary monument the world has ever seen. Perhaps it was because he was so firmly rooted in the world that is beyond time, multiplicity and passion that he wrote with such superb authority and compassion about the miseries, the passions, and the infinite diversity of the world we know only too well. In his own words he can be said to have belonged to 'the spiritual world which is static in its

---

[1] See W. Montgomery Watt, *The Faith and Practice of Al-Ghazālī*, London, George Allen & Unwin, 1953, p. 64.

essence though mobile in its faculties'[1] and which separates and unites the natural world of man where all is mobile and in flux with God's world where all is static, still, and one. This, it seems to me, is where 'natural religion' starts: it is a half-way house between the 'fixed, still state of Brahman', as the Bhagavad-Gītā (2: 72) puts it, the Nirvāna of the Buddhists, and the pantheistic cosmic consciousness which Bucke experienced and which seems to have been induced by the reading of Whitman who, according to Bucke, expresses it more perfectly than any of his chosen thirteen.

The first of these was Gautama the Buddha, the last Walt Whitman. A strange pair! In their own way, certainly, both of them are mystics, if by a mystic we mean one who has caught a glimpse of eternity. And yet what a colossal difference between the two!

In the case of Buddhism Bucke was at a disadvantage because he had to rely on second-hand interpretations of the early texts; and human nature, whether moving in an atmosphere of cosmic consciousness or merely in one of self-consciousness, being what it is, he was bound to choose the interpretation that was most congenial to his own temperament. The views of early Buddhism, however, as they emerge from the Pāli canon are now well known, and they stand in stark and frigid contrast to the materialistic pantheism of Walt Whitman. In the whole of mystical literature there are no two characters more uncompromisingly opposed. For Whitman there is nothing in the whole wide world he will not embrace and make his own, nothing with which he will not claim kinship, even identity. No wonder Dr. Bucke adored him (the word is scarcely too strong), for what he had experienced for so brief a moment seemed to be confirmed by everything Whitman had written in *Leaves of Grass*.

'This consciousness shows the cosmos to consist not of dead matter', Bucke had written, 'governed by unconscious, rigid and unintending law; it shows it on the contrary as entirely immaterial, entirely spiritual and entirely alive.' The phrasing is unfortunate, for Whitman is above all things the body's worshipper because he can see no distinction between body and soul, spirit and matter: both are equally divine because in the last resort eternal:

> Strange and hard that paradox true I give,
> Objects gross and the unseen soul are one.[2]

Was somebody asking to see the soul?
See, your own shape and countenance, persons, substances, beasts, the trees, the running rivers, the rocks and sands.

---

[1] *Louis Lambert*, ed. Pléiade, Balzac, *La Comédie humaine*, vol. x, p. 452.
[2] Walt Whitman, *A Song of Occupations*, 5.

All hold spiritual joys and afterwards loosen them;
How can the real body ever die and be buried?
Of your real body and any man's or woman's real body,
Item for item it will elude the hands of the corpse-cleaners and pass to the
   fitting spheres,
Carrying what has accrued to it from the moment of birth to the moment of
   death. . . .

Behold, the body includes and is the meaning, the main concern, and includes and is the soul;
Whoever you are, how superb and how divine is your body, or any part of it![1]

Whitman indeed is the pantheist poet of all material things. For if cosmic
consciousness destroys sin and shame and the sense of good and evil,
then Whitman is surely its finest prophet; for he is the unashamed advocate of life lived in its fullness and the source of life, sex. Like Bucke he
is in full reaction against the Puritanism of his times and the whole life-
denying tradition which, with its horror of sexuality, can be traced back
to Augustine of Hippo, the converted Manichee.

In his masterpiece characteristically entitled *Song of Myself* he sings:[2]

I am the poet of the Body and I am the poet of the Soul,
The pleasures of heaven are with me and the pains of hell are with me,
The first I graft and increase upon myself, the latter I translate into a new
   tongue.

I am the poet of the woman the same as the man,
And I say it is as great to be a woman as to be a man,
And I say there is nothing greater than the mother of men.

In the cult of the great God Śiva in India, Śiva and his *Śakti* or creative
power are inseparable. Śiva is the static principle that is forever and
unalterably the same, Śakti the power by and through which all things are
made, cohere, pass away, only to be made again. In mythology Śiva is the
Male, Śakti, personified as a goddess, the Female, the fecund womb from
which all material things proceed. Philosophically considered, however,
the two are inseparable, Śiva subsuming into himself both the male and
the female principles. So too in the *Song of Myself*, in which Whitman
identifies himself with the All (for in 'natural religion' the microcosm, the
individual self, and the macrocosm, the ensouled universe, are seen as one),
soul and body are, in the words of an Indian text, 'close-linked companions',[3] so closely linked indeed as ultimately to be one; and this one,

---

[1] Whitman, *Starting from Paumanok*, 13.
[2] Id., *Song of Myself*, 21.
[3] *Śvetāśvatara* Upanishad 4: 6.

as in all Hindu religion again, is called the 'self', 'myself'. Hence Whitman's poem opens with the words:

I celebrate myself, and sing myself,
And what I assume you shall assume,
For every atom belonging to me as good belongs to you.

I loafe and invite my soul,
I lean and loafe at my ease observing a spear of summer grass.

So speaks the gross body to the subtle soul, inviting it to union. There can, however, be no union if the soul persists in despising the body; and so the body goes on to say:

I believe in you my soul, the other I am must not abase itself to you,
And you must not be abased to the other.[1]

For body and soul are equal, each being an aspect of the same vital principle which, for Whitman, is shamelessly and sinlessly sex. So body summons his eternal lover and says:

Loafe with me on the grass, loose the stop from your throat,
Not words, not music or rhyme I want, not custom or lecture, not even the best,
Only the lull I like, the hum of your valvèd voice.

I mind how once we lay such a transparent summer morning,
How you settled your head athwart my hips and gently turn'd over upon me,
And parted the shirt from my bosom-bone, and plunged your tongue to my bare-stript heart,
And reach'd till you felt my beard, and reach'd till you held my feet.

Swiftly arose and spread around me the peace and knowledge that pass all the argument of the earth,
And I know that the hand of God is the promise of my own,
And I know that the spirit of God is the brother of my own,
And that all the men ever born are also my brothers, and the women my sisters and lovers.

As in the mystical poetry of the Persians the imagery is so frankly sexual that one wonders whether it is imagery at all. We know that in the case of the Persian Sūfīs what started as the mystical love of God sometimes degenerated into something all too human, the love of a human boy.[2] This was a development of which the orthodox did not approve, yet even the

[1] Whitman, *Song of Myself*, 5.
[2] See R. C. Zaehner, *Hindu and Muslim Mysticism*, London, Athlone Press, 1960, p. 179.

great Al-Ghazālī conceded that the contemplation of youthful male beauty
was a legitimate first step on the way to the contemplation of the divine.[1]
In Whitman's case sex *is* divine, and by sex he means not the so-called
Hieros Gamos or 'sacred marriage' of the soul with God, the constant
theme of the Christian mystics to which we shall return, but the physical
act in all its sacred squalor:

> Give me now libidinous joys only,
> Give me the drench of my passions, give me life coarse and rank,
> To-day I go consort with Nature's darlings, to-night too,
> I am for those who believe in loose delights, I share the midnight orgies of
> young men,
> I dance with the dancers and drink with the drinkers,
> The echoes ring with our indecent calls, I pick out some low person for my
> dearest friend,
> He shall be lawless, rude, illiterate, he shall be one condemned by others for
> deeds done,
> I will play a part no longer, why should I exile myself from my companions?[2]

The symbol of the great Hindu God, Śiva, is the *lingam* or phallus, and
for his devotees it is just this that proves that he is the true God, for the
whole universe coheres through the conjunction and reconciliation of the
opposites, and the most fundamental of all the pairs of opposites is that of
male and female, the *yang* and *yin* of the Chinese. Śiva's *lingam* is the
symbol of the eternal which, unchanging itself, never ceases to generate
life. But whereas in the cult of Śiva the goal of life is to escape from merely
physical life, to return from time to eternity, for Whitman eternity and the
world of time are inseparable: eternity is bodily activity and bodily joys
transported into a timeless sphere, something not unlike the Muhammadan
heaven as depicted in the Koran. It is unity in diversity, the 'true knowledge' as defined by the Bhagavad-Gītā:

> That [kind of] of knowledge by which one sees
> One mode of being, changeless, undivided
> In all contingent beings, divided [as they are],
> Is Goodness' [knowledge]. Be sure of this.[3]

In other words, what unites is good, and what is good is creative. In
the words of Teilhard de Chardin, 'Creation comes about by uniting; and
true union can only be achieved by creating: these two propositions are

---

[1] See R. C. Zaehner, *Hindu and Muslim Mysticism*, London, Athlone Press, 1960, p. 179.
[2] Whitman, *Children of Adam*, 'Native Moments'.
[3] Bhagavad-Gītā 18: 20

correlative.'[1] For Whitman *pro*creation comes about by uniting. This may seem a truism; but what he means and what his most frankly sexual poems express is that the sexual act not only symbolizes the union of the opposites and the harmony of the spheres but in a sense *is* them:

A woman waits for me, she contains all, nothing is lacking,
Yet all were lacking if sex were lacking, or if the moisture of the right man were lacking.
Sex contains all, bodies, souls,
Meanings, proofs, purities, delicacies, results, promulgations,
Songs, commands, health, pride, the maternal mystery, the seminal milk,
All hopes, benefactions, bestowals, all the passions, loves, beauties, delights of the earth,
All the governments, judges, gods, follow'd persons of the earth,
These are contain'd in sex as parts of itself and justifications of itself.[2]

Sex unites, and what unites is creative and therefore good:

Urge and urge and urge,
Always the procreant urge of the world.
Out of the dimness opposite equals advance, always substance and increase, always sex,
Always a knit of identity, always distinction, always a breed of life.[3]

Sex is the source of life, even of immortality, for death itself is the final union, the sting of passion that lasts for ever:

O hymen! O hymenee! why do you tantalize me thus?
O why sting me for a swift moment only?
Why can you not continue? O why do you now cease?
Is it because if you continued beyond the swift moment you would soon certainly kill me?[4]

Whitman, like all pantheists, identifies himself with the whole wide universe in all its diversity, but this does not mean that by doing so he excludes personal relationships, for sex and death are both the most vivid of personal relationships, each uniting him with the ideal lover from eternity without beginning to eternity without end:

Afar down I see the huge first Nothing, I know I was even there,
I waited unseen and always, and slept through the lethargic mist,
And took my time, and took no hurt from the fetid carbon.

Long was I hugg'd close—long and long.[5]

---

[1] Teilhard de Chardin, *Écrits du temps de la guerre*, Paris, Grasset, 1965, p. 178.
[2] Whitman, *Children of Adam*, 'A Woman waits for me'.
[3] Id., *Song of Myself*, 3.   [4] Id., *Children of Adam*, 'O Hymen! O Hymenee!'
[5] Id., *Song of Myself*, 44.

So Whitman sees himself as existing from the beginning of time, and yet he remains eternally young:

> O span of youth! ever-push'd elasticity!
> O manhood, balanced, florid and full.
> My lovers suffocate me,
> Crowding my lips, thick in the pores of my skin,
> Jostling me through streets and public halls, coming naked to me at night, . . .
> Noiselessly passing handfuls out of their hearts and giving them to be mine.[1]

All this is good, and Whitman is perpetually returning to the theme of rank physical love because in sex spirit and matter are indissolubly linked, merging into one, making whole and therefore holy. And so he passes on the final and abiding love-affair, death. Though 'there is no stoppage and never can be stoppage',

> My rendezvous is appointed, it is certain,
> The Lord will be there and wait till I come on perfect terms,
> The great Camerado, the lover true for whom I pine will be there.[1]

If by a mystic we mean one who has tasted of an eternal mode of being, then Whitman was certainly a mystic, but he is essentially a mystic of the earth, of Nature, and of matter:

> I accept Reality and dare not question it,
> Materialism first and last imbuing.[2]

He is a mystic in revolt against the cult of pure spirituality, and so he does not hesitate to say that *Leaves of Grass* 'is avowedly the song of Sex and Amativeness, and even Animality',[3] for he sees and knows that there is a mysticism of the body just as much as there is a mysticism of the soul, of matter as well as of spirit. He is—

> Walt Whitman, a kosmos, of Manhattan the son,
> Turbulent, fleshy, sensual, eating, drinking and breeding.[4]

With cosmic consciousness all things are possible: the fleshy man of Manhattan feels himself coterminous with the cosmos and indwells all material things:

> I find I incorporate gneiss, coal, long-threaded moss, fruits, grains, esculent roots,
> And am stucco'd with quadrupeds and birds all over.[5]

[1] Whitman, *Song of Myself*, 45.   [2] Ibid., 23.
[3] Id., *A Backward Glance* in *Walt Whitman*, London, Nonesuch Press, 1938, p. 871.
[4] Id., *Song of Myself*, 24.   [5] Ibid., 31.

This feeling of identity he has with human beings too in all their animality, their sufferings which he transmutes into joy, and their uncouth pleasures, but he most emphatically does not identify himself with what we usually call civilization, and in this he allies himself with the equally 'animal' mysticism of the Taoists. Chuang Tzŭ, the Taoist sage, might well have written the following lines:

> I think I could turn and live with the animals, they're so placid and self-contain'd,
> I stand and look at them long and long.

> They do not sweat and whine about their condition,
> They do not lie awake in the dark and weep for their sins,
> They do not make me sick discussing their duty to God,
> Not one is dissatisfied, not one is demented with the mania of owning things,
> Not one kneels to another, nor to his kind that lived thousands of years ago,
> Not one is respectable or unhappy over the whole earth.[1]

This is an almost primitive hankering for that state of original innocence man is supposed to have possessed before he became conscious as an individual.

Matter in itself is neither good nor evil, and so he is 'not the poet of goodness only, I do not decline to be the poet of wickedness also':[2]

> I make the poem of evil also, I commemorate that part also,
> I am myself just as much evil as good, and my nation is.[3]

But, he immediately adds, 'there is in fact no evil'; for where self-consciousness is transcended nothing can be evil, for everything is in its place. Here, whether it be in what Bucke calls 'simple consciousness' or in 'cosmic consciousness', Whitman finds something that 'is not chaos or death—it is form, union, plan—it is eternal life—it is Happiness'. Death, however, for Whitman does not mean annihilation or disintegration into chaos; rather it is a new form of life in a new form of body:

> Death is beautiful from you, (what indeed is finally beautiful except death and love?)
> O I think it is not for life I am chanting here my chant of lovers, I think it must be for death,
> For how calm, how solemn it grows to ascend to the atmosphere of lovers,
> Death or life I am then indifferent, my soul declines to prefer,
> (I am not sure but the high soul of lovers welcomes death most.)[4]

[1] Ibid. 32. [2] Ibid., 22.
[3] *Starting from Paumanok*, 7. [4] Id., *Calamus*, 'Scented Herbage of my Breast'.

Or, sometimes, it is an ascent to the steady centre of the vast and swirling universe of sex—the sleep that follows the transports of love, the sleep that prolongs that love for ever:

> I ascend from the moon, I ascend from the night,
> I perceive that the ghastly glimmer is noonday sunbeams reflected,
> And debouch to the steady and central from the offspring great or small.

> There is that in me—I do not know what it is—but I know it is in me. [He is referring to Bucke's cosmic consciousness.]

> Wrench'd and sweaty—calm and cool then my body becomes,
> I sleep—I sleep long.[1]

In death the body is not annihilated but transformed, and this is

> The real life of my senses and flesh transcending my senses and flesh,
> My body done with materials, my sight done with my material eyes,
> Proved to me this day beyond cavil that it is not my material eyes which finally see,
> Nor my material body which finally loves, walks, laughs, shouts, embraces, procreates.[2]

> For not life's joys alone I sing, repeating—the joy of death!
> The beautiful touch of Death, soothing and benumbing a few moments, for reasons,
> Myself discharging my excrementious body to be burn'd, or render'd to powder, or buried,
> My real body doubtless left to me for other spheres,
> My voided body nothing more to me, returning to the purifications, further offices, eternal uses of the earth.[3]

For a man who has transcended space and time, who has surmounted death and feels his identity with all living and existent things, for whom body, soul, and cosmos are his own self ('I celebrate myself, and sing myself'[4]), for such a man all institutional religion must be meaningless, 'they were alive and did the work of their days'. These so-called revelations, taken on trust, are worth no more than the most ordinary things of life lived in the raw:

> Not objecting to special revelations, considering a curl of smoke or a hair on the back of my hand just as curious as any revelation,
> Lads ahold of fire-engines and hook-and-ladder ropes no less to me than the gods of the antique wars.[5]

---

[1] Whitman, *Song of Myself*, 49–50.
[2] Id., *A Song of Joys*, Nonesuch, p. 167.   [3] Ibid., p. 169.
[4] Id., *Song of Myself*, 1.   [5] Ibid., 41.

His is a faith that embraces all others because it comprises and experiences them all. He is not opposed to institutional religion, but regards
it as enshrining at most a mere fragment of truth. *His* religion is universal
because it is always and everywhere valid and comprises all things:

> I do not despise you priests, all time, the world over,
> My faith is the greatest of faiths and the least of faiths,
> Enclosing worship ancient and modern and all between ancient and modern.[1]

Such, then, is the mysticism of Walt Whitman, one mysticism among
many. This variety of mystical experience I shall be discussing in some
detail later, but I must to some extent anticipate now. To my way of
thinking there are three types of mystical experience. First, there is nature
mysticism, of which Whitman is an almost perfect example: it sees the
human self as encompassing all Nature, the subjective 'I' is merged into
the cosmic All, and all distinction between subject and object seems to be
obliterated. Secondly, there is the mysticism of 'isolation'—the isolation of
the eternal soul from all that has its being in space and time, 'to isolate
eternity from origination'[2] as Al-Junayd, the tenth-century Muslim
mystic, puts it. Lastly, there is the mysticism of the love of God in an
ecstasy of eternal love. Whitman clearly belongs to the first class; and it
seems to be a fact that nature mystics, as a result of their own self-authenti-
cating experience, come to regard all organized religion as being simply a
way, and not a very satisfactory one at that, of attaining the mystical
state they have themselves achieved and in which they see themselves as
eternally merged in the All. Whitman is an extremist in that he tends to see
it the other way round: mystical happiness is 'the efflux of the soul'[3]—his
soul. Hence each must find it for himself:

> No one can acquire for another—not one,
> Not one can grow for another—not one. . . .
>
> And no man understands any greatness or goodness but his own.[4]

I have spoken of Whitman at some length because he is, if anyone, the
mystic of matter; for it is in matter that he finds a 'discordant concord' and
a 'concordant discord'. And Marx himself tells us that 'the first and most
important of the inherent qualities of *matter* is *motion*, not only *mechanical*
and *mathematical* movement, but still more *impulse, vital life-spirit,
tension*, or, to use Jacob Boehme's expression, the *throes* of matter'.[5]

[1] Ibid., 43.   [2] See R. C. Zaehner, *Hindu and Muslim Mysticism*, p. 135.
[3] Whitman, *Song of the Open Road*, 8.   [4] Id., *A Song of the Rolling Earth*, 2.
[5] K. Marx and F. Engels, *The Holy Family*, Moscow, 1956, p. 172.

Whitman is also the last of Bucke's thirteen paragons of whom Gautama
the Buddha is the first. The contrast between the two could scarcely be
greater. Whitman seeks to comprise all existing beings within himself, to
realize unity in diversity and diversity in unity in and through material
things. The Buddha rejects the whole world of matter out of hand; it is
impermanent, it has no substance, no identity, no self: it is subject to
origination and decay, and there can be no salvation in it or through it.
Sex as the source of becoming is the arch-enemy of eternal peace: the flesh
is the devil. All attachment to the things of this world, all love of them,
enslaves. Hence there is only one virtue necessary to salvation—detachment
and withdrawal from both world and cosmos. Only so can you reach
Nirvāna, the ultimate peace beyond space and time. Here there is eternal
rest, for all becoming will have been brought to an end, all activity stilled.
Here there is no further contact with the world, here there is only disgust
at the world, the extinction of the flame of passion and attachment to earthly things. You cannot by any stretch of the meaning of words call this
'cosmic consciousness', because the cosmos, both the 'microcosmos', man,
and the 'macrocosmos', the universe, is utterly and completely transcended, left behind, cast off with a fine disgust.

This is a deep and fundamental cleavage within the worldwide mystical
tradition itself. Both types are represented in all religions; to say that *this*
is simply a matter of interpretation is manifestly untrue, for it cannot be
claimed that either Whitman or the Buddha was in any way conditioned
by the particular religious environment into which he was born. Both
are *original* geniuses reacting against the dominant religious trend of their
day, the Buddha against the 'Whitmanism' of the Brāhmans, Whitman
against the world-denying puritanism of his day. Both considered that they
had received an 'enlightenment' and an 'awakening' which was self-
authenticating. Both were convinced that theirs was a truer vision of
reality than was to be found in the religions of their day. And yet, if words
have only so much as a symbolic meaning, their messages flatly contradict
each other. For Whitman the world of matter, of flesh and blood and sex,
is as divine as is the soul, because in a sense it *is* the soul: for the Buddha
the same world, in its miserable impermanence, is hateful and an object of
contempt, and the only sensible thing to do is to say goodbye to it for ever.
To proclaim this parting of the ways and to show just how this world of
wretched living and wretched dying could be transcended was the Buddha's
compassionate mission to man.

IV

SPIRIT AND MATTER

THE sixth century B.C. was a time of intense religious ferment in India. It witnessed the birth of Buddhism and the rebirth of Jainism, the two great heretical movements that separated themselves from the main stream of orthodox Brahmanism, while within Brahmanism itself it was probably during this period that the Upanishads, those speculative treatises which constitute the end of the Veda, as the Hindu scriptural canon is called, were taking shape. Orthodox Brahmanism had itself developed out of all recognition since the time of the Rig-Veda, the earliest scripture of the Aryan invaders of India which can be vaguely dated somewhere towards the end of the second millennium B.C.

These Aryan invaders were, of course, of Indo-European or 'Aryan' stock, and their language, Sanskrit, belongs to the Indo-European group which includes almost all the European languages whether derived from Latin or Greek or not. Their mythology and their religion too are recognizably akin to the mythologies of Greece and Rome and those of the Germanic peoples. Their religion was frankly polytheistic, as was the religion of Homeric Greece, but whereas in Greece one god, Zeus, in due course emerged as the supreme deity on whom all the rest depended, no such development can be observed in India. On the contrary, the gods, never so sharply defined or mythologically developed as their opposite numbers in Greece, tended to associate freely together, gradually losing their individual characteristics and finally coming to be identified with each other.

In what seem to be the earliest parts of the Rig-Veda the various gods have a distinct personality: they have their own characteristic weapons, associations, and associates. Some of them are clearly personifications of natural phenomena—*Ushas*, the dawn, *Dyāvā-prithivī*, heaven and earth, *Agni*, the fire, and so on. Others combine naturalistic characteristics with a social function. Indra, for instance, the most prominent god in the Rig-Veda, is both a storm-god and the god of battles who leads the Aryan warriors in their struggle to crush the resistance of the indigenous population. Varuna is both the impassive lord of the starry heavens and the guardian of cosmic law and 'magic power' (*māyā*, a word that was to

assume a tremendous importance in later Hinduism)—a power by which
he rules the universe in a mysterious way. Slowly, however, the gods tend
to lose their individuality, and wholesale identifications take place. In
Rig-Veda 2: 1: 3, for instance, Agni is successively identified with Indra,
Vishnu (a god who was later to assume a tremendous importance), with
Brahmanaspati, the divine priest, with Varuna and his associates, with
Tvashtri, the creator, with Rudra, the precursor of the great god Śiva, and
the Maruts, gods of the storm, with Savitri, a sun-god, and a host of others.
This 'kathenotheistic' tendency, as Max Müller called it, is summed up
in Rig-Veda 1: 164: 46 where we read: 'They call [the ultimate reality]
Indra, Mitra, Varuna, Agni, or again it is called the celestial bird Garut-
mat. What is but one the wise call [by] manifold names. They call it Agni,
Yama, Mātariśvan.'

As the gods lost their individuality, they also lost their power. Power was
transferred from them to the apparatus of sacrifice. This became all-
important, for the sacrifice (which was of enormous complexity) came to
have efficacy of itself: it compelled the gods to accede to the will of man.
Thus, through the sacrifice, man himself had become a god: given the
correct performance of the ritual he could become the master of Nature.
This was not disputed. But already Indian man was beginning to feel
deeper aspirations, deeper dissatisfactions. What was the use of all the
good things that sacrifice was believed to procure, what was the use of
riches, an abundance of sons, or a long life, if life itself must end? Man is
miserable because he must die, and 'for all his toil, his toil under the sun,
what does he gain by it'?[1] For, as the Psalmist says:

> Our days dwindle under your wrath,
> our lives are over in a breath
> —our life lasts for seventy years,
> eighty with good health,
>
> but they add up to anxiety and trouble—
> over in a trice, and then we are gone.[2]

So too in India man became increasingly dissatisfied with the human
condition as such. He did not, indeed, doubt that there was life of some
sort beyond the grave, but this, at best, could only be a prolongation of
earthly life in another form; and this too the correct performance of the
sacrifice could procure. But this was no longer enough: the search for the
Absolute had begun in India: this alone was the 'pearl of great price',
the 'hoard of gold hidden beneath a field',[3] that could alone bring total

---

[1] Ecclesiastes 1: 3.   [2] Psalm 90: 9–10.   [3] *Chāndogya* Upanishad 8: 3: 1.

satisfaction to the human heart. Sacrifice had been tried, but in the one
thing that mattered it had been found wanting:

> 'Come, come!' the oblations say, full-glorious,
> Carrying the sacrificial priest on the sun's [bright] rays,
> Addressing him with pleasing speech and praising him:
> 'This is the Brahman-world, pure and well made for you.'

> *But* unstable are these barks, the eighteenfold,
> In the form of sacrifice,
> In which an inferior [ritual] act is uttered:
> Deluded men who hail it as the best
> Return again to old age and death.

> Self-wise, puffed up with learning,
> Passing their days in the midst of ignorance,
> They wander, the fools, doing themselves much hurt,
> Like blind men guided by the blind.[1]

To the Vedic Indian it seemed not so much that the sacrifice had failed;
it was simply that the *goal* of sacrifice had proved to be inadequate. It
fell short of the ultimate, of the Absolute, and this, nothing less, was what
he now demanded. Neither the good things of this world nor the joys of
paradise which the sacrifice could infallibly supply could satisfy him, for
both must come to an end, and the wretched, futile business of living would
have to start all over again:

> Thinking that sacrifice and merit are the highest good,
> Deluded men, they nothing better know:
> On heaven's vault they'll first enjoy their works well done
> But then come back to this world—or to another—worse![2]

What had caused this intense dissatisfaction with life in a people that had
once revelled in the good things of this world and avidly sought out its joys?
The answer is simple. Between the age of the Rig-Veda and that of the
Upanishads the belief in the transmigration of souls had struck deep roots
in the Indian mind. How and why this happened we do not know; but the
common-sense explanation would seem to be that his belief was firmly
rooted in the religion of the aboriginal population and that the Aryan
invaders had in the course of time succumbed to it. In the earlier Upanishads the belief is still in the process of development. What survives a man
at death? a sage asks; for death is a dispersion in which, according to the
theories of sympathetic magic current at the time, a man's faculties are
reabsorbed into the cosmic entities from which they had in the first

---

[1] *Mundaka* Upanishad 1: 2: 6–8.   [2] Ibid. 1: 2: 10.

instance emerged—the voice entering the fire, the breath the wind, the eye the sun, mind the moon, and so on. What is left of a 'person' then? Does anything that can be called personality remain, and if so, of what is it made up? The great sage, Yājñavālkya, knew the answer, but as yet it was a secret; so he takes his friend by the hand and draws him apart:

'We two alone will know about this. It is not for us [to speak of this] in public.'
Together they went away and conversed together. What they were discussing was works (*karma*): what they were praising was works. By good works a man becomes holy, by evil [works] evil.[1]

In other words a man's 'personality' is the sum total of the works he performs. This is what survives the dissolution of the body and conditions man's future existence, whether this be in a new incarnation on earth or in one of many heavens and hells. The doctrine had, however, not yet been formulated with any clarity; so the same Upanishad goes on to speak more clearly:

As a caterpillar, drawing near to the tip of a blade of grass, prepares its next step and draws itself up towards it, so does this self, striking the body aside and dispelling ignorance, prepare its next step and draw itself up [for the plunge into a new life in a new body].[2]

Or again:

As a goldsmith, making use of the material of a [golden] object, forges another new and more beautiful form, so does this self, striking the body aside and dispelling ignorance, devise another new and more beautiful form—be it [the form] of one of the ancestors or of a Gandharva or of a god or of one in the Prajāpati[-world] or of one in the Brahman[-world] or of any other being.[3]

Hindus have often shown impatience at the excessive dogmatism of Christianity: they have reproached the Christians for putting blind faith in a series of credal propositions which are unprovable or irrelevant. And yet Hinduism, from the time of the Upanishads on, and Buddhism and Jainism, from their very beginnings until this day, have accepted not so much as an article of faith as a matter of fact the theory of the transmigration of souls; and it is this belief, which for them is a certainty, that conditions their approach to salvation, by which I understand the final goal and good of man.

It obviously makes a tremendous difference what one believes about death. If death is final, if it is simply the stoppage of the process of change and therefore of life as we know it, then surely there is nothing to worry

---

[1] *Brihadāranyaka* Upanishad 3: 2: 13.   [2] Ibid. 4: 4: 3.   [3] Ibid. 4: 4: 4.

about. All that matters is that life, so long as it lasts, should be as pleasant as possible, and any sensible man will see to it that it is. Yet so incurably religious an animal does man appear to be that he has rarely been able to accept the fact of death as final. This would be comprehensible if he had always sought to comfort himself with visions of a fuller life in another world. In fact he has rarely done this. For the Mesopotamians, for instance, the after-life was far worse than the mere cessation of life. And so in the *Epic of Gilgamesh* the hero's wild friend, Enkidu, has a vision of the underworld when he is about to die. It terrifies him:

I stood alone before an awful being [he tells his anxious friend]; his face was sombre like the black bird of the storm. He fell upon me with the talons of an eagle and he held me fast, pinioned me with his claw, till I smothered; then he transformed me so that my arms became wings covered with feathers. He turned his stare towards me, and he led me away to the palace of Irkalla, the Queen of Darkness, to the house from which none who enters ever returns, down the road from which there is no coming back. There is the house whose people sit in darkness; dust is their food and clay their meat. They are clothed like birds with wings for covering, they see no light, they sit in darkness.[1]

This gloomy picture of the after-life was inherited both by the Jews of the Old Testament and by the Homeric Greeks. For the Jews all men, whether good or evil, went down to the pit of Sheol where 'there is neither achievement, nor planning, nor knowledge, nor wisdom'.[2] Only at a very late stage were they to learn a doctrine of heaven and hell from the Zoroastrians. So too for the Greeks, life after death was a shadow-play; all that was left was like a shadow or a dream,[3] and the shade of the great Achilles reproaches Odysseus for trying to sugar the bitter pill and tells him bluntly that to live as even the hireling of a poor farmer is better than to rule over the kingdom of the dead.[4]

If one lives but once, one will cling to the vigour and joy of life, for there is no certainty of what lies beyond the grave. The Mesopotamians, whom both the Jews and Greeks followed in this, foresaw nothing but misery and darkness, while the Egyptians and Zoroastrians assumed that there was indeed an after-life and that its quality was pre-conditioned by the quality of a man's moral life on earth. This belief was shared by the Vedic Indians.

Things, however, do not look quite the same when once a belief in reincarnation has become firmly established in the minds of men. *Requiem aeternam dona eis, Domine*: 'Give them eternal rest, O Lord' is what

---

[1] *The Epic of Gilgamesh*, tr. N. K. Sandars, Penguin Books, 1960, p. 89.
[2] Ecclesiastes 9: 10.   [3] *Odyssey* 11. 207.   [4] Ibid. 11. 488–91.

Catholics ask for the souls of their dead: and this is a universal longing of the human spirit, for man has never believed in the finality of death. If death really were the end, this would be eternal rest and eternal peace, the 'cessation of becoming', as the Buddhists put it. This condition or, perhaps we should say, this absence of condition, which the materialist takes for granted and which he views with an irrational horror and anguish, the Mesopotamians would have welcomed with joy: and it is at least arguable that the Buddhist Nirvāna means nothing less than death, final and complete, the final extinction of the flame of life.

Eastern religions, and particularly Indian religions, are not easy to understand, and in order to understand them at all you must try to see through their eyes: you have to try to understand what 'life everlasting' for which Christians pray can possibly mean to *them*. Unfortunately they take it for granted, and it appals them. The process of transmigration has no beginning and, unless there are in the universe secrets not normally accessible to the human mind, it can have no end either. The prospect of endless birth, endless decline, endless death, of endless rebirth, re-decline, and re-death repeated for unending ages in the same monotonous cycle is daunting indeed; and it was precisely this that appalled the Buddha and impelled him to seek a solution to this ghastly problem of life lived for ever and an escape from this world where nothing is stable, nothing abiding, and to adopt a life of a religious mendicant through which he hoped, simply by giving up the things of this world, to escape from its bondage. This was for him a strictly practical affair: there must be a *way*, he thought, which led to release, and this way, he felt, was not to be found by speculation: it could only be found by actual experience. But how to promote the experience, that was the question.

The Buddha lived in the sixth century B.C., a time of great philosophical activity. To judge from the Pāli canon metaphysics was all the rage. Is the self eternal or not? Is the world eternal or not? Is it infinitely extended or not? Is there another world apart from the one we know? Do good and evil produce good and evil fruits or do they not? Does a Buddha, after he has won Enlightenment, continue to exist after death or not? Is the world due to chance? Does consciousness continue after death? If so, does the conscious self have form or not? It is happy or unhappy? Or is it completely annihilated?

All such speculations, according to the Buddha, were futile, even though they may be based on experience. Mystical experience as described in the Upanishads was itself futile too, for it is all ultimately based on sense-perception, on contact with the outside world: this must be ruthlessly suppressed, for salvation does not consist in cosmic consciousness, but in excluding the cosmos and all its works *from* consciousness.[1] It is Nirvāna, the 'blowing out' of the flame of desire, disgust with the world, total detachment, the cessation of becoming, the stilling of passion, wisdom, an awakening to an abiding reality, seeing things as they really are.[2] Above all it is 'release' (*vimutti*)—release from passion and all sense of self, immortality in the sense that time is transcended and rebirth as well as death are thereby abolished. It is the end of death, but it is also the end of life. The most common description of this state is that 'there is something set free in what is free' (*vimuttasmiṁ vimuttam*). It is not cosmic consciousness, for cosmic consciousness sees the human self as in some way identical with the whole universe; and this view is emphatically and specifically denied.[3] It is in fact the very opposite, for it is the total exclusion of the whole cosmos from the liberated consciousness—and naturally so since the cosmos is composed of matter, and the principle of matter, as Marx saw, is movement: in Nirvāna there is no movement. Nirvāna is a reaction against and a curt dismissal of the whole idea of cosmic consciousness.

The Brahmanical thought against which the Buddha was reacting was deeply concerned with consciousness and the possible transformation of self-consciousness into cosmic consciousness. This is in part due to a tendency, which appears even in the earliest parts of the Veda and is strongly developed in the sacrificial texts called the *Brāhmaṇas*, to identify everything with more or less everything else. 'A very striking feature of these works', Franklin Edgerton rightly pointed out, 'is their passion for identification of one thing with another, on the slenderest possible basis; indeed, often on no basis at all that we can discover. The purpose was strictly practical; more specifically, magical. It was to get results by setting cosmic forces in motion. To this end a cosmic force was said to "be" this or that other thing, which other thing we can control. . . . It required only a slight extension of this to arrive at the notion that if we can only "know" the one principle of the whole universe, the one which is to be *identified* with "all", with everything that is, we shall then control all, and be able to deal with the universe as we please.'[4] Thus to take but one example among scores, man himself is identified with the year[5] and each part of him corresponds to a part of the year. This tendency the Upanishads continue, and in the earliest of them this passion for identification passes all bounds. Thus

[1] *Digha Nikāya* i. 1. 1–46.
[2] *Majjhima Nikāya* i. 165, 485; ii. 82; iii. 113, etc.   [3] Ibid. i. 135.
[4] Franklin Edgerton, *The Beginnings of Indian Philosophy*, London, George Allen & Unwin, 1965, pp. 21–2.
[5] *Śatapatha* Brāhmana 12: 3: 2.

the longest and probably the earliest of them starts with the following words (and how many Western readers must have been put off by this apparent gibberish!):

> The dawn is the head of the sacrificial horse; the sun is its eye, the wind its breath, universal fire its mouth. The year is the self of the sacrificial horse, the sky its back, the atmosphere its belly, the earth the underside of its belly, the cardinal points of the compass its flanks, the intermediate points its ribs, the seasons its limbs, the months and half-months its joints, day and night its feet, the stars its bones, the clouds its flesh. Sand is the food in its stomach, rivers are its entrails, the mountains its liver and lungs, plants and trees its hair. The east is its fore part, the west its hind part. When it yawns, then there is lightning. When it shakes itself, then there is thunder. When it urinates, then it rains.[1]

The idea behind these fantastic identifications is that the sacrificer, by gaining control of the sacrificial horse, thereby gains control of the whole cosmic process, and by *knowing* this process he *becomes* it. By knowing these magical correspondences in detail he comes to know the total correspondence of the sacrifice with the sum total of the universe. And since the only proper sacrifice is man himself—the 'male person' (*purusha*) who is the victim of the cosmic sacrifice in Rig-Veda 10: 90—man comes to see himself as identical with the 'All'.

Ātman is *Brahman*; and *Brahman* is *Ātman*. This, it is generally conceded, is the main purport and teaching of the Upanishads, those strange speculative treatises that bring the Vedic canon to an end. The word *ātman*, the original meaning of which is still uncertain, very soon came to be used as a reflexive pronoun, and so it is very properly translated as 'self', either the self of an individual or the Self of the entire universe. *Brahman* seems originally to have meant 'sacred word' or 'sacred power'; and so it comes to mean the sacred in general, that is to say, the eternal and timeless reality that sustains the transient universe.

This search for the One Reality behind and beyond all phenomenal existence had preoccupied the ancient Indian sages from a very early period; and the first metaphysical question they asked was: 'How did the universe come into existence?' On this subject there are a series of hymns in the tenth and last book of the Rig-Veda which set the tone for all later speculation. In Rig-Veda 10: 129 the whole subject is swathed in mystery, and various answers are tentatively put forward, only to be immediately questioned:

> Then neither Being nor Not-being was,
> Nor atmosphere, nor firmament, nor what is beyond.

[1] *Brihadāranyaka* Upanishad 1: 1: 1.

What did it encompass? Where? In whose protection?
What was water, the deep unfathomable?

Neither death nor immortality was there then,
   No sign of night or day.
That One breathed, windless, by its own energy:
   Nought else existed then.

In the beginning was darkness swathed in darkness;
All this was but unmanifested water.
Whatever was, that One, coming into being,
   Hidden by the void,
Was generated by the power of heat.

In the beginning this [One] evolved,
Became desire, first seed of mind.
Wise seers, searching within their hearts,
Found the bond of Being in Not-being.

Their cord was extended athwart:
Was there a below? Was there an above?
Casters of seed there were, and powers;
Beneath was energy, above was impulse.

Who knows truly? Who can here declare it?
Whence it was born, whence is this emanation.
By the emanation of this the gods
   Only later [came to be].
Who then knows whence it has arisen?

Whence this emanation has arisen,
Whether [God] disposed it, or whether he did not—
Only he who is its overseer in highest heaven knows.
[He only knows,] or perhaps he does not know.

St. Paul might well have had the ancient Hindus in mind when he said
that God created the whole human race 'that all nations might seek the
deity and, by feeling their way towards him, succeed in finding him'.[1]
Here, if anywhere, men were groping their way towards God and, beautifully obscure though the hymn is, one thing at least emerges: even in
a chaos there is and must be a principle of unity. 'That One breathed,
windless, by its own energy.' We are immediately reminded of the opening
words of Genesis: 'Now the earth was a formless void, there was darkness
over the deep, and God's spirit hovered over the water.' The symbolism is
the same—water and darkness representing chaos, the spirit, the 'breathing'
One, representing emergent life. In Genesis the spirit is God's spirit; in the

---

[1] Acts 17: 27.

Rig-Vedic hymn God is the 'overseer in highest heaven' who may be responsible for creation or not. '[He only knows,] or perhaps he does not know.'

The leading ideas of this hymn can be briefly summarized. The manifold cosmos evolves from a unitive principle already present in chaotic and unorganized matter. Matter and spirit are indissolubly linked. Over above the world process there is God who is 'overseer in highest heaven'. This last idea was to lose ground in the Upanishadic period and, as we shall see, it was only in the late *Śvetāśvatara* Upanishad and the Bhagavad-Gītā that it was to return with renewed emphasis. There the immanent and transcendent God will be one: here they appear to be two—the Father, one might almost say, and the Holy Spirit.

In another hymn, Rig-Veda 10: 121, equally evocative and equally seminal, the transcendent and the immanent coalesce in what is called the 'Golden Embryo', probably representing the sun:

> In the beginning the Golden Embryo
>   [Stirred and] evolved:
> Once born he was the one Lord of [every] being;
> This heaven and earth did he sustain . . .
> What God shall we revere with the oblation?

Strictly speaking the Golden Embryo is not the supreme Being, for since he is an embryo there must be something or someone prior to him; and so we read:

> When the mighty waters moved, conceived the All
> As an embryo, giving birth to fire,
> Then did he evolve, the One life-force of the gods . . .
> What God shall we revere with the oblation?

Child of the waters, the One in the womb of chaos, he has to be born in order to exercise his sovereignty. Only then can he sustain heaven and earth; only then does he become

> Giver of life, giver of strength,
> Whose behests all [must] obey,
> Whose [behests] the gods [obey],
> Whose shadow is immortality,
> Whose [shadow] death . . .
>
> Who by his might has ever been the One
> King of all that breathes and blinks the eye,
> Who rules all creatures that have two feet or four . . .

By whom strong heaven and earth are held in place,
By whom the sun is given firm support,
By whom the firmament, by whom the ether
Is measured out within the atmosphere . . .

May he not harm us, father of the earth,
Who generated heaven, for truth is his law,
Who gave birth to the waters—shimmering, strong . . .
What God shall we revere with the oblation?

The God is as yet unnamed. Son of primeval chaos—the 'mighty waters'—he is yet father of an ordered cosmos whose law is truth. In the last stanza he is triumphantly named:

Lord of Creatures! None other than thou hath comprehended
All these [creatures] brought to birth.

Prajāpati, the 'Lord of Creatures', is a late arrival in Vedic literature. The old gods had failed: none had succeeded in becoming the undisputed creator and disposer of the universe. Prajāpati, the 'Lord of Creatures', seems to have been invented specifically to fill this gap. He is the answer to the question: 'What God shall we revere with the oblation?' Yet even he is not the ultimate principle which is the 'mighty waters', primal chaos from which he evolves. The waters represent primal matter in all its chaotic multiplicity; Prajāpati is the spirit that emerges from them. Or again, it would be fair to say that the waters represent pre-conscious life and inanimate matter from which life arises, while the birth of Prajāpati represents the birth of consciousness in man, for it is consciousness or rather self-consciousness which gives man his power over Nature.

Alongside Prajāpati another god came into prominence—Viśvakarman, the 'Maker of All'. In him again the Vedic seers thought they had found the answer to the question: 'Who made the world, and out of what did he make it?' He is 'our father'[1] who begat heaven and earth[2] by sacrifice. He is

Maker of All, exceeding wise, exceeding strong,
Disposer, Ordainer, highest Exemplar, . . .
    . . . the One . . .[3]

His eyes on every side, on every side his face,
On every side his arms, his feet on every side—
With arms and wings he together forges
Heaven and earth, begetting them, God, the One![4]

[1] Rig-Veda 10: 81: 1.   [2] Ibid. 10: 82: 1.
[3] Ibid. 10: 82: 2.   [4] Ibid. 10: 81: 3.

But what of the matter from which the universe is formed? Is it a
separate substance or is it, as later writers were to suggest, the 'body' of
this one God?

> What was the primal matter? What the beginning?
> How and what manner of thing was that from which
> The Maker of All, see-er of all, brought forth
> The earth, and by his might the heavens unfolded?[1]

> What was the wood? What was the tree
> From which heaven and earth were fashioned forth?
> Ask, ask, ye wise in heart, on what did he rely
> That he should [thus] support [these] worlds?[2]

But Viśvakarman, the 'Maker of All', is no more than Prajāpati, the
'Lord of Creatures', independent of matter; for he too is the 'first embryo'
who emerges from primal matter, but who, once he has emerged therefrom,
takes control of the universe and sets it in order:

> Beyond the heavens, beyond this earth,
> Beyond the gods, beyond the Asuras,
> What was the first embryo the waters bore
>   To which all the gods bore witness?

> He was the first embryo the waters bore
>   In whom all gods together came.
> The One implanted in the Unborn's navel
> In which all the worlds abode.[3]

Yet he is still the unknown God, for the whole polytheistic tradition of
the first nine books of the Rig-Veda, so far from bringing man nearer to the
ultimate reality, had rather brought confusion on him. And so the hymn
ends on a note of almost disgusted scepticism:

> You will not find him who [all] these begat:
> Some other thing has stepped between you.
> Blinded by fog and [ritual] mutterings
> Wander the hymn-reciters, robbers of life!

All these hymns are 'monist' in the sense that they regard the whole of
existence, conscious and unconscious, spirit and matter, as being reducible
to one cause and one cause only; and this cause is primal matter from which
spirit—the One—wells forth.

In the hymn to Primal Man[4] there is a shift of emphasis. *Purusha*,

---

[1] Rig-Veda 10: 81: 2.   [2] Ibid. 10: 81: 4.
[3] Ibid. 10: 82: 5–6.   [4] Ibid. 10: 90.

Primal Man, the male principle in the universe, is sacrificed in order that the world may come into being. He both *is* the universe, the 'All', and also extends beyond it:

> A thousands heads had [Primal] Man,
> A thousand eyes, a thousand feet:
> Encompassing the earth on every side,
> He exceeded it by ten fingers' [breadth].

> [That] Man is this whole universe—
> What was and what is yet to be,
> The Lord of immortality
> Which he outgrows by [eating] food.

> This is the measure of his greatness,
> But greater yet is [Primal] Man:
> All beings form a quarter of him,
> Three-quarters are the immortal in heaven.

> With three-quarters Man rode up on high,
> A quarter of him came to be again [down] here:
> From this he spread in all directions,
> Into all that eats and does not eat.

In this hymn the idea is quite different. Spirit is not the outgrowth of matter as in the other hymns we have cited. On the contrary the whole material universe forms but a quarter of Primal Man who is the supreme Being: 'three-quarters are the immortal in heaven.' This means that in the totality of existence matter and what derives from it, that is, mortal life of which conscious human life is the highest manifestation, is only of secondary importance. The greater part of existence is concealed from us, all that is 'immortal in heaven', the world of ideas as we might say which, being immortal, is exempt from the passage of time. Matter is subject to perpetual change, spirit (that is, three-quarters of macrocosmic as of microcosmic Man) is changeless. The process of change starts when Primal Man gives birth to Virāj (probably meaning extended space which is the *locus* of matter), and Virāj in turn gives birth to a second Man who must be sacrificed in order that the cosmos in all its variety may come to be. From this second Man, when sacrificed, beasts and birds, the Vedas, the four classes of Vedic society, sun, moon, the gods, atmosphere, sky, and earth came into existence. But this is still only a quarter of Primal Man, three-quarters are the 'immortal in heaven', beyond the reach of the senses and mind of merely mortal man.

This hymn had more influence on subsequent Hindu thought than any other, for it is both monist and dualist—monist in the sense that all being is one in Primal Man, yet within this one Being there is a clear dichotomy between the 'whole universe' of matter and the 'immortal in heaven' which is changeless spirit. Matter is Virāj, a noun of fluctuating gender, while Primal Man himself, the Male, remains unperturbed in three-quarters of his being as the 'immortal in heaven'. Later there was a tendency to see this dichotomy in sexual terms, for Purusha, the Male, came to be the synonym for pure spirit, and alongside of him there was the Female, *prakriti*, who is matter. However that may be, the hymn to Primal Man marks a change of outlook in Vedic man. The other creation hymns see in primal matter the first cause: they are dialectically materialist. The hymn to Primal Man reverses this trend, for it gives the primacy to the immortal and unchanging which accounts for three-quarters of existence, the remaining quarter being the cosmos as we know it. With this change of emphasis the whole trend of Indian religion changes: the quest for immortality has begun. Typical of this new trend is the moving prayer we meet with in the *Brihadāranyaka* Upanishad (1: 3: 28):

> From the unreal lead me to the Real!
> From darkness lead me to the Light!
> From death lead me to Immortality!

It would, however, be wrong to suppose that the Upanishads are solely concerned with the pursuit of immortality. Every religion, it is true, sooner or later comes face to face with the problem of death and how to transcend it, but none treats it quite as the Indians of the Upanishads did, not simply as a matter of speculation (as in Mesopotamia and Greece) or as a matter of divine revelation of some sort (as in Egypt and Israel), but as a matter of empirical inquiry. True, the empirical method is not nearly so developed in the Upanishads as it is in the early Buddhist texts, for it is all the time accompanied by another strand which runs like a golden thread throughout these absorbing texts: What is the nature of ultimate reality? What is the ground of the universe, and what is the inner essence of man?

In all the hymns of the final section of the Rig-Veda we have considered hitherto, all but one see matter as being the primal source of all things, and in this they are at one with Darwin and Marx. Spirit emerges from matter, consciousness from the unconscious, and once it is born it takes control of all things, it becomes the Lord of all things. In the creation myths of the Upanishads this tendency is largely reversed. The universe was originally one only, without a second: from this duality and multiplicity arise. Let us make a rapid survey of the various creation myths in the *Brihadāraṇyaka* Upanishad, the longest and perhaps the oldest of these venerable treatises.

In the beginning nothing at all existed here. This [whole world] was enveloped by Death—by Hunger. For what is death but hunger? And Death bethought himself: 'Would that I had a self!'[1]

What follows is as confused—some would say as childish—as anything in the Upanishads: but the meaning seems clear. In the beginning nothing at all existed to which you could give a name: you could only call it Death or Hunger, dead matter in a state of indeterminate desire groping after some kind of determination, some kind of individuality or personality. 'Would that I had a self.' Here we are still in the 'materialist' atmosphere of the creation hymns of the last book of the Rig-Veda.

So too the *Taittirīya* Upanishad says:

> In the beginning this [universe] was Not-being only,
>   Therefrom was Being born:
> [And Being] itself made [for itself] a self:
> Hence is it called 'well-done'.[2]

Here again 'Being' and 'Not-Being' are best interpreted as spirit and matter. Spirit arises from matter, the One, changeless and eternal, from the indeterminate many, and once it has become conscious of itself it pervades the world of matter and multiplicity as the taste of salt pervades the sea.[3] For as that Upanishad goes on to explain:

What that 'well-done' really is, is the [essential] savour [in all things]. Once a man has tasted this savour, he tastes bliss. For who could breathe, who could live, were this bliss not [diffused] throughout space? For this [savour] alone brings bliss.

For when a man finds security from fear and permanence in this invisible, insubstantial, unspecified, uncontainable universe, then does he achieve [full] security from [all] fear. But when he excavates a hole in it and splits it into different parts, then will he experience fear—the fear of a man who thinks he knows.

Spirit is one, and it has the same 'flavour' in man, the microcosm, as it has in the world of Not-being, the constantly changing universe. It is still matter that is the first cause: Being arises from Not-being.

The *Chāndogya* Upanishad (3: 19) tries to have it both ways: there is no distinction between Being and Not-being, the first inheres in the second.

[1] *Brihadāraṇyaka* Upanishad 1: 2: 1.   [2] *Taittirīya* Upanishad 2: 7.
[3] *Brihadāraṇyaka* Upanishad 2: 4: 12.

'In the beginning this [universe] was Not-being: [Yet] it was Being [too].
It developed. It turned into an egg.' And the egg split into two halves, one
of which was the sky and the other the earth. Both this idea and the earlier
one, that Not-being or an infinitely diffuse and indeterminate matter
precedes Being which increasingly comes to mean the principle of unity,
are summarily rejected later in the same Upanishad (6: 2):

In the beginning [it is firmly stated] this [universe] was Being only—one only—
without a second. True, some say that in the beginning this [universe] was
Not-being only—one only—without a second, and that from Not-being Being
was born.

But . . . whence could this be? . . . How could Being be born from Not-being?
No, it was Being alone that was this [universe] in the beginning—one only,
without a second.

There, as in the *Brihadāranyaka* Upanishad, 'it had this thought:
"Would that I were many; fain would I procreate" ', and so out of Being
are produced the three elements from which the whole world was supposed
to derive—fire, water, and food, that is to say, gaseous, liquid, and solid
matter.

This Being, which 'in the beginning' alone exists, 'one only, without a
second', corresponds to the Self and Brahman in similar myths in the
early chapters of the *Brihadāranyaka* Upanishad. There Self, *Purusha*, the
Primal Male of Rig-Veda 10: 90, and Brahman, the sacred power that
pervades all and gives reality to all, are used indiscriminately for the first
principle which *Chāndogya* Upanishad 6: 2 calls simply 'Being'.

By now the original principle is single, simple, One. In this purely
mythological phase this state of oneness is regarded as being an unconscious
state: it is beyond all dualities and all distinctions including sex. When
consciousness is attained there is discontent: the One desires variety. In
one of the most evocative creation myths the supreme Principle attains
consciousness and is afraid. Being afraid he wants companionship, and so
the unity of Being is shattered:

In the beginning this [universe] was the Self alone—in the likeness of a human
male. Looking around he saw nothing other than himself. First of all he said:
'This is I.' Hence the name 'I' came to be. . . . He was afraid. So, [even now] a
man who is all alone is afraid.

He thought and said [to himself]: 'Since nothing exists other than I, of whom
(or what) am I afraid?' And his fear then departed [from him]; for of whom (or
what) should he have been afraid? It is of a second that one is afraid.

He found no pleasure at all. So, [even now] a man who is all alone finds no
pleasure. He longed for a second.

Now he was of the size of a man and a woman in close embrace. He split this self in two; and from these arose husband and wife. . . . He copulated with her, and thence were human beings born.[1]

The first duality has now appeared, that of male and female, and from the conjunction of the two the universe in all its variety and multiplicity comes to be. This is felt to be a fall from a higher state, though not necessarily so, for the Upanishads are far from being consistent in this respect, as we shall see.

In the same chapter of the same Upanishad (1: 4: 10) we find another creation myth in which Brahman is the first principle. The conclusion, however, is different, for Brahman passes straight from self-consciousness to cosmic consciousness—he becomes simultaneously conscious of his own self, his *ātman*, and of himself as the All:

In the beginning this [universe] was Brahman alone, and he truly knew [him]self (*ātman*), saying: 'I am Brahman.' And so he became the All. . . . This is true even now. Whoso thus knows that he is Brahman, becomes this whole [universe]. Even the gods have not the power to cause him to un-Be, for he becomes their own self.

So, whoever reveres any other deity, thinking: 'He is one, and I am another', does not [rightly] understand. . . .

For where there is any semblance of duality, then does one smell another, then does one see another, then does one hear another, then does one speak to another, then does one think of another, then does one understand another. But when all has become one's very self, then with what should one smell whom? With what should one see whom? With what should one hear whom? With what should one speak to whom? With what should one think of whom? With what should one understand whom? With what should one understand him by whom one understands this whole universe? With what indeed should one understand the Understander?[2]

This is cosmic consciousness with a vengeance: the individual self realizes itself as being Brahman, and since Brahman is both the One and the All it sees and feels itself to be co-terminous with the universe. Outside this there is nothing, since time and space are abolished, birth and death are done away with; the man who has 'become Brahman' thereby lives the life of the All, and in the All there is room for matter as well as spirit. Indeed, it seems to be a characteristic of cosmic consciousness that it appears to comprise all *matter*, and Teilhard de Chardin, who knew from personal experience just what cosmic consciousness means, thought it could be explained in terms of electro-magnetic waves: 'Thanks to the prodigious biological event', he writes, 'represented by the discovery of

---

[1] *Brihadāranyaka* Upanishad 1: 4: 1–3.   [2] Ibid. 2: 4: 14.

electro-magnetic waves, each individual finds himself henceforth (actively and passively) simultaneously present, over land and sea, in every corner of the earth.'[1] Whether this makes scientific sense or not I am in no position to say, but it certainly represents the intuitive feeling of the Upanishads.

Brahman is the All. As such it is not just a timeless, static, and totally unchanging eternity. Rather it is both the universe as we know it and the unseen world that forever abides beyond all change:

There are two forms of Brahman, the formed and the unformed, the mortal and the immortal, the static and the moving, the actual and the beyond.[2]

It is everywhere and it is nowhere: 'More minute than the minute, [yet] greater than the great, the Self is hidden in the heart of creatures [here].'[3] Whether the ultimate principle is called Brahman, Self, or the human Male, it is macrocosmic being suffused with eternal life, the still, static silent ground that is wholly present in every living and conscious being which is itself subject to perpetual change. Man's own self is identical with the great Self which is Brahman in that it too 'is conformed to infinity':

> Think of this living self as but a part
> Of a hundredth part of the tip of a hair
>   Divided a hundred times!
> And [yet] to infinity is it conformed.[4]

For the infinite and the infinitesimal, the 'abyss of the infinite and that of nothingness', as Pascal puts it,[5] meet in the heart of man. To contemplate the human being as being simply poised between these two abysses can only cause terror and despair, but, Pascal adds: 'I think that as his curiosity turns into astonishment (*admiration*), he will be inclined to contemplate them in silence rather than presumptuously to investigate them.' This was the way of the Upanishads, for the knowledge or wisdom of which they speak is in no scientific sense knowledge at all, their 'omniscience' is not the knowledge of the totality of scientific truth, rather it is an intuitive apperception of the oneness of being which is 'an infinite sphere having its centre everywhere and its circumference nowhere',[6] because every single conscious being is the centre of its own field of consciousness, and that field is infinite. Infinite circumference and

[1] Pierre Teilhard de Chardin, *The Phenomenon of Man*, E.T., London, Collins, 1959, p. 240.

[2] *Brihadāranyaka* Upanishad 2: 3: 1.

[3] *Katha* Upanishad 2: 20; *Śvetāśvatara* Upanishad 3: 20.   [4] Ibid. 5: 9.

[5] Pascal, *Pensées*, ed. Pléiade, p. 1106.   [6] Ibid., p. 1105.

infinitesimal centre meet in the 'point without magnitude' and the 'timeless moment' of the human heart. This was beautifully and miraculously expressed in one of the earliest passages of the Upanishads—miraculously, because the texts in which it is embedded are a farrago of puerile sympathetic magic that made no sort of sense even to the medieval commentators in India itself. From all this the following stanza stands out like a beacon:

> This whole universe is Brahman. . . .
> He who consists of mind, whose body is the breath of life, whose form is light, whose idea is the real, whose self is space, through whom are all works, all desires, all scents, all tastes, who encompasses all this universe, who does not speak and has no care—he is my Self within the heart, smaller than a grain of rice or a barley-corn, or a mustard-seed, or a grain of millet, or the kernel of a grain of millet; this is my Self within my heart, greater than the earth, greater than the atmosphere, greater than the sky, greater than all these worlds. All works, all desires, all scents, all tastes belong to it: it encompasses all this universe, does not speak and has no care. This my Self within the heart is that Brahman. When I depart from hence I shall merge into it. He who believes this will never doubt.[1]

Man is the microcosm, and in some mysterious sense he is identical with the universe, the macrocosm; but this is not the absolute unity-in-identity of a later philosophy since both the microcosm and the macrocosm are unities in diversity, the one infinitely great, the other infinitely small. As Nicolas of Cusa, philosopher and cardinal of the Roman Church in the fifteenth century, put it, man is not only the *imago Dei*, the image of God, he is also the *imago mundi*, the image of the world: *Homo enim Deus est, sed non absolute, quoniam homo. Humane igitur est Deus. Homo etiam mundus est, sed non contracte omnia, quoniam homo. Est igitur homo μικρό-κοσμος*: 'for man is God, though not absolutely, for he is man. He is therefore God in a human way. Man is the world too, not indeed all things compressed into a small compass, since he is man. He is therefore man as microcosm.'[2]

What the Upanishad and Nicolas of Cusa seem to be saying is that the human spirit has an infinite dimension which, once freed from the bodily senses, sees that all things interpenetrate one another since they are all held together and made to cohere in and by their changeless ground, whether you call this *Brahman* which is the All, or *ātman*, the 'self within the heart'. None of this is, I fear, easy to understand, and perhaps I may be allowed to quote Whitman again, for Bucke is quite right when he

[1] *Chāndogya* Upanishad 3: 14.
[2] Quoted by C. G. Jung, *Collected Works*, vol. xvi, p. 317.

singles him out as the poet of cosmic consciousness *par excellence*; and cosmic consciousness is indeed the principal theme of the Upanishads:

> O the joy of my soul leaning pois'd on itself, receiving *identity* through
>   materials and loving them, observing characters and absorbing them,
> My soul vibrated back to me from them, from sight, hearing, touch, reason,
>   articulation, comparison, memory, and the like,
> The real life of my senses and flesh transcending my senses and flesh,
> My body done with materials, my sight done with my material eyes,
> Proved to me this day beyond cavil that it is not my material eyes which finally
>   see,
> Nor my material body which finally loves, walks, laughs, shouts, embraces,
>   procreates . . .
>
> O to realize space!
> The plenteousness of all, that there are no bounds,
> To emerge and be of the sky, of the sun and moon and flying clouds, as one
>   with them.[1]

'The plenteousness of all.' Perhaps that is as good a translation as any of the Sanskrit word *bhūman* which we find in *Chāndogya* Upanishad 7: 23–5, a word derived from the root *bhū*- meaning 'to become' or less correctly 'to be', the same root from which the Greek φύσις, 'physical nature' is derived:

> Happiness [the Upanishad says] is nothing less than *bhūman* (the plenteous-ness of all): there is no happiness in what is petty (and finite). Only *bhūman* is happiness. . . .
> Where one sees nothing else, hears nothing else, knows nothing else, that is *bhūman*—'the plenteousness of all'. But where one sees something else, hears something else, knows something else, that is something petty; . . . the petty is the same as what is mortal.

Bhūman is indeed 'the plenteousness of all', and it is immortal; it is omnipresent and it is joy, 'security from fear and permanence' as the *Taittirīya* Upanishad puts it (2: 7); it is the Self of all things, and so it is you and it is I:

> This *bhūman* is below, it is above, it is to the west, to the east, to the south, to the north. Truly it is this whole universe. . . .
> I am below, I am above, I am to the west, to the east, to the south, to the north. Truly I am this whole universe. . . .
> The Self is below, the Self is above, the Self is to the west, to the east, to the south, to the north. Truly the Self is this whole universe.

[1] Whitman, *A Song of Joys*, Nonesuch, pp. 167–8.

Bhūman, the 'plenteousness of all', which is Brahman, can only be described in paradox. It is not quite the 'unmoved Mover' of Aristotle; rather it is the 'unmoved *moving* mover':

> Unmoving—One—swifter than thought—
> The gods could not seize hold of it as it sped before [them]:
> Standing, it overtakes [all] others as they run;
> In it the wind incites activity.

> It moves. It does not move.
> It is far, yet it is near:
> It is within this whole universe,
> And yet it is without it.[1]

This God, this One, this 'plenteousness of all', is within one's own heart. There it is 'exempt from evil, untouched by age or death or sorrow, untouched by hunger or thirst: its desire is the real, its idea is the real'.[2] And because it dwells fully in the 'city of Brahman'[3] which is the human heart,

> Those who see all beings in [this] Self,
> And the Self in all beings,
> Will never shrink from it.

> When once one understands that within oneself
>   The Self's become all beings,
> When once one's seen the unity,
> What room is there for sorrow? What room for perplexity?[4]

This is the state in which all the opposites, male and female, good and evil, are merged and united. Bucke, you may remember, said that one of the things cosmic consciousness showed was that 'the universe is God and that God is the universe, and that no evil did or ever will enter into it'. He oversimplified. Neither his hero, Walt Whitman, nor the Upanishads deny the existence of evil; for Whitman, as he himself said, did 'not decline to be the poet of wickedness'. To say, as Bucke does, that cosmic consciousness leads to moral elevation is to disregard the facts. Cosmic consciousness *transcends* good and evil, a fact which the Upanishads do not attempt to deny:

> That from which [all] words recoil together with the mind,
>   Unable to attain it—
> That is the bliss of Brahman; knowing it,
> A man has nothing to fear from anywhere.

[1] *Iśā* Upanishad 4–5.   [2] *Chāndogya* Upanishad 8: 1: 5.
[3] Ibid. 8: 1: 1–5.   [4] *Iśā* Upanishad 6–7.

G

Such a man is not worried [by the thought]: 'Why did I not do good? Why did I do evil?' Knowing [good and evil] in this way he saves [him]self.[1]

These two thoughts [simply] do not occur to him, 'So I have done evil', or 'So I have done what is [good and] fair'. He shrugs them off. What he has done and what he has left undone does not torment him.[2]

This may sound shocking, but it is natural enough, for in this timeless and spontaneous form of existence there is neither birth nor death, neither time nor space, and action as we understand it can therefore have no meaning; and the man who has passed beyond the temporal world, though living still, cannot be affected by what he does. He is free: and he has passed beyond good and evil. He is as Adam was in Paradise. If, then, cosmic consciousness is really the only form of mysticism, and if this mysticism represents the truth of which the religions are only partial facets, then it makes nonsense of every moral code. This is the real challenge of mysticism so interpreted: the authors of the Upanishads faced it, and it seems not to have worried them at all.

---

[1] *Taittiriya* Upanishad 2: 9.   [2] *Brihadāranyaka* Upanishad 4: 4: 22.

V

THE PARTING OF THE WAYS

Now, in this city of Brahman there is a dwelling-place, a tiny lotus-flower; within that there is a tiny space. What is within that is what [you] should seek: that is what [you] should really want to understand. . . .

As wide as is this space [around us], so wide is this space within the heart. In it both sky and earth are concentrated, both fire and wind, both sun and moon, lightning and the stars, what a man possesses here on earth and what he does not possess: everything is concentrated in this [tiny space within the heart]. . . .

[This city of Brahman] does not grow old with [the body's] ageing nor is it slain when [the body] is slain. This is the true city of Brahman; in it are concentrated [all] desires. This is the self, exempt from evil, untouched by age or death or sorrow, untouched by hunger or thirst: [this is the self] whose desire is the real, whose idea is the real. . . .

As here on earth the worldly station that is won by work must perish, so too must the [heavenly] state won by merit perish in the next world.

[All] those who go hence without having found the self and these real [objects of] desire, will have no freedom or movement in any state of being. But those who go hence, having found the self and these real [objects of] desire, will have freedom of movement in every state of being.[1]

IN the earlier Upanishads there is no distinct difference between matter and spirit; there is rather identity of the infinitesimal and the infinite, of all that cannot be measured. In the 'tiny lotus-flower' within the heart of man the whole universe is contained. Origen too had said: 'Know that you are another world in miniature and that in you there is a sun, a moon, and the stars too.'[2] To realize this, as one may by a flash of intuition which in its suddenness is like a flash of lightning,[3] is to realize that one is free—free from the bondage of the material body and from the ordinary processes of thought; this is 'freedom of movement in every state of being'. It is not, as it was to be in the later monistic philosophy, a totally undifferentiated and static oneness, because Brahman, though unmoving and One, is yet 'swifter than thought':[4] it is to taste of a mode of being in which there is no distinction between the moving and the static, the transient and the

---

[1] *Chāndogya* Upanishad 8: 1: 1–6.
[2] Origen, *Homilia in Leviticum*, 126. 5. 2 in C. G. Jung, *Collected Works*, vol. xvi, p. 196.
[3] *Kena* Upanishad 4: 4.   [4] *Iśā* Upanishad 4.

permanent. This is at least how the *Chāndogya* Upanishad understood it
in the passage with which we opened this lecture.

The main trend of the Upanishads is not monistic, rather is it what
is sometimes called 'qualified monism', what St. François de Sales calls
'unity in diversity or diversity in unity'. Of course, there are passages in
the Upanishads which are purely monistic, but these are of much less
frequent occurrence than many commentators would have us believe.
And this is natural, for diversity and multiplicity are all too obvious: they
stare us in the face here, there, and everywhere. Only a minute proportion
of a privileged few can see the unity that binds it all together, and since they
see it with a clarity that will not be denied, they tend to assert and proclaim it to the exclusion of all difference and multiplicity at all in defiance
of what passes for common sense and sound reason:

> Descry This with your mind:
> Herein there's no diversity at all.
> Death beyond death is all the lot
> Of him who sees in This what seems to be diverse.

> Descry It in its Oneness,
> Immeasurable, firm,
> Transcending space, immaculate,
> Unborn, abiding, great—
>   [This is] the Self![1]

> What [we see] here is also there beyond;
> What there, that too is here:
> Death beyond death does he incur
> Who sees in This what seems to be diverse!

> Grasp This with your mind:
> Herein there's no diversity at all.
> Death beyond death is all the lot
> Of him who sees in This what seems to be diverse.[2]

These are extreme positions and it would seem that they were deliberately taken up since the unity of all things is *not* apparent to the ordinary
man, and yet it is of immensely more signification than the multiplicity,
for through it and through it only can one experience immortality. In the
last analysis it is impossible to define it with any precision. 'This Self—
[what can one say of it but] "No, no!" It is impalpable, for it cannot be
grasped; indestructible, for it cannot be destroyed; free from attachment,

---

[1] *Brihadāranyaka* Upanishad 4. 4. 19–20.
[2] *Katha* Upanishad 4. 10–11.

for it is not attached [to anything], not bound. It does not quaver, nor can it be hurt.'[1]

It is true that perhaps the principal teaching of the Upanishads is that the infinitesimal within the human heart is, from the eternal point of view, identical with the infinite that comprises the whole universe, and that this unity which exists between the two is what we would call God in his essence. It would, however, be wrong to conclude from this that the human self is identical with God in all respects. A favourite simile, as in all mystical traditions, is that of rivers flowing into the sea or of a drop of water merging into a larger mass of water. In either case this implies a loss of individual personality and participation in a universal form of existence. And so we read:

> As rivers flowing [downwards] find their home
> In the ocean, leaving name and form behind,
> So does the man who knows, from name and form released,
> Draw near to the divine Person who is beyond the beyond.[2]

Or again:

> As water pure into pure [water] poured
> Becomes even as [that pure water] is,
> So too becomes the self of him—
> The silent sage who knows.[3]

Christian writers, including Teilhard de Chardin, dislike the idea of depersonalization in the Absolute, and yet it is as typical of the Christian mystics as it is of the Upanishads themselves, as it is bound to be; for how can you savour the infinite unless your own finite personality is swallowed up in it? One would have thought that this would be particularly obvious to Christians, since Christ himself teaches that 'unless a grain of wheat falls on the ground and dies, it remains only a single grain; but if it dies, it yields a rich harvest'.[4] Without the death of the 'ego' there can be no resurrection of the true 'self', and so we find in the Christian mystics too the simile of the drop and the ocean turning up again and again. Indeed, St. François de Sales might have been commenting on the Upanishadic passage we have just quoted when he wrote:

Suppose a drop of plain water, thrown into an ocean of orange-flower water, were alive and could speak, could describe the state in which it found itself, would it not cry out in great joy: 'True, I am living, yet it is not myself who lives, but this ocean lives in me, and my life is hidden away in its depths.' The

---

[1] *Brihadāranyaka* Upanishad 4. 4. 22.　　[2] *Mundaka* Upanishad 3: 2: 8.
[3] *Katha* Upanishad 4: 15.　　[4] John 12: 24.

soul that flows out into God does not die, for how could she die through being drowned in life? Rather, she lives though not living in herself.[1]

So too the Hindu sage becomes 'an ocean, One, without duality',[2] and this is the highest bliss that, according to the Upanishads, it is possible to reach.

This, however, is not just a realization of self, it is also a true union, and this is expressed in terms of sexual union in which the self of man, even when it sees itself as co-terminous with the All, is yet able to experience intercourse with the supreme Self who is greater than the All; for this 'One' of whom the Upanishads speak, though 'abiding in all beings, is other than all beings', and though all beings are his body, they do not know him since he controls them from within: 'he is the Self within you, the Inner Controller, the Immortal.'[3] And yet he is other than you, for even when a man sees himself as the whole universe, which 'is his highest state of being, that form of his which is beyond desire, free from evil, free from fear',[4] he still knows the ecstasy of union with him who is 'other than all beings':

Just as a man, closely embraced by his loving wife, knows nothing without, nothing within, so does this person, closely embraced by the Self that consists of wisdom, know nothing without, nothing within. This is his [true] form in which [all] his desires are fulfilled, in which Self [alone] is his desire, in which he has no desire, no sorrow.[5]

In this union he 'is not followed by good, not followed by evil; for then he will have passed beyond all sorrow of the heart'.[6]

There is plenty of sexual imagery in the Christian mystical writers, but with the Hindus this imagery is more robust. For them sexual union is the most natural image of the union of the soul with God. So long as it lasts good and evil are transcended, for all action is concentrated in it.

So too in the passage from the *Chāndogya* Upanishad I quoted in my last lecture[7] in which the ego is identified with both the Infinite and the universal Self, this apparent identification does not exclude relationship of the most intimate kind. For—

The man who sees and thinks and understands in this way has pleasure in the Self, plays with the Self, copulates with the Self, and has joy with the Self: he becomes an independent sovereign. In all the worlds (and in every state of being) freedom of movement is his. But [all] those who understand [reality] in any way

[1] *Traité de l'amour de Dieu*, 6. 12. [2] *Brihadāranyaka* Upanishad 4: 3: 32.
[3] Ibid. 3: 7: 15. [4] Ibid. 4: 3: 20–1.
[5] Ibid. 4: 3: 21. [6] Ibid. 4: 3: 22. [7] Above, p. 80.

that is different from this, are subjects of another sovereign: their states of being are perishable, and in all the worlds (and states of being) they have no freedom of movement.[1]

There is threefold paradox here; for in this liberation of the spirit man sees himself as identical with the whole universe because he has transcended space and time—everything is now present in the 'now' and the 'here'. At the same time he is united with the universal Self, with the Being we call God, in what is frankly described as a sexual ecstasy. And this is not surprising, for even St. François de Sales, not generally considered to be an immodest writer, says that there is a genuine similarity between our spiritual emotions and our physical passions.[2] This union, however, is at the same time complete 'freedom of movement'—a total release from the restraints that our material nature imposes on us. This is a 'rest' which is unity but which yet contains movement within itself; it is an eternal 'now' in which all the past and all the future are present.[3] It seems to me that in these two passages the Upanishads are saying rather confusedly what St. François de Sales was to put very much more clearly. Their paradox is this: the individual self both desires the universal Self or God and is yet free from desire; it is at rest and yet has complete freedom of movement. This is how St. François puts it:

In a good that is infinite desire can exist with possession, and possession with desire; for the infinite is rich enough to satisfy desire by its sacred presence while all the time quickening it by the excess of its perfection, fostering in those who have it a desire that is always satisfied and a satisfaction that yet ever desires. . . . When our [human] will meets with God, it rests in him, finding in him its highest delectation, yet this does not stop it from giving movement to its desire. . . . Peace of heart does not consist in staying absolutely still, but in having need of nothing, not in a simple lack of movement, but in having no need to move.[4]

Here, as in the Upanishads, there is no contradiction between desire and fruition, between eternal rest and freedom of movement. There is, as the same author says, unity in diversity and diversity in unity.

---

[1] *Chāndogya* Upanishad 7: 25: 2. [2] *Traité de l'amour de Dieu*, 6. 13.
[3] Cf. Nicolas of Cusa, *De docta Ignorantia*, 2. 3.
[4] *Traité de l'amour de Dieu*, 5. 3: 'Le bien infini fait régner le désir dans la possession, et la possession dans le désir, ayant de quoi assouvir le désir par sa sainte présence, et de quoi le faire toujours vivre par la grandeur de son excellence, laquelle nourrit, en tous ceux qui la possèdent, un désir toujours content et un contentement toujours désireux. . . . Quand notre volonté a rencontré Dieu, elle se repose en lui, y prenant une souveraine complaisance, et néanmoins elle ne laisse pas de faire le mouvement de son désir. . . . Le repos du cœur ne consiste pas à demeurer immobile, mais à n'avoir besoin de rien; il ne gît pas à n'avoir point de mouvement, mais à n'avoir point d'indigence de se mouvoir.

Identity between the Absolute (Brahman) and the individual self there certainly is in the Upanishads, but it is an identity from which relationship is not excluded. If we are thinking of the universe then the Absolute is far greater than it. If, however, we think of the human heart, then the indwelling God is far smaller. If the human self can be said to be 'of the measure of a thumb', then the indwelling God is no larger than the fine point of an awl:

> Of the measure of a thumb, the sun's equal in appearance—
> Such is he when conjoined with will and ego,
> With the attribute of soul and the attribute of self:
> [But there is also one] no larger than the fine point of an awl,
>   He is Another.[1]

The universal Self is certainly defined as 'the Immortal, Brahman, the All':[2] it is, then, not only the sum total of matter but also the permanent substratum of matter, that which gives to matter its coherence. Hence it is not too far-fetched to say that it is Lord and King:

> This Self is indeed the Lord of all beings, king of all beings. Just as the spokes of a wheel are together fixed on to the hub and felly, so are all beings, all gods, all worlds, all vital breaths *and all these selves* together fixed in this Self.[3]

In the Upanishads monism, pantheism, and monotheism coexist: they are not regarded as being mutually incompatible. To me there is an obscure consistency in what they say—a consistency quite beyond all logic, certainly, but a consistency none the less, since the authors of these texts are trying to see reality from every angle and in all its aspects, excluding nothing. The Absolute is pure Being: 'He IS—so must we understand him',[4] and in so far as anything *is* it is the Absolute: it is Brahman. Yet there are also degrees of being, and in so far as this is so, Brahman or the universal Self must be king and Lord of all beings. Thus for the authors of the Upanishads there is no inconsistency in first promising 'death beyond death' to him who 'sees in This what seems to be diverse',[5] and then going on to proclaim that this one true Self in whom there is no diversity is also 'Lord of all':

> This is indeed the great unborn Self which consists of understanding among the human faculties. In the space within the heart lies the Ruler of all, the Lord of all, the King of all. He neither increases by good works nor does he diminish by evil ones. He is the Lord of all, he the King of beings, he their Protector. He is the causeway which holds these worlds apart lest they should split asunder.[6]

[1] *Śvetāśvatara* Upanishad 5: 8.   [2] *Brihadāranyaka* Upanishad 2: 5: 1–14.
[3] Ibid. 2: 5: 15.   [4] *Katha* Upanishad 6: 13.
[5] *Brihadāranyaka* Upanishad 4: 4: 19.   [6] Ibid. 4: 4: 22.

This Self is both the unknown and unknowable God of negative theology and also the Ruler of the universe; he is both transcendent, immanent, and active in the universe which can perhaps even at this stage be regarded as his 'body'. On him the whole universe is 'woven, warp and woof':[1]

It is not coarse nor fine; not short nor long; not red (like fire) nor adhesive (like water). It casts no shadow, is not darkness. It is not wind nor is it space. It is not attached to anything. It is not taste or smell; it is not eye or ear; it is not voice or mind; it is not light or life; it has no face or measure; it has no 'within', no 'without'. Nothing does it consume nor is it consumed by anyone at all.

And yet 'at the behest of this Imperishable . . . sun and moon are held apart and so abide, . . . sky and earth are held apart and so abide'. Yet, though the Imperishable sustains the universe, it remains in its essence 'the unseen seer, the unheard hearer, the unthought thinker, the ununderstood understander' in which 'space is woven, warp and woof'.[2]

Speculation on the nature of the universe, speculation on the nature of the self: these were the twin concerns of the Upanishads. Creation can be regarded as an expansion of the One into what is outside itself. But what is outside itself is perishable; in it alone is immortality. Macrocosm and microcosm are essentially one, and so man too must return to what is within himself:

> The self-existent [Lord] bored holes facing the outside world;
> Therefore a man looks outward, not into [him]self.
> A certain sage, in search of immortality,
> Turned his eyes inwards and saw the self within.[3]

The Upanishads never say that the external world is an illusion, but their preoccupation with dream and dreamless sleep does indicate that they attached more importance to what goes on inside a man than to the people and things that surround him. The external world is given; man cannot do with it what he likes. In sleep, however, things are different, for when a man 'falls asleep, he takes with him [all] the materials of this all-embracing world. Himself, he destroys them and himself builds them up [again]; and he dreams [in a world lighted] by his own brilliance, by his own light'.[4] So, in dream a man is freed at least from the bondage of gross matter: what matter there is, is of his own contriving, but even so he is not fully in control:

> In the realm of dream aloft, beneath, he roams,
> A god—how manifold the forms he fashions!

[1] Ibid. 3: 8: 11. [2] Ibid. 3: 8: 8–11.
[3] *Katha* Upanishad 4: 1. [4] *Brihadāranyaka* Upanishad 4: 3: 9.

With women he takes his pleasures, laughs—or else
Sees dreadful sights: so does it seem to him.[1]

But beyond dream there is the state of dreamless sleep in which, as in death,[2] he touches the Infinite:

When a man is properly asleep, then . . . is he suffused in Being—he will have returned to his own. . . . Just as a bird, tied to a string, will fly around in all directions and finding no resting-place anywhere else, will resort to the very [string] that keeps it captive, so too . . . the mind will fly around in all directions and, finding no resting-place anywhere else, will come to rest in the breath of life.[3]

Dreamless sleep is the brother of death, for in death as in dreamless sleep a man 'becomes one',[4] and

When all desires which shelter in the heart
Detach themselves, then does a mortal man
Become immortal: to Brahman he wins through.[5]

If dreamless sleep is the nearest approach to the immortality of Brahman in this life, does this, then, not mean that the ultimate state of total oneness is simply another way of describing total death from which there is no return—the total stoppage of the whole process of *samsāra*, of ever-repeated rebirth and re-death? This is in fact precisely the question that European scholars asked themselves about the Buddhist Nirvāna when they first started to study the Buddhist texts, and it was also a question which exercised the authors of the Upanishads themselves.

In the eighth book of the *Chāndogya* Upanishad there is a dialogue between the ancient god Indra (himself once Lord of the gods) and Prajāpati who had succeeded him in this capacity. Here, however—and this is typical of how radically Indian religion had changed—Indra appears as a student of sacred knowledge, Prajāpati as his preceptor. Neither, however, now makes any claim to be the supreme God, let alone the Absolute. What they are discussing is the supreme Self—the subject *par excellence* to which all other beings are objects and which itself stands in an objective relationship to nothing:

'The Self is exempt from evil, untouched by age or death or sorrow, untouched by hunger or thirst: its desire is the real, its idea is the real. This is what [you] must seek, this is what [you] must want to understand. Whoso has found this

[1] *Brihadāranyaka* Upanishad 4: 3: 13.   [2] Cf. ibid. 4: 4: 2.
[3] *Chāndogya* Upanishad 6: 8: 1–2; cf. *Brihadāranyaka* 4: 3: 19; *Praśna* Upanishad 4: 7.
[4] *Brihadāranyaka* Upanishad 4: 4: 2.   [5] Ibid. 4: 4: 7.

Self and understands it, wins all states of being and all [objects of] desire.' Thus spake Prajāpati.[1]

Indra, the chief of the gods, and Virocana, the foremost of the demons, overheard him and approached him with a view to receiving instruction in the royal science of Brahman. Prajāpati bade them look at their own reflections in a dish of water. They dressed up in gorgeous apparel, and Virocana came back well satisfied, saying: 'This is the Self, this the Immortal, [this] the free from fear: this is Brahman.' But the more prudent Indra had his doubts, for if the reflection were, as it seemed to be, in all respects identical with the body it reflected, would it not then be sick when the body is sick and die when the body dies? So he returned to Prajāpati, and Prajāpati said: 'He who roams abroad in dream, glorying in himself— this is the Self, this the Immortal, this the free from fear: this is Brahman.'

Again Indra reflected on this, and still he was not satisfied. Certainly the dreamer is unaffected by the body's ailments, but even so 'it does have the impression of being killed, of being stripped, of undergoing unpleasant experiences. I see nothing enjoyable in this', said Indra. Then Prajāpati spoke again:

Now, when a man is sound asleep, integrated within himself and quite serene, and when he is not conscious of dreaming—this is the Self, this the immortal, [this] the free from fear: this is Brahman!

Indra was not taken in. 'Such a man', he thought, 'has no present knowledge of [him]self so that he could say, "This I am", nor, for that matter, [has he any knowledge] of these creatures [here]. Surely he might as well be a man annihilated. I see nothing enjoyable in this.'

And Prajāpati revealed to him the state that was beyond dreamless sleep, beyond death:

Bountiful one! [he said] For sure the body is mortal, held in the grip of death. Yet it is the dwelling-place of the immortal, incorporeal Self. [And this Self,] while still in the body, is held in the grip of pleasure and pain; and so long as it remains in the body there is no means of ridding it of pleasure and pain. But once it is freed from the body, pleasure and pain cannot [so much as] touch it.

The wind has no body. Clouds, thunder, and lightning—these too have no body. So, just as these arise from [the broad expanse of] space up there and plunge into the highest light, revealing themselves each in its own form, so does this deep serenity arise out of this body and plunge into the highest light, revealing itself in its own form. Such a one is a superman; there he roves around laughing, playing, taking his pleasure with women, chariots, or friends, remembering no more that excrescence [which was] his body.[2]

---

[1] *Chāndogya* Upanishad 8: 7: 1.   [2] Ibid. 8: 12: 1–3.

To win immortality one must be freed from the body. All agree about this; and even St. Paul, Jew though he was and as such brought up in a tradition in which man was regarded as being a unitary whole of soul and body for whom bodily death could only mean that he ceased to be a man— even he realized that the resurrected body of which Christ's resurrected body was the first-fruits must be quite different from the body we know. For, according to him, 'The thing that is sown is perishable but what is raised is imperishable; the thing that is sown is contemptible but what is raised is glorious; the thing that is sown is weak but what is raised is powerful. The thing that is sown is a physical body, the thing that is raised is a spiritual body.'[1]

How many of us must have wondered what on earth a spiritual body can be. Well, perhaps the *Chāndogya* Upanishad gives us a hint of the answer. It is a body which, like wind, cloud, and lightning, exists in a milieu in which 'gross' matter is transcended and which it is free to traverse at will in the twinkling of an eye: it has 'freedom of movement in every state of being[2] in what the Upanishads call the 'Brahman-world' and, though 'merged into Brahman',[3] it gains the status of a 'superman,' free to love, worship, and rejoice 'in its own form'; for in the Brahman-world, like the gods, it 'reveres this Self',[4] that is, the supreme Self whom we call God:

Shaking off evil as a horse [shakes off] its hairs, shaking off the body as the moon delivers herself from the eclipse, with self perfected, I merge into the unmade Brahman-world.[5]

This is the state that was later called *moksha* or *mukti*, 'liberation, release, emancipation, or freedom' from all dependence on matter, freedom from the bondage of rebirth and from the good and evil works that condition it.

However, let us not suppose that this great sequence in the last book of the *Chāndogya* Upanishad is typical of the general teaching of these deeply emotive works. Far more typical is the identification of the One with the All, of the spirit that indwells the soul of man (the 'more minute than the minute') with Him who encompasses both spirit and matter in all their infinite variety,[6] and the union, expressed in sexual terms, between the two.

In this same *Chāndogya* Upanishad there is another and much more famous sequence[7] which, long though I have lingered over the Upanishads, can scarcely remain unmentioned. This is the much-quoted sequence, the

---

[1] 1 Corinthians 15: 42–4.   [2] *Chāndogya* Upanishad 7: 25: 2.
[3] Ibid. 3: 14: 5; *Śvetāśvatara* Upanishad 1: 7.
[4] *Chāndogya* Upanishad 8: 12: 6.   [5] Ibid. 8: 13.
[6] *Īśā* Upanishad 8.   [7] *Chāndogya* Upanishad 6: 8–16.

refrain of which is: 'This finest essence—the whole universe has it as its Self: that is the Real: that is the Self: that *you* are.' This was regarded by the great monist philosopher, Śankara, as being one of the four 'great sayings' of the Upanishads because it seems to identify outright the soul of man with the very ground of the universe. In fact the sequence is not nearly so monist as it seems, for this refrain has too often been dragged out of its context and the nuances of this remarkable text have therefore been lost.

The author of the Upanishad in fact gives eight examples to explain his meaning. First, he compares the absorption of individual selves into Brahman to bees collecting the pollens of many trees and reducing them all to a unity in honey. This may be pantheism, but it certainly is not monism; it is what St. François de Sales means when he says; 'There is beauty in music when voices, which are true, clear, distinct, blend to produce perfect consonance, perfect harmony, to achieve unity in diversity or diversity in unity'[1]—a harmony in which, in the case of the Upanishad, each type of pollen contributes its own 'true, clear, distinct' flavour to the whole mass of honey. True, once merged into Being the individual beings or 'flavours' do not know that they have been so merged any more than St. François's drop, once merged into the ocean dares to claim life for itself, for 'it is not myself who lives, but this ocean lives in me, and my life is hidden away in its depths'.[2] And, as might have been expected, the *Chāndogya* Upanishad's second simile is precisely the merging of rivers into the sea.

So too the self is like a tree which, however much you may hack it about, still lives on. 'Strengthened by the living Self it still stands, drinking in the moisture and exulting.' To merge into Brahman means not to die but to partake of eternal life. It is only the branches hacked off that are consigned to death, just as the branches which bear no fruit are cut away from the 'true vine' in the Gospel according to St. John.[3]

Again, if you cut up the seed of a fig finely enough, the pieces will ultimately be so small that you will not be able to see them. So too 'it is true that you cannot perceive this finest essence [which is yet the Self and the Real], but it is equally true that this huge fig-tree grows up from this same finest essence'. Or again it is compared to salt dissolved in water, pervading it all equally. Or it is like a blindfold man who has lost his way; a kindly stranger takes off the bandage and directs him home; for his only true home is Being, the Self.

It is this Self again into which a man merges at death when his senses and his mind are extinguished and all his faculties are peeled away.

[1] Above, p. 1.   [2] Above, p. 85.   [3] 15: 2.

Finally, this Self is the Truth in the sense not only of ultimate Reality but of that Reality as reflected among us as true speech here on earth.

What, then, is this Self which indwells man as something more intimate to himself than what he normally calls his self? It is the unity to which all diversity tends; it is eternal life on which all individual life depends; it is the invisible principle, apparently non-existent, from which the tree of the world grows up; it is the fine and imperishable essence that pervades all things, the salt that never loses its savour; it is our true home; it is the oneness of our faculties which we call death; it is Reality and Truth manifesting themselves among us as true speech, which means seeing and describing things as they really are in relation to the one Reality itself. This is not what most people understand by monism.

There is, however, one Upanishad, very short and probably very late, in which a fully monistic position is taken up. This is the *Māndūkya*. To the Western mind it appears very peculiar. The themes of sleep and the microcosm–macrocosm correspondence are here combined, each state of consciousness in man being equated with a corresponding state of matter in the macrocosm. In the waking state a man experiences 'what is gross' and this is 'common to all men', that is to say, the objective world appears the same to all who experience it. In a state of dream, however, one is conscious of what is within rather than of what is without. What is here experienced is 'subtle' matter which is 'created' by the dreamer.[1] This is regarded as being a more perfect state since it is more unified. Beyond this, of course, is dreamless sleep, and this is described as 'unified, a very mass of wisdom, composed of bliss, experiencing bliss, with thought as its mouth, wise'. That an *unconscious* state should be described as 'a very mass of wisdom' is surprising enough, but when we are told that this state of dreamless sleep is 'the Lord of all', 'the omniscient', 'the Inner Controller', and 'the source of all, for it is both the origin and the end of contingent beings', we are surely entitled to a high degree of astonishment, for what is here described is the highest Principle of the *Brihadāranyaka* Upanishad— the highest Self which is 'Lord of all',[2] the 'Inner Controller',[3] and the origin and end of all[4]—in other words, what we call God.

Given the macrocosm–microcosm equivalence, however, the equation of dreamless sleep with God is not quite so strange as it would seem; for God is primal matter as well as pure spirit, and just as dreams emerge from dreamless sleep and the waking consciousness out of dream, so does subtle matter issue from primal matter, and gross matter from subtle matter.

---

[1] *Brihadāranyaka* Upanishad 4: 3: 10.   [2] Ibid. 2: 5: 15; 4: 4: 22.
[3] Ibid. 3: 7: 3 ff.   [4] Ibid. 2: 1: 20; *Mundaka* Upanishad 2: 1: 1.

Beyond dreamless sleep, however, there is yet another state of being, the 'fourth state' or 'fourth quarter of Brahman' which is identical with the Self. This state is

Conscious of neither within nor without, nor of both together, not a mass of wisdom, neither wise nor unwise, unseen, one with whom there is no commerce, impalpable, devoid of distinguishing mark, unthinkable, indescribable, its essence the firm conviction of the oneness of itself, bringing all development to an end, tranquil and mild, devoid of duality. Such do they deem this fourth to be. That is the Self: that is what should be known.

It may be remembered that in the Rig-Vedic hymn describing the Primal Man, it was said of him:

> [That] Man is this whole universe—
> What was and what is yet to be,
> The Lord of immortality
> Which he outgrows by [eating] food.
>
> This is the measure of his greatness,
> But greater yet is [Primal] Man:
> All beings form a quarter of him,
> Three-quarters are the immortal in heaven.[1]

In another Upanishad the fourth state beyond dreamless sleep is said to be identical with the three-quarters of the macrocosm which 'are the immortal in heaven', the three other states of consciousness being identi-fied with his first quarter only, which comprises 'all beings', that is to say, the whole phenomenal world:

> He who sees with the [waking] eye, and he who roves in dream,
> He who [dreamless] sleeps, and he who transcends the dreamless—
> These are the four states [of mortal man]:
>   Of these the greatest is the fourth.
> In the three [first] a quarter of Brahman moves,
>   Three-quarters in the last.[2]

Here we have moved a long way from cosmic consciousness and from the idea of unity in diversity. What we have is rather either a pure monism or an uncompromising dualism. The three states of consciousness, to which the world of matter including wisdom, bliss, and God corresponds, together form the phenomenal world. The fourth state is wholly other, for its essence is absolute oneness, devoid of duality, and it brings all develop-ment to an end: it negates the phenomenal world completely, for there is

---

[1] Rig-Veda 10: 90: 2–3.   [2] *Maitri* Upanishad 7: 11.

no 'commerce' between the two. This either means that there are two orders
of reality, the absolutely Real, the One, on the one hand, and the world of
coming to be and passing away, the phenomenal world, on the other; or it
means, as that of the prince of monists, Śankara, was to maintain, that the
One, devoid of duality, unfractionable, and indescribable, is alone real,
and that therefore the phenomenal world together with its ruler, God, must
be from the absolute point of view illusory. The One is traditionally granted
the essential attributes of Being, Consciousness, and Joy, but as it is in its
essence it is devoid of all attributes and qualities.

To experience absolute oneness means to experience an eternity which
is wholly static and in which there is and can be no change—to experience
what Eckhart called the Godhead which is beyond God and the three
Persons of the Trinity. But need it necessarily be so interpreted? Martin
Buber, who himself had had the experience, said that he knew well that a
state existed in which the bonds of the personal nature of life seem to fall
away and in which an undivided unity is experienced. Once you have had
this experience, you are practically bound to think that you have attained
to union with the Primal Being or the Godhead. This, however, he came
to regard as an exaggeration. All you have a right to infer from the experience is that you have reached the 'undifferentiable unity' of yourself
'without form or content'. This may be interpreted as an 'original pre-
biographical unity', meaning, I suppose, the simple unity of the soul of a
new-born babe or even of the embryo in the womb. This, he says, is the
basic unity of a single soul 'beyond the reach of all the multiplicity it has
hitherto received from life, though not in the least beyond individuation,
or the multiplicity of all the souls in the world of which it is one: . . . one
of the human souls and not the "soul of the all"; a defined and particular
being and not Being.'[1]

This is the alternative interpretation of this experience of pure oneness
of which the *Māndūkya* Upanishad speaks; and even in the Indian
tradition Buber's pluralistic interpretation of the experience receives
considerable support.

The Upanishads are in the main speculative treatises, but it can, I think,
be assumed that their pantheism, their identification of the individual self
in its eternal ground with the All, must be based on a direct experience of
what Bucke calls 'cosmic consciousness'. The experience to which the
Māndūkya Upanishad testifies, however, is the exact opposite of cosmic
consciousness: it is the experience of absolute oneness to the exclusion of
all plurality, the severance of spirit from all commerce with matter, of

[1] Martin Buber, *Between Man and Man*, London, Routledge, 1947, p. 24.

eternity from time, of placelessness from place. It is what one of the greatest Muslim mystics, Al-Junayd, who flourished in the ninth and tenth centuries A.D., called the 'isolation of eternity from origination'. And, strangely enough, 'isolation' is precisely the word used by the Sānkhya-Yogin school of philosophy in India.

Traditionally there are six schools of philosophy in India. Of these by far the most important is the Vedānta, the philosophy that claims to be based on the 'end of the Veda' (for that is what the word *Vedānta* means), that is to say, the Upanishads. Next in importance are the Sānkhya and the Yoga. *Sānkhya* is a word meaning 'enumeration', and the school of philosophy bearing this name is so called because it divides all existent things into categories. The word *Yoga* is, of course, familiar to most people as meaning a specific physical technique pursued with the view to attaining a purely spiritual end: it is a practical method serving a philosophical discipline. Theoretically Sānkhya and Yoga are distinct philosophies: in practice, however, they coalesce, Sānkhya providing the theoretical background and Yoga providing the technique for realizing the theoretical principles on which Sānkhya is based.

The basic text of the Sānkhya is the *Sānkhya-kārikā* of Iśvarakrishna, that of the Yoga is the *Yoga-sūtra*s of Patañjali. The Sānkhya system is fundamentally dualist: it makes a hard and fast distinction between spirit and matter. Matter or material Nature includes everything in the universe as we know it. It is not matter in the Aristotelian sense, something wholly indeterminate that only achieves real existence once it combines with 'form': it is rather matter in the Marxian sense of the word, 'the first and most important of the inherent qualities of [which] is motion, not only mechanical and mathematical movement, but still more impulse, vital life-spirit, tension, or, to use Jacob Boehme's expression, the throes of matter'.[1] Such too is matter in the Sānkhya system. Time, as in all Indian systems, is cyclic, starting from a state of quiescence and rest, then differentiating itself into the universe as we know it, and finally returning to its original state of rest from which the same process is ever again renewed. The highest and most subtle form of matter is *buddhi*, more or less what we would call soul since it is the seat of cognition, determination, and right conduct.[2] Next to this comes the ego which includes both self-consciousness and *amour-propre*, and from this proceeds the mind (*manas*), corresponding more or less to the *sensus communis* of the Schoolmen, and along with the mind the five organs of sense and the five so-called organs

[1] Marx and Engels, *The Holy Family*, Moscow, 1956, p. 172.
[2] *Sānkhya-kārikā* 23.

of action, that is, speech, the hands, the feet, the anus, and the genitals. In addition there are five 'subtle elements' corresponding to the five senses (the objects of sight, hearing, smell, taste, and touch), and the five gross elements which are supposed to be the *locus* in which the five senses operate (ether or space corresponding to sound, air to touch, fire to sight, water to taste, and earth to smell). These elements, if you include primal matter itself, add up to twenty-four. There is, however, a twenty-fifth, and that is spirit.

The word used for spirit in the Sānkhya system is *purusha*, meaning 'a human male'. This is confusing, for the same word is used in Rig-Veda 10: 90 for the Primal Man, the macrocosm, who is sacrificed to bring the universe into being. The Sānkhya *purusha* has nothing to do with this, for in the Sānkhya system *purusha* is not one but many. There are as many *purusha*s as there are human beings, but *purusha* or spirit alone does not constitute a human being. For this it must be combined with matter, whether gross or subtle.

As it is in itself *purusha* or spirit is eternal, timeless, unlocalized, and inactive. Matter, usually called *prakriti* (which is feminine in gender just as *purusha* is masculine), is also eternal but in quite another sense: it has no beginning and no end, it is the perpetual flux of Heraclitus. Spirit and matter, as distinct principles, should never have got mixed up together, but somehow they did. How, when, and why this unnatural state of affairs came to be is not explained. This, however, according to the Sānkhya, is the human condition as we know it. It is an unsatisfactory condition, for it is out of joint with the radical dualism which the system assumes. Each individual spirit is ideally a self-contained monad but, unlike the monads of Leibniz, in itself devoid of perception and appetition and therefore incapable of development. Only when it is conjoined with and imprisoned in matter can it seem to act or do anything. The goal of both spirit and matter is to reach a final separation—the 'isolation' (*kaivalyam*) of spirit in its own timeless essence. Since spirit is of its very nature incapable of action, it is matter that must help it to freedom.

Matter is not evil as it is in another dualist system better known in the West, Manichaeism. Rather, it is a compound of three elements called *sattva*, *rajas*, and *tamas*, which can best be translated as 'goodness' or 'purity'; 'energy', 'passion', or 'activity'; and 'darkness' or 'lethargy'. The first of these helps spirit to become disentangled from matter, while the second two hinder it. These three 'strands' or 'constituents' of matter are of great importance both in the Sānkhya system and in the Bhagavad-

Gītā, and through the Gītā in all subsequent literature. Their properties are most clearly described in the Gītā itself:[1]

Purity—energy—lethargy: these are the [three] constituents from Nature sprung that bind the embodied [self] in the body though [the self itself] is changeless. Among these purity, being immaculate, knowing no sickness, dispenses light, [and yet] it binds by [causing the self] to cling to wisdom and to joy. Energy is instinct with desire, [this] know. From craving and attachment it wells up. It binds the embodies [self] by [causing it] to cling to works. But from ignorance is lethargy born: mark [this] well. All embodied [selves] it leads astray. With fecklessness and sloth and sleepiness it binds. Purity causes [a man] to cling to joy, energy to works; but lethargy, stifling wisdom, attaches to fecklessness.

The union of spirit and matter is compared to a lame man mounted on the shoulders of a blind one. Spirit is the lame man since he must rely on another to carry him around, his sole function being to see: it is the contemplative intellect. Matter is the blind man: it acts but it cannot contemplate. The purpose of the union is that spirit shall have the opportunity to contemplate material Nature in all its variety and that matter shall then gradually work to free spirit from its involvement with itself.[2] Since spirit, of itself, is completely static and timeless, it cannot be the subject of the process of transmigration, and you cannot say of it with any truth that it is either bound to matter or released from it: it is the subtle body that transmigrates, and each individual spirit continues to be associated with that subtle body until the latter leaves it. To make its meaning clear the *Sānkhya-kārikā* resorts to a simile:

[Spirit] is like a spectator at a play, [matter] brings [the play] to an end. . . .[3] As a dancer stops dancing once she has shown herself to the audience, so does material Nature stop once she has shown herself to spirit. By divers means material Nature works for spirit's sake though he has no purpose at all, ministering to him though he does not minister to her, possessed of [many] attributes though he has none himself. There is nothing more chivalrous than Nature, or so I think, for, content that she has been seen, she never again comes within the range of spirit's sight.[4]

This is the end of the drama: material Nature bows herself out, and spirit is left (as in fact he always is) in splendid isolation. He has come to understand that in reality he and material Nature have nothing in common, and he thereby achieves 'perfect and absolute isolation',[5] a '[holy] indifference and [pure] contemplation'.[6] But what, one may ask, does he

---

[1] 14: 5–9. [2] *Sānkhya-kārikā* 21. [3] Ibid. 66.
[4] Ibid. 59–62. [5] Ibid. 68. [6] Ibid. 19.

contemplate? It cannot be God, for in the Sānkhya system there is no
God. It cannot be other spirits, for he is as isolated from them as he is
from material Nature. He can then only be contemplating himself in his
total and ultimate oneness.

Now it would seem clear that the experience described in the *Sānkhya-
kārikā* is identical with that described in the *Māndūkya* Upanishad.
Spirit in its ultimate purity has no commerce with anyone or anything:
it is one, and it is free from all development and any contact with the
phenomenal world. The interpretation of the experience, however, is
entirely different. In the case of the Upanishad it is interpreted as meaning
that the man who has realized this condition has in fact realized himself as
the Absolute which is beyond God, just as the Neoplatonic One is beyond
the creative Nous. In the *Sānkyha-kārikā* on the other hand, as with
Buber, it is merely the realization of the oneness of one's own eternal core.
It must be clearly understood, however, that this being, this core, has
nothing whatever to do with the ego, the centre of everyday self-consciousness: on the contrary, true knowledge consists in spirit's realization
that there is no such thing as 'I' or 'mine'.[1] Spirit is totally other than our
ordinary self-conscious ego; hence you cannot rightly say that it is either
bound to or released from matter, for it exists in another sphere altogether.
As Jung has repeatedly pointed out, there are two selves in man—the ego
which is the centre of the conscious mind, and the 'self' as he calls it,
borrowing the Sanskrit term *ātman*, which is the centre of the total personality, both conscious and unconscious.[2] It is the latter that corresponds
to the Sānkhya *purusha*, but in the Sānkhya system salvation consists in the
total detachment of this higher 'self' from everything which has its origin
in matter, including mind, the conscious ego, and what we would call
'soul'. This distinction has also been drawn by the late Thomas Merton, a
modern Trappist monk:

Contemplation [he writes] is not and cannot be a function of this external
self. There is an irreducible opposition between the deep, transcendent self that
awakens only in contemplation, and the superficial, external self which we commonly identify with the first person singular. We must remember that this
superficial 'I' is not our real self. It is our 'individuality' and our 'empirical self'
but it is not truly the hidden and mysterious person in whom we subsist before
the eyes of God. This 'I' that works in the world, thinks about itself, observes
its own reactions and talks about itself is not the true 'I' that has been united to
God in Christ. It is at best the vesture, the mask, the disguise of that mysterious
and unknown 'self' whom most of us never discover until we are dead. Our

---

[1] *Sānkhya-kārikā* 64.
[2] C. G. Jung, *The Integration of the Personality*, London, Routledge, 1940, p. 96.

external, superficial self is not eternal, not spiritual. Far from it. This self is doomed to disappear as completely as smoke from a chimney. It is utterly frail and evanescent. Contemplation is precisely the awareness that this 'I' is really 'not I' and the awakening of the unknown 'I' that is beyond observation and reflection and is incapable of commenting upon itself. It cannot even say 'I' with the assurance and the impertinence of the other one, for its very nature is to be hidden, unnamed, unidentified in the society where men talk about themselves and about one another. In such a world the true 'I' remains both inarticulate and invisible, because it has altogether too much to say—not one word of which is about itself.[1]

This, surely, is an exact description of the Sāṅkhya *purusha*. It cannot say a word about itself because it is not the subject of such propositions as 'I am' or 'I have'. Because it is eternal and spiritual, it cannot even describe itself in words, even if it wanted to, for words can only describe material things, their properties, and ideas deriving from those properties: they can only hint at spiritual things. This accounts for what is usually described as the 'negativism' of early Buddhism. It is asserted that a state called Nirvāna exists, and this state can be and has been reached by persons called Buddhas, Tathāgatas, and Arahats, but who or what these persons really are cannot be expressed in words. Hence, though early Buddhism agrees in many respects with the Sāṅkhya system, it cannot be identified with it because the Buddhists were extremely reluctant to discuss the question of who or what enters into Nirvāna.

It has been endlessly discussed whether or not the early Buddhists admitted a 'transcendent' self. That they denied the existence of what Merton calls the 'empirical self' there is no doubt at all. Throughout the Pāli canon it is repeatedly stressed that you cannot identify the 'self' with anything at all in the phenomenal world, for that world is by definition painful, impermanent, and devoid of self. Hence you cannot in any significant way speak of 'personality', for 'personality', like a chariot, is no more than the sum total of its parts.[2] This does not mean, however, that there is no such thing as a 'transcendent' self, otherwise there would be no one and nothing to experience Nirvāna, no one and nothing that could be 'liberated'— 'liberation' or spiritual freedom being a synonym for Nirvāna. Moreover, the early Buddhist texts speak of a 'self which has become Brahman'[3] which must surely point to a transcendent self of some kind—whether individual or universal is left quite unclear.

When the Buddha was asked point-blank whether or not there was such

---

[1] Thomas Merton, *New Seeds of Contemplation*, London, Burns & Oates, 1962, pp. 5–6.
[2] *Milinda*, p. 27 (2: 1: 1.).
[3] See R. C. Zaehner, *The Bhagavad-Gītā*, Oxford, 1968, pp. 214–15.

a thing as a self, he is said to have remained silent, for had he said 'yes' he would have been classed as an 'eternalist' or one who believes in the eternity of the soul, while had he said 'no' he would have been classed as an 'annihilationist' or one who believes that nothing survives bodily death.[1] In either case he would have increased the questioner's confusion; for had he replied that there is a 'self', how would this square with his teaching that all things (*dhamma*) were devoid of self? And had he said that there was not, then the questioner would have gone away in still greater confusion, thinking that while he had previously thought that he had a 'self' or 'spirit' in the Sānkhya sense of the word, even this was now taken away from him. This must surely mean that the 'self' which can 'become Brahman', not being a 'thing', a *dhamma*, must nevertheless exist, though in an altogether different mode of existence. Similarly, when the Buddha was asked whether a Tathāgata (that is, a Buddha) existed after death, he would not commit himself[2] and for the same reason, for this form of existence has nothing to do with survival after death in the vulgar sense of those words, since survival, like birth and death, has no meaning in a form of existence where there is no time. All such questions are meaningless because the answer cannot be put into words that are unambiguous. Of this state it can only be said that it is deathless and uncompounded, the final stopping of the process of becoming, that is to say, of human life as we know it.[3] The most positive thing that can be said about it is that 'there *is* an unborn, not become, not made, uncompounded, and were it not for this unborn, not become, not made, uncompounded, no escape could be shown from what is born, has become, is made and compounded. But since there is an unborn, not become, not made, uncompounded, therefore an escape can be shown from what is born, has become, is made and compounded'.[4]

For the early Buddhists this is the whole point. There *is* a state of being which is unconditioned by time, space, causation, and the endless process of transmigration. The proof of it is the Buddha's own Enlightenment. If this eternal state of being did not exist, then Buddhism would have as little meaning as Christianity would have if Christ had not risen from the dead. In their very different ways the Buddha's Enlightenment and Christ's Resurrection guarantee immortality in some sense. There is, of course, an enormous difference between them. The Buddha's Enlightenment means

---

[1] *Saṁyutta Nikāya* iv. 400–1.   [2] Ibid. iv. 401–2.

[3] For a representative collection of descriptions of Nirvāna see A. K. Coomaraswamy and I. B. Horner, *The Living Thoughts of Gotama the Buddha*, London, Cassell, 1948, pp. 210–19, and R. C. Zaehner, op. cit., pp. 159, 213–14.

[4] *Udāna*, pp. 80–1.

that he has freed himself from everything that could possibly attach him to the world of *saṁsāra*, the world of matter in the Marxian sense, the world of movement, of physical life, and of thought. As in the *Sānkhya-kārikā* he can now be compared to a potter's wheel no longer propelled by anything: it will spin for a while, but then it will stop.[1] So too for the Buddha: once he had attained enlightenment the whole process of *saṁsāra* came to an end though he still lived. He might just as well have been dead, however, for final death in which all desire is quenched, unlike vulgar death which is only the prelude to rebirth, means the total cessation of becoming, which is Nirvāna. Whatever the Resurrection of Christ means, it does not mean this: it does not mean the negation of becoming in that which does not become, it means rather the assumption and transformation of the transient into the 'unborn, not become, not made, uncompounded'.

Both in the Sānkhya and in Buddhism salvation means 'liberation' *from* our human condition as we know it into an absolute form of existence which is simple, since it is not compounded of anything, being beyond time and space and causation. Indian religion in practically all its forms claims that man in his essence is a pure spirit: he is an angel and must be done with matter once and for all. There is, however, a danger here, for, as Pascal saw: 'Man is neither angel not beast, and it is his misfortune that whosoever would play the angel plays the beast.'[2] This is certainly not always so, but the danger is there; for in seeking a form of consciousness which eliminates the ego it is very possible that one will not rise to an angelic state but fall to that elemental state of consciousness which must have existed before man learnt to say 'I'.

Both the Sānkhya and Buddhism get on very nicely without a personal God. Man's liberation from his earthly condition is in his own hands, the Buddha can do no more than point the way; and this way includes techniques of meditation akin to the Hindu Yoga. But, as we have already pointed out, Yoga is not only a technique but also a school of philosophy closely akin to Sānkhya. How, then, does it differ from Sānkhya? The main difference is that it does admit a God of sorts. This God, however, is not the Creator of heaven and earth: he is merely 'a special type of *purusha* who is untouched by care, works, the fruits of works, or desire. . . . He is the teacher even of the ancients since he is not limited by time'.[3] He is the exemplar of man in that he serves as an object of contemplation. Being permanently free from matter he is what every *purusha* or spirit by nature is, though he cannot realize himself as such because he is gripped in the

---

[1] *Sānkhya-kārikā* 67.   [2] Pascal, *Pensées*, ed. Pléiade, p. 1170.
[3] *Yoga-sūtras* 1 : 24–6.

benevolent bondage of matter. Contemplation, however, does not lead to union with God, for the goal of Yoga as much as of Sānkhya is the isolation of the spirit not only from matter but also from all other spirits including God. In Buddhism the Buddha himself replaces the God of the Yoga system: a historical figure, who has won Enlightenment by his own unremitting efforts and who is his own guarantee, replaces a divine Being, who must be accepted by faith alone, as the one pure spirit who is never affected by matter in any way, although he has the power to control it and to assist imprisoned spirits out of their sensuous bondage. Thus in the *Yoga-sūtras* Yoga does not mean union with God, as is so often erroneously maintained, any more than Nirvāna means union with the Buddha; it simply means, as the very first *sūtra* plainly states, the stopping of conceptual thought, and its final goal, as in the Sānkhya proper, is the isolation of the spirit from all else—from matter, from other spirits, and from God.

Buddhism, Sānkhya, and Yoga, then, agree in this, that there is an absolute cleavage between spirit and matter, and that the goal of life is to use life, both physical and psychic, to win a peace so perfect in its abiding changelessness as to be almost indistinguishable from what we call death—the *requiem aeternam*, 'eternal rest', for which Catholics pray. This the *Māndūkya* Upanishad interprets as an unfractionable oneness underlying even the state of dreamless sleep in man, the microcosm, and, in the macrocosm, as the same oneness transcending even God, the Lord and Inner Controller of all. Sānkhya-Yoga will have none of this, for this, it maintains, is no more than the basic unity of a single soul 'beyond the reach of all the multiplicity it has hitherto received from life, or the multiplicity of all the souls in the world of which it is [but] one'. This is how the Sānkhya-Yoga explained the experience of unqualified oneness which, in one form or another, turns up in every mystical tradition. The prudent Buddha, on the other hand, considered that it was profitless to define what is of its very nature indefinable.

VI

THE BIRTH OF GOD

IN the sacred books of the Jews and Muslims there is no question at all as to who is the principal *dramatis persona*. It is God. There is both a *drama*, an 'action', and there are *personae*, persons acting in it. In Buddhism *drama* is *karma* and persons are merely aggregates of sensations, conations, and mental processes which emerge from the universal flux: they have no permanence and no inner coherence in themselves. Moreover, *karma*, 'action', is precisely what binds the transcendent element in man and lends it a specious appearance of personality. There is no personal God in the Hebraic sense, and even if there were, he would have no particular relevance. Buddhism, in this respect, is remarkably consistent and 'pure'. In Hinduism there is always a metaphysical ferment at work, a thirst for metaphysical ultimates which not only did the Buddha not feel: he actively discouraged all such speculation.

In Ātman and Brahman the authors of the Upanishads thought they had found a satisfactory representation of what the neo-Confucians in China called the 'Great Ultimate'. It is often alleged that the Hindu Absolute is essentially impersonal and that, therefore, no personal relationships are possible with it. This view is, at most, a partial one, for, as we have seen, two passages in the Upanishads speak of a sacred marriage with this supreme Self which is not at all unlike the spiritual nuptials between Christ and the soul that was to become a commonplace among the Christian mystics. Moreover, the passages in the Upanishads which have been taken to show that Brahman is less than personal have either been based on inadequate translations or have been imperfectly understood.

Take, for example, *Brihadāranyaka* Upanishad 3: 8: 8; there R. E. Hume's standard translation has: 'without eye, without ear, without voice, without mind,[1] without energy, without breath', etc. This certainly suggests something very much less than personal, but it is better translated: 'it is not eye or ear; it is not voice or mind; it is not light or life', etc., that is, it is none of these things because it transcends them all. Moreover, the very next verse makes it quite clear what is meant:

At the behest of this Imperishable . . . sun and moon are held apart and so abide. At the behest of this Imperishable . . . sky and earth are held apart and so

[1] Misprinted 'wind' in the text.

abide. At the behest of this Imperishable . . . seconds and minutes, days and nights, fortnights and months, seasons and years are held apart and so abide.

In other words, this 'Imperishable', of which nothing positive can be justly predicated, is also that which sustains the whole universe of space and time. This is the same Self which the same Upanishad describes as 'the Lord of all contingent beings, king of all beings'.[1] It is both the hub and the felly of the cosmic wheel, and individual selves are the spokes.[2]

There is no real contradiction between passages like this and those passages in which identity is proclaimed between the human self and the transcendent Reality which indwells the whole universe. They are one in so far as they *are*, but they are not by any means identical from the empirical point of view since the Imperishable Self is also Lord, and human selves depend on him as does everything else:

> For fear of it the wind doth blow,
> For fear [of it] the sun doth rise,
> For fear of it the gods of fire and storm
> And Death, the fifth, [hither and thither] fly.[3]

This, 'the great fear', 'the upraised thunderbolt',[4] is menacing so long as you do not know it in its timeless essence; once you know it as indwelling your own heart, all fear must cease:

> That from which [all] words recoil together with the mind,
>   Unable to attain it—
> That is the bliss of Brahman; knowing it,
> A man has naught to fear from anywhere.[5]

In some of the later Upanishads Sānkhya-Yoga ideas begin to make themselves felt. In the earlier ones, however, there was no hard and fast line between the contrasting worlds of time and eternity. Rather it was the cosmic Self which preserved both the distinction between them and their basic unity; for 'the Self is a causeway which holds these worlds apart lest they should split asunder. On this causeway there passes neither day nor night, neither old age nor death nor sorrow, neither deeds well done nor deeds ill done. All evils recoil from it, for in this Brahman-world evil has ever been laid low.'[6]

The salient difference between the religion of the Upanishads and early Buddhism is, that the first sees the eternal as a principle dwelling in the heart, whose unchanging ground it is and through which the heart

---

[1] *Brihadāranyaka* Upanishad 2: 5: 15.   [2] Ibid.
[3] *Taittirīya* Upanishad 2: 8.   [4] *Katha* Upanishad 6: 2.
[5] *Taittirīya* Upanishad 2: 9.   [6] *Chāndogya* Upanishad 8: 4: 1.

sees the same principle in all existent things; while in the second the Buddha's scepticism and mistrust of dogmatic and metaphysical formulations is so extreme, that he is content to formulate all that is necessary to salvation from this life-in-death and death-in-life which is our human condition, in four basic propositions:

(i) the phenomenal world is 'un-ease' because transient and devoid of all essence or self;

(ii) this un-ease which characterizes all life is due to desire, the 'thirst' for life and worldly happiness; and therefore

(iii) this un-ease cannot be cured unless and until it is eliminated at its source, unless and until desire is totally suppressed and absolute detachment achieved.

(iv) The royal road to this is the Noble Eightfold Path discovered by the Buddha through his own experience as being the one sure way to Nirvāna or perfect peace. The Path comprises right views, right resolve, right speech, right action, right livelihood, right effort, right mindfulness, and right contemplation.

This amounted to a religious revolution in India, and its reflexion within Hindu orthodoxy is the Sānkhya-Yoga which we discussed in our last lecture; for both Buddhism and Sānkhya-Yoga dispense with a single first cause, whether you wish to call it Brahman, Ātman, or God. The Buddhists, however, retained the term *brahma-bhūta*, 'one who has become Brahman', but the word *brahman* in this compound means simply the condition of Nirvāna: it is not a metaphysical principle.

The *Brihadāranyaka* Upanishad[1] had said that 'the great, unborn Self, that knows neither age nor death nor fear, is Brahman . . . free from fear', and that 'whoso knows this becomes Brahman, free from fear', for fear is a synonym for the Buddhist 'un-ease' which is identical with our human condition as normally understood. It does not, however, mean that one in some way becomes the Absolute or realizes oneself as the Absolute, for the simple reason that in Buddhism there is no Absolute and these prodigious identifications are quite foreign to the system.

It has often been said, as we have seen, that Brahman or the supreme Self is not a personal God. This has been exaggerated, but it is none the less true that in the Upanishads there is rarely any sense of communion with Brahman or the supreme Self except in the two passages which speak of it in terms of sexual intercourse and to which we have had occasion to refer. As Sānkhya ideas began to make themselves felt, the infinite and the

[1] 4: 4: 25.

finite, the absolute and the relative, tended to drift apart: the causeway between them of which the *Chāndogya* Upanishad speaks tends to disappear. This dualism, however, was felt to be contrary to the whole tenor of the earlier teaching, and so the 'causeway' comes to be reconstructed in the shape of a personal God or 'Lord'. Hence one of the shortest, and in some respects the most important, of the Upanishads bears the title *Iśā* —'by a Lord'. This is the first word of the Upanishad, and it is of immense significance in the development of Indian religion:

> This whole universe must be pervaded by a Lord—
> Whatever moves in this moving [world].
> Abandon it, and then enjoy:
> Covet not the goods of anyone at all.[1]

Thus we are told that there is a Lord and that there is the world. Of the 'Lord' nothing further is said for the moment. The world, on the other hand, must be renounced as the Buddhists would renounce it; yet it must also be enjoyed, but without clinging to it. Hence—'covet not the goods of anyone at all':

> Some worlds there are called 'devilish'
>   In blind darkness swathed:
> To these at death such folk pass on
>   As [seek to] slay the Self.[2]

Who is this Self? Is it the cosmic Self or the individual self? Perhaps it does not matter very much, for the 'Imperishable' indwells both. It is both the static and the moving, and it can be grasped in a flash of intuition in both its forms; for this is 'cosmic consciousness' which transports the human spirit into another dimension. It is

> Unmoving—One—swifter than thought—
> The gods could not seize hold of it as it sped before [them]:
> Standing, it overtakes [all] others as they run;
> In it the wind incites activity.

> It moves. It does not move.
> It is far, yet it is near:
> It is within this whole universe,
> And yet it is without it.[3]

And then the unitary vision of cosmic consciousness is described:

> Those who see all beings in the Self,
> And the Self in all beings,
> Will never shrink from it.

---

[1] *Iśā* Upanishad 1.   [2] Ibid. 3.   [3] Ibid. 4–5.

When once one understands that in oneself
  The Self's become all beings,
When once one's seen the unity,
What room is there for sorrow? What room for perplexity?[1]

The Self is here the sum-total of phenomenal existence grounded in the Imperishable, the eternal rest and peace over which the whole universe is 'woven, warp and woof'.[2] But the Lord 'encompasses' this Self even as the Self encompasses the whole universe:

He, the wise Sage, all-conquering, self-existent,
Encompassed that which is resplendent,
  Incorporeal, invulnerable,
Devoid of sinews, pure, unpierced by evil:
[All] things he ordered each according to its nature
  For years unending.[3]

This 'Lord', then, encompasses what is 'resplendent, incorporeal, invulnerable, . . . unpierced by evil', that is, Ātman-Brahman in so far as it is an eternal mode of being. Because he 'encompasses' it, he is prior to it in the order of reality, just as he is prior to the world of space and time which he 'orders' in all its variety, 'each [thing] according to its nature'.

As for the Buddhists and the Sānkhya-Yoga there are two forms of existence, the eternally static and the constantly moving, the compounded and the uncompounded; yet each has an existence and a value of its own. This the following stanza makes abundantly clear:

Blind darkness enter they
Who revere the uncompounded:
Into a darkness blinder yet
[Go they] who delight in the compounded.

Existence is not to be wrenched apart, diversity is not to be separated from unity, for the two cohere in 'Another' who is the Lord:

Other, they say, than what becomes,
Other, they say, than what does not become:
So from wise men have we heard
Who instructed us therein.[4]

This 'other' is the Lord in whom the compounded and the uncompounded meet; they must be known both together:

Coming to be and perishing—
Who knows these both together,
By 'perishing' surpasses death,
By 'coming to be' wins deathlessness.[5]

[1] Ibid. 6–7.   [2] *Brihadāranyaka* Upanishad 3: 6; 3: 8: 3–8.
[3] *Iśā* Upanishad 8.   [4] Ibid. 10.   [5] Ibid. 11.

To experience immortality, not just to accept it on faith, is the core of Indian religion: for early Buddhism and for the Sānkhya-Yoga this immortality can only be experienced by completely transcending the world of space and time. The *Iśā* Upanishad will not accept this, for 'blind darkness' is the lot of both the materialists and the 'spiritualists'.

In the later literature 'wisdom' or 'knowledge' is equated with timeless eternity, 'unwisdom', 'ignorance', or 'nescience', as it is sometimes called, with this world, with matter, and with action (*karma*). This curious equivalence has its origin in this same Upanishad, for in the very next stanza we read:

> Blind darkness enter they
> Who reverence unwisdom:
> Into a darkness blinder yet
> [Go they] who delight in wisdom.

And the corollary is the same:

> Wisdom and unwisdom—
> Who knows these both together,
> By 'unwisdom' surpasses death,
> By 'wisdom' reaches deathlessness.[1]

The importance of the *Iśā* Upanishad consists in this: while it accepts the division of existence into a 'perishable' and an 'Imperishable' half (the two parts representing different aspects of Brahman-Atman in the earlier Upanishads), it does not accept the uncompromising dichotomy of the Buddhists and Sānkhya-Yoga. Further, the two halves of existence, though together they may be legitimately described as the Self or Brahman, are nevertheless subject to the 'Lord', who is 'other' than both in that he 'encompasses' them. This is clear enough already in the *Iśā*: in the frankly theistic *Śvetāśvatara* Upanishad this emerges with absolute clarity:

> In the imperishable, infinite city[2] of Brahman
>   Two things there are—
> Wisdom and unwisdom, hidden, established there:
> Perishable is unwisdom, but wisdom is immortal:
> Who over wisdom and unwisdom rules, he is Another.[3]

This is something quite new in Hinduism. For the first time a personal God emerges who is superior not only to the transient world but also to the changeless, eternal world which the Buddhists call Nirvāna. This God is the Vedic Rudra now in the process of being transformed into the Śiva

[1] *Iśā* Upanishad 14.   [2] Reading *pure*.   [3] *Śvetāśvatara* Upanishad 5: 1.

of classical Hinduism, whose salient traits he is already beginning to
assume; for he is both the ideal Yogin, and therefore perfectly chaste, and
at the same time he is ithyphallic, and the phallus is the symbol in which he
delights and under which he is normally worshipped. Both aspects of him
are already present in the *Śvetāśvatara* Upanishad. Sānkhya dualism is
adopted: on the one side there is *purusha*, the male—spirit—on the other
prakriti, the female—matter: but beyond them is Śiva, the Lord, who
unites and sustains them both. He it is who brings about the union of
individual *purusha*s with material Nature, and he it is who brings about
their ultimate release:

> What is here conjoined together—
> Perishable and imperishable,
> Manifest and unmanifest—
> All this does the Lord sustain;
> But for lack of mastery the self is bound,
> Its [very] nature to enjoy experience:
> [But] once it knows [its] God,
> From all fetters is it freed![1]

The individual self, spirit, or *purusha* has no function but to experience.[2]
It is bound to matter which alone acts, and this union is decreed by God
who is 'the Beginning, the efficient cause of the conjoining'.[3] God is
distinct from the individual self or spirit: 'one is the self, another he who
impels to action'. Both have intercourse with matter, but the one becomes
involved in the experience, the other does not. The one is bound, the other,
though controlling matter, remains unaffected by it, aloof and alone:[4]

> Two unborn [males] there are: one knows, the other knows not;
> One Master, Lord, the other lacking mastery.
> One unborn female there is too, close linked
> To what enjoys experience and to the experience enjoyed.
> And there is the self unbounded
> Of universal form: it neither works nor acts.
> Find out [this] trinity. That is Brahman.[5]

For the Sānkhya the whole of existence could be divided into matter
and spirit: the two, though mixed, are utterly distinct in nature. In the
Śvetāśvatara Upanishad, however, there is a third principle—God, who
is both he 'who impels to action'[6] and the absolutely aloof and alone. This
trinity forms the triple Brahman—a word that has by now come to assume
a bewildering number of meanings. Here it has come to mean the sum

---

[1] Ibid. 1: 8.   [2] Ibid. 1: 2.   [3] Ibid. 6: 5.
[4] Ibid. 6: 11.   [5] Ibid. 1: 9.   [6] Ibid. 1: 6.

total of existence—God, the Lord; the whole world of spirit; and the universe of matter. 'This is the triple Brahman.'[1]

The attributes of God are fully described in chapter vi, but only three need detain us now: these are his absolute transcendence—he is 'the Eternal, Self-subsistent'[2] 'witness, observer, absolute, alone, devoid of attributes'[3]—secondly his omnipotence:

> Maker of all is he, all-knowing, source of selves;
> He knows, he the architect of time,
> Possessed of [all] attributes, omniscient:
> Lord of primeval Nature, [Lord of all] knowers of the field,[4]
> Lord of the constituents of Nature,[5]
> Cause of the round of birth and death,
> [Cause of] deliverance,
> [Cause of] our sojourn here and of [our] imprisonment.[6]

Thirdly, despite his transcendence, he is wholly immanent both in individual selves and in matter:

> This is the God who pervades all regions:
> He is the first-born, he is in the womb.
> He is born indeed and will be born again.

But—

> Over against [his] creatures does he stand,
> His face turned every way.[7]

In his complete transcendence Śiva is beyond all categories of being[8] and beyond all attributes,[9] and yet he initiates all action, he starts the world process and puts a stop to it: he abides when all else perishes and at the same time he is higher than the Imperishable itself.[10] Since in his transcendence there is nothing he need do, it can be said of him that 'he neither works nor acts'.[11] Like the 'Lord' of the *Iśā* Upanishad he 'encompasses' both time and eternity, both space and spacelessness:

> From all eternity this whole universe
>   Doth he encompass:
> He knows, he the architect of time,
> Possessed of attributes, omniscient:
>
> By him are works commanded
> [By him do works] evolve . . .

---

[1] *Śvetāśvatara* Upanishad 1: 12.   [2] Ibid. 1: 12.   [3] Ibid. 6: 11.
[4] i.e. *purushas*.   [5] The three 'constituents' of Nature, pp. 98–9.
[6] *Śvetāśvatara* Upanishad 6: 16.   [7] Ibid. 2: 16.   [8] Ibid. 2: 15; 6: 4.
[9] Ibid. 6: 11.   [10] Ibid. 5: 1.   [11] Ibid. 1: 9.

His work accomplished he takes his rest,
Then once again conjoins himself
With principle after principle—
With one, with two, with three or eight,
With time, and the subtle attributes of self.

[All] works does he initiate,
[And works] are never free from quality:
All modes of being he directs.
When once these cease to be, the work once done must perish.
When works have perished, he goes on:
Other than essence is he,
[Other than anything even as it really is].

He is the Beginning, the efficient cause of the conjoining,
Seen as beyond the three times—partless too:
Of old did men worship him, this God adorable,
Become becoming, in his thought subsisting, omniform![1]

If God is both transcendent and immanent, so too is man; both are
*purusha*s, males, and as such both stand over against *prakriti*, material
Nature, which is the *one* female.[2] Man is bound by matter and enmeshed
in it; by nature he is 'without mastery',[3] and it is only by knowing God that
he can be freed. God, on the other hand, is Lord. Though he consorts
with matter he is never affected by it, since he is always free, 'absolute,
alone, devoid of attributes'.[4] Man's salvation, as in the *Yoga-sūtra*s, is
won by meditating on God and by the practice of Yoga techniques (mentioned here for the first time in some detail[5]). Matter or Nature is the same
as *māyā*, the phenomenal world, *not* illusion as in later monist thought:
like the individual selves it is not independent but subject to God. Individual selves are metaphorically spoken of as 'parts' of him, though elsewhere it is categorically stated that he has no parts:[6] perhaps they are best
regarded as the seeds he constantly injects into Nature (for the imagery is
sexual throughout this Upanishad). And so we read:

Māyā is material Nature, this must be known,
And he who possesses it is the mighty Lord:
By things that are but parts of him
This whole world is pervaded.

It is he alone who approaches every womb,
In him [alone] does this universe grow together and dissolve;
He is the Lord who grants [us] favours,
    God, the adorable:
Discerning him a man wins peace for ever.[7]

[1] Ibid. 6: 2–5.   [2] Ibid. 1: 9.   [3] Ibid. 1: 2, 9.   [4] Ibid. 6: 11.
[5] Ibid. 2: 8–13.   [6] Ibid. 6: 5.   [7] Ibid. 4: 10–11.

'Peace', the Buddhist Nirvāna, then, is won by discerning God as he really is, both as utterly transcendent and beyond all categories, and as 'dwelling in the heart': only so does a man become immortal.[1]

The individual self's resemblance to and dissemblance from Śiva, the One God, is well illustrated in two similies. Both are concerned with matter, but the one is deeply enmeshed, the other sublimely detached:

> With the one unborn female, red, white, and black,
> Who gives birth to many a creature like unto herself,
> Lies the one male unborn, taking his delight.
> Another unborn Male forsakes her, for she has had her pleasure.

> Two birds, close-linked companions,
>   Cling to the selfsame tree;
> Of these the one eats of the sweet fruit,
> The other, nothing eating, looks on intent.

> On the selfsame tree a person is plunged in [grief],
> Mourning his lack of mastery, perplexed;
> When he sees the other, the Lord, rejoicing
> In his majesty, his sorrow melts away.[2]

'By knowing God a man is from all fetters freed':[3] this is the refrain of the *Śvetāśvatara* Upanishad. But 'knowing' does not mean loving or being united with him: rather one attains to that 'isolation' that is always his and to 'mastery', that is to say, freedom from the bondage of matter, what the *Chāndogya* Upanishad[4] calls 'freedom of movement in all states of being'. Three things seem to be involved in this condition:

(i) the individual spirit is freed from matter;
(ii) it achieves 'mastery' and 'isolation' in complete independence; and
(iii) it knows and sees God as supremely isolated because devoid of attributes and beyond all categories.

This triple knowledge constitutes the triple Brahman. It is not to experience immortality by participation, Bucke's 'cosmic consciousness', but to achieve a personal 'isolation' of an independent spirit by the contemplation of the only spiritual monad which is eternally unaffected by matter and which is therefore its eternal exemplar. The whole mystical theology of the *Śvetāśvatara* Upanishad is summed up in two passages (1: 10–12 and 2: 14–15). In both passages the absolute supremacy of Śiva, the personal God and Lord, shines through, but because both passages

---

[1] *Śvetāśvatara* Upanishad 4: 20.   [2] Ibid. 4: 5–7.
[3] Ibid. 2: 15; 4: 16; 5: 13; 6: 13.   [4] 7: 25: 2.

have, in my opinion, been consistently mistranslated, I shall have to quote them in full. In any case their importance in the history of Indian religion fully warrants this. In the first passage the trinity of God, individual selves or spiritual monads, and material Nature is roundly affirmed, and the experience of 'liberation' is interpreted in terms of it:

> Perishable is material Nature;
> Immortal and imperishable [the self]:
> Both the perishable and the self
> Doth the one God Hara rule.
> By meditating on him, by constant striving,[1]
> By becoming what one really is,[2]
> The whole world of appearance (*māyā*) will once again
> Be lost to sight at last.

> Once God is known, all fetters fall away,
>   [All] cares dissolve,
> Birth and death are left behind;
> And thirdly, by meditating on him
> At [the time of] the body's breaking up
> There is mastery supreme: his desires fulfilled
> [A man is then] absolute, alone (*kevala*).

> This must be known—the Eternal, Self-subsistent:
> For than that there's nothing higher to be known.
> The enjoyer of experience—the thing experienced—
> The one who provides the impulse—
> Know these! and all is said.
> This is the triple Brahman.

So much for the metaphysical explanation.

Now, in the *Śvetāśvatara* Upanishad as in the Bhagavad-Gītā, the word *Brahman* is used in a variety of ways which we need not enumerate here. In the second passage which we are about to quote, however, there is an upward gradation—self, Brahman, God. Neither 'Brahman' nor 'God' is a Sānkhya category, and it is not quite clear how we should understand the word here. It seems, however, that we should understand it as the 'Imperishable', which in this Upanishad stands for the totality of spirit or, if you like, the aggregate of all spiritual monads. The previous verses have been describing for the first time the techniques of Yoga—posture, breath-control, and so on—and the immediate benefits these techniques are alleged to produce. The first major result here as in the

---

[1] *Yojanāt.* Most translations have 'union', which the word scarcely ever means.
[2] Much less likely, 'by becoming [his] essence'.

Bhagavad-Gītā is the unification or integration of the personality around the immortal self; but this is not the end, as it would have to be in any monist scheme of things. Once again I quote, for in this case the words speak for themselves:

Even as a mirror with dirt begrimed
Shines brightly once it is well cleaned,
So too the embodied [self], once it has seen
  Self as it really is,
Becomes one, its goal achieved, from sorrow free.

Then by means of self as it really is as with a lamp
An integrated man sees Brahman as it really is.
[Then will he know] the unborn, undying God, the Pure,
Beyond all essences as they really are,
[And] knowing him, from all fetters he'll be freed.

The *Śvetāśvatara* Upanishad is almost wholly and consistently theistic throughout. The personal God, Rudra-Śiva, emerges as the principle from which both the main Sānkhya categories, both spirit, or the sumtotal of spiritual monads, and matter, or material Nature, arise. Sometimes this God is thought of as Brahman, hitherto the highest principle by definition, sometimes he stands beyond it.

This is one of the things that makes Hinduism so maddeningly difficult to understand; I mean, the extreme fluidity of its terminology. St. Anselm defined God as that than which one can think of nothing higher; and in the Upanishads this is what Brahman usually means. Alternatively the same principle is called Self or *Purusha*, the [Supreme] Male. Sometimes they are simply alternative terms for the same thing; at other times they are graded, as in the last passage we quoted. What is new in the *Iśā* and *Śvetāśvatara* Upanishads is that the personal 'Lord', in the case of the latter, Rudra-Śiva, is exalted over and above Brahman understood as the totality of eternal being and temporal becoming—a transcendently immanent and immanently transcendent personal Absolute who 'encompasses' not only the world of appearance but also the world of eternal, unchanging essence—the world of 'wisdom' (*jñāna*) as well as the world of 'action' (*karma*). In Aristotelian terminology this God is the unmoved *moving* Mover, beyond both movement and rest, of both of which he is the apex and ground. This personal Absolute is identified with the Vedic God Rudra, from now on more generally to be known as Śiva.

In the West, since Bultmann, demythologization has been all the rage. In the Upanishads demythologization had become a fact: the Upanishadic

Brahman had come to have as much substance as the abstractions of Pseudo-Dionysius and Nicolas of Cusa: it could only be hinted at in paradox. The Rig-Veda and the Brāhmanas had been fully mythological; in them we find myth interpreted and re-presented as ritual. The Upanishads both start and bring near to completion the process of demythologization. Hinduism properly so called, that is, the religion of the Great Epic and the Purānas remythologizes with a vengeance. This is their weakness; for whereas it may be true to say that absolute truth (whatever that may be) can only be presented to the average human being in mythological terms, the fact remains that some myths are more striking—strike us as more true—more arresting, and more thought-provoking than others. To go no further than Christianity for the moment, the nineteenth-century myth of 'Gentle Jesus, meek and mild' is trivial; the myth of the agony of the Son of God in Gethsemane rings so terrifyingly true that few can bear to contemplate it seriously. None of the Vedic myths had any such evocative power, and so they were quietly and rightly forgotten. They were, however, succeeded by myths about other gods who, though they bore the names of minor Vedic deities, were nevertheless quite new gods, so utterly had they changed in the course of the centuries that had elapsed between the time of the Rig-Veda and the compilation of the Great Epic and the Purānas. In fact, by the time the Epic came to be written—let us say in the third century B.C., though everyone agrees that there are strata of antiquity in it, the earliest of which may be separated from the latest by as much as six hundred years—two gods and two gods only had emerged whose devotees claimed for them the title of *Parabrahman* and *Paramātman*, the 'highest Brahman' and the 'highest Self', thereby identifying them both with the God who 'encompasses' all things in time and eternity and with the God in the human heart who is 'no larger than the fine point of an awl'.[1] These gods were Rudra-Śiva, the God of the *Śvetāśvatara* Upanishad, and Vishnu, who in his incarnation as Krishna is the God of the Bhagavad-Gītā, a religious classic which is not only by far the best known and by far the most influential text within the Hindu tradition, but also, to my mind, ranks as the most significant sacred text in the whole history of religion.

In the Gītā, as in the *Śvetāśvatara* Upanishad, myth plays only a small part, and yet it cannot be ignored. Śiva, as we have seen, is the ithyphallic Yogin who combines all the opposites within himself. There are, of course, plenty of myths about him around which his devotees were later to play. Symbolically, however, he is the union of the male and

---

[1] *Śvetāśvatara* Upanishad 5: 8.

female principles, and because they are the very foundation of the physical universe, he claims that they are not mere symbols but the very stuff of reality;[1] and it is in him and in him alone that this discordant pair of opposites, and all other pairs of opposites, meet in perfect concord.

Vishnu can make no such claim; but Vishnu is far more deeply involved in mythology than Śiva, for he is essentially a god who takes on human or animal form in order to restore the just balance of things on earth. Ten such incarnations or 'descents' (*avatār*s) are usually recognized—as fish, tortoise, boar, man-lion, and dwarf; as Rāma 'with the axe' who exterminated the warrior class; as Rāma or Rāmacandra, the hero of the shorter Sanskrit Epic, the *Rāmāyana*; as Krishna, one of the heroes of the Great Epic or *Mahābhārata*; surprisingly enough as the Buddha; and finally as Kalkin, who is yet to come. It is, however, Krishna alone who will concern us in these lectures, for it is he who is the teacher in the Bhagavad-Gītā to which we now turn.

The Bhagavad-Gītā is one episode out of hundreds in India's colossal Epic, the Mahābhārata. As such it does not rank as *śruti*, as primary revelation, for the Epic is not and never has been part of the Veda, although it claims itself to rank as the 'fifth Veda'. The Bhagavad-Gītā is a didactic poem, but there are literally hundreds of such poems in the Epic. How, then, did it come to enjoy the unrivalled prestige it has consistently held at least since the ninth century A.D. at the very latest? How has it come about that no single philosopher of any note, either medieval or modern, has failed to comment on it, though many have not commented on the Upanishads themselves which, forming as they do the end of the Veda, should theoretically command a far greater authority? Why is the rest of the didactic matter in the Mahābhārata almost entirely neglected although, in theory, it should rank equally with the Gītā as coming from the semi-sacred source? If it is because the teacher is Krishna, who had come to be accepted as an incarnation of Vishnu, then why is it that Krishna's second discourse, the *Anugītā* or 'supplementary Gītā', remains neglected and almost unknown? None of these questions is easy to answer.

Can it be, then, that the Gītā introduces an entirely new type of religion that had a more popular appeal than the Upanishads? To this the answer must be at least a qualified 'Yes', if only because the whole course of Indian religion changed after it. The 'Yes', however, must remain qualified, for the new type of religion it introduces is *bhakti*, a religion of love and loyalty and devotion, but there is plenty about love and devotion to both Śiva and Vishnu in the rest of the Epic. Certainly, the Gītā appears

---

[1] Mahābhārata 13: 14: 102 and additional lines in footnote.

in the Epic narrative at a crucial turning-point of the story, and it is also very much a self-contained whole, although its beginning and its end and many allusions in the middle to the actual situation it occupies in the Epic would not be comprehensible except in the context of the Epic. When all is said and done, however, the only satisfactory explanation is that the Gītā contains religious teachings that almost all men who have read it have recognized to be of abiding value. Its impact on the West has been almost as great as its impact on India, and I doubt whether any other book has been so often translated into English. Again, it has a certain timeless quality since the Krishna of the Gītā, like the Jesus of the Sermon on the Mount, has stepped out of mythology or history as the case may be: his personality is of no consequence. It is enough to know that he is God incarnate, and that, not his character as portrayed in the Epic, is what gives authority to his teaching. This the Hindus have always admitted, for religion to them would and could have no meaning unless its message were timeless. The Protestant idea of the 'Lord of history' is meaningless to them, for they do not stem from the Jews, and the subject-matter of their religion is not history but eternity and immortality.

The *dramatis personae* of the Bhagavad-Gītā are Krishna and Arjuna. Arjuna is the third of the five Pāndava brothers who are about to go to war with their cousins, the Kauravas, because the latter refuse to hand over to them any part of the kingdom to which they are entitled. The kingdom had indeed been theirs by right, but Yudhishthira, the eldest of the brothers and the incarnation of Dharma, the god of righteousness, driven on by fate, had rashly gambled against his cousins and lost everything. The family elders, however, came to an agreement according to which the Pāndava brothers were to spend thirteen years in exile. They were then to be allowed to have at least part of their kingdom back. Duryodhana, however, the eldest of the Kaurava brothers, had tasted power and had no intention of giving it up. His cousin, Yudhishthira, on the other hand, despised power. An ascetic by nature, he would have much preferred to go on living in the forest, but Krishna thought otherwise. In the end a compromise was reached: Yudhishthira asked for only five villages, one for himself and one for each of his four brothers. Even this Duryodhana was not prepared to concede, and so Yudhishthira reluctantly prepared for war. All was now ready: the two armies stood facing each other in their opposing ranks, the conches sounded, and it seemed as if the struggle had already begun. At this critical moment Arjuna's nerve failed him; and yet of all the five brothers Arjuna was the most chivalrous and brave. It was not, then, out of cowardice that he suddenly announced he would not fight, but out of a conviction that it was wrong to go to war with one's own kith and kin, many of whom he respected and loved, however just the cause might appear to be. Krishna, who had elected to act as his charioteer, remained coldly unimpressed, for not only was this war just, but it was also his divine will that it should be fought to a victorious finish. With a stern admonition to Arjuna not to play the coward, he then proceeds to advance a variety of reasons why Arjuna should fight. It is at this point that the Bhagavad-Gītā, the 'Lord's Song', begins.

The occasion for the discourse is, then, to urge Arjuna to fight. Krishna advances two main reasons why the fight should go on. First there is the purely mundane consideration of caste-duty and honour. Arjuna belongs to the *kshatriya* class of royal warriors, and it is therefore his duty to fight. Quite apart from this, however, he is making an absurd fuss about this business of killing and being killed; for you can only kill the body, you cannot kill the soul. This the *Katha* Upanishad[1] had already made clear:

> Should the killer think, 'I kill',
> Or the killed, 'I have been killed',
> Both these have no [right] knowledge:
> He kills not, is not killed.

In the *Katha* Upanishad this refers to the eternal essence in man which is identical in all. In the Gītā, which draws a clear distinction between the individual self which is 'part' of God[2] and God himself, it refers to the individual self, which you can regard in one of two ways. Either you can see it as a spiritual monad as in the Sāṅkhya system, in which case it can neither be born nor die since it does not exist in time; or you can regard it as the transmigrating subject, and in that case there is no cause for worry either, for, as Krishna says:

Even if you think that it is constantly [re-]born and constantly [re-]dies, even so you grieve for it in vain. For sure is the death of all that is born, sure is the birth of all that dies: so in a matter that no one can prevent you have no cause to grieve.[3]

Reincarnation, you will notice, is now taken completely for granted and the quality of your incarnation rigorously follows the law of *karma*: what you sow, that you will reap. 'By good works a man becomes holy, by evil [works] he becomes evil',[4] and evil is the incarnation of the man whose works are foul, for 'those whose conduct on earth has been foul can expect to enter a foul and stinking womb, that is, the womb of a bitch or a sow or

---

[1] 2: 19.   [2] Bhagavad-Gītā 15: 7.   [3] Ibid. 2: 26–7.
[4] *Brihadāranyaka* Upanishad 4: 4: 5.

an outcaste'.[1] If, however, Arjuna does his caste-duty, he cannot lose; for if he is killed in battle he will go straight to paradise, and if he wins his family will regain an empire. Even so, actions bring their own rewards and punishments, and, for the author of the Gītā as for the Buddhists, ultimate salvation consists not in the attainment of one of the heavens but in total deliverance from phenomenal existence as such—in 'Nirvāna that is Brahman too'.[2]

The author of the Bhagavad-Gītā was certainly familiar with the Upanishads, particularly the *Katha* and *Śvetāśvatara*, but the background he takes for granted is partly Sānkhya-Yoga and partly Buddhist. In the first six chapters, particularly ii, v, and vi, he is consciously using Buddhist terminology, the most obvious examples of which are *nirvāna* itself and *brahma-bhūta*, 'having become Brahman', used in the Buddhist sense of simply transcending phenomenal existence. It is important to bear this in mind. The idea of Nirvāna is not rejected, rather is it taken for granted, but it is not the ultimate goal. It is, however, a necessary stage on the way. All action, whether good or evil, binds: hence a way must be found which will put a stop to the effects of action or works for ever, for there is no salvation in works. To achieve this an attitude of complete detachment from what you do must be cultivated; you must 'hold pleasure and pain, profit and loss, victory and defeat to be the same'.[3] You must hold them to be the same because *sub specie aeternitatis* they *are* the same; for Brahman, the stuff of eternity, remains always the same, however much phenomena may change, and, in the case of the individual, whatever he may do or leave undone. Fools may not understand this, the wise do:

Wise men see the selfsame thing in a Brāhman wise and courteous as in a cow or an elephant, nay, as in a dog or outcaste. While yet in this world they have overcome [the process of] emanation [and decay], for their minds are stilled in that which is ever the same: for devoid of imperfection and ever the same is Brahman: therefore in Brahman [stilled] they stand.[4]

Total detachment means the loss of all sense of ego, all sense of possessing anything—and this again is a typically Buddhist idea. And so:

The man who puts away all desires and roams around from longing freed, who does not think, 'This I am', or 'This is mine', draws near to peace. This is the fixed, still state of Brahman; he who wins through to this is nevermore perplexed. Standing therein at the time of death, to Nirvāna that is Brahman too he goes.[5]

[1] *Chāndogya* Upanishad 5: 10: 7.   [2] Bhagavad-Gītā 2: 72.
[3] Ibid. 2: 38.   [4] Ibid. 5: 18–19.   [5] Ibid. 2: 71–2.

And yet, even in outlining the principles of the contemplative life, Krishna impresses on Arjuna that work alone is his proper business. This, however, he immediately qualifies by saying that the fruit of what he does is *not* his proper business: 'let not your motive be the fruit of works nor your attachment to [mere] worklessness. Stand fast in Yoga, surrendering attachment; in success and failure be the same and then get busy with your works. Yoga means sameness and indifference.'[1]

'Yoga' is the keyword of the Bhagavad-Gītā. It is both the *way* to Brahman, the 'spiritual exercise' or technique of self-control centred on the twin virtues of detachment and indifference, and it is also the goal itself; for in so far as it is defined as 'sameness' it is identical with Brahman, whereas the same word when applied to a man still working in the world means 'indifference', the 'sainte indifférence' of St. François de Sales.

But *yoga* also means the 'integration' of the personality around its immortal centre, the individual self, as well as 'skill in performing works'. Yet even in this sense *yoga*, a term which always implies action, does not mean pursuing action for its own sake; 'for lower far is [the path of] active work [for its own sake] than the Yoga (spiritual exercise) of the soul (*buddhi*)'—the term *buddhi* meaning in the Gītā almost exactly what we understand by the soul, the seat of intellect and will and the responsible element in man. So 'seek refuge in the soul! How pitiful are they whose motive is the fruit [of works]! Whoso is integrated (*yukta* from the same root as *yoga*) by the soul discards here [and now] both good and evil works: brace yourself then for [this] Yoga; for Yoga is [also] skill in [performing] works.'[2] And yet, having said this much, Krishna then goes on to describe not the man of action who is at the same time detached, but rather the 'man of steady wisdom' whose soul is integrated (*yukta* again) and who 'draws in on every side his senses from their proper objects as a tortoise [might draw in] its limbs'.[3] *This* is the man who goes to Nirvāna that is Brahman too.

Small wonder that Arjuna is perplexed, for Krishna has not explained why he should engage in a bloody war. All he seems to have said is that it does not matter whether you go to war or not so long as you dissociate yourself entirely from what you do. So Arjuna, with an impatience characteristic of his own warrior class, replies:

If you think that [the contemplative life of] the soul is a loftier [course] than [the mere performance of] acts, then why do you command me to do a cruel deed? You confuse my soul, or so it seems, with distinctly muddled words: so tell me with authority the one [simple way] whereby I can attain the better part.[4]

---

[1] Bhagavad-Gītā 2: 47–8.   [2] Ibid. 2: 49–50.   [3] Ibid. 2: 58.   [4] Ibid. 3: 1–2.

To this Krishna has two answers. First, without work of some sort it is impossible even to keep the body in good trim; and this is desirable, for so long as men are in this world, they have to act in accordance with the duties laid down for their various classes and castes. Indeed, this is the purpose of the various divine incarnations, for, as he himself says: 'Whenever the law of righteousness withers away and lawlessness arises, then do I generate myself [on earth]. For the protection of the good, for the destruction of evildoers, for the setting up of the law of righteousness I come into being age after age.'[1] That this world should continue is God's will; and later writers will usually describe the whole world process as God's 'sport', and as such it must go on. Though salvation consists in escape from the world, suicide is not a legitimate way out, for this would denote attachment to 'worklessness'.[2] Secondly, God himself is engaged in ceaseless activity, and who is man that he should seek to be more perfect, more uncommitted and free, than God himself? There is nothing God need do, nor does he lack any perfection after which he need strive, yet work is the element in which he moves. 'If I were not to do my work', Krishna says, 'these worlds would fall to ruin, and I should be a worker of confusion, destroying these [my] creatures.'[3] God, then, is to be imitated not only in his eternal rest, but also in his tireless activity. It is up to Arjuna to set an example to less enlightened people. These are attached to what they do, but the wise should work on without attachment 'longing to bring about the welfare of the world';[4] for even the fully integrated man who has won liberation from the world and has no further interest in it[5] takes pleasure in the welfare of his fellow men.[6]

In its analysis of being the Gītā follows the Sānkhya system. The true self is not the agent. In the *Katha* Upanishad[7] man's body is compared to a chariot: what we understand by soul is the charioteer, mind is the reins, senses the horses, the object of sense the tract before them, while the true self, the *ātman*, is merely the owner of the chariot. The soul is entirely responsible for keeping the rebellious senses under control, while the self, though it owns the body, can merely observe the skill of the charioteer or his lack of it. So too in the Gītā it is most emphatically asserted that the self is not the agent;

All works renouncing with the mind, quietly he sits in full control—the embodied [self] within the city with nine gates: he neither works nor makes another work. Neither agency nor worldly works does [the body's] lord engender,

[1] Ibid. 4: 7–8.   [2] Ibid. 2: 47.   [3] Ibid. 3: 24.
[4] Ibid. 3: 25.   [5] Ibid. 3: 18.   [6] Ibid. 5: 25.
[7] *Katha* Upanishad 3: 3–4.

nor yet the bond that work to fruit conjoins: it is inherent Nature that initiates the action.[1]

Nature or matter alone acts through its three constituents of purity, energy, and lethargy. The whole world process and all the interplay of human actions the one upon the other are simply the changing relationships of these three constituents. It is man's ego that fools him into the belief that it is he, not they, who acts;[2] 'but he who knows how constituents and works are parcelled out in categories, seeing things as they are, thinks thus: "Constituents on constituents act", [and thus thinking] remains unattached.'[3]

This is pure Sānkhya. But in the Gītā there is, apart from matter and spirit, also God. God, as we are gradually to learn, is the source of both, and hence the source of the three constituents themselves and through them of all agency. He is the doer, but he is never affected by what he does because he has no yearning for its fruits: hence he is never bound by the works he himself initiates.[4] As in the *Svetāśvatara* Upanishad material Nature is also God's *māyā*, his creative power, which, by the mere fact that it is the source of multiplicity, tends to hide God in his changeless essence from man. The relationship between God and the constituents of Nature is most clearly set out in 7: 12–14:

Know too that [all] states of being whether they be of [Nature's constituent] purity, energy, or lethargy proceed from me; but I am not in them, they are in me. By these three states of being inhering in the constituents this whole universe is led astray and does not understand that I am far beyond them and that I neither change nor pass away. For [all] this is my *māyā*—my creative power—composed of the constituents, divine, hard to transcend.

God initiates all change: he emanates and reabsorbs the whole universe in vast cosmic cycles of time:

Subduing my own material Nature ever again I emanate this whole host of beings—powerless [themselves], from Nature comes the power. These works [of mine] neither bind nor limit me: as one indifferent I sit among these works, detached. [A world of] moving and unmoving things material Nature brings to birth while I look on and supervise: this is the cause [and this the means] by which the world revolves.[5]

The universe, then, is the work of God, but it is also a snare and a delusion to the individual self who, like the spiritual monad of the Sānkhya system, has his real home outside the whole created order. Salvation still means transcending all contingent existence and reaching that changeless state

---

[1] Gītā 5: 13–14.   [2] Ibid. 3: 27.   [3] Ibid. 3: 28.
[4] Ibid. 4: 13–14.   [5] Ibid. 9: 8–10.

which man shares with God. This is what the Buddhists call Nirvāna, which the Gītā had identified with Brahman (but in the Buddhist, not the Upanishadic sense) or more accurately with the 'fixed, still state of Brahman'.[1] This is, of course, an experience of changeless, timeless, abiding eternity, the 'higher' mode of being that Krishna claims is his. This is, however, not emphasized in the first six chapters where God plays no part in the process of liberation at all.

There are three passages in the first six chapters which deal directly with the attainment of this changeless state. As in the *Śvetāśvatara* this is not interpreted as union with God. What we learn of God is essentially that he is, through material Nature, the source of all action, though his essence, like that of the individual self, is changeless. As in the *Yoga-sūtras*, then, he is a fit object of contemplation,[2] something on which to concentrate one's attention in order to be rid of outside distractions, but, again as in the *Yoga-sūtras*, once full integration has been achieved and no sense of ego remains, there is no sense of God's presence at all—only a perfect peace, the 'fixed, still state of Brahman' which is Nirvāna.

In a similar passage in chapter v there is no reference to God at all until the very last verse—only to Nirvāna and Brahman, the principle that has no characteristic except to be 'ever the same'. This alone is the goal of the man who has attained to complete detachment and integration:

While yet in this world they have overcome [the process of] emanation [and decay], for their minds are stilled in that which is ever the same: for devoid of imperfection and ever the same is Brahman: therefore in Brahman [stilled] they stand. Winning some pleasant thing [the sage] will not rejoice, nor shrink disquietened when the unpleasant comes his way: steadfast and still his soul, [all] unconfused, he will know Brahman, in Brahman [stilled] he'll stand. [His] self detached from contacts with the outside world, in [him]self he finds his joy, [his] self in Brahman integrated by spiritual exercise (*yoga*), he finds unfailing joy. . . . His joy within, his bliss within, his light within, the man who is integrated in spiritual exercise becomes Brahman and draws near to Nirvāna that is Brahman too. Nirvāna that is Brahman too win seers in whom [all] taint of imperfection is destroyed; their doubts dispelled, with self controlled, they take their pleasure in the weal of all contingent beings. Around these holy men whose thoughts are [fast] controlled, estranged from anger and desire, knowing [at last] the self, fares Nirvāna that is Brahman too. . . . With senses, mind, and soul restrained, the silent sage, on deliverance intent, who has forever banished fear, anger, and desire, is truly liberated.[3]

This is the peace of the Buddhist Nirvāna, this is to become Brahman which is ever the same in all beings, and therefore to know it: this is to

---

[1] Ibid. 2: 72.   [2] Ibid. 2: 61.   [3] Ibid. 5: 19–28.

realize one's own inner self as partaking in that very sameness which is Brahman, this is liberation and freedom of the spirit. There has been no mention at all of Krishna, the personal God. In the last strophe of the chapter, however, Krishna says:

Knowing me to be the proper object of sacrifice and mortification, great Lord of all the worlds, friend of all contingent beings, he reaches peace.

This again, quite plainly, does not mean union with God, but simply the recognition of Krishna's consistent teaching that he is the sole object of sacrifice and the sole agent. Krishna does the work, the human self, released from work of any kind, stands fixed and still in timeless bliss. This is why Krishna had already said: 'Cast all your works on me, your thoughts [withdrawn] in what appertains to self; have neither hope nor thought that "This is mine": cast off this fever! Fight!'[1] God works and disposes: man contemplates and accepts.

The sequel in chapter vi is very much the same, but there is one crucial difference. Let us see what it is:

When thought is checked by spiritual exercise and comes to rest, and when of [one]self one sees the self in self and finds content therein, that is the utmost joy which transcends [all things of] sense and which soul [alone] can grasp. When he knows this and [knowing it] stands still, moving not an inch from the reality [he sees], he wins a prize beyond all others—or so he thinks. Therein he [firmly] stands, unmoved by any suffering, however grievous it may be. This he should know is what is meant by spiritual exercise (*yoga*)—the unlinking of the link with suffering and pain. This is the act of integration (*yoga*) that must be brought about with [firm] resolve and mind all undismayed. . . . By soul held fast in steadfastness he must make his mind [too] subsist in self; then little by little will he come to rest; he must think of nothing at all. Wherever the fickle mind unsteady roves around, from thence [the soul] will bring it back and subject it to the self. For upon this athlete of the spirit whose mind is stilled the highest joy descends: [all] passion laid to rest, free from [all] stain, Brahman he becomes. [And] thus [all] flaws transcending, the athlete of the spirit, constant in integrating self, with ease attains unbounded joy, Brahman's [saving] touch. With self integrated by spiritual exercise [now] he sees the self in all beings standing, all beings in the self: the same in everything he sees. Who sees me everywhere, who sees the All in me, for him I am not lost, nor is he lost to me.[2]

What does this mean? First when it is said that the Yogin, the 'athlete of the spirit', sees self in self, it means that he sees the eternal self, which in Christian theology is called the 'image of God', in himself, and 'this is his utmost joy, transcending [all things of] sense—*or so he thinks*.

---

[1] Gītā 3.30.   [2] Ibid. 6: 20–30.

Secondly, it is his utmost joy because he has become Brahman—he has reached a mode of existence which is ever the 'same', because unchanging and unchangeable, in all transient and changing things. And thus, thirdly, by 'seeing the self in all beings standing, all beings in the self', the bonds of individuality are broken asunder and he can sing with Schiller, 'Seid umschlungen, Millionen', for he has become the All. If this is so, must it not mean that all relationships are forever done away with? No, says Krishna, for the man 'who sees the self in all beings standing, all beings in the self', will then see me everywhere, will see the All in me; and yet 'for him I am not lost, nor is he lost to me'. Arjuna cannot yet understand how this can be.

VII

GOD TRANSCENDING TRANSCENDENCE

'ATTACH your mind to me.' These are the opening words of the seventh chapter of the Bhagavad-Gītā: and they come as a real shock. Throughout the first six chapters the one virtue repeatedly and tirelessly preached as being necessary to salvation was detachment. Until a man has wholly detached himself from the world and the things of sense he cannot 'become Brahman' nor can he enter Nirvāna, the final goal of the Buddhists. Attachment binds: detachment frees. Hence the earlier Hindu and Buddhist term for man's spiritual end is *vimukti* or *moksha*, 'liberation' or 'freedom of the spirit'. To love is to be bound with the bonds of affection: hence love must be ruthlessly excluded from the human consciousness. This is a strictly inhuman doctrine, since the aim of Indian religion has always been the transcendence of the human condition as such. Indian man has rarely been ready to accept human nature as he finds it, he has always sought to raise himself to the high estate of the angels even at the risk of falling to the level of the 'simple consciousness' of the beasts.

Every mystical tradition, in so far as it remains strictly religious, recommends detachment from the world and, in the theistic religions, from creatures. This is the indispensable condition for attaining to enlightenment in the case of the Buddhists, or of realizing a love of God that is in any sense worthy in the case of the Christians and Muslims. 'All that impels us to attach ourselves to creatures', Pascal says, 'is evil because it prevents us either from serving God if we know him, or from seeking him out if we do not.'[1] This is a typically Christian formulation of the religious quest, for it assumes the existence of a personal God who is in himself lovable. The Buddhist makes no such assumption: in Nirvāna, which means, among other things, the extinction of passion, there can be no room even for love of the Buddha: there is only complete impassibility and passivity.

Now, it has sometimes been maintained that what Christians mean by union with God in love is identical with the Buddhist Nirvāna. This is surely more than questionable, and the Bhagavad-Gītā seems to disprove this too facile identification; for the Gītā does not deny or reject the

---

[1] *Pensées*, ed. Pléiade, p. 1204.

Buddhist concept of Nirvāna, rather it accepts it but claims to carry it a stage further: it claims to transcend the transcendent itself. For in the Gītā there are two forms of *bhakti*, two forms in which the love of God may manifest itself—and it is all too easy to confuse them. There is the lower form which consists in simple acts of devotion, and there is a higher form which is strictly mystical, since it is a stage beyond that 'Nirvāna which is Brahman too' into which divine love is introduced to fill the vacuum left by the extrusion of the love of earthly things.

The Buddhists, as we have seen, do not define Nirvāna at all clearly except as the passing beyond phenomenal existence; but it is worth pointing out that, when using similes, they speak of a cooling down, never of a 'flame of love' as do all the other mystical traditions. Nirvāna is the end of the 'purgative way', it is not yet even the beginning of the 'unitive way'. That this is so the Gītā makes very clear. Yoga, meaning the 'integration of the personality', is the essential preparation for 'liberation'—the breaking through of the barriers of space and time into a mode of being in which there appears to be room for all kinds of experience which no amount of interpreting away can reduce to one single experience. True, it is perfectly reasonable to maintain that the experience of complete oneness we find in the Sānkhya system is experientially the same as that described in the *Māndūkya* Upanishad, and that therefore the interpretation of either the one or the other must be wrong: the experience may either mean that the mystic has realized his identity with transcendent Being as such beyond space and time, or it may mean no more than the simple oneness of his own essential self. These are alternative interpretations of the same experience.

On the other hand, when the *Chāndogya* Upanishad describes a total 'freedom of *movement*' in this same timeless mode of being, it can scarcely be talking about the same thing, for in the Absolute One of the *Māndūkya* Upanishad, as in the spiritual monad of the Sānkhya system, there is by definition neither motion, nor relationship, nor interconnectedness. In the *Chāndogya* all these things are present, and it makes this very clear:

The wind has no body. Clouds, thunder, and lightning—these too have no body. So, just as these arise from [the broad expanse of] space up there and plunge into the highest light, revealing themselves each in its own form, so too does this deep serenity arise out of this body and plunge into the highest light, revealing itself in its own form. Such a one is a superman; and there he roves around, laughing, playing, taking his pleasure with women, chariots, or friends and remembering no more that excrescence [which was] his body.[1]

[1] *Chāndogya* Upanishad 8: 12: 2–3.

Now, if words have any meaning at all and if they serve in any way to point to a reality which cannot be precisely defined, plainly there are here two distinct experiences—that of spiritual oneness, unfractionable and beyond all change, on the one hand, and that of spiritual plurality, beyond 'that excrescence [which was] the body', but in which relationship remains, on the other. Both, it will be remembered, are said to be states beyond that of deep, dreamless sleep—and yet they could scarcely be more different. In the Upanishads there seems to be no obvious link between the two. In the Gītā things are different, for the process is defined with some clarity. The first stage, Nirvāna, is the result of detachment from all worldly things, of spiritual integration. This results in the loss of all sense of ego (the 'empirical self' as Thomas Merton calls it). This must entirely disappear; and once the ego is lost, then one *sees* the eternal shining in and illuminating the whole phenomenal world: one 'sees the selfsame thing' everywhere, in the ritually impure as much as in the ritually pure.[1] This is the 'sainte indifférence' of St. François de Sales which we shall be discussing later. For, as the Gītā says:

> Winning some pleasant thing [the sage] will not rejoice, nor shrink disquietened when the unpleasant comes his way: steadfast and still his soul, [all] unconfused, he will know Brahman, in Brahman [stilled] he'll stand. [His] self detached from contacts with the outside world, in [him]self he finds his joy, [his] self in Brahman integrated by spiritual exercise, he finds unfailing joy.[2]

This is 'Yoga', and its immediate result is the 'unlinking of the link with suffering and pain',[3] and through this 'he sees the self in all beings standing, all beings in the self', because all things are shot through with one single eternal essence which is Brahman. By unifying and integrating one's own spirit, by withdrawing all the faculties into the self within, one realizes the unity of the macrocosm *through* the unity of the microcosm. This, as the fourteenth-century Flemish mystic, Ruysbroek, saw, is a 'rest' that can be achieved by purely natural means,[4] and it is this 'natural rest', perhaps, that the Zen Buddhists call *satori*.

The great achievement of the Buddha was surely just this, that he discovered an infallible method whereby this state of perfect peace and rest could be won without reference to any supernatural explanation. This is a state of changeless peace and rest which is the foundation of man's very being; this, as the Mahāyāna was to say, was the Buddha-nature that is in

---

[1] Bhagavad-Gītā 5: 18.   [2] Ibid. 5: 20–1.   [3] Ibid. 6: 23.
[4] Blessed Jan van Ruysbroek, *The Spiritual Espousals*, London, Faber & Faber, 1952, p. 167.

all of us and that it is up to us to discover. For this no God is necessary, only a Buddha, one 'fully awakened', who is there to point the way. This peace is not 'cosmic consciousness': indeed it would appear to be quite the reverse, yet it is not wholly unconnected with it, for in this mode of existence nothing is really separate from anything else, because there is a connecting link between all things which the Hindus call Brahman and Jung called 'God's world'.[1] So too in the Gītā the sage sees first all beings in himself (for he has 'become Brahman') and then in God, because God is the *foundation* of Brahman.[2] This means that though all things are one in Brahman, they are at the same time dependent on God. Hence the man 'who sees me everywhere, who sees the All in me, for him I am not lost, nor is he lost to Me'. God is not lost to his devotee even in that state in which he sees the unity of all things converging in and on himself. On the contrary, until the unity of the self is realized, there can be no immediate communion with God. Hence Krishna goes on to say: 'Who standing firm on unity communes in love with me as abiding in all beings, in whatever state he be, that athlete of the spirit abides in me.' Here, for the first time in the Hindu scriptures, a personal God speaks directly to man. In this respect the Gītā must surely rank as revelation in the Christian sense of that word, for here God reveals something about himself that could scarcely have been arrived at by mystical intuition alone.

In both the Christian and the Muslim mystical traditions knowledge and love are regarded as being the two things necessary to achieve union with God. 'Knowledge' seems to me to be a most inadequate term for what the mystics attempt to describe; and I much prefer the unknown English mystic's term, the 'Cloud of *Unknowing*', and the 'Docta *Ignorantia*' of Nicolas of Cusa. For this is not 'knowledge' as understood in everyday language but an intuition of ultimate reality, of that 'unity in diversity' and 'diversity in unity' of which St. François de Sales speaks. So too in the Iśā Upanishad, 'knowledge' is equated with the 'uncompounded', with the Buddhist Nirvāna, that is—'ignorance' with the 'compounded'—with the phenomenal world. It has nothing whatever to do with discursive thought, nothing to do with philosophy as traditionally understood in the West, let alone with what contemporary British philosophers understand by that word. It has everything to do with what Jung calls 'God's world', a world he was lucky enough to discover when still a boy. This is the world of infinity, and to it 'belonged everything superhuman—dazzling light, the

[1] C. G. Jung, *Memories, Dreams, Reflections*, London, Collins & Routledge, 1963, p. 79, etc.
[2] Bhagavad-Gītā 14: 27.

darkness of the abyss, the cold impassivity of infinite space and time, and the uncanny grotesqueness of the irrational world of chance. "God", for me, was everything—anything but "edifying" '.[1]

This is the world with which mystical 'knowledge' is concerned—or at least it is part of it. It is the 'imperishable city of Brahman'[2] of which the Upanishads speak and which is in the heart of man.[3] And this world can be reached by a 'knowledge' that is yet no knowledge but rather a direct intuition. It is simply another mode of being—lovable in so far as it is eternal and can never suffer change, but in no other sense. The originality of Krishna's teaching in the Gītā is that it questions not the value, let alone the reality, of the Buddhist Nirvāna, but its ultimacy. This he does very gradually, but ever more clearly throughout his dialogue with Arjuna. To 'become Brahman' is not enough; for this is a 'knowledge' that must be fulfilled in *bhakti*, in an unquestioning love of God.

Love and devotion, of course, assume a relationship with someone who is other than yourself; but if Brahman is all and you are identical with it as some of the Upanishads teach, then whom or what are you to love? Krishna gives the answer. He alone, as personal God and ruler of the universe, is worthy of such love. This does not mean that he denies the necessity of 'knowledge', an intuitional glimpse of reality; quite the contrary, for God can only be adequately worshipped and loved by one who is freed from all other attachments by that wisdom which sees things as they really are. Only such a man can love really disinterestedly, for 'wisdom' frees from the bondage of *karma* which attaches him ever more closely to the world. 'Wisdom' means seeing all things in oneself,[4] and this realization of the interconnectedness of all things brings freedom and independence. It 'reduces all works to ashes'[5] so that they 'will never bind him more'.[6] But though the man of wisdom is independent of this world, he is still not perfect, for he has no right knowledge of God, and unless you know God in some sense, it is impossible to love him. This, to the author of the Gītā, was the great defect of the old idea of Brahma–Nirvāna, for this is a state that seems to preclude love of any kind. Hence, before he even mentions the word *bhakti*, he points out gently but firmly that 'that peace which has Nirvāna as its end' also 'subsists in' God.[7] This means that the state of Nirvāna which a man can reach by his own efforts, if he is properly directed, is itself a mode of God's being: it is not itself independent but simply the impassible aspect of God's dual nature. To

---

[1] C. G. Jung, op. cit.,   [2] Śvetāśvatara Upanishad 5: 1.
[3] Chāndogya Upanishad 8: 1.   [4] Gītā 4: 35.   [5] Ibid. 4: 37.
[6] Ibid. 4: 41.   [7] Ibid. 6: 15.

enter Nirvāna is simply to imitate God in his eternity; it is not to imitate him in his totality.

Now, it has been a fairly constant criticism of both Hinduism and Buddhism from the Christian side that both are wholly other-worldly and pay all too little attention to what goes on in this world. There is no doubt that this criticism has gone home and that the reform Hinduism of the last two centuries has tried to remedy this defect, if indeed defect it be. Again it has been to the Gītā that the Hindu reformers have turned, reinterpreting it in a more activist sense. This is particularly true of Aurobindo's commentary, which is perhaps the best modern commentary on the work in that it does least violence to its spirit. Thus Aurobindo does not try to pretend that the Gītā has anything to do with social service, as others have done. This idea he rightly dislikes, since he sees in it a misguided attempt to read purely modern ideas into a traditional and traditionally Hindu book:

We are told continually [he writes] by many authoritative voices that the Gita, opposing in this the ordinary ascetic and quietistic tendency of Indian thought and spirituality, proclaims with no uncertain sound the gospel of human action, the ideal of disinterested performance of social duties, nay, even, it would seem, the quite modern ideal of social service. To all this I can only reply that very patently and even on the very surface of it the Gita does nothing of the kind and that this is a modern misreading, a reading of a modern mind . . . into a thoroughly antique, a thoroughly Oriental and Indian teaching.[1]

Yet this does not prevent Aurobindo from saying that 'undoubtedly, the Gita is a Gospel of Works', though he immediately qualifies this by saying that this is a gospel of works 'which culminate in knowledge, that is, in spiritual realization and quietude, and of works motived by devotion, that is, a conscious surrender of one's whole self first into the hands and then into the being of the Supreme, and not at all of works as they are understood by the modern mind'.[2]

And yet can one go the whole way with Aurobindo even in this? He is certainly right in his rejection of the traditional division of the teaching of the Gītā into three 'ways'—the way of work, the way of wisdom, and the way of devotion;[3] but does it make any sense to say that works (karma) can ever be a 'way' in themselves? How can works have merit of themselves when the ideal is always to perform them in a spirit of pure detachment? Certainly Arjuna is told that work is his proper business, in his case the unlovely work of war, as Aurobindo frankly recognized, but only on the

[1] Sri Aurobindo, *Essays on the Gita* (1st ser.), Calcutta, Arya Publishing House, 1922 and reprints, p. 38.
[2] Ibid.   [3] Ibid. p. 108.

condition that he takes no interest in the results it may produce.[1] This is
ultimately God's business and man cannot know his ultimate purpose. As
far as Arjuna is concerned it matters very little whether he conforms himself to the will of God or not, for if he but possess wisdom, his works will
be 'burnt up in wisdom's fire'[2] and 'entirely melt away',[3] for 'all works
without exception find their consummation in wisdom'.[4] Works are all
very well for the man who is on the way to liberation, but once this is won
they cease to have any relevance.[5]

There seems to me to be a genuine dilemma in both Hinduism and
Buddhism here. It is true that right living can help on the way to final
liberation, but liberation in the end means the transcendence of all works:
once it is won all work is pointless. Moreover, there is very little that man
can do about it, and Krishna's final argument is that God's will cannot be
resisted. 'If', Arjuna is told, 'relying on your ego, you should think, "I
will not fight", vain is your resolve, [for] Nature will constrain you. You
are bound by your own works which spring from your own nature; [for]
what, deluded, you would not do you will do perforce. In the region of the
heart of all contingent beings dwells the Lord, twirling them hither and
thither by his uncanny power [like puppets] mounted on a machine.'[6]

In the Great Epic itself of which the Gītā forms a minute part, this
dilemma, this tension between action and repose, between righteous
action and that state which, because it is beyond good and evil, 'reduces all
works to ashes' comes out very forcefully and is never satisfactorily
resolved. In the Gītā itself too no real attempt is made to bring right action
into harmonious relationship with the eternal rest that can only be won by
detaching oneself from all action. There is only one straight answer and
that is to leave all action to God: leave it where it ultimately belongs, for
man, at least in his deepest essence, is not a responsible being. Action
can only take place in a material context, and the human spirit does not
control matter. Though the soul in a sense owns the body while it is yet
incarnate, it does not control it: 'it neither works nor makes another
work',[7] this is the function of material Nature alone, and Nature is identical
with *māyā*, which in the Gītā is both God's creative energy and the power
that enslaves spirit to matter and prevents it from seeing the spiritual
world as it really is. Only one who is fooled by his own ego thinks that he
does anything at all, in reality it is the three constituents of Nature reacting
on one another;[8] and these are in turn dependent on God who thus both
binds man to matter and liberates him from it:

[1] Gītā 2: 47.   [2] Ibid. 4: 19.   [3] Ibid. 4: 23.   [4] Ibid. 4: 33.
[5] Ibid. 6: 3.   [6] Ibid. 18: 59–61.   [7] Ibid. 5: 13.   [8] Ibid. 3: 28.

[All] states of being whether they be of [Nature's constituent] purity, energy, or lethargy proceed from me. . . . By these three states of being inhering in the constituents this whole universe is led astray and does not understand that I am far beyond them and that I neither change nor pass away. For [all] this is my *māyā*, composed of the constituents, divine, hard to transcend. Whoso shall put his trust in me alone, shall pass beyond this [my] *māyā*. Doers of evil, deluded, base, put not their trust in me; their wisdom swept away by *māyā*, they cleave to a devilish mode of existence.[1]

It is, then, not only wisdom that saves, but faith and trust in a transcendent God who freely grants that knowledge of the true nature of things which is necessary to salvation. The paths of *jñāna* and *bhakti*, 'knowledge' and love, complement each other. Trustful love of God may show itself in the humblest acts of devotion, and so long as the intention is right God will lead the soul to liberation, the Buddhist Nirvāna, and beyond it to a personal experience of him in all his immanence and transcendence:

Be it a leaf or flower or fruit or water that a zealous soul may offer me in love's devotion, that do I [willingly] accept, for it was love that made the offering. Whatever you do, whatever you eat, whatever you offer in sacrifice or give away in alms, whatever penance you may perform, offer it up to me. So from [those] bonds which works [of their very nature forge], whose fruits are fair and foul, you will be freed: yourself [now] integrated by renunciation and spiritual exercise, set free, you will draw nigh to me. In all contingent beings the same am I; none do I hate and none do I fondly love; but those who commune with me in love's devotion [abide] in me and I in them.

However evil a man's livelihood may be, let him but worship me with love and serve no other, then shall he be reckoned among the good indeed, for his resolve is right. Right soon will his self be justified and win eternal rest. Arjuna, be sure of this: none who worships me with loyalty and love is lost to me. For whosoever makes me his haven, base-born though he may be, yes, women too and artisans, even serfs, theirs it is to tread the highest way. How much more, then, Brāhmans pure and good, and royal seers who know devoted love. Since your lot has fallen in this world, impermanent and joyless, commune with me in love. On me your mind, on me your loving service, for me your sacrifice, to me be your prostrations: now that you have thus integrated self, your striving bent on me, to me you will [surely] come.[2]

There are three things to be noticed here. First, Krishna claims to be the 'same' in all creatures, 'none does he hate and none does he dearly love'; and yet he adds in the same breath, 'those who commune with me in love's devotion [abide] in me and I in them'. This is certainly a paradox, but it is paradox that ought to be familiar to Christians; for the Christian God too rains alike on the just and the unjust, but he also has his own

[1] Ibid. 7: 12–15.   [2] Ibid. 9: 26–34.

particular friends—first the children of Israel, and secondly the twelve
apostles, the fathers of the new Israel, and singled out among them all 'the
disciple whom Jesus loved', traditionally held to be St. John. God offers an
equal love to all, but his love cannot be felt or appreciated unless there is an
answering love in man. It does not matter how evil your conduct may have
been, for much is forgiven to those who love much. Without love it is
perfectly possible to reach Nirvāna or to become Brahman, but it is not
possible to reach the God who *is* love.[1]

Secondly, the fruits of salvation are open to all classes of society, to
'women, artisans, even serfs'. In the Upanishads scripture and the
doctrine of salvation that it contained had to be closely guarded from
women and serfs. True, this did not mean that they would be forever
excluded from the supreme goal of liberation since there was always hope
that by virtuous living they could be reborn in a 'twice-born' caste; but it
did exclude them from any chance of salvation in this life. Krishna opens
the doors of salvation to all.

This was not particularly new in India, for all castes were admitted into
the Buddhist monastic community which was the organism through which
liberation and Nirvāna could normally be achieved; but it *was* new in
Hinduism which firmly insisted on the separation of the four great classes
and on the difference of the duties assigned to each. Krishna does not do
away with the existing social system any more than the Buddha did. On the
contrary, he reaffirms it since he claims to be the source of it;[2] but he does
offer salvation even to the lowest classes of society.

Thirdly—and this is most important—in order to draw near to God it is
assumed that the aspirant is already *yukta*, already integrated in himself,
and *vimukta*, 'set free' from the bonds of mortal existence. In the early
stages devotion to God is a short cut to the attainment of liberation, for
God's responding grace raises man out of the ocean of recurring death,[3]
but in the later stages, even after liberation, love becomes more intense, for
the individual self is now free to attach himself exclusively to God since
he has cut himself loose from all else.

To attain to complete detachment from the world and thereby to
spiritual freedom is never easy; without God's grace it is very difficult
indeed. 'Among thousands of men but one, maybe, will strive for [self-]
perfection and even among [these] athletes who have won perfection['s
crown] but one, maybe, will come to know me as I really am.'[4] So says
Krishna, and he implies that even to achieve the Buddhist ideal of Nirvāna
is exceedingly difficult without divine assistance. To get to know the God

---

[1] 1 John 4: 8.   [2] Gītā 4: 13.   [3] Ibid. 12: 7.   [4] Ibid. 7: 3.

who is beyond Nirvāna is almost impossible, for to know God means to know him not only in his fathomless peace in which the human self participates by nature, but also in his activity. Hence one must conform to his will, which is nothing else than the cosmic process itself. Thus self-will is not only wrong: it is stupid since it is a delusion thought up by the ego. God has set the wheel of existence in motion, and man has to 'match his turning [with the turning of the wheel]': if he does not, 'he lives out his life in vain'.[1] Since man is in fact helpless, he must at least make the gesture of casting all his works on God,[2] for it is really God who is the agent. He is the sole agent, for, as Protestants would say, he is the Lord of history, but, much more essentially, he is the Lord of eternity. As in the *Śvetāśvatara* Upanishad he is beyond both the perishable and the Imperishable.

The man of God is the man who has achieved a 'sainte indifférence' to all worldly things, who has passed beyond the three constituents of Nature and become Brahman. So too St. François de Sales writes:

Indifference must be practised towards all things concerned with material life, such as sickness and health, beauty and ugliness, strength and weakness; towards the things of social life—honours, rank, and riches; towards the vicissitudes of spiritual life, such as aridity and consolations, delectation (*goûts*) and dryness; towards [all] actions and sufferings—in a word, to whatever may happen.[3]

In exactly the same spirit the Gītā says:

Radiance—activity—yes, delusion too—when these arise he hates them not; and when [in turn] they cease he pines not after them. As one indifferent he sits, by the constituents unruffled: 'So the constituents are busy': thus he thinks. Firm-based is he, unquavering. The same in pleasure as in pain and self-assured, the same when faced with clods of earth or stones or gold; for him, wise man, are friend and foe of equal weight, equal the praise or blame [with which men cover him]. Equal [his mind] in honour and disgrace, equal to ally and to enemy, he renounces every [busy] enterprise: 'He has transcended the constituents': so must men say.

And as to those who do me honour with spiritual exercise, in loyalty and love undeviating, passed [clean] beyond these constituents, to becoming Brahman they are conformed. For I am the base supporting Brahman—immortal [Brahman] which knows no change— [supporting] too the eternal law of righteousness and absolute beatitude.[4]

Now the word *brahman* in the Gītā is used in three senses: first, in the Buddhist sense of 'becoming Brahman', which means to pass clean beyond

[1] Ibid. 3: 16.   [2] Ibid. 3: 30.   [3] *Traité de l'amour de Dieu*, 9. 5.
[4] Gītā 14: 22–7.

the phenomenal world; secondly, in the sense of the eternal in the sacrifice; and thirdly, in the sense of primal matter into which Krishna injects his seed.[1] In the last sense it is equivalent to the Sānkhya *avyakta*, the 'unmanifest' form of material Nature which precedes all differentiation.

When we come to study the thought of Pierre Teilhard de Chardin we will find that he distinguishes between a mysticism of diffusion into matter —Bucke's cosmic consciousness—and a mysticism of concentration on to a single centre which for him is the cosmic Christ. In the Hindu mysticism we have studied so far we have been able to distinguish two similar poles— diffusion throughout the All on the one hand and the isolation of the One on the other. The first is most typically and astonishingly expressed in *Chāndogya* Upanishad 7: 25: 1 where it is said: 'I am below, I am above, I am to the west, to the east, to the south, to the north. Truly I am this whole universe.' The second is represented by the Sānkhya system and by the *Māndūkya* Upanishad, though their interpretations of what the 'One' is are very different.

Now, in the Gītā, after the terrific theophany in chapter xi to which we shall return, Arjuna asks:

Of those who are ever integrated and serve you with loyal devotion, and those who [revere] the Imperishable Unmanifest, which are the most experienced in spiritual exercise?[2]

To this Krishna answers:

Those I deem to be the most integrated who fix their thoughts on me and serve me, ever integrated [in themselves], filled with the highest faith. But those who revere the indeterminate Imperishable Unmanifest, unthinkable though coursing everywhere, sublime, aloof, unmoving, firm, who hold in check the complex of the senses, in all things equal-minded, taking pleasure in the weal of all contingent beings, these too attain to me. [But] greater is the toil of those whose thinking clings to the Unmanifest; for difficult [indeed] is it for embodied men to reach and tread the unmanifested way.

Now, in the context of the Gītā, this can only mean that the man who 'becomes Brahman' and enters the Nirvāna that is Brahman too must also reach God in his abiding essence. There are three stages in the process; first, the process of integration (*yoga*) which either immediately precedes or is identical with liberation, the entry into the 'indeterminate Imperishable Unmanifest'; second, liberation itself; and third, direct contact with the personal God. This in fact corresponds exactly to what we have already noticed in the *Śvetāśvatara* Upanishad.[3] The human psyche, likened to a

---

[1] Gītā 14: 3.   [2] Ibid. 12: 1.   [3] 2: 14-15.

mirror which has been cleansed, becomes one in the essential self, and by means of this self as with a lamp throws light on Brahman as it is in its essence; that done, it comes to know God who is beyond all essences. The same scheme of things is found in the *Katha* Upanishad[1] where it is stated that beyond the 'great self', which here must mean the individual self, there is the Unmanifest, and higher than that the 'Person' than whom there is nothing higher.

Given that the *Katha* Upanishad is influenced by Sānkhya ideas and terminology, it would seem clear that the 'Unmanifest' means what it means in the Sānkhya system—primal, undifferentiated matter; but in the place of the Sānkhya spiritual monads you have 'selves' which are graded *below* primal matter: they are not totally independent of it as they are in the Sānkhya system. Above both matter and these 'selves' stands the 'Person', God. The process of salvation in all three passages would, then, seem to be this. By detachment and indifference to all worldly things the essential oneness of the self is realized (as in the Sānkhya system), but in order to break through to pure spirit which is God the purified soul plunges into the 'indeterminate Unmanifest'—undifferentiated matter—in order to emerge into the pure light of God.

In the Gītā, as in Thomas Merton, two selves are recognized, the carnal self which drags a man down towards sensual pleasures, and the higher one which raises him up.[2] The lower self, as all mystical traditions agree, must be subdued if not completely eradicated in order to release the higher, eternal self; but this too must be plunged back into the Unmanifest— must dissolve in primal matter—in order to re-emerge into the presence of God.

Christians, it seems to me, talk a great deal of rather confused nonsense when they insist that Christian mysticism above all others safeguards the human personality over against God. Why then do they use similes of melting and fusion as much as do all other mystics? This 'melting' must surely mean that all trace of self must pass away through unconsciousness into a more perfect form of spiritual life in which any new 'personality' will be so different from what we normally understand by personality as not to merit the same name. In any case this self which has lost all sense of 'I' and 'mine' could hardly want its sense of separateness restored. After all, Christian baptism is a baptism into death,[3] that is, into matter—water as so often symbolizing matter—in order that the baptized may rise again, not with their own life, but with Christ's, for it is Christ who is alive in them, not they.[4]

[1] 3: 10–11; 6: 7–8.   [2] Gītā 6: 5–6.   [3] Romans 6: 3.   [4] Galatians 2: 20.

In the common mystical tradition of mankind the Bhagavad-Gītā represents the Middle Way, the way of St. François de Sales, of 'unity in diversity, or diversity in unity, . . . of discordant concord or, better still, concordant discord'. Let us see how the Gītā defines true knowledge.

Like everything else 'knowledge' can be classified according to the three constituents of Nature—purity, energy, and lethargy. The first will be nearest to truth, the second will accord with sturdy common sense, while the third will tend towards the brutish. This is what the Gītā has to say on these three types of knowledge:

> That [kind of] knowledge by which one sees one mode of being, changeless, undivided in all contingent beings, divided [as they are], is [the knowledge of] purity. . . . But that [kind of] knowledge which in all contingent beings discerns in separation all manner of modes of being, different and distinct—this is knowledge born of energy. But that [kind of knowledge] which sticks to one effect as if it were all—irrational, not bothering about the Real as the [true] object [of all knowledge, thinking of it as] finite—this [knowledge] belongs to lethargy.[1]

The first two types of knowledge are readily recognized. The second is normal human consciousness in which we see the universe in all its diversity and in which we distinguish the subjective 'I' from the objective world of 'things'—all that is not 'I'. The first is more or less what Bucke called 'cosmic consciousness'. This is what the Upanishads understood by Brahman in which knower, known, and knowledge are all one; and to know Brahman is to become Brahman and to see as Brahman sees, to see from the standpoint of eternity. This is the essential teaching of the Upanishads; and just as the Gītā does not deny the main teachings of Buddhism, least of all Nirvāna, but fits them into a new framework, so does it adopt this central Upanishadic teaching in all its fullness. True, in most of the Gītā the word *brahman* is used in three specialized ways, but a 'total' Brahman is also admitted, and this total Brahman is simply an older word for what we would call God: indeed in chapters xii and xiii it is quite indistinguishable from him. For when we are again told that 'when once a man can see [all] the diversity of contingent beings as abiding in One [alone] and their radiation out of it, then to Brahman he attains',[2] we do not know whether by the One we should understand Brahman or Krishna himself, for both have been extolled in almost identical terms. It is ridiculous to argue, as Christians tend to do, that Brahman is an impersonal Absolute while Krishna, as *Iśvara*, the 'Lord', is a highly personal God, for what they seem to be arguing is that because Brahman

---

[1] Gītā 18: 20-2.   [2] Ibid. 13: 30.

is of neuter gender in Sanskrit it must therefore be impersonal. To this one can only reply that on these premises the Holy Spirit in Christianity must be both personal and impersonal, both masculine, feminine, and neuter— masculine in Latin, feminine in Hebrew, and neuter in Greek; and with none of these purely symbolic representations would I disagree. For does not the *Śvetāśvatara* Upanishad say: 'Thou art woman, thou art man: thou art the lad and the maiden too'?[1] And then again, as if to right the balance, 'It is not male, not female, nor yet hermaphrodite'.[2] All this talk of safeguarding the personality of either God or man means very little indeed when we begin to concern ourselves with mystical religion. Nothing could be more impersonal than the God of the Pseudo-Dionysius, and it is fair to say that it is *this* God, this interloper from Neoplatonism, this pale intellectual substitute for the 'God of Abraham, God of Isaac, God of Jacob' who moved Pascal to tears of joy, that has drained so much Christian mysticism of life and colour and depersonalized the Deity far more than the Upanishads ever did. The word 'person' as applied to God, however, has become a fetish, for if we really think about this matter at all, we will see that we use the word 'person' because we thereby understand someone at least analogous to a human being, and the God of the Old Testament is so overwhelmingly human in all his passionate outpourings, his fury, and his rueful tenderness, so outsize a *human* being that 'person' is the natural word to apply to him. If, however, we are content with Boethius' definition of a 'person' as 'an individual substance of rational nature',[3] then the Upanishadic Brahman as redefined in the Gītā is most certainly a 'person'. What then has the Gītā to say of this 'All-Highest Brahman'?

The highest Brahman it is called—beginningless—it is not Being nor is it Not-being. Hands and feet it has on every side, on every side eyes, heads, mouths, and ears: in the world all things encompassing [changeless] it abides. Devoid of all the senses, it yet sheds light on all their qualities, [from all] detached, and yet supporting all; free from Nature's constituents, it yet experiences them. Within all beings, yet without them; unmoved, it yet moves indeed; so subtle is it you cannot comprehend it; far off it stands, and yet how near it is! Undivided in beings it abides, seeming divided: this is That which should be known—[the one] who sustains, devours, and generates [all] beings. Light of lights, 'Beyond the Darkness' it is called: [true] knowledge, what should be known, accessible to knowledge, established in the heart of all.[4]

This plainly is a description of the supreme Being both in its transcendence, its creative, sustaining, and destructive activity, and in its

[1] *Śvetāśvatara* Upanishad 4: 3.   [2] Ibid. 5: 10.
[3] Thomas Aquinas, *Summa Theologica*, Pars 1: Q. 29, Art. 1. 1.   [4] Gītā 13: 12–17.

immanence. This is the 'Highest Lord' or 'Person' described later in the same chapter[1]—'the same in all contingent beings, abiding [without change], the Highest Lord, when all things fall to ruin, [himself] is not destroyed: who sees him sees [indeed]'.

The terms 'Brahman', 'Self', and 'Person' are sometimes identical, sometimes distinguished in the Upanishads. In chapter xiii of the Gītā which we have just quoted Brahman is clearly identical with Krishna, the personal God; and yet, as we have seen, Krishna is nevertheless exalted above Brahman understood both as an eternal mode of being experienced in Nirvāna and as primal matter.[2] This is because the author of the Gītā here wants to emphasize that Krishna, the personal God, transcends both eternity and time in that he acts purposively *from* the one *in* the other, and is thus the 'causeway' between the two mentioned in the *Chāndogya* Upanishad, the 'mediator' who welds time and eternity together into that single whole which Sānkhya dualism had split asunder. He is time, and he is eternity, and he is the causeway that links the two; and yet he infinitely transcends all three.

Again the world of spirit can be conceived of in Sānkhya terms as being composed of an infinite number of spiritual monads, some of them still bound to matter, others released, isolated, and free, become Brahman in the Nirvāna that is Brahman too—'perishable' *purusha* and 'imperishable' *purusha*, as the Gītā puts it.[3] The 'perishable' is all sentient beings as we know them, the 'imperishable' is utterly aloof, 'standing on a mountain peak', to use the Gītā's own phrase. And the phrase is significant, for it indicates a state of detached contemplation of the phenomenal world, a state in which one is immovably suspended between heaven and earth. The phrase is not uncommon in those other parts of the Epic which are later than the Gītā, and was obviously considered particularly apt. It is significant because the same phrase, presumably for the same reasons, occurs in Richard of St. Victor, the great Scottish mystic of the twelfth century; for Richard saw, as did the Gītā, that the 'fixed, still state of Brahman' with which his predecessor Hugh had been obsessed was not the end of the mystic quest but only the beginning. The parallel is remarkable and we shall be considering it in some detail in lecture xv. For the present, however, we must leave the Victorines aside and reaffirm, with Krishna, God's unequivocal transcendence:

In the world there are these two persons—perishable the one, imperishable the other: the 'perishable' is all contingent beings, the 'imperishable', they say, stands high upon a peak. But there is [yet] another Person, the [all-]Sublime,

[1] Gītā 13: 27.   [2] Ibid. 14: 27.   [3] 15: 16.

surnamed 'All-Highest Self': the three worlds he enters and pervades, sustaining them—the Lord who passes not away. Since I transcend the perishable and am more exalted than the imperishable itself, so am I extolled in Vedic as in common speech as the 'Person [All-]Sublime'. Whoever thus knows me, unconfused, as the Person [All-]Sublime, knows all and [knowing all] communes with me with all his being, all his love. And so have I [at last] revealed this most mysterious doctrine: let a man but understand it, for then he will be a man who [truly] understands, his [life's] work done.[1]

To a Christian it may seem strange that the doctrine of the love of a God who is both supremely transcendent and intimately immanent, and who is at the same time incarnate in a man, should seem so strikingly novel and mysterious; for to worship a God 'with all one's being, all one's love' is the essence of the Christian religion. To the Hindu, however, who was familiar only with the traditional teachings of the Upanishads and perhaps also with the heresies of the Buddhists and Jains who knew nothing of either God or Absolute, it must have seemed well-nigh incomprehensible.

This God, Krishna, not only transcends transcendence but is also a God of love. But like any God who claims to be more than merely the sum-total of existence he has a terrible as well as an 'auspicious' aspect. This is only too apparent in the Old Testament and the Koran. So too in the Bhagavad-Gītā the climax of the poem is not any description of the love of God nor is it a revelation of God's timeless peace: it is a direct vision of God in his awful aspect as all-devouring Time. In the chapter before this theophany Arjuna had asked Krishna to describe to him his 'far-flung power'. Not content with this, however, he now asks whether he may not be allowed to *see* him in his form of 'Lord' and 'All-Highest Person'. Krishna grants his request and promises to show him 'this whole universe . . . centred here in One, with all that it contains of moving and unmoving things; [behold it] in my body'.[2] Such a vision, however, cannot be seen with ordinary mortal eyes, so Krishna bestows on Arjuna a 'celestial' eye, and:

So saying Hari, the great Lord of power and the skilful use of it, revealed to the son of Prithā his highest sovereign form. . . .
If in [bright] heaven together should arise the shining brilliance of a thousand suns, then would that perhaps resemble the brilliance of that [God] so great of Self. Then did the son of Pāndu see the whole [wide] universe in One converged, there in the body of the God of gods, yet divided out in multiplicity.[3]

But this is not to be just a philosophical vision of the truth the Gītā had been patiently preaching—the age-old mystical vision of a multitudinous universe held together in the One who, in the formula of the later texts,

[1] Gītā 15: 16–20. [2] Ibid. 11: 7. [3] Ibid. 11: 9–13.

consists of Being, Consciousness, and Joy—but a vision of God as power,
the ruthless destroyer of all he generates. And so:

Filled with amazement Arjuna, his hair on end, hands joined in reverent
greeting, bowing his head before the God, [these words] spake out.
'O God, the gods in your body I behold and all the hosts of every kind of
being; . . . End, middle, or again beginning I cannot see in you. O Monarch
Universal, [manifest] in every form! . . . You are the Imperishable, [you] wisdom's highest goal; you, of this universe the last prop and resting place, you the
changeless, [you] the guardian of eternal law, you the primeval Person; [at last]
I understand. Beginning, middle, and end you do not know—how infinite your
strength! How numberless your arms—your eyes the sun and moon! So do I see
you—your mouth a flaming fire, burning up this whole universe with your
blazing glory. By you alone is this space between heaven and earth pervaded—
all points of the compass too; gazing on this, your marvellous, frightening form,
the three worlds shudder, [All-]Highest Self!'[1]

So this is the Self, the highest principle of the Upanishads, but seen
not as it is in its eternal rest but as the terrible principle that devours all
it has created. All must return to God (and this is one of the great themes of
the Koran even more than of the Gītā), but the manner of the return will
seem very different to God's enemies and to his friends. For the supreme
Principle is now seen not as the deep ocean into which the rivers of individual life must flow and find their rest, but as a flaming fire:

As rivers flowing [downwards] find their home [the *Mundaka* Upanishad[2] had
   said]
In the Ocean, leaving name and form behind,
So does the man who knows, from name and form released,
Draw near to the divine Person who is beyond the beyond.

This is the 'light of lights beyond the darkness' of which the Gītā[3]
speaks elsewhere, the light that is at the same time a consuming fire. Just
as in the Zoroastrian account of the last days all flesh is made to pass
through a sea of molten metal in order to be cleansed, 'and it will seem to
him who was saved as if he were walking through warm milk, but to the
man who was damned it will seem exactly like walking through molten
metal',[4] so in the Gītā some are utterly terrified at the vision of the Lord,
others accept and enter reverently in; and so Arjuna exclaims:

Lo! these hosts of gods are entering into you: some, terror-struck, extol you,
hands together pressed; great seers and men perfected in serried ranks cry out,
'All hail', and praise you with copious hymns of praise. . . . Ablaze with

---

[1] Gītā 11: 14–20.   [2] 3: 2: 8.   [3] 13: 17.
[4] R. C. Zaehner, *The Teachings of the Magi*, London, Allen & Unwin, 1956, p. 148.

many-coloured [flames] you touch the sky, your mouths wide open, [gaping], your eyes distended, blazing: so do I see you and my inmost self is shaken: I cannot bear it, I find no peace, O Vishnu.[1]

'My inmost self is shaken . . .': this is very revealing, for according to the Upanishads and the Gītā itself the 'inmost self' is identical with that Brahman which is 'established in the heart of all'.[2] And yet, if we are to believe this passage, even that still centre of the human being can be shaken out of its deep peace by the God who not only indwells it but governs and pursues it. For the God who dwells in the heart is not only the serene tranquillity of Nirvāna but also the Lord of *māyā*, the Lord of uncanny power, who twirls his recalcitrant creatures hither and thither like puppets mounted on a machine.[3] Between God and man as they are in eternity there is a 'sameness' which is Brahman, but man, so long as he is in this world, needs to attain not only to this sameness but also to an identification of his will with the will of God. If he does not, he will be shaken out of the complacency he had found in Nirvāna and made to do things he hates to do. His 'inmost self is shaken': if this is possible, then man's identity of being with God can be no more than an identity in dependence which God, who is the source of it, can break at any time and whenever he so wills. This he will do whenever man asserts his own individuality and personality in defiance of the world order which is nothing less than the will of God. God is by definition *purushottama*, the 'Highest Person', and no one else has the right to call himself a person at all, for a 'person' implies an independent will, and this is no more than an illusion of the ego which, being derived from material Nature, is unable of itself to see things as they really are.

The world is not merely transient, Arjuna now sees, it is madly reeling and tottering to its own destruction. The vision is almost unbearable in its intensity:

I see your mouths with jagged, ghastly tusks reminding [me] of Time's [devouring] fire: I cannot find my bearings, I cannot find a refuge; have mercy, God of gods, home of the universe! Lo, all these sons of Dhritarāshtra accompanied by hosts of kings . . . rush [blindly] into your [gaping] mouths that with their horrid tusks strike [them] with terror. Some stick in the gaps between your teeth—see them!—their heads to powder ground. As many swelling, seething streams rush headlong into the [one] great sea, so do these heroes of the world of men enter your blazing mouths. As moths in bursting, hurtling haste rush into a lighted blaze to [their own] destruction, so do the worlds, well trained in hasty violence, pour into your mouths to [their own] undoing.[4]

---

[1] Gītā 11: 21, 24. [2] Ibid. 13: 17.
[3] Ibid. 18: 61. [4] Ibid. 11: 25–9.

As we have seen, the simile of the rivers and the sea recurs in all mystical traditions to denote the merging or melting of the individual self into the supreme Principle. So too the moth which destroys itself in the fire is another symbol particularly dear to the Muslims, meaning that the ego must entirely disappear in the divine fire. The fire is, of course, the 'living flame of love' of which St. John of the Cross wrote *and* the cleansing fires of Purgatory—the same fire, but seen and experienced very differently by the man who clings to his personal ego and the man who sees in it only what transmutes him into something divine. The divine fire is a raging furnace which destroys everything that cannot conform to it completely. We find the same thing in the Christian tradition where we read:

Just as death is so strong that it separates the soul from everything, even from its body, so does the love of God, when it has reached the stage of zeal, divide and separate the soul from all other affections and purify it from all alloys. For not only is it as strong as death, but it is also harsh, inexorable, hard, and merciless in punishing the wrong done to it by one who admits rivals along with it, just as hell is violent in its punishment of the damned. And just as hell, filled as it is with horror, rage, and treachery, admits of no blend of love, so does jealous love admit of no admixture of any other affection, since it wills that all should be for the Beloved.[1]

This jealous love which, in its violence, can scarcely be distinguished from hate, Krishna knows too. For there is one thing that God, once he assumes a personal form, hates more than anything else, and that is egoism, the combination of self-love and personal interest as Balzac rightly defined it.[2] This is the 'I' and 'mine' so roundly condemned by the Buddhists and, following them, the Gītā—the root sin of mankind on the one hand and the cardinal virtue of bourgeois society on the other. Man has not changed much, and the human devils described in the Gītā are very much with us still:

Insatiate desire is their starting-point—maddened are they by hypocrisy and pride, clutching at false conceptions, deluded as they are: impure are their resolves. Unmeasured care is theirs right up to the time of death, [for] they have no other aim than to satisfy their lusts, convinced that this is all. Bound by hundreds of fetters forged by hope, obsessed by anger and desire, they seek to build up wealth unjustly to satisfy their lusts.
'This have I gained today, this whim I'll satisfy; this wealth is mine and much more too will be mine as time goes on. He was an enemy of mine, I've killed him, and many another too I'll kill. I'm master [here]. I take my pleasure [as I will]; I'm strong and happy and successful. I'm rich and of good family. Who else can

---

[1] St. François de Sales, *Traité de l'amour de Dieu*, 10. 13.
[2] Balzac, *Eugénie Grandet*, ed. Pléiade, vol. iii, p. 556.

match himself with me? I'll sacrifice and I'll give alms: [why not?] I'll have a marvellous time!' So speak [fools] deluded in their ignorance.

[Their minds] unhinged by many a [foolish] fancy, caught up in delusion's net, obsessed by the satisfaction of their lusts, into foul hell they fall. Puffed up with self-conceit, unbending, maddened by their pride in wealth, they offer sacrifices that are but sacrifice in name and not in the way prescribed—the hypocrites! Selfishness, force and pride, desire and anger, [these do] they rely on, envying and hating me who dwell in their bodies as I dwell in all.[1]

Krishna too is a jealous God, and the words 'You cannot worship God and Mammon' would come appropriately from his lips. Jealous love in God, then, seems like hate to the worshippers of Mammon and desire. This is a fact, and Krishna makes no bones about it:

Birth after birth in this revolving round, these vilest among men, strangers to [all] good, obsessed with hate and cruel, I ever hurl into devilish wombs. Caught up in devilish wombs, birth after birth deluded, they never attain to me: and so they tread the lowest way.[2]

This is the terrible side of God,—his loathing of human egoism, status-seeking, acquisitiveness, and pride. The obverse we have already quoted:

However evil a man's livelihood may be, let him but worship me with love and serve no other, then shall he be reckoned among the good indeed, for his resolve is right. Right soon will his self be justified and win eternal rest. Arjuna, be sure of this: none who worships me with loyalty and love is lost to me.[3]

Krishna demands devoted love directed to him alone. So too did Yahweh in the Old Testament and so does Allah in the Koran; but both these (who are unmistakably the same God) detest idolatry above all things and punish it accordingly. To our human eyes Krishna must appear both more civilized, more wise, and more indulgent to our human capacity to err; for, though he does demand an exclusive devotion, he does not for that reason condemn the worship of other gods since all devotion is really directed to him and it is he who dispenses and even encourages it:

Whatever form, [whatever god,] a devotee with faith desires to honour, that very faith do I confirm in him [making it] unswerving and secure. Firm-stablished in that faith he seeks to reverence that [god] and thence he gains his desires, though it is I who am the true dispenser. But finite is the reward of such men of little wit: whoso worships the gods, to the gods will [surely] go, but whoso loves and worships me, to me will come indeed.[4]

[1] Gītā 16: 10–18.   [2] Ibid. 16: 19–20.
[3] Ibid. 9: 30–1.   [4] Ibid. 7: 21–3; cf. 9: 23–5.

Krishna reveals himself as a God of love, but at the same time he demands a total renunciation of the things of this world. This the early Buddhists had also demanded, because for them this world and the next, *saṁsāra* and Nirvāna, were incompatible. In the later Mahāyāna parlance Nirvāna is also the Void—void, that is, of all *dharma*s, of all that has individual existence in space and time. Krishna, however, is a God of grace, and grace, it seems, abhors a vacuum as much as does Nature. Hence he says that even those who revere the 'indeterminate Imperishable Unmanifest' also attain to him.[1] By voiding himself of all purely human content man can by his own natural powers reach the perfect peace of Nirvāna, but he does not always understand, as the Zen Buddhists were later to teach, that the Void which is Nirvāna is also the plenitude of Brahman, the body of the Lord, in which Arjuna saw 'the whole [wide] universe in One converged . . ., yet divided out in multiplicity',[2] nor does he know that beyond this there is a stage in which he achieves a personal union with the God who 'transcends the perishable and is more exalted than the Imperishable itself, . . . the Person [All-]Sublime'.[3] This is the prerogative of grace, the divine 'favour' so abhorrent to Michelet, which God bestows on whom he will.

The whole of the teaching of the Gītā is triumphantly summed up at the end of the book. There are four stages through which the human self must pass from the world of action through the imperishable Brahman right up to God. The first and most humble is very Anglican—to do your duty in that estate to which God has called you:

By [doing] the work that is proper to him [and] rejoicing [in the doing], a man succeeds, perfects himself. . . . By dedicating the work that is proper [to his caste] to him who is the source of the activity of all beings, by whom this whole universe was spun, a man attains perfection and success. Better [to do] one's own [caste] duty, though devoid of merit, than [to do] another's, however well performed. By doing the work prescribed by his own nature a man meets with no defilement. Never should a man give up the work to which he is born, defective though it be: for every enterprise is choked by defects, as fire by smoke.[4]

The second step is to detach yourself from all you do:

With soul detached from everything, with self subdued, [all] longing gone, renounce: and you will find complete success, perfection, works transcended.[5]

And now the third step, 'becoming Brahman':

Let a man be integrated by his soul [now] cleansed, let him restrain himself with constancy, abandon objects of sense—sound and the rest—passion and hate

---

[1] Gītā 12: 3–4.   [2] Ibid. 11: 13.   [3] Ibid. 15: 18.
[4] Ibid. 18: 45–8.   [5] Ibid. 18: 49.

let him cast out; . . . let him give up all thought of 'I', force, pride, desire and anger and possessiveness, let him not think of anything as 'mine', at peace;—[if he does this,] to becoming Brahman is he conformed.[1]

Now that he has become Brahman he enters into God:

Brahman become, with self serene, he grieves not nor desires; the same to all contingent beings, he gains the highest love and loyalty to me. By love and loyalty he comes to know me as I really am, how great I am and who; and once he knows me as I am, he enters [me] forthwith. Let him then do all manner of works continually, putting his trust in me; for by my grace he will attain to an eternal, changeless state.[2]

But there is still one last word of assurance to the spellbound Arjuna:

And now again give ear to this my highest word, of all the most mysterious: 'I love you well.' Therefore will I tell you your salvation. Bear me in mind, love and worship me, sacrifice, prostrate yourself to me: so will you come to me, I promise you truly, for you are dear to me. Give up all things of law, turn to me, your only refuge, [for] I will deliver you from all evils; have no care.[3]

Such is the gospel that Krishna preached to his friend, Arjuna, on the field of Kurukshetra. It was something radically new in Hinduism, and Hinduism was never to be quite the same again.

[1] Ibid. 18: 51–3.   [2] Ibid. 18: 54–6.   [3] Ibid. 18: 64–6.

VIII

GOD IS LOVE AND GOD IN LOVE

THE Bhagavad-Gītā is the great divide in Hinduism, and through the Bhagavad-Gītā Hinduism becomes the *via media* between the 'atheistic' mysticism of early Buddhism and the theistic mysticism that grew up in the religions of Semitic origin. It represents as radical a break with the past as does Catholic Christianity with the older prophetic Judaism. The parallelism with nascent Christianity is close, for both are revolutionary. Both revolt, consciously or unconsciously, against an *ancien régime* which seemed to have outgrown its usefulness, and in so doing both were laying the foundations of a bridge which might one day unite the two totally dissimilar types of religion which dispute the allegiance of mankind—the transcendental, severely ethical monotheism of the Judaeo-Arab Semites on the one hand and the immanent pantheism of the Sino-Indians on the other. In Christianity it is the transcendent Lord of history who becomes man, in the Bhagavad-Gītā it is the immanent principle of the universe. God transcendent and God immanent meet in man, the middle point between the 'greater than the great' and the 'more minute than the minute'. This is not the 'causeway which holds apart the worlds [of time and eternity] lest they should split asunder' of which the *Chāndogya* Upanishad speaks;[1] rather it is the laying of the foundations of the bridge that may come to unite and bring into concord the apparently irreconcilable poles of total immanence and total transcendence, however discordant these may appear to be.

The Bhagavad-Gītā, not the Vedānta, is the starting-point from which any fruitful converse between Eastern immanentism and Western transcendentalism can begin. It is the eastern end of the great religious bridge, the building of which should be our ideal; the western end is Catholic Christianity—and both ends are built on the foundation of God made man. That God should be made man is not only unthinkable in the Judaeo-Arab tradition—it is blasphemous, and Caiaphas did well, as high priest of Yahweh, to rend his robes when Jesus made the unheard-of claim to be the Son of God. In India the reaction would have been somewhat different, for in the time of the Upanishads God, or rather the

[1] 8: 4: 1.

divine, was felt to interpenetrate everything, and it would not occur to anyone that it was particularly wrong to claim to be a god or even God since
God is all things and all things are God—or so at least the Hindus would
have expressed themselves. Certainly the 'heretical' Buddhists and Jains
would have phrased things differently, but even they would admit that
every man had it in him to rise above his purely temporal state so that he
might experience what is totally beyond the senses and the mind—a state
of pure being which makes death, and with it birth, a meaningless impossibility. For the Hindus, however, except in so far as they were affected
by classical Sānkhya dualism, there was nothing so very extraordinary in
God, in this case Vishnu, becoming man; for Vishnu himself had hitherto
been little more than a concretization of the Absolute in the divine sphere.
How, then, should it seem strange that he should be further concretized
in a specific human being? What, however, must have seemed strange and
well-nigh blasphemous is that the God-Man should claim to transcend
transcendence itself, should claim to be 'the base supporting Brahman—
immortal [Brahman] which knows no change',[1] and that this utterly
transcendent being should offer his love to man.

It is a truism to say that there is always a pantheistic element in Hinduism
even in its most theistic manifestations, and that the Hindu idea of salvation remains *moksha*, 'liberation' or 'deliverance'. But here, surely, there
is room for what the Confucians call the 'rectification of names'. Among
Christians, and particularly among Protestants, 'pantheism' has almost
become a dirty word, and part of the originality and importance of Teilhard
de Chardin for the understanding of Eastern religion is that he does not
hesitate to describe his own religious temperament as 'pantheistic'.[2] What
he means by 'pantheist' and in what way he distinguishes between different
pantheistic trends we shall have occasion to discuss later. The *Shorter
Oxford Dictionary* defines 'pantheism' as 'The belief or theory that God
and the universe are identical (implying a denial of the personality and
transcendence of God); the doctrine that God is everything and everything is God'. It is true that this definition would fit some Upanishadic
passages, but not very many: it would be truer to say that the general
view of the Upanishads is that God is 'over all, through all, and within all',[3]
as St. Paul puts it. If we speak of Hindu pantheism, then let it be clear that
this is what we mean.

[1] Gītā 14: 27.
[2] Pierre Teilhard de Chardin, *Hymne de l'univers*, Paris, Seuil, 1961, p. 56; E.T.
(*Hymn of the Universe*, London, Collins, 1965), p. 53 and *passim*.
[3] Ephesians 4: 6.

Again when we speak of 'liberation' or 'deliverance' in Hinduism, we must be clear as to what we mean, just as in Christianity we should be clear as to what we mean by 'salvation'. 'Liberation' means primarily liberation from *saṁsāra*, freedom from the round of birth and death, of rebirth and re-death, and from attachment to works and their fruits which bind us to the wheel of *saṁsāra*. Theoretically good works bind as much as evil ones; but this is an extreme view. The more usual view is that by the dutiful performance of your caste-duty you will in the long run attain to liberation, though it is essential to detach yourself from any desire for personal advancement in what you do. Hence Krishna comes to restore Hindu caste-law, not to destroy it: in particular he is insistent that warriors should fight when the occasion demands; and this, as everyone knows, is the starting-point of the Gītā. We are at liberty to say, if we like, that the Gītā remains pantheistic and that its ideal remains liberation: but again it is a question of 'rectification of names'. The 'pantheism' of the Gītā is one of unity in diversity and diversity in unity, of seeing 'the whole [wide] universe in One converged, there in the body of the God of gods'.[1] True, liberation still means liberation from all attachment to the world and a total freedom of the spirit, but this is now completed by *at*tachment to a living and active God and a community of being with him. The words remain the same, but they have been given a new content by the introduction of a quite new concept—the concept of love. This is a development in Hinduism which transcends all others in importance and which Western scholars have on the whole preferred to ignore. Teilhard de Chardin himself has done this, and this does him little credit, for he had ample opportunity to know better. In a little treatise of his, 'Pour y voir clair', written in 1950, he distinguishes between two types of pantheism (the word and the idea obsessed him)—'a pantheism of identification, at the very antipodes of love: God [is] All. And a pantheism of union, beyond love: God, All in all'.[2] This is a valid and valuable distinction, but Teilhard goes on to generalize grandly and says:

On the oriental or Hindu side there is no doubt that from the very beginning the ideal of diffusion and identification prevailed, individual egos being regarded as anomalies to be reduced (or holes to be filled in) in the universal Being; or, what comes to the same thing, the biological evolution of the world appearing to the eyes of the sage as no more than an illusion or an unimportant eddy. That is the unchangeable essence however much secondary patching up you may do and ... the irremediable weakness of all mysticisms akin to the Vedānta.[3]

[1] Gītā 11: 13.
[2] In *L'Activation de l'énergie*, Paris, Seuil, 1963, pp. 231–2.
[3] Ibid., p. 233.

This is a monstrous generalization and a travesty of Hindu mysticism as it developed in history. Teilhard, in his anxiety to prove the superiority of the Christian West,[1] ignores not only the Bhagavad-Gītā but the whole luxuriant flowering of theistic mysticism to which it gave birth. And so, in his ignorance, he can exclaim: 'The hour has indeed come when, at the very antipodes of an out-of-date orientalism, a new mysticism which is at once fully human and fully Christian can and must emerge—the way of the West, the way of the world of tomorrow.'[2]

He may be right, but at least he should have made himself familiar with how much of the way the East had already traversed without his knowing it; for had he studied the Gītā in depth he would have realized that here you have a mysticism not of diffusion and identification but rather precisely what he asks for and what he himself so magnificently proclaimed, a 'pantheism of union, beyond love: God, All in all'.

The Gītā, as we have seen, is the watershed between the pantheistic monism of the Upanishads and the still pantheistic theism of post-Vedic Hinduism as represented in those bulky, amorphous, yet fascinating treatises, the *Purānas*, and in the later Hindu sects. Its hero, Krishna, is God incarnate, more or less fully demythologized, for we learn very little about Krishna the man in the Gītā: rather it is the God we meet, the point of convergence of the whole universe. Among the Hindu scriptures the Gītā corresponds in a sense to the fourth Gospel in the New Testament canon: in both it is the God aspect of the God-Man that is emphasized. And just as in Christianity, despite the demythologizers, we turn to the synoptic gospels to find out what we can about the man Jesus, so must we turn to Mahābhārata, the Great Epic, of which the Gītā forms a minute episode, if we would learn about the man Krishna.

In the Gītā[3] Krishna says that his successive incarnations occur 'whenever the law of righteousness withers away and lawlessness arises . . . for the protection of the good, for the destruction of evil-doers, and for the setting up of the law of righteousness'. This is not at all the impression we get from reading the Mahābhārata. Rather, it would seem, he is inexorably resolved on the destruction of the whole warrior class on the somewhat frivolous grounds that the earth can no longer bear the burden of an over-populated world. In the Gītā he declares that he neither hates nor loves anyone,[4] though he immediately qualifies this statement. In the bulk of the Epic, however, his love for Arjuna is such that they are time and again referred to in the dual number as the 'two Krishnas', and so close is

[1] Ibid., p. 235.   [2] Ibid., p. 236.
[3] 4: 7–8.   [4] Gītā 9: 29.

the bond between them that neither can live without the other,[1] for Arjuna is Krishna's very self.[2] He favours the Pāndavas against their cousins and enemies, the Kauravas; and this is very natural, for they recognize him as God while the Kauravas either do not or do so grudgingly. Krishna in the Mahābhārata belongs to a stage of Hinduism that is as yet unaffected by Buddhism: his is a hunting and drinking tribe, and it is no disgrace to him to get drunk.[3] Worse than this, he is not above deceit, and this comes out all too clearly in the course of the war.

Once, when things were going badly for the Pāndavas because Drona, who had been the well-loved preceptor of both them and the Kauravas, but who had sided with the latter for reasons that are not altogether clear, when Drona was making havoc of their forces and could not, even with the help of Krishna himself, be certainly defeated, Krishna devised a stratagem. He bade Bhīma, Arjuna's brother and the family tough, kill an elephant whose name was Aśvatthāman. Now Aśvatthāman was also the name of Drona's son, and Krishna calculated that once Drona thought that his son was dead, he would abandon the battle. The plan was that Bhīma, after killing the elephant, should tell Drona that Aśvatthāman was dead. Drona, however, did not believe him, for Bhīma's renown rested on his enormous strength, not on his veracity. If, however, thought Krishna, the eldest of the Pāndava brothers, Yudhishthira, the 'king of righteousness', were to confirm what Bhīma had said, then Drona would surely believe him. Seeing that Yudhishthira was torn between his instinctive horror of untruthfulness and a desire for victory, he persuaded him that in some circumstances it is better to lie than to tell the truth, certainly when one's life is at stake. Though Krishna was God, Yudhishthira still hesitated until, 'egged on by Krishna and because it was fated so to be', he said the fatal words but added the word 'elephant', though indistinctly. At this Yudhishthira's chariot, which hitherto had remained poised a few inches off the ground in token of his saintliness, subsided on to the solid earth. Krishna had triumphed: Drona was slain and the honour of the righteous one was tarnished.[4]

So too at the end of the war, when the Kauravas had been routed and when their leader, Duryodhana, stood alone against his enemies and Yudhishthira would spare him, Krishna again egged Bhīma on to destroy him with a foul blow.[5] Bhīma complied; and it was not only Yudhishthira who raised his voice in protest, but Krishna's own brother, Balarāma, while the immortals in heaven showered down celestial flowers in honour

[1] Mahābhārata (MBh.) 2: 18: 14, etc.   [2] Ibid. 3: 13: 37, etc.
[3] Ibid. 1: 214.   [4] Ibid. 7: 164: 96–107.   [5] Ibid. 9: 57: 4 ff.

of the vanquished Duryodhana, the victim of foul play, and 'seeing these marvels and the honour paid to Duryodhana Krishna and his followers were filled with shame'.[1]

The Krishna of the Mahābhārata is a puzzling character because his exaltation as an incarnation of Vishnu seems to be secondary, and traces of an earlier and all too human hero have not been erased in much the same way as the priestly redaction of the Old Testament willy-nilly was unable to obliterate all traces of an earlier polytheism. So too in the Gītā, Vishnu's incarnation as Krishna is supposed to inaugurate a new era of justice. In actual fact its immediate result is the devastation of the known world, and the heritage into which the Pāndava brothers enter is one of desolation. Krishna himself retires to his own tribe which destroys itself in a drunken orgy. The incarnate God, alone and apparently powerless, retires to the forest to prepare himself for death. He falls into a Yogic trance, and while he is thus withdrawn from the world a huntsman appears, mistakes him for a gazelle, and shoots him in the heel. Such was the miserable end of Vishnu's eighth incarnation. Admittedly Krishna's soul ascends into heaven, there to resume its rightful place, but the welcome it receives from the gods seems to be less than whole-hearted. In the Mahābhārata read simply as literature Krishna is a god who failed; and this failure seems to be due to his own moral defects, his trickery, and his disregard of those very moral standards he had himself proclaimed in the Gītā. As a moral character he is utterly dwarfed by the righteous Yudhishthira, the just man and reluctant servant of an unjust God.

How then did Krishna become the chosen God of a vast company of adoring Hindus? The answer is twofold; for, in religion, there are two Krishnas: there is the Krishna of the Bhagavad-Gītā, lording it over the Absolute itself, and there is the Krishna of popular devotion. The first we have already discussed at length; let us now consider the second.

The Krishna of popular theology is not the Krishna of the Mahābhārata: he is not the passionate ally of the Pāndavas who is prepared to stoop to any trick in their supposed interests: he is not the God who consoles them after the appalling carnage of war by telling them that there is no cause for remorse or grief because, however many living creatures are killed or die, life nevertheless goes on. He is not a teacher, but a lover. He is not the God-Man of the Mahābhārata but the comely young cowherd of the *Bhāgavata Purāna*. If it is true to say that the Bhagavad-Gītā demythologized the Krishna of the Mahābhārata, it is equally true to say that the

[1] Ibid. 9: 60: 54.

Bhāgavata Purāna remythologized him—for living religion demands myth of some sort. Demythologize it, and it dies.

The Purānas are vast treatises in verse containing an immense variety of cosmological and mythological material designed to exalt one or other of the two great gods, Vishnu and Śiva. The latest of them, though by far the most influential, is the Bhāgavata, particularly its tenth book which tells of the loves of Krishna and the cowherd girls who are his attendants. The dalliance of Krishna with these young women who are all passionately in love with him is the myth on which the mysticism of the Vaishnavite sect plays. It is their 'Song of Songs': and if Europeans find the frankly erotic imagery of much of this writing excessive, they might do well to reread the 'Song of Songs', a frankly secular love-poem which has yet given rise to some of the finest mystical writing in Christendom, from Origen through Gregory of Nyssa to St. Bernard of Clairvaux and beyond.

Philosophy and religion are inextricably mixed up in Hinduism, and this applies as much to popular devotion as it does to the more refined theistic mysticism of the Bhagavad-Gītā. *Bhakti* in the Gītā is still a passion rigorously controlled, and God's love goes out pre-eminently not to the ecstatic who has lost all self-control, but to the man who has brought his body and senses under rigorous control and yet has learned how to love God with all his concentrated, integrated, and liberated being. Specifically God loves the man 'who is free from exaltation, fear, impatience, and excitement.'[1] He is not interested in enthusiasts.

The Muslim mystics divide mystical experience into two categories— the sober, and the intoxicated. They dispute endlessly as to which is the more perfect, the orthodox wing coming down somewhat naturally in favour of the sober variety. So long as man's approach to Reality is directed towards the timeless peace of Nirvāna, obviously the question does not arise. Nirvāna is by definition cold, since in it the flame of desire is forever extinguished. Hence the 'way' of Nirvāna can be regarded as a progressive 'sobering up' of all our human faculties: it brings them to a total stop. Once, however, you introduce the idea of a personal God who is at the same time the supreme object of love, you introduce a new perspective, for love implies both attachment and commitment: and this seems to make nonsense of *de*tachment, the great ascetic virtue. The Muslims, however, were and are uncompromising monotheists, and this dilemma did not therefore arise, and so they devised the formula *inqitā' 'an al-khalq ilā'l-ḥaqq*, 'cutting oneself off *from* creatures *towards* God'—total *de*tachment from creatures and *at*tachment to God.

[1] Gītā 12: 15.

In India, however, the whole process leading up to liberation had been based on *de*tachment and *dis*passion, and even in the Gītā these are regarded as essential and abiding stages on the way towards God. It is never suggested that one's love of and devotion to God should contain an element of passion—rather it is a quiet delectation. True, God has a stormy, terrible, and passionate aspect, but when at Arjuna's own request he shows this, it strikes him with terror, and he pleads that God will once again resume his comforting human form since he cannot bear the other, let alone love it. But, by introducing the idea of love at all into the divine economy, the author of the Bhagavad-Gītā had introduced something into Hinduism that was utterly to transform it. It is true that the monist philosophers of the school of Śankara, who dismissed the whole phenomenal world including its Lord and Ruler, God, as being, from the standpoint of the 'man who has attained the highest', illusory, continued to dominate the philosophical scene, but nevertheless every single original philosopher of note who followed Śankara made love the centre, if not of his philosophy, then at least of the religion which his philosophy was supposed to clarify. Thus the great names which follow Śankara in the history of Indian philosophy, although they may call themselves monists or rather 'non-dualists' in some qualified sense, are primarily concerned with the *experience* of the love of God; and it is their philosophical task to relate this devoted love and loving devotion to the sacred texts they claim to elucidate, and to harmonize them in a single synthesis. Since in the Upanishads Brahman or God is never wholly distinct from matter nor essentially different from the transcendental self of man, the result is rarely adequate either as philosophy or as theology. This is much to their credit, for neither is of the essence of religion. And so it is that we have heard so little about Indian devotional religion in the Middle Ages; for writers on Indian religion have usually been content to describe the 'systems' of the various Vedānta philosophers and have told us almost nothing of the devotional attitudes they presuppose and which alone have religious importance.

In all the theistic systems, whether the supreme personal God is called Vishnu or Śiva, that God is at the same time the highest Brahman. This does not mean that he is at the same time *im*personal unless we concede that the God of Pseudo-Dionysius and his followers is equally impersonal: it means simply that, as the *Śvetāśvatara* Upanishad says and as any theologian ought to know, God, as he is in his essence, cannot be described in words. The whole question of personal as against impersonal deities is then largely irrelevant. The God of the Vedāntin philosophers who succeeded Śankara—of Rāmānuja, Madhva, Nimbārka, Vallabha, and Caitanya—is, however, personal by any standards. He differs from the Judaeo-Arabic God, however, in that he is never entirely divorced from his creation. Though different in kind he is none the less committed. According to Rāmānuja he transcends the spiritual monads as much as he does matter and is therefore different in kind from both, but, being wholly devoid of evil, he is not only good but compassionate and tender. 'His divine form is the depository of all radiance, loveliness, fragrance, delicacy, beauty, and youth—desirable, congruous, uniform, unthinkable, divine, marvellous, eternal, indefectible, perfect. His essence and nature are not to be limited by word or thought. He is an ocean of boundless compassion, moral excellence, tenderness, generosity, and sovereignty, the refuge of the whole world without distinction of persons. The one ocean of tenderness to all who resort to him, he takes away the sorrows of his devotees' and he becomes incarnate simply out of compassion, 'to give light to the whole world with his indefectible and perfect glory and to fill out all things with his loveliness'.[1]

This is taken from Rāmānuja's commentary on the Gītā. There is no longer any trace of the terrible aspect of God: he is now all compassion and tenderness. Perhaps this shows a lack of balance, for the maxim that 'the fear of the Lord is the beginning of wisdom',[2] even if 'fear' means little more than 'devotion', seems to be true unless we wish to equate mystical religion with emotional excess. Rāmānuja was almost certainly influenced by the Ālvārs, a sect of enthusiasts which originated in the Tamil lands of south India probably in the sixth century A.D. and whose ecstatic devotion to their God went to such lengths that they were some-times believed to be mad[3]—an accusation often brought against the so-called 'intoxicated' mystics in Muslim lands. Rāmānuja's Krishna is not the Krishna of the Mahābhārata nor even of the Bhagavad-Gītā: he is the Krishna of the Bhāgavata Purāna—the handsome cowherd boy who ravishes the hearts of all who hear the sweet sound of his flute. This God has no terrors; the worst he can do and does is to play hide and seek with his devotees who are rapt in ecstasy when he is near them, forlorn and distracted when he hides himself. This he does in order to revive the intensity of their desires.[4]

Hindus have always maintained that the erotic imagery contained in the Bhāgavata Purāna is to be understood metaphorically and mystically,

---

[1] Rāmānuja on Bhagavad-Gītā 6: 47.   [2] Proverbs 1: 7.
[3] Jan Gonda, *Die Religionen Indiens* II, Stuttgart, Kohlhammer, 1963, p. 127.
[4] Bhāgavata Purāna 10: 32: 21.

though the imagery is often sensuously concrete. Krishna embraces his adoring devotees, touches their breasts, scratches them, and so on,[1] despite the fact that most of them are respectably married, and they in turn leave their homes and husbands for his sake.[2] All this has from time to time deeply shocked Protestant Christians, and this puritan reaction is quite natural, for orthodox Protestantism has always regarded mysticism of any kind with the deepest suspicion. And yet the simile of the spiritual nuptials between Christ and his Church[3] is easily transferred to the human soul, and the total surrender demanded is clearly expressed in the words of Jesus: 'Anyone who prefers father or mother to me is not worthy of me. Anyone who prefers son or daughter to me is not worthy of me.'[4] This is what Krishna demands in the Bhāgavata Purāna too, developing further what he had said in the Gītā: 'Give up all things of the law, turn to me, your only refuge, [for] I will deliver you from all evils; have no care.'[5] Devoted love means an exclusive love even to the abandonment of duty.

If taken literally Krishna's relations with the cowherds' daughters and wives are adulterous, or at best fornication; but even the Bhāgavata Purāna does not take itself literally. God delights in his elect through their spiritual senses (an idea to be found in Christian mysticism too), for 'he indwells (and moves among) the cowherds' daughters *and their husbands* as he does among all embodied creatures, looking after them the while and partaking of a body here on earth in the exuberance of his being (*krīḍanena*). It is out of sheer grace towards his creatures that he takes on a human body.'[6] Krishna is the lover of all and he multiplies himself so that he may be all in all to each, so that none may be jealous of another.[7]

Once mysticism admits the existence of a God who is distinct from the self and who is felt to be supremely lovable, erotic imagery cannot be avoided, for there is a certain harmony between the physical and spiritual worlds. This being so, it is always possible that spiritual ecstasy will seek a physical outlet in a purely human relationship. This is particularly true when ascetic techniques are abandoned and song and dance—and nowadays drugs—are used to induce violent ecstasies characterized by weeping, trembling, sweating, and finally loss of consciousness. All these phenomena appeared in the Krishna cult in India as they did among the Sūfīs in Islam. In India it was Caitanya who set this particular ball rolling, though he himself drew a sharp distinction between the love of God (*preman*) and earthly passion (*kāma*).[8]

[1] Ibid. 10: 29: 46. [2] Ibid. 10: 32: 21. [3] Ephesians 5: 23 ff.
[4] Matthew 10: 37. [5] Gītā 18: 66. [6] Bhāgavata Purāna 10: 33: 36-7.
[7] Ibid. 10: 33: 38. [8] J. Gonda, op. cit., pp. 159-60.

In the Bhāgavata Purāna Krishna has no special favourites: he offers himself equally to all. But in the later literature, and outstandingly in the *Gītagovinda* of Jayadeva who wrote towards the end of the twelfth century, a single figure comes into prominence as Krishna's especial beloved. Her name is Rādhā; and just as Krishna is the incarnation of Vishnu, so is Rādhā the incarnation of Vishnu's heavenly spouse, Lakshmī, who is at the same time his creative power through which all things are made. Mystically, however, Rādhā represents the human soul in its relationship to God. The soul, as is normal in mystical literature, is seen as female: she abandons herself entirely to God who is the male. The soul is passive, God alone is active and does with the soul what he will. The soul thereby experiences *rasa*, 'relish', a strong emotional response of which sexual love is the reflection, and sexual love is thereby sanctified and caught up into the divine.[1]

This erotic mysticism of Krishna and Rādhā reached its climax in Caitanya, who seems to have spent his life in almost continuous ecstasy sometimes verging on madness. His followers regarded him as being an incarnation not only of Krishna but of Rādhā too. In him were united the male and the female principles in the godhead—God and his *hlādinī śakti*, his infinite capacity for imparting ravishing sweetness; but in so far as Caitanya remains a human being he is Rādhā, for the human role in relationship to God is always that of the female to the male. Liberation as it had hitherto been understood no longer has any significance; all that matters is the ecstasy of being loved, possessed, and ravished by God. To arouse this violent emotion Critanya instituted the *Sankīrtana*, which consisted in dancing to the music of drums and cymbals and hymns in praise of Rādhā and Krishna. All this was deliberately designed to provoke an ecstasy in which the soul, so far from being negated, was deemed to expand and flower in the embrace of the divine lover.

In all mystical traditions the love of bride for bridegroom is taken as the most satisfying symbol for the love of the soul for God. There are, however, other relationships for which the Krishna cult makes ample provision— the love of servant for master, of friend for friend, of son for father, and even of mother for son (the cult of the infant Krishna so strikingly similar to the cult of the child Jesus in popular Catholicism); but it is always the love of the bride for her spouse that is deemed to be the most adequate symbol of the human–divine relationship—the 'spiritual marriage' of the Christian mystics. Here all sense of awe disappears: God is no longer Lord but solely and simply the lover. According to S. Cakravarti, however,

---

[1] J. Gonda, op. cit., p. 154.

'this love is the opposite pole of earthly passion, free from any kind of eroticism, without end or beginning, yet ever new'.[1] This can scarcely be true, for the kind of love depicted is simply sexual passion transported on to the spiritual plane; and this is surely what we would expect once we admit the possibility of love between the Creator and his creature. Moreover, the 'higher' may slip over into the 'lower', and the Caitanya movement was later to become notorious for erotic practices in which the flesh was allowed its due part. In this respect Caitanya's erotic mysticism bears a family resemblance to the 'carnal' cosmic consciousness of Walt Whitman. The body is no longer the enemy that must be quelled, but a friend whose co-operation is sought and who is invited to share with the soul in the raptures of the divine embrace.

The Bhagavad-Gītā had said that for the man 'whose wisdom is firm-stablished', 'objects of sense must disappear—save only the recollected relish (*rasa*)—and that too must vanish at the vision of the highest'.[2] For Caitanya liberation means the development of this 'relish' to its highest possible degree, for this is to taste the infinite sweetness that only an infinite Lover can supply.

In Hinduism the mysticism of the love of God as it develops in the Krishna cult is characterized by passion: it is the very opposite of the Buddhist Nirvāna, one of the principal characteristics of which is *vairāgya*, 'passion*less*ness'. It has the closest possible affinity with sexual love, and many would maintain and have maintained that it is simply a sublimation of the sexual instinct. This we shall have to discuss later, since all kinds of factors enter in here which we cannot deal with in our present context. This much must suffice for the moment. In human love, as opposed to human lust, sexual intercourse is the normal climax of the whole process of self-giving which is love: it is a sacrament, the seal of divine approval set on a life of self-dedication. In the very nature of things it is the woman who sacrifices herself and gives herself to the man because this is the instinct of the female in the whole natural order. Similarly in divine love the soul abandons herself entirely to the will of the divine Lover who is therefore necessarily conceived of as male—*Purusha*, a 'male Person'. So too in Christian mysticism one speaks of 'ravissement' and 'rapture', both of which are euphemisms for rape.

In sexual intercourse as in ecstasy the human ego melts away and is, so to speak, lifted out of itself; the senses cease to operate in the ordinary way and all are fused into the sense of touch, but this sense too is so heightened and transformed as to seem to have very little to do with the sense of touch

---

[1] J. Gonda, op. cit., p. 160.   [2] Gītā 2: 59.

as normally experienced. It is perhaps because the raptures of divine love
have so close an affinity with purely sexual love that Augustine condemned
the latter with a bigotry as disastrous as it was ferocious. This, indeed, is
just what would be expected from one who had for so long been a Manichee.
St. François de Sales, however, who was both more sane and more civilized, himself realized this awkward resemblance between the raptures of
divine love and sexual orgasm: both involve the total suspension of the
rational faculty and both take one outside oneself. Both, one might add,
involve the total concentration of the whole personality on to one point:
both are a kind of 'yoga' or integration. But here the resemblance ends, for
the point on which the whole personality is concentrated is in the one case
the point without magnitude within the heart through which one has access
to the life of the spirit and to God, the giver of life, in the other it is the
sexual act itself—in crude, physical terms, the phallus—the source of
physical life. St. François was still too much of an Augustinian to see that
the two are both naturally and logically connected since both are steeped
in life—and life more abounding—life in eternity on the one hand and the
recreation of life in the material world on the other. The one is the 'fixed,
still', spiritual self, the other what Marx, following Boehme, called 'the
throes of matter'. In both cases the human psyche is taken outside its
natural condition, raised above itself in the one case, St. François maintains, degraded below itself in the other:

Ecstasy [he says] is called rapture (*ravissement*), for it is by means of ecstasy
that God attracts us up to himself: and rapture is called ecstasy, for it is by
means of rapture that we take leave of ourselves and remain outside and above
ourselves in order to be united with God. Wonderfully sweet, gentle, and
delightful are the attractions by which we are drawn towards God. If we think of
the [sheer] power that God's beauty and goodness have to attract the soul's
attention and diligence towards him, then it will seem that it does not only lift
us up but ravishes us and carries us away. If, on the other hand, we think of the
free consent of our will and the fervid movement by which the ravished soul flows
out in the wake of God's power of attraction, then it will seem that not only does it
rise and ascend, but that it hurls itself out of itself, rushing into the Godhead itself.
The very same thing happens in that basest of ecstasies, that abominable rapture, which the soul experiences when it is drawn out of the spiritual dignity
proper to it, enticed away by carnal pleasures and [dragged] below its natural
state; for in so far as it follows this ill-omened sensory bliss (*volupté*) of its own
free will and rushes out of itself, that is to say, out of the spiritual condition [as
such], it can be said that it is in a state of sensual ecstasy; but in so far as sensual
enticements draw it on with power and, so to speak, carry it off by force into this
low and miserable condition, it can be said that it is ravished and carried out of
itself because these gross, sensory joys deprive it of the use of reason and intelli-

gence with so furious a violence that . . . a man in this condition seems to have been overcome by epilepsy, so absorbed is his mind and as it were lost.[1]

Thus, for St. François there is a real analogy between mystical ecstasy and sexual orgasm; but they are opposite and contrary poles of that oddest of human instincts, self-transcendence, the very negation of the instinct of self-preservation, the longing to have done with all sense of individual personality for ever. Both sex and mysticism are manifestations of this instinct, endemic to the human race, to merge into a greater whole. The two are complementary, not black and white alternatives. The black and white version is basically a Manichaean distortion for which we have Augustine to thank. In India things do not look quite the same.

Hinduism has been much misunderstood in the West since it has been introduced in one or other of its exaggerated forms. One image of it is that of the starveling *sannyāsin* who by dint of extravagant austerities claims to have realized himself as the soul of the All. This is a gross over-simplification which we have been at some pains to correct. The other is that of a religion of unbridled sexuality which the publication of the *Kāmasūtras* as a paperback has done nothing to dispel. This too is an absurd distortion which nevertheless contains a grain of truth. Rather Hinduism is the religion of the 'coincidence of opposites', to borrow the phrase of Nicolas of Cusa, sometime cardinal of the Roman Church; and nowhere is this more plain than in the great God Śiva.

Hindus are divided into worshippers of Śiva (Śaivites), worshippers of Vishnu (Vaishnavites), and worshippers of Śakti (Śāktas). With Vishnu we are now familiar. He is the God who becomes incarnate from time to time to restore right order in the world. *Śakti* is the 'power' or 'active, creative principle' in both Śiva and Vishnu: she is feminine in gender and therefore appears in mythology as the consort of one or other of the two. Usually she is Śiva's consort, and her devotees worship her rather than Śiva himself because Śiva is thought to be so infinitely transcendent as to have no possible interest in this wretched world. His 'active principle' or 'consort', however, is directly concerned with the management of the world and is therefore open to intercession.

For the worshippers of Śiva, however, Śiva alone is God. In him several gods seem to have coalesced. In the Vedic tradition he is identified with Rudra, the one god in the Vedic pantheon who is primarily terrible. This aspect of him remains in the later literature—in the Mahābhārata and the Purānas—and it is this that principally distinguishes him from Vishnu. Śiva always retains his majesty; and it is perhaps for this reason that his

[1] St. François de Sales, *Traité de l'amour de Dieu*, 7. 4.

worshippers never seem to have fallen into the excesses associated with the devotees of Krishna and Rādhā. This seems odd, for, as everyone knows, Śiva's emblem is the *lingam*—the phallus. And yet, so strange a god is he, he is also the perfect Yogin, the perfect ascetic forever lost in trance, and in mythology he shows a particular antipathy towards Kāma, the god of sensuous love. He is the total paradox—perpetually ithyphallic yet perpetually chaste.

It is true that in devotional literature neither Śiva nor Vishnu ever escapes from the often unedifying mythology that surrounds them, but this is only to be expected, as the history of Christian devotion as opposed to Christian theology clearly shows. The Śiva of theology, however, is not the Śiva of mythology, and it is with the Śiva of theology with which Śaivite mysticism is primarily concerned.

In these lectures I shall only have time to deal with the Śiva of south India—more specifically with the Śiva of the *Śaiva Siddhānta*, if for no other reason than that of all the religions and sects of India it approximates most closely to Christianity. All that is lacking is the Incarnation. Until very recently the Śaiva Siddhānta has been sadly neglected in the West. Literally scores of books on the non-dualist Vedānta pour out of the presses, while only a trickle on this crowning achievement of Indian spirituality from time to time seeps out of India. It is to be hoped that this unbalance will shortly be corrected by the forthcoming publication of Fr. M. Dhavamony's definitive and sympathetic study, *Love of God according to 'Śaiva Siddhānta'*, to which I am heavily indebted.

It seems probable that the theistic cults of both Śiva and Vishnu originated in the Dravidian south of India. The literature of the Śaiva Siddhānta, indeed, is almost entirely in Tamil, and the theology that underlies the whole literature, though it may owe something to the *Śvetāśvatara* Upanishad, seems to be quite free from the pervasive pantheism that is characteristic of the Upanishads in general.

In the Śaiva Siddhānta existence is classified under three headings: *pati, paśu,* and *pāśa*—the Lord, the herd, and fetters. Let us see what is meant by these terms.

The Lord is Śiva who alone is God, the Lord of all things, endowed with wisdom, love, and grace, wholly transcendent and wholly immanent, wholly independent of all that is not he. He has his centre everywhere, his circumference nowhere; he is the inner principle of all things, self of all selves. He is the soul of the soul, indwelling it just as the soul indwells the body. He is a God in trinity—he is love, he is the Absolute (*Śivam* (neut.)), and he is creative power (*śakti*). Love, however, is the essence of his nature, for it is love that causes all things to cohere. This follows from the mythological representation of Śiva who unites within himself both the male and female principles, both the *lingam* and the *yoni*. Śiva is the union of the two. God is inseparably united with his creative power as the sun is with sunlight. In his essence he is ever at peace, but through his creative power he never ceases to work. As one of the texts puts it: 'Śiva generates Śakti, and Śakti generates Śiva. Both in their happy union produce the worlds and souls. Still Śiva is [ever] chaste and the sweet-speeched Śakti is [ever] a virgin. It is only the true lovers of God who comprehend this mystery.'[1] The Śaivite trinity, then, is one of male and female and the love that unites them, each deriving from the other in an eternal ebb and flow. Yet the Śaiva Siddhānta insists as much as does the Christian mystic that this union and this 'generation' are essentially chaste, and it is a curious fact that the Lingāyats, a Śaivite sect that wore the phallic symbol round their necks, were the most puritanical of all the Śaivites.

The unity of the Godhead rests squarely on love: for God *is* love. And so we read:

> The ignorant think that love and God are two;
> They do not know that love is God.
> After knowing that love is God,
> They remain possessed of the love which is God.[2]

If God is love in essence, the world is the outpouring of his love, and love is its bond of union with God and with its own members:

> [The Lord] is in love; he forms the body of love outside.
> He is [love] before and after [he acts outside]; as the Lord of the mystics
> He dwells within love, the supremely Real;
> He is the help of those who love him.
> As love, wisdom, and good conduct he abides:
> As bliss and the blissful union between lovers he abides:
> In time and *karma* he abides:
> With love in his fivefold function he abides.

The very essence of God is love both within himself and in relation to 'created' beings.

Already in the Atharva-Veda, the latest of the canonical Vedic *saṁhitās*, Rudra-Śiva was known as *paśu-pati*, the 'lord of cattle'; and this term was

---

[1] P. Nallaswami, *Sivajñāna Siddhiyār*, Madras, 1913, 3. 2. 77.

[2] This and the other quotations from Śaiva Siddhānta sources are taken from Dhavamony's forthcoming book.

retained in the developed Śaiva Siddhānta, Śiva being regarded as the Good Herdsman very much as Jesus saw himself as the Good Shepherd. He is, of course, not only the herdsman but also the owner of the herd, the herd being composed of human souls. The 'form' of Śiva indwells every human soul and is thereby distinguished both from matter and from Absolute Being, since Śiva in the soul is always accompanied by his creative energy and grace. The soul, however, is unaware of God's presence within it, for it is triply fettered: it is fettered by *karma*, it is fettered by *māyā*, and it is fettered by *āṇava*. With *karma* and *māyā* we are already familiar. *Karma*, as in all other Hindu sects and systems, is the accumulation of past actions which accrue to the soul as it transmigrates from body to body: *māyā* again is *not* illusion but the material world as it affects the embodied self or soul. *Āṇava* seems to be peculiar to the Śaiva Siddhānta. Literally it means 'the quality of being minute'. Perhaps it is best translated as 'egoism', but if so, it must be understood as egoism in an unimaginably pure form. It is the Śaivite original sin, for it separates the soul from everything including its 'self' and the God who is within it. If God is the 'soul of the soul', then *āṇava* is, like Mephistopheles, 'der Geist der stets verneint'—it denies and shuts itself off not only from the outside world (*māyā*) and its own experience accumulated in past lives (*karma*) but also from its existence as a self-conscious subject. It is neither spirit nor matter: it is a pure non-entity, but a non-entity that is furiously self-centred. It is the quality that adheres to the soul in its lowest state in which its alienation from God is complete. This state is called *kevalam*, 'solitary and isolated': 'It is non-intelligent, it is formless, imperishable . . . devoid of parts or categories or attributes, has no distinguishing mark, it is not itself an agent nor can it experience the fruits of action, it is immersed in *āṇava* and everywhere present.'

Here again we seem to have a head-on collision between two different types of mysticism, for what is described here seems to be what the *Māndūkya* Upanishad considered to be the 'fourth' state of the self beyond dreamless sleep, the state of absolute Oneness which is identical with what we would call the Godhead. The use of almost identical terminology would seem to be deliberate, and one is reminded of Indra's laconic criticism of the alleged blissfulness of the state of dreamless sleep: 'Such a man, it seems to me, has no present knowledge of himself . . . nor of these creatures here. Surely he might as well be a man annihilated. I see nothing enjoyable in this.'[1] For the Śaiva Siddhānta too, it would appear, the monist's description of this state of the complete oneness of the self is

---

[1] *Chāndogya* Upanishad 8: 11: 2.

simply a retrogression to a pre-natal state, for it not only precludes all
sense-perception and discursive thought but also excludes love and
therefore God: it is not salvation at all but eternal damnation, or rather
perdition, since it 'loses' all things including its self and the God who
indwells it. Whether or not this is a true interpretation of the purely
monistic experience, or is what used to be called the diabolic counterfeit
of it, we shall have to discuss in a later lecture. Suffice it to say that a
'return to the womb' type of mysticism is amply attested particularly in
Chinese Taoism. For the Śaiva Siddhānta, however, this is the lowest
possible state of the soul, prior to all experience and not in the least
transcending experience, the most intractable of all fetters and not by any
means the final liberation of the spirit. If I understand this doctrine
correctly, ānava is individuality or the ego-principle. 'Liberation' is
fusion with the divine—a fusion so intimate and intense that the soul may
and does cry out 'So 'ham', 'I am he'; but this must not and cannot be
taken literally because ānava is indestructible and continues to exist even
when all consciousness of it has been lost, just as the stars continue to
exist when their light has been absorbed into the light of the sun. Ānava is
a spiritual darkness ever present in the soul side by side with the inner
spiritual light which is the wisdom or 'form 'of God in the soul: its nature
is to reject and to deny.

God, however, does not leave the soul in the state of pure isolation, but
uses the other two fetters to break down the worst. These are māyā and
karma, the objective world and what you do with it. Through these the
soul acquires a body through which it can experience what is other than
itself. This is the state of ordinary consciousness and is called sakala,
'possessed of parts', meaning an awareness of multiplicity but not of the
underlying unity of all things. In this state the mere perception of the
objective world, of māyā, like a lamp removes a little of the darkness of
ānava. Māyā, then, is not at all, as it is in the non-dualist Vedānta, an
illusion which stands between the soul and God but one of the instruments
which God uses to rid the soul of its ingrained egoism. Māyā and karma
are thus not so much obstacles that stand between the soul and God as
manifestations of divine grace; for it is grace that sheds its light everywhere, enabling the soul to act (karma) and to enjoy the fruits of what it
does. Man has to act because it is only by acting that in the long run he
realizes that action is a fetter; but under the grace of God it is a fetter that
slowly shakes itself loose, though the soul is as yet quite unaware of it.
Slowly, however, the soul realizes that it is being guided by divine grace
and that all its actions are dictated by grace. Once the soul comes to

recognize grace for what it is, it yearns for the author of grace and for union with him; for this is the true end of the mystic's path.

As in the sect of Caitanya, the soul is regarded as the bride, God as the bridegroom. This is always so when the symbolism of the spiritual espousals is used. To say that mysticism of this type is no more than a sublimation of sex is really rather absurd since the majority of mystics in all traditions—a vast majority in the case of the Muslims—have in fact been men. Anyone rash enough still to put forward this theory must carry his theory to its logical conclusion, namely, that all male mystics must be, whether they know it or not, pathic homosexuals. If you believe this, you can believe anything. It would be difficult to imagine anyone more virile than Meister Eckhart, and yet it is he who tells us that not only must we become virgins, that is, free from all earthly attachments, but that we must also become women in the full sense of the word—wives, *Weib*—so that we can conceive Jesus in the soul and bring forth fruit.[1]

So too for the Śaiva Siddhānta, marriage is the highest form of union because the most intimate; and this union, as with St. John of the Cross and the mystics of the Eastern Church, means nothing less than deification. 'The process of deification', Fr. Dhavamony writes, 'consists of alienation and integration.' The first stage consists of alienation from the outside world, the 'detachment' of the Buddhists and the Bhagavad-Gītā and the integration of the self. This, like everything else in the spiritual ascent, is brought about by the grace of God, whether the soul realizes it or not. The second stage will then be realization by the soul that it is what it is not through anything it has of itself but through the operation of God's grace. This Fr. Dhavamony calls 'alienation from the egoism of the self and the realization of the divine form of grace'. Thirdly there is what he calls the 'alienation from the dual objective realization of God and the non-dual subjective realization of God.' This is a dark saying, but it is important that we should try to understand it. As one of the texts puts it: 'Just as the two words *tāl* and *talai* combine into one word *tātalai*, the *bhakta* is mystically united to the Lord as one. If the *bhakta* and God were identically one in substance, then no union would be possible between them, for union presupposes two beings; if they were to remain two, there would be no fruition; hence in the mystical union they are neither identically one nor two.' 'The condition of such a *bhakta*', Fr. Dhavamony adds, 'must be a combination of duality and non-duality; after release the soul is not merged into the supreme Being (there is no non-duality); yet they are not separate (no duality either). Hence the mystical union does imply

---

[1] Meister Eckhart, *Predigt* 2.

both duality and non-duality but at different levels of being and [of] experience.'

To express this experience words can only mislead, for such words as 'one and many', 'dual and non-dual', are only applicable to sensible things as the twelfth-century Andalusian Muslim mystic, Ibn Tufayl, points out; between liberated souls, or 'separate essences' as he calls them, and God there is both difference and identity: there is oneness of spirit but difference in degree, God being cause, the soul effect. In his own words:

> Much and little, unity and multiplicity, concentration and diffusion are all of them attributes of the body. But we cannot say of these separate essences which know the essence of this true One, that they are many or one, because they are immaterial. . . . But the explication of things in this place is very strait and difficult; because if you go about to express what belongs to these separate essences, by way of multitude, or in the plural, according to our present way of speaking, this insinuates a notion of multiplicity, whereas they are far from being many; and if you speak of them by way of separation, or in the singular, this insinuates a notion of identity, and this is impossible.[1]

In the experience of union with God the sense of unity predominates over that of separateness, but to interpret this as absolute identity Ibn Tufayl calls a 'misgrounded conceit' (*shubha*), and both the author of the Bhagavad-Gītā and the Śaiva Siddhānta would agree with him, for where there is love there must be both duality and unity. This may be incomprehensible to the intellect: to the lover it is self-evident.

In the Śaiva Siddhānta man of himself can do nothing: everything depends on grace. Hence man is overcome with a sense of utter unworthiness when confronted with the holiness of God. On the whole this is not typical of Indian religion: the south Indian Śaivites are the exception. Let me quote an example from the Tamil poet Appar:

> Evil, all evil, my race, evil my qualities all,
> Great am I only in sin, evil is even my good.
> Evil my innermost self, foolish, avoiding the pure,
> Beast am I not, yet the ways of the beast I can never forsake.
> I can exhort with strong words, telling men what they should hate,
> Yet I can never give gifts, only to beg them I know.
> Ah! wretched man that I am, whereunto came I to birth?[2]

Without God's grace nothing is possible, and just as Krishna in the Bhāgavata Purāna withdraws his presence from his devotees in order to

---

[1] See R. C. Zaehner, *Hindu and Muslim Mysticism*, p. 186.
[2] F. Kingsbury and G. E. Phillips, *Hymns of the Tamil Śaivite Saints*, Calcutta, 1921, p. 47.

stir their ardour up anew, so does Śiva withdraw his grace in order to make his devotees realize that he alone is their supreme good. The loss is unbearable, and Mānikka Vāśagar, the greatest of these mystical poets, returns to this theme again and again:

> Through ignorance I have Thy grace refused; and Thou, my Gem,
> Hast loathed me! Lo, Thou'st forsaken me! My throng of 'deeds'
> Suppress and make me thine . . .
> Will not the great-soul'd bear, though little curs are false?
> False me Thou mad'st Thine own, as though some worth I had; didst mend
> Me, O Thou True! Lo, Thou'st forsaken me! Thy throat is black
> With swallowed poison! . . .
> O roseate One, Śivan, who putt'st away my mortal pains![1]

'Thy throat is black with swallowed poison': This is a reference to a well-known Hindu myth in which Śiva drinks a draught of deadly poison to save the world from destruction. These and other myths which are not always edifying turn up again and again in the Śaivite devotional literature, but they are always used to illustrate the main theme of this remarkable sect—man's total dependence on the grace of God and God's tender love for man in all his weakness and misery. God is the saviour and he draws man to himself so that at last he may be one with him for ever.

For the Śaiva Siddhānta salvation means a gradual growing into God. 'Let my unchanging great love grow towards him,' one of the most important texts says. This 'growing into God' takes place in four stages, each of which corresponds to some specific form of religious activity. Acts of external worship, caring for the temples and so on, show the love of the servant for his master and are rewarded by participation in the 'world' of God (sālokya). To perform the same acts, but with an inner conviction that Śiva is actually present in his images and symbols as pure wisdom and light, is to achnowledge him as father: this is the trusting love of a son for his parents and it brings the worshipper into the proximity of God (sāmīpya). Thirdly, when the devotee turns from acts of external worship to Yogic meditation, subduing his senses and fixing his mind on God alone, he passes beyond the spheres of māyā and karma and wins fellowship with God—the love of friend for friend, paralleled in the Krishna legend by Arjuna's love for Krishna. In the last phase God and the soul are inextricably united in knowledge and love. This is called sāyujya, 'yoking together' or 'interpenetration' which, as the texts repeatedly point out, is not simple identity: it is not a total loss of consciousness such as we meet with in the more ecstatic among the Muslim mystics, but a

---

[1] G. U. Pope, *The Tiruvāçagam*, Oxford, 1900, pp. 87–8.

conscious realization of a oneness with and in God which yet does not abolish the existence of the soul. The essence of the experience is love saturated in knowledge, and it is symbolized by the union of bride with groom. It is a melting away into the divine Being—a simile that is used time and again: 'You made me yours, thrilling my frame through every pore: you are the Lord who, melting my bones, entered my [inmost] self as one might enter a shrine.' Now the mystic no longer lives, acts, and enjoys the supreme bliss, but it is Śiva who lives, acts, and enjoys within him. This seems to echo the words of St. Paul: 'It is no longer I who live, but Christ who lives in me',[1] so close is the Śaiva Siddhānta to the Christianity of St. Paul and St. John.

To describe the ineffable union with God, the Siddhānta uses similes which always point to transformation, not to identity, to deification, not to ontological deity. The soul melts into God as iron is melted by and transformed into fire: it is not destroyed, for it continues to experience the ineffable union. Again it is transmuted into the divine as copper is transmuted into gold by the philosopher's stone, or it is drawn to God by the power of magnetism which both share in common. United with God it is united to all other beatified souls in something not unlike what Christians call the Communion of Saints.

Theologically the Śaiva Siddhānta stands closer to Christianity than any other Hindu system or sect. Moreover, while northern Europeans might find Caitanya's cult of Krishna and Rādhā frivolous and be shocked at the frank sexuality it displays, they could scarcely withhold their admiration from the exalted spirituality of the Śaiva Siddhānta in which sensuality has no part. And yet Śiva's symbol is and always has been the phallus. Once again we are faced with a discordant concord and a concordant discord; but perhaps it is Hinduism that sees the concord more clearly than does Augustinian Christianity, which has been too hasty in its rejection of the 'throes of matter' from which life and consciousness ultimately derive.

[1] Galatians 2: 20.

IX

THE GREATNESS OF MAN AND
WRETCHEDNESS OF GOD

PERHAPS some of you will be feeling by now that you have had enough of both mysticism and the Hindus. This would be very comprehensible, for the Hindu way of thinking is very different from our own and is not always easy to follow; but it is precisely because Hindu presuppositions are so radically different from our own that Hinduism and its daughter religion, Buddhism, have aroused such interest today. Moreover, Hinduism is the only one of the world religions that has no known founder: in this sense it is a 'paganism', if by that we mean a traditional religion peculiar to a given nation. Apart from Judaism, which is a very special case indeed, it is the only 'national' religion that has survived with undiminished vigour; and it is worth while inquiring why this should be so.

Hinduism, like the two other great Indian religions usually associated with it, Buddhism and Jainism, is a religion of escape: all three of them see in this world only transience and emptiness. Buddhism put all its emphasis on this, but at the same time it taught that the world can only be transcended if one pursues a moral way of life on earth. The goal is Nirvāna, the complete severing of all links with this transient world, but the way to that goal is *dharma*, the Buddhist way which, as the Buddha said before he passed into his final peace, was to replace him when he was gone. Thus we find the phrase *dhammabhūto*, 'become *dharma*', used in the Pāli canon as a synonym for *brahmabhūto*, 'become Brahman'. To identify oneself with the Buddhist *dharma* is, then, the only sure way of reaching Nirvāna. There is an essential link between the two, and this the Hindus had not always realized, for their sacred books not infrequently speak of transcending good and evil. This is not the way the Buddhists talk, for moral training and the cultivation of the ascetic and Stoic virtues are essential in primitive Buddhism, as they are in the Zen Buddhism practised in Japan today. Moral living, for the Buddhist, means dying to self, as it does for mystics always and everywhere. Here there is no dichotomy between moral development and final emancipation: the one is not considered possible without the other. The contradiction in Buddhism is not between the moral law, which is one of detachment and self-abnegation, and Nirvāna which is its result: rather it is between the Buddhist denial of personality in any real sense and the Buddhist compassion. This is illustrated with particular vividness in the story of the Buddha's temptation before and after he had attained enlightenment.

Māra, the Evil One, whose name means death, first tries to persuade the Buddha to give up his ascetic practices and return to an ordinary life—the kind of life recommended by the Hindu law-books, the purpose of which was to accumulate merit. The Buddha, however, was no longer interested in merit but only in transcending the world, and he well knew that this meant death:

Faith have I [the Buddha says] and steadfastness and wisdom. Why do you prate of life to me now that I have made up my mind? The wind dries up the rivers' floods: why should it not dry up my blood, for I have made up my mind? . . . When the flesh is wasted away, the mind (*citta*) becomes yet more serene: yet more firmly do mindfulness and wisdom and inner contemplation abide in stillness. While this is the way I live and since I have transcended all sensations, my mind pays no heed to desires. See to what purity a man may attain.[1]

Māra, seeing that he cannot turn the Buddha from his path, dejectedly slinks away. This, however, was a vulgar temptation, for the Buddha, on the verge of enlightenment as he was, was scarcely likely to throw everything up at the last moment. It is after he has attained enlightenment that the real temptation is to come; for with enlightenment he realized that he was finally released from the three root evils of desire, becoming, and ignorance. 'The knowledge arose: "There is something released in what is [permanently] released and free." I realized that birth was destroyed, the ascetic life had been lived [and done with], what had to be done was done, and there was nothing further for me in this world.'[2]

Having realized this he was sorely tempted to keep his saving doctrine to himself since it was quite beyond the comprehension of ordinary men:

If I were to teach this doctrine [he thought] and others did not understand it, it would be so much trouble wasted, so much tiresomeness. . . . How much trouble I took to win it! There is no point in proclaiming it. How should people wracked with lust and hate understand this teaching? How should they see it? for it goes against the stream [of life], is clever, deep, difficult to discern, and subtle— and they are wracked with lust and enveloped in darkness.[3]

The great god Brahmā Sahampati, however, read his thoughts and, thoroughly alarmed, he thought: 'This is the end of the world, the destruction of the world, for now that the Tathāgata has become thoroughly

---

[1] *Suttanipāta* 432-5.   [2] *Majjhima Nikāya* i. 249 and *passim*.
[3] Ibid. i. 168.

enlightened, he seems to care precious little and has no thought of teaching the doctrine.' He therefore appeared before the Buddha and begged him to teach the doctrine, for there surely would be some people who would understand:

Open the door of immortality and let them hear the doctrine in all its purity. As a man standing on a peak at the top of a mountain might survey the people round about, so do you, greatly wise as you are . . . look down on the people plunged in grief—[look down on them] for they are stricken with birth and old age. Rise up, O hero, victorious in battle, leader of the caravan; you have repaid your debt [to the world], stride through the world, teach the doctrine: some there are who will understand.

The Buddha relents because he has compassion on the people, and so he says:

Paying attention to Brahmā's request and because I had compassion on the people, I looked down upon the world with a Buddha's eye and I saw . . . that some had little impurity, others much, some had keen faculties, others dull, some had good dispositions, others evil, some were easy to teach, others difficult, while yet others saw the dangers that were to be avoided in another world. Just as among lotuses there are some that are born in water, grow up in it, but do not rise out of it and grow fat submerged in it, while others are born in it, grow up in it, remaining on a level with it; others again are born in it, grow up in it, but grow beyond it and cannot be splashed by it; so I saw that some creatures had but little impurity, others much, some had keen faculties, others dull, some had good dispositions, others evil, some were easy to teach, others difficult, while yet others saw the dangers that were to be avoided in another life.

Of the two protagonists in this scene it was the Buddha who at first showed himself the more logical. Enlightenment had shown him the world was an utter sham—transient, unsubstantial, a place of un-ease: and what is true of the world is true of mankind too. There is nothing in a human being that is permanent, neither his body, nor his sensations, nor his emotions, nor his habitual ways of behaving, nor yet his consciousness. Of none of these can you legitimately say: 'This I am, this is mine, this is the self, this belongs to the self.' If this is really so, then what sense can there be in teaching or saving beings who are simply bundles of sensations without any abiding substance? Moreover, Brahmā's argument, that if he did not teach the doctrine the world would perish, could scarcely have much meaning for a fully enlightened Buddha, who by his very enlightenment had seen that the world of its very nature cannot be saved, because even a Buddha cannot confer abiding reality on what is of its very nature an impermanent flux. Surely to do this would be to attempt to do the impossible. The Buddha, however, has second thoughts because he is moved by compassion. This is the paradox of every type of Buddhism, and in the later schools of the Mahāyāna it becomes more, not less, marked. Basically it is a metaphysical paradox, not a moral one; for if human beings are utterly unsubstantial, then what is there to be saved, what is there to be guided into the timeless peace of Nirvāna? Perhaps the answer is to be sought in the Buddha's own description of his enlightenment. It is not just extinction as some of the earlier students of Buddhism supposed, but rather 'something is released in what is [always] released [and free]'. In this formula the 'something released' always appears in the neuter gender because, whatever it is, it has nothing to do with anything we normally take to be ourselves. It may be spoken of as a 'self' that has 'become Brahman' or 'become *dharma*', but 'self' in these contexts is what Thomas Merton understands by the 'transcendent self' of which nothing positive can be predicated. It has neither individuality nor personality. This being so, there still seems to be no reason why the Buddha or anyone else should have compassion either for it or for the miserable and ever-changing bundle of sensations that is emphatically not it.

This seems to be the contradiction that is ingrained in Buddhism, and it is a contradiction that Hinduism tends to avoid. The Buddhist contradiction is accepted in the Bhagavad-Gītā, but there it is solved and dissolved in a personal and transcendent God who gives permanence to the transient by his compassionate love. Again, in Buddhism there is another and closely related paradox. Life is transient and worthless, and yet it is held to be sacrosanct. No man is entitled to take the life of a sentient being even if provoked. This too is anomalous, for Nirvāna is the total cessation of becoming; and it is difficult to see how one can conceive of life except in terms of change. Moreover, the similes used by the Buddhists all point to what we would call death—the drying up of a tree or of the body and so on. Why then is physical life held sacred? There seems to be no answer. The Hindus were more logical. To win spiritual freedom means to transcend morality, and Krishna himself says: 'Were a man to slaughter [all] these worlds—he slays nothing, he is not bound.'[1] He is not bound because he has transcended all sense of 'I' and 'mine' and what he does cannot then affect him. This is the thin end of the wedge, for it bears all too close a resemblance to the so-called *acte gratuit* which André Gide proposed for our consideration in his novel, *Les Caves du Vatican*. Is it possible to commit an act generally thought to be morally evil, in this case murder, with an unruffled conscience? The question had long ago been

[1] Bhagavad-Gītā 18: 17.

answered by the *Kaushītakī* Upanishad in the affirmative. The man who has won spiritual freedom, who is 'liberated', 'loses nothing . . . even though he should slay his mother or his father, even though he steal or procure an abortion. Whatever evil he does, he does not blanch.'[1] This attitude is supported by Krishna in the Bhagavad-Gītā. There he argues that Arjuna must fight because it is God's will and whatever he does God will relieve him of the responsibility. Admittedly, this is to emphasize one tendency in the Gītā at the expense of others, but, such as it is, it is a dangerous and ultimately amoral doctrine, for if everything that happens is God's will, then man is relieved of responsibility and can do as he pleases. To obviate any excesses that such a doctrine might encourage, a whole corpus of Hindu law came into being. This law was at best a *pis aller* and was in any case based on the distinction of class which, in theory at least, was the basis of Hindu society. This was the law that Vishnu became incarnate as Krishna to restore, and among its tenets was the duty prescribed to members of the warrior class to kill and to be killed. Buddhist compassion and the Buddhist aversion from the taking of life had, however, bitten deeply into Hinduism during the period in which the Great Epic was written, and Hinduism was beginning to have a guilty conscience.

The Mahābhārata has many themes, but it seems to me that the main theme is the inner tension that exists between Krishna, who is God incarnate, and Yudhishthira, 'the King of Righteousness', who is himself the incarnation of the god Dharma, 'righteousness and justice'. Krishna, as he himself says in the Gītā, had become incarnate 'for the protection of the good, for the destruction of evil-doers, for the setting up of the law of righteousness'.[2] His chosen weapon for this purpose was the five Pāndava brothers of whom Yudhishthira was the eldest, Arjuna the third. From the very beginning there was a bitter feud between the Pāndavas and their cousins, the Kauravas, the hundred sons of Dhritarāshtra, the blind and stubborn king who always followed the worst advice. Yudhishthira, as we mentioned in our last lecture, was tricked into a game of dice by his cousins: he lost—and in losing the game he lost everything and was deprived of his kingdom for thirteen years.

Yudhishthira must be unique—and uniquely Indian—among Epic heroes, for he is a pacifist who hates war above all things. He is a gentle saint whose instinct is always to forgive. And yet he is a member of the *kshatriya* class—the class of princes and warriors for whom the law-books prescribe the duty of killing and being killed in war. None of this is to Yudhishthira's liking, and it is quite clear that for him the years of exile in

---

[1] *Kaushītakī* Upanishad 3: 1.   [2] Gītā 4: 8.

which he lived a beggar's life in the forest were more congenial than the days of his royal prosperity. He was outstanding in virtue, but his virtues were those normally associated with a Brāhman, not with a *kshatriya*. Wise beyond his years, he had ever been tender and compassionate.[1] In him were 'fortitude, compassion, long-suffering, truth, and courage securely planted'.[2] These are not the virtues of a fighter but rather of a man who has felt the attraction of the Buddha's gentle creed. Yet this is the man who is to lead his people into the most titanic struggle ever described in literature. Krishna, however, is there to see that he does his 'duty'.

Yudhishthira knows that Krishna is God, the 'omniscient Creator and Ordainer'[3] of all things, and knowing him to be God he loves him. Each knows the other as he really is[4] and this makes the inner tension between them the more poignant. This tension is almost imperceptible at first, but becomes ever more plain as this mighty Epic unfolds; for the God Krishna represents the old order in which the *kshatriya dharma* and all that it entails of trickery and violence has an honourable place, whereas the man Yudhishthira, the King of *dharma*, starting from the premisses of the religion of his time, slowly comes to realize that it is fraught with injustice and plain stupid in that to seek vengeance is to bring vengeance on oneself. But Krishna is God. His will is to go to war, and his will cannot be withstood. It was his will that Yudhishthira should lose the game of dice and go into exile. All this Yudhishthira accepts without a murmur since it relieves him of the responsibility of killing. Draupadī, his wife, however, who had been publicly insulted by the Kaurava brothers and who cannot understand Yudhishthira's 'holy indifference' which seems to extend even to herself, will not or cannot take things so quietly. Whether or not she remembers at the time that Krishna, the family friend, is God, she proceeds to denounce the deity in scathing terms: in her humiliation and despair she can see only senseless cruelty in God:

As a man splits log with log, stone with stone, iron with iron—things that [of themselves] can neither move nor think—so does the Lord God, the Self-subsistent, the primal Grandsire, hurt one creature by means of another, establishing for himself an alibi. Joining things together only to disjoin them again the Lord acts at his own good pleasure, playing with his creatures as children play with dolls. He does not treat his creatures as a father or a mother would but acts in raging anger; and since he acts so, others follow his example.[5]

In this terrible indictment of God Draupadī rubs in the consequences of what Krishna himself says in the Gītā: God is the sole agent, and, if this

---

[1] Mahāthārata (MBh.) 1: 129: 7.   [2] MBh. 1: 197: 19.
[3] Ibid. 5: 149: 33, 36.   [4] Ibid. 3: 120: 26.   [5] Ibid. 3: 31: 34–7.

is so, he is seen to act irresponsibly, without rhyme or reason; the law of *karma* is so much moonshine, for it is perfectly obvious that good deeds are not rewarded and that the evil triumph. Yudhishthira, who has not yet come to question the validity of the old order, is shocked and wounded. Desperately he defends the established order and the God who presides over it, for he cannot face the alternative. He cannot believe that the universe is run by 'a genius as wily and deceitful as he is powerful and who uses all his industry to deceive us', as Descartes, in a moment of doubt, had suggested.[1] And this is just what Draupadī is challenging him to believe. This will not do, he says, it is incumbent on all of us to do our duty without worrying too much about what this will lead to. Duty leads to immortality, and the man who disregards his duty is worse than a thief— he is a *nāstikya*, an atheist, Buddhist, or Jain. Yudhishthira will not as yet face the predicament of Job: the consequences are too frightening. It is *dharma*, doing your duty in that station of life to which God has been pleased to call you, that leads to Nirvāna: to deny this would be to make nonsense of all human existence. For:

> *Dharma* is the bark: there is no other for men who go to heaven. It is the ship that ferries the merchant to the other side of the ocean. For if *dharma* performed by men who live the life of *dharma* were to go unrewarded, this world would be submerged in darkness without basis or support. None would draw nigh to Nirvāna and men would lead the life of beasts. They would be struck down and never attain any object.[2]

If, moreover, the stock virtues commended by religion—asceticism, chastity, sacrifice, scriptural study, generosity, and honesty—did not produce results, why should people have practised them from time immemorial? For Yudhishthira the law of *karma* is not so much an automatic process: it is under the control of God and God must infallibly reward good deeds. That good and bad deeds receive their appropriate reward is a matter of faith: this is a mystery that only the gods can understand. 'No one knows these things and all creatures are misled therein. These are secrets in the keeping of the gods, and the gods are deeply cunning.'[3] Only seers among men who have mortified themselves and purified their mind of all worldly dross can *see* that this is so. It is they who testify to the rightness and righteousness of the world order, and their living experience of it must be trusted. They *see*, as we do not, and because we have not seen, we have no right to question their vision. That deeds are rewarded and that God disposes over the rewards are at this

---

[1] Descartes, *First Meditation.*   [2] MBh. 3: 32: 22–4.
[3] Ibid. 3: 32: 34.

stage articles of faith for Yudhishthira. There is no hope unless we trust and love God despite the injustice we see perpetrated everywhere. And so in conclusion he thus admonishes Draupadī:

Do not slander the Lord who disposes of all beings: learn to know him, prostrate yourself to him: do not harbour thoughts like these. For it is by his grace that a mortal man who is loyally devoted to him will come to transcend mortality. Do not exaggerate when speaking of the highest Deity.[1]

Yudhishthira does his best to defend the traditional *dharma* against Draupadī. Like Job he has to justify the ways of God in the eyes of men. In a way his task is harder, for Job can rebut his friends' facile charges that somehow he must have sinned because he has a clear conscience. Yudhishthira's conscience can never be entirely clear since he had allowed himself to be tricked into a game of dice and had gambled his kingdom and family away. Yet he is oddly blind to his fault here, for he is ascetic by nature and loss of property therefore means nothing to him: rather the reverse. What he seems never fully to understand is that neither his wife nor his brothers are in the least like him. His very nature is to give up, to be detached and indifferent to all worldly things. At heart he does not want his kingdom back, and he is, though infinitely patient, curiously lacking in sympathy with his more earthy brothers and wife. In a way he reminds us of Jesus among his disciples: his kingdom is not of this world. Though he is a worldly king by right he cannot think that he is of this world at all; and in so far as he is forced to live in it, then let his life be lived in exile, and let his arch-enemy, Duryodhana, administer the kingdom since in any case he enjoys the job and can therefore do it better than he. None of this appeals to his brothers, and Bhīma, the roughest of the five, is never tired of reminding him that he is a *kshatriya*, not a Brāhman, and that begging and playing the eunuch,[2] as he puts it, are not consistent with the warrior's code. But for Yudhishthira the virtues ascribed to the Brāhmans (which they all too rarely possessed) were the only ones worth having—truth, open-handedness, long-suffering, uprightness, mercy, self-control, and compassion.[3]

The halcyon days in the forest, however, could not last for ever, and when the thirteen years are up Yudhishthira is forced by both his brothers and Krishna himself to ask for the kingdom back. Rather than risk a war, however, he lets it be known that he would be content with only five villages, one for himself and one for each of his brothers. Duryodhana, however, who hated Yudhishthira for his ridiculous unmanliness, refused

[1] Ibid. 3: 32: 39–40.   [2] Ibid. 3: 34: 13.   [3] Ibid. 3: 177: 16.

to yield even so much land as could be pierced by a needle. Left to himself
Yudhishthira would no doubt have accepted, so greatly appalled was he
at the prospect of [war. With passionate earnestness he pleads with
Krishna, the incarnate God—*his* God—denouncing the whole business of
war and the legal system which makes war inevitable. He is the King of
Righteousness, the King of *dharma*, and should therefore above all others
have acquiesced in the *dharma* prescribed for his class. Yet he cannot, for
he knows that a higher *dharma* dwells in his conscience and that it is this
dharma that he must obey. But though he may be *dharma* incarnate,
Krishna is God incarnate: and Krishna wills that there shall be war: right
is on Yudhishthira's side though he knows that Duryodhana will never give
way. This is Yudhishthira's dilemma: is he to obey his own conscience or
is he to obey the incarnate God in whom he has unquestioning faith?
Bitterly he argues with his God:

> Even if our enemies had not blood ties with us, even if they were not
> Aryans, even so should we not fight them, let alone in a case like this. [Our so-
> called enemies] are for the most part our relatives, comrades, and elders, and to
> kill them is the extremity of wickedness. What possible good can there be in
> war? The caste-duty of warriors is evil, and we are warriors. So our caste-duty
> (*dharma*) is no *dharma* at all—and yet not to do it would be reprehensible! A
> Śūdra's duty is obedience, Vaiśyas live by trade, but we live by killing while
> Brāhmans choose a beggar's bowl. Warrior kills warrior as fish lives on fish or
> dog kills dog. Krishna, don't you see to what a pass *dharma* has come? War
> means killing, battle means the taking of life. . . . War is always wrong, for the
> killer will in his turn be killed, and for one who has been killed victory and
> defeat are all the same. . . . Victory breeds hatred, . . . and hatred can never be
> extinguished by hatred. . . . Once gentleness has been set aside, then cruelty
> sets in, and wise men have compared this to a dog-fight in a puddle. First they
> wag their tails, then one barks and the other barks back; then they whirl around
> together, biting each other and snarling. And then the fight to the finish begins.
> The stronger wins and eats the other's flesh. Krishna, there is no difference at all
> between men and dogs.[1]

These are bitter words, but even before the slaughter Yudhishthira is
beginning to understand that Hindu *dharma*, the Hindu moral code as set
down in the law-books, is a hollow sham and has its roots in violence. But
Krishna will have none of this Buddhistical nonsense. Beggary, he snorts,
is no part of a Kshatriya's *dharma*. 'Victory or death in battle is the eternal
decree of the Creator. This is the *dharma* appropriate to a warrior. Compassion is not prescribed.'[2] 'What a warrior does not take by force he will
never get at all.'[3] Everybody understands this, surely. But Yudhishthira is

---

[1] MBh. 5: 70: 44–72.   [2] Ibid. 5: 71: 4.   [3] Ibid. 5: 73: 23.

obstinate, and the seed of doubt has entered into his mind. He already sees that the warrior's caste-duty is no *dharma* at all—rather is it *adharma*, rank injustice.[1] Somewhere there is real *dharma*, true justice and righteousness, and this is more important to him than any kingdom, more important than life and even immortality itself.[2] But Krishna is God: 'In victory or defeat he is our very root,' Yudhishthira confesses, 'in him is life and royalty, Being and Not-being, pleasure and distress. He is the Creator and Ordainer; in him is prefection and success.'[3] He is God and must be obeyed: so Yudhishthira mobilizes the army. But in so doing he protests again:

> That goal for the sake of which I dwelt in the forest and suffered hardship, now turns out to be no goal at all, utterly futile. So this is what we strive for. The goal for which we strove, we have now lost by our very striving; and even if we had not striven at all, a great disaster would have befallen us. How can we go to war with innocent men? What kind of victory will that be if we slay our aged preceptors?[4]

Nobody is impressed—and Krishna smiles.

Battle is joined and for several days the issue is in the balance. So far both sides have loyally obeyed the rules of war, but now Drona is making havoc of the Pāndava hosts and it looks as if the war cannot be won by valour alone: it can only be won by trickery, and it is God who is to be the trickster. Krishna, however, is not content with this: the righteous Yudhishthira must be made his accomplice, he must be made to make Krishna's wrong-doing seem right. Always, however, Yudhishthira follows Krishna's lead under duress, for he still cannot face the fact that this God is indeed what he seems to be.

As we have seen, in the heat of the battle Krishna made him tell a lie, and the moment the false words fell from his lips his chariot, which, on account of his righteousness, had hitherto been suspended in the air, sank to the ground. And then again at the very end of the war when all the sons of Dhritarāshtra had been killed with the single exception of Duryodhana, Yudhishthira is overcome with compassion. All along Duryodhana had done everything in his power to cheat and humiliate him; but now that he is at bay Yudhishthira refuses to let him be mown down by the mob of his enemies. Let him pick whichever of the Pāndava brothers he will and kill or be killed in single combat. Krishna is furious at this mad act of generosity, for he knows that unaided none of them is a match for Duryodhana, and Yudhishthira, not content with sparing his life, has promised to

---

[1] Ibid. 5: 70: 46.
[2] Ibid. 3: 35: 21.
[3] Ibid. 5: 149: 35-6.
[4] Ibid. 5: 151: 20-2.

allow him to keep the kingdom should he emerge the victor. In the event
it is Bhīma who is selected to fight the last decisive fight. Krishna is
rattled. True, Bhīma is superior in strength, but Duryodhana is the more
skilful fighter. Krishna, however, is taking no chances. With Arjuna's
connivance he tells Bhīma to smash Duryodhana's thighs with a foul blow
contrary to the *kshatriya dharma* itself. Bhīma obeys, and when his enemy
is at his mercy he kicks him savagely on the head and dances a war-dance
round his prostrate body. Yudhishthira is icy in his scorn. 'Once,' he says,
'people used to say, "Bhīma is just". You are still Bhīma. Why then do you
gloat over the king?'[1] From Yudhishthira that is enough. But Krishna's
own elder brother, Balarāma, is less restrained and he curses Krishna for
his betrayal of all known moral codes.

Krishna, as yet undaunted, makes every possible excuse for his hench-
man and accuses Yudhishthira of all people of condoning unrighteousness
in that he had wished to spare Duryodhana the fate he so richly deserved.
But Yudhishthira is not only compassionate but fair: he realizes that
Bhīma has suffered much and is no saint. He says:

> Krishna, it gives me no pleasure that Bhīma, in his anger, should kick the
> king's head, nor do I rejoice in the destruction of [our] family. True, time and
> again we were cheated by the sons of Dhritarāshtra, and many a harsh word did
> they speak when they exiled us to the forest. Bhīma has endured more grief than
> his heart can bear. If I think of it in this way, I can condone it. All right, he has
> killed a man who never cultivated wisdom, was covetous and a slave to his
> desires. Let him reap [the fruits of his] desire, whether it is justice or injustice
> that has been done.[2]

With these words Yudhishthira bids farewell to the code of morality on
which he had been brought up. The kind of *dharma* Krishna condones
is not his *dharma*: the words *dharma* and *adharma*, righteousness and
unrighteousness, justice and injustice, no longer have any meaning for
him. Everything has to be thought out anew.

Worse, however, is yet to happen, and there is poetic justice in what
ensues. Yudhishthira, it will be remembered, had, on Krishna's instigation,
told Drona that his son, Aśvatthāman, was dead; and Drona, on hearing
this from the lips of one who had never been known to tell a lie, lost heart
and was killed. But Aśvatthāman was still alive and bent on vengeance. He
appeals to the great God Śiva—still in the Epic very much the rival of
Vishnu and his incarnation, Krishna—and Śiva hears his prayer. With
Śiva's blessing he attacks the Pāndava armies in their sleep and slaughters
them almost to a man. This too was contrary to the code that regulates the

---

[1] MBh. 9: 58: 17.   [2] Ibid. 9: 59: 31–4.

conduct of war, but had not the Pāndavas flouted the rules of war first, and did not the law-books themselves say that one who lived according to the *kshatriya-dharma* was entitled to do what the world reproved?[1] The Pāndavas' victory, then, turned out to be no victory at all, for the destruction on both sides had been almost total, the toll of the dead amounting to 1,660,020,000 souls while the survivors numbered no more than 24,165.[2] As Yudhishthira had prophesied, in war there is neither victory nor defeat. Now that his prophecy has come true he curses the whole mad business of war:

> In defeat our enemies triumph, and we, the victors, are vanquished. We have killed brothers, comrades, fathers, sons, friends, relatives, counsellors, and grandsons, and having conquered all, ourselves are conquered. For what is profitless appears in the guise of profit, and profit turns out to be loss. Our victory is transformed into defeat: therefore victory *is* defeat. The conqueror who lives to regret his victory is no more than an afflicted fool. What sort of victory is this in which we are doubly defeated by the foe? Cursed be this evil victory of those for whose sakes we slew our friends; for we, apparently victorious, have been vanquished by the vanquished, for it was they who were alert.[3]

Draupadī, turbulent as ever, demands vengeance for the slain, but Yudhishthira has had enough and turns on her with some severity: 'Just is their death,' he says, 'and in accordance with justice. *You* have no reason to bemoan your sons and brothers.'[4] The Pāndavas, he considers, had brought the disaster on themselves, but he, as the eldest brother, must accept full responsibility. And so, when Gāndhārī, the mother of Dhritarāshtra's hundred slaughtered sons, threatens to curse him, he does not blanch. Yes, he says, 'I, Yudhishthira, am the pitiless murderer of your sons. I deserve to be cursed, for it is I who am responsible for the destruction of the world. Curse me, for I have no interest in life or kingship or in wealth. Such friends as these have I killed, deluded as I was and false to friends.'[5]

Gāndhārī knows, however, that Yudhishthira is the least responsible of all. She relents and turns upon the real villain—Krishna. She curses *him* and prophesies his miserable end—the slaughter of his tribe, an inglorious death for himself, and the rape of his women.[6] The incarnate God accepts his sentence, for what he had promised in the Gītā has not come to pass. He had come 'for the protection of the good, for the destruction of evildoers, for the setting up of the law of righteousness'.[7] In actual fact both

[1] Ibid. 10: 5: 16–23; 10: 1: 47–52. [2] Ibid. 11: 26: 9–10.
[3] Ibid. 10: 10: 10–13. [4] Ibid. 10: 11: 18. [5] Ibid. 11: 15: 3–4.
[6] Ibid. 11: 25: 40–1. [7] Gītā 4: 8.

good and evil have been relentlessly destroyed and as yet there is no sign
of the restoration of the law of righteousness. Truly, as the Upanishad says,
'The gods, it seems, love the obscure and hate the obvious'.[1]

The war is now over, but Yudhishthira's struggle with himself has only
just begun. What he had always suspected he now sees to be true: war is
not only wicked but also futile, and war is the business of the *kshatriya*
class to which kings belong. Now, it appears, he is to resume his royal
duties. How can he, since he now realizes that the duties of kingship as
interpreted by the law-books are incompatible with *dharma* as he understands it? Though Krishna is responsible for all that has happened, he
never accuses or criticizes him directly, for he is God—and he is also the
friend he has cherished right up from his childhood days even more than
his own brother Arjuna.[2] And Yudhishthira is loyal. Yet every word he
says carries an implied condemnation of everything that Krishna stands
for. On a warrior's duty to kill, which Krishna applauds,[3] he could scarcely
be more scathing:

Cursed be the *kshatriya* code, cursed be physical strength, cursed be violence
through which we have been brought to our present pass. Blessed be long-
suffering, self-control, purity, freedom from strife and slander, refusal to do
another harm, truthful speech, the constant virtues of forest-dwellers. But we—
through greed, delusion, and stubborn pride, have come to our present pass, so
eager were we to eat the bait called sovereignty. Let no one now seek to gladden
our hearts with sovereignty even over the three worlds, now that we have seen
our relatives struck down upon the earth because we were eager for the bait.
Are we to abandon these innocents whom, for the sake of [mastering] the earth,
we have levelled with the earth, and yet live on cheated of our goal, though our
relatives are slain? We are not dogs, yet we behave like dogs fighting for a piece
of meat. Now we have lost the meat as well as those who once enjoyed it.[4]

Yudhishthira has reached the end of his tether. The very idea of ruling
a kingdom sickens him, and he announces that he will go to the forest to
lead a hermit's life. In solitude he will renounce all his possessions, for
possessions make the perfect pursuit of justice impossible; he has no
interest in either the kingdom or the ordinary amenities of life.[5] The whole
family is now up in verbal arms against him. One after another they urge
the traditional Hindu arguments against this saintly crypto-Buddhist.

Arjuna, losing all patience, leads the attack. Yudhishthira has only
fulfilled his duty as a warrior and now he is playing the eunuch. Think
what the people would say: a king turned beggar of his own volition!

[1] *Brihadāranyaka* Upanishad 4: 2: 2.   [2] MBh. 12: 29: 5.
[3] Ibid. 11: 26: 5.   [4] Ibid. 12: 7: 5–10.   [5] Ibid. 12: 7: 40.

Poverty for the noble is shameful and a sin, whereas private property is the source of *dharma* itself, leads to heaven, and promotes joy. '*Dharma* flows out from property as mountain streams flow forth from a mountain.'[1] Besides, had he not read the Veda where the gods themselves win their high position by violence and lying? Moreover, even if he has an uneasy conscience, he has only to perform the horse-sacrifice which eliminates every sin.[2]

To reprove Arjuna is to reprove Krishna indirectly—and Yudhishthira does not hesitate to do so with frosty scorn:

> Try to be single-minded if only for a moment, . . . and be so good as to listen to me. I have no intention of embarking on a career of self-interest once again to please you; rather will I give up vulgar pleasures and go my own way. Ask me rather about the path of peace that hermits follow. And if you prefer not to ask, well don't; but listen to me all the same.[3]

Nostalgically he then describes the life of a forest-hermit who lives on whatever fruits and roots may come his way in the company of beasts. There he will quietly await the disolution of his body 'neither grieving nor rejoicing, holding praise and blame to be of equal weight, hoping nothing, thinking of nothing as mine, devoid of all dualities, possessing nothing, with self my pleasure-ground, with self serene, like a lifeless thing, blind and deaf, having commerce with nobody whatever, injuring none.'[4] 'Then will I be freed from all attachments, . . . subject to no one, I shall be as free as the wind. All passion spent I shall win eternal satisfaction—for by craving and ignorance I was made to do a monstrous evil thing.'[5]

'Craving and ignorance'; *tṛṣṇā* and *ajñāna*: these are the twin roots of evil, according to the Buddhists, which bind you to the cycle of transience and rebirth. 'How [then] could a man who knows causality as it really is make physical life (*bhava*) his goal?'[6] This is Buddhist talk, and Yudhish-thira is bent on Nirvāna; but for him Nirvāna is the symbol and reality of despair. For since he has rejected the world and rejected life, he has rejected *dharma* too, because, whether *dharma* means the letter of the law-books or the dictates of a good man's conscience, it belongs to life as lived in this world and must fade away into nothingness once life and the temporal process are brought to a final stop.

Bhīma, not usually the most percipient of the brothers, sees that Yudhishthira is beginning to toy with dangerous ideas. In trampling under foot his duties as a warrior he shows that his faith now derives from

---

[1] Ibid. 12: 8: 23.   [2] Ibid. 12: 8. 35.   [3] Ibid. 12: 9: 1–3.
[4] Ibid. 12: 9: 14–16.   [5] Ibid. 12: 9: 28–9.   [6] Ibid. 12: 9: 34.

outside sources:[1] he is adopting the way of the *nāstikas*[2]—atheists, Buddhists, and Jains. Yudhishthira has travelled a long way, for this is precisely the accusation he had levelled against Draupadī at the moment of *her* humiliation and despair. His despair, however, is very different from hers. *She* sought only revenge against palpable injustice: *he* cannot seek revenge even if he wanted to, for he sees the world as injustice incarnate. *In* what is unjust of its very nature there can be no salvation. Perhaps, as the Buddhists say, there is a way of escape *from* it.

It is now the turn of the youngest of the five brothers, Sahadeva, who prided himself on his cleverness. His arguments are more subtle, and Krishna will take them up at a later stage. Giving up possessions is all very well, but this must apply to the inner man as well as to externals. Yudhishthira is now once again a king in his own right and the principal duty of a king in peacetime is the protection of his subjects: this should be an acceptable duty. Instead Yudhishthira, in spite or perhaps because of his righteous indignation, is simply shirking his duty for what are ultimately selfish reasons. It is easy enough for him to give up external possessions because he has never been attached to them, but he seems to have no intention of giving up his internal proclivities, and this is not what is meant by the term *nirmama*, 'counting nothing as mine', a concept that Krishna himself had taken over in the Bhagavad-Gītā from the Buddhists. As to the *dharma* that bids a man give up his external possessions but encourages him to cling to his own foibles, 'may that be the *dharma* of those who hate us'.[3] Yudhishthira is silent.

This gives the egregious Draupadī her chance. The trouble with Yudhishthira, she says, is that he is not normal. If he only had normal instincts, he would be only too pleased to reap the rewards of his and his brothers' actions: he must be mad. This is serious, for, she says, 'In a family in which the eldest son is a lunatic, all the others will follow him, and thanks to this lunacy of yours all the [other] sons of Pāndu are going mad too. Yes, if your brothers were not mad, they would lock you up with the heretics (*nāstika*) and rule the earth [themselves]. . . . [After all] a man who goes off the rails has to be treated with drugs.'[4]

Arjuna now weighs in again, pressing the traditional arguments of carnal man in their crudest form. Not only must Yudhishthira accept the kingdom, he must rule in the only sensible way—by inspiring terror. Look at the gods: they all kill except Brahmā, and no one worships him. Their behaviour is in accord with the laws of nature, and, says Arjuna, 'I

[1] MBh. 12: 10: 19.   [2] Ibid. 12: 10: 20.
[3] Ibid. 12: 13: 2.   [4] Ibid. 12: 14: 32–4.

have never seen any creature keep alive except by taking life. All living creatures live on one another, the stronger on the weaker. The mongoose eats mice, the cat eats the mongoose, dog eats cat, and wild beasts eat the dog. Man eats them all. That is the way *dharma* operates. The whole universe, whether stationary or moving, is the food of life. This is the divinely appointed order and a sensible man should not be upset by it. Do try to behave in the way that nature intended. Only fools repress anger and exultation, repairing to the forests, but even ascetics cannot keep alive without taking life. There are plenty of living creatures in water, the earth, and in fruits. These are killed by absolutely everybody if for no other reason than that they have to keep alive.'[1]

The arguments of 'natural' man do not impress Yudhishthira, and he tells Arjuna curtly to stick to his own speciality which is arms and not to prattle about *dharma* which he might in decency leave to *him*. All this arguing upsets the simple Bhīma because he can now no longer understand his elder brother. He is, after all, the 'King of *dharma*', and now he seems to have lost all interest in *dharma* even as understood by himself, he is no longer interested in the right thing to do but only in escaping from doing—from *karma*—altogether. This is what upsets them all, and Yudhishthira confirms them in their worst suspicions when he roundly asserts that 'the scriptures are all confused and ambiguous thanks to rationalist interpretations'.[2] The deadlock is now complete. Yudhishthira is determined to commit suicide both out of genuine despair and to atone for the carnage of the war: his family insists that he perform the horse-sacrifice both to set his mind at rest and because it infallibly erases any guilt that they might collectively have incurred. In any case, they say, only Fate is responsible; and this is a view that Yudhishthira emphatically rejects.

Finally, however, he is persuaded to accept the crown, and he is taken off to receive instruction from Bhīshma, the much-revered grandsire of the whole clan, who lies dying on a bed of arrows. Bhīshma proceeds to expound the traditional *dharma* of kings which includes not only wars of aggrandisement but also lying, cheating, and spying on the grandest possible scale. He expatiates further on the sanctity of the Brāhmans who are gods on earth and whose actions must never be questioned. And Yudhishthira is told how the great sage Viśvāmitra, during a great famine, had tried to force an outcaste to give him the flesh of a dog to allay his hunger and how the outcaste had said that it ill beseemed a Brāhman to accept forbidden food from an unclean man. So Viśvāmitra helped

[1] Ibid. 12: 15: 20–5.   [2] Ibid. 12: 19: 2.

himself saying that even evil deeds could not hurt a Brāhman. This was too much for Yudhishthira, for he now understood that there was more righteousness and genuine moral worth in this outcaste than in so great and holy a Brāhman as Viśvāmitra was alleged to be. 'If', he says, 'this frightful deed which is contrary to faith and truth is indeed prescribed, then why should I not follow the standards of [this righteous] slave? If *dharma* has become as flabby as this, then am I utterly at sea and sunk in depression. Search as I may I can see no sense in even trying.'[1] For Yudhishthira the old order has passed away and there is as yet nothing to put in its place.

Bhīshma then approaches the subject of liberation, going into every aspect of this obsessional subject. Yudhishthira, who only a few hours earlier had himself been extolling the ascetic's life as the prelude to this liberated state of Brahma-Nirvāna, now begins to question this too. Like any Christian critic of Hinduism and Indra in the *Chāndogya* Upanishad, he sees clearly that these sublime, transcendent states that Bhīshma has been describing leave no room for personality and therefore no room for *dharma*. 'This seems to be the great defect in that liberation which ascetic sages attain to and which is the crown of their endeavour,' he says, 'if it means that there they move in an atmosphere of transcendent wisdom. For my part, I cannot conceive of the highest *dharma* except in terms of activity, for what could be more irksome (*duḥkha*) than to be drowned in transcendent wisdom?'[2] In one flash of insight Yudhishthira sees the weakness at the core of Hindu mysticism. In the hands of the traditional sages the bridge between morality and transcendent truth has been allowed to collapse: the peace of eternity has no connection with justice on earth. In the Gītā the two poles seemed to meet in God; but in the bulk of the Epic Krishna, the God of the Gītā, is not a God of justice as Yudhishthira understands it. Nor can the dying Bhīshma help him, and his reply is ambiguous and evasive.

Bhīshma's life had been preserved so that he might instruct Yudhishthira in statecraft and in the mysteries of time and eternity. In both he had failed to give satisfaction. None the less he had done his best. He dies quietly and his soul is liberated for ever from the bondage of matter.

Once again Yudhishthira is filled with despair and once again he threatens to become a forest-hermit. This time Krishna realizes that it is useless to go on talking about the so-called merits of the warrior's *dharma* which Yudhishthira hates with all his being. No, he will attack the apostle of renunciation in his Achilles' heel: he will show him that his renunciation,

---

[1] MBh. 12: 140: 1–2.   [2] Ibid. 12: 290: 78–9.

high-minded though it may be, is not devoid of hypocrisy. For Yudhishthira is renouncing something to which, of his very nature, he feels no
attachment and he is opting for a way of life which accords with his own
instincts. Had he not, when still in exile, asked his heavenly father, the
god Dharma, for one thing only, 'that I may ever vanquish greed, delusion,
and anger, and that my mind may always dwell on giving, austerity, and
truth',[1] and had not this boon been granted and his erring brothers
raised from the dead because he had exalted the virtue of mercy over what
was supposed to be the highest good of man, liberation from his purely
human state, and because he had promised to practise it?[2] Was it not,
then, sheer selfishness to want to lead a hermit's life when as the ruler of
a devastated kingdom he could effectively exercise all the virtues he so
highly prized and which came so effortlessly to him? This was the issue he
must face, for this was the battle he must now wage against himself, the
battle between egoism, however cleverly disguised, and that selflessness
which is of the essence of Brahman. And so Krishna bids him face the
issue squarely:

Just as you had to fight against Drona and Bhīshma, so now has the time come
to fight against your own mind. So you must enter into the battle, harnessing
(*yuktvā*) your highest faculties (?) to what you do. There neither arrows nor
servants nor kinsmen can help. With your own self alone you must fight: this is
your battle now. If you do not win this battle what will your condition be?
Understand this, and you will have done your duty. Make your decision,
bearing in mind the ebb and flow of all contingent beings, and rule the kingdom
even as your father and forefathers did before you. There is no salvation in
giving up external goods: in giving up what is within you (*śarīra*) there may or
may not be salvation. Whatever *dharma*, whatever pleasure the man may enjoy
who has divested himself of external goods though he still clings to what is
within him, may that be the lot of those who hate you. Death is spelt out in two
syllables, the eternal Brahman in three. Death in two syllables is *mama*—'this
is mine'—the eternal is *na mama*—'this is not mine'. So death and Brahman
reside within the self. Unseen they bring strife on [all] creatures: have no doubt
of that. If it is true that the soul cannot be destroyed, then to slay the body of
others must be the same as to refrain from injury. If a man were to gain the whole
earth with all that it contains of moving and unmoving things and yet have no
thought that it was his, what then would he do with it? Or if a man were to
choose to live in the forest, subsisting on forest herbs, yet consider things as his
own, then would he be ripe to enter into the jaws of death. Consider the nature
of your outward and inner enemies. Only the man who sees the truth of this
will be freed from the great terror [of recurring death].[3]

[1] Ibid. 3: 298: 23.　　　　　　　[2] Ibid. 3: 297: 71.
[3] Ibid. 14: 12: 11–14: 13: 8.

Here we seem to have the Krishna of the Bhagavad-Gītā speaking again. He speaks with authority, and his message is much the same. What is new, however, is that he now goes on to assure Yudhishthira that liberation, whatever it may be, is not the annihilation of *dharma*, it is rather the fulfilment of *dharma* as each man understands it, for in God there is not only peace but also desire: and just as Krishna describes himself in the Gītā as 'desire that does not conflict with *dharma*',[1] so too is that same desire present in the world of pure spirit which the Buddhists call Nirvāna. And so he goes on to say:

A man whose self is all desire receives no praise in this world and yet without desire there can be no activity. For it is through desire that a man gives alms, studies the Veda, performs penance, and [all] Vedic exercises. [Is there anyone] who undertakes a vow, performs sacrifice or any other religious observance, or engages in the spiritual exercise of meditation without desiring it and knowing that [full well]? For whatever a man desires is *dharma*: it cannot be sound to curb one's *dharma*. These are the verses sung by Desire which knowers of ancient lore celebrate. Listen to them as I sing them to you, Yudhishthira, missing nothing.

'I cannot be slain by any being whatever since none has the means to do so. If a man should seek to slay me, putting his trust in the power of a weapon, then do I appear again in the very weapon he uses. If a man should seek to slay me by offering sacrifices and paying all manner of fees, then do I appear again in "the self that indwells all action" in moving things. If a man should seek to slay me by means of the Vedas and the ways of perfection inherent in the Vedas' end, then do I appear again as the "stilled, quiet self" in unmoving things. If a man should seek to slay me by steadfastness, a very paladin of truth, then do I become his very nature, unaware of me though he be. If a man should seek to slay me by ascetic practice, firm in his vows, then do I appear to him again in his very austerities. If a man should seek to slay me, wise and bent on liberation, then do I dance and laugh in him as he abides in the ecstasy of liberation. There is no being that can slay me, for I am the One Eternal.'[2]

At this Yudhishthira takes comfort. But he has yet, at Krishna's instance, to perform the horse-sacrifice which is incumbent on every triumphant monarch. The details of this tiresome affair, always costly and usually violent, he leaves to Arjuna; but when it is all over and he is receiving the congratulations of Brāhmans and others for the lavish gifts he had bestowed, a blue-eyed mongoose, one half of whose body was pure gold, appears and says to him in a human voice: 'Your sacrifice is not worth as much as a barley-corn.'[3] Then the mongoose told its astonished audience of Brāhmans and kings the story of a family of poor Brāhmans

---

[1] Gītā 7: 11.   [2] MBh. 14: 13: 9–17.   [3] Ibid. 14: 92: 4–7.

who gave away their whole pitiful stock of food to entertain a greedy stranger, leaving nothing for themselves. And then he explained: 'Dharma takes no pleasure in gifts given in expectation of great rewards; he delights in little gifts honestly come by and purified by faith.'[1] Then the mongoose revealed itself as the god Dharma, Yudhishthira's heavenly father. And Yudhishthira knew that just as the so-called sacrifice of war was abominable in his father's sight, so too were the blood-sacrifices of the ancient dispensation.

The roles are now reversed; for of the two protagonists in this enormous Epic it is Yudhishthira, the King of Righteousness, who emerges justified and morally victorious, Krishna, the god of tradition, who is seen to have failed. In the last books this becomes absolutely clear, for Krishna meets an ignominious end while Yudhishthira is received up into heaven, body and soul.

Krishna returns to his tribe but he cannot escape Gāndhārī's curse. No sooner has he reached home than his tribe goes berserk and the tribesmen slaughter one another in a drunken orgy in which Krishna himself participates. Retiring to the forest he is shot in the heel by a fowler called Jarā, 'Old Age', who mistakes him for a gazelle. The fowler's name is surely significant, for Krishna's *dharma* had indeed grown old. All godly dignity has now left him, for shortly before his death the sound of his divine conch is answered by the derisive braying of asses, and the emblems of his divinity, sovereignty, and power mysteriously disappear. All the able-bodied males of his tribe had been killed and he leaves the women in the protection of Arjuna. Arjuna is Krishna's *alter ego*, but he too has lost all his prowess; for as he is escorting the women and children back to his capital city they are attacked and carried off by robbers while Arjuna looks helplessly on. The mission of the incarnate God is over: it has failed and it is seen to have failed. Yudhishthira's code of compassion and mercy has been completely vindicated; and so, having nothing more to do, he anoints his grandson king, and sets out once again with his four brothers and their common wife to live the life of a hermit in the forest. One by one they fall by the way until Yudhishthira is left alone—and yet not quite alone, for ever since he left his capital city he has been followed by a dog who will not leave his side. As he approaches the Himalayas the great god Indra appears in his chariot and bids Yudhishthira mount it. But Yudhishthira has no desire to go to heaven now that his brothers and wife are dead. Indra, however, assures him that they are already there. Yudhishthira is still not satisfied, for *dharma* still holds him back. Even

[1] Ibid. 14: 93: 73.

now when all earthly ties seem to have fallen away he is bound by the tie of compassion he feels for this dog who is faithful till the end. He says:

This dog is ever loyal to me. Let him come with me, for I have compassion on him.

Indra: You have cast off mortality and are now my equal. All glory and great fulfilment have you now won. Today will you taste of the joys of paradise. Renounce the dog, there is nothing cruel in that.

Yudhishthira: Difficult indeed is it for a man of chivalry to do an unchivalrous deed. Such glory do I in no wise covet for which I must renounce a creature loyal to me.

Indra: In paradise there is no place for men with dogs. . . . Renounce the dog, there is nothing cruel in that.

Yudhishthira: It has been said that to renounce one who is loyal to you is an infinite evil—as evil as the slaying of a Brāhman. Hence will I by no means whatever, seeking my own pleasure, renounce [this] dog today.

Indra: Dogs are ever swayed by anger. No sooner do they see a gift [offered to the gods], or the sacrificial meat, or the oblation, if these are uncovered, than they carry it off. Do you then renounce this dog, for by renouncing it you will attain to the world of the gods. By renouncing your brothers and the well-loved Draupadī you gained a world by your own deeds. How is it, then, that you will not renounce this dog, bent on total renunciation though you are. Indeed you are distraught today.

Yudhishthira: Among dead men there is neither peace nor war, or so we believe on earth. Never can I bring them to life again. While yet they lived I did not renounce them. To abandon a loyal [friend], methinks, is as bad as to frighten off one who seeks sanctuary with you, as the murder of a woman, as the theft of a Brāhman's goods, or to violate a compact.[1]

Indra is right: for throughout the Epic Yudhishthira has been the very embodiment of dispassion and renunciation. Why, then, will he not renounce this dog which has so recently attached itself to him? It is the dog that gives the answer, for it too reveals itself as the great god, Dharma, Yudhishthira's heavenly father. To be loyal to those one loves—to one's brothers and one's wife—there is nothing remarkable in this, nor is renunciation in itself necessarily the highest virtue, as Krishna had pointed out, but to renounce a great good for the sake of one who is devotedly loyal to you, though you may have no feelings at all for him, is something new in Hinduism, and it is for this that Yudhishthira is exalted above all the saints in heaven. And so the god Dharma is right to say: 'Because you said, "This dog is loyal and loves me", and renounced thereby the godly chariot, therefore, O king, is there none in heaven who equals you. And so you will attain to imperishable worlds in your own body and tread the divine way than which there is none higher.'[2]

[1] MBh. 17: 3: 7–15.　　[2] Ibid. 17: 3: 20–1.

This Yudhishthira accepts, for he now understands that loyalty and love have an infinite value in themselves, and he therefore says: 'Whether my brothers' lot is good or bad, that is the lot I wish for myself. I do not wish for any other worlds.'

Indra, however, now as ever the tempter, seeing that Yudhishthira is still fast attached to compassion and mercy, protests:

> Stay on in this state which you have won by your own fair works. Why do you even today drag human love around with you? You have won perfections' highest prize such as no other man has won before. . . . Yet even today human affection [has the power to] touch you. This is heaven: look at the divine sages and the perfected who dwell in paradise.

But Yudhishthira only said: 'Without them I cannot live anywhere. I want to go where my brothers have gone and . . . Draupadī and my dearest friends.'

If the Bhagavad-Gītā is the crucial landmark in the history of Hindu religion in that it transfers the attention of mortal man from the bare idea of immortality and liberation to a God who transcends both, then, it seems to me, Yudhishthira's refusal to enjoy any state of being, however exalted, unless it be shared with those whom he had loved on earth, marks a second and scarcely less significant turning-point. In Yudhishthira alone does the 'holy indifference' of St. François de Sales comprise, as it does in St. François himself, a love of God that yet does not exclude the love of one's neighbour. This is most unusual in Hindu spirituality which is mystical to the core: but then, dare I say, 'Thank God', Yudhishthira was not a mystic.

X

THE DEATH OF SELF

THE bulk of this year's Gifford Lectures has, I am afraid, been devoted to Indian religion, particularly to Hinduism. And yet I cannot think that the time allotted to the subcontinent has been disproportionate; for Hinduism is both the fountain-head and the typical manifestation of mystical religion in all its forms. It gives the lie, as no other religion does, to the facile assumption that 'mysticism is essentially one and the same whatever may be the religion professed by the individual mystic: a constant and un-wavering phenomenon of the universal longing of the human spirit for personal communion with God'. This assertion concerning the nature of mysticism was made by the late Professor A. J. Arberry in the preface to his little book on Sūfism published in 1950. On the lips of a scholar who had devoted so much of his life to the popularization of *Islamic* mysticism the assertion is pardonable and indeed in harmony with what has traditionally been understood by mysticism or mystical theology in the West until quite recent times, when the publication of the mystical treasures of the Hindu and Buddhist traditions led to a radical reappraisal of the nature of mystical experience. In the West, that is to say, in the three religions which arose in the near *East*—for no world religion has originated in Europe—we have until quite recently started from God as our major religious assumption, and the Christian and Muslim mystics therefore quite naturally see in the love of God the centre and core of their experience. Hence Professor Arberry was justified in speaking of the 'universal longing of the human spirit for *personal communion* with *God*'. No Christian or Muslim mystic would quarrel with this. St. François de Sales called it 'a conversation of the soul with God', and this, he says, is the essence of prayer which in turn is the essence of mystical theology:

If prayer is a colloquium, a talk, or conversation of the soul with God, then it is in prayer that we speak to God and God on his side speaks to us: we aspire to him and breathe in him; and he, on his side, inspires us and breathes upon us (*nous aspirons à lui et respirons en lui; et mutuellement il inspire en nous et respire sur nous*).

But what do we speak about in prayer? What is the subject of our conversation? We speak about God and nothing else. For about what could love talk and con-verse except the Beloved? And so prayer and mystical theology are one and the same thing. It is called theology because, just as the subject-matter of speculative theology is God, so does mystical theology speak of nothing but God. Only there are three differences. First, speculative theology deals with God *qua* God, while mystical theology speaks of him as the supremely lovable: that is to say, the first considers the divinity of supreme goodness, the second the supreme goodness of the Divine. Secondly, speculative theology deals with God [in his dealings] with men and among men, mystical theology speaks about God to God, nay, in God. Thirdly, speculative theology tends towards knowledge of God, mystical theology towards the love of God. The first makes its pupils learned scholars and theologians, the second makes its own into fervent, devoted lovers of God, whether they be Philotheas or Theophiluses. [Once again the female is mentioned before the male because in this divine love-affair the soul must play the female part.]

This theology is called mystical because in it the conversation is wholly secret and all that passes between God and the soul is from heart to heart in a communion that cannot be communicated to anyone except to the participants themselves.[1]

This is a fine description of Christian and Muslim mysticism, classically the mysticism of the love of God. It cannot, however, be said that it fits the kind of mysticism with which we became acquainted in the Upanishads, let alone with the experience of Nirvāna as described in the early Buddhist texts. Only one thing do the Buddhists and Christian-Muslim traditions seem to have in common, and that is that the mystical experience, however expressed, is essentially an individual and personal affair that cannot be directly communicated to anyone else. In the Buddhist tradition this is made very clear. Teaching Buddhas are exceedingly few and far between, and even they, as we have seen, on the rare occasions when they arise, are sorely tempted to keep their enlightenment to themselves, so difficult is the teaching of it and so incurably blind and spiritually ignorant is the generality of mankind.

This seems to be both the strength and the weakness of the Indian tradition—and indeed of the contemplative life in general: it simply cuts itself off from the community and is content, or so it appears, to let the world stew in its own juice. It probably deserves to do just that, but that is not the point at issue. For the moment I would merely summarize for you the various points I have been making in these lectures while at the same time anticipating what I shall have to say next year.

In my last lecture I introduced into my survey of the varieties of Indian mysticism a discordant note sounded not by me but by the most august figure in Indian mythology, Yudhishthira, the King of Righteousness, who saw precious little righteousness in the moral code accepted in

[1] St. François de Sales, *Traité de l'amour de Dieu*, 6. 1.

his day. The *dharma*, the sense of right and wrong, that indwelt his conscience considered the *dharma*, the 'law' laid down by the Brāhmans in
society, and found it not only wanting but in many respects abominable.
So too with the ways of salvation expounded to him at enormous and
wearisome length by Bhīshma, his venerable grandsire, from his bed of
arrows, he sees that they too, because they are concerned only with final
peace and not with activity, must put paid to any ideal of right conduct, for
conduct (*karma*) of any kind is obliterated in the fathomless abyss of pure,
transcendental wisdom. Thus, for him the religion of his day seemed to
have failed both in the sphere of action and in the sphere of contemplation.
It had failed because it had found no middle term between the two—
righteousness, the right way of doing, on the one hand, and the deep
serenity of 'holy indifference', the right way of being, on the other. In this
Yudhishthira was well ahead of his time. Alone among the heroes of
mythology and indeed among Indian religious thinkers of historical times
until the appearance of Mahatma Gandhi, he hungered and thirsted after
righteousness. He had the originality to regard justice on earth as being
at least as important as liberation from the bonds of earthly existence in
which alone justice could be exercised.

The doctrine of reincarnation is, of course, fundamental to all Indian
religion. It is not so much a dogma as an assumed and undisputed axiom
of existence. This, combined with the caste system, has not made for
active charity (in any sense of the word) among the Hindus. Theoretically
the caste system as it developed in history is supposed to have derived
from an original fourfold division of society into Brāhmans or priests;
*kshatriya*s, warriors and princes; *vaiśya*s, peasants and artisans; and
lastly the *śūdra*s or serfs, these last probably representing the indigenous
population enslaved by the Aryan invaders. According to the distinguished French scholar, Georges Dumézil, the three upper classes or
castes were a common feature of all Indo-European society, and in Great
Britain this division may be seen even today in the structure of Parliament
where we have the lords spiritual and the lords temporal on the one hand
sitting in the House of Lords, and the common people (not, it is true,
overwhelmingly either peasants or artisans) sitting in the House of Com-
mons on the other. Similarly in the *ancien régime* in France you had the
three 'estates' of clergy, nobility, and commoners, each deriving from the
three ancient Indo-European classes. Be that as it may, the ancient
systems in India, if it ever really existed in practice, soon broke down into
a proliferation of castes and sub-castes, each socially separated from the
other. Such a system assumes the inequality of man, and what is unequal

is inequitable and therefore unjust, as Yudhishthira very clearly saw. For his fellows, however, it seemed to belong to the natural order of things, for a man is born into a station of life which he has earned for himself in former lives which stretch back to eternity without beginning. Below even the lowest castes there are, of course, the outcastes, the refuse of society, who were, at least until Gandhi challenged this particular abuse with all the force of his spiritual prestige, a source of pollution to caste society, just as physical refuse befouls everything with which it comes into contact. This intolerable condition they had brought upon themselves through the wicked deeds they were supposed to have committed in former lives. Hence the attitude of society towards them could only be one of reprobation: they were criminals whose only salvation lay in a meek acceptance of their lot, which was of their own devising, and, through this cheerful acceptance, in the hope of a better incarnation in future lives.

Buddhism, it is true, did much to correct this mechanistic view of the transmigrating process, for it strongly and repeatedly asserted that a true Brāhman is not one who is born into that caste but the man whose conduct is consistently upright, merciful, selfless, and compassionate. If a man lacks these virtues, then he is no better than a *śūdra*. In the *bhakti* sects too, among the devotees of both Śiva and Vishnu, there was no distinction of caste within the sect itself, though in everyday life caste barriers naturally remained. This was the situation that the British found when they came to India, and the puritanical mind of the Evangelical missionaries quite rightly found it appalling.

Between Evangelical Protestantism and Hinduism as it existed in the eighteenth century a head-on collision was inevitable. No religion, I suppose, could be less in sympathy with mysticism than Evangelical Protestantism. Mysticism, in any case, is not a phenomenon that can be observed, and what the Evangelicals observed was to them the most degraded form of idol-worship, superstition, and social injustice. There was the inequality and iniquity of the caste-system itself, what Gandhi was to call the 'ineffaceable blot' of 'untouchableness', widow-burning, child marriage, and so on. Yet all these practices found their justification in the Hindu *dharma* itself. Take the case of the immolation of widows, for instance. It is the wife's duty according to the Hindu *dharma* to serve her husband, and it is therefore most meritorious for her to immolate herself on his pyre when he dies, for, by so doing, not only does she gain great merit for herself but she will also be able to continue to serve her husband who is to her a god in another life. Not unnaturally the Christian missionaries could not see things quite in this way.

It is generally believed these days that good and evil are relative terms; and so perhaps they are. And yet the fact remains that the arrival of the Christian missionaries did arouse in India a social conscience that had not been present before, and it was under their influence that the Indians themselves, without actually accepting conversion, pressed for the suppression of age-old abuses.

It is customary nowadays to denigrate the missionaries; and there is no doubt that few of them showed tact or made any attempt to make sense of the immensely complicated mosaic that is Hinduism. Yet, for all that, they did stir the Indian conscience into an awareness of what all enlightened Indians have long since regarded as being evils; and in this I for one cannot believe that they did wrong.

That such evils did deface Hindu society as it had been moulded by the Brāhmans was perhaps inevitable, for if one is a specialist in matters concerning the Absolute, one tends to shrug off the relative as being of little or no importance: and, unfortunately, it is only in the sphere of the relative that right and wrong have any meaning. Buddhism had tried to bridge the gulf by making the attainment of Nirvāna dependent on the Buddhist *dharma*, the minimum requirements of which were purely ethical—not to take life either human or animal, not to steal, not to commit fornication, not to lie, to abstain from intoxicants, to which are added abstention from malicious, frivolous, and harsh talk, and so on. These are binding on everyone; they are the firm base from which the ascent to Nirvāna must begin. As to the man who has achieved the final freedom and peace which is Nirvāna, there is no question that he is thereby freed from moral obligations as Krishna suggests in the Bhagavad-Gītā ('A man who has reached a state where there is no sense of "I", . . . were he to slaughter [all] these worlds, slays nothing. He is not bound'[1]). Rather he should suffuse the whole world with love, compassion, joy, and equanimity.[2] This is typical of all forms of Buddhism, including Zen; and it is perhaps the greatest positive contribution that Buddhism made to the religion of India. There can be no salvation or liberation or spiritual freedom or Nirvāna unless this is based on the Buddhist *dharma*—on the Noble Eightfold Path which consists of right views, right intention, right speech, right action, right livelihood, right effort, right mindfulness, and right concentration—the emphasis always being on 'right'. The Buddha knew full well that mystical states could be attained without moral training, states in which a man passed beyond good and evil, as the Hindus put it; but this he did not countenance. And so, although he was not prepared to

---

[1] Gītā 18: 17.   [2] *Dīgha Nikāya* i. 251; ii. 186 and *passim*.

define Nirvāna except in negative terms, he was quite clear that this timeless immortality could not be validly achieved except by practising his moral code and by a total detachment from all things of sense. For him, at least as we know him from the Pāli canon, Nirvāna means the 'cessation of becoming', the severing of all links with carnal man and with life as lived in this world. The Mahāyāna in general and the Zen sect in particular was to change all that, and to them we shall return next year.

Meanwhile let us recapitulate what of mystical religion we have learnt from the Hindus. We started with a discussion of R. M. Bucke's concept of 'cosmic consciousness' which he claimed to be a new phase of consciousness[1] which showed that 'death is an absurdity, that everyone and everything has eternal life; . . . that the universe is God and that God is the universe, and that no evil ever did or ever will enter into it'.[2] Now it would be a waste of time and a trial of your patience to refute Bucke's thesis in detail, although there are still people who believe that all mystical experience is the same and ultimately reducible to Bucke's formula of cosmic consciousness. Our original confrontation of primitive Buddhism (for Bucke the first known manifestation of cosmic consciousness) with Walt Whitman, the last and, for him, the most perfect, demonstrated that this could not, except by the wildest stretch of the imagination, be true; for the mysticism of Walt Whitman is a thoroughly pantheistic identification of spirit with matter ('Objects gross and the unseen soul are one'),[3] and this is frequently expressed in terms of a very earthly sexuality. The mysticism of Gautama, the Buddha, on the other hand, is wholly dualist: it puts an end to all becoming, to all life as we know it, in order that the mystic may enter a world of pure spirit which is deathless, unborn, unbecome, uncompounded, utterly beyond space and time. To the Buddhists, as to the Manichaeans who imitated them in this, sexuality is utterly repellent, since it not only ensures that the whole wretched business of becoming should go on, but also, more than anything else, distracts one from the awareness of any spiritual reality.

There have been many attempts to classify the elements that go to make up a mystical experience, the most notable of which are perhaps those of Bucke himself and of William James in his *Varieties of Religious Experience*. More recently we have had Professor W. T. Stace in his *Mysticism and Philosophy* and Miss Marghanita Laski in her book *Ecstasy*. Needless to say they do not agree among themselves, and it would be unprofitable to discuss their different analyses now. A word, however, must be said about Stace.

---

[1] R. M. Bucke, *Cosmic Consciousness*, p. 79.   [2] Ibid., p. 17.
[3] Walt Whitman, *A Song of Occupations*, 5.

Stace does not even mention love as a possible ingredient in his recipe for mystical experience. This is interesting; for in the Western tradition love has always been regarded as *the* essential ingredient. As far as the Christian and Muslim traditions are concerned, to analyse mystical experience without so much as mentioning love is like analysing a *bouillabaisse* without mentioning fish or a haggis without mentioning offal. Professor Stace is very keen on unmasking doctrinal bias in others, even going so far as to attribute Martin Buber's interpretation of his own experience after mature reflection to 'the environmental pressure of the culture to which he belongs':[1] in other words he is accusing him of intellectual dishonesty, whether conscious or unconscious. Yet Stace is far more guilty of bias than Buber ever was, for at least Buber had had an experience and, so far as is known, Stace had not. His failure to mention love can only be due to an obvious anti-Christian bias reinforced by a massive ignorance of the whole tradition of love-mysticism within Hinduism itself.

Bidding farewell to Stace, then, let us see just what Indian mysticism has to tell us. In this tradition alone it would appear that we can distinguish four types of mystical experience.

1. First, we have Bucke's cosmic consciousness, to which would correspond the formula, 'I am the Cosmos', or 'I am the All'. This is a common concept in the Upanishads, and is perhaps best exemplified in the following passages:

> Whoso thus knows that he is Brahman becomes this All. Even the gods have not the power to cause him to un-Be, for he becomes their own self.[2]

And again:

> What is other than the organs of sense (*deva*) and the vital breaths is [called] *sat* ('what is'), the organs of sense and the vital breaths are [called] *tyam* ('this'). [All] this is expressed in the [one] word *satyam*, the Real. It comprises this whole universe: thou art this whole universe.[3]

This is the transcendence of space. The same idea can be expressed in the formula 'without and within are one'. This is clearly expressed in the *Chāndogya* Upanishad:[4]

> In this city of Brahman there is a dwelling-place, a tiny lotus-flower; within that there is a tiny space. . . . As wide as this space [around us], so wide is this space within the heart. In it both sky and earth are concentrated, both

---

[1] W. T. Stace, *Mysticism and Philosophy*, Philadelphia and New York, 1960, p. 157.
[2] *Brihadāranyaka* Upanishad 1: 4: 10.   [3] *Kaushitaki* Upanishad 1: 6.
[4] 8: 1: 1–3.

fire and wind, both sun and moon, lightning and the stars, what a man possesses here on earth and what he does not possess: everything is concentrated in this [tiny space within the heart].

Or to turn to a modern author, Pierre Teilhard de Chardin, who seeks to explain this enigma scientifically:

Thanks to the prodigious biological event represented by the discovery of electro-magnetic waves, each individual finds himself henceforth (actively and passively) simultaneously present, over land and sea, in every corner of the earth.[1]

So much for the transcendence of space. What of time?

2. The transcendence of time would seem to be the second type of experience, often accompanying the first as it would be reasonable to expect, but not always so. The classic formulation of this is perhaps Bhagavad-Gītā 2: 12–21:

Never was there a time when I was not, nor you, nor yet these princes, nor will there be a time when we shall cease to be—all of us hereafter. . . . Of what is not there is no becoming; of what is there is no ceasing to be: for the boundary-line between these two is seen by men who see things as they really are. . . . Finite, they say, are these [our] bodies [indwelt] by an eternal embodied [self]— [for this self] is indestructible, incommensurable. . . . Never is it born nor dies; never did it come to be nor will it ever come to be again: unborn, eternal, everlasting is this [self]—primeval. It is not slain when the body is slain. If a man knows it as indestructible, eternal, unborn, never to pass away, how and whom can he cause to be slain or slay?

This is the eternal Now of Meister Eckhart which is shared between man and God, in which there is neither before nor after and in which the soul is single (*ledig*) and free and receives God's gifts ever anew.[2] It is the same Now of which Richard Jefferies speaks as well and as beautifully as anyone:

I cannot understand time [he writes]. It is eternity now. I am in the midst of it. . . . Nothing has to come: it is now. Now is eternity; now is the immortal life. . . . To the soul there is no past and no future; all is and will be ever, in now. . . .
There is no separation—no past; eternity, the Now, is continuous. When all the stars have revolved they only produce Now again. The continuity of Now is for ever.[3]

The 'now' and the 'here' are at the same time the 'always' and the 'everywhere', and this is of the essence of Zen Buddhism as it is interpreted in Japan today. When these two experiences—the transcendence of

[1] Pierre Teilhard de Chardin, *The Phenomenon of Man*, E.T., p. 240.
[2] Eckhart, *Predigt* 1.   [3] Richard Jefferies, *The Story of my Heart*, chapter iii.

space and the transcendence of time—combine, they may converge in yet another experience.

3. And this is the experience of absolute oneness. The classic formulation of this is perhaps that of Parmenides: 'It never was, nor shall it ever be; for it is now, together, all, one, continuous.'[1] Here 'I am this All' combines with the eternal Now in a static One. At the height of this experience no sense remains of anything except this One: all else has fallen away. It is the *Māndūkya* Upanishad which expresses this state in all its denudation:

Conscious of neither within nor without, nor of both together, not a mass of wisdom, neither wise nor unwise, unseen, one with whom there is no commerce, impalpable, devoid of distinguishing mark, unthinkable, indescribable, its essence the firm conviction of the oneness of itself, bringing all development to an end, tranquil and mild, devoid of duality, such do they deem this fourth to be. That is the self: that is what should be known.[2]

The only positive thing said about this state is that it is 'tranquil (*śānta*, 'brought to a full stop') and mild'—wholly static and indivisibly One. Or again, even more emphatically:

Descry This with your mind:
Herein there is no diversity at all.
Death beyond death is all the lot
Of him who sees in This what seems to be diverse.

Descry It in its Oneness,
Immeasurable, firm,
Transcending space, immaculate,
Unborn, abiding, great,—
    [This is] the self![3]

This is an 'infinite' Oneness—and let there be no mistake about it, it seems to be of the very essence of this Hindu experience that what is experienced is not only unfractionably One but also infinite. This is as true of the individual self (the apex of the soul of the Rhenish mystics and St. François de Sales) as it is of the universal self of the Godhead; for as the *Śvetāśvatara* Upanishad[4] says:

Think of this living self as but a part
Of a hundredth part of the tip of a hair
Divided a hundred times!
And [yet] to infinity is it conformed.

[1] Fragment 8.
[2] *Māndūkya* Upanishad 7.
[3] *Brihadāranyaka* Upanishad 4: 4: 19–20.
[4] 5: 9.

Now, it seems that this experience can be interpreted in one of three ways. Either you may interpret it in a strictly monistic sense: the individual soul, when stripped of all its attributes, is simply identical with the Absolute; or it is, in Buber's terminology, 'the basic unity of my own soul, . . . beyond the reach of all the multiplicity it has hitherto received from life, . . .—existing but once, single, unique, irreducible, this creaturely one: one of the human souls and not the "soul of the All" '.[1] This is what Louis Gardet misleadingly calls a 'finite absolute':[2] rather it is the Absolute reflected in finite things, the 'image of God' of the Christian and Muslim traditions as well as of the theistic Vedāntin philosophers, the wax that is capable of receiving every possible form, though itself formless, as Nicolas of Cusa[3] says. Or, thirdly, it is an independent and infinite because undefinable entity, sufficient unto itself, a pure spiritual monad, separate from all other spiritual monads as it is from matter, as the Sānkhya holds.

Well, you are very welcome to choose whichever interpretation you will, but if you opt for the purely monistic one, then it is clear that this state must be the absolute Truth beyond which it is impossible to go. For if you are the One, the Absolute, then plainly there is nowhere to go from there since in the Absolute there can be no movement, no 'going' of any kind, as Parmenides clearly saw. So did the Gītā: but for the Gītā this was not the end but in a sense only a beginning. The danger of thinking it is the end is very great. This is what Buber once thought and indeed, he says, was bound to think, so crushingly convincing is this sense of absolute oneness. In India, however, things are very different, for *this* is an experience that the Gītā takes for granted; but it gently points out that this is in fact *not* the end. What lies beyond is our fourth category of mystical experience.

4. This is the infinite love of God. In a crucial passage the Gītā[4] says:

When thought by spiritual exercise (Yoga) is checked and comes to rest, and when of [one]self one sees the self in self and finds content therein, that is the utmost joy which transcends [all things of] sense and which soul [alone] can grasp. When he knows this and [knowing it] stands still, moving not an inch from the reality [he sees], he wins a prize beyond all others—*or so he thinks*. Therein he [firmly] stands, unmoved by any suffering, however grievous it may be. This he should know is what is meant by spiritual exercise (Yoga)—the unlinking of the link with suffering and pain. . . . Upon this athlete of the spirit whose mind is stilled the highest joy descends: [all] passion laid to rest, free from [all] stain, Brahman he becomes.

[1] Martin Buber, *Between Man and Man*, E.T., p. 24.
[2] Louis Gardet, *Expériences mystiques en terres non-chrétiennes*, Paris, Alsatia, 1953, p. 37.
[3] *De docta ignorantia*, ii. 8.   [4] 6: 20–7.

This is the Buddhist Nirvāna. This is the final denudation, the final stripping away from spirit of all material, mental, and affective adjuncts, of all difference and diversity. Whether this is a unity that is identical in each separate spiritual monad or whether it is the unity of all things in God, it is merely a stepping-stone to a higher state in which the liberated soul comes to commune with God. 'Who standing firm on unity communes in love with me as abiding in all beings, in whatever state he be, that athlete of the spirit abides in me.'[1] This is the higher *bhakti*, the love of God that is awakened only after the soul's liberation from the world of sense and discursive thought. In Indian spirituality this is a revolutionary doctrine which was to change the whole course of Hindu mysticism.

In Hinduism, then, *four* types of mysticism can be distinguished:

1. The transcending of spacial limitations and the consequent feeling that one is the All.
2. The transcending of temporal limitation and the consequent realization that one cannot die.
3. The intuition of oneness outside both space and time in a realm in which there is no becoming, only Being. This state is normally achieved by a process of *Yoga*—of introspection and integration of all the faculties into a timeless inner core. This is a 'contraction' into the One rather than an 'expansion' into the All. All three experiences invariably bring peace and joy: sometimes they are considered to transcend good and evil. Of love there has hitherto been no hint.
4. The love of God in the context of pure spirituality beyond space and time and beyond the 'One'. In the Hindu tradition this first appears in the Bhagavad-Gītā.

It is often said that the alleged ideal of the Upanishads which is supposed to be pure monism was too exalted to leave any room for 'religion' as normally understood, and that the *bhakti* cults are therefore compromises—*ersatz*-monism, if you like—devised by merciful teachers for the spiritually immature. This would be to impute to the great teachers of both the Śaiva Siddhānta and the theistic Vedānta a benevolent dishonesty—but dishonesty none the less. This is certainly uncharitable and probably untrue.

In the case of the Gītā it is certainly untrue, for it accepts all the main premises of Upanishadic and Buddhist mysticism and shows how these can be complemented and consummated in a mysticism of divine love—a transcendent and timeless love because love itself is seen to be infinite.

[1] Gītā 6: 31.

As the Tamil Vaishnavite saint, Namm'alvar, says: the mystic, 'through the cessation of all inclination to other things and the increase of longing for God in a timeless and spaceless manner, and through the pangs of separation in not realizing him constantly, considers himself as a woman, and through the pangs of love loses his consciousness'.[1] Yet even in the later theistic writings the idea of liberation is rarely lost sight of, but it is invariably supplemented by a burning love of God which culminates in a union so close and so intense that it is sometimes spoken of in terms of identity. Well then, it will be objected, is this not simply a more round-about way of reaching the absolute Oneness proclaimed by the *Mandukya* Upanishad?

The short answer to this is the Bhagavad-Gita itself which, alone among the classical Hindu scriptures, claims to be a direct revelation from God. In the Gita the mystical stages are clearly defined. First there is the inte-gration of the personality into its immortal ground which is the same in all beings, and this leads to 'liberation', that freedom of the spirit implied in the phrase 'to become Brahman'. Then, *after* becoming Brahman the mystic communes with Krishna in love and so finally enters into him. But both Krishna's love and the love of the mystic remain, as the last chapter of the Gita makes abundantly clear. This means that in eternity personal relationships at least as between the soul and God remain, though transformed on to a higher plane. Monists are free to explain this away if they will, but this is the doctrine of the Gita and there is no getting round it. It is, of course, the doctrine of all theistic mysticism too.

'This is not I: this is not mine: this is not the self: this has nothing to do with a self.' So runs the refrain in the Buddhist text, *Samyutta Nikaya* iv. This is of the very essence of Theravada Buddhism, and it is this abdication of personality that many find attractive today. It stands at the opposite pole from modern Christianity's wearisome insistence on the inviolability and sanctity of the human 'person', which, we are given to understand, is in some mysterious way distinct from 'individuality'. This emphasis on the 'person' seems to me to be at its best misleading and at its worst corrupt. For Christianity, little less than Buddhism, preaches self-denial as perhaps the one essential virtue. This, surely, is what the Sermon on the Mount is about; and this is why it is the Sermon on the Mount that has appealed so strongly to the Indian mind, and to Gandhi in particular, for in India renunciation is the queen of all the Virtues: and what does the Sermon on the Mount say except 'Renounce'?

[1] S. N. Dasgupta, *A History of Indian Philosophy*, Cambridge, 1952, vol. iii, p. 72.

It says it very tersely: and this, for the student of religion, is one of the great beauties of the Gospels and particularly of the synoptics: they enunciate the highest truths in the fewest possible words. Buddhism, on the other hand, is handicapped by the sheer size and wearisome repetitiveness of the texts: the message is lost in a welter of categorized lists of virtues, vices, psychic states, 'impediments', 'limbs of enlightenment', and so on. Only the shorter independent treatises have a freshness and spontaneity that cannot fail to impress; but the bulk of the Pāli canon is already infected with a scholastic dryness that must test the patience of the uncommitted reader. The Upanishads, the Gītā, and the Gospels are at least of a manageable size. They can be read at a session, yet they can serve as themes for meditation as wide and as deep as is the capacity of whoever chooses to approach them in this way. To my mind the whole of Buddhism and half of Hinduism is summed up in Matthew 16: 24–6 and its parallels in Mark and Luke:

Then Jesus said to his disciples, 'If anyone wants to be a follower of mine, let him renounce himself and take up his cross and follow me. For anyone who wants to save his self (ψυχή = ātman) will lose it; but anyone who loses his self for my sake will find it. What, then, will a man gain if he wins the whole world at the cost of his self? Or what has a man to offer in exchange for his self?

As the editors of the Jerusalem Bible say, the 'self' that must be lost and refound is 'life', 'soul', and 'person'. It is not only the 'ego' but also the *ātman*, the timeless self of the Bhagavad Gītā, the immortal centre and core of one's whole personality, what La Rochefoucauld calls the 'truth' (*le vrai*) of each and all of us which is the same in all, in the greatest as in the smallest.[1] Even this must be given up if you would follow the Christ or, for that matter, the Buddha. There is no other way. For, although according to the Gītā[2] and the Buddhist *Dhammapada*[3] there are two selves in man—the *nafs* or carnal self and the *rūḥ* or spiritual self of the Muslims— you must not *want* to save either, since the mere desire to do so leads to the loss of both. This seems to me to be of crucial importance for the understanding of all Indian religion: everything must be given up which ties you to this life. Only so can you win through to Nirvāna, the state of Brahman, the *requiem aeternam*, the 'eternal rest', for which Catholics

[1] La Rochefoucauld, *Réflexions diverses*, i.—'Du vrai', ed. Pléiade, p. 503 'Le vrai, dans quelque sujet qu'il se trouve, ne peut être effacé par aucune comparaison d'un autre vrai, et quelque différence qui puisse être entre deux sujets, ce qui est vrai dans l'un n'efface point ce qui est vrai dans l'autre: ils peuvent avoir plus ou moins d'étendue et être plus ou moins éclatants, mais ils sont toujours égaux par leur vérité, qui n'est pas plus vérité dans le plus grand que dans le plus petit.'   [2] 6: 5–6.   [3] 160.

pray on behalf of the faithful departed. 'Eternal rest', be it noted, not 'eternal *life*'. And in this the liturgy for the dead is very Buddhist indeed; for this is precisely what the Theravāda Buddhists sought—the 'cessation of becoming', the extinction of the flame of desire which is at the same time the flame of life as we understand it, the cooling off and drying up of all affections—the unutterable peace of death. To the Buddhists of the early dispensation this was the end: for the Bhagavad-Gītā and for Christianity as it was understood and lived by the early martyrs it was no more than a beginning. Why should this be?

The short answer is, as we said in an earlier lecture, that to cling to life is natural if you believe that you only live once: it is *unnatural* to desire death as Christ tells us we must. If, however, life is an endless re-becoming and re-decaying to which there is neither beginning nor end, then the prospect becomes overpowering in its horror: it can only lead to despair of all things worldly and a desperate longing for liberation and release. To one schooled in this way of thought death can only appear as a blessed release, and under these circumstances to desire death is *natural*. The difference between the two religions would appear to be this: Buddhism diagnoses the human condition as being impermanent, devoid of substance, and therefore as a state of unending un-ease and tension (*dukkha*), and the Buddha claims to have found a sure way out of this hateful condition. Hence despair is a Buddhist virtue and 'eternal rest' is the final goal. Christianity agrees with Buddhism that life as we know it is a mess (this is what is meant by the Fall) and that *this* life must be sacrificed. Like the Buddhist the Christian too must die. Hence in all three synoptics the passage we have just quoted follows immediately on Christ's first prophecy of his Passion. As Christ must die on the Cross, so must the Christian die to self just as the Buddhist does. The Buddha conquers un-ease, tension, and sorrow by demonstrating their hollowness and insubstantiality: Christ accepts humiliation, insult, and spiritual agony as having a mysterious worth in themselves just as he had accepted the unpretentious joys of life and life itself. Hence the Agony in the Garden which is quite literally inconceivable in any other religion. The Buddha rejects matter, the source of that fungus which is life, as being unredeemable: Christ takes to himself matter and life and promises Christians life eternal. Hence the Resurrection.

In the synoptics, in St. John, in St. Paul the same message repeats itself: Deny yourself, die to self, face what the Buddhists have always faced with calm and joy, face death, final and complete: *requiem aeternam dona eis, Domine.* Forget about yourself and forget about the Resurrection as the Buddhists do. And so in the fourth Gospel too we read[1] again with reference to the Passion:

> I tell you, most solemnly,
> unless a wheat grain falls on the ground and dies,
> it remains only a single grain;
> but if it dies,
> it yields a rich harvest.
> Anyone who loves his self loses it;
> anyone who hates his self in this world
> will keep it for eternal life.

This is a text that any Buddhist could readily understand; for though the death of self is the core of Buddhist teaching, the Buddha also speaks of Nirvāna being attained *brahmabhūtena attanā*, 'with a self that has become Brahman', that has become transcendent and free. True, this self is totally devoid of characteristics and not at all what modern Christians understand by a 'person'. Yet the use of the word implies some form of existence, not simply annihilation.

In Christianity it is Baptism that corresponds to Nirvāna—the death of carnal man before his allotted time. 'When we were baptized in Christ Jesus,' St. Paul writes, 'we were baptized in his death; in other words, when we were baptized we went into the tomb with him and joined him in death.'[2] So too does the perfected Buddhist join the Buddha in his *parinirvāna*, his final farewell to all things worldly, but for the Buddhist there seems to be nothing corresponding to the Resurrection. And yet the Buddhist insight that death of self is the only true gateway to an eternal mode of being, to immortality (let us not call it eternal life), is, I should have said, basic to Christianity too. What we should ask of our theologians is not a theology of the Death of God (Nietzsche had already given us that and he went mad), but a theology of the death of self, the death of the human 'person', who is not only our old enemy, the ego, 'gorgeously attired, clad in fine raiment and [richly] adorned', as the *Chāndogya* Upanishad[3] so charmingly and so pertinently puts it, but also the ego who has 'got religion' because he thinks he has found or even has found the 'true' self.

This much at least we can learn from Buddhism. The Hinduism of the Bhagavad-Gītā and above all of the Śaiva Siddhānta takes us beyond this, for it takes us out of our 'selves', out of our own 'truth', into God. Thus, in its later stages Hindu mysticism converges on Christian mysticism— converges through what La Rochefoucauld calls our individual 'truths'

---

[1] John 12: 24–5.   [2] Romans 6: 3–4.   [3] 8: 8: 3.

which in Christianity, Islam, and the theistic Vedānta are the reflections of God in us, the *imago Dei*. The principal difference between Indian mysticism and its Christian counterpart is that salvation is understood by the Indians, both Buddhist and Hindu, as necessarily implying liberation from matter—matter in the Marxian sense understood as the basis of all that moves and strives, acts and thinks; while for the Christian mystic salvation ultimately means union with a God who is not only a static Absolute (as in Śankara and the other Indian monists) but also being *in act*. This is true of the Bhagavad-Gītā too, and therein lies its importance.

India is the classical land of mysticism—both the mysticism of eternal rest which seems indistinguishable from total death and that of eternal life in a living God: but mysticism is only one aspect of religion. It is fashionable today, particularly in the United States, because it offers an alternative to the Protestant God of Luther, Calvin, and Barth—the God of *sola gratia*, of pure gratuitous grace arbitrarily given and arbitrarily withheld, the God of favouritism as Michelet put it, the God who is 'totally other', the God 'out there' whose credibility Dr. John A. T. Robinson so forcefully questioned. It is true that this God no longer convinces and in that sense he is dead, but this has never been the Catholic God, nor for that matter the Quaker God, but it is this image of God that has been presented to the Anglo-Saxon world during the last two centuries, and it is now so tarnished that no amount of polishing will ever restore it in its original form.

The present interest in Zen Buddhism is quite clearly a reaction against this Old Testament image of God; and because the image had become not only irrelevant but also repulsive, the reaction has been extreme. Not only this God but all gods have been thrown on the rubbish-heap, and so the religious *avant-garde* has turned to the monistic Vedānta of Śankara and to 'godless' Zen, not to the far deeper insights of the Bhagavad-Gītā. Moreover, both Zen and Yoga as vulgarized in the West have become popular not only because they put paid to that useless and essentially unlikeable God 'out there', but also because they are 'do it yourself' religions, the purpose of which is to uncover an eternal dimension within yourself, what Jesus called 'the kingdom of God within you'. That this 'kingdom' can be revealed by psychedelic drugs as well as by more traditional methods has long been maintained by people as serious-minded as Aldous Huxley and Christopher Mayhew who has claimed to have experienced timelessness under the influence of mescalin. There seems to be nothing particularly surprising in this since this is not an experience peculiar to religious mystics but can happen to anyone, as the cases of, for instance, Proust and Richard Jefferies show. Whether this is what the Zen Buddhists mean by *satori*, only they can say. On the whole they resent the comparison.

Mysticism is, of course, a purely personal affair, as even the Buddhists, despite their emphatic rejection of the ego, admit; and even when the existence of a personal God is allowed, it is a personal relationship between the soul, the bride, and God, the bridegroom, in which obviously no one else can share. It is all a question of loving God 'with all your heart, with all your soul, with all your strength': in Indian mysticism there is rarely any question of loving 'your neighbour as yourself'. This is true to some extent of Christian mysticism too, St. François de Sales being an outstanding exception. Again Indian mysticism is not interested in 'fruits': Christian mysticism not infrequently is, witness St. Catherine of Siena, St. Bernard, and St. Ignatius Loyola whose active life welled out of their contemplative experience. Whether or not these fruits seem pleasing to us today is not for the moment the point. The point is that with them contemplation and action are no longer divorced, because union with God meant for them not only union with his eternal Being but also union with his will (St. Bernard is very insistent on this). For St. François de Sales God's will and his love are synonymous, and this love of God not only overflows into the daily life of the mystic in his relationship with his fellow men, but also bears fruit in heaven in constant *active* love. Deeds are not reduced to ashes as they are in the Bhagavad-Gītā,[1] but transformed into the purest love: and this means activity and life, for love implies both.

In Buddhism and particularly in the later Mahāyāna school, the highest virtue and the highest state of being conceivable is called *prajñā*, usually translated 'wisdom'. This means an intuitive apprehension of eternal Being, the corollary of which is *śūnyatā*, 'emptiness'—being emptied, that is, of all *dharma*s, of all that can be defined as a 'thing'. If this experience is devoid of love, however, St. François de Sales warns us, we must regard it with deep suspicion:

The first mark of a truly *holy* ecstasy [he says] is that it never engages or attaches itself to the understanding as much as it does to the will, which it moves, warms, and fills with a powerful affection for God; so that if an ecstasy is more beautiful than good, more luminous than warm, more speculative than affective, it is highly dubious and much to be distrusted. I do not say that one cannot have raptures, or even prophetic visions, without charity; for I am well aware that just as one can have charity without being enraptured and without prophecy, so too can one be enraptured and prophesy without possessing

[1] 4: 37.

charity. But I do say that when a man enraptured has more clarity in his understanding with which to wonder at God than he has warmth in his will with which to love him, then he had better be on his guard; for there is a danger that this ecstasy may be false, inflating rather than edifying his spirit, ranking him indeed among the prophets like Saul, Balaam, and Caiaphas, but leaving him none the less among the outcast (*reprouvés*).[1]

For St. François passive contemplation is not enough, for 'love is the first act (*karma!*) and principle of our spiritual life of devotion (*bhakti!*) by which we live and feel and move (*émouvons*). Our spiritual life must correspond to our affective impulses (*mouvements*), and a heart which has neither impulse nor affection has no love, just as, on the other hand, a heart which has love cannot be devoid of affective impulse.'[2]

Raptures in themselves are suspect—and among these raptures I have no doubt that St. François would have included the pure 'wisdom' of Yogic trance and the Zen Buddhist *satori*, *if* these bore no fruits in one's daily life:

If, then, [he goes on to say,] you see someone experiencing raptures in prayer which bring him out of himself and raise him above himself into God, and yet having no ecstasy in his [daily] life—that is to say, if he does not lead an exalted life attached to God by the renunciation of worldly lusts, by mortification of natural desires and inclinations, by an inward sweetness, simplicity, and humility, and above all by unceasing charity, then you may be sure that these raptures are highly dubious, even dangerous. Such raptures are apt to win the admiration of men, they do nothing for their sanctification. For how can it profit a soul to be rapt in God through prayer, if, in its dealings with its fellows (*conversation*) and its [daily] life it is rapt in affections which are earthly, low, and natural? To rise above self in prayer, but to sink below self in one's [daily] life and activity (*opération, karma!*), to be angelic in meditation and bestial in one's dealings with one's fellows, is 'to hobble on one leg then on another',[3] 'to swear by God and to swear by Milcom'.[4] In short it is a sure sign that such raptures and such ecstasies are nothing but the playthings and wiles of the Evil Spirit.

This is going a little far, perhaps; but it does show at least how strongly a highly intelligent, civilized, and saintly Christian felt about mystical states and the differences he discerned between them. St. François, of course, speaks the language of his age, and to us it must seem odd that he should attribute to the Devil a rapture 'which raises a man above himself into God'. Against the Hindu background, however, with which, I hope, we are now to some extent familiar, his meaning is clear. 'Liberation', if it is in the understanding only, if it is pure 'wisdom' and nothing else, is

[1] *Traité de l'amour de Dieu*, 7. 6.   [2] Ibid. 7. 7.   [3] 1 Kings 18: 21.
[4] Zephaniah 1: 5.

'fraught with defect', as another saint, Yudhishthira, saw; for it bears no
fruit. As the Buddha himself said, the tree of life must dry up, or, as the
uncanonical *Nāradaparivrājaka* Upanishad[1] says, the perfected sage will
behave like an inanimate object, a lunatic, a dumb man, or an idiot. This is
one type of mysticism and it would seem to be quite profitless even to the
mystic himself.

Mysticism, as interpreted, experienced, and lived by St. François de
Sales, however, overflows into daily life: it can, then, to a certain extent be
shared, for the essence of love, whether mystical or otherwise, is participation—and this is the original meaning of the Sanskrit word *bhakti*.
Normally, however, the mystic, as the Buddha says,[2] fares 'like the horn of
a rhinocerous, alone'.

Teilhard de Chardin was a mystic no less than the Buddha, yet he is a
mystic of solidarity, not of solitude, a mystic of 'togetherness' and harmony, not an existentialist contemplating the bleakness of his own soul.
He is a mystic in the tradition of the Gītā, not of the Buddhists, whether
Zen or otherwise. If he has a consistent theme, it is this: ever since man
reached the stage of self-consciousness he has been torn between two
diametrically opposed types of mysticism which, on the surface, seem
almost identical. The one he calls a 'unity at the base, by dissolution', the
other the 'unity of the summit, by ultra-differentiation'; the one is the
'pantheism of identification, the very antithesis of love: God is all'
(the monism of Śankara), the other the 'pantheism of unification beyond
love: God is all in all *(tout en tous)*'.[3] The one looks backwards towards
the days before man reached the stage of self-consciousness, the other
looks forwards and upwards towards a single point of convergence to which
all evolution seems (to Teilhard) to be tending. The one dissolves into the
All, the cosmic consciousness of Bucke, the other concentrates itself on to
the One, the *yoga*, that is, the 'integration' preached by the Bhagavad-Gītā.
And just as in the Gītā it is never possible to draw a hard and fast line
between the microcosm and the macrocosm, so does Teilhard de Chardin
regard personal integration as but a prelude to the integration of all things
into what he calls Omega and what I call God. And just as the body is an
organism in which each member has its allotted place in the service of the
whole, so has each individual his allotted place in the structure of human
society. This is one of the basic tenets of Marxian Communism as it was
of imperial Confucianism, the religion of solidarity *par excellence* to which
we shall be turning in next year's lectures.

---

[1] *Upadeśa.* 4, 8; Schrader, vol. i, p. 184.   [2] *Suttanipāta* 35 ff.
[3] Pierre Teilhard de Chardin, *L'Activation de l'énergie*, Paris, Seuil, 1963, pp. 231-2.

Meanwhile, before we bid farewell to the 'solitary' mysticisms of India, let us turn for the last time to the Bhagavad-Gītā. Its message is roughly this: integrate yourself around the immortal core that is within you and then you will be free, seeing yourself in all things and all things in yourself. Having seen this, you will see all things in God and God as the ground of all things; and seeing him thus, you will not be lost to him, nor will he be lost to you. And just as your whole personality—body, mind, and soul— is centred on that timeless 'fraction' of God which is you as you are in eternity, so are all 'I's' and 'thous' and 'hes' and 'shes' centred on the one centre of centres which is God. The first preoccupation of the Gītā and indeed of all Indian religion is the liberation of this eternal particle in man from the shackles of temporal existence; but the Gītā is further concerned with the harmony of these individual 'particles of God', the 'divine sparks' of Meister Eckhart, within the transcendent God himself. Like all Eastern religions the Gītā seeks out the concord behind the discord, the One beyond the many. In the end it sees a concord in which discord is dis- solved, in which all the opposites blend and meet. This it sees primarily in the human individual. In China the same harmony was seen rather in the ordered hierarchy of Confucian society. The Indians are 'solitary', the Chinese 'solidary'. In the West the Catholic Church is or should be both— making room both for the 'togetherness' of our mechanized age and for the solitude in which all of us would do well from time to time to renew our spiritual life if we have one, and in which, in any case, we must all of us die. This is a tension and at the same time a reconciliation, a 'discordant concord' and a 'concordant discord', in which we may hope, with Marx and Engels, that 'we shall have an association'—a concord—'in which the free development of each'—a discord—'is the condition of the free develop- ment of all'[1]—a discordant concord and a concordant discord. Perhaps, as Teilhard de Chardin said,[2] the age of Religion as opposed to the age of religions is only just beginning, and that religion may yet, in Marx's beautiful words, become 'the heart of a heartless world' and 'the spirit of a spiritless situation'.[3] In next year's lectures we shall be considering how, in the light of the religious history of the world, this might conceivably come about.

---

[1] *The Communist Manifesto*, ii. end. [2] *L'Activation de l'énergie*, p. 247.
[3] K. Marx, *Contribution to the Critique of Hegel's Philosophy of Right*, quoted in K. Marx and F. Engels, *On Religion*, Moscow, 1957, p. 42.

XI

THE WAY OF HEAVEN AND EARTH

The Way that can be told is not an Unvarying Way;
The names that can be named are not unvarying names.
It was from the Nameless that Heaven and Earth sprang;
The named is but the mother that rears the ten thousand creatures, each
after its kind.[1]

THESE are the opening words of the great Taoist classic, the *Tao Tê
Ching*, 'The Way and its Power'.

Taoism is one of what used to be called 'the three religions of China'.
We also speak of the 'three religions' of the United States, meaning
Protestantism, Catholicism, and Judaism. The parallel is misleading, for
in this case we are speaking of three separate religious organizations which
necessarily exclude one another. This is not true of the 'three religions' of
China, for in China there has always been a syncretistic tendency, a
willingness to absorb and a drive to harmonize different 'ways' of life,
different ways of assessing our human condition of living and dying.
These ways are not thought to exclude each other: rather they complement each other. Of these three 'ways' two are native to China—Confucianism and Taoism—while the third is an intruder from India,
Buddhism, with which we became reasonably familiar in last year's
series of Gifford Lectures. Buddhism was indeed an intruder, but so
skilful did it prove itself to be in adapting itself to alien ways that, apart
from one major persecution in 845/6, it succeeded in striking deep roots
in China from where it was transplanted to Korea and Japan. Buddhism
came to China in its Mahāyāna form and in Taoism it found a religion
strikingly similar to itself. Each interacted on the other, but it would
seem that Taoism penetrated Buddhism rather more deeply than Buddhism influenced Taoism. This is particularly true of the Ch'an sect
which has been popularized in the West under its Japanese name, Zen.

Buddhism, like all Indian religion, is primarily concerned with the
individual rather than with the community; and this broad generalization
is not invalidated by the so-called 'Three Refuges' to which all Buddhists
subscribe: 'I take refuge in the Buddha, I take refuge in the *dharma*, I

[1] *Tao Tê Ching*, 1; E.T., Arthur Waley, *The Way and its Power*, London, Allen &
Unwin, 1934 and reprints, p. 141.

take refuge in the *sangha*.' In this context *dharma* means the doctrine laid down by the Buddha, and the *sangha* means the 'community' he founded; but it is a community only in the sense that we speak of a monastic community, and it is in fact just that. It is not a 'church' of which the laity form the mass and the clergy the élite, much less is it the community of all the faithful bound together by simple beliefs and ritual practices as is Islam. Rather is it the 'community' of celibate monks and nuns who have given up the world and have committed themselves to the search for Nirvāna under rigorous monastic discipline. It is the community of the 'elect', and the elect have never been more than a tiny minority of those who call themselves Buddhists.

In China things were very different; for the religion of China *par excellence* is Confucianism, not Taoism, the religion of an ordered *society*, harmoniously constructed and owing allegiance to the Emperor, the Son of Heaven, and God's representative on earth. It is a religion that looks back to a golden age when all things were supposed to have been held in a balance of perfect harmony, man himself co-operating effortlessly and spontaneously with the powers of Heaven and Earth, with which he formed a coequal triad. Taoism looks back even beyond this to a time when what it calls the Great Unity was still unbroken, and man lived in perfect harmony with birds and beasts, perfectly content because he had not yet learnt to differentiate. He had not learnt to differentiate between life and death, right and wrong, pleasure and pain, profit and loss: he was still perfect and whole because his life was merged in the uninterrupted flow of all natural things. This was man as he was before the Fall, and Taoism is very conscious that there *was* a Fall, and it conceives of it very much in the terms of the Book of Genesis. Man falls by acquiring *knowledge*; and knowledge means the ability to make distinctions—to divide, to separate, and to classify. For the Confucians this means that man learns to use and to improve on Nature: for the Taoists it is rather a profanation of Nature, a hacking away at the 'Uncarved Block' of reality, a desecration of the holy.

Before the Fall man had the innocence of a child or an animal: he had consciousness, but not *self*-consciousness: he had not learnt to say 'I am', and so he had not learnt to fear death, for he was at one with the All which never dies. Hence for the Taoists the acquisition of knowledge was a disaster—a Fall in very truth.

In all other mystical traditions the word 'knowledge' is used to mean an intuitive apperception of transcendent reality. The exceptions are the anonymous author of the 'Cloud of *Unknowing*', and Nicolas of Cusa, who prefers to speak *de docta ignorantia*, of 'learned *ignorance*'. All mystical traditions again agree that the discursive intellect is powerless to grasp, let alone to describe, the timeless reality experienced in mystical rapture, yet reason is allowed its due place in the cosmic order. The Taoists will have none of this: 'knowledge', reason, and the arts of civilization are a decadence, a falling away from the pristine simplicity of the Tao, a meddling with and an outrage against the effortless yet active Quiet which is the still source of all mutability and change. If Taoism has a message, it is this: stop meddling, let things be, relax (as the Americans would say), and then all things will miraculously but automatically be added to you. 'Do not worry about tomorrow: tomorrow will take care of itself.'[1]

In Confucianism the key virtues are *jên*, the quality that distinguishes man as man, his human-ness and therefore his humane-ness, and *yi*, 'rightness, righteousness, morality'. For the Taoists these are human inventions, human interferences in the Tao—in what we might call the divine order—and these, so far from being an advance and however well intentioned, are the acknowledgement of separateness and the beginning of evil: they are the fruit of the tree of the knowledge of good and evil:

> Banish wisdom, discard knowledge,
> And the people will be benefited a hundredfold.
> Banish human kindness (*jên*), discard morality,
> And the people will be dutiful and compassionate.
> Banish skill, discard profit,
> And thieves and robbers will disappear.
> If when these three things are done they find life too plain and unadorned,
> Then let them have accessories;
> Give them Simplicity to look at, the Uncarved Block to hold,
> Give them selflessness and fewness of desires.[2]

For:

> It was [only] when the Great Way (*Tao*) declined
> That human kindness and morality arose;
> It was [only] when intelligence and knowledge appeared
> That the Great Artifice began.
> It was only when the six near ones[3] were no longer at peace
> That there was talk of 'dutiful sons';
> Nor till fatherland was dark with strife
> Did we hear of 'loyal slaves'[4].[5]

---

[1] Matthew 6: 34. [2] *Tao Tê Ching*, 19.
[3] i.e. father and son, elder brother and younger brother, husband and wife.
[4] i.e. Ministers. [5] *Tao Tê Ching*, 18.

No religion is so uncompromisingly anti-intellectual as is Taoism. The Tao is incomprehensible to the intellect: it is the 'Way' of Heaven rather than the Word, the Logos, of God; and yet Christian missionaries could find no better translation for this Logos, which in the beginning was with God and which was God, than Tao, the 'Way'. In this they were perfectly right, for the Tao is the Way in which all things behave according to their own natures because it is the source from which their being proceeds, the path they instinctively follow, the element which effortlessly supports them. If the word Logos strikes too intellectual a note, then it is the Way and the Truth and the Life,[1] for it is beyond rationality and reason itself. Hence Taoism is not only un-theological, it is anti-theological: it is the religion of 'Behold the lilies of the field', not of the Epistle to the Romans; the religion of 'unless you change and become like little children you will never enter the kingdom of heaven',[2] not of 'Now that I am a man, all childish ways are put behind me':[3] it is the religion of ignorance, not of learning, for it 'does not study nor does it labour to cram itself with useless knowledge (*vanité*) unable to resist [idle] curiosity'.[4] It is the Way of the 'men of old' who had not yet learnt to be clever:

> In the days of old those who practised Tao with success did not, by means of
>   it, enlighten the people, but on the contrary sought to make them ignorant.
> The more knowledge people have, the harder they are to rule.
> Those who seek to rule by giving knowledge
> Are like bandits preying on the land.
> Those who rule without giving knowledge
> Bring a stock of good fortune to the land.
> To have understood the difference between these two things is to have a test
>   and standard.
> To be always able to apply this test and standard
> Is called the mysterious 'power',
> The mysterious 'power', so deep-penetrating,
> So far-reaching,
> That can follow things *back*—
> All the way back to the Great Concordance.[5]

Always in Taoism the way to the Tao, the 'Great Way', the 'Great Concordance', the 'state of the Uncarved Block',[6] the way to 'harmony' and the 'always so',[7] to the 'Mother of all things'[8] 'which was the beginning of all things under heaven',[9] is a way *back*—a return to the womb, if you

[1] John 14: 6.   [2] Matthew 18: 3.   [3] 1 Corinthians 13: 11.
[4] François de Sales, *Traité de l'amour de Dieu*, 6. 2; cf. E.T., p. 222.
[5] *Tao Tê Ching*, 65.   [6] Ibid. 57; cf. 19, 28, 32.   [7] Ibid. 16, 51, 52, 55.
[8] Ibid. 25, 52, 59.   [9] Ibid. 52.

like. In biblical terms it is a return to the original innocence of the Garden of Eden before man reached the age of reason and had tasted of the tree of the knowledge of good and evil.

In one sense the God of the Book of Genesis is the Tao personified—the *vis inertiae* that would hold up the evolutionary process by which man must emerge into full *self*-consciousness and face the grim fact that 'the original substance of all things' has indeed been 'shattered and divided'.[1] Both for the Taoists and for the Book of Genesis the acquisition of knowledge is a *fall*: it is not the first rung on the ladder of spiritual ascent. The Uncarved Block of Taoism is like the fourth state of consciousness of the *Māndūkya* Upanishad[2] which is beyond even the bliss of dreamless sleep—the state of ultimate and undifferentiated unity, to lose which is to lose that security in irresponsibility which is the privilege of the animal world and in which there is knowledge of neither good nor evil, neither right nor wrong, neither life nor death. This is the fall from the heaven of spontaneity into the hell of responsibility.

As Pascal saw, man is midway between an animal and an angel, and this constitutes both his misery and his grandeur. But, alas, we now know that there never was an age of angelic innocence; there was only the innocence of the beasts and of very little children who are still near to the beasts. Instinctively the Taoists sensed this and desperately tried to undo what could never be undone—the emergence of man from group-consciousness into self-consciousness, individual consciousness, which brings with it a sense of separation and responsibility and a now unavoidable confrontation with the brute fact of individual physical death. The Taoist ideal was to restore the idyllic state when men were still brutes, but, with men as they had come to be with their ideas of good government and civilization, they realized that this would have to remain an ideal perhaps for ever. For them the best government was no government, letting things be as they wish to be and are, a no-government in which everything falls into its proper place under the kindly but creative inactivity of the Tao. It had been said:

> 'Kingdoms can only be governed if rules are kept;
> Battles can only be won if rules are broken.'[3]

This is the debased counsel of the worldly-wise. The true sage knows better, for:

> The adherence of all under heaven can only be won by letting-alone.
> How do I know that this is so?

---

[1] *Chuang Tzŭ* 11: 4 (James Legge's translation, pp. 297–8, see below, p. 224, n. 2).
[2] Above, p. 95.   [3] *Tao Tê Ching*, 57.

By this.
The more prohibitions there are, the more ritual avoidances,
The poorer the people will be.
The more 'sharp weapons' there are,
The more benighted will the whole land grow.
The more cunning craftsmen there are,
The more pernicious contrivances will be invented.
The more laws are promulgated,
The more thieves and bandits there will be.
Therefore a sage has said:
So long as I 'do nothing' the people will of themselves be transformed.
So long as I love quietude, the people will of themselves go straight.
So long as I act only by inactivity the people will of themselves become prosperous.
So long as I have no wants the people will of themselves return to the 'state of the Uncarved Block.'[1]

Heaven and Earth do nothing, and it is by their doing nothing that everything prospers and grows. It is because man, with his ridiculous 'human kindness' and 'morality' so dear to the Confucians, has broken away from the Tao, has opted out of the natural law, that all evils have arisen. The true sage will, then, imitate the Tao in its serene inactivity by effacing himself in silent protest against the busy morality and moralism of organized society, and by his example, maybe, all things will right themselves. Like the Tao itself and the Tao of the Christians, the sage is 'gentle and humble in heart'[2] and his humility makes him the laughing-stock of the clever. He is humble even as water is humble, seeking always the lowest place, for 'the highest good is like that of water, [and] the goodness of water is that it benefits the ten thousand creatures; yet itself does not scramble, but is content with the places that all men disdain. It is this that makes water so near to the Way'.[3] And so too in quite another context the Persian poet, Rūmī, sings:

The way (Tao!) of love is all lowliness and intoxication:
For the torrent makes for the lowlands, how should it flow uphill![4]

The power of water lies in its very weakness and inconspicuousness. This too must be the way of the sage: he must be humble before he can be exalted:

How did the great rivers and seas get their kingship over the hundred lesser streams?

[1] Ibid.   [2] Matthew 11: 29.   [3] Tao Tê Ching, 8.
[4] Dīvāni Shamsi Tabrīz, ed. R. H. Nicholson, Cambridge, 1898 (reprint 1952), pp. 4–5.

Through the merit of being lower than they; that was how they got their
    kingship.
Therefore the Sage
In order to be above the people
Must speak as though he were lower than the people.
In order to guide them
He must put himself behind them.
Only thus can the Sage be on top and the people not be crushed by his weight.
Only thus can he guide, and the people not be led into harm.[1]

Only thus will they 'find rest for their souls, for the yoke of [the Christian
as well as the Taoist Tao] is easy and its burden light'.[2]

The parallelisms with Christianity are striking; and if Christianity is the
religion of humility, then Taoism has much to teach us. It is a wholesome
antidote to the poison of so-called existentialist 'anxiety', for it speaks of
spontaneity and of letting things be. And yet its ideal is in a past that never
was, and the utopia it would build it can never build because man, though
he may and must recapture the spirit of childhood, can never be a child
again. It is no good telling him that 'there is a bourn where there is neither
right nor wrong, in a realm where every straight is doubled by a crooked,
and every good by an ill', and that 'mankind has gone long enough astray',[3]
for the way back to Paradise Lost is guarded by an angel with a flaming
sword who bars the way back to the Garden of Eden which was after all
his *Kindergarten*.

The *Tao Tê Ching* is the gospel of spontaneity: it is the most elusive of
all the religious classics of the East, and it repeatedly warns us against
trying to define what cannot and should not be defined. It is a protest
against the instinct to order things aright which from the very beginning
seems to have been endemic with the Chinese, a protest against system-
atization and conventional morality which it sees as an infraction of
natural law.

It is mystical in the sense that it seeks a direct contact with the divine—
with the Tao which is the ultimate principle of all things—and like all
mystical traditions it sees mystical experience as the transcending of all
the opposites, including good and evil. As we saw last year this is typical
of the Upanishads and even of the Bhagavad-Gītā; it is not wholly absent
from the *Tao Tê Ching*, but the emphasis is very different. It does not
condone evil: rather it seeks to understand what it is that makes people do
wrong, and this cannot be achieved by moral indignation or by judging

[1] *Tao Tê Ching*, 66.   [2] Matthew 11: 30.
[3] *Tao Tê Ching*. 58.

from outside but only by putting yourself in the place of the evil-doer. You must accept others on their own terms, not on your own:

> The Sage has no heart of his own;
> He uses the heart of the people as his heart.
> Of the good man I approve,
> And of the bad I also approve,
> And thus he gets goodness.
> The truthful man I believe, but the liar I also believe,
> And thus he gets truthfulness.
> The Sage, in his dealings with the world, seems like one dazed with fright;
> For the world's sake he dulls his wits.
> The Hundred Families all the time strain their eyes and ears,
> The Sage all the time sees and hears no more than an infant sees and hears.[1]

Just as the Cross was 'foolishness to the Greeks',[2] so was the Taoist wisdom 'foolishness' to the Confucians—and for the same reason. Deliberate self-humiliation is to deny man's human nature at its very centre; it is a denial of his natural self-assertiveness, of that very *amour-propre* which La Rochefoucauld and Rousseau saw as the root-sin of mankind, indeed of what Christians all too often mistake for the 'infinite dignity of the human person'—that kind of 'dignity' of which Christ 'emptied himself to assume the condition of a slave and became as men are'[3] and which is apparently natural to the Tao. *This* is the foolishness that is an abomination to the scribes, whether Christian or Confucian. It is, then, natural that—

Every one under heaven says that our Way is greatly like folly. But it is just because it is great, that it seems like folly. As for things that do not seem like folly—well, there can be no question about *their* smallness.[4]

So true is it that 'he who lives without folly is not as wise as he thinks'.[5] And so, having condemned the wisdom of the world, Lao Tzŭ, the putative author of the *Tao Tê Ching*, goes on to offer his 'three treasures' which are of more value than all the 'wisdom' of men:

Here are my three treasures. Guard and keep them! The first is pity; the second, frugality; the third, refusal to be 'foremost of all things under heaven'.

> For only he that pities is truly able to be brave;
> Only he that is frugal is truly able to be profuse.
> Only he that refuses to be foremost of all things
> Is truly able to become chief of all Ministers.[6]

---

[1] Ibid. 49.   [2] 1 Corinthians 1: 23.   [3] Philippians 2: 7.   [4] *Tao Tê Ching*, 67.
[5] La Rochefoucauld, ed. Pléiade, p. 430 (no. 209).   [6] *Tao Tê Ching*, 67.

These 'treasures' sound like counsels of perfection, for the times are evil and men are greedy and 'would gain what is under heaven by tampering with it'.[1] They do not succeed because it is always dangerous to tamper with what is of itself whole and therefore holy:

> For that which is under heaven is like a holy vessel, dangerous to tamper with.
> Those that tamper with it, harm it.
> Those that grab at it, lose it.[2]

And because they do this, all their virtues crumble away to dust: they are not using the 'three treasures' rightly:

> At present your bravery is not based on pity, nor your profusion on frugality, nor your eminence on self-effacement; and this is death. But pity cannot fight without conquering or guard without saving. Heaven arms with pity those whom it would not see destroyed.[3]

Why should the absence of these self-effacing virtues spell death? Because it is by clinging to life that the fear of death arises and because it is literally true that 'anyone who wants to save his life will lose it',[4] as Jesus says, and in the words of the *Tao Tê Ching*, 'he who aims at life achieves death';[5] in the last analysis life and death are but the positive and negative aspects of the same Tao, which, though apparently 'gentle and humble' and weak, is nevertheless the source from which all life and all strength proceed. Hence the Tao is deserving of all worship though it makes no claims, and it becomes the object of the veneration of all even though they do not know that they are venerating it:

> Tao gave them birth;
> The 'power' of Tao reared them,
> Shaped them according to their kinds,
> Perfected them, giving to each its strength.
> Therefore of the ten thousand things there is not one that does not worship Tao and do homage to its 'power'. No mandate ever went forth that accorded to Tao the right to be worshipped, nor to its 'power' the right to receive homage.
> It was always and of itself so.
> Therefore as Tao bore them and the 'power' of Tao reared them, made them grow, fostered them, harboured them, brewed for them, so you must
> Rear them, but not lay claim to them,
> Control them, but never lean upon them,
> Be chief among them, but not manage them.
> This is called the mysterious power.[6]

---

[1] *Tao Tê Ching*, 29.   [2] Ibid.   [3] Ibid. 67.   [4] Matthew 16: 25.
[5] *Tao Tê Ching*, 50.   [6] Ibid. 51.

The *Tao Tê Ching* is nothing if not elusive because, as we are told in its very first words, 'The Way that can be told is not an Unvarying Way'; and since this is so, then to speak about it is to distort it. In this we are reminded of the Brahman of the Upanishads of which we read:

> That from which [all] words recoil together with the mind,
>   Unable to attain it—
> That is the bliss of Brahman; knowing it,
> A man has naught to fear from anywhere.[1]

But whereas the Upanishads, though imprecise, strive increasingly after a certain precision, the *Tao Tê Ching* makes of imprecision a virtue. What is the point, after all, of giving a name to what is of its very nature unnameable, of attempting to pigeon-hole what is essentially fluid and to define and limit what is essentially infinite and limitless?

The second great Taoist classic, the *Chuang Tzŭ*, is very much longer, and though retaining to the full the typical Taoist flavour of effortless spontaneity and spontaneous creativity, it does occasionally seek to place landmarks in the vast ocean of the Tao and to chart the uncharted Way. It is a later work than the *Tao Tê Ching*, and most of it seems to be the work of one man, Chuang Tzŭ, tentatively dated at 369–286 B.C., who, even in translation, has a quite distinctive flavour of his own—bantering, slyly humorous, and urbane. Attacks on Confucianism are frequent, and Confucius himself is often represented as denying his own philosophy, admitting his errors, and accepting conversion to the true Tao, the true primeval Way of heaven which is not the way of men. The *Chuang Tzŭ* pleads for a return to a state of original innocence in which men will have done with the artificialities of civilized life and the ordered morality which civilization seeks to impose. It is a nostalgia for a vanished age when the Tao had not yet been lost. Already the *Tao Tê Ching* had said:

> After Tao was lost, then came the 'power';
> After the 'power' was lost, then came human kindness.
> After human kindness was lost, then came morality,
> After morality was lost, then came ritual.
> Now ritual is the mere husk of loyalty and promise-keeping
> And is indeed the first step towards brawling.[2]

This is one of the main themes of the *Chuang Tzŭ* too; and it can indeed be regarded as a more philosophical, more urbane, and more 'modern' version of the first chapters of Genesis from which, however, the Lord God has been excluded. In Genesis the Lord God represents the old order,

---

[1] *Taittiriya* Upanishad 2: 9.   [2] *Tao Tê Ching*, 38.

the serpent, 'the most subtle of all the wild beasts', the spirit of inquiry and progress, the Confucian tempter. How unreasonable is God's command to our first parents not to eat of the tree of the knowledge of good and evil, the tree of intellectual enlightenment, he says, and how vindictive is his threat to condemn them to death if they do not obey! ' "No," he says to the woman, "You will not die! God knows in fact that on the day you eat it your eyes will be opened and you will be like gods, knowing good and evil." The woman saw that the tree was good to eat and pleasing to the eye, and that it was desirable for the knowledge that it could give. So she took some of its fruit and ate it. She gave some also to her husband who was with her, and he ate it. Then the eyes of both of them were opened and they realized that they were naked.'[1]

What, then, according to Genesis was this original sin? Ostensibly disobedience, but more basically the desire to know—the desire to rise above the level of the beasts and thence to be 'like gods, knowing good and evil'. This is not a 'Fall' at all from the human, humane, humanistic, Confucian point of view, but a break-through from group-consciousness into self-consciousness, the winning of that ability to distinguish and compare which is what distinguishes man from the beasts. This is man's refusal to form one piece for ever with the 'Uncarved Block', even though this participation means a blissful unawareness of physical death because the Block itself can never die. This is how the Confucians saw it. They accepted the challenge and tried to adapt themselves to the new conditions. For the Taoists, however, it was a disaster—a 'fall' from unity into multiplicity, from concord into discord, from spontaneity into artifice: it was the root calamity of mankind. For them it was 'the knowledge of the ancients [that] was perfect. . . . They were not yet aware that there were things. This is the most perfect knowledge; nothing can be added. Then, some were aware that there were things, but not yet aware that there were distinctions among them. Then, some were aware that there were distinctions, but not yet aware that there was right and wrong among them. When right and wrong became manifest, the Tao thereby declined. With the decline of the Tao came the growth of (partial) love.'[2]

[1] Genesis 3: 4–7.
[2] The translation is from the admirable Columbia University production *Sources of Chinese Tradition*, p. 72, edited by Wm. Theodore de Bary, Wing-tsit Chan, and Burton Watson, Columbia University Press, 1960 and reprints. This, of course, only contains selections from the *Chuang Tzŭ* as does Burton Watson's *Chuang Tzŭ, Basic Writings*, Columbia University Press, 1964. In addition there are massive selections in Wing-tsit Chan's compendious *Source Book in Chinese Philosophy*, Princeton University Press, 1963. The present passage (*Chuang Tzŭ* (2: 5)) appears on pp. 36–7 in Burton Watson, p. 185 in Wing-tsit Chan. In addition there are the two 'classic' translations of the whole work by

The Tao 'declines' or 'is injured' by the 'growth of (partial) love' because, whatever it may be, it is impartial: it 'causes its sun to rise on bad men as well as good, and its rain to fall on honest and dishonest men alike'.[1] And as the Tao is, so too must you be:

> Be benign and impartial like the god of the soil at the sacrifice—he grants no private blessing. Be broad and expansive like the endlessness of the four directions—they have nothing which bounds or hedges them. Embrace the ten thousand things universally—how could there be one you should give special support to? This is called being without bent. When the ten thousand things are unified and equal, then which is short and which is long?[2]

The Tao is 'gentle and humble',[3] loving all things with an impartial love and showing favour to none: it is the 'sainte indifférence' of St. François de Sales on a cosmic scale. In the ancient days before man became self-conscious, or, to translate this typical Taoist idea into another idiom, before Adam fell, the Way of Heaven, the Great Tao, and the ways of man did not diverge: God and man walked together in the Garden, and there was a great peace. There was no conflict between the human and the heavenly[4] or, as another translation has it, between the artificial and the natural,[5] and man had not yet done violence to the Tao. But with the 'Fall', the ways of man became separated from the Way of Heaven, the artificial tampered with the natural, discord broke into the great Concord. The 'True Man' who was at one with Heaven and the Tao had ceased to exist, for he had learnt to discriminate between the 'heavenly' and the

---

James Legge in *Sacred Books of the East*, vols. xxix and xl, 1891 and reprints, and Herbert A. Giles, London, George Allen & Unwin, revised ed. 1926 and reprint. The present passage is to be found on pp. 185–6 in vol. xxix of Legge and on p. 40 in Giles. There is considerable discrepancy between the available translations. On the advice of Sinologists and relying to some extent on my own judgement, I usually quote either from Burton Watson or from the *Sources of Chinese Tradition*, both because they are more recent and because they read better and seem to be more successful in transmitting the flavour of the original. The student of comparative religion who has no Chinese has no alternative except to compare the available translations and to select the one that seems to be nearest to what the spirit of the original seems to be. In this passage there are no greater variations in the translations than one would expect in a book of this kind except in the last sentence, 'With the decline of the Tao came the growth of love'. Here Burton Watson has 'because the Way was injured, love became complete', which is even more confusing. Wing-tsit Chan, however, has 'Because Tao was reduced, individual bias was formed', which gives a very different impression. Similarly Legge has 'the formation of (partial) preferences' and Giles again 'individual bias'. By comparing the five translations one is perhaps justified in settling for 'partial love'.

[1] Matthew 5: 45.
[2] *Chuang Tzŭ* 17: 6, Burton Watson's translation, p. 103.
[3] Matthew 11: 29.
[4] *Chuang Tzŭ* 17: 7 Burton Watson, p. 104; cf. Legge, p. 383.
[5] *Sources of Chinese Tradition*, p. 79; cf. Giles, p. 166.

'human', the 'natural' and the 'artificial'. He had learnt to discriminate between life and death. But:

The True Man of ancient times knew nothing of loving life, knew nothing of hating death. He emerged without delight; he went back in without a fuss. He came briskly, he went briskly, and that was all. He didn't forget where he began; he didn't try to find out where he would end. He received something and took pleasure in it, he forgot about it and handed it back again. This is what I call not using the mind to repel the Way, not using man to help out Heaven. This is what I call the True Man. . . .[1] Therefore his liking and his not liking was one. His being one was one and his not being one was one. In being one, he was acting as a companion of Heaven. In not being one, he was acting as a companion of man. When man and Heaven do not defeat each other, then you have the True Man.[2]

Life and death are fated—constant as the succession of dark and dawn, a matter of Heaven. There are some things which a man can do nothing about— all are a matter of the nature of creatures. If a man is willing to regard Heaven as a father and to love it, then how much more should he be willing to do for that which is even greater! If he is willing to regard the ruler as superior to himself and die for him, then how much more should he be willing to do for the Truth.[3]

There is something tantalizingly Christian about the Taoist classics, one is tempted to exclaim with Tertullian, *O testimonium animae naturaliter christianae*. But let us temper our excessive zeal, for *t'ien*, which Burton Watson literally and correctly translates as 'Heaven', Wing-tsit Chan translates as 'Nature'—the God of Spinoza, then, rather than the God of the Christians. And yet 'Heaven' is surely the better translation, for though Tao and *t'ien* are frequently identified, in this passage Tao is clearly 'that which is even greater' than our 'father', Heaven, whom we are exhorted to love. For if Heaven is our father, then Earth is our mother: 'Heaven and earth are the father and mother of the ten thousand things.'[4] Though Taoism avoids precision like the plague, it might approximate to the truth to say that Heaven represents the regularity of natural law, earth the flux of life and death here as it affects you and me. For it is earth,

the Great Clod [that] burdens me with form, labours me with life, eases me in old age, and rests me in death. So if I think well of my life, for the same reason I must think well of my death.[5]

---

[1] *Chuang Tzŭ* 6: 2; Burton Watson, p. 74.

[2] For the last clause Watson has: 'then he may be said to have the true man'. For the whole sentence Wing-tsit Chan has: 'Neither Nature nor man should overcome the other. This is what is meant by a pure man.'

[3] *Chuang Tzŭ* 6: 5; Watson, p. 76; Chan, p. 193.

[4] Ibid. 19: 1; Watson, p. 119.

[5] Ibid. 6: 6; Watson, p. 76.

It is natural for man in his present state to rejoice in life and shrink from death, but this is because he has fallen out of the stream of the Tao which is infinite and comprises all things. And so the sage must reintegrate himself into the Tao again. Once there 'he wanders in the realm where things cannot get away from him, and all are preserved'. And so he not only delights in life, 'he delights in early death; he delights in old age; he delights in the beginning; he delights in the end'.[1] He is invulnerable because, as the Bhagavad-Gītā would say, he 'treads the highest Way'— the highest Tao—which is itself the parent of man's first parents, Heaven and earth—the Way which is 'its own source' and 'its own root', which 'was there before Heaven and earth existed, firm from ancient times. . . . It exists beyond the highest point, and yet you cannot call it lofty; it exists beneath the limit of the six directions, and yet you cannot call it deep. It was born before Heaven and earth, and yet you cannot say it has been there for long; it is earlier than the earliest time, and yet you cannot call it old.'[2]

Once he has realized this infinite Tao within himself, the sage can have no care, for nothing can hurt him, nothing affect him: he has become like the 'True Man of old', and the True Man of old

did not rebel against want, did not grow proud in plenty, and did not plan his affairs. Being like this, he could commit an error and not regret it, could meet with success and not make a show. Being like this, he could climb the high places and not be frightened, could enter the water and not get wet, could enter the fire and not get burned. His knowledge was able to climb all the way up to the Way like this.[3]

This 'knowledge' is not, of course, the knowledge condemned by the *Tao Tê Ching*;[4] it is the intuitive knowledge of the Tao by which a man becomes the Tao, just as in the Gītā by knowing Brahman one goes to Brahman[5] and becomes Brahman.[6] In this state too—

Weapons do not cut him nor does fire burn him, the waters do not wet him nor does the wind dry him. Uncuttable, unburnable, unwettable, undryable is he—eternal, roving everywhere, firm-set, unmoved, primeval. Unmanifest, unthinkable, immutable is he called: then realize him thus and do not worry.[7]

A man like this is in harmony with all things. But whereas the Hindus and Buddhists tend to stress such a man's transcendence of all that comes to be and passes away, the *Chuang Tzŭ* stresses his unity with all life, both with heaven and the beasts and with all living and growing things; and

---

[1] Ibid.   [2] Ibid. 6: 7; Watson, p. 77.   [3] Ibid. 6: 2; Watson, p. 73.
[4] Above, pp. 216–17.   [5] Gītā 8: 24.   [6] Ibid. 6: 27.
[7] Bhagavad-Gītā 2: 23–5.

yet he does not deny his self-consciousness but lets it take its place naturally in the whole. This is how things were in the 'age of perfect virtue' before man fell:

[Then] the people had their regular and constant nature: they wove and made themselves clothes; they tilled the ground and got food. *This was their common faculty. They were all one in this, and did not form themselves into separate classes*; so were they constituted and left to their natural tendencies. Therefore in the age of perfect virtue men walked along with slow and grave step, and with their looks steadily directed forwards. At that time, on the hills there were no foot-paths, nor excavated passages; on the lakes there were no boats nor dams; *all creatures lived in companies*; and the places of their settlement were made close to one another. Birds and beasts multiplied to flocks and herds; the grass and trees grew luxuriant and long. In this condition the birds and beasts might be led about without feeling the constraint; the nest of the magpie might be climbed to, and peeped into. Yes, in the age of perfect virtue, men lived in common with birds and beasts, and were on terms of equality with all creatures, *as forming one family*;—how could they know among themselves the distinctions of superior men and small men? *Equally without knowledge*, they did not leave (the path of) their natural virtue; *equally free from desires*, they were in the state of pure simplicity. In that state of pure simplicity, the nature of the people was what it ought to be. But when the sagely men appeared, limping and wheeling about in (the exercise of) human kindness, pressing along and standing on tiptoe in the exercise of morality,[1] then men universally began to be perplexed. (Those sages also) went to excess in their performances of music, and in their gesticulations in the practice of ceremonies, *and then men began to be separated from one another*. If the raw materials had not been cut and hacked, who could have made a sacrificial vase from them? If the natural jade had not been broken and injured, who could have made the handles for the libation-cups from it? If the attributes of the Tao had not been disallowed, how should they have preferred human kindness and morality? If the instincts of nature had not been departed from, how should ceremonies and music have come into use? . . . The cutting and hacking of the raw materials to form vessels was the crime of the skilful workman; the injury done to the characteristics of the Tao in order to exercise human kindness and morality was the error of the sagely men.[2]

In this passage Chuang Tzǔ tells us a little more about the Fall of man, and it seems to me very relevant to this central Christian dogma. In the very nature of things man had to emerge from a state of group-conscious-ness into individual self-consciousness and responsibility: he was in no position to fight against the imperious 'immanent will' of the evolutionary process. It was right and proper that he should weave himself clothes and

---

[1] 'morality' (*yi*); Legge: 'righteousness'; Giles: 'duty to one's neighbour'. See below, p. 240 ff.

[2] *Chuang Tzǔ* 9: 2 (Legge, pp. 277–9; Giles, pp. 97–8).

till the ground for food and thereby cease to plague the birds and beasts. His 'sin' was that once he had learnt to support himself without having to hunt his brothers, the animals, for food, he should seek a superfluity for himself and those nearest to him, that he should not rest content with what little knowledge he *needed* and with the few desires which Nature itself bade him satisfy, but that he should seek to multiply his knowledge and, once he had done that, to use his knowledge to multiply his desires. This surely was his original sin and it is the sin that is ubiquitously and acutely present with us today.

For the Taoist the two basic Confucian virtues, human kindness and morality or righteousness, are innate to man: they are natural to him. The original sin (which was also the sin of the Confucians) was to place them on a pinnacle, to objectivize them as something separate both from man and the Tao. Once these natural attributes of man became a duty, his link with the Tao was broken and 'men began to be separated from one another'. So was *amour-propre* born, the objectivization and deification of what Rousseau called *amour de soi*, the individual personality.

Amour-propre is the imposition of a false personality on to a man's natural self: it is the inevitable result of the differentiation of man from man which is one of the marks of a nascent civilization. Taoism is the declared enemy of civilization and all that it implies—the loss of spontaneity and the sense of wonder, the cutting off of the individual consciousness from the life-stream of the Tao, the invention of political and social institutions, the substitution of morality and duty for the spontaneous outflow of an innate goodness derived from heaven, the complication of life by the pursuit of knowledge, the regimentation of society, and the substitution of art and artefacts for Nature and the 'characteristics of the Tao'.

Philosophy, the idol of yesterday, and technology, the idol of today, are abominations, and despicable abominations at that. It is legitimate for men to 'have accessories', but these must be few; and so does the Taoist gardener condemn the innovations of his day:

He put on an angry look, laughed, and said, 'I have heard from my teacher that, where there are ingenious contrivances, there are sure to be subtle doings; and that, where there are subtle doings, there is sure to be a scheming mind. But, when there is a scheming mind in the breast, its pure simplicity is impaired. When this pure simplicity is impaired, the spirit becomes unsettled, and the unsettled spirit is not the proper residence of the Tao. It is not that I do not know (the contrivance which you mention), but I should be ashamed to use it.[1]

[1] *Chuang Tzŭ* 12: 11 (Legge, p. 320).

So much for technology. As for philosophy, that is the very fountain-head of confusion and disorder:

[The philosophers'] versatility shown in artful deceptions becoming more and more pernicious, . . . is [indeed] great, but the common people are perplexed by all this sophistry. Hence there is great disorder continually in the world, and the guilt of it is due to that fondness for knowledge (that is, to philosophy). Thus it is that all men know to seek for the knowledge that they have not attained to; but do not know to seek for that which they already have (in themselves); and that they know to condemn what they do not approve (in others), and do not know to condemn what they have allowed in themselves;—it is this which occasions the great confusion and disorder. . . . Great indeed is the disorder produced in the world by the love of knowledge.[1]

'On the day that you eat [of the tree of the knowledge of good and evil], you shall most surely die,' God had told the 'True Men of old'. They did not listen, and so they suffered not only physical death but also a creeping paralysis of all the spontaneity that should well up from life. What was wrong with the Confucian Way or Tao was not that the virtues inculcated by it were wrong: it was that they were practised self-consciously and thereby lost their value. Charity, or disinterested and unaffected human kindness, lost its savour and became organized and depersonalized charity (than which, as we all know, there is nothing colder), and righteousness became self-righteousness. This was because simple consciousness had turned into self-consciousness, *amour de soi* into *amour-propre*:

In the age of perfect virtue men attached no value to wisdom, nor employed men of ability. Superiors were (but) as the higher branches of a tree; and the people were like the deer of the wild. They were upright and correct, without knowing that to be so was righteousness (*yi*, morality); they loved one another, without knowing that to do so was human kindness; they were honest and loyal-hearted, without knowing that it was loyalty; they fulfilled their engagements, without knowing that to do so was good faith; in their simple movements they employed the services of one another, without thinking that they were conferring or receiving any gift. Therefore their actions left no trace, and there was no record of their affairs.[2] This was what is called the state of Perfect Unity. At this time, there was no action on the part of anyone, but a constant manifestation of spontaneity.[3]

After the Taoist 'Fall', the great Tao, the cosmic rhythm of the universe, and the individual Tao, the 'way' of man, became out of joint. The times were against the sages whose function was always seen, both among the Taoists and among the Confucians, as being to restore a pristine unity

[1] *Chuang Tzŭ* 10: 4 (Legge, p. 289).
[2] Ibid. 12: 13 (Legge, p. 325).
[3] Ibid. 16: 2 (Legge, p. 370).

which had somehow been shattered. What, then, could they do? They could only restore the shattered Tao within themselves—there they could find the same unity in diversity and the apparently discordant concord which had once been present in the human race at large. 'The conditions laid on them by the times were very much awry. If the conditions of the times had allowed them to act in the world on a great scale, they would have brought back the state of unity without any trace being perceived (of how they did so). When those conditions shut them up entirely from such action, they struck their roots deeper (in themselves), were perfectly still and waited. It was thus that they preserved (the Way in) their own persons.'[1] It is precisely this 'stillness' of mind that the Buddhists understand by Nirvāna and *citta-vimutti*, the 'freeing of the mind'; and this is all that 'fallen' man can hope to achieve by his own efforts. Once the mind has achieved a 'holy indifference' to all seeming opposites, to birth and death, good and evil, right and wrong, then 'it is still; [and] being still, it is pellucid; being pellucid, it is free from preoccupation, . . . it is in the state of inaction, in which it accomplishes everything'.[2]

Indifference is one of the great themes of the *Chuang Tzŭ*—indifference to life and death, good and evil, right and wrong; but this does not mean that it condones evil. It has none of the brutal frankness of the Hindu scriptures and could never have said, as the Bhagavad-Gītā[3] does:

A man who has reached a state where there is no sense of 'I', whose soul is undefiled—were he to slaughter [all] these worlds—slays nothing. He is not bound.

This is an extremely dangerous doctrine, and André Gide's account in *Les Caves du Vatican* of a totally unmotivated murder committed by one whose mind is 'still, pellucid, and free from preoccupation' is not simply a clever phantasy of a clever man as recent unmotivated crimes in the United States and elsewhere have shown. It may be the act of a man who has 'transcended good and evil', but it is not part of the Taoist Way; for one of the characteristics of the Tao is that, though it is never censorious of others, it never leads the sage who has rediscovered its freely roving spontaneity within himself to do violence either to himself or to others. This is because—

The sage comprehends the connexions between himself and others, and how they all go to constitute him of one body with them, and he does not know how it is so;—he naturally does so. In fulfilling his constitution, as acted on and acting, he (simply) follows the direction of Heaven; and it is in consequence of

[1] Ibid. 16: 3 (Legge, pp. 371–2).
[2] Ibid. 23: 11 (Legge, vol. ii, p. 88).   [3] 18: 17.

this that men style him (a sage). . . . When (the sage) is born with all his excellence, it is other men who see it for him. If they did not tell him, he would not know that he was more excellent than others. And when he knows it, he is as if he did not know it; when he hears it, he is as if he did not hear it. His source of joy in it has no end, and men's admiration of him has no end;—all this takes place naturally. The love of the sage for others receives its name from them. If they did not tell him of it, he would not know that he loved them; and when he knows it, he is as if he knew it not; and when he hears it, he is as if he heard it not. His love of others never has an end, and their rest in him also has no end: all this takes place naturally.[1]

This is the Way of selflessness as it is with the Buddhists, the Way of 'holy indifference' of St. François de Sales. It is because the sage sees himself to be at one with the Tao, and sees thereby the interconnectedness of all things, that he forgets himself, because he has identified himself with Heaven.[2] And so 'he is united with the great community of existences. He belongs to that great community, and has no individual self. Having no individual self, how should he have anything that can be called his? . . . [Such a one] is the friend of heaven and earth.'[3]

The Taoist sage is as free as the air: the Confucian scholar has about as much freedom as a frog in a well, and 'you can't discuss the ocean with a frog in a well—he's limited by the space he lives in'. No more can you 'discuss the Way with a cramped scholar—he's shackled by his doctrines. [But] once you have come out beyond your banks and borders and have seen the great sea, you will realize your own pettiness. From now on it will be possible to talk to you about the Great Principle.'[4]

The Way of the Ocean, the Way of the 'Great Principle', is the Way of Heaven, of Nature, and of God: the ways of men are the ways of 'civilization'—of man trying to improve on the handiwork of God:

Horses and oxen have four feet—this is what I mean by the Heavenly. Putting a halter on the horse's head, piercing the ox's nose—this is what I mean by the human. . . . Do not let what is human wipe out what is Heavenly . . .; do not let [the desire for] gain lead you after fame. Be cautious, guard [the Tao], and do not lose it—this is what I mean by returning to the True.[5]

Stop meddling and let yourself be carried away into the Ocean of the Tao; and even if, in so doing, you may feel that you have become the Ocean itself,[6] this has nothing to do with you. 'I have never for this reason

---

[1] *Chuang Tzŭ* 25: 2 (Legge, vol. ii, pp. 115–16).
[2] Ibid. 12: 9.
[3] Ibid. 11: 6 (Legge, vol. i, p. 305).
[4] Ibid. 17: 1 (Watson, p. 97; Legge, vol. i, p. 375).
[5] Ibid. 17: 7 (Watson, p. 104; Legge, p. 384).
[6] Cf. above, p. 85.

THE WAY OF HEAVEN AND EARTH

prided myself on it,' says the sage. 'I take my place with heaven and earth and receive breath from the *yin* and *yang*.[1] I sit between heaven and earth as a little stone or a little tree sits on a huge mountain. Since I can see my own smallness, what reason would I have to pride myself?'[2]

Man has indeed no reason to pride himself on anything; in himself he is but one of the 'ten thousand things', poised between the infinite and the infinitesimal. 'Compared to the ten thousand things, is he not like one little hair on the body of a horse?'[3] Since man is so insignificant and since all his philosophizing only makes confusion worse confounded, let him accept things as they are. Then 'in his actions he will not harm others, but he makes no show of human kindness or charity. He will not move for the sake of profit, but he does not despise the porter at the gate. He will not wrangle for goods or wealth, but he makes no show of refusing or relinquishing them. . . . The Man of the Way wins no fame, the highest virtue wins no gain, the Great Man has no self.'[4]

The Great Man has no self because he has reintegrated himself into the Tao—he has returned to the 'Great Beginning', to that 'sameness [which] is pure vacancy, and the vacancy is great'.[5] And again we are reminded of the Bhagavad-Gītā where we are told: 'devoid of imperfection and ever the same is Brahman'[6]—and of the philosophy of the Mahāyāna Buddhists for which 'Brahman', unconditioned Existence, is also *śūnyatā*, 'Emptiness, Vacancy, Vacuity, the Void'. If a man can but empty himself of all that is purely 'human' while still in this world, he can free himself from anxiety and disquiet; only so can he 'enjoy himself with the Tao in the land of Great Vacuity'.[7] Only so can he overcome his alienation from the stream of the Tao and become as he was in the beginning:

Let the little children come to me; do not stop them; for it is to such as these that the kingdom of God belongs. I tell you solemnly, anyone who does not welcome the kingdom of God like a little child will never enter it.[8]

The child is near to the kingdom of God because he is near the 'beginning', near to the ineffable simplicity of the Tao. So Chuang Tzŭ asks: 'Can you maintain an entire simplicity? Can you become a little child?' You must do this because, like a child, you must 'walk you know not

---

[1] The basic pair of opposites, female (passive) and male (active).
[2] *Chuang Tzŭ* 17: 1 (Watson, p. 97; Legge, vol. i, p. 376).
[3] Ibid. (Watson, p. 98; Legge, p. 376).
[4] Ibid. 17: 3 (Watson, pp. 99–100; Legge, pp. 378–9).
[5] Ibid. 12: 8 (Legge, pp. 315–16).
[6] Gītā 5: 19.
[7] Chuang Tzŭ 20: 2 (Legge, vol. ii, p. 31).
[8] Mark 10: 14–15; Luke 18: 16–17; cf. Matthew 18: 2–4.

whither; rest where you are not placed, not knowing why; be calmly indifferent to things, and follow their current'.[1]

Becoming like a child involves 'the breaking up of the ice, and the dissolving of the cold'.[2] All the jagged edges of what we are pleased to call personality must be melted away so that the sage will have shed all that is purely 'human' in order that he may enter into the 'Heavenly'; for, as we have seen, what is human is artificial, what is 'natural' is of Heaven, and Heaven is of the Tao. And so the *Chuang Tzŭ* goes on to say:

> He whose mind is thus grandly fixed emits a Heavenly light. In him who emits heavenly light men see the (True) man. When a man has cultivated himself (up to this point), thenceforth he remains constant in himself. When he is thus constant in himself, (what is merely) the human element will leave him, but Heaven will help him. Those whom their human element has left we call the people of Heaven. Those whom Heaven helps we call the Sons of Heaven.[3]

'Son of Heaven' was, of course, the official title of the Chinese emperors, but Taoism pays no attention to rank or title: of all the religions it is the least a respecter of persons. What it teaches is what primitive Buddhism teaches, but, to my mind, it goes a little further than Buddhism, for primitive Buddhism says no more than that you must be utterly done with 'I' and 'mine': you must lose your 'self', but there is no guarantee that you will find it again. Taoism too teaches that self must be quite transcended, but, this done, another 'self', another entity emerges which is at one with the Tao, and it is this, not the old self, that becomes a 'Son of Heaven', an emperor, and an incarnation of the Tao.

Do not, however, think that we have finished with paradox. In Taoism, as in the Upanishads, we never have. The Tao is both one *and* many; and the 'True Man', though he may have vanished in the Void, has yet a real existence of his own. 'He is extinguished'—he has entered Nirvāna, as the Buddhists would say—'and yet he has a real existence. . . . He has a real existence, but it has nothing to do with place, such is his relation to space; he has continuance, but it has nothing to do with beginning or end, such is his relation to time; he has life; he has death; he comes forth; he enters; but we do not see his form;—all this is what is called the door of Heaven, [and] the door of Heaven is Non-Existence.'[4]

This is not logic, and it is not sense: but what Chuang Tzŭ is hinting at is what both the Hindus and the Buddhists endlessly repeat: beyond the phenomenal world there is another world which is eternal in the sense that it knows nothing of space and time, and which can therefore, in our

---

[1] *Chuang Tzŭ* 23: 5 (Legge, vol. ii, pp. 80–1).   [2] Ibid. 23: 6.
[3] Ibid. 23: 7 (Legge, vol. ii, p. 82).   [4] Ibid. 23: 9 (Legge, vol. ii, p. 85).

inadequate terminology, only be described as 'constant', 'still', 'permanent', 'unmoving', and so on. This is admitted in all mystical traditions,
but according to Chuang Tzŭ in this state which is the 'Great Unity' and
the 'Great Mystery', there is diversity as well as unity, and in this realm
the 'True Man' is an 'emperor' just as in the *Śvetāśvatara* Upanishad[1] the
man who knows God enjoys 'mastery supreme'. And just as in the Gītā a
personal God emerges who is yet higher than Brahman, so too in the
Chuang Tzŭ both existence and non-existence are transcended by the
'One Keeper' who is beyond both:

> Of those who acknowledge that existence and non-existence, death and life,
> are all under the One Keeper, we are the friends.[2]

The One Keeper is also Heaven—the Great Unity, the Great Mystery,
the Great Illuminator, the Great Framer, the Great Boundlessness, the
Great Truth, the Great Determiner. Only the sage can know him thus;
and knowing him thus:

> As the Great Unity, he comprehends it; as the Great Mystery, he unfolds it;
> as the Great Illuminator, he contemplates it; as the Great Framer, it is to him
> the Cause of all; as the Great Boundlessness, all is to him his embodiment; as
> the Great Truth, he examines it; as the Great Determiner, he holds it fast.[3]

Heaven and the Tao are one; and as is evident from the texts both are
what we would call God—God immanent rather than God transcendent,
yet also God incarnate in what Chuang Tzŭ calls the 'True Man'. But, a
Christian might well ask, is this God a personal God or merely an impersonal force which animates all Nature? This is an un-Taoist question,
and I am sure that Chuang Tzŭ would have given no answer; or had he
answered he would have done so in paradox. And this is in fact what he
does, for he goes on to say:

> Thus Heaven is to him all; accordance with it is the brightest intelligence.
> Obscurity has in this its pivot; in this is the beginning. Such being the case, the
> explanation of it is as if it were no explanation; the knowledge of it is as if it were
> no knowledge. (At first) he does not know it, but afterwards he comes to know it.
> In his inquiries, he must not set himself any limits, and yet he cannot be without
> a limit. Now ascending, now descending, then slipping from the grasp, (the
> Tao) is yet a reality, unchanged now as in antiquity, and always without defect:
> may it not be called what is capable of the greatest display and expansion?
> Why should we not inquire into it? Why should we be perplexed about it? With

---

[1] 1: 11.   [2] *Chuang Tzŭ* 23: 10 (Legge, vol. ii, p. 86).
[3] Ibid. 24: 14 (Legge, vol. ii, p. 112).

what does not perplex let us explain what perplexes, till we cease to be perplexed. So may we arrive at a great freedom from all perplexity![1]

And so we come back again to where we began:

> The Way that can be told is not an Unvarying Way;
> The names that can be named are not unvarying names.
> It was from the Nameless that Heaven and Earth sprang.[2]

The Way is all concord; in it there is no discord. Discord is the fruit of human meddling. The Way is all meekness and humility, and yet it is the source of all virtue and power. It is quite inactive, and yet it activates everything. This is the model that men should follow, and so they would be foolish to 'worry about their life and what they are to eat, or about their body and how they are to clothe it![3] Rather let them guard and keep the three Taoist treasures—pity, frugality, and a refusal to be 'foremost of all things under heaven'.[4] Above all, accept things as they are, including yourself; for, seen from the vantage-point of the Tao, all things are good and right because each and all of them are in their right place, just where they ought to be. Is the Tao, then, God? How can we answer this except by saying 'Yes' and 'No'—the God of *justesse*, not of *justice*, if you like—of what is right, but not of righteousness: the God of self-denial and abnegation, but not, I think, the God of Grace.

---

[1] *Chuang Tzŭ* (Legge, pp. 112–13). Giles's translation is very different and the reader would do well to compare him with Legge.

[2] Above, p. 214.   [3] Matthew 6: 25.   [4] *Tao Tê Ching*, 67.

XII

THE WAY OF MAN

TAOISM is the Way of Heaven or of Nature. Its God is the God of Spinoza since it makes no distinction between God and the natural processes through which he operates. It is the classic expression of what Lord Gifford meant by 'natural religion'. Its counterpart in the West is Rousseau. It is an essential ingredient in what came to be the official philosophy and cultus of the later Chinese Empire, neo-Confucianism; and it transformed the philosophical aridities of Chinese Mahāyāna Buddhism into the irrational, almost anti-rational, enigmas of Zen. It is not peripheral to Chinese religion as a whole, but at the same time it is not central; for the central figure of Chinese religion is Confucius, and its core is the 'Five Classics' of which he was reputed to be the editor.

As we saw last year Indian religion in all its forms is primarily concerned with the salvation or rather 'liberation' of the individual 'self'. However much it may deny the existence of anything that can properly be called a 'person', it is none the less concerned with individual liberation from the power of matter—with enlightenment—not with the destinies of a concrete human community living out its life here on earth. Its approach is individualistic, not corporate; its concern is with a mode of being quite different from, and indeed incomprehensible to, our world of space and time. With it Taoism has much in common, as we have seen. Confucianism differs from it in all respects.

The primary concern of Confucianism is with *this* world: in its early stages it interests itself but little in the next. It is not interested either in those states of absolute awareness so dear to the Buddhists and Hindus or in what may or may not be the lot of the human spirit after the body's dissolution. 'Till you know about living,' Confucius had said, 'how are you to know about the dead?'[1] Man's concern is not with how to escape from this world but with how to live *in* it, since, when all is said and done, it is the only one we know.

When Buddhism came to China in the early centuries A.D., it found a sympathetic audience among the Taoists. No such fruitful contact, however, was possible with the Confucians, for between the two parties

[1] *Analects* 11: 11 (E.T., Arthur Waley, London, George Allen & Unwin, 1938 and reprints).

there was no common ground. Though he lived in the eighth century A.D., the neo-Confucian Hu Yin might have been speaking for all Confucians when he laid bare the gulf that yawned between the two religions:

Man [he said] is a *living* thing; the Buddhists speak not of life but of death. Human affairs are all visible; the Buddhists speak not of the manifest but of the hidden. After a man dies he is called a ghost; the Buddhists speak not of men but of ghosts. What man cannot avoid is the ordinary Way; the Buddhists speak not of the ordinary but of the marvellous. That by which the ordinary Way is as it is is principle; the Buddhists speak not of principle but of illusion. It is to what follows birth and precedes death that we should devote our minds; the Buddhists speak not of this life but of past and future lives. Seeing and hearing, thought and discussion, are real evidence; the Buddhists do not treat them as real, but speak of what the ear and eye cannot attain, thought and discussion cannot reach.[1]

In other words, all that was of passionate concern to the Buddhists appeared both irrelevant and fantastic to the this-worldly Confucians; for what they were interested in was man as a concrete being, both in himself and in his relationship to his fellow men, and beyond this in his relationship to the cosmic Tao. For them the universe was a harmonious and well-regulated visible whole, and man had his due place in it. What allegedly lay outside this universe was no concern of his: it was merely a matter of idle speculation. The universe was a concrete whole expressed in Chinese by the words 'heaven and earth', and in this concrete whole man had a central role to play, for together with heaven and earth he formed a triad; and by his participation in the cosmic pattern he elevated the cosmos itself on to a higher plane—the plane of thought and ethics. The Taoists had sought salvation in the dehumanization of man in the ineffable Tao: the Confucians sought to adapt human values to the Tao. Taoism is 'natural' religion at its purest: Confucianism is humanism at its most self-confident, for its overriding concern is with man as he lives his life out from birth to death and in the regulation of that life in accordance with principles which he believes to be implicit in Nature itself, or, if you prefer, as they are dictated by a God who makes those principles known. Thus one can quite understand how the Buddhists, with their superior metaphysics and their contempt of this world, must have infuriated the Confucians; for Buddhism, before it made contact with the Chinese, remained basically dualistic: there was *saṁsāra*, the round of birth and death, life as we know it, on the one hand, and there was Nirvāna, unconditioned existence, on the other. The two modes of existence were not compatible: you had to

[1] A. C. Graham, *Two Chinese Philosophers*, London, Lund Humphries, 1958, p. 84.

choose one or the other. In spite of the fact that they called themselves the Middle Way, this merely meant the middle way between the extremes of asceticism and self-indulgence: it did not mean the middle way between, and the reconciliation of, time and eternity. This it was only later to discover but it was not what the Buddha had originally preached. The Chinese, however, both Taoists and Confucians, had an intimate feeling of kinship with all natural things. To them Nature was sacred: it was the manifestation of the Tao, the Way of Heaven; and to feel oneself at one with the ebb and flow of the universe, accepting without cavil whatever might happen to you, this was the ultimate bliss. Union and harmony in, among, and with the ten thousand things and with the Tao that was the source of them all, this was true wisdom, not the brutal, and to them unnatural, separation of the eternal from the fleeting loveliness of a lovely world.

Taoism, however, even more than Buddhism, refused to face the fact that man had emerged from the state of a nebulous collective conscious-ness, a primitive 'cosmic consciousness', into full self-consciousness; and this implied not only responsibility, but an organized *collective* responsi-bility which should also be in harmony with the primitive Tao. This is the starting-point of Confucianism. Man is neither an angel nor a beast: he is, as he is in the Hebrew tradition, a unitary being with instincts, desires, reason, and intuition. As such he is human—*jên*—the keyword of Con-fucianism; and to be truly human means to be humane.

The word *jên*, Arthur Waley tells us, 'in the earliest Chinese means freemen, men of the tribe, as opposed to *min*, "subjects, the common people". The same word, written with a slight modification, means "good" in the most general sense of the word, that is to say, "possessing the qualities of one's tribe". For no more sweeping form of praise can be given by the men of the tribe than to say that someone is a "true member" of that tribe. . . . *Jên*, "members of the tribe" show a forbearance towards one another that they do not show to aliens, and just as the Latin *gens*, "clan", gave rise to our own word "gentle", so *jên* in the Chinese came to mean "kind", "gentle", "humane". Finally, when the old distinction between *jên* and *min*, freemen and subjects, was forgotten and *jên* became a general word for "human being", the adjective *jên* came to be under-stood in the sense "human" as opposed to "animal", and to be applied to conduct worthy of a man, as distinct from the behaviour of mere beasts.'[1]

Taking all this into consideration it seemed to me that perhaps the best translation of *jên* was 'human kindness', and of the adjective, 'humane', since Confucianism is essentially a 'humanist' religion. Though it started

[1] Arthur Waley, op. cit., p. 27.

with a fairly clear conception of 'Heaven' or God as the ultimate arbiter of
human destiny, this was allowed to become blurred and sank into the background while the centre of the stage came to be increasingly occupied by
man. Like the religion of Rousseau Confucianism is a pietistic humanism,
the pillars of which are Nature, reason, and human kindness. Unlike Rousseau, however, and more like the *philosophes* of the Enlightenment, it was
very much a religion of scholars, usually known as the *literati*, who drew
their inspiration from the 'Five Classics' which Confucius was supposed
to have edited. Thus in its fully developed form Confucianism looked less
like a religion than a School of *litterae humaniores* which, however, also
claimed to hold the secret of statecraft and the right and duty to guide and
direct the policies of the ruling house. It was a very eighteenth-century
affair, and in Europe the closest parallel to it is perhaps the position of
Voltaire at the court of Frederick the Great.

For the Taoists, as for the Book of Genesis, man's emergence into
self-consciousness was a 'Fall'—a disastrous severing of the umbilical
cord which united man to his mother Nature. This was not the Confucian
view. For them the Fall was no Fall at all but a challenge to modify the
Way of Heaven in accordance with the new situation, to create a purely
human Way which would yet be in harmony with heaven and earth and in
which man would assume his allotted place as the central member of a
triad of which heaven and earth were the poles. Though partially independent, he would still be drawing his life, his sustenance, and his equilibrium
from them, for after all they were his father and mother. Hence in ancient
times 'the illustrious kings served heaven intelligently because they were
filial in the service of their fathers. They served earth discreetly because
they were filial in the service of their mothers.'[1] By honouring your father
and your mother you acknowledge your sonship of heaven and earth:
hence filial piety is the very 'trunk of human kindness'.[2] And human
kindness, together with the ancillary virtues, justice and morality (*yi*),
propriety (*li*), wisdom (*chih*), and (a later addition) good faith (*hsin*), is
seen as an extension of the Way of Heaven into the sphere of grown-up
and self-conscious humanity. It is as natural for men to practise these
virtues as it is for the sun and moon to rise and set and the four seasons to
succeed each other at their appointed times. They are indeed man's
natural and correct response to the influence of the Tao: they are the Tao
as it manifests itself in man.

---

[1] *Hsiao Ching*, 16 (E.T., Mary L. Makra, New York, St. John's University Press,
1961, p. 35).
[2] *Analects* 1: 2.

The Taoists had said:

> After Tao was lost, then came the 'power',
> After the 'power' was lost, then came human kindness.
> After human kindness was lost, then came morality,
> After morality was lost, then came ritual.
> Now ritual is the mere husk of loyalty and promise-keeping
> And is indeed the first step towards brawling.[1]

To the Confucian this would appear to be a stupid caricature of the Tao: it would preclude any development in it, any adjustment to the new situation. Even so, both 'Ways', the Taoist and the Confucian, are conservative, both look backwards, not forwards. But if Confucianism can be described as conservative, Taoism, despite its iconoclasm, is frankly reactionary; for whereas Confucianism looks to a golden age of three purely legendary 'culture heroes' and the three 'sage kings', Yao, Shun, and Yü, Taoism looks back far beyond to a time when men 'lived in common with birds and beasts'[2] in a generalized form of consciousness that was not yet fully human, not yet *jên*.

'Do not imagine that I have come to abolish the Law or the Prophets. I have come not to abolish but to complete them,'[3] Christ had told the Jews. Similarly Confucius came not to abolish the ancient Tao, but to adapt it and interpret it in terms appropriate to a civilized state. He had invented nothing, but had simply tried to learn from the ancients, from written and oral tradition, and to pass on what he had learnt to future generations:

> I have transmitted what was taught to me without making up anything of my own. I have been faithful to and loved the Ancients. . . . I have listened in silence and noted what was said, I have never grown tired of learning nor wearied of teaching others what I have learnt. These at least are merits which I can confidently claim. . . . The thought that I have left my moral power (*tê*) untended, my learning unperfected, that I have heard of righteous men, but been unable to go to them; have heard of evil men, but been unable to reform them—it is these thoughts that disquiet me.[4]

Confucian virtue is seen to well up from the Tao, and just as the Tao is the inactive source of all activity, so should the Emperor, the 'Son of Heaven' and God's viceroy on earth, rule simply by being what he is—by being *jên*, a truly *human* being and therefore a good man. If he does this, his influence will effortlessly leaven the lump of the Empire, all his officials will fulfil their duties automatically, the people will be contented,

---

[1] *Tao Tê Ching*, 38.   [2] Above, p. 228.   [3] Matthew 5: 17.
[4] *Analects* 7: 1–3.

and the Empire will be at peace. Consider the case of the Emperor Shun, Confucius implores us, for 'among those who ruled by inactivity surely Shun may be counted. For what action did he take? He merely placed himself gravely and reverently with his face due south; that was all.'[1]

How had Shun reached this state of radiant equanimity? He had learnt to accept the evils of this world without complaining and so to accept the splendour of Empire without exulting. For not only was he no relative of the former Emperor Yao; he belonged to the common people. And not only this, 'he was the son of a blind man. His father was stupid, his mother deceitful, his half brother Hsiang arrogant. Yet he was able to live in harmony with them and to be splendidly filial.'[2] That was enough: Yao chose him as his successor. For *jên* has nothing to do with noble birth, everything to do with nobility of character. Shun possessed filial piety and was thus supremely *jên*.

Harmony, filial piety, and self-cultivation: these are of the essence of *jên*. Harmony: this is the golden thread that runs through all Chinese religion, whether Taoist or Confucian. Hence the Confucian obsession with the importance of rites and music, the external manifestation of the virtue of 'ritual' or 'propriety'; for it is through rites and music that the precarious balance of the Tao is preserved among men, as it had been said:

> In the usages of ritual it is harmony that is prized; the Way of the Former Kings from this got its beauty. Both small matters and great depend upon it. If things go amiss, he who knows the harmony will be able to attune them. But if harmony itself is not modulated by ritual, things will still go amiss.[3]

Filial piety: this is the root from which all the other virtues spring: 'it is the foundation of virtue and the root of civilization.'[4] It is the virtue on which the whole hierarchical structure of the Empire is built. It explains both why we should make the most of ourselves and why we should extend the reverence we owe to our parents to those placed in authority over us:

> We develop our own personality and practice the Way so as to perpetuate our name for future generations and to give glory to our parents. . . . Thus, begun in the service of our parents, continued in the service of the prince, filiality is completed in the building up of our character.[5]

The building up of individual character in its turn is the firm foundation on which society rests. Hence, 'from the Son of Heaven down to the

---

[1] *Analects* 15: 4.
[2] *Book of Documents* 1: 3 (translation from *Sources of Chinese Tradition*, ed. de Bary, etc., p. 11).
[3] *Analects* 1: 12.　　　　　[4] *Hsiao Ching*, 1.　　　　　[5] Ibid.

common people, all must regard the cultivation of the personal life as the root or foundation.'[1]

Buddhism and Confucianism have at least this much in common: they both teach the suppression of the passions. But what a difference between the two! Whatever modern Zen Buddhists may say, this is a purely negative ideal in Buddhism; it is a process designed to uncover man's eternal being by sweeping away all that may have accrued to it in time. In Confucianism it is rather a matter of removing blemishes in one's character which obstruct the growth of virtue. By practising the cardinal virtues the Confucian develops and fulfils himself: he multiplies his talents, and even if he has only one, he will not bury it in the ground but make the most of it if only to honour his parents thereby.

Human kindness, benevolence, love, goodness (for *jên* is all of these) should be extended to all; the gentleman (the man who is *jên*) is open to all. But there are degrees. His first duty is to his parents and to the family in general: he is not required to extend his affection equally to all as Mencius' contemporary Mo Ti had taught, for this is the prerogative of Heaven on the one hand and the Way of the beasts on the other. 'Mo Ti speaks of "loving all equally",' Mencius had said, 'as though the family did not exist. It is only among wild animals that a state is found in which neither the prince nor the family is of any account.'[2] If human kindness must be open to all, 'propriety' and 'wisdom' nevertheless demand that there should be distinctions.

The Taoists too had looked back with nostalgia to the days when men and beasts lived together in harmony and understanding, and the Buddhists, like the whole Indian tradition from which they sprang, felt themselves to be very near to the beasts since there was always a possibility that they might be reincarnated in animal form. For the Confucians, however, man is different in kind from the beasts by the mere fact that, simply by being a man, he possesses at least the rudiments of human kindness and justice. Among men, of course, there are differences of endowment, and there is therefore an immense gap between the highest—the true gentleman—and the common people. This Shun, though of humble birth himself, clearly understood:

The difference between a man and an animal is slight. The common man disregards it altogether, but the True Gentleman guards the distinction most carefully. Shun understood all living things, but saw clearly the relationships

[1] *The Great Learning* (translation from Wing-tsit Chan, *A Source Book in Chinese Philosophy*, Princeton University Press, 1963, p. 87).
[2] *Mencius*, 3B. 9 (3. 3 in the translation of W. A. C. H. Dobson, Oxford University Press, 1963, p. 58).

that exist uniquely among human beings. These relationships proceed from
human kindness and justice. It is not because of these relationships that we
proceed towards human kindness and justice.[1]

It is, then, not human relationships as such that give rise to human
kindness and justice, but human kindness and justice that regulate human
relationships; for these two virtues are natural to the Way of man just as
instinct is natural to the animals. There is, however, a difficulty here; for
though Mencius maintained that human nature is good in itself, the fact
remains that both he and Confucius ceaselessly inculcate self-discipline.
Goodness, summed up by Mencius in the four cardinal virtues—human
kindness, justice, propriety, and wisdom—is *latent* in all men, but strict
self-discipline is necessary if it is to become fully apparent. Not everyone
is a Shun: not everyone can sit facing due south and expect everything to
turn out for the best. Even the sage has to struggle to achieve that poise
and contentment which are his outward distinguishing mark. And yet,
Mencius was to insist, the four cardinal virtues are inborn in every man;
they constitute his true nature, and what conflicts with them comes from
outside. So, in a well-known passage, Mencius claims that it is an ingrained trait in the human character to go to the help of the distressed.
No *human* being would simply watch a child drown without trying to do
anything about it. For the Confucian to 'love your neighbour as yourself'
is not a divine command but the natural tendency of the human heart:
'Treat others as you would like them to treat you'[2] is not so much the
'meaning of the Law and the Prophets' as the natural corollary of *jên*—of
the mere fact that we are human:[3]

It is a feeling common to all mankind [Mencius tells us] that they cannot bear
to see others suffer. The Former Kings had such feelings, and it was this that
dictated their policies. One could govern the entire world with policies dictated
by such feelings, as easily as though one turned it in the palm of the hand.

I say that men have such feelings because, on seeing a child about to fall into
a well, everyone has a feeling of horror and distress. They do not have this
feeling out of sympathy for the parents, or to be thought well of by friends and
neighbours, or from a sense of dislike at not being thought a feeling person. Not
to feel distress would be contrary to all human feeling. Just as not to feel shame
and disgrace and not to defer to others and not to have a sense of right and
wrong are contrary to all human feeling. This feeling of distress (at the suffering
of others) is the first sign of human kindness. This feeling of shame and disgrace
is the first sign of justice. This feeling of deference to others is the first sign of
propriety. This sense of right and wrong is the first sign of wisdom. Men have

[1] *Mencius* 4B. 19 (Dobson, 6. 19).   [2] Matthew 7: 12.
[3] Cf. *Analects* 12: 2.

these four innate feelings just as they have four limbs. To possess these four things, and to protest that one is incapable of fulfilling them, is to deprive oneself. To protest that the ruler is incapable of doing so is to deprive him. Since all have these four capacities within themselves, they should *know how to develop and fulfil them*. They are like a fire about to burst into flame, or a spring about to gush forth from the ground. If, in fact, a ruler can fully realize them, he has all that is needed to protect the entire world. But if he does not realize them fully, he lacks what is needed to serve even his own parents.[1]

Humans are to be distinguished from animals not only by the fact that they are self-conscious, but also by the fact that they have a conscience. Conscience expresses itself in the four cardinal virtues which are enshrined, so Mencius thought, in every man's heart. No *human* being is unaffected by the sufferings of others; no human being again is unable to distinguish right from wrong.[2]

If this is so, then why do men so obstinately go against their natural bent? Mencius has no real answer to this problem. The four cardinal virtues 'do not soak in from without,' he says, 'we have them within ourselves. It is simply that we are not always thinking about them. So I say, "Seek them and you have them. Disregard them and you lose them." [But] men differ, some by twice, some by five times, and some by an incalculable amount, in their inability to exploit this endowment.'[2]

Mencius' faith in the natural goodness of man was by no means shared in his day, some maintaining, more sensibly, that he was naturally neither good nor bad,[2] while Hsün Tzŭ, Mencius' junior and a Confucian, maintained that man's nature was downright evil. Neither was prepared to face the fact that in man there are two forces equally 'natural' to him, yet pulling in different directions. St. Paul realized this only too well and attributed his evil actions to the 'sin which lives in' him but which is alien to his true self, 'with the result that instead of doing the good things I want to do, I carry out the sinful things I do not want. When I act against my will, then, it is not my true self doing it, but sin which lives in me'.[3] To this extent Paul agrees with Mencius; but neither Mencius nor any Confucian, perhaps not even Hsün Tzŭ, could agree with him in identifying the 'law of sin' with the body, nor would they cry out in agony to be rescued from 'this body doomed to death'.[4] For in Confucianism, as in Taoism, there is no sharp differentiation between spirit and matter: the two act in harmony, they are not at war. In Christian terms the Chinese religions are serenely synoptic in outlook; Buddhism, before it

---

[1] *Mencius*, 2A. 6 (Dobson, 6. 1).   [2] Ibid. 6A. 6 (Dobson, 4. 11).
[3] Romans 7: 19–20.   [4] Ibid. 7: 24.

was 'civilized' by the Chinese, was discordantly Pauline. The first saw the world as it ought to be and devised means by which it might become so: the latter saw things as they are, found them hopeless, and could find no solution except escape from 'this body doomed to death'.

Mencius saw things as they ought to be, maintaining that the nature of man was good. Hsün Tzŭ took the darker view: he saw things as they seemed to be, and from what he saw he concluded that man is by nature evil, and that whatever goodness he exhibited was due to 'conscious activity':

Man's nature is evil; goodness is the result of conscious activity. The nature of man is such that he is born with a fondness for profit. If he indulges this fondness, it will lead him into wrangling and strife, and all sense of courtesy and humility will disappear. He is born with feelings of envy and hate, and if he indulges these, they will lead him into violence and crime, and all sense of loyalty and good faith will disappear. Man is born with the desires of the eyes and ears, with a fondness for beautiful sights and sounds. If he indulges these, they will lead him into licence and wantonness, and all ritual principles (*li*) and correct forms will be lost. Hence, any man who follows his nature and indulges his emotions will inevitably become involved in wrangling and strife, . . . and will end up as a criminal. Therefore, man must first be transformed by the instructions of a teacher and guided by ritual principles, and only then will he be able to observe the dictates of courtesy and humility, obey the forms and rules of society, and achieve order. It is obvious from this, then, that man's nature is evil, and that his goodness is the result of conscious activity.[1]

It may be remembered that the Bhagavad Gītā[2] speaks of two selves in man: one of them raises him up, the other drags him down. So too in Islamic mysticism these two selves are clearly differentiated: there is the *rūḥ* or 'spirit', which is of God, and the *nafs* or 'carnal ego', which is of the flesh. The total disagreement between Mencius and Hsün Tzŭ on what constitutes the original nature of man seems, then, to be based on an arbitrary one-sidedness; and Hsün Tzŭ seems to realize this himself in his criticism of Mencius:

Mencius [he says] states that man's nature is good, and that all evil arises because he loses his original nature. Such a view, I believe, is erroneous. It is the way with man's nature that as soon as he is born he begins to depart from his original naïveté and simplicity; and therefore he must inevitably lose what Mencius regards as his original nature. It is obvious from this, then, that the nature of man is evil.[3]

[1] *Hsün Tzŭ* 23: 1 (translation from Burton Watson, *Hsün Tzu, Basic Writings*, Columbia University Press, 1963, p. 157). Cf. the complete translation by H. H. Dubs, *The Works of Hsüntze*, Taipei, Ch'eng-Wen Publishing Co., 1966, p. 301.
[2] 6: 5-6.   [3] *Hsün Tzŭ* 23: 2 (Watson, p. 159; Dubs, pp. 303-4).

Mencius had, in fact, said that 'the great man is one who never loses his child-like touch',[1] while Hsün Tzŭ seems to imply that evil though man's nature may be, he is nevertheless born into a state of original Taoist innocence which, however, he immediately loses. Mencius accepts the myth of a pristine state of innocence, the age of the Garden of Eden when man is said to have walked with God: Hsün Tzŭ rejects this as unrealistic, and, given what we now know of the evolutionary origins of man, he is unquestionably right. Both agree that there was a stage of original innocence which preceded the rise (or fall) of man into self-consciousness—the ancient Tao when men were at one with the animals. Hsün Tzŭ, knowing nothing of evolution, nevertheless saw that man in his beginnings must have been barely distinguishable from the beasts: there was nothing angelic about him at all, only a 'naïveté and simplicity' commonly associated with domestic animals. His 'angelic' characteristics had come to him from outside, and these he had somehow to 'acquire'. The *deus ex machina* is the Confucian sage.

If left to himself man, like any other animal, will follow his instincts. Advancing a little in the arts of civilization he will want to own things, and, since others will be doing the same, this will inevitably lead to strife. He will develop a sense of beauty, and this will inflame his lust—what St. John calls the 'lust of the eyes'.[2] Why is it, then, that Confucian man eschews all this? Why does he accept the restraint of the Confucian virtues so that he will not even eat first when in the presence of elders? None of this is natural. 'For a son to yield to his father or a younger brother to yield to his elder brother, for a son to relieve his father of work or a younger brother to relieve his elder brother—acts such as these are all contrary to man's nature and run counter to his emotions. And yet they represent the way of filial piety and the proper forms enjoined by ritual principles.'[3]

You may well ask how this comes about. The answer is that 'all ritual principles are produced by the conscious activity of the sages; essentially they are not products of man's nature. A potter moulds clay and makes a vessel, but the vessel is the product of the conscious activity of the potter, not essentially a product of his human nature. A carpenter carves a piece of wood and makes a utensil, but the utensil is the product of the conscious activity of the carpenter, not essentially a product of his human nature. The sage gathers together his thoughts and ideas, experiments with various forms of conscious activity, and so produces ritual principles and sets

---

[1] *Mencius*, 4B. 12 (Dobson, 7: 12).   [2] 1 John 2: 16.
[3] *Hsün Tzŭ* 23: 3 (Watson, p. 160; Dubs, p. 304).

forth laws and regulations. Hence, these ritual principles and laws are the products of the conscious activity of the sage, not essentially products of his human nature.'[1]

In the Old Testament we read:

> Yahweh, you are our Father;
> We the clay, you the potter,
> We are all the work of your hand.[2]

Here it is God who moulds the human clay into the shapes of civilization: in Confucianism it is the sage. One thing, however, remains unexplained: where does conscious activity come from? It does not come from God, for Hsün Tzǔ regards Heaven or God as little more than a synonym for Nature. It can only be, then, that this 'conscious activity' which is 'acquired', not 'given', must be a principle of some kind independent of human nature; and yet it only manifests itself in human beings. And Hsün Tzǔ himself says: 'In respect to human nature the sage is the same as all other men and does not surpass them; it is only in his conscious activity that he differs from and surpasses other men.'[3]

Although Mencius and Hsün Tzǔ seem to represent diametrically opposite points of view, there is really very little difference between them. For Mencius human nature is good, but it is latent and must be brought out into the open by an effort of the will: for Hsün Tzǔ it is evil and virtue must be imposed on to it by the will so that it becomes almost a second nature. In either case human nature is a battle-field between good and evil, between the angel and the beast. In practice it makes very little difference which is considered to be the fundamental nature of man, since, if it is the angel, it is submerged beneath extraneous qualities which are evil, and if it is the beast, there is always an angel at its side to train it for higher things.

Both Confucius and Mencius stand nearer to Taoism than does Hsün Tzǔ, for both regard the 'Way of Man' as being a natural outgrowth of the 'Way of heaven'. All three of them, however, look *back* to the golden age of the sage kings when perfect virtue was effortlessly and harmoniously exercised and man formed a triad with heaven and earth. Both heaven and earth have their own Tao or Way. The Way of man manifests itself in the four cardinal virtues: it is the 'norm' appropriate to human beings. Thus *jên* or human kindness is simply that virtue by which man is truly man; *yi* or justice is also *justesse*, 'rightness' as well as 'righteousness'; *li*, 'propriety, seemliness, and ritual principles', is that virtue

---

[1] *Hsün Tzǔ* 23: 3.   [2] Isaiah 64: 8; cf. *Hsün Tzǔ* 29: 16 (Dubs, p. 305).
[3] *Hsün Tzǔ* 23: 4 (Watson, p. 161; Dubs, p. 306).

through which the relationships of men are regulated both among themselves and with the Way of heaven and earth; while *shih*, 'wisdom', is
conscience, the unique privilege of the human animal which enables him
to choose between right and wrong. For Mencius these virtues develop
naturally along with the emergence of self-consciousness from group-
consciousness; for Hsün Tzŭ they have somehow to be laboriously
acquired.

Even the Confucians at their most optimistic, however, realized that in
human affairs no state of ideal harmony in fact exists. This is scarcely surprising since their founding fathers all lived in what Professor Toynbee
has called a 'time of troubles' before the Empire was united not by the
Confucians but by brute force. Hence they looked back nostalgically to a
golden age during which perfect harmony was believed to have reigned.
In a degenerate age this harmony could not be restored except by *li*,
'propriety', that is, by the inculcation of good and deferential manners and
their codification in 'rites' in which music and dancing played an all-
important part.

The importance in Confucianism of ritual decorum can scarcely be
exaggerated, and this is not surprising; for ritual in all its forms, from the
common courtesies of everyday life to the elaborate prescriptions for the
mourning of the dead, was held to express that harmony among human
beings which reflects the harmony between heaven and earth. Ritual puts
individual man back again into the cosmic pattern: it is the great harmoni-
zer, eschewing extremes and vanquishing discord. Of the four cardinal
virtues it is clearly the most artificial, the product of 'conscious activity'
rather than of 'human nature'. And it is for this reason that Hsün Tzŭ
lays such tremendous emphasis on the importance of rites and music, for
it is they, in their very artificiality, that can endow even the common man
with some of the poise of the gentleman:

What is the origin of ritual? [he asks.] I reply: man is born with desires. If his
desires are not satisfied for him, he cannot but seek some means to satisfy them
himself. If there are no limits and degrees to his seeking, then he will inevitably
fall to wrangling with other men. From wrangling comes disorder and from
disorder comes exhaustion. The ancient kings hated such disorder, and therefore they established ritual principles in order to curb it, to train men's desires
and to provide for their satisfaction. They saw to it that desires did not over-
extend the means of their satisfaction, and material goods did not fall short of
what was desired. Thus both desires and goods were looked after and satisfied.
This is the origin of rites.[1]

----

[1] *Hsün Tzŭ* 19: 1 (Watson, p. 89; Dubs, p. 213).

The basic function of ritual, then, is the satisfaction, regulation, and canalizing of legitimate desire. This must be in accordance with the Way not only of heaven and earth but also of man, the partner of heaven and earth in the cosmic triad. 'Rites', then, 'have three bases. Heaven and earth are the basis of life, the ancestors are the basis of the family, and rulers and teachers are the basis of order.'[1] Ritual, then, is founded on Nature, the family, and the hierarchical social system, which is both an extension of the family and the cosmic order on a human scale. It is the human expression of the unity of all things: it does not destroy emotion, not even emotions normally considered discordant and disruptive, nor does it reduce forms to the formless as would be the case in classical Indian religion: rather it sets everything in its proper place. It is the magical restoration of that unity in diversity which is of the essence of the Tao.

Ritual is a profound mystery and is in a very real way the Tao of Confucianism, because ritual and music are not only essentially human activities but also communal human activities which, without seeking to deprive man of his individuality and consciousness of self, reintegrate him into the cosmic harmony on a higher, because a human, level. Hsün Tzŭ identifies the sounds of musical instruments with various emotions, all of which contribute to the universal harmony. Hitherto the harmony of the spheres had lacked any human contribution because man had not yet emerged from the womb of Nature. In Confucian ritual the human voice is added to Nature's orchestra and sings out in concord with the music of heaven and earth:

Through rites heaven and earth join in harmony, the sun and moon shine, the four seasons proceed in order, the stars and constellations march, the rivers flow, and all things flourish; men's likes and dislikes are regulated and their joys and hates made appropriate. Those below are obedient, those above are enlightened; all things change but do not become disordered; only he who turns his back upon rites will be destroyed. Are they not wonderful indeed? When they are properly established and brought to the peak of perfection, no one in the world can add to or detract from them. Through them the root and the branch are put in proper order, beginning and end are justified, the most elegant forms embody all distinctions; the most penetrating insight explains all things. In the world those who obey the dictates of ritual will achieve order; those who turn against them will suffer disorder. Those who obey them will win safety; those who turn against them will court danger. Those who obey them will be preserved; those who turn against them will be lost. This is something that the petty man cannot comprehend.[2]

[1] *Hsün Tzŭ* 19: 3 (Watson, p. 91; Dubs, p. 219).
[2] Ibid. 19: 7 (Watson, p. 94; Dubs, pp. 223–4).

The function of ritual is to harmonize all things into a 'middle state' in which nothing is left out, not even what is ugly and distressing. Confucianism, then, as much as Buddhism, is a Middle Way—it abhors extremes:

Beauty and ugliness, music and weeping, joy and sorrow are opposites, and yet rites make use of them all, bringing forth and employing each in its turn. Beauty, music, and joy serve to induce an attitude of tranquillity and are employed on auspicious occasions. Ugliness, weeping, and sorrow induce an attitude of inquietude and are employed on inauspicious occasions. But though beauty is utilized, it should never reach the point of sensuousness or seductiveness, and though ugliness is utilized, it should never go as far as starvation or self-injury. Though music and joy are utilized, they should never become lascivious and abandoned, and though weeping and sorrow are utilized, they should never become frantic and injurious to health. If this is done, then rites have achieved the middle state.[1]

Ritual is the means by which man not only restores the unity and harmony of the cosmos but actually improves on it. God can create, but he cannot perfect: this only the sage can do. This rather surprising doctrine is perhaps peculiar to Hsün Tzŭ; for human nature, which for him is evil, is the natural outcrop of heaven and earth: it is the evolute of Heaven, that is, of God. And so in his discussion of rites we get back to his fundamental distinction between human nature and conscious activity. For him, much more than for Confucius or Mencius, it is man who perfects the Way. It is not divine grace that perfects Nature as in Catholic Christianity, it is man who orders to his own liking the raw material of Nature which he has inherited:

Human nature [he says] is the basis and raw material, and conscious activity is responsible for what is adorned, ordered, and flourishing. If there were no human nature, there would be nothing for conscious activity to work upon, and if there were no conscious activity, then human nature would have no way to beautify itself. Only when nature and conscious activity combine does a true sage emerge and perform the task of unifying the world. Hence it is said that when heaven and earth combine, all things are born, when the *yin* and the *yang* act upon each other, all changes are produced, and when nature and conscious activity join together, the world is well ordered. Heaven can give birth to creatures but it cannot order them; earth can bear man up but it cannot govern him. All creatures of the universe, all who belong to the species of man, must await the sage before they can attain their proper places.[2]

---

[1] Ibid. 19: 12 (Watson, pp. 100–1; Dubs, pp. 232–3).
[2] Ibid. 19: 14 (Watson, pp. 102–3; Dubs, pp. 234–5).

In Hsün Tzŭ the perfected sage who is yet to come takes the place of God. This is the first step in the dethronement of the God of Confucius, for in the Five Classics, in the *Analects*, and in Mencius 'Heaven' is still supreme, and Heaven is also *Shang Ti*, the 'Supreme Ancestor or Lord', or *T'ien Ti*, the 'Heavenly Ancestor' or 'Lord of Heaven'. In the Classics and particularly in the *Book of Songs* the existence of a personal God who is the Lord of Heaven is taken for granted. There are, of course, nature spirits and spirits of the dead as well, but the supremacy of the Lord of Heaven is unquestioned. So far as God is concerned the Confucian scene is almost the exact obverse of the Indian. In India an original polytheism gives way to either philosophic monism or dualism, and this in turn gives way to the monotheism of the *Śvetāśvatara* Upanishad. Finally, with the Bhagavad-Gītā and the Śaiva Siddhānta, this God emerges as a Saviour God who pursues man with his grace. In Confucian China, on the other hand, we start with God transcendent, the Lord of Heaven, the God 'out there' so displeasing to Dr. J. A. T. Robinson and this God remains virtually unchanged in the *Analects* and in Mencius, though his association with man as well as with mother Earth makes him both more approachable and more immanent. In Hsün Tzŭ his stature is further diminished, for though he can create he cannot perfect: this is the prerogative of the Confucian sage. Lastly in the neo-Confucian philosophy, which was the official 'religion' of China from the fourteenth until the beginning of the twentieth century and the dominant philosophy long before, God ceases to be personal at all; he becomes rather the principle of rationality that informs all Nature; Pascal's 'God of Abraham, God of Isaac, God of Jacob' has become the God of the philosophers: he has lost all reality. And perhaps this is why it was so easy for the Nationalist revolutionaries and for the Communists who followed them to make so utterly clean a sweep of the whole Confucian heritage.

In the Classics the words 'Will of Heaven' and 'Decree of Heaven' occur again and again. Kingship is in the 'charge of Heaven':[1] Heaven commands,[2] judges,[3] cherishes,[4] protects,[5] and blesses.[6] Yet Heaven may also be displeased,[7] taking from us 'all our good men',[8] and once it is even said that 'it is Heaven, not I, that is bad'.[9] In the *Book of Songs* God is the God of Majesty 'out there' who surveys all that goes on between heaven and earth and takes note of the wickedness of man.

---

[1] *The Book of Songs*, 229, etc.   [2] Ibid. 246, 247, 248, etc.
[3] Ibid. 282.   [4] Ibid. 221.   [5] Ibid. 245.
[6] Ibid. 248, 251, 254.   [7] Ibid. 271.   [8] Ibid. 278.
[9] Ibid. 283.

Sometimes we almost feel that here in China it is the Lord God of Israel who is speaking to a people which does not know him:

> Mighty is God on high,
> Ruler of his people below;
> Swift and terrible is God on high,
> His charge has many statutes.
> Heaven gives birth to the multitudes of the people,
> But its charge cannot be counted upon.[1]

And again:

> God on high in sovereign might
> Looked down majestically,
> Gazed down upon the four quarters,
> Examining the ills of the people.
> Already in two kingdoms
> The governance had been all awry;
> Then every land
> He tested and surveyed.
> God on high examined them
> And hated the laxity of their rule.
> So he turned his gaze to the west
> And here made his dwelling-place.[2]

More remarkable still, perhaps, is the song attributed to the boy king Ch'êng who is overwhelmed with the 'charge' that Heaven has laid upon him:

> Reverence, reverence!
> By Heaven all is seen;
> Its charge is not easy to hold.
> Do not say it is high, high above,
> Going up and down about its own business.
> Day in, day out it watches us here.
> I, a little child,
> Am not wise or reverent.
> But as days pass, months go by,
> I learn from those that have bright splendour.
> O radiance, O light,
> Help these my strivings;
> Show me how to manifest the ways of power.[3]

These hymns, however, are the exception rather than the rule. Heaven or the Lord of Heaven remains the somewhat remote dispenser of destiny.

---

[1] Ibid. 242 (E.T. Arthur Waley, *The Book of Songs*, London, George Allen & Unwin, 1937 and reprints, p. 252).
[2] Ibid. 243 (Waley, p. 255).   [3] Ibid. 229 (Waley, p. 234).

Heaven's will is identical with the 'Way', and what happens must there-fore necessarily be the will of Heaven. Among men, however, things are rather different, for only in the time of the sage kings did the will of Heaven exactly correspond with the Way of men. It is the function of the sage to find it out for himself and then to teach it to others. This is a long and arduous process, and Confucius himself claimed no special revelations, only a patient ascent to what he thought was Truth.

'At fifteen', he said, 'I set my heart upon learning. At thirty, I had planted my feet firm upon the ground. At forty, I no longer suffered from perplexities. At fifty, I knew what were the biddings of Heaven. At sixty, I heard them with docile ear. At seventy, I could follow the dictates of my own heart; for what I desired no longer overstepped the boundaries of right.'[1] For Confucius Heaven is not simply fate or the 'Way' of the Taoists, the *deus sive natura* of Spinoza, though it is this too, for it mani-fests itself silently and without fuss in the succession of the four seasons.[2] In Nature it is the natural law, among men it is *jên*, the same law applicable specifically to *human* beings, and *yi*, the right relationships that should exist between them: it is the moral law that arbitrates between right and wrong. Confucius knows this and is once moved to cry out: 'Whatsoever I have done amiss, may Heaven exorcise it, may Heaven exorcise it!'[3]

Heaven disposes of both life and death, of wealth, rank, and moral excellence, for, Confucius says, 'Heaven begat the moral excellence (*tê*) that is within me'.[4] As a sage and a counsellor of kings Confucius was a failure, but this like everything else he accepted with equanimity: it was enough to know that Heaven did not despise him. 'The studies of men here below', he had said, 'are felt on high, and perhaps after all I am known; not here, but in Heaven.'[5] Heaven, then, is not indifferent to the lot of man; and yet the Will of Heaven transcends even the Way of Heaven, for, as in Taoism, it is a 'Way' that cannot be told and cannot be named and may at times seem to run contrary to the Way that even the most enlightened sage can discern. Confucius was convinced that the true Way was his Way, and yet he had failed to win its acceptance; and so, with characteristic resignation, he says: 'If it is the will of Heaven that the Way shall prevail, then the Way will prevail. But if it is the will of Heaven that the Way shall perish, then it must needs perish.'[6] In any case it would be presumptuous to 'accuse Heaven' and pointless to 'lay the blame on men'.[7]

[1] *Analects* 2: 4.   [2] Ibid. 17: 19.   [3] Ibid. 6: 26.
[4] Ibid. 7: 22.   [5] Ibid. 14: 37.   [6] Ibid. 14: 38.
[7] Ibid. 14: 37.

In his teaching about Heaven Mencius is true to Confucius. The will of Heaven is to be sought in one's own conscience. This is man's 'true nature' just as sight is the 'true nature' of the eye.[1] It may be true that nothing happens that is not in accord with the will of heaven, but this may not be used as an alibi for neglecting one's duty; and so 'we should accept obediently our rightful lot. Therefore he who understands Heaven's ordinances, does not walk below high walls'—does not take unnecessary risks—'but when he dies in the full discharge of his principles he has fulfilled the lot that Heaven has ordained for him. He who dies, however, in a felon's chains cannot be said to have fulfilled the lot that Heaven has ordained for him.'[2]

What is true for the individual is also true for the community and even for the supreme head of the community, the Emperor, the Son of Heaven. Should an Emperor prove to be unworthy, by that same token he morally ceases to be Emperor, and the people are justified in overthrowing him. Thus, concerning the impious Chou who, Emperor though he was, had been put to death, Mencius says: 'A man who despoils humanity I call a robber; a man who despoils justice, a ruffian. Robbers and ruffians are mere commoners. I was aware that that commoner Chou was slain, but unaware that a prince was slain.'[3] This is a case in which Heaven denies its own 'son' and makes its will known through the people. So too in the case of Shun, 'Yao having recommended him to Heaven, Heaven accepted him. He presented him to the people and the people accepted him. . . . We may say that both Heaven and man gave the Empire to him.'[4] The people owe allegiance to the Emperor as the Son of Heaven and God's representative on earth, but only so long as he follows the Confucian Way. Once he deviates from it, God inspires the people to overthrow him, and the voice of the people becomes the voice of God. Such at any rate is the theory of it.

Mencius' attitude to Heaven or God may be summed up thus: because man's nature is good he will *naturally* co-operate with Heaven, thereby fulfilling its will. So too collective man, the 'people', being good, will co-operate with Heaven in the choice of a worthy 'Son of Heaven' on earth. This was so in the idyllic days of Yao and Shun, but it was no longer true in Mencius' day when it seemed that Heaven's Way was incomprehensibly at variance with the way of human kindness and justice as pursued on earth. Hsün Tzŭ saw things differently. For him the will of Heaven means little more than the laws of Nature which are constant though they appear to be haphazard. It is the function of the sage to

[1] *Mencius*, 7B. 24 (Dobson, 6. 25).   [2] Ibid. 7A. 2 (Dobson, 6. 26).
[3] Ibid. 1B. 8 (Dobson, 1.1).   [4] Ibid. 5A. 5 (Dobson, 3. 10).

improve on this not very promising raw material (the Taoists would say to 'meddle' with it). Of itself the Way of Heaven is morally neutral: its 'ways are constant. It does not prevail because of a sage like Yao; it does not cease to prevail because of a tyrant like Chieh. Respond to it with good government, and good fortune will result; respond to it with disorder, and misfortune will result.'[1]

The Way, for Hsün Tzŭ, is not a unity in quite the same sense as it is for Confucius and Mencius: for there are two ways which are not identical, the Way of Heaven and the Way of Man; and just as man is an amalgam of the nature he receives from Heaven, which is evil, and 'conscious activity', which in the last resort also derives from Heaven and tends towards a greater good, so Heaven itself is the source of good and evil. Man, however, is required to co-operate only with that in Heaven which manifests itself in conscious activity. Morality is his business, not philosophy and theology. Leave the study of Heaven to the philosophers and theologians, for such pursuits do not become a gentleman: 'the experts may study Heaven; the ruler himself should concentrate on the Way [of government by moral power].'[2] Order and disorder, good and bad government, have nothing to do with Heaven: they are the responsibility of man, and so 'the gentleman cherishes what is within his power and does not long for what is within the power of Heaven alone'.[3] 'God helps those who help themselves' some of us were told in our nurseries, and this might have been the moral of Hsün Tzŭ too. He is uncompromisingly on the side of Martha (as is Confucianism in general); he has no use at all for Mary who, according to Jesus, had chosen the better part. In a series of rhetorical questions he asks:

> Is it better to exalt Heaven and think of it,
> Or to nourish its creatures and regulate them?
> Is it better to obey Heaven and sing hymns to it,
> Or to grasp the mandate of Heaven and make use of it?
> Is it better to long for the seasons and wait for them,
> Or to respond to the seasons and exploit them?
> Is it better to wait for things to increase of themselves,
> Or to apply your talents and transform them?
> Is it better to think of things but regard them as outside you,
> Or to control things and not let them slip your grasp?
> Is it better to long for the source from which things are born,
> Or to possess the means to bring them to completion?[4]

[1] *Hsün Tzŭ* 17: 12 (Watson, p. 79: Dubs, p. 173).
[2] Ibid. 17: 15 (Watson, p. 82: Dubs, p. 177).
[3] Ibid., 17: 16 (Watson, p. 83; Dubs, p. 179).
[4] Ibid. 17: 19 (Watson, p. 86; Dubs, p. 183).

This does not mean that one should go against the Way of Heaven, since the Way of Heaven is simply things as they are, the given subject-matter of scientific inquiry; nor should one try to manipulate the Way, for that would be irreverent. It means that you should *develop* the Way in the best interests of mankind, that you should seek out a new harmony in a human context, and for this you need a little common sense. And so, 'if you harmonize with what is best in the Way, all will go well; if you distort what is best in the Way, you cannot govern effectively; if you mistake what is best in the Way, you will be led into grave error.'[1] In short, you can and must worship both God and Mammon.

[1] Ibid. (Watson, p. 87; Dubs, pp. 183-4).

XIII

THE GRAND SYNTHESIS

BOTH Confucius and Mencius lived in a 'time of troubles'. Neither succeeded at all significantly in influencing the ruling houses of their time. The function of the sage was to harmonize society in accordance with moral principle, and this he could not even begin to do until he had harmonized the warring elements within himself. This is the precondition for the establishment of that state of society in which 'the free development of each is the condition for the free development of all'.[1] The good ordering of human affairs must be the ultimate concern of the sage. But this can only start with the individual, and in practice this means the ruling class with the Emperor at its head, which alone is in a position to influence the behaviour of the common man.

The Confucians thought that good government could only be achieved by good example. In principle they deplored excessive legalism and the ruthless enforcement of law to 'harmonize' society: they stood for a golden mean between the cynical pragmatism of the Legalists, with their fine contempt both for the all-too-idealist sage, and for the impossible *laisser-faire* of the Taoists, which in practice meant withdrawal from this wicked world of human artifice and artificiality. Confucianism stood for government in accordance with moral principle. It had, however, to bide its time, and it was not until the foundation of the Han dynasty in the third century B.C. that Confucian ideas received official recognition. From then on, however, right up to the Nationalist revolution in 1905 it remained the dominant philosophy of China. The Buddhists and Taoists might and did rise to greater metaphysical heights on the one hand and minister more effectively to the practical religious needs of the people on the other, but it was the Confucian scholars, men immersed in the Confucian Classics, who were the chosen guides of the Emperor. This alliance worked out to the advantage of both, each becoming indispensable to the other. In theory it should have been the sage—the man who had normally perfected himself—who was entrusted with supreme power, but Confucianism was an essentially practical philosophy. Hence Confucian scholars were content to act as advisers and ministers to dynastic

---

[1] K. Marx and F. Engels, *The Communist Manifesto*, ii, end.

Emperors, and the value of their teaching was recognized by the introduction of a civil service examination in the second century B.C. which was entirely based on the Confucian Classics. It is true that in the course of time Confucianism absorbed much Taoist and Buddhist thought, and in so doing became less narrow; but it also became less practical, the actual contents of the examination becoming more and more literary and less and less concerned with the business of running a state. Theory and practice were no longer one, and it seems to have been the sharpening of this dichotomy between learning and its practical application that brought the whole system crashing down, never to be restored.

In addition to the 'Five Classics',[1] the ancient legacy on which the Confucians built, four books were added to the canon in the twelfth century A.D. Two of these were, understandably enough, the *Analects* of Confucius himself and the *Book of Mencius*. The remaining two were two chapters extracted from the *Book of Rites*, now figuring as treatises in their own right: these were the *Great Learning* and the *Mean*. Both were to exercise enormous influence on later Confucian thought.

There is, of course, plenty in Confucius and Mencius about the Way of Heaven and the Way of Man and how the two interact and reciprocate each other, but in these two short treatises their essential interconnectedness is more clearly etched. Heaven, man, and earth together form a triad, but the central position is occupied by man. At the centre of the human group, of course, stands the Emperor, the Son of Heaven, in theory the embodiment of *jên*—of human kindness; but in practice, in China as elsewhere, the ruler habitually fell far short of the impossible ideal. Even so his central position is never questioned: he is the apex of a hierarchical society in which everyone, whether noble or commoner, has his allotted place. Hence the idealization of the Sage Kings of the golden age: they were the true Sons of Heaven and the incarnations of the Way of Heaven among men. They 'led the world by human kindness and the people followed them'.[2] As Mencius had said, the endowment man receives from Heaven is good, and he has only to follow this in order to fulfil his destiny. To do this is to adhere to the Mean which is simply another word for the Way. But to leave matters there would be Taoist talk, for though the Mean is indeed the Way of Heaven as it applies to man, very few men have been able to find it, let alone to put it into practice. And so Confucius is quoted as saying: 'Perfect is the Mean. [But] for a long time few people have been

---

[1] The *Book of Changes*, the *Book of History*, the *Book of Songs*, the *Book of Rites*, and the *Spring and Autumn Annals*.

[2] *Great Learning*, 9. See Wing-tsit Chan, *A Source Book in Chinese Philosophy*, Princeton University Press, 1963, p. 91.

able to follow it.'¹ This is the human dilemma as it had been the dilemma of Yudhishthira in India: we know that there is a cosmic law and that the moral law of men as enshrined in the cardinal virtues of the Confucians reflects this cosmic law, but we cannot see how, and are therefore constantly false to it: in so doing we miss the Mean. 'Humanity', after all, as usually understood, is not the same as human kindness, and if, like the Chinese, you have only one word for the two, confusion is likely to arise. The Way that is the same as the Mean can be understood as moral principle, but since the Way is also simply things as they are, and since things as they are in human affairs frequently diverge from things as they ought to be, what, then, has happened to the Mean? The answer is that the Way itself must be cultivated so far as we understand it. In theory it can never be separated from us, but wrong-doing makes us unconscious of it:

What Heaven bestows on man is called human nature; to follow our nature is called the Way. Cultivating the Way is called education [or culture]. The Way cannot be separated from us for a moment. What can be separated from us is not the Way.²

There seems to be an element of make-believe or, if you prefer it, double-think in this as in all Confucian ethical thinking. From the Taoists they had learnt that what *is*, is right; but from their own tradition and its profound concern for ethical values as well as from daily experience, they saw that from the purely human point of view this is really nonsense. Being and the good are simply not interchangeable terms as the Taoists, the Bhagavad-Gītā, and Thomas Aquinas would have us believe. To sin is rather to be separated from God, from the ultimate Principle which the Taoists and the Confucians call the Way: this is the inevitable result of human wickedness which Christians seek to explain by the doctrine of the Fall. Confucianism acknowledged but could not explain man's inability to do what he knew to be right. The Confucian, like Rousseau in a later age, knew intuitively that between Heaven and earth there was a mysterious concord, an unerring Way: he felt that this Way should and must be reflected in man who was their partner, but he saw and experienced that his own nature as it had come to develop in time was no more than a distorting mirror of the ideal Mean. He could not and would not accept the Taoist and Buddhist way of escape into another form of existence in which all action, whether good or evil, was irrelevant and in which all human relationships thereby became meaningless, because right human relationships were the very basis on which his religion rested.

¹ *Mean*, 3; Chan, op. cit., p. 99; de Bary, op. cit., p. 133.
² *Mean*, 1; Chan, op. cit., p. 98; de Bary, op. cit., p. 132.

The *Mean*, which, together with the *Great Learning*, was the seed from which the Grand Synthesis of neo-Confucianism was to spring, taught that the indefectible principle inherent in the universe was equilibrium and harmony, and that in human affairs this harmony showed itself in the Mean between the opposite poles of excess and deficiency as in Aristotle. Before man became self-conscious, that is, 'before the feelings of pleasure, anger, sorrow, and joy were aroused', the Way manifested itself as equilibrium (*chung*) and centrality. But 'when these feelings were aroused and had all attained due measure and degree, it was called harmony'. Thus 'equilibrium is the great foundation of the world, and harmony its universal path. When equilibrium and harmony are realized to the highest degree, heaven and earth will attain their proper order and all things will flourish'.[1]

Equilibrium is thus the natural state of the cosmos: harmony is the extension of equilibrium on to the human plane. But whereas the equilibrium of the cosmos is effortless, harmony among human beings which is its reflection and perfection can only be maintained by conscious effort—by education, the conscious bringing out into the open and development of the Mean which is the endowment of Heaven, which functions everywhere and yet is hidden in man.[2] To educate—to draw man's true nature out of himself so that it can shine forth in its native brilliance—is the function of the sage: it is the Great Learning, which Professor Wing-tsit Chan disconcertingly translates as 'higher education':

The Way of Great Learning consists in manifesting the clear character [which is our endowment from Heaven], in loving the people, and in resting in the highest good.[3]

Tranquillity is of the essence of the Way since it is the creative source of everything. So too in the human being it is only from a calm mind that unbiased deliberation can proceed, and this in turn will result in right action and achievement. This is the very opposite of Buddhism and indeed of the whole tradition of world-denial that we found to be so characteristic of Indian religion in last year's lectures. Even in the Gītā there is no real fruition of action in this world: rather action must be 'reduced to ashes' by wisdom or at the best be 'consummated' in it.[4] For the Confucian, wisdom or intuitive apperception of the Way is not an end in itself but rather the starting-point from which right action can proceed. Right action again

---

[1] *Mean*, 1; Chan, loc. cit., de Bary, loc. cit.
[2] *Mean*, 12; Chan, loc. cit., p. 100.
[3] *Great Learning*, opening words; Chan, op. cit., p. 86; de Bary, op. cit., p. 129.
[4] Bhagavad-Gītā 4: 37, 33.

must start from yourself. Until you are clear what you are and what you are here to do, you cannot hope to lead a life in accordance with the Way. This is true at all levels—from the Emperor to the common people. And so we read in the *Great Learning*:[1] 'From the Son of Heaven down to the common people, all must regard cultivation of the personal life as the root [and foundation].' Character-building again is dependent on the 'rectification of the mind', sincerity of the will, and the extension of knowledge by the 'investigation of things'. In fact the 'investigation of things' did not mean the disinterested pursuit of objective knowledge, since the neo-Confucianists never seem to have been interested in science at all: it meant rather the search for the same principle in the outside world as was to be found in oneself—the discernment of that 'equilibrium' in Nature which is reflected as harmony in the human mind. This is the starting-point, for unless you are at peace with yourself you will scarcely promote concord even in your own family. 'When', however, 'the personal life *is* cultivated, the family will be regulated; when the family is regulated, the state will be in order; and when the state is in order, there will be peace throughout the world.'[2]

Thus it is quite clear that the Way of Man as opposed to the Way of Heaven is very far from being an automatic affair. On the contrary it would seem to be uncommonly like the predicament of the Red Queen in *Alice through the Looking-Glass*: you have to run as fast as you can in order to stay in the same place. The 'Way' indeed is hedged in by 'ifs', and these 'ifs' assume menacing proportions when the subject of them is the Son of Heaven. For *if* he fails in the 'investigation of things', if he fails to recognize the Way both in himself and in Nature, if he gets things wrong, the whole Empire will suffer. There is no easy way round this. The only safe way is to do your duty in accordance with the principles of human kindness, justice, propriety, wisdom, and good faith in that state of life to which it has pleased Heaven to call you. Whatever your position in the social hierarchy, it is for the gentleman—the man of *jên*—to set the tone. To seek to better oneself is obviously to transgress the Mean. No gentleman would do this: rather, 'he acts according to the situation he is in and does not desire what is outside it. If he is wealthy and honourable, he acts like one wealthy and honourable; if poor and lowly, he acts like one poor and lowly.'[3] This is to accept things as they are, and that is the Mean.

[1] *Great Learning*; Chan, op. cit., p. 87; de Bary, op. cit., p. 129.
[2] *Great Learning*; Chan, op. cit., pp. 86–7; de Bary, op. cit., p. 129.
[3] *Mean*, 14; de Bary, op. cit., p. 133; Chan, op. cit., p. 101.

But, when all is said and done, everything depends on the Emperor himself. If he is a good Confucian and observes human kindness, then the Empire will flourish; for government is like agriculture which is indeed its material basis. Earth, rain, and seed are the gifts of Nature, but it is man's function and duty to tend the plant and bring it to fruition. If he fails in his duty the plant will be ruined:

If there are the right men, then the government will prosper; if the right men are lacking, the government will collapse. Men must be keen in matters of government, as the earth is keen in making things grow, and then their government will be like a growing reed. Therefore the administration of government depends upon the right men. One gets the right men by the force of one's own personality. One trains one's personality by means of the Way. And one learns the Way through practice of human kindness. Human kindness is what it is to be a human being, and loving one's relatives is the most important part of it. Justice is doing what is right [and proper], and honouring the worthy is the greatest part of it. The degree to which one loves one's different relatives and the grades to which one honours various worthy men are dictated by the rules of propriety [and ritual]. . . . Therefore the gentleman may not neglect the training of his personality. If he would train his personality, he must serve his parents. If he would serve his parents, he must understand men. And if he would understand men, he must understand Heaven.[1]

In the last resort filial piety is the source from which human kindness springs; for the cultivation of one's own personality is something one does not in isolation but in association with the whole nation and in dependence on Heaven which is God. Man does not stand aloof from Nature, nor is he totally immersed in it as the animals are: he is bound to his own kind by ties of family and through his own kind to all things. This is what the Confucians call sincerity—the ability to develop one's own talents to the full. The development of one's own potentialities should contribute to the development of the community through 'an association in which the free development of each is the condition for the free development of all'.

The Confucian goal is to restore an organic system of interconnection and interdependence within the human polity and through the human polity and its head, the Son of Heaven, with the whole natural order; for it was Mencius' estimate of human nature that triumphed, not that of Hsün Tzŭ. What is truly human is good and therefore in accord with the Way. Evil results from an abuse of human nature, from selfishness. Human desires are in themselves natural and good, but they must be controlled, holding fast to the Mean. A human being is bound to feel pleasure, anger, sorrow, and joy: this is all bound up with being human. You cannot

[1] *Mean*, 20; de Bary, op. cit., pp. 133–4; Chan, op. cit., p. 104.

prevent the passions from arising, but once they have arisen they must not be allowed to pass beyond their 'due measure and degree'. If they do not deviate from the Mean, they can be integrated into a new harmony, more fruitful and more rational, because more human, than the original 'equilibrium' could ever have been.

Rousseau held strangely similar views about an original innocence and an original harmony, but, at least in his political writings, he had sense enough to see (as the Taoists did not) that the original innocence of the Garden of Eden in which 'men found security in their being able to interpenetrate one another'[1] could not be prolonged once man had learnt to 'meddle', as the Taoists put it—once he had in his pride 'emerged from the state of happy ignorance to which eternal Wisdom had consigned him'.[2] This was a period of human history which had gone for ever (if it had ever existed), and willy-nilly man would have to try to organize society in accordance with human justice and law.

It was in fact according to Legalist principles of strict *law* savagely enforced that the Chinese Empire had been unified, and no one had enjoyed the experience. But the times had changed since Confucius had commended the Sage King Shun not for anything that he had done but for the fact that he had *appeared* to do nothing. 'For what action did he take? He merely placed himself gravely and reverently with his face due south; that was all.'[3] With the advance of civilization and sophistication, however, things had changed. Virtue no longer came naturally to man, so it had to be humanely enforced. The Five Classics embodied all wisdom. Let them then form the basis for the training of the civil service, and let the civil servants prove their understanding of them by competitive examination. If it was not possible to guarantee that the Son of Heaven himself would be a scholar and a gentleman, it would yet be possible to ensure that the members of the ruling class would be just that. Such a system is no doubt repulsive to the modern mind: none the less it lasted for more than two thousand years. Every system thinks it has found the Mean, but, such is human frailty, each and all of them are liable to fall into whatever 'excess' is potentially present within them. Taoism deviated into its own typical excess—antinominalism, occultism, and alchemy. So too did Confucianism drift into the excess of conformism, pedantry, and a pathological aversion to innovation.

'The ruler is the basis of the state'[4] and the 'executor of Heaven', the focal point where Heaven, earth, and human kind meet, patterning his

---

[1] J.-J. Rousseau, *Discours sur les sciences et les arts*, ed. Pléiade, vol. iii, p. 8.
[2] Ibid., p. 15.   [3] *Analects* 15: 4.   [4] De Bary, op. cit., p. 178.

action on Heaven's commands and causing the people to follow them.[1] The people's response to him should be one of reverence. If this is forth- coming, he will 'transform the people as though by supernatural power, but if the basis is not revered the ruler will have nothing with which to lead the people'.[2] Between ruler and ruled there is a social contract, the ruler representing, as in Rousseau, the general will of the community: once the general will is withdrawn and the ruler is no longer revered, the contract ceases to be binding. Such an eventuality had been provided for by Mencius, but it was none the less most repulsive to the Confucian mind, for the Emperor was sacrosanct and the people's infallible guide. He it is who makes actual that human kindness which is Heaven's gift to man not only in himself but also in his subjects:

> Heaven begets the people; their nature is that of potential good, but has not yet become actual good. For this reason it sets up the king to make real their goodness. This is the will of Heaven. From Heaven the people receive their potentially good nature, and from the king the education which completes it. It is the duty and function of the king to submit to the will of Heaven, and thus to bring to completion the nature of the people.[3]

This is the theory of it, but in practice things do not always follow the Mean. Hence the necessity for a morally trained bureaucracy. Just as in the great Tao there are the principles of *yin* and *yang*, repose and activity, so too in the state there is the Emperor, the serene and inactive source of human kindness; and the bureaucracy, which transforms his virtue into administrative action. It is for the Emperor to *be*, for his ministers to act:

> The craft of the ruler consists in disposing of affairs without action and issuing orders without speaking. The ruler remains still and pure without moving, impartial without wavering. Compliantly he delegates affairs to his subordinates and without troubling himself exacts success from them. . . . Thus among his policies are none that fail and among his plans none that go awry.[4]

In this the Emperor realizes the Taoist Way within himself—the Way which 'never does, yet through it all things are done'.

'Perfect consonance, perfect harmony':[5] this is what both Taoism and Confucianism dimly descry and long to achieve. But there is discord too which turns the consonance into a 'discordant concord' and the harmony into a 'concordant discord'. This discord Taoism attributes to purposeful human activity, the fruits of which are civilization and private property. It is man himself who has deliberately shattered the primal unity; and it is futile to suppose that it can be restored except *in parvo*, in the person of the

[1] Ibid., p. 179.   [2] Ibid., p. 178.   [3] Ibid., p. 183.
[4] Ibid., p. 174.   [5] Above, p. 1.

Taoist sage. This involves withdrawal from the world: hence the affinity of the Taoists with the Buddhists. Confucianism cannot accept this: it is not only impracticable but also immoral to return to a state of original innocence, for it is man's function to develop the Way itself and to help it forward on to a higher plane. Hence the Son of Heaven must rule by moral power alone, remaining inactive himself and acting through his ministers. In so doing he imitates the regular processes of Nature, or, in more theistic terms, he fulfils God's plan for man. In God or Nature there can never be disharmony: in man there *is* disharmony and discord: but man forms a triad with Heaven and earth, with Nature and the universe: *ergo* man must restore the Mean. The processes of government are fallible: music and rites are not: *ergo* only by rites and music can man be reintegrated into the Mean. This is his contribution to the harmony of the spheres; for rites and music are the outward and visible sign, through corporate and collective action, of man's continuing unity with the ten thousand things between Heaven and earth:

Man is born in stillness, for stillness is his nature given by Heaven. In response to external things he becomes active, activity being the expression of the desires of his nature. He comes to know external things, and with this knowledge his likes and dislikes take form. If these likes and dislikes are not controlled within him and his understanding is beguiled by the external world, then he cannot return to his true self and the principle of Heaven within him will be destroyed. . . . Therefore the former kings set up rites and music that men might be controlled by them. . . . Music comes from within, rites from without. Music coming from within is characterized by stillness, while rites which are from without are characterized by order. Great music must be easy, great rites simple. Music induces an end to anger, rites an end to strife. . . . Music is the harmony of Heaven and earth, rites are their order. Through harmony all things are transformed; through order all are distinguished. Music arises from Heaven; rites are patterned after earth. . . . Therefore the sage creates music in response to Heaven, and sets up rites to match earth. When music and rites are fully realized, Heaven and earth function in perfect order.[1]

There is a certain consistency about the Confucian system which one cannot but admire. Heaven itself is pervaded with human kindness, justice, propriety, wisdom, and good faith, and these are transmitted through the Emperor and the bureaucracy to the people. Through rites and music the people themselves re-enact the grand and beneficent harmony of the universe. But the Chinese are a practical people, and good government is not always possible. And because you cannot fool all the people all the time, and because the inevitable disharmonies that are

[1] De Bary, op. cit., pp. 184–5.

bound to appear in even the best-run state cannot be concealed, then let harmony be re-established and be seen to be re-established in the concert-hall. Confucianism, based as it is on the fallacy that human nature is good, was a sublime exercise in make-believe: rites and music were called in to make the people believe—to make them believe that Paradise Lost had really been regained. It had not solved the problem of human evil, but at least it had faced it. So too had the Buddhists—but in a totally different way.

Buddhism had come to China in its Mahāyāna form; but the Mahāyāna, despite its deviations from the primitive doctrine (if we may speak of such a thing) remained true to the Buddha's central teaching, namely, that *this* world, because it is transient and without substance, is the cause and *locus* of human un-ease and distress. There can be no salvation in it, only escape *from* it. It is true that the Mahāyāna schools tried to bridge the gulf the Buddha had fixed between matter and spirit, and even went so far as to identify them on a 'higher' plane; but this did not affect the Buddhist practice. It doggedly remained a monastic religion, the ideal Buddhist remaining always the monk who has turned his back on the world and all worldly values, which in China meant Confucian values—the sanctity of the family and of filial piety which held the family together, and the extension of the unselfish family virtues throughout the Empire through an orderly and co-ordinated hierarchy. Hence the Buddhist ideal of total withdrawal from the world into what the Mahāyāna had come to call 'Emptiness, Vacuity, the Void' could only be anathema to the Confucians. The self-styled Mahāyāna or 'Great Vehicle' differed from the Theravāda or 'School of the Elders' which we discussed last year in that it accused the latter of concentrating entirely on individual salvation or liberation without bothering very much about the liberation of others. This, according to the Mahāyāna, was selfish. The unselfishness of the Mahāyāna, on the other hand, was held to consist in its throwing open the doors of salvation to all. The goal of human endeavour remained Nirvāna—the snuffing out of human life as we know it—but no one was entitled to enter Nirvāna without doing his utmost to bring as many of his fellow men as he could along with him into that beatific state. Those who did so were known as Bodhisattvas, 'Beings of Enlightenment', who willingly deferred their own Nirvāna in order to save others. In fact a whole host of these beings sprang up to form what was in fact a whole new pantheon in a religion that had once paid scant attention to the traditional gods and had denied both God and the Absolute. The Buddha himself had now become the Absolute, and the Bodhisattvas, who were for the most part imaginary beings and not men at all, were his apostles whose function it was to deliver men from time into eternity, from their carnal nature into the one true Buddha-nature.

The School of the Elders or, as the Mahāyāna preferred to call them, the 'Defective Vehicle' (*hīnayāna*), had regarded 'liberation' as being final deliverance from this world and all its works, the separation of the eternal from the transient, of spirit from matter. It was a thoroughly gnostic dualism of spirit and matter which in the West was to seep into Christianity and later into Islam through the mediation of the Manichees, traditionally regarded by the Christians themselves as the *pessima haeresium*. In China it represented the complete antithesis of Confucianism.

The Buddha himself had been sensible enough to avoid metaphysics like the pest on the very reasonable ground that theorizing in the void about the Void was not conducive to liberation: it was simply a waste of time. The Mahāyāna did not follow him in this, but preferred to elaborate systems of metaphysics, the very obscurity of which was designed to make nonsense of metaphysics itself and together with it all rational (or, as they would say, dualist) thought. Of them I can only say what St. François de Sales said in another context: 'I cannot criticize authors or authorize criticism of a doctrine I do not understand.'[1] All that need be said is that this extremely irksome variety of what is really anti-metaphysics, by declaring all dualities to be unreal, had to admit the unreality of the ultimate duality of Nirvāna and *saṁsāra*—eternity and time—too. This considerable modification of the Buddha's message brought the Buddhists very much closer to the nature mysticism of the Taoists: it did not bring them any nearer to the Confucians. For even the Confucians, in a characteristic attempt to 'harmonize' Taoist and Buddhist ideas within a 'grand synthesis' of their own, could not stomach the hard core of Buddhism— escape from the world and refusal to allow it any importance or reality at all. To choose this way of escape for oneself might be selfish: to try to inflict it on others, the Confucians thought, as Yudhishthira had also thought in the Hindu context, was doubly selfish. And so the Mahāyāna, which had not scrupled to accuse the perfected monks of the School of the Elders of selfishness, was in its turn subjected to the same accusation by the outraged humanity and human kindness of the Confucian *litterati*.

The charge was not unjustified, for however much the Buddhists might deny the reality of a self, they nevertheless attached exclusive importance to the inner life (the life 'of the self', *ajjhattaṁ* as it is called in Pāli), not to the promotion of a harmony based on human relationships and human

[1] *Traité de l'amour de Dieu, préface.*

kindness within the totality of human kind. They did not seek to develop their personality in the context of sense, emotion, and reason: all this they ruthlessly suppressed. They did not seek to transform the 'equilibrium' inherent in Nature into a 'harmony' in which man helped Nature to achieve a higher stage of evolution: they merely 'became disgusted and wanted to get rid of sense-perception . . . and be like dry wood and dead ashes. But this is impossible,' the neo-Confucian Ch'êng Hao exclaims,[1] 'it is only possible with death'. Buddhism, instead of reinforcing human relations, destroyed them. 'When it comes to Zen, however,' Chu Hsi, himself the author of the Confucian 'Grand Synthesis', said, 'from the very start it wipes out all moral principles completely. Looked at this way, Zen has done the greatest harm.'[2] This may or may not be true, but given the resurgence of Zen in our times it is worth bearing in mind.

Once Confucianism had become the official cult and once the new religion from India had become firmly rooted in China, Confucianism itself could scarcely remain unaffected; for Buddhism was concerned with an aspect of reality that Confucianism had left largely out of account— the timeless ground of all existent things which the Mahāyāna called the 'Buddha-nature' and which they had come to regard as the One Absolute Principle in which Nirvāna itself inhered and over against which the phenomenal world should be viewed. The essential dualism of the Buddha's original teaching had now been bridged, and Nirvāna and *samsāra* were reconciled in the Great Emptiness which was itself identical with the Buddha-nature, equally present and equally absent in the objective world and in the deep places of the human heart. This was not unlike the Taoist 'Way': and Buddhism and Taoism thus converged on what seems to be the core and goal of all 'natural' religion, that Infinite Being which is or should be the subject of all Gifford Lectures, that 'unity in diversity' which constitutes order, harmony, proportion, integrity, and beauty, of which St. François de Sales had spoken, that 'one mode of being' which is 'changeless and undivided in all contingent beings, divided as they are' which the Bhagavad-Gītā[3] had discerned.

Buddhism and Confucianism had started from two opposite poles of the religious spectrum, the first seeing reality only in the 'unborn, not made, not become, not compounded', the second granting reality only to the natural order as manifested in the regularities of a reasonable cosmos and in the human order of harmonious and virtuous living which had grown out of it. The one, because it accepted the transmigration of souls as a fact, rejected all the mutability of life for the glacial immortality of perfect

[1] Chan, op. cit., p. 533.   [2] Ibid., p. 647.   [3] 18: 20.

death, the other accepted and welcomed life and sought to perfect it. Between the two stood the Taoists in that they affirmed life as the permanent principle of existence in which the death of the individual was no more than the transformation of one mode of life into another and its reabsorption into the whole.

Neo-Confucianism sought to integrate the Way of Man and the ethical system that it enshrined into the broader context of the Way of Heaven. Its problem was the same as Yudhishthira's had been in India: how to reconcile the moral imperative of which Yudhishthira was the Hindu incarnation with an Absolute which seemed to have no care for human affairs. The easy way out was to identify the two and to attribute to the Absolute, to Heaven, or to God human characteristics he or it did not obviously possess. This was central in early Confucianism and it could be said: 'The highest human kindness rests with Heaven, for Heaven is human kindness itself.'[1] In other words, everything that exists must be good and work together for the good.

It is true that within the Confucian tradition itself there had always been a tendency to trace the origin of all existence back to a first cause which they called the 'Great Ultimate',[2] but since this had little bearing on the conduct of human affairs here on earth, the idea remained undeveloped until the eleventh century A.D., the great century of neo-Confucian thought. The first of these neo-Confucian thinkers was Chou Tun-yi who was so influenced by Taoist and Buddhist ideas that one of his contemporaries referred to him contemptuously as a 'poor Zen fellow'.

With Chou Tun-yi the process of syncretism that was to result in the Grand Synthesis of Chu Hsi becomes apparent. The Great Ultimate, which, out of deference to the Buddhists, he also calls the 'Non-Ultimate', is the source of motion and rest, the *yang* and the *yin*, which together give rise to all things in their myriad transformations. 'It is', however, 'man alone who receives these in their highest excellence, and therefore he is the most intelligent. His corporeal form appears, and his spirit develops consciousness. The five cardinal virtues of his nature are aroused by, and react to, the external world and engage in activity; good and evil are distinguished and human affairs take place.'[3]

The Great Ultimate is not a spiritual principle, rather it is the source of all change, the unmoved Mover from which all dualities, including good and evil, arise. Chou Tun-yi's successor, Chang Tsai, is more specific.

---

[1] De Bary, op. cit., p. 179.

[2] It first appears in the so-called 'Great Appendix' to the *Book of Changes*: see de Bary, op. cit., p. 212.

[3] Ibid., p. 513.

The 'Great Vacuity', as he prefers to call it, in consonance with the Buddhists and Taoists again, is matter[1] in its most subtle form. Material things come together from this Great Vacuity and disintegrate into it again. 'When, in the midst [of this universal operation] the sage fulfils the Way to the utmost, and identifies himself [with the universal processes of appearance and disappearance] without partiality, his spirit is preserved in the highest degree.'[2] The sage, then, identifies himself with the whole universe of matter in its perpetual flux. This is, of course, the cosmic consciousness of R. M. Bucke which we discussed last year and which crops up again and again in the Upanishads:

> It moves [it is *yang*]. It does not move [it is *yin*].
> It is far, yet it is near.
> It is within this whole universe,
> And yet it is without it.
>
> Those who see all beings in [this] Self,
> And the Self in all beings,
> Will never shrink from it.[3]

The first duality to arise out of the Great Vacuity is that of male and female: Heaven is the male, earth the female. Therefore 'Heaven is my father and earth my mother, and even such a small creature as I finds an intimate place in their midst'.[4] Thus it is filial piety that binds the universe together in equilibrium and harmony. Heaven or God is the father of all, and 'even such a small creature as I' will 'rejoice in Heaven and have no anxiety. This is filial piety at its purest.'[5] Filial piety, because it is love at its purest, enables the sage to identify himself with what he loves. 'Therefore that which extends throughout the universe I regard as my body and that which directs the universe I consider as my nature. All people are my brothers and sisters, and all things are my companions',[6] the Emperor thus being no more than the first-born of Heaven and my eldest brother.

Because the universe is man's 'body', nothing in it is alien to him, and to renounce the world as the Buddhists do or to write it off as an illusion is to blaspheme against the Way: only 'he who puts his moral nature into practice and brings his physical existence to complete fulfilment can match [the Way]'.[7]

---

[1] This seems to be the obvious translation of the Chinese word *ch'i*. In his book *Two Chinese Philosophers* (London, Lund Humphries, 1958), Dr. A. C. Graham translates it as 'ether' which, he disarmingly says, 'means so little that it cannot be positively misleading' (p. 31). The word, however, seems to mean precisely what Marx understood by 'matter' —matter in motion from which life and consciousness develop.

[2] De Bary, op. cit., pp. 521–2.   [3] *Īśā* Upanishad 5–6.
[4] De Bary, op. cit., p. 524.   [5] Ibid., p. 525.
[6] Ibid., p. 524.   [7] Ibid., p. 525.

Chang Tsai was a friend of the brothers Ch'êng Hao and Ch'êng Yi who contributed more than anyone else to the Grand Synthesis of Chu Hsi which was to become the norm of neo-Confucianism for six centuries— the same six centuries during which, in Europe, the philosophy of Thomas Aquinas became the norm for Catholic philosophy. Ch'êng Yi accepted the teaching of Chang Tsai in its main outlines, but to the concept of *ch'i*, the matter-in-motion of Marx, he added that of *li*, usually translated as 'principle'. Superficially this 'dualism' bears some resemblance to the dualism of the Sānkhya-Yoga in India which made the sharpest distinction between matter (*prakriti*) and spirit (*purusha*). With Ch'êng Yi, however, the distinction is an intellectual one only; *li* and *ch'i* are not as 'spirit' and 'matter' are in the Sānkhya, totally separate principles which combine fortuitously and unnaturally to form an uneasy mixture in man only to be separated again for ever. Rather *li* is the principle according to which *ch'i* operates. 'All things under Heaven can be understood by their *li*,'[1] Ch'êng Yi writes. *Li*, then, is the *ratio*, the 'Logos', of *ch'i*, that by and according to which things are as they are. *Li* is both the Logos of Johannine Christianity and the unchanging laws of Nature that remain unchanged in and behind the material flux, on which Engels insisted so much in his later works. *Li* or principle is one—eternally good and the same in all men. The obvious inequalities in the physical, mental, and spiritual endowment of men are not due to any difference in principle, they are due to what in him derives from matter, for it is matter that differentiates, not principle. 'All that has form is matter; only the Way is without form.'[2]

Principle is one: it does not and cannot change; matter is the source of multiplicity and variety. It is shot through with the cosmic duality of *yin* and *yang*, rest and motion, female and male, soft and hard, and so on. It is a continuum like water,[3] the perpetual flux of Heraclitus, the *saṁsāra* of the Buddhists and Hindus. Yet if *ch'i* corresponds to *saṁsāra*—matter in the Marxian sense—*li* is not Nirvāna, for it is never divorced from *ch'i*. You can separate principle from matter in thought, you cannot do so in practice. 'There is only one principle in the world', and this principle is identical in all things. 'You may extend it over the four seas and it is everywhere true.'[4] Like Brahman in the Indian tradition it is one, but it appears to be divided. 'All things have principles, for example that by which fire is hot and that by which water is cold',[5] but these apparently contradictory principles are in the last analysis reducible to one, and this

---

[1] De Bary, op. cit., p. 527.
[2] Quoted by A. C. Graham, op. cit., p. 34.
[3] Graham, ibid.
[4] De Bary, op. cit., p. 527.
[5] Graham, op. cit., p. 8.

is equally present in the human heart and in the objective world. 'There is a *single* principle in outside things and in the self; as soon as "that" is understood "this" becomes clear. This is the way to unite external and internal. The scholar should understand everything, at one extreme the height of heaven and thickness of earth, at the other *that by which* a single thing is *as it is*.'[1] This is simply the *tathatā*, the 'suchness' or 'thusness' of Mahāyāna Buddhism, appearing in Confucian dress; but in neo-Confucianism it is given a positive and concrete content.

As the one principle of all things *li* is identical with Tao, the 'Way'; but when the two are contrasted Tao means the Great Ultimate seen as the principle in all principles, while *li* means the apparently distinct principles inherent in individual things. In this case 'principle' corresponds more or less to the Platonic 'forms' or 'ideas', Tao to the 'idea of the Good'. 'The word *Tao* is all-embracing; the *li* are so many veins inside the *Tao*: . . . the word *Tao* refers to the whole, the word *li* to the detail.'[2] To take a concrete example from Chu Hsi: 'This armchair is an object [or instrument]; that it can be sat in is its principle; the human body is an object, that it speaks and moves is its principle.'[3] *Li*, then, is both that in virtue of which a thing is what it is and that *for* which it exists. In Aristotelian parlance it is both the 'formal' and the 'final' cause of a thing. Yet ultimately all principles are reducible to one. In the words of Dr. Graham 'the great innovation of the Ch'êng brothers is to claim that "the innumerable principles amount to one principle", for which "heaven", the "decree", and the "Way" are merely different names, thus transforming a natural order conceived after the analogy of human society into a rational'—and one might add, a moral—'order'.[4]

Principle in man manifests itself as 'human nature' which, in the Ch'êng brothers as in Mencius, is good. This nature is identical with the cardinal virtues of human kindness, justice, propriety, and wisdom. There is no evil in it: this can only come from matter which is not evil in itself but contains the potentiality or capacity for evil. 'Human nature comes from Heaven'[5] and is therefore 'universally good':[6] 'capacity'[7] comes from matter',[8] and 'in cases where there is evil it is because of one's capacity. Human nature is the same as principle, and principle is the same whether in the sage Emperors Yao and Shun or in the common man in the street. Matter, which may be either clear or turbid, is the source of capacity. Men

---

[1] Ibid.   [2] Ibid., p. 12.   [3] Ibid., p. 17.
[4] Ibid., p. 11.   [5] De Bary, op. cit., p. 528.   [6] Ibid., p. 529.
[7] So de Bary: Graham prefers 'talent'. Aristotelians would say 'potency' or 'potentiality'. 'Principle' is good in itself, 'matter' has the potentiality of both good and evil.
[8] De Bary, op. cit., p. 528.

endowed with clear matter are wise, while those endowed with turbid matter are stupid.'[1] It is matter and only matter that accounts for the unequal endowment of different men. You might compare principle to water in a stream and matter to what happens to it in the stream. 'The nature of water is to be clear, still, and smooth like a mirror, but when it strikes sand and stone, or when the ground underlying it is not level, it immediately begins to move violently. Or when the wind blows over it, it develops waves and currents. But are these the nature of water?' Of course not. And so just 'as without water there cannot be waves, so without nature there cannot be feelings'.[2] In other words, principle in human nature is the substance for which matter provides the accidents: without principle matter is unthinkable. The substance being perfectly good, it follows that any acquired accidents cannot make it better: they can only make it worse.

In the Gospel Jesus says: 'Why do you call me good? No one is good but God alone.'[3] This has been interpreted as meaning that the 'goodness' of God so far transcends goodness as understood by human beings that to speak of him as 'good' can only mislead. Ch'êng Yi was one of the few neo-Confucian philosophers who did not make this distinction. For most of them principle and human nature, which is principle as it appears in the human sphere, can only be called good in a very special sense, for in ordinary speech good and evil are a pair of opposites like male and female, soft and hard, hot and cold, and so on, whereas in the Way—in the Great Ultimate—there is no duality.

It had been said in the *Mean*:

> What Heaven bestows on man is called human nature; to follow our nature is called the Way. Cultivating the Way is called education. The Way cannot be separated from us for a moment. What can be separated from us is not the Way.[4]

Evil, then, is that which *appears* to separate us from the Way. In the ideal world it cannot be said to exist, but in human affairs it is very active. Chu Hsi, the author of the Confucian 'Grand Synthesis', solves the dilemma in this way:

> Original human nature is an all-pervading perfection not contrasted with evil. This is true of what Heaven has endowed in the self. But when it operates in man, there is the differentiation of good and evil. When man acts in accord with it, there is goodness. When man acts out of accord with it, there is evil. . . . We fall into evil only when our actions are not in accord with our original nature.[5]

---

[1] De Bary, op. cit., p. 529.   [2] Ibid., p. 528.
[3] Mark 10: 18; Luke 18: 19.   [4] Above, p. 260.
[5] De Bary, op. cit., p. 547.

But, Chu Hsi adds, 'I hold that the good at the source of our being and the good in the process of life involving both good and evil are not two different things. They merely refer to two different states before and after it has merged into activity.'

Evil derives from 'turbid' matter which seems to distort the nature of principle itself just as mud seems to change the nature of water. Principle, however, remains ever the same as does Brahman in the Bhagavad-Gītā. You might put it like this: principle is the blueprint of human nature, but it needs matter to be actualized as a machine. The actual character of a man will therefore vary in accordance with the matter that goes into his making just as the quality of the actual machine will depend on the quality of the materials of which it is made and of the workmen who put it together. So too with men, if the matter of which they are composed is defective, they will incline towards evil; if it is of good quality, they will be good. The variety in the actualizations of the blueprint does not affect the excellence of the blueprint itself.

It has been said that Ch'êng Yi's philosophy is a dualism while his brother Ch'êng Hao's was a monism. This is not quite true since Ch'êng Yi never says that principle can be wholly divorced from matter. He did not, however, recognize the 'Great Ultimate' of his predecessors as being an entity higher than both principle and matter. Ch'êng Hao not only accepted it but was bold enough to identify it with the great Confucian concept of *jên*, 'human kindness' or humanity.

Chang Tsai had said: 'That which extends throughout the universe I regard as my body, and that which directs the universe I consider as my nature.'[1] This all-pervading principle Ch'êng Hao identifies with *jên*, in this context probably best translated simply as 'humanity'. And so it is 'the human man [who] forms one body with all things comprehensively. Justice, propriety, wisdom, and good faith are all [expressions of] humanity. [One's duty] is to understand this truth and preserve [this] humanity with sincerity and seriousness. That is all. There is no need to avoid things or restrict oneself. . . . It is necessary to avoid things when one is mentally negligent, but if one is not negligent, what is the necessity for avoidance? . . . This is the way to preserve humanity. As humanity is preserved, the self and the other are then identified.'[2] You have but to realize the oneness of all things in this ultimate principle of human goodness and thereby see that nothing can be alien to you; then there will be no need for self-abnegation as the Buddhists seemed to think. But then the Buddhists were not gentlemen. 'For the training of a gentleman,'

[1] Above, p. 271.   [2] De Bary, op. cit., pp. 559–60.

however, 'there is nothing better than to become broad and impartial and to respond spontaneously to all things as they come.'[1] These sentiments are more Taoist than Confucian, nor are they at all foreign to Zen Buddhism. This is not surprising, for neo-Confucianism, despite its frequent attacks on the Buddhists, was more or less consciously absorbing into itself the basic metaphysical principles of the rival schools and transforming them into a 'Grand Synthesis' which still remained characteristically Confucian, human, and humane.

It was Chu Hsi (1130–1200) who was to give the Grand Synthesis its definitive form. From Ch'êng Yi he inherited the 'dualist' analysis of existence into *li*, 'principle', or, as we shall now call it, Logos, and *ch'i*, matter-in-motion: from Ch'êng Hao he inherited the concept of the Great Ultimate. This Great Ultimate is the Logos of all *logoi*, the 'principle of the highest good'. It is one, single, and entire, and yet it is wholly present in each one of the 'ten thousand things', just as in the Bhagavad-Gītā the God, Krishna, indwells wholly every single soul,[2] or, as in Catholicism, the God-Man, Christ, is held to be wholly present in every single consecrated wafer throughout the world:

The Great Ultimate is simply the Logos (*li*) of Heaven and earth and the ten thousand things. . . . Fundamentally there is only one Great Ultimate, yet each of the ten thousand things has been endowed with it and each in itself possesses the Great Ultimate in its entirety.[3]

As in the Indian tradition the relationship of the highest Principle as it is in itself to that same Principle indwelling individual souls is compared to the moon and its reflection. 'There is only one moon in the sky but when its light is scattered upon rivers and lakes, it can be seen everywhere. It cannot be said that the moon has been split.'[3] This, in the Christian and Muslim traditions, is the distinction between God and the image of God in man. This may not be the God of devotional Christianity, but it is certainly the 'God of the philosophers' of whom Pascal spoke but whom he did not claim to know because he seemed not to be a living God: it is the God of Plotinus and Pseudo-Dionysius and all the Christian metaphysical mystics who depend on them. It is essentially the God of all apophatic theology; but Confucianism could not leave things quite as imprecise as that, for the Great Ultimate is also *jên*, 'an appellation for all virtues and the highest good in Heaven and earth, man and things'.[4] It is, then, not only that in virtue of which a thing is what it is and that for which

[1] De Bary, op. cit., p. 561. [2] Gītā 18: 61, etc.
[3] De Bary, op. cit., p. 539. [4] Ibid., p. 540.

a thing is; it is also the moral law that is the blueprint for man. Individual men are born and die, but death means absorption not simply into Nature but into the Logos or principle of absolute Goodness; for 'the nature of man and things is nothing but Logos and cannot be spoken of in terms of integration and disintegration. That which integrates to produce life and disintegrates to produce death is only matter, and what we call the spirit, the soul, and consciousness are all the effects of matter.'[1]

As in early Hinduism, Buddhism, and Marxism death—which in Confucianism is final since there is no reincarnation—means the extinction of anything that can be called personality, since what we call soul and spirit have their origin in matter. What 'survives' is human nature only—the Logos of man and all things, which is also human kindness.

What the neo-Confucians had tried to do, and what Rousseau was to try to do long after them, was to equate the mystic vision of the oneness and goodness of all things with human virtue and conscience. They did not and could not succeed because the vision of the mystics does not correspond to life as we experience it. If, absolutely, it is true, empirically it is a lie.

If, however, the *grand siècle* of neo-Confucianism left the strait and practical Way of their founder, the last of the great Confucians, Wang Yang Ming (1472–1529), did his best to bring them back a little nearer to the Mean. In India it had been said that 'all works without exception in knowledge find their consummation',[2] and this summed up the dominant trend in both Hinduism and Buddhism. Not only does life on earth have no point or purpose: it is foolish even to look for such a purpose since 'knowledge' of the eternal annuls and abolishes all man's striving. Wang Yang Ming turned this maxim upside-down: for him 'knowledge is the crystallization of the will to act and action is the task of carrying out that knowledge; knowledge is the beginning of action and action is the completion of knowledge'.[3]

After all, mystics are few and far between and the men who are unfortunate enough to be burdened with 'turbid' matter are the great majority. As to the mystic, he 'has already accomplished his task as soon as he apprehends the original substance, penetrating the self, other people, things internal and things external at the same time. On the other hand, there are inevitably those whose minds are dominated by habits so that the original substance of the mind is obstructed. I therefore teach them definitely and sincerely to do good and remove evil in their will and thoughts. When they become accomplished at this and the impurities of

---

[1] Ibid., p. 538.   [2] Bhagavad-Gītā 4: 33.   [3] De Bary, op. cit., p. 579.

the mind are completely eliminated, the original substance of the mind will become wholly clear.'[1]

It is to the credit of the neo-Confucians that they squarely faced the problem of evil, which is more than the Hindus or Taoists ever did. Like the Buddhists, St. Paul in the Epistle to the Romans, the Gnostics, and the Manichees, they saw in matter the origin of evil, but, being Confucians, they could not identify the two. Evil was an ultimately inexplicable deviation from the Mean. Had their thesis that the Way of Heaven and the Way of Man were simply two facets of the same Perfection been not only true but seen to be true, then all our problems would have been solved and religion itself would have become superfluous. Unfortunately their thesis remained a thesis, and what might have been a magnificent ideal was slowly and inexorably strangled to death by being made the obligatory subject in the examination of bureaucrats-to-be. For ideas, for literature, for art, and indeed for life itself this is the kiss of death.

[1] De Bary, op. cit., pp. 580-1.

XIV

WHAT IS ZEN?

FOR six hundred years neo-Confucianism remained the official philosophy of Imperial China. For the same number of years Thomism remained the official philosophy of the Catholic Church—from the fourteenth to the twentieth century. Neo-Confucianism disappeared with the collapse of the Empire because the one was dependent on the other. Throughout the nineteenth century it was the hope and reasoned belief of all shades of progressive opinion that the Roman Church would perish under the dead weight of its own conservatism and its blank opposition to the forces of revolution just as the neo-Confucian establishment was to do in China. This has not yet happened—for two reasons, it would appear. First, unlike China, Europe, since the collapse of the Roman Empire, was a peninsula of barbarians lacking any principles of coherence. With its 'conversion' to Christianity the Roman Church sought to impose on it a unity based on the Christian religion and the memory of an officially Christian Roman Empire. This rather artificial uniformity, however, had no deep roots among the barbarian peoples, it had not the immemorial tradition on which the Confucians could draw in China: it was 'apparent, verbal, and therefore fictitious',[1] a Latin crust imposed on a 'Gothic' reality. That this imposing façade had been smashed in the sixteenth century may have been a disaster, but it was scarcely surprising. The Church, not content with its allotted role of being the mystical body of Christ on earth, had also become a secular 'establishment' with all the trappings of secular pomp and power; and a Christian 'establishment' seems to me at least as contrary to Nature as a dissenting Confucianism: for Confucius thought always in terms of the state and of man's place in the state. Had neo-Confucianism developed more in accordance with its own principles and had it been less eager to absorb and adapt Taoist and Buddhist ideals, it might quite naturally have moved towards a Marxist solution in which 'the free development of each [would have been] the free development of all'. The early Christians too thought in terms of individual salvation within the framework of a Church which was in this world but not of it. That the world should persecute the Church had been

---

[1] Above, p. 6.

foreseen by Jesus himself; but that, with the conversion of Constantine, the Church of God should have all but identified itself with the Empire of Caesar, and that the greatest doctor of the Christian West should have preached the persecution not only of pagans but of dissenters too, he could, humanly speaking, scarcely have foreseen: for this was indeed, in Nietzsche's words, an *Umwertung aller Werte*—a revaluation of all Christian values. For a Christian establishment, whether it be of throne and altar, of bourgeoisie and altar, or even of proletariat and altar, would seem to me to be a contradiction in terms. In Confucianism such a development follows naturally on the Confucian premises: in Christianity it turns the original premises upside-down.

The second reason why after six hundred years the neo-Confucian domination collapsed irretrievably and the Roman Church did not would seem to be that Confucianism had ceased to be a religion in any real sense: it was simply the dominant philosophy rather like Stoicism in the Roman Empire. It had lost its roots in the everyday practice of religion and had not, on the more esoteric level, developed techniques of contemplation which could rival or supplant those of the Buddhists. It had become a mystical philosophy largely divorced from both mystical practice and mystical superstition. With the abolition of the famous civil service examination and the class of the *litterati* which had produced it and which it had in its turn produced, it died of inanition, just as Buddhism died in India once the Muslims had suppressed the physical centre of their faith, the monasteries. Roman Catholicism, on the other hand, did not die because Thomism, though the official philosophy of the Church, was never much more than an intellectual game played with zest and rancour and small regard for fair play by theologians for theologians. The spectators, whether Catholic or Protestant, might applaud or boo; but the children of the Enlightenment, the precursors of our present secular society, were already saying with Voltaire, 'Oh, those fat volumes of theology—of course I never open them, nor does anyone else'.[1] For them, as for most of us, theology, which once had the impudence to call itself the 'queen of the sciences', had become the plaything of desiccated mandarins. As to the Roman Catholic faithful, then as now, they went to mass; and it was there that, for them, time and eternity met; from there they could catch a glimpse of a world that did not pass away. The average Confucian was not thus provided for. This was the Confucian weakness.

And yet neo-Confucianism was perhaps the most serious attempt ever made in Eastern Asia to solve Yudhishthira's dilemma—how to bring

---

[1] Voltaire, *Candide*, ch. xxv.

together what the Confucians called 'wisdom', that is, the ability to distinguish right from wrong, with 'wisdom' as defined by the Buddhists and Hindus, namely, the *transcending* of right and wrong and all the opposites. It did not fully succeed perhaps because this is a dilemma which cannot be perfectly resolved; but at least, despite the pantheistic mysticism of its latterday saints, it never doubted that the dilemma was real.

If we compare the history of Confucianism with that of Hinduism we can say that Confucianism starts with a clear idea of a personal God, whether he is called Heaven or the Supreme Lord, and ends in a qualified monism in which 'God' is dismissed as a popular term for the 'principle' or Logos which unifies all *logoi* and all material things into a natural and moral whole; while Hinduism, if we discount its earliest beginnings, starts with a full-fledged pantheism in which God and the material world, God and the human self, are gloriously intermingled and intertwined, and only then proceeds to disentangle this God from both matter and spirit and to elevate him to a position in which he both transcends transcendence and indwells immanence, thus becoming the one true object of love, for he is both the principle of your own being within you and the totally other without. The movement of Hinduism is from pantheism to theism, that of Confucianism is from theism to pantheism. But to state the matter thus baldly is to miss the point of Confucianism.

What neo-Confucianism was trying to do was to recreate within the context of the Chinese Empire that equilibrium and harmony which were seen to hold sway in all natural things: it was trying to translate into a political context the Taoist mystical insight of the unity of all things in the self. This was a social and collective concern that remained foreign to both the Taoists and the Buddhists. In Buddhism mystical experience which, for the 'School of the Elders', meant simply the transcendence of matter and of time and space which condition matter, and which, for the 'Great Vehicle', meant the discovery of the Buddha-nature which is the Absolute in oneself, was and can only be an individual experience (Pāli *ajjhattaṁ*, Sanskrit *adhyātmam*); it cannot be a shared experience, let alone a collective one. It matters not at all that the Buddhists of all schools deny to the self all that is specifically human: the fact remains that your Nirvāna, your *samādhi*, and your Satori (as the Japanese call it) can never be my Nirvāna, *samādhi*, and Satori. Buddhism, like all contemplative religion, is and must be a religion of solitary salvation, not a bond of union which unites individuals in and around a divine centre. And this is precisely what Confucianism had tried to achieve.

Neo-Confucianism, however, owed much to Buddhism which appeared in China in its Mahāyāna form. Buddhism had always been adaptable; and the Mahāyāna or 'Great Vehicle' far exceeded the old-fashioned Theravāda or 'School of the Elders' in this respect. As the *Great* Vehicle it was capacious enough to make room for all who were prepared to mount it in its course towards Nirvāna and beyond. And just as in India Hinduism divided into an absolutist and monist wing on the one hand and a theistic and devotional one on the other, so too in China did the Great Vehicle follow this twofold course. On the one hand the Buddha, who knew nothing of the Absolute, was himself elevated to that supreme eminence and manifested himself from there as the omniscient, self-subsistent, and compassionate Lord of all the worlds: on the other he became the inner principle of all things, identical in all things, the 'Buddha-nature' in each and every man which can burst through in a liberating flash if one only strives with sufficient earnestness and in accordance with a recognized spiritual discipline to attain to it. This Buddha-nature is indistinguishable from the 'principle' or Logos of the neo-Confucians. The first, the theistic, tendency finds its most complete expression in a scripture called *The Lotus of the Wonderful Law*, the second in the 'meditation' school nowadays known to most of us under its Japanese name 'Zen'. The first is a conscious reaction against the apparent self-centredness of the School of the Elders; the second claims on the contrary to be the purest distillation of the early teaching.

In its own way the *Lotus Sūtra* is as important a development within Buddhism as is the Bhagavad-Gītā within Hinduism. In it the Buddha is not only the infallible teacher but God, the 'self-subsistent' and 'Highest Person', as Krishna is in the Gītā. And just as in the Gītā Nirvāna is only a stage on the way to the final bliss which consists in loving and being loved by God and in entering into his being, so too in the *Lotus Sūtra* Nirvāna is represented as being only a rest on the way to the ultimate goal which is the Buddha-nature itself. What is meant by the 'Buddha-nature' we shall have to consider when we come to discuss Zen.

Like the synoptic gospels the *Lotus Sūtra* teaches in parables. There is, however, nothing particularly arresting in this since parables had always been a favourite didactic method with the Buddhists. What is arresting, however, is that one of these parables is so like that of the prodigal son that we cannot help suspecting that we have here a case of direct borrowing. This should not surprise us, for in the first centuries A.D. central Asia was a great melting-pot of religions—the Buddhists being followed by the Nestorian Christians and then by the Manichees who were open to ideas from both sides and were wittingly or unwittingly the mediators of ideas between the other two. Moreover, borrowings from Buddhism into Christianity are well known. The story of the Buddha's 'Great Renunciation'—his refusal of his royal inheritance and his adoption of the life of a religious mendicant in search of enlightenment—reappears, through Manichaean and Muslim mediation, in a wholly Christian and Trinitarian setting in the delightful tale of *Barlaam and Josaphat*[1] which gained immense popularity in both Eastern and Western Christianity in the Middle Ages. The story has been enlarged and embellished from a variety of sources, but the frame-story remains unmistakably Buddhist, and, despite the theistic and Trinitarian trappings, its message too is unmistakably Buddhist, not Christian—the impermanence and worthlessness of the world, the evil of passion, the loathsomeness of the body, the elimination of the ego, and the exaltation of death as 'rest from the troubles of this world'.[2] So popular did the story become that Josaphat, who is no less a person that the Buddha himself (his name being a corruption of *Bodhisattva*, the Buddha's title before he attained Buddahood), came to be acknowledged as a saint of the universal Church both in its Eastern Orthodox and its Roman Catholic branches.

Conversely, in the *Lotus Sūtra* the story of the prodigal son is recognizably the same as the parable preserved in St. Luke. There are differences, of course—the envious elder brother has disappeared and the circumstances of the prodigal's return are different—but the point of the story remains: the rejoicing of the father at the return home of his wayward son and the son's realization of the folly of his ways.

The Buddhist version runs something like this:

Once upon a time there was a rich man who had only one son, but he left his father's house and stayed away for many, many years. Fortune, however, did not smile on him, and so in the end he returned to his father's house, saw his father living in great pomp and luxury, but did not recognize him. Overawed by so much splendour he said to himself: 'This must be a king, or someone of royal rank; it is no place for me to obtain anything for the hire of my labour. I had better go to some poor hamlet, where there is a place for letting out my labour, and food and clothing are easier to get. If I tarry here for long, I may suffer oppression and forced service.'[3]

---

[1] See particularly D. M. Lang, *The Wisdom of Balahvar*, London, Allen & Unwin, 1957; id., *The Balavariani*, do., 1966.

[2] Lang, *The Balavariani*, p. 64.

[3] W. E. Soothill, *The Lotus of the Wonderful Law* (tr. from the Chinese version), Oxford, 1930, p. 108.

The king meanwhile had recognized his son, was overjoyed, and sent his servants to fetch him back. They laid hold of him and would have carried him off by force, but the young man, fearing for his life, fell fainting to the ground. His father, seeing this, sent other messengers to him, telling him that he was free to do as he would. The young man, still overawed, preferred to go off to a poor hamlet in search of food and clothing. There he was hired as a scavenger, for which he received a daily wage. Seeing this, his father had compassion on him, went to him, won his confidence, and told him: 'From this time forth you shall be as my own begotten son.'[1] So the young man was made the steward of the rich man's goods, and the rich man, sensing the nearness of his own death, summoned all his attendants and declared to them that the young man was in truth his own begotten son and the rightful heir to all his riches.

The moral of the story is, however, not only as it is in Luke that the prodigal 'was dead and has come to life; he was lost and is found': it is rather that he, not knowing anything better, had, as a scavenger, been content 'to receive a day's wage of Nirvāna, . . . never having a mind to seek after the Great Vehicle',[2] which is the ultimate Buddha-wisdom. As in the Gītā, Nirvāna, the 'eternal rest' associated with death, seems to be the end of the mystic path. In this state, which is surely the 'prayer of quiet' of St. Teresa, 'there seems nothing left to desire',[3] so great is the peace and so tranquil is the joy. But, the Lotus Sūtra insists, this state, in which the senses and the mind are laid to rest and in which there is no consciousness except of changeless Being (or Not-Being, if you will; in this context it makes no difference), must be superseded if the Buddha-wisdom and the Buddha-nature are to be realized in their fullness. This Buddha-wisdom is that which transcends and negates all the opposites, including time and eternity, bondage and release, samsāra and Nirvāna: it is the ultimate Nirvāna (parinirvāna) beyond which it is impossible to go. Here, as in the great Tao, all things that can be named (dharmas) are seen as magic, or a dream, or an echo, devoid of substance as a plantain is devoid of pith. In reality there is neither bondage nor liberation; nothing really exists except the Buddha's 'transcendent body'. 'All things (dharmas) are the same and forever identical. He who knows this, knows Nirvāna, deathlessness, and peace.'[4]

This seems to mean exactly what the Gītā means when it speaks of the spiritually perfected whose 'minds are stilled in that which is ever the

[1] Soothill, op. cit., p. 110.   [2] Ibid., p. 113.
[3] St. Teresa of Avila, The Way of Perfection, ch. xxxi.
[4] Lotus Sūtra, 5: 78–82: Sanskrit text Saddharma-puṇḍarīkasūtram, Bibliotheca Indica, Calcutta, 1952, p. 101: E.T., H. Kern, Oxford, 1909, pp. 140–1.

same: for devoid of imperfection and ever the same is Brahman: therefore in Brahman stilled they stand'.[1] This is not just the perfect peace which is the privilege of individuals (*pratyātmam*) only,[2] but the complete vision of reality, the 'ultimate wisdom', which belongs to the Buddha alone but which can be shared by all since the one Buddha-nature indwells us all. In other words, to realize the Buddha-nature means to experience the eternal in oneself and at the same time to *see* it in and through everything else. And this, it seems to me, is what the Zen Buddhists mean by Satori.

What is Zen? This is a question that is almost certain to turn up in any book on Zen Buddhism. It is not a rhetorical question; for a rhetorical question usually implies the answer 'Yes' or 'No'. 'What is Zen?' on the other hand seems to be a question that expects both these answers and neither. Nor are the Zen Buddhists themselves very helpful, for, in theory at least, they abominate theory; and in this they are at one with the earliest tradition of the School of the Elders. In his book *Buddhism in China* Professor Kenneth Ch'en sure enough asks the question 'What is Ch'an (the Chinese form of Japanese "Zen")?' And for once he attempts to answer the question in more or less intelligible terms:

Zen [he says][3] has been described as an intuitive method of spiritual training aimed at the discovery of a reality in the innermost recesses of the soul, a reality that is the fundamental unity which pervades all the differences and particulars of the world. This reality is called the mind, or the Buddha-nature that is present in all sentient beings. In common with other Mahāyāna systems Zen teaches that this reality is *śūnya*, empty or void, inexpressible in words and inconceivable in thought. To illustrate this the Zen masters often resorted to silence or negation to express the truth. Being inexpressible and inconceivable, this reality or the Buddha-nature can only be apprehended by intuition directly, completely, and instantly. Intellectual analysis can only divide and describe and scratch the surface but cannot apprehend the fundamental reality. In order to apprehend it one must calm the mind and have no conscious thought. In any conscious thought there is the ego at work, making for the distinction between subject and object. Conscious thought also begets karma, which ties one down to the endless cycle of birth and death and breeds attachment to external objects. Such conscious efforts as heeding the teachings of the Buddha, reciting the sutras, worshipping the Buddha images, or performing the rituals are really of no avail and should be abandoned. Instead, one should allow the mind to operate freely, spontaneously, and naturally.

It was in accordance with this emphasis on freedom and spontaneity that the Zen master I-hsüan [founder of the Rinzai sect] called upon his disciples to 'kill everything that stands in your way. If you should meet the Buddha, kill the

---

[1] Gītā 5: 19.   [2] *Lotus Sūtra*, Kern, p. 81.
[3] I have substituted the more familiar 'Zen' for 'Ch'an' throughout the quoted passage.

Buddha. If you should meet the Patriarchs, kill the Patriarchs. If you should meet the arhats on your way, kill them too.' Another Zen master Hsüan-chien (782–865) called upon his followers to do just the ordinary things in life—to drink when thirsty, to eat when hungry, to pass water and move the bowels, and, when tired, to take a rest. 'There are neither Buddhas nor Patriarchs; Bodhidharma [the founder of Zen] was only an old bearded barbarian. Śākyamuni [the historical Buddha] and Kāśyapa [to whom he was supposed to have passed on his supreme teaching, that is, Zen] . . . are only dungheap coolies. . . . Nirvāna and bodhi (enlightenment) are dead stumps to tie your donkeys [to]. The twelve divisions of the sacred teachings are only lists of ghosts, sheets of paper fit only for wiping the pus from your boils.[1]

As we have seen, the Mahāyāna had defined the Buddha both as the Absolute and as the self-subsistent Lord, thereby reversing the whole sceptical trend that the Buddha had initiated. Zen, then, merely claimed to be reviving the original teaching in which there are only two things necessary—the end, which was enlightenment, and the means, the Law (*dharma*), the Buddha's noble eightfold path. In Islam two types of mysticism were contrasted—the 'drunken' and the 'sober'. The first was iconoclastic and antinomian, the second outwardly orthodox and inwardly controlled. So too in Zen two sects developed, Rinzai and Sōtō— the school of sudden enlightenment and that of gradual enlightenment. So far it has been the Rinzai sect that has been popularized in the West: it has been represented as being thoroughly iconoclastic and destructive of all traditional values: hence its appeal to a rootless and disillusioned generation. Add to this that it claims to be a 'do it yourself' religion from which God and his grace, the King 'up there' and his favouritism, have been rudely excluded, and its appeal to a generation for which the word 'God' has ceased to have any meaning is all the more readily comprehensible. And yet it *is* a religion in the sense that it claims to release us from all our nagging worries and to transport us into a condition in which we are utterly independent and free, unified in ourselves and united to all things, blessedly released from the ego, the source of *amour-propre*, and dissolved into the 'All'.

The iconoclastic teachings of the Zen Patriarchs which Professor Ch'en quotes, however, are to be taken with very much more than a pinch of salt. For Rinzai Zen, it may be, the Buddha and the Patriarchs and what they teach are no more than symbols; but they are traditionally Buddhist symbols and must be used when one is still on the way to enlightenment. Once the reality of enlightenment is experienced, however, the symbols will have served their purpose and can be quietly swept under the carpet.

[1] Kenneth K. S. Ch'en, *Buddhism in China*, Princeton, 1964, pp. 357–8.

The matter has been well summed up by a recent American convert to Zen:

> To be sure [he writes], Buddhism inspires in us the utmost respect for all Buddhas. But at the same time it admonishes us that eventually we must free ourselves from attachment to them. When we have experienced the mind of Shakyamuni Buddha and cultivated his incomparable virtues, we have realized the highest aim of Buddhism. Then we bid him farewell, shouldering the task of propagating his teachings, I have never heard of such an attitude in religions teaching belief in God.[1]

Mr. Kapleau, the author of these lines, seems in his innocence to have been unfamiliar with the phenomena of 'religionless Christianity', the 'death of God' theology, and the 'Christian atheism' with which Messrs. Hamilton and Altizer have made us familiar. The two phenomena, however, have this much in common. They, like the more readable and likeable Voltaire, denounce both traditional beliefs and the conventional 'bourgeois' ethos that these beliefs are held to sanction. Both represent the revolt of an apparently irrepressible 'religiosity' that claims to be done with 'religion'. With the Christian atheists we are not at present concerned: we are concerned with Zen, and in this lecture I propose to say a few words about Zen as interpreted by two Westerners who are yet thoroughly steeped in it and who hold that Zen can do much to revive and reanimate the flagging spirituality of the West. These two are Mr. Philip Kapleau and Fr. Enomiya-Lassalle. The first is an American journalist who has been converted to Zen and who has received from his teacher a certificate guaranteeing the genuineness of his enlightenment; the second is a German Jesuit who has for decades lived in Japan, has practised Zen in Zen monasteries under the supervision of Zen masters, and has taken Japanese nationality. Both are Zen enthusiasts and both agree that Zen is in rapid decline in Japan itself (according to Mr. Kapleau there are only ten genuine Zen masters left).[2] Despite this both see in Zen a saving power that can be utilized to infuse a little spirit into the materialism of the modern world. Mr. Kapleau would like to press it into the service of 'Americanism': Fr. Enomiya would introduce its contemplative techniques into the Roman Catholic Church. Both, interestingly enough, studied under the same master, Yasutani Roshi, himself a disciple of Harada Roshi who had sought to combine the more 'orthodox' and conscientiously ethical Sōtō school with the often violent and irrational methods of Rinzai.

[1] Philip Kapleau, *The Three Pillars of Zen*, New York, Harper & Row, 1966, p. 81.
[2] Ibid., p. 226.

The word 'Zen' derives from the Sanskrit *dhyāna*, meaning 'meditation' or 'contemplation': it is a contemplative technique with a minimal doctrinal content. What content there is is negative, as can be seen from Mr. Kapleau's proud boast that whereas the enlightened Buddhist can happily bid his saviour, the Buddha, farewell, he has 'never heard of such an attitude in religions teaching belief in God'. Hence, we are given to understand, the superiority of Zen.

Zen does, however, make certain assumptions, and in so far as these assumptions are retained and respected, it remains authentically Buddhist. It accepts the doctrines of reincarnation and of the unfailing operation of the law of *karma*—the law according to which all deeds, all thoughts, all emotions, and all aspirations, however 'good' they may be, bind us to this impermanent and unsubstantial world: it accepts the doctrine that there is a state of absolute freedom from *karma* and its effects in which the ego is forever left behind, and in which any action the body or mind may still engage in will be seen not to be the work of the ego but the free operation of the Buddha-nature, which is also the fathomless abyss of the Void. All this Mr. Kapleau seems to accept and in that he has every right to style himself a Buddhist.

In the School of the Elders *dharma* is the one royal road to Nirvāna: the Law which was devised by the Buddha himself from his own experience when he was still a Bodhisattva or Buddha-to-be is the one sure way to Nirvāna, the Buddha's own experience of enlightenment. So too in Zen, Zen techniques of meditation, of correct sitting, of correct breathing, and so on, practised under the experienced eye of a master both kindly and severe who is already enlightened, are the necessary discipline that will lead to enlightenment provided the aspirant's dispositions are right.

Zen, then, is a discipline of controlled and supervised meditation which claims to go back to the Buddha himself. So much for its alleged spontaneity. Its second founder was Hui-nêng, the sixth Patriarch of the sect who lived in the seventh century A.D., and his *Platform Scripture* is still the theoretical basis over against which the Zen techniques must be seen. On the retirement of the fifth Patriarch the monks of the community were invited to compete in writing a verse describing the true nature of man. The author of whichever verse the retiring Patriarch should judge to be the best would thereby succeed him. Accordingly the favourite in the line of succession wrote the following lines:

> The body is the tree of Perfect Wisdom,
> The mind is the stand of a bright mirror.

At all times diligently wipe it.
Do not allow it to become dusty.[1]

The symbol of the grimy mirror is more familiar to the early Christian and above all to the Muslim mystical tradition than it is in either India or the Far East, the mirror being the image of God in man and the dust and rust being the accumulation of sin that obscures it. At this stage, however, Hui-nêng, an intruder from the south, produced the following verses and they won him the succession:

> Fundamentally Perfect Wisdom has no tree.
> Nor has the bright mirror any stand.
> Buddha-nature is forever clear and pure.
> Where is there any dust?

Or again:

> The mind is the tree of Perfect Wisdom.
> The body is the stand of the bright mirror.
> The bright mirror is originally clear and pure.
> Where has it been defiled by any dust?[2]

The verses of Hui-nêng and those of his rival represent two different philosophical positions with which we are already familiar from the Indian tradition—an absolute monism equivalent to that of Śankara on the one hand, and a qualified monism corresponding to the system of Rāmānuja on the other. Hui-nêng, however, like his followers, attached little importance to theory, for in another passage, changing his metaphor, he says that the 'self-nature' (which is the same as the Buddha-nature) is in fact obscured by 'erroneous thoughts' just as the light of the sun is obscured by clouds. The only difference between the two positions would appear to be that the one denies all real existence to the 'clouds' while the other accepts them at their face value, as an opaque substance that effectively blinds the inner eye to the sun of the Buddha-nature,[3] in other words, as the 'turbid matter' of the neo-Confucians.

It would, however, be a waste of time to look for consistency either in Zen in general or in the *Platform Scripture* in particular. What, however, is interesting in Hui-nêng is the distinction he draws between true and false enlightenment—of Satori from what was later called the 'Zen sickness'.

One thing is certain and that is that there can be no enlightenment without total detachment from all things. We have met this in the Gītā and

---

[1] *The Platform Scripture*, tr. Wing-tsit Chan, New York, St. John's University Press, 1963, ch. vi (p. 35).

[2] Ibid., ch. viii (p. 41).   [3] Ibid., ch. xx (p. 59).

it is common to all mystical traditions. The difference between Zen, however, and theistic mysticism in general is that whereas for the latter detachment from all things has as its corollary *at*tachment to and in-herence in God, for Hui-nêng it is even more important to be detached from the tranquillity of Nirvāna than it is to be from the turmoil and shiftiness of this world of space and time. Vulgar attachment to the world is relatively harmless, but once you become attached to enlightenment itself, then you must beware, for that way lies madness:

> Good and learned friends, [the master warns,] I also know some who teach people to sit and look into the mind as well as to look at purity, so that the mind will not be perturbed and nothing will arise from it. Devoting their efforts to this, deluded people fail to become enlightened; consequently they are so attached to this method as to become insane. There have been several hundred such cases.[1]

'Right mindfulness' is one of the steps on the Noble Eightfold Path to which all Buddhists in theory subscribe: so you must be on the watch. When in the company of men, wish them well but remain detached: when active be detached from what you do: when inactive and totally absorbed in the practice of meditation, remain detached from your meditation. And 'while in the midst of Emptiness be free from Emptiness. To be attached to Emptiness merely means to increase ignorance.'[2] This is the Zen sickness described by Fr. Enomiya.[3] How to tell it from the true Satori or enlightenment, that is the question. And perhaps it is a question that only a qualified Zen master can answer. Or can he? For while he may have real insight within the limits of his own spiritual milieu, can we trust him when he says that 'seeing *Mu* ['Nothing' with a very big capital letter] is seeing God'?[4] Or what are we to make of a Jesuit who says that while for the Buddhist enlightenment means being one with Nature, it is for the Christian being one with God?[5] The Bhagavad-Gītā describes both these experiences and does not confuse them: though closely related they re-main distinct, as we saw last year[6] and shall see once again next week.[7]

There is no doubt that Zen Buddhists today interpret the experience of Satori or enlightenment as the realization of the oneness of all things[8] with oneself, and this brings with it a feeling of utter peace, tranquillity, and

---

[1] *The Platform Scripture*, ch. xiv (p. 49).   [2] Ibid., xlvi (p. 127).
[3] Hugo M. Enomiya-Lassalle, S.J., *Zen-Buddhismus*, Köln, J. P. Bachem, 1966, p. 68.
[4] Kapleau, op. cit., p. 254.
[5] H. M. Enomiya-Lassalle, S.J., *Zen — Weg zur Erleuchtung*, Wien, Herder, 1960, p. 94; E.T., London, Burns & Oates, 1967, p. 81.
[6] Above, pp. 132 ff.   [7] Below, p. 313.
[8] Enomiya, *Zen-Buddhismus*, p. 81, etc.; Kapleau, op. cit., pp. 96, 135, 137, 154, 191, 301, etc.

joy,[1] quite different, we are assured, from the 'Zen sickness'. This is, after all, the prime characteristic of the Nirvāna of the School of the Elders too: it is the 'fixed, still state of Brahman' of the Bhagavad-Gītā,[2] the 'Brahman that is ever the same'[3] through which one 'sees the self in all beings standing, all beings in the self'.[4] This is an absolute 'rest' that transcends the duality of motion and rest just as the 'Good' of the neo-Confucians transcends the duality of good and evil. So too Hui-nêng, bidding his last farewell to his disciples, says:

Sit still correctly for a while, so long as there is neither activity nor tranquillity, neither production nor annihilation, neither coming nor going, neither right nor wrong, and neither remaining nor going away. So long as you are quiet and tranquil, that is the great Way.[5]

This is to realize the Buddha-nature in oneself.

According to Yasutani Roshi there is a lesser enlightenment and a greater enlightenment. The lesser enlightenment or Nirvāna is, as I suggested last year, the *requies aeterna* or eternal peace of death: it is the snuffing out of life without hope or desire for eternal life, whatever we may understand by those mysterious words: it is 'death without rebirth'.[6] 'I see nothing enjoyable in this,' Indra had said in the *Chandogya* Upanishad. Nor did the Mahāyāna. Hence its reversion to the 'cosmic consciousness' of the Upanishads; for the Mahāyāna dogma of the identity of all things in an eternal Now and a ubiquitous Here, of the eternal flux of *samsāra* with the changeless peace of Nirvāna—the 'greater' enlightenment—is clearly what R. M. Bucke understood by 'cosmic consciousness' which, in his own words, 'shows the cosmos ... as entirely immaterial, entirely spiritual and entirely alive; it shows that death is an absurdity, that everyone and everything has eternal life; it shows that the universe is God and that God is the universe, and that no evil did or ever will enter into it'.[7] 'God', for Bucke, is of course the pantheistic God, the One which pervades the many. Given this difference, his 'cosmic consciousness' seems to be exactly what the Zen masters understand by Satori or enlightenment. Freud called it the 'oceanic feeling', and for Hui-nêng too 'sudden enlightenment ... is like the great ocean receiving the rivers and streams. The big body of water and the small bodies of water merge to form one body. This is seeing [one's own] nature.'[8] That this 'oceanic feeling experienced by certain types of neurotics has ... been confused with enlightenment'

[1] Enomiya, op. cit., p. 75, etc.; Kapleau, op. cit., pp. 135, 191, etc.
[2] Gītā 2: 72.   [3] Ibid. 5: 19.   [4] Ibid. 6: 29.
[5] *Platform Scripture*, ch. liii (Chan, p. 147).   [6] Kapleau, op. cit., p. 45.
[7] Above, pp. 42–3.   [8] *Platform Scripture*, ch. xxix (Chan, p. 77).

upsets Mr. Kapleau. If, however, descriptions mean anything, then the two experiences are clearly the same; and in any case the 'oceanic feeling' is not by any means confined to neurotics any more than Zen enlightenment implies madness.[1] The common characteristic of all these experiences is that they are sudden, unexpected, and unheralded, just as Rinzai Zen enlightenment is 'sudden'. The difference between 'cosmic consciousness' or nature mysticism on the one hand and Zen enlightenment on the other is that natural mystical experiences occur without preparation of any kind, last usually only a very short time, and are rarely repeated, whereas Zen enlightenment, if it comes at all, comes often only after a long, rigorous, and painful training—whether by shock treatment and sermons as in the Rinzai sect or by moral training and catechism as in Sōtō. *Zazen* is the technique of meditation that is designed to produce enlightenment: it includes the adoption of bodily postures often very painful to the beginner, breath-control, beatings, scoldings, and so on. Even when enlightenment is won it must not be given up, otherwise the enlightenment, as in the case of nature mysticism, will simply fade away. It would then seem clear that Zen is a technique designed to achieve a natural mystical experience by purely natural means.

' "Every man has his own Satori," say the Zen masters.'[2] Those who have undergone a rigorous moral training will accordingly show every sign of sanctity. 'Truly enlightened monks are not proud,' Fr. Enomiya assures us. 'On the contrary, they are very humble and congenial. Anyone who lives in a Zen monastery for a short time will confirm this. In a monastery there prevails an atmosphere of benevolence and charity which is not often found elsewhere.'[3] This cannot be said of the eight cases of enlightenment which Mr. Kapleau reports in full. In many of these one detects a touch of madness and a triviality that are exasperating. There is plenty of joy, but how much of it seems to be merely silly! Truly, 'every man has his own Satori'. If the good become better, then is it not at least possible that the bad will become worse? This is not likely to happen in a Zen monastery where aspirants after enlightenment are under the constant supervision of an experienced master, because, as in any religious order in Christendom, the chaff would be very soon sifted out from the wheat; but what of what Mr. Kapleau calls 'beat' Zen?

In the fourteenth century Europe was plagued by an epidemic of strange antinomian sects with chiliastic and mystical tendencies.

---

[1] Cf. Kapleau, op. cit., p. 206. 'My son told me later he thought I had gone mad.'

[2] Enomiya, *Zen-Buddhismus*, p. 84.

[3] Enomiya, *Zen—Way to Enlightenment*, E.T., p. 46.

Prominent among these were the Brethren of the Free Spirit who claimed that the 'enlightened' man—the man who thought he had reached unity with the Godhead—was free in every sense of the word, not only 'liberated' from the bonds of matter but also freed from all laws human and divine— free therefore to do what he liked, free, as often as not, to indulge in sexual practices of any and every kind.[1] They were, it seems, the 'beat' generation of the declining Middle Ages and effected what we would now call their own 'sexual revolution'. Their argumentation too was much the same. 'If, as "beat" Zen had led us to believe,' Mr. Kapleau quotes some earnest young Americans as saying, 'Satori reveals the unreality of the past and the future, is one not free to live as one likes here and now, without reference to the past and without thought for the future?'[2] The question seems fair enough, and the Zen master's answer does not seem satisfactory. Because, he said, the 'present moment' of the enlightened man embraces all dimensions of time and space, this 'Satori-realization . . . unavoidably carries with it a sense of fellowship and responsibility to one's family and society as a whole, alike to those who came before and those who will follow one'. When one remembers that the whole Confucian tradition is at one in its criticism of Buddhism—and particularly Zen—for causing precisely the opposite result, the word 'unavoidably' seems exaggerated. Freedom from *karma*, after all, means freedom not only from the actions you perform but also from any responsibility for them, since *sub specie aeternitatis* they do not exist. As Hui-nêng himself says: 'So long as there is . . . neither right nor wrong, . . . and so long as you are quiet and tranquil, that is the great Way.'[3]

This is, of course, the attraction of Zen as it is of all Eastern mysticism, if improperly and incompletely understood. For what are the 'beats' looking for? They are not content to abandon religion altogether because, having once jettisoned all the tenets of a moralistic, 'thou shalt not', Christianity, they have not the courage or simply the strength to live in a religious vacuum. What, then, if they find a religion that appears to offer them a glimpse into an eternal world, in which all things are harmonized into an eternal Now and Here, and from which not only do no moral imperatives proceed, but in which there is a tranquillity that puts a stop to all this moral carping and raises you to a sphere in which there is neither right or wrong? This surely is irresistible and, in its apparent hostility to all formalized religion, irresistibly 'modern'. It is an escape back into

[1] For the Brethren of the Free Spirit see Gordon Leff, *Heresy in the Later Middle Ages*, Manchester University Press, 1967, pp. 308–407.
[2] Kapleau, op. cit., p. 15.   [3] Above, p. 291.

the Garden of Eden, into 'God's world', without the disagreeable necessity
of having to meet God.

'Beat' Zen may be a caricature of Zen, but it is a caricature to which Zen
all too easily lends itself, just as the antinomianism of the Free Spirit was
a caricature of Meister Eckhart's mystical theology. Moreover, Zen, so
far as it has a basis in theory at all, tends to interpret the experience of
Satori in terms of nature mysticism—the interpenetration and interdependence of all natural things in which evil as much as good must find
its allotted place. It does not speak of God, of love, of union with God, let
alone of a spiritual marriage; and since it does not do so, then it is presumably
because these symbols are inappropriate, not because, as Fr. Enomiya
suggests,[1] the Japanese do not understand how an inferior can possibly
love a superior. Odd, one would have thought, in a country so thoroughly
imbued with the Confucian spirit.

In the West it is Jung, more than anyone else, who has familiarized the
intelligent reader with Eastern mysticism. This was easy for him because,
right up from his childhood, his religious *experience* had been of an
entirely mystical kind. The God he sensed in Nature and in himself was
so different from the God his Protestant upbringing had proposed for his
earnest consideration that the latter had to be put into inverted commas.
'God's world' was to him an intensely lived experience, whereas the God
he had learnt about from his pastors and masters seemed to be no more than
a disagreeable figment of the collective imagination of the Swiss bourgeoisie in whose image he had been made. The God of 'God's world' was
the God of Zen and Rousseau; and this God had made the institutionalized
religion of which the other God was the centre seem to be a pointless
and badly acted charade. Jung had, indeed, expected too much: he had
actually expected something to happen at his first Communion for which
he had been so laboriously prepared. The fact not only that nothing
happened, but that all those earnest people who had so carefully prepared
him plainly never expected anything to happen and were only too glad to
get the whole thing out of the way, convinced him that the whole thing
was a sham. He could not be fooled because at the age of twelve he had
first seen into 'God's world' and found his true self therein.

He was walking to school when he had the overwhelming impression of
having just emerged from a dark cloud:

I knew all at once: now I am *myself*! It was as if a wall of mist were at my back,
and behind that wall there was not yet an 'I'. But at this moment *I came upon
myself*. Previously I had existed too, but everything had merely happened to me.

[1] Enomiya, *Zen—Way to Enlightenment*, p. 80.

Now I happened to myself. Now I knew: I am myself now, now I exist. Previously I had been willed to do this and that; now I willed. This experience seemed to me tremendously important and new: there was 'authority' in me.[1]

This is not unlike many contemporary accounts of Zen enlightenment: the ego either dies or is pushed from the scene altogether and 'another' takes over who is also at one with the 'All'.

Then, [Jung goes on to say,] to my intense confusion, it occurred to me that I was actually two different persons. One of them was the schoolboy who could not grasp algebra and was far from sure of himself; the other was important, a high authority, a man not to be trifled with.[2]

Jung had in fact discovered that in him there were two selves, the one the empirical self of everyday experience, the other an inhabitant of a strange world from which 'the human mind looked down upon Creation simultaneously with God'.

Somewhere deep in the background I always knew that I was two persons. One was the son of my parents, who went to school and was less intelligent, attentive, hard-working, decent, and clean than many other boys. The other was grown up—old, in fact—sceptical, mistrustful, remote from the world of men, but close to nature, the earth, the sun, the moon, the weather, all living creatures, and above all close to the night, to dreams, and to whatever 'God' worked directly in him. I put 'God' in quotation marks here. For nature seemed, like myself, to have been set aside by God as non-divine, although created by Him as an expression of Himself. Nothing could persuade me that 'in the image of God' applied only to man. In fact it seemed to me that the high mountains, the rivers, lakes, trees, flowers, and animals far better exemplified the essence of God than men with their ridiculous clothes, their meanness, vanity, mendacity, and abhorrent egotism—all qualities with which I was only too familiar from myself, that is, from personality No. 1, the schoolboy of 1890. Besides his world there existed another realm, like a temple in which anyone who entered was transformed and suddenly overpowered by a vision of the whole cosmos, so that he could only marvel and admire, forgetful of himself. Here lived the 'Other', who knew God as a hidden, personal, and at the same time suprapersonal secret. Here nothing separated man from God; indeed, it was as though the human mind looked down upon Creation simultaneously with God.

What I am here unfolding, sentence by sentence, is something I was then not conscious of in any articulate way, though I sensed it with an overpowering premonition and intensity of feeling. At such times I *knew* I was worthy of myself, that I was my true self. As soon as I was alone, I could pass over into this state. I therefore sought the peace and solitude of this 'Other', personality No. 2.

[1] C. G. Jung, *Memories, Dreams, Reflections*, London, Collins and Routledge & Kegan Paul, 1963, p. 44.
[2] Ibid., p. 45.

The play and counterplay between personalities No. 1 and No. 2, which has run through my whole life, has nothing to do with a 'split' or dissociation in the ordinary medical sense. On the contrary, it is played out in every individual. In my life No. 2 has been of prime importance, and I have always tried to make room for anything that wanted to come to me from within. He is a typical figure, but he is perceived only by the very few. Most people's conscious understanding is not sufficient to realise that he is also what they are.[1]

This, as the Upanishad says, is 'what you should seek, what you should really want to understand',[2] for 'this is the Self, exempt from evil, untouched by age or death or sorrow, untouched by hunger or thirst, [the Self] whose desire is the real, whose idea is the real'.[3] This is the 'self' that is the subject of the Zen experience too, the Buddha-nature as they call it, since the Zen Buddhists are as bound by their own dogma of there being no such thing as a 'self' as are the Christians by their obsession with personality.

That Jung's 'personality No. 2' is what the Hindus mean by the *ātman* and the Buddhists by the 'Buddha-nature' is scarcely open to doubt. The great difference is that Jung's personality No. 2 has a sense of destiny, of a divine task that it has to fulfil here on earth. 'God's world' is not merely a timeless eternity, it is also a categorical imperative, and it is in this world that personality No. 2 has its being; hence its *karma*, its acts and volitions, are rooted in eternity. And so Jung goes on to say:

From the beginning I had a sense of destiny, as though my life was assigned to me by fate and had to be fulfilled. This gave me an inner security, and, though I could never prove it to myself, it proved itself to me. *I* did not have this certainty, *it* had me. Nobody could rob me of the conviction that it was enjoined upon me to do what God wanted and not what I wanted. That gave me the strength to go my own way. Often I had the feeling that in all decisive matters I was no longer among men, but was alone with God. And when I was 'there', where I was no longer alone, I was outside time; I belonged to the centuries; and He who then gave answer was He who had always been, who had been before my birth. He who always is was there. These talks with the 'Other' were my profoundest experiences: on the one hand a bloody struggle, on the other supreme ecstasy.[4]

'The struggle of the spirit is as brutal as the battle of men; but the vision of justice is the good pleasure of God alone.'[5]

Jung stresses that this second personality 'outside time' is perceived by the very few. Most people are never aware of it at all, just as only a very

---

[1] Jung, op. cit., p. 55.   [2] *Chāndogya* Upanishad 8: 1: 1.
[3] Ibid. 8: 1: 5.   [4] Jung, op. cit., pp. 57–8.
[5] Arthur Rimbaud, *Une saison en enfer*, ed. Pléiade, p. 244.

few Buddhists ever realize the Buddha-nature within them. And just as
the initial experience is as sudden as a flash of lightning but grows ever
deeper if one persists in *zāzen*, so too in Jung's case did it deepen throughout his life, but always at the base of it was 'cosmic consciousness',
embracing all time and pervading all space:

> At times [he says] I feel as if I am spread out over the landscape and inside
> things, and am myself living in every tree, in the plashing of the waves, in the
> clouds and the animals that come and go, in the procession of the seasons. . . .
> Here everything has its history, and mine; here is space for the spaceless
> kingdom of the world's and the psyche's hinterland.[1]

How familiar it all is! In the course of these lectures alone we have
met it in Bucke, in Whitman, in the Upanishads, in Taoism, in neo-
Confucianism, in Zen, and now in Jung. In Western literature it turns up
sporadically: in the East it is all-pervasive, and it has come to be the
dogma of Zen. In the words of Yasutani Roshi:

> Our supreme faith . . . is in the Buddha's enlightenment experience, the
> substance of which he proclaimed to be that human nature, all existence, is
> intrinsically whole, flawless, omnipotent—in a word, perfect.[2] With perfect
> enlightenment we apprehend that our conception of the world as dual and
> antithetical is false, and upon this realization the world of Oneness, of true
> harmony and peace, is revealed.[3]

This is the 'God's world' of which Jung speaks—the world in which his
personality No. 2 has its being: but, he warns us elsewhere,[4] 'even the
enlightened person remains what he is, and is never more than his own
limited ego before the One who dwells in him, whose form has no knowable boundaries, who encompasses him on all sides, fathomless as the
abysms of the earth and vast as the sky'.

Ecumenism nowadays is all the rage, and Christian attempts to equate
what all theists proclaim to be the love of God with Zen enlightenment,
which, in its essentials, seems to be identical with Bucke's cosmic consciousness and Freud's oceanic feeling, deserve every sympathy. But let
us, like the neo-Confucians, hold fast to the Mean. Both the Trappist
Thomas Merton[5] and Fr. Enomiya have recently tried to close the gap between the two, but without having resort to the Hindu bridge which is there
for the asking. This rash enterprise lands Merton in a quagmire of contradiction made none the more endearing by an *odium theologicum* we do not

[1] Jung, op. cit., p. 214.   [2] Kapleau, op. cit., p. 59.   [3] Ibid., pp. 48–9.
[4] C. G. Jung, *Answer to Job*, London, Routledge & Kegan Paul, 1954, p. 180.
[5] Thomas Merton, *Mystics and Zen Masters*, New York, Farrar, Straus, & Giroux, 1967.

expect to find in the mystics, while Fr. Enomiya, Jesuit though he is, sometimes reads more like a disciple of Spinoza. The problem that faces him
is this: if the essence of Christian mysticism is the love of God, and if
Zen Buddhism is also authentic religious mysticism, then why does it
speak of neither God nor love? Here is his attempted solution:

> There are certainly some monks who, according to their own interpretation
> of their experience of enlightenment, become one with nature and the universe
> and in this union experience an immense joy. This joy is so deep that it cannot
> be diminished but is, rather, strengthened through suffering and adversity. On
> speaking to such people one gets the impression that there is only a difference
> of words, not of matter. When they use the words 'nature and universe' is it not
> really 'God' whom they mean?[1]

This seems to be begging the question; for what does Fr. Enomiya
understand by 'God'? Is it the God with whom St. Teresa communes
with such personal intensity, or is it not rather Jung's personality No. 2
which cannot be diminished by suffering because it is outside time? Is it
not the *ātman*, the 'Self', of the Upanishads which, before the 'new
dispensation' of the Bhagavad-Gītā, Hindu sages found difficulty in
distinguishing from what we would call God? For this too is 'untouched
by age or death or sorrow' and—

> When once one understands that in oneself
> The Self's become all beings,
> When once one's seen the unity,
> What room is there for sorrow? What room for perplexity?[2]

Perhaps in the light of what we learnt from the Upanishads last year
we could say that by 'Nature' and the 'universe' the Zen Buddhist means
'Nature' and the 'universe' seen against its eternal background, Brahman,
which, 'though undivided, abides in [all] beings, seeming divided'.[3] This
is 'the prize beyond all others—*or so he thinks*. Therein he [firmly] stands,
unmoved by any suffering, however grievous it may be'.[4] So speaks the
Bhagavad-Gītā. And it adds: this is a state in which 'by self one sees the
self in self and finds content therein',[5] the 'fixed, still state of Brahman'[6]
which must be reached *before* one can safely approach the personal God,
Krishna. In the Christian tradition this corresponds in some respects to
the 'prayer of quiet' of St. Teresa.

Like Teresa the Bhagavad-Gītā then goes on to speak of love. The Zen
Buddhists do not because 'this is *the prize beyond all others—or so they*

---

[1] Enomiya, *Way to Enlightenment*, E.T., p. 80.   [2] *Iśā* Upanishad 7.
[3] Bhagavad-Gītā 13: 16.   [4] Ibid. 6: 22.
[5] Ibid. 6: 20.   [6] Ibid. 2: 72.

think'. So did Hugh of St. Victor as we shall very soon see, but Fr. Enomiya still prefers to equate the two experiences, and continues:

There is another reason for the silence the enlightened ones in regard to their expressing their love of God. The Japanese consider it disrespectful for an inferior person to love a superior person. This attitude is rooted in a misunderstanding, and when the non-Christian Japanese understands what is meant by the love of God, this difficulty disappears. A Japanese layman told me (he had practised Za-zen for many years and was enlightened) that after reading a book of St. John of the Cross he understood for the first time what the love of God meant. A very old monk once told me that enlightenment was being one with nature.[1] Spontaneously, I replied: 'For us it is being one with God.' He bowed his head with a glance of agreement. This does not mean that Buddhist monism is to be equated with Christian monotheism. It only means that there are some outstanding monks who in their experience of enlightenment succeed in meeting us.[2]

This proves nothing. The Japanese are a very polite people, and they would be unlikely to disagree openly with a Western friend who obviously so very much wanted to identify the transports of Teresa with the calm certainties of Zen. Moreover, it is surely a little naïve to suggest that a Japanese does not speak of the love of God because he thinks it disrespectful for an inferior to love a superior. This seems incredible in a race imbued with the Confucian tradition of graded love, the highest manifestation of which is the relationship of son to father. Surely it is obvious that in a religion the highest good of which is to realize the Buddha-nature as being one's own true nature, there can be no room for love of even a Buddha who is in any way external to ourselves. In the Christian tradition things are very different. The highest good is conceived of in terms of a 'spiritual marriage', and I cannot believe that this is meaningless to a Japanese.

Further, it is misleading to generalize about 'Buddhist monism' even in the Mahāyāna, more misleading still to generalize about 'Christian monotheism'. The untypical Eckhart, for instance, is frequently cited as being a Christian monist; and this, though a simplification, is not absurd. As pantheistic monists we might, with greater justification, cite Angelus Silesius and even Teilhard de Chardin. Eckhart certainly lays great stress on the eternal Now and the ubiquitous Here, and the close similarities between him and the great Indian monist, Śankara, have been meticulously noted by Rudolf Otto in his *Mysticism, East and West*; but, even so,

---

[1] E.T. has 'the becoming-conscious-of the oneness of nature'. The original German has only 'Einssein mit der Natur' (p. 94).

[2] Enomiya, *Zen—Way to Enlightenment*, pp. 80–1.

as Otto shows, there is a dynamism in Eckhart that is quite foreign to his Indian counterpart. Nothing ever corresponds quite as closely as we could wish. Let us then be content with Angelus Silesius who not surprisingly forsook the Lutheran Church for a wider Catholicity. For him too the human soul, like the Buddha-nature and Jung's personality No. 2, encompasses all space and all time:

> Die Welt ist mir zu eng, der Himmel ist zu klein;
> Wo wird doch noch ein Raum für meine Seele sein?[1]

It is man who makes time, for in reality there is no distinction between time and eternity:

> Du sprichst: Versetze dich aus Zeit in Ewigkeit.
> Ist denn an Ewigkeit und Zeit ein Unterscheid?
>
> Du selber machst die Zeit, das Uhrwerk sind die Sinnen;
> Hemmst du die Unruh nur, so ist die Zeit von hinnen.[2]

In the soul all things are one and all the opposites transcended:

> Ich weiß nicht, was ich soll! Es ist mir alles ein:
> Ort, Unort, Ewigkeit, Zeit, Nacht, Tag, Freud und Pein.[3]

But, just as in the Bhagavad-Gītā the soul must become the 'All' before it can draw near to God, so too, according to Angelus Silesius, in order to see God you must first be the 'All':

> Wer selbst nicht alles ist, der ist noch zu geringe,
> Daß er dich sehen soll, mein Gott, und alle Dinge.[4]

The message of Angelus Silesius is the same as that of the Gītā: you cannot 'see' God and all things in God until you have yourself 'become the All'. But, the Gītā adds, you cannot love God until you see him in and through the universe: without love even this 'wisdom' must remain incomplete, for love splits open what seems self-sufficient and whole in order that it may enter in. Hence, as St. François de Sales says, 'the first stirrings (traits) that we receive from love are called wounds because the heart which had seemed whole (sain), entire, and sufficient to itself

---

[1] *Cherubinischer Wandersmann*, 1. 187: 'The world is too narrow for me, heaven too small; where then will there be room for my soul?'

[2] Ibid. 1. 188–9: 'You say: Move from time into eternity. But is there any difference between eternity and time? You yourself make time, the senses are the clockwork. If you will but restrain disquiet, then time will disappear.'

[3] Ibid. 1. 190: 'I know not what to do! All is one to me: space, spacelessness, eternity, time, night, day, joy and sorrow.'

[4] Ibid. 1. 191: 'Who is not himself the All, he is still too small to see thee, my God, and all things.'

(*tout à soi-même*) while it did not love, begins, once it is smitten by love, to be separated and divided from itself in order to give itself to the Beloved'.[1] And what is this *cœur qui semblait sain, entier et tout à soi-même* if not the man who, 'with self by Yoga integrated, sees the self in all beings standing, all beings in the self'.[2] He 'knows' the All because he has 'become' the all: the butterfly has emerged from the chrysalis and thinks that its goal is achieved. But, St. Teresa warns, 'if anyone told me that after reaching this state he had enjoyed continual rest and joy, I should say that he had not reached it at all, but that if he had got as far as the previous Mansion [the prayer of recollection, that is, the 'integration' of the Gītā], he might possibly have experienced some kind of consolation the effect of which was enhanced by physical weakness, and perhaps even by the Devil, who gives peace to the soul in order later to wage a far severer war upon it'.[3]

It was not then for nothing that Krishna commanded the Yogin, who has 'become Brahman' and thought himself sufficient unto himself, to attach his mind to him, the personal God:

Attach your mind to me: engaged in Yogic exercise put your trust in me.[4]

For Krishna, being God, knew that to become one with Nature or the universe is not the same as becoming one with himself in the bond of love. Did we really need a God to tell us this?

---

[1] *Traité de l'amour de Dieu*, 6. 13.   [2] Bhagavad-Gītā 6: 29.

[3] Teresa of Avila, *Interior Castle*, 5. 2 (tr. E. Allison Peers, London, Sheed & Ward, 1946, p. 256).

[4] Bhagavad-Gītā 7: 1.

XV

STANDING ON A PEAK

IN our last lecture it was argued that despite the well-meaning efforts of some Christian contemplatives to equate the Christian concept of the union of the soul with God in love with the Zen Buddhist formula of oneness with Nature or the 'All', such an equation was precluded not only by common sense but much more by the evidence supplied by the Hindu mystical tradition which, wholly unrestricted as it is by the apparatus of dogma, nevertheless moves serenely on from pantheism to theism. It is as well to recall again the distinction that Teilhard de Chardin draws between two distinct forms of pantheism—and he is not frightened of using the word, for he knows that the mystical temperament is by nature pantheistic in that it sees God everywhere. These are the 'pantheism of identification, at the antipodes of love: "God [is] all." And the pantheism of unification, beyond love: "God, all in all (*tout en tous*)" '. These he defines as 'unity at the base, through dissolution' on the one hand and 'unity at the summit, through ultra-differentiation'[1] on the other. The one is a 'regression, even if only partial, of consciousness (*le réfléchi*) towards the unconscious', the other 'a position of equilibrium situated not below (*en deça*) but beyond all organization and all thought'.[2] And Teilhard admits that these two extreme poles share a certain number of common properties which make them 'terribly alike'.[3]

Let us not make the mistake of comparing and contrasting Christian mysticism with its Hindu and Buddhist counterparts as if they were self-contained wholes. In each tradition you will find the same types of mysticism which I have sought to classify, but, even so, you will find a difference of emphasis. On the Indian side the keyword is *mukti*, *moksha*, *vimutti*, 'liberation, emancipation, freedom of the spirit': on the Christian side it is union with God. The key to the relationship between the mysticism of eternal repose—Nirvāna—and that of the unitive love of God is to be found pre-eminently in the Bhagavad-Gītā. First comes detachment from the world perceived through the senses, second the perfect peace you find in the still depths of your own self, third *at*tachment to God, and lastly a loving communion with God which enables you to 'enter' him.

[1] *L'Activation de l'énergie*, Paris, Seuil, 1963, pp. 231–2.
[2] Ibid., p. 233.   [3] Ibid., p. 231.

The Buddha's enlightenment was a state of absolute peace in which he achieved total detachment from all things and independence of all things: this dispensed him from having to occupy himself any more with the problems of an unreal world. This was his temptation. 'Like a man standing on a peak at the top of a mountain' so had he 'ascended the palace of the doctrine, surveying all things on every side'.[1] The temptation simply to stay on the top of the mountain was great. But the Buddha relents and returns to the world out of compassion in order to teach the doctrine.

The word 'standing on a peak' is familiar to the Gītā too. It is *kūṭa-stha*, and in my translation of the Gītā I have rendered it 'sublime, aloof'. This is intended to convey the idea of reaching a state so high and so sublime that it is not possible to pass beyond. It is, then, the highest point in the spiritual ascent that a man can reach by his own efforts. This is the Buddhist Nirvāna and it is a state of transcendent stillness and rest. It is the state which the Gītā describes in these words:

When thought by spiritual exercise is checked and comes to rest, and when of [one]self one sees the self in self and finds content therein, that is the utmost joy which transcends [all things of] sense and which soul alone can grasp. When he knows this and [knowing it] stands still, moving not an inch from the reality [he sees], he wins a prize beyond all others—or so he thinks.[2]

The point of the passage is that once a man reaches this sublime state, he thinks, indeed he is bound to think, that this is his journey's end, for here all is unchanging peace, quiet, and utter stillness. And so

The higher self of the self-subdued, quietened, is rapt in enstasy—in cold as in heat, in pleasure as in pain, likewise in honour and disgrace. With self content in wisdom learnt in holy books and wisdom learnt from life, with sense subdued, *standing on a peak*, [this] athlete of the spirit [stands]: 'Integrated', so is he called; the same to him are clods of earth, stones, gold.[3]

The simile is quite common in the didactic parts of the Great Epic and is used in precisely similar contexts. For example:

Once you have crossed this [stream of *saṃsāra*] you will be freed on every side, your self made clean and pure; firmly relying on the highest part of your soul you will become Brahman, for you will have transcended all defilements, your self serene, immaculate. As *one standing on a mountain* survey those beings still living in the plain.[4]

The state of 'being Brahman', it may be noted, is said to have been the state of man at the beginning of every cosmic cycle, the state of original

---

[1] *Majjhima Nikāya* i. 168.   [2] Bhagavad-Gītā 6: 20-2.
[3] Ibid. 6: 7-8.
[4] *Mahābhārata* 12: 242: 16-18; cf. ibid. 12: 17: 19; 12: 172: 6.

innocence that Adam is said to have enjoyed before the Fall, the original
purity of the Tao.[1] Thus the 'one who stands on the peak' may refer either
to the individual liberated soul or to the sum-total of such souls. And so
again we read in the Gītā:[2]

> In the world there are two 'persons'—perishable the one, imperishable the
> other: the 'perishable' is all contingent beings, the 'imperishable' they call *'the
> one who stands on the peak'*. But (the text significantly adds) there is [yet] another
> Person, the [All-]Sublime, surnamed 'All-Highest Self': the three worlds he
> enters and pervades, sustaining them—the Lord who passes not away.

Here 'all contingent beings' must mean all souls or selves that are still
involved in matter, while the 'one who stands on the peak' is the totality
of liberated selves which, all being 'the same' in that they have all 'become
Brahman', can be spoken of in the singular number.[3] What is significant,
of course, is that God, the 'Person [All-]Sublime', is superior to and other
than they. God, even if he is considered as an impersonal Absolute,
transcends the perfect stillness and tranquillity of eternity itself. But—and
here perhaps we can see a clear link between the Buddhist Nirvāna and
the Zen Satori on the one hand and the Christian and Hindu concept of
'union with God' on the other—the man who reaches this state of absolute
calm and peace also 'attains to' God; for

> Those who revere the indeterminate Imperishable Unmanifest, unthinkable
> though coursing everywhere, *standing on the peak*, unmoving, firm, who hold in
> check the complex of the senses, in all things equal-minded, taking pleasure in
> the weal of all contingent beings, these too attain to me.[4]

This surely is the missing link between what the Zen Buddhists mean
by 'being at one with Nature' and the union with God in love of the
theistic traditions. The first is to experience and see the Eternal One as
pervading all Nature and oneself, whereas the 'man standing on the peak'
inheres in the eternal, unchanging, timeless, static, inert, and 'dead'
essence of this One, seeing the world and himself from its utterly sublime
point of view—seeing them *sub specie aeternitatis*. This man does not
experience love nor does he say he does so: he experiences Being. This
may happen to theists too and this would seem to be what St. François de
Sales is describing when he says: 'There are times when the soul neither
hears its beloved nor speaks to him, *nor feels any indication of his presence.*'[5] It simply knows, he adds, that it is in God's presence, and that

---

[1] *Mahābhārata* 3: 181: 12.   [2] 15: 16.
[3] See R. C. Zaehner, *The Bhagavad-Gītā*, Oxford, 1968, pp. 366–7.
[4] *Gītā* 12: 3–4.   [5] *Traité de l'amour de Dieu*, 6. 11.

is where God wants it to be. But this surely a Christian *interpretation* of a universal mystical experience: as in Nirvāna there is no *experience* of the presence of God. The saint makes his meaning clear in a simile. 'Supposing', he says, 'the glorious apostle St. John had fallen into a bodily sleep on his dear Lord's breast at the Last Supper. . . . In that case he would certainly have been in his Master's presence, but without being aware of it in any way.' This is what the Gītā means by saying that those who revere the Imperishable Unmanifest also attain to God: they attain to an Absolute that is devoid of attributes, but they do not know that this is also a personal God.

The Christian mystics on the whole are very much less preoccupied with 'liberation' from our human condition as such—with the eternal peace of Nirvāna—than they are with love, communion, and union with God. This, we may freely admit, is conditioned by the very nature of Christianity itself which, having defined God as Love, was bound to admit plurality in God himself—the eternal Lover, the eternal Beloved, and the mutual love that unites them. In so far as this love is identified with the Holy Spirit, it seems to me to be almost nonsensical to speak of it as a 'Person'. Christian mysticism, however, is quite as much influenced by the Pseudo-Dionysius and, through Augustine, by Plotinus as it is by the New Testament; and so we have Christian 'monists' like Eckhart, Christian 'pantheists' like Angelus Silesius, and Christian 'qualified monists' of whom perhaps the most interesting are Hugh and Richard of St. Victor, who between them constitute a kind of Christian Bhagavad-Gītā. Of the two, Richard, a Scotsman, is the more obviously interesting since he saw clearly that merely to stand stock-still on a mountain-peak was not enough; and in this he clarifies and develops Hugh who, of all the Christian mystics I have read, seems to be the most Buddhistic, in that he thirsts above all things for the changelessness and unmoving peace of Nirvāna—what the Gītā[1] calls the 'fixed, still state of Brahman'. Hence his predilection for Ecclesiastes, itself by far the most 'Buddhist' book of the Old Testament. He too, like the Buddha, takes his stand upon a peak, and, just as Arjuna receives a 'divine eye' from Krishna in the Gītā, so does his soul receive the 'heart's eye' from Reason, the Western equivalent of the divine Wisdom.[2]

And so, like the Buddha, Hugh looks down on the phenomenal world and sees that all things pass away. He sees the ocean of *saṁsāra*, the relentless ebb and flow of earthly life and death, and what had once seemed

---

[1] 2: 72.
[2] *Hugh of Saint-Victor, Selected Spiritual Writings*, p. 158.

pleasing now seems terrible. All this is 'vanity, and vanity of vanities'.[1]
This applies to everything—riches, friendship, the deceptive joys of
married life and the tiresomeness of rearing a family, the world of learning
and the acquisition of new skills, the arts and sciences and all they have
achieved. All this is vanity because it does not abide,[2] or, as the Buddhists
would say, it is impermanent, it has no self, and therefore it is fraught with
suffering. And just as the Buddha saw that beyond all this flux there was
an 'unborn, not made, not become, uncompounded', so did Hugh of St.
Victor seek a dwelling beyond this world 'in order to remain *unmoved*
ourselves when all things in the world pass on'[3]—unmoved because he
too knew that 'with God', as he puts it, 'there is a perpetual, unshakable
stability'[4] in which 'we attain even to that simple oneness, that true
simplicity and everlasting changelessness'[5] which the Buddhists call
Nirvāna.

Thus there are two contrasted worlds—'God's world', as Jung would
call it, and this world—'God as it were in the heights, and this world in the
depths', God 'in the changeless condition of his eternity', 'this world . . .
in a state of flux and instability'. Between them is the human soul: 'by a
certain native excellence it rises above the mutability below it, but it has not
yet attained to that true changelessness that is above it.'[6] The soul is thus
suspended between God's world where all is a unified and changeless
whole and this world which is ruled by perpetual change and dis-traction.
It is of the nature of the soul of fallen man to be distracted and dispersed.
As the Upanishad says:

> As rain that falls in craggy places
> Loses itself, dispersed throughout the mountains,
> So does the man who sees things as diverse
> [Himself] become dispersed in their pursuit.[7]

This is the danger, but the soul can recover its fundamental unity 'if
he will pick himself up[8] and, shaking off base attachments,[9] learn to be
with himself once more.[10] The more a man gathers himself together in
spirit,[11] the more, forsaking lower things, is he raised in thought and desire;
until at last, when he comes to that one supreme changelessness, he is

---

[1] *Hugh of Saint-Victor, Selected Spiritual Writings*, p. 161.
[2] Ibid., p. 171.   [3] Ibid., p. 174.   [4] Ibid., p. 126.
[5] Ibid., p. 127.   [6] Ibid., pp. 174-5.   [7] *Katha* Upanishad 4: 14.
[8] Cf. Bhagavad-Gītā 6: 5: 'Raise self by self, let not the self droop down.'
[9] Cf. *Chāndogya* Upanishad 8: 13: 'Shaking off evil as a horse [shakes off] its hairs . . .'
[10] Cf. Gītā 6: 20: 'When of [one]self one sees the self in self . . .'
[11] Cf. Gītā 2: 58: 'He draws in on every side his senses from their proper objects as a
tortoise [might draw in] its limbs.'

altogether unchangeable[1].'[2] This is the Nirvāna that is Brahman too, and the way to achieve it, as in Hinduism and Buddhism, is by recollection and contemplation. Contemplation is what the Indians call *jñāna* ('wisdom'). According to Hugh of St. Victor it 'embraces the complete understanding of . . . everything. . . . It is the alertness of the understanding which, finding everything plain, grasps it clearly with entire comprehension.'[3] This is the Zen Satori, which is 'beyond objectization and the senses, . . . purely spiritual, . . . cosmic, . . . comprehending all (*ganzheitlich*)',[4] the vision of all things in all their diversity as being one and undivided in changeless Being.[5] And here I cannot refrain from quoting Hugh at some length, for he seems to be describing exactly the process by which the sudden enlightenment of Zen is classically attained and which involves a ceaseless struggle:

In meditation [he writes] a sort of wrestling-match goes on between ignorance and knowledge [how utterly Indian that is!], and the light of truth somehow flickers in the midst of the darkness of error. It is then rather like a fire in green wood, which gets a hold at first only with difficulty; but, when it is fanned by a stronger draught and begins to catch on more fiercely, then we see great billows of black smoke arise, and smother the flame, which so far is still only fairly bright and leaping out here and there, until at last, as the fire gradually grows, all the smoke clears, the darkness is dispelled, and a bright blaze appears. Then the conquering flame, spreading throughout the crackling pyre, gains ready mastery and, leaping round the fuel, with lightest touches of its glancing tongues consumes and penetrates it. Nor does it rest until, reaching the very centre, it has so to speak absorbed into itself everything that it had found outside itself.[6]

Finally the fire, 'having brought everything beneath its own control and bound it up together in a sort of friendly likeness to itself, sinks down in deep peace and silence. For it no longer finds anything other than itself, nor anything in opposition to itself.' This is the fire of contemplative wisdom which, according to the Gītā, 'reduces all works to ashes'.[7] For Hugh of St. Victor, however, it is also the fire of love, but it is a strange sort of fire, for 'it sinks down to rest in utter peace from every conflict and disturbance. . . . Then, the whole heart being turned into the fire of love, God is known to be truly all in all. For he is received with a love so deep that apart from Him nothing is left to the heart, even of itself.'[8]

With Hugh love seems to be an afterthought, for what he has been seeking all along is the utter peace of changelessness, and this is symbolized

[1] Ibid. 2: 25: 'Unmanifest, unthinkable, unchangeable is it called.'
[2] *Hugh of Saint-Victor, Selected Spiritual Writings*, p. 175.
[3] Ibid., pp. 183–4.   [4] Enomiya, *Zen-Buddhismus*, pp. 101–2.
[5] Gītā 13: 16; 18: 20.   [6] Hugh of St. Victor, ibid., p. 184.
[7] Gītā 4: 37.   [8] Hugh of St. Victor, ibid., p. 185.

by the 'sinking down', that is, the extinction of the fire, and that is precisely what the Sanskrit word 'Nirvāna' means. Moreover, his God is the God of the pantheists: 'this one is all, and this all is one.'[1] One has, then, the impression that he introduces love simply because he is a Christian. The experience itself is one of utter peace and changelessness: love is the Christian interpretation imposed on the experience. As Aelred Squire says, Hugh of St. Victor has a positive terror of time:[2] what he is groping after is not love but rather the abolition of time, the peace of the man 'standing on a peak'.

His successor, Richard of St. Victor, realized that this is not quite enough. The peak has to be reached all right, but the peak is only the spring-board from which the soul must leap forward into God. The peak is what Jung calls personality No. 2, the *ātman* or 'self' of the Bhagavad-Gītā.

It will be remembered that the Gītā, in speaking of the 'Imperishable Unmanifest', described it not only as 'standing on a peak, unmoving, firm', but also as 'coursing everywhere'.[3] So too Richard of St. Victor says that 'the liveliness of the intelligence in the soul of the contemplative sometimes comes and goes with wonderful quickness, sometimes it circles around, sometimes it draws itself into a point and remains motionless'.[4] It both 'roams at will', as in the *Chāndogya* Upanishad,[5] and gathers itself up into a single point, as in the Gītā.[6]

For Hugh contemplation meant primarily the realization of the unchanging stillness that is present in the depths of the soul: for Richard it is a more boisterous affair, 'it flies around and when it wills, it hovers upon the height'.[7] It involves no effort and it is fruitful. What is much more important, however, is that Richard distinguishes two degrees of contemplation—the contemplation of self as the image of God and the contemplation of God himself. Richard makes the clearest possible distinction between these two, dealing with the first in a treatise called *Benjamin Minor* and with the second in another called *Benjamin Major*. Joseph represents the contemplative who sees the self as the image of God, but it is Benjamin alone who is privileged to contemplate God himself:

By Joseph the soul is carefully taught and eventually it is brought to full *self-knowledge*, just as by his half-brother Benjamin, it is at length brought to the contemplation of God. For as by Joseph we understand the grace of discretion [Sanskrit *viveka*!], so by Benjamin we understand the grace of contemplation.

---

[1] Hugh of St. Victor, op. cit., p. 51.   [2] Ibid., p. 28.   [3] Above, p. 304.
[4] *Richard of Saint-Victor, Selected Writings on Contemplation*, London, Faber & Faber, 1957, p. 140.   [5] 7: 1: 5; 8: 1: 6, etc.
[6] 6: 12.   [7] Richard of St. Victor, op. cit., p. 136.

Both are born of the same mother, for both the knowledge of God and of one-self are perceived by reason [Sanskrit *jñāna*!]. Benjamin is born long after Joseph. For the soul which has long been exercised in self-knowledge and is not yet fully taught cannot be raised up to the knowledge of God. In vain does the eye of the heart which is not yet fit to see itself, try to see God. First man must learn to know his own invisible nature [his Buddha-nature!] before he presumes to approach the invisible things of God.[1]

This is exactly what the Gītā teaches too: only by knowing the *ātman*, the self, can you come to know God. So too in Madhva and the Vaishnavite philosophers that follow him as in the neo-Confucians, the soul is the mirror or reflection of God or the 'Great Ultimate'. So, 'let him who desires to see God wipe his mirror and cleanse his heart', says Richard of St. Victor.[2] And the Zen master, Shen-hsiu:

> The body is the tree of Perfect Wisdom,
> The mind is the stand of a bright mirror.
> At all times diligently wipe it.
> Do not allow it to become dusty.[3]

And again the *Śvetāśvatara* Upanishad:

> Even as a mirror with dirt begrimed
> Shines brightly once it is well cleaned,
> So too the embodied self, once it has seen
> Self as it really is,
> Becomes one, its goal achieved, from sorrow free . . .
>
> [Then will he know] the unborn, undying God, the Pure,
> Beyond all essences as they really are,
> [And] knowing him, from all fetters he'll be freed.[4]

The self is a mountain-peak and therefore a single point. The ascent is difficult, but until you have made it you cannot hope to pass beyond the image to the reality of God:

The soul which is attempting to rise to the height of knowledge must make *self-knowledge* its first and chief concern. The high peak of knowledge is perfect self-knowledge. The full understanding of a rational spirit is as it were a high and great mountain. This mountain rises far above the top of all earthly learning and looks down from on high upon all philosophy and all the learning of this world. . . . By as much as you make daily progress in self-knowledge by so much

---

[1] Ibid., p. 109.   [2] Ibid., p. 110.
[3] *Platform Scripture*, ch. vi (Wing-tsit Chan, p. 35).
[4] *Śvetāśvatara* Upanishad 2: 14–15.

you will be reaching out to higher things, for he who attains perfect self-knowledge has reached the top of the mountain.[1]

As in Zen and in Yoga the ascent of the mountain is arduous, demanding, as does the Buddhist Eightfold Path, right conduct, right effort, right mindfulness, and right concentration.[2] As in Zen again there are pitfalls on the way, for it is always possible that you will think you have reached the top when in fact you have only got as far as the foothills;[3] and this is what we have learnt to recognize as the 'Zen sickness'. If these pitfalls are avoided, however, the top of the mountain will be reached: it is Mount Tabor and there you will see Christ transfigured, but everything you see is really yourself, the Buddha-nature and the image of God:

Would you see Christ transfigured? Climb this mountain, *learn to know yourself*. Would you see and recognize Moses and Elias without any sign? Would you understand the law and prophecy without a teacher or commentator? Climb this mountain, learn to know yourself. Would you have the privacy of the Father's secrets? Climb this mountain, learn to know yourself. He came down from heaven who said 'Know thyself'.[4]

For, as the Muslim tradition has it: 'Who knows himself, knows his Lord.'

Once a man has learnt to know himself and 'seen the self in all beings standing, all beings in the self',[5] then:

Let him rise up by himself above himself, and from self-knowledge to the knowledge of God. Let a man first learn from the image of God, let him learn from the likeness of God what he ought to think about God. . . . A mind which does not raise itself to consideration of its own nature, how can it fly away on the wings of contemplation to that which is above itself. . . . If [the mind] has not yet been able to gather itself together into a unity, and does not yet know how to enter into itself, when will it be able to ascend by contemplation to those things which are above itself?[6]

This reads like a paraphrase of the Gītā, for there too we read:[7] 'Let a man sit and make his mind a single point . . . and practise integration to purify the self . . ., then will he approach that peace which has Nirvāna as its end and which subsists in Me.' For this mountain-peak is Nirvāna, 'the unmoving, firm, though coursing everywhere',[8] which was the highest aspiration of Hugh. This is the 'Emptiness' or 'Great Vacuity' of the Mahāyāna and the neo-Confucians 'in which rest is sufficient and great, and it is in itself no sin, if one knows how to make oneself empty'. But, as

[1] Richard of St. Victor, op. cit., p. 114.   [2] Ibid., p. 117.
[3] Ibid., p. 118.   [4] Ibid., pp. 116–17.   [5] Bhagavad-Gītā 6: 29.
[6] Richard of St. Victor, op. cit., p. 122.   [7] 6: 12–15.
[8] Gītā 12: 3.

the Blessed Jan van Ruysbroek warns us, as does the *Lotus Sūtra*, 'when men wish to exercise and possess this rest without works of virtue, then they will fall into spiritual pride, and into a self-complacency from which they seldom recover. And at such times they believe themselves to have and to be that which they never achieve.'[1] This 'first contemplation', as Richard of St. Victor calls it, is symbolized by Rachel, and she—the 'transcendent', not the 'empirical' self—must die if Benjamin, 'a youth in ecstasy of mind',[2] is to be born, for it is Benjamin alone who can be lifted off the mountain-peak of the self which is the image of God into the wide expanse of God himself.

To learn to know oneself as the image of God is a laborious affair, but once the soul reaches the top of the mountain, 'it goes forth a freeman':[3] liberated from the trammels of space and time it 'has freedom of movement in all states of being'[4] and 'circles around with great nimbleness wherever the impulse takes it'.[5] For this purpose it must be supplied with wings: for if one is to rise up beyond the peak, then one cannot do so without wings. The metaphor is extraordinarily apt, for while it is perfectly possible to reach the top of the mountain by one's own unaided efforts, you cannot take off into the atmosphere unless someone gives you wings: these are the gift of grace.

Hugh of St. Victor was bound by the Platonic idea that the good is the changeless, evil is mutability. In this he was at one with Origen, Augustine, and the whole line of Christian Platonists, he was at one with the Theravāda Buddhists and the monism of the *Māndūkya* Upanishad and Śankara. Richard, like Indra in the *Chāndogya* Upanishad, saw that this changeless state was only the necessary stillness that precedes a new and wholly spiritual life. St. Gregory of Nyssa had seen this too: the pure image of God which Adam was supposed to have possessed before the Fall must be restored before a man could ascend to the living God. Among the Muslims too Al-Junayd of Baghdad had said that man must learn 'to be as he was before he was', to be as he ideally *is* in the mind of God. Human nature as it was before man fell was what the Mahāyāna Buddhists call the 'Buddha-nature': it 'seemed to be another good of the same sort [as God], fashioned in the most exact likeness in the image of its prototype. For man then possessed all those gifts about which we now speculate: incorruptibility, happiness, independence and self-determination, a life without toil or sorrow, absorption in divine things, a vision of the Good with a mind

---

[1] Blessed Jan van Ruysbroek, *The Spiritual Espousals*, London, Faber & Faber, 1952, pp. 167–8.
[2] Richard of St. Victor, op. cit., p. 123.   [3] Ibid., p. 134.
[4] *Chāndogya* Upanishad 8: 1: 6.   [5] Richard of St. Victor, op. cit., p. 136.

unclouded and pure of any interference'¹—a state exactly corresponding to what the Hindus call 'being Brahman'. It is possible to restore this state by our own efforts, and this is precisely what Yoga and Zen are about. 'By our human efforts,' Gregory says, 'we can merely clear away the accumulated filth of sin and thus allow the hidden beauty of the soul to shine forth.'² This incorruptibility, independence, and self-determination, this 'being Brahman', is the air you naturally breathe on the mountain-peak, the apex of the soul. We need not worry about the spacial image of the peak 'up there', which Dr. J. A. T. Robinson saw as a stumbling-block to a true understanding of Christianity, for the apex of the soul and the deepest places of the heart coalesce in one:

When speaking of spiritual and unseen things, something is said to be 'the highest', it is said to be so not as if it were some place above the topmost peak of heaven, but as deepest of all within us. To ascend to God means, therefore, to enter into oneself, and not only to enter into oneself, but in some ineffable manner to penetrate even into one's own depths. He, then, who . . . enters really deeply into himself and, penetrating deep within, transcends himself, he of a truth ascends to God.³

This is because 'in the human soul, the apex is the same as the inmost point, and the deepest place is one with the highest. And we mean the same thing by the top of the mountain as by the mercy seat in the tabernacle of the covenant.'⁴ The point of the simile is clear: whether you ascend to the peak of the mountain or withdraw into the inmost recess of the heart, you will reach a point without magnitude, the 'more minute than the minute' of the Upanishads, 'no larger than the fine point of an awl'.⁵ This is the point of convergence between time and eternity, what the Gītā calls the 'mouth of Brahman' where the sacrifice is consumed by the fire and transmuted into the divine. It is the prayer of quiet and the prayer of recollection of St. Teresa, while in St. John of the Cross it is the dark night of the senses which must precede the dark night of the soul, and this in turn must precede the spiritual nuptials of the soul with God. If you think of the peak as some existent thing, then it is the 'self' of the Hindus, the 'Buddha-nature' of the Mahāyāna, the personality No. 2 of Jung, the still apex or gound of the soul of the Christian mystics, the unsullied image of God. If you think of it as a state of being, then it is Nirvāna, the 'fixed, still state of Brahman', the 'immortal, devoid of fear'.⁶ On reaching this the soul thinks that it has won the 'prize beyond all others',⁷ for this

¹ *From Glory to Glory, Texts from Gregory of Nyssa's Mystical Writings*, ed. Jean Daniélou, S.J., E.T., London, John Murray, 1962, p. 88.
² Gregory of Nyssa, ibid., p. 114.   ³ Hugh of St. Victor, op. cit., p. 176.
⁴ Richard of St. Victor, op. cit., p. 179.   ⁵ *Śvetāśvatara* Upanishad 5: 8.
⁶ *Chāndogya* Upanishad 8: 3: 4, etc.   ⁷ Gītā 6: 22.

is that Brahman which is 'ever the same'[1]. Here all is peace, tranquillity, rest, and quiet; here 'rest is sufficient and great'. This is what the Muslim mystics call 'sobriety', what Louis Gardet and others have appropriately called 'enstasy'—standing still within oneself oblivious to the senses and the world. Here, as the Gītā says, a man 'draws in on every side his senses from their proper objects as a tortoise [might draw in] its limbs';[2] and so great is the concord and harmony between the different mystical traditions that St. Teresa, who could not possibly have been familiar with the Gītā, nevertheless applauds. In connection with the prayer of recollection she says: 'I think I have read that [such people] are like a hedgehog or a tortoise withdrawing into itself; and whoever wrote that must have understood it well.'[3] This is the prayer of recollection which must precede the prayer of union—the 'enstasy' within yourself from which you emerge into the ec-stasy which takes you out of yourself into God. The danger is that you will remain fixed and, as it were, frozen on the frosty peak of solitude, that you will be tempted to rest here for ever as the Buddha would have done had he followed his own inclination. This, it seems, you are bound to do unless God himself intervenes: and the miracle of the Gītā is surely this, that in a religious tradition the ideal of which had hitherto been to attain to the 'fixed, still state of Brahman', 'standing on a peak, unmoving, firm', a personal and incarnate God intervenes with the astonishing words, '*At*tach your mind to me'.[4]

'Who knows himself, knows his Lord', so runs the Muslim tradition. This is the message of Richard of St. Victor too: but, he warns, if this is to happen, then Rachel, the self you have learnt to know as the image of God, must die too, if Benjamin, 'a youth in ecstasy of mind', is ever to be born. St. Teresa knew this too: 'It is absurd to think', she writes, 'that we can enter Heaven without first entering our own souls.'[5] But knowing the image does not mean knowing the author of that image. On the contrary, it may prove a bar to further progress, and beginners on this dangerous path had better beware:

Some souls, at the beginning of the spiritual life, or even when well advanced in it, get as far as the Prayer of Quiet, and are about to enjoy the favours and consolations given by the Lord in that state, and then think it would be a very great thing to be enjoying these gifts all the time. Let them take my advice, and become less absorbed in them.[6]

---

[1] Ibid. 5: 19.   [2] Ibid. 2: 58.
[3] *Interior Castle*, 4. 3 (E. Allison Peers's translation, London, Sheed & Ward, 1946, p. 241).
[4] Gītā 7: 1.   [5] *Interior Castle*, 2. 1 (Peers, p. 218).
[6] Ibid., 6. 7 (Peers, p. 308).

Ruysbroek is yet more emphatic:

All those men are deceived whose intention it is to sink themselves in natural rest, and who do not seek God with desire nor find Him in delectable love. For the rest which they possess consists in an emptying of themselves, to which they are inclined by nature and by habit. . . . In this emptiness rest is sufficient and great, and it is in itself no sin, for it is in all men by nature, if they know how to make themselves empty. But when men wish to exercise and possess this rest without the works of virtue, then they fall into spiritual pride, and into a self-complacency from which they seldom recover. And at such times they believe themselves to have and to be that which they never achieve.[1]

This is the Nirvāna in which love is not present, that 'deep sleep' of which St. François de Sales speaks[2] in which the soul, though united to God, is yet unaware of it. Or rather it is that fourth state of consciousness beyond deep, dreamless sleep of which the *Māndūkya* Upanishad speaks and which is 'conscious of neither within nor without, nor of both together, not a mass of wisdom, neither wise nor unwise, unseen, one with whom there is no commerce, impalpable, devoid of distinguishing mark, unthinkable, indescribable, its essence the firm conviction of the oneness of itself, bringing all development to an end, tranquil and mild, devoid of duality. . . . That is the self.'[3]

For Richard of St. Victor this is the sleep of self-forgetfulness—forgetfulness of the self which is the image of God and an awakening to the wholly divine. He is still on a mountain-peak, but this time it is Sinai, and it is Moses who is ascending it:

Moses enters the cloud when the human mind, absorbed by the immensity of divine light, falls asleep in complete forgetfulness of itself. So that you may well wonder and you ought rightly to wonder how the cloud agrees here with the fire and the fire with the cloud; the cloud of unknowing with the fire of the enlightened intelligence; unknowing and forgetting of things known and experienced, with the revelation and understanding of things previously unknown and not experienced hitherto. For at one and the same time the human intelligence is illuminated with regard to divine things and darkened in respect of human things. This peace of the uplifted soul, this darkness and illumination is described by the Psalmist in a few words when he says: 'In peace in the selfsame I will sleep and I will rest.'[4]

All this is in the Gītā too; what is night for ordinary mortals is broad daylight for the sage who sees:

In what for all [other] folk is night, therein is the man of self-restraint awake. When all [other] folk are awake, that is night for the sage who sees. . . .[5] For [his]

---

[1] *The Spiritual Espousals*, pp. 167–8.   [2] Above, pp. 304–5.
[3] *Māndūkya* Upanishad 7.   [4] Richard of St. Victor, op. cit., p. 176.
[5] Gītā 2: 69.

mind is stilled in that which is ever the same: for devoid of imperfection and ever the same is Brahman: therefore in Brahman [stilled he] stands. . . .[1] With self integrated by spiritual exercise [now] he sees the self in all beings standing, all beings in the self: the same in everything he sees.[2]

This is possible because, as Richard says, when 'the soul "sleeps in the selfsame", . . . it rests in him . . . to whom it is one and the same thing to be everything that is, who alone can truthfully say: "I am who am" '.[3] Because the soul now rests in God it dilates into God's Being, but this does not mean that either loses its identity:

Who sees Me everywhere, who sees the All in Me, for him I am not lost, nor is he lost to Me.[4]

This is as true for Richard of St. Victor as it is for the Gītā. For both there can be no experience of the infinite until the life of the senses has been destroyed. Only then is it possible to enter into 'God's world' in which time and space are transcended. From here the soul can now ascend 'on the wings of a dove', as St. Gregory of Nyssa puts it, into the very being of God himself. There, Krishna says, 'he gains the highest love and loyalty to Me',[5] and this is the spiritual marriage of which the Christians speak.

For Richard there are four stages in the mystical ascent—knowledge of self, ascent to God, absorption in God, and finally going forth from God:

In the first degree, God enters into the soul and she turns inward into herself. In the second, she ascends above herself and is lifted up to God. In the third the soul, lifted up to God passes altogether into Him. In the fourth the soul goes forth on God's behalf and descends below herself. In the first she enters into herself, in the second she goes forth from herself. In the first she reaches her own life, in the third she reaches God. In the first she goes forth on her own behalf, in the fourth she goes forth because of her neighbour. In the first she enters in by meditation, in the second she ascends by contemplation, in the third she is led into jubilation, in the fourth she goes out by compassion.[6]

The first stage, as we have seen, corresponds to the Nirvāna of the Buddhists, and there is great danger in it because everything is for self. The soul 'turns inward into herself', 'enters into herself', 'reaches her own life', 'goes forth on her own behalf'.

'The struggle of the spirit is as brutal as the battles of men, but the vision of justice is the good pleasure of God alone,' as the poet Rimbaud said. It is brutal because the way is strewn with pitfalls. The first is that in

---

[1] Ibid. 5: 19. [2] Ibid. 6: 29. [3] Richard of St. Victor, op. cit., p. 177.
[4] Gītā 6: 30. [5] Ibid. 18: 54. [6] Richard of St. Victor, op. cit., p. 224.

reaching the 'truth' of yourself you should suppose that you have thereby reached the 'truth' of God and exhausted the inexhaustible. The second is to become so obsessed with God as totally to neglect and even to hate your neighbour: this is the besetting temptation of the mystics and one which they rarely overcome. This is, I think, what St. François de Sales means when he says that 'our hearts, at the threshold of their devotion, love God in order to become one with him, . . . but gradually, when they become proficient in the practice of love, an imperceptible change comes over them, . . . and instead of being in love with God, they fall in love with their own love for him, . . . finding contentment in this love in so far as it is theirs, in their own mind (*esprit*), proceeding from themselves. For although we call this holy love the love of God since it is through it that God is loved, it does not cease to be ours since we are the lovers who love through it. That is the point at which the change comes about; for instead of loving this sacred love because it tends towards God who is the Beloved, we love it because it proceeds from ourselves who are the lovers.'[1]

Not only is this 'struggle of the spirit' 'as brutal as the battles of men': it would also appear that you cannot win it if you forget for one moment the Buddhist precept that you may call nothing 'I', nothing 'mine'. In perfect love the soul is merely the *locus* of the divine love, the love of the Father for the Son *in* the Holy Spirit, as the Christians would put it, or, in Hindu terms, the love of Śiva for his Śakti, his Logos, *in* the essence of both which is love.[2]

It is at the top of the mountain-peak that all temporal things are put aside, and that the image of God, now perfectly clean, is ready to ascend towards God himself. This is pure contemplation, and it consists of 'enlarging the mind', 'raising the mind', and 'abstracting the mind'.[3]

'Enlargement' of the mind we are already familiar with: it is the 'cosmic consciousness' of R. M. Bucke, what the Muslims call *basṭ*, 'expansion'. This is still a matter of nature, not of grace; for, as Richard says: 'The enlarging of the mind is when the gaze of the soul expands widely and is intensely sharpened, but this in no way goes beyond the limit of human effort.'[4] It is natural to man, for it is perhaps the most common experience of the nature mystics, the 'seeing of all beings in the self and the self in all beings', the intuitive vision of the interpenetration and reconciliation of all things, both within and without, in the self. This coincides with the integration of the self into its original oneness because, according to popular mystical belief, man is a microcosm in which are reflected both the

[1] *Traité de l'amour de Dieu*, 9. 9 (E.T., pp. 379–80).   [2] Above, p. 165.
[3] Richard of St. Victor, op. cit., p. 185.   [4] Ibid., p. 183.

world and God. This produces an impression of almost limitless dilation, and this too was familiar to St. Teresa:

> It is clear [she says] that a dilation or enlargement of the soul takes place, as if the water proceeding from the spring had no means of running away, but the fountain had a device ensuring that, the more freely the water flowed, the larger became the basin.[1]

More strikingly it is related of the ninth-century Muslim mystic, Abū Yazīd, who seems to have been influenced by Hindu ideas, that he said:

> I raised my head from the valley of Lordship, and quaffed a cup the thirst for which could never, never be quenched. Then for thirty thousand years I flew in the atmosphere of his unity, and for another thirty thousand years I flew in deity, and for another thirty thousand years [I flew] in isolation. When these ninety thousand years were completed, I saw Abū Yazīd. Whatever I saw, all that was I. Then did I traverse four thousand deserts, and reached the end. When I looked, I saw that I had [only] reached the starting-off point of the prophets.[2]

This is the realization of the 'more minute than the minute' in 'the greater than the great' of which the Upanishads speak; and this too can be a pitfall, for 'it is only the *starting-off point* of the prophets'.

And so a slightly later mystic, Al-Qushayrī, warned in his turn:

> The expanded man experiences an expansion great enough to contain [all] creation; and there is practically nothing that will cause him fear. He is so 'expanded' that nothing will affect him in whatever state he may be. . . . Expansion comes suddenly and strikes the subject unexpectedly, so that he can find no reason for it. It makes him quiver with joy, yet scares him. . . . There is the greatest danger in this mood, and those who are open to it should be on their guard against an insidious deception. . . . [Moreover, it] must be considered a poor thing and a harmful one if compared with the [spiritual states] which are above it, such as the [apparent] annihilation of the servant [of God] and his gradual progress in the truth.[3]

'Upward progress in the truth' is what Richard of St. Victor calls 'raising the mind', and Gregory of Nyssa the flight 'upon the wings of the dove above all the lowly strivings of the world and, indeed, above the entire universe'.[4] This is possible because in the spiritual world motion and rest, like all the opposites, are not incompatible: the one thing that is constant, but constant in increase, is the soul's thirst for God. Because we can conceive of no limit to an infinite Being, and because what is limitless cannot by definition be understood, 'every desire for the Beautiful . . . is

---

[1] *Interior Castle*, 4. 3 (Peers, p. 244).
[2] R. C. Zaehner, *Hindu and Muslim Mysticism*, London, Athlone Press, 1960, p. 216.
[3] Ibid., p. 119.   [4] Gregory of Nyssa, op. cit., p. 109.

intensified by the soul's very progress towards it. And this is the real meaning of seeing God: never to have this desire satisfied.'[1]

The 'enlarging of the mind' in turn gives way to the 'raising' and 'abstracting of the mind', to an ecstasy in which the soul is drawn out above itself and alienated from itself:

> The human soul is led up above itself by wonder, when radiant with infused heavenly light and lost in wonder at the supreme beauty of God, she is torn from the foundation of her being. Like flashing lightning, the deeper she is cast down in self-depreciation in the face of the beauty she sees, so much the higher and the more rapidly does she rebound in her desire for the highest, and carried away above herself, she is lifted up to the heavens. The mind of man is abstracted from itself by excess of joy and exultation, when *its inmost self*, drunk with the abundance of interior sweetness, indeed wholly inebriated, *forgets altogether what it is and what it will be*, and is brought forth to this going forth of ecstasy by the greatness of its religious fervour, and in this condition of wonderful happiness, is suddenly transformed into a heavenly state.[2]

Here the 'image of God' is shattered so that it may melt into the very being of God. For this shattering Richard is prepared and the experience is therefore for him one of joy. In the Gītā Arjuna had the experience when he was shown Krishna's 'universal form'—and it terrified him:

> I see thee [he cries out], and *my inmost self is shaken*:
> I cannot bear it, I find no peace, O Vishnu![3]

But his terror is inseparable from his joy, for just as the justice of God is tempered by mercy, so is his violence tempered by sweetness:

> Things never seen before I've seen, and ecstatic is my joy;
> Yet fear and trembling possess my mind . . .
> Have mercy, Lord of gods, Home of the universe.[4]

In the Hindu tradition the terrible side of God—even of Śiva whose awful aspect is so prominent in mythology—is rarely emphasized. The Gītā is the one notable exception; and there is no doubt that the tremendous theophany of chapter xi puts one into the presence of God, as St. François de Sales would say, far more effectively than all the previous discourses on the integration of the soul, its liberation, and its 'detached attachment' to God. Here we come face to face with the Living Flame of Love of which St. John of the Cross speaks; and this is both the purifying fire of purgatory, in which the burning hope of an ultimate union with God outweighs the violence of the pains that have actually to be endured, and the flames

---

[1] Gregory of Nyssa, op. cit., pp. 147–8.   [2] Richard of St. Victor, op. cit., p. 189.
[3] Gītā 11: 24.   [4] Ibid. 11: 45.

of hell in which the self-willed are destroyed and lost. This 'sameness' and this contrast, this 'concord' and this 'discord' are here magnificently brought out:

> Lo, the hosts of gods are entering into thee:
> Some, terror-struck, extol thee, hands together pressed;
> Great seers and men perfected in serried ranks
> Cry out, 'All hail', and praise thee with copious hymns of praise.[1]

These are the blessed, but even they cannot escape the terror of the 'harsh, inexorable, hard, and pitiless'[2] love of God. As to God's enemies, they are swallowed up as rivers are in the ocean or as a moth is burnt to death in the fire. These similes, used in *this* context, are striking, for usually, in all mystical traditions, they are used to express the *joy* the mystic feels in having done for ever with all sense of self. This is true of the mystic, but for the ordinary natural man this loss of personality means an agonizing disruption and dissolution in death:

> Lo, all these sons of Dhritarāshtra
> Accompanied by a host of kings, . . .
> And those foremost in battle in our party too,
>
> Rush [blindly] into thy [gaping] mouths
> That with their horrid tusks strike [them] with terror.
> Some stick in the gaps between thy teeth,
> See them! their heads to powder ground! . . .
>
> As moths, in bursting, hurtling haste
> Rush into a lighted blaze to their destruction,
> So do the worlds, well-trained in hasty violence,
> Pour into thy mouths to their own undoing.
>
> On every side thou lickest, lickest up—devouring—
> Worlds, universes, everything—with burning mouths;
> Vishnu! thy dreadful rays of light fill the whole universe
> With flames of glory, scorching [everywhere].[3]

To discover one's own self, the unflecked mirror of absolute peace, is hard enough in itself since it runs wholly counter to the habits of 'natural' man born of the flesh. The struggle has been brutal. Small wonder, then, that the mystic should seek to sink himself in this 'natural rest', in this 'emptiness in which rest is sufficient and great'[4] and which he takes to be the journey's end. But the final stage when the soul comes face to face with

---

[1] Gītā 11: 21.
[2] François de Sales, *Traité de l'amour de Dieu*, 10. 13 (E.T., p. 436).
[3] Gītā 11: 26–30. [4] Above, p. 314.

the living God is the most dreadful of all, and Al-Junayd of Baghdad put the whole thing in a nutshell when he said:

> The journey from this world to the next is easy and simple for the believer, but to separate oneself from creatures for God's sake is hard, and the journey from self to God is exceedingly hard, and to bear patiently with God is the hardest of all.[1]

In the Dark Night of the Soul as opposed to the Dark Night of the Senses, God assaults and wounds the soul—he shatters the unity of his own image in man that he may prepare it for the spiritual marriage. These first assaults of love 'are called wounds,' says St. François de Sales, 'because the heart that seemed whole, integrated (*entier*), and sufficient to itself (*tout à soi-même*) while it did not love, comes . . . to be separated and divided from itself in order to give itself to the Beloved'.[2] St. John of the Cross speaks of these wounds as arrows or as a fiery spear. St. Teresa uses the same symbol to the great satisfaction of the Freudians. She sees an angel, and

> In his hands I saw a long golden spear and at the end of the iron tip I seemed to see a point of fire. With this he seemed to pierce my heart several times so that it penetrated to my entrails. When he drew it out, I thought he was drawing them out with it and he left me completely afire with a great love for God. The pain was so sharp that it made me utter several moans; and so excessive was the sweetness caused me by this intense pain that one can never wish to lose it, nor will one's soul be content with anything less than God. It is not bodily pain, but spiritual, though the body has a share in it—indeed, a great share.[3]

So too François de Sales speaks of 'the pitiless sword that pierced the Virgin Mother's sacred breast on the day of the Passion'[4] and which in turn pierced the heart of St. Francis of Assisi. To deny that the symbolism is phallic is quite unrealistic, for this is clearly the consummation of the spiritual marriage which is itself the climax of a long betrothal. Both in India and in Europe the soul's union with God has been conceived of in sexual terms, and it is no accident that some of the best Christian mystical writing has taken the form of a commentary on the 'Song of Songs'. Origen was well aware of this, and it upset him since he saw no interconnection between spirit and flesh:

> If [then] any man who lives only after the flesh should approach it, to such a one the reading of this Scripture will be the occasion of no small hazard and danger. For he, not knowing how to hear love's language in purity and with

[1] Zaehner, *Hindu and Muslim Mysticism*, p. 153.
[2] *Traité de l'amour de Dieu*, 6. 13 (E.T., p. 262).
[3] *Life*, tr. E. Allison Peers, pp. 192–3.   [4] *Traité* etc., 6. 15 (E.T., p. 262).

chaste ears, will twist the whole manner of his hearing of it away from the inner spiritual man and on to the outward and carnal; and he will be turned away from the spirit to the flesh, and will foster carnal desires in himself, and it will seem to be the Divine Scriptures that are thus urging and egging him on to fleshly lust.[1]

St. François de Sales too contrasts mystical ecstasy and rapture with the 'most infamous and abominable rapture'[2] of the flesh, but he is sane enough to recognize the genuine similarity, the 'discordant concord', between 'the affections of the heart and the passions of the body'.[3] In French 'rapture' is *ravissement*, and this also means 'rape'. As in India God is the male, the soul the female, and in the union there is violence as well as joy. Eckhart, as we have seen, says that the soul must become a woman, and not only become a woman but bring forth much fruit.[4] Here there is a difference of emphasis between what is most Christian in Christian mysticism and the main Indian tradition: 'By their fruits shall ye know them.' If the mystic forgets this, then however sublime his ecstasies may be, however much he may annihilate both his sensual and his spiritual self in God, however much he may be melted and consumed in the divine fire, however selfless his love for that Love which is God, he is still not a Christian unless his ecstasies, raptures, and transports bear fruit in this world:

> Unless a wheat grain falls on the ground and dies,
> it remains only a single grain;
> but if it dies, it yields a rich harvest.[5]

Contemplation and action—*jñāna* and *karma*—these should never be divorced. Even when one has left the mountain-peak of one's self and has soared aloft in the wide expanse of God, a man has still a duty to perform on earth; for, as Richard of St. Victor saw, there are four stages in this life: 'In the first [the soul] enters in [to herself] by meditation, in the second she ascends by contemplation, in the third she is led into jubilation, in the fourth she goes out by compassion.'[6]

The soul is female: but it must be doubly female—it must be Martha as well as Mary; and the pair of them 'must work together when they offer the Lord lodging. . . . And how can Mary give him anything, seated as she is at his feet, unless her sister helps her?'[7]

St. Teresa is right; for, as we have seen in our analysis of the major mystical traditions, even in the most sublime raptures you can never be

[1] *Origen, The Song of Songs, Commentary and Homilies*, tr. R. P. Lawson, London, Longman's, 1957, p. 22.
[2] *Traité* etc., 7. 4 (E.T., p. 282).   [3] Ibid. 6. 13 (E.T., p. 253).
[4] *Predigt.* 2.   [5] John 12: 24.   [6] Above, p. 315.
[7] St. Teresa, *Interior Castle*, 7. 4 (Peers, p. 348).

sure you have put behind you the sin of Lucifer—spiritual pride. This is Satan's last and most deadly weapon, for he too, the good saint assures us, can simulate raptures. And so let us say good-bye to the mystics in her own words:

'May God free you from pride and vainglory and grant that the Devil may not counterfeit these favours.'[1]

[1] St. Teresa, *Interior Castle*, 4. 3 (Peers, p. 245).

XVI

THE SERPENT'S GIFT

IN our survey of the Indian and Chinese traditions during the last year and a half, mysticism of one sort or another has never been far from us. Even when we had thought that we had safely landed on terra firma among the Confucians, we found that we were very soon ascending again to the heights of metaphysical mysticism which culminated in the 'Grand Synthesis' of Chu Hsi. Then, passing on to Christianity, I left you at the end of last term 'standing on a peak' with Hugh and Richard of St. Victor. Perhaps I have been wasting your time, for all are agreed that the mystic path is reserved for the very few. And so the greatest mystical classic of them all, the Bhagavad-Gītā, itself warns:

> Among thousands of men but one, maybe, will strive for [self]perfection, and even among [these] athletes who have won perfection['s crown] but one, maybe, will come to know Me as I really am.[1]

This is daunting enough, but it becomes even more so when we are authoritatively told by St. Teresa that these mystical states may well be counterfeited by the Devil. During our last five lectures we shall try to descend from the rarified air of the mountain-peak into the polluted atmosphere of the cities of the plain in which most of us are condemned to live. Both William James and Aldous Huxley thought that mystical states could be induced by drugs; but the more we have come to learn about these, the clearer it becomes that while it seems quite possible that the state of what Bucke called 'cosmic consciousness' can be induced by these, this may be the prelude not only to what Aldous Huxley took to be the Beatific Vision, but also to states of pure dissociation and disintegration which would seem to belong to Satan's infernal realm, not to the Kingdom of God. There is no short cut to these beatific states which is not fraught with peril; and, in any case, as a modern author has warned, 'meditation takes time, and time takes unearned income'.[2] On these grounds it is open to the same criticism as is psycho-analysis.

Of all the great religions of the world it is Judaism alone that fights shy of mysticism. What is called Jewish mysticism is rather visionary

---

[1] Bhagavad-Gītā 7: 3.
[2] Holmes Welch, *The Practice of Chinese Buddhism 1900–1950*, Harvard, 1967, p. 47.

experience or gnostic speculation as in the Kabbalah and Isaac Luria: it is certainly not the integration of the personality around its immortal core as in the Gītā, or the separation of spirit from matter as in early Buddhism, nor is it union with God. 'Not only is there for the mystic no divine immanence,' Professor Gershom Scholem writes, 'there is also almost no love for God. . . . Ecstasy there was, and this fundamental experience must have been a source of religious inspiration, but we find no trace of a mystical union between the soul and God. Throughout there remained an almost exaggerated consciousness of God's *otherness*, nor does the identity and individuality of the mystic become blurred even at the height of ecstatic passion. The Creator and His creature remain apart, and nowhere is an attempt made to bridge the gulf between them or to blur the distinction.'[1]

In my inaugural lecture I wrote:

It is then only too true that the basic principles of Eastern and Western, which in practice means Indian and Semitic, thought are, I will not say irreconcilably opposed; they are simply not starting from the same premises. The only common ground is that the function of religion is to provide release: there is no agreement at all as to what it is that man must be released from. The great religions are talking at cross purposes.[2]

And yet even this is not true, for the prime characteristic of the Jewish religion is not release—not even release from sin, for that is secondary— but living in accordance with the revealed will of God. That the Indian and Semitic religions are talking at cross purposes seems to me to be entirely true; and this hits one with quite appalling force and clarity when one returns from the 'concord' and 'harmony' so characteristic of the East to the 'discord' engendered by the literally furious activity, concern, and passion of the Lord God of Israel.

'J'ai dit: Dieu,' exclaims the poet Rimbaud in his *Saison en enfer*: 'je veux la liberté dans le salut.'[3] This is what the Jews were saying and still say: God and the liberty in salvation that can only come from God. And this is not the 'God of the philosophers and scientists' (*savants*), but 'the God of Abraham, the God of Isaac, the God of Jacob', whom Pascal experienced in ecstasy and who is a concrete and alarming force that conjures, begs, threatens, abjures, and loves the Jewish people with an exceedingly jealous love, who chastises them terribly and yet always repents! This God bears no resemblance whatever to the impassible Brahman of the Hindus or to the calmly aloof 'Heaven' of the Chinese: only in the Gītā does one catch a glimpse of this 'dark' side of the living God.

[1] Gershom G. Scholem, *Major Trends in Jewish Mysticism*, London, 1955, pp. 55–6.
[2] See Appendix, p. 439.   [3] *Œuvres complètes*, ed. Pléiade, p. 225.

Kierkegaard was right: this God can only be approached in fear and trembling.

I am sometimes amazed at the blindness of those often not very well-informed rationalists who brush aside the Jewish claim to be the chosen people. Their sacred book is like none other, for it is little concerned with eternal values but with human life and human misery as lived out on this earth in time. It is written in the form of a history book: it is the story of God and his people, of his covenant with them, their constant inability to live up to it, and the terrible retribution that overtakes them when, through pride, they choose to set it aside. Not even the Koran is comparable, for it simply repeats the Old Testament story in a discontinuous form mixing Old and New Testament themes and introducing matter deriving from the apocrypha of both. It is not the Koran that, as the Muslims claim, is a miracle in its own right, but the Jewish scripture on which, humanly speaking, it is based: for the Allah of the Koran is simply the Yahweh of Jewish scripture delivering the Old Testament message of 'promise and threat' to the Arab Ishmaelites, the traditional kinsmen of the Jews. The essential message is the same: God is totally other than man, and man is his servant whose sole function is to hear and to obey.

On the creation of man too the two books agree: he is created 'in God's image and likeness' on the one hand and is thereby God's 'viceroy on earth';[1] and on the other he is drawn out of the dust of the ground. It has now been established that in Genesis 1–3 two different accounts of the creation, usually called the Priestly and the Yahweistic, exist side by side: there seems to be little agreement between them. This, however, was not suspected until the so-called 'higher criticism' was launched on its erratic course. Hitherto it had been the task of successive generations of theologians to produce a more or less coherent account that reconciled the two stories. Sometimes the 'angelic' nature of man has been emphasized, sometimes the 'bestial'; but the consensus of the tradition as a whole is that man created 'in the image of God' must have been perfect in all respects and that he must have been immortal. So great is his glory that, for St. Gregory of Nyssa, he is all but the equal of God; for, as he says:

[God] did not make the heavens in His image, nor the moon, the sun, the beauty of the stars, nor anything else which you can see in the created universe. You alone are made in the likeness of that nature which surpasses all understanding; you alone are a similitude of eternal beauty, a receptacle of happiness, an image of the true Light; and if you look up to Him, you will become what He is, imitating Him Who shines within you, Whose glory is reflected in your purity.

[1] Koran 2: 28.

Nothing in all creation can equal your grandeur. All the heavens can fit into the palm of God's hand; the earth and the sea are measured in the hollow of His hand. And though He is so great that He can grasp all creation in his palm, you can wholly embrace Him; He dwells within you, nor is He cramped as He pervades your entire being. . . . If you realize this you will not allow your eye to rest on anything of this world. Indeed you will no longer marvel even at the heavens. For how can you admire the heavens, . . . when you see that you are more permanent than they? For the heavens pass away, but you will abide for all eternity with Him.[1]

Augustine's vision of primal man is less exalted:

Man lived in paradise as he desired, whilst he only desired what God commanded. He enjoyed God, from whence was his good. He lived without need, and had life eternal in his power. . . . Height of health was in his flesh, and fullness of peace in his soul. . . . There was no true sorrow, nor vain joy. Their joy continued by God's mercy, whom they loved with a pure good conscience and an unfeigned faith.[2]

This dream of an original innocence of man no longer makes sense, except in Taoist terms. Man's innocence was the innocence of an animal because, not being conscious of himself outside the group, he shared in the common life of the group, and through the group in the life of all living things. If indeed he was created 'in the image of God', then he was certainly not aware of it, for he had no self-consciousness with which he could be aware of himself or of anything else as being distinct from himself.

The discovery of evolution hit the Christian churches hard, and for a long time they kicked against the evolutionary pricks. This they can no longer do, and the Genesis story has to be interpreted against the background of our evolutionary origin. Once we do this, then the Fall begins to look more like an ascent than a degradation. For self-consciousness which transforms man into a *rational* animal is a qualitative leap in the evolutionary process which adds a new dimension to life: life becomes conscious of itself. Hence, as Pascal says, 'though man may be only a reed and the weakest one in all nature, he is none the less a thinking reed. It is quite unnecessary for the whole universe to be mobilized to crush him; a vapour or a drop of water is quite enough to kill him. But even if the universe were to crush him, man would still be more noble than what kills him because he knows he dies, and of the advantage that the universe has over him the universe knows nothing.'[3]

---

[1] Gregory of Nyssa, *Commentarius in Canticum Canticorum, Oratio II*, 807–8: E.T. in Jean Daniélou, *From Glory to Glory*, tr. Herbert Masurillou, pp. 162–3.

[2] Augustine, *City of God* (tr. John Healey), 14. 26.

[3] Pascal, *Œuvres complètes*, ed. Pléiade, pp. 1156–7.

Every generation has its own interpretation of these perennially fascinating first chapters of Genesis, and R. M. Bucke's seems to me still to have some relevance. This is how he sees the drama:

Man's progenitor was a creature (an animal) walking erect but with simple consciousness merely. He was (as are to-day the animals) incapable of sin or of the feeling of sin and equally incapable of shame (at least in the human sense). He had no feeling or knowledge of good and evil. He as yet knew nothing of what we call work and had never labored. From this state he fell (or rose) into self consciousness, his eyes were opened, he knew that he was naked, he felt shame, acquired the sense of sin (became in fact what is called a sinner), and learned to do certain things in order to encompass certain ends—that is, he learned to labor.

For weary eons this condition has lasted—the sense of sin still haunts his pathway—by the sweat of his brow he still eats bread—he is still ashamed. Where is the deliverer, the Saviour? Who or what?[1]

For Bucke, of course, the 'Saviour' was 'cosmic consciousness'. This, he maintained, could for a long time be the privilege of only a few individuals. But what if it should spread to the masses, become a *shared* experience, and destroy in them 'sin, shame, the sense of good and evil as contrasted one with the other, and annihilate labor, though not human activity', as Bucke had prophesied?[2]

Well, some of us are old enough to remember how Hitler succeeded in stirring up what can only be described as a collective 'cosmic consciousness' through which he was indeed able to 'destroy sin, shame, the sense of good and evil as contrasted one with the other'. The Devil, St. Teresa assures us, can counterfeit mystical states: he can also, it would appear, produce cosmic consciousness on a collective scale, and this is sometimes called mass hysteria. But let that pass; for it is with Bucke's interpretation of the Fall that we are now concerned. His approach is broadly evolutionary, and he is therefore unhampered by the difficulties that the myth presents to the theologian. This is easy for him, for the myth lends itself to evolutionary interpretation, but with embarrassing results for the theologian; for it is not God who personifies the forward thrust of evolution, but the serpent: it is the serpent who propels man into a state of self-consciousness, and Yahweh who would hold him back.

The Genesis account of the Fall which shows Yahweh up in such a bad light has always been a grave embarrassment to the orthodox, but a godsend to critics of both Judaism and Christianity from Marcion, the Gnostics, and the Zoroastrians to Voltaire and C. G. Jung. It is not my

---

[1] R. M. Bucke. *Cosmic Consciousness*, p. 6.   [2] Ibid., pp. 6–7.

purpose to trace the vicissitudes of the doctrine of the Fall in the orthodox Jewish and Christian traditions, for this has recently been admirably summarized by Dr. J. M. Evans in his *Paradise Lost and the Genesis Tradition*; but it is worth pointing out that interpretations of Adam's nature before the Fall oscillate between what are called the 'maximal' and 'minimal' views. The maximal we have already met with in St. Gregory of Nyssa and Augustine: man is the image of God and exhibits the perfection of all virtues and happiness. The minimal view, which alone is consonant with the evolutionary theory of the origin of man, emphasizes not man's angelic perfection but his childlike innocence and ignorance. The Fall indeed was not a 'fall at all. On the contrary, it was an over-abrupt *rise*, a momentary transition from a state of naïve innocence to one of precocious maturity; it was a cautionary tale of a child who grew up too quickly, not of a demi-god who fell.'[1]

But what of the roles of Yahweh and the serpent in all this? For Marcion and the Gnostics the answer was simple: Yahweh is not the true God at all, but an underling who is not only ignorant of the existence of the true God and of his own subordinate nature, but also pusillanimous, unjust, and malicious.[2] He is the demuirge, but through his own stupidity he botches his own creation and chastises his own creature, man, for his own mistakes. The serpent, on the other hand, is the spirit of rationality, the immanent will inherent in the evolutionary process, if you like, which urges the human race to grow up. In Genesis there is no indication at all that he is Satan, for this identification first appears in Revelation 20: 2. It is only said of him that he was 'the most subtle of all the wild beasts that Yahweh God had made'—so subtle indeed that he seemed to be privy to God's counsels just as Satan himself, the 'accuser', serves God's inscrutable purpose in the Book of Job:

The serpent was the most subtle of all the wild beasts that Yahweh God had made. It asked the woman, 'Did God really say you were not to eat from any of the trees in the garden?' The woman answered the serpent, 'We may eat the fruit of the trees in the garden. But of the fruit of the tree in the middle of the garden God said, "You must not eat it, nor touch it, under pain of death."' Then the serpent said to the woman, 'No! You will not die! God knows in fact that on the day you eat it your eyes will be opened and you will be like gods, knowing good and evil.' The woman saw that the tree was good to eat and pleasing to the eye, and that it was desirable for the knowledge that it could give. So she took some of the fruit and ate it. She gave some also to her husband who

[1] J. M. Evans, op. cit., p. 19.
[2] Adolf von Harnack, *Marcion: das Evangelium vom fremden Gott*, Leipzig, 1924, p. 101.

was with her, and he ate it. Then the eyes of both of them were opened and they realized that they were naked.[1]

They had, in fact, become self-conscious as individual and responsible human beings. Civilization had begun: they had passed above the level of the beasts, and seeing themselves naked like the beasts they were ashamed. To distinguish themselves from the beasts they clothed themselves: they were now separate from Nature and began to use Nature for their own purposes—they began to think in terms of 'I' and 'mine', according to the Buddhists the root-delusion of mankind. In Western terminology they had become 'persons', that is, 'individual substances of a rational nature' as St. Thomas, following Boethius, puts it,[2] and in the Western tradition it is our rationality that constitutes our superiority to the beasts. Hence, according to our Western way of thinking, the hero of the story can only be the serpent: it is Yahweh who is the enemy of the progress of mankind. And so even the Church fathers who took a minimal view of Adam's original nature were forced to say that the tree of knowledge was not in itself evil, most of them understanding by it scientific knowledge, while Gregory Nazianzen regards it as contemplation for which mankind was not yet ripe.[3] I cannot, however, help feeling that the most natural interpretation of the myth of the Fall is a Taoist one. Knowledge is in itself evil because it automatically leads to misery. Of its very nature it distinguishes— meddles with the 'Uncarved Block', brings discord into the original harmony of the Tao. No amount of humanly contrived virtue will put this right, for virtue, so long as it is objectivized as virtue and therefore no longer spontaneous, is the mother of vice. The Fall was not sudden— and in evolutionary terms it must represent tens of thousands of years—it was a gradual but inexorable *chute à l'abîme*:

> After Tao was lost, then came the 'power';
> After the 'power' was lost, then came human kindness.
> After human kindness was lost, then came morality,
> After morality was lost, then came ritual.
> Now ritual is the mere husk of loyalty and promise-keeping
> And is indeed the first step towards brawling.[4]

In the Western tradition, so far as I know, it is only Rousseau who approximates to this position: for him too it is reason, and along with reason its offspring *amour-propre*, that is responsible for all our ills, for, as he disconcertingly says, 'the state of reflective thought is a state that is contrary to Nature and meditating man is a depraved animal'.[5] Rousseau does not

[1] Genesis 3: 1–7.   [2] *Summa Theologica*, xxix. i, obj. 1.
[3] J. M. Evans, op. cit., p. 81.   [4] *Tao Tê Ching*, 38.
[5] *Discours sur l'origine . . . de l'inégalité . . .*, ed. Pléiade, vol. iii, p. 138.

confuse God with Nature as Spinoza had done: rather God is the principle of unity within all things and the intelligence that directs 'the
harmony and concord of all things'.[1] Hence, Rousseau would have us
believe, to see all things as one and to see the One as the all is the natural
state of primitive man; but once reason starts 'to enter into details, the
greatest marvel of all escapes it, that is, the harmony and concord of the
All'.[2] As in Taoism, to live in harmony with the All means that one has no
sense of distinction between oneself and others; death itself is not a
catastrophe since the *idea* of death has not yet arisen. 'Men die, and nobody
even notices that they have ceased to exist, and they themselves are scarcely
aware of it.'[3] And yet primitive man is both distinct from and superior to
the beasts because he is self-conscious in the sense that he sees himself and
feels himself to be an integral part of the whole, fulfilling his appointed role
in the universal design in harmony and concord with all other created
things: he sees himself and loves himself in the context of the whole
because he, like the whole and all the other parts that make it up, is made
in the image of God. Hence *l'amour de soi*, love of self, is inseparable from
love of one's neighbour because both have their allotted parts to play in
the fulfilment of the whole: together they go to make up the 'image of
God'. For Rousseau, though he had broken with both Calvinism and
Catholicism and then with Calvinism again, remained very conscious that
man is made in the image of God and that he has miserably fallen. 'God of
my soul,' he exclaims in a moving passage in the 'Profession de foi du vicaire
savoyard', 'I shall never hold it against you that you have made my soul in
your image so that I could be free, good, and happy like you.'[4]

As for Mencius, so for Rousseau, man was originally free and good and
happy like the God in whose image he was made; and so 'eternal wisdom'
had created him not only innocent but ignorant, wishing thereby to
'preserve him from knowledge (*science*) just as a mother would wrench a
dangerous weapon from the hands of her child'.[5] For knowledge and happiness are incompatible. Knowledge distinguishes and therefore separates;
only much later can it strive after synthesis and cohesion. Happiness, on
the other hand, is scarcely conceivable without communication, expansion,
and interpenetration; and so the first men 'found security in their ability
to penetrate each other reciprocally, and this faculty (*avantage*), the value
of which we can no longer appreciate, spared them many a vice'.[6] Because
there was this *participation mystique* among these 'men of old', love of self

[1] *Émile*, ed. Garnier–Flammarion, 1966, p. 359.   [2] Ibid.
[3] *Discours sur l'origine . . .*, p. 137.   [4] *Émile*, p. 366.
[5] *Discours sur les sciences et les arts*, ed. Pléiade, vol. iii, p. 15.
[6] Ibid., p. 8.

necessarily meant love of one's neighbour in and through a 'unique intelligence', the existence of which is guaranteed by the felt certainty that 'All is One' though infinitely and mysteriously diversified.[1] Of course, every human being is from his own point of view the centre of the universe of which he is a part, but this can only be really true if he is indwelt by the 'unique intelligence' which is the centre of centres and the focus of love. For

> In the whole universe there is no being which cannot be considered, from some point of view, as being the common centre of all the rest around which they are set in due order so that they are all and reciprocally both ends and means to one another. The mind loses its bearings and goes astray in this infinity of relationships of which, nevertheless, not one is [really] lost in the crowd.[2]

All these relationships cohere in God who is the centre of centres but nevertheless always inaccessible to the senses and the mind. 'The more I think of him,' says Rousseau, 'the more perplexed do I become. I know absolutely for sure that he exists and exists of himself: I know that my existence is subordinated to his and that this is true of all things known to me. I see God everywhere in his works; I feel him within me, I see him all around me; but once I would contemplate him as he is in himself, . . . he escapes me and my troubled spirit is no longer aware of anything.'[3]

For Rousseau this was as true of primitive man as it was of himself; and primitive man or 'Adam' was, of course, the human race as he supposed it to have existed in its pristine innocence. No more than for Julian of Norwich and many other Christian writers was Adam a single man: he was what Julian calls 'All-man', the human race in its infancy. Like the Taoists Rousseau projected his own experience of a blissful oneness with all Nature on to our mythical and as yet unsullied ancestors. Of himself he says in the *Rêveries du promeneur solitaire*:

> The more the soul of a contemplative is sensitive, the more does he abandon himself to the ecstasies aroused in him by this [natural] concord. A sweet and profound *rêverie* then takes hold of his senses and, delightfully intoxicated, he is lost in the immensity of this beauteous system with which he feels himself identified. Then all individual objects elude him; he sees and feels nothing except in the All.[4]

This was the paradise from which Adam strayed—a paradise in which God was a living presence, a loving father (and mother), walking with a child who trusted him but who was content not to understand him or question his ways. The serpent, however, intervened: he ate of the fatal

---

[1] *Émile*, p. 360.   [2] Ibid., p. 359.   [3] Ibid., p. 360.
[4] *Rêveries du promeneur solitaire*, 7. Ed. Pléiade, vol. i, pp. 1062–3.

tree, and then, with knowledge, evil entered into the world of man. Having tasted of the bitter-sweet fruit, Adam looked round and found that the harmonious concord in which his soul had bathed, and from which it had drawn its sustenance, was irretrievably marred and wracked with an inexplicable discord; for the All-man has now become many men each with an individual consciousness, and all are baffled by what they see; and this is how Rousseau describes their situation:

> Wishing henceforward to know my individual place among my own kind, and contemplating the various orders [of existence] and the men that constitute them, what happens to me? What do I see? What has happened to the order which I had previously observed? Nature had once shown me a picture in which there was only harmony and due proportion; but in the picture of the human race I saw only confusion and disorder! Among the elements concord reigns supreme, but men live in chaos. The animals are happy, only their king is wretched! Wisdom, where are your laws? Providence, is it thus that you govern the world? O beneficent Being, what has happened to your power? I see evil on the face of the earth.[1]

Rousseau had rejected what he considered to be the crude mythology of the first chapters of Genesis, but he yet preserved its inner meaning and its abiding Catholic truth. With the appearance of knowledge and primitive science evil had entered the world of man. Like the Taoists he saw that 'where there are ingenious contrivances, there are sure to be subtle doings; and that, where there are subtle doings, there is sure to be a scheming mind. But, when there is a scheming mind in the breast, its pure simplicity is impaired. When this pure simplicity is impaired, the spirit becomes unsettled, and the unsettled spirit is not the proper residence of the Tao.'[2]

For the Taoist, however, there was no problem, for the Tao is an impersonal flow, rebellion against which could in no wise affect or offend it. Man had strayed from it through his own cleverness and fatuous pride. Even so it would not occur to him to doubt the existence of the Tao or that it could be other than good; for the Tao is not a person, it has no conscious will such as man had come to have: it simply is, and you do not kick against the pricks of what *is* and is simply given. Not even the Confucians would do this; for the Confucian too accepts the fact of the 'Fall', but he cannot accept it as irreparable. Man, by the very use of his conscious intellect and the human kindness and morality which are innate to his nature, can restore that order from which he had unknowingly strayed. He is, or should be, master in his own house: he must recreate the Tao in his own image.

---

[1] *Émile*, pp. 361–2.   [2] Above, p. 229.

In the Hebrew tradition things are very different. Man's sin was to disobey the command of a very personal God: the child has rejected the authority of the father, not knowing the result of what he does. Through the temptation of the serpent and the eating of the forbidden fruit his eyes are opened, and he knows that every advance in knowledge brings new problems to be solved and new and more acute suffering to be undergone. The image of God has become obscured: it has sunk deep down below the level of consciousness, and what should have been the ruler and director of the whole man has become the slave of a mortal, animal frame. And here, in Genesis, the Fall of man is depicted in starkly tragic terms, far more moving—and far more depressing—than anything we meet with in India or China. For both in India and in China the possibility of restoring the image was never wholly lost to sight. For the Hindu it was always possible to recover the image in each individual person; you have only to detach your gaze from the outside world and contemplate your inner essence. There you will find the image. This may not seem natural, but it can be done:

> The self-existent [Lord] bored holes facing the outside world;
> Therefore a man looks outward, not into himself.
> A certain sage, in search of immortality
> Turned his eyes inward and saw the self within.[1]

This was the way of India: it was not the way of China. True, there had been a break in the Tao, but this did not mean that Heaven had abandoned man, for its image in man remains. It is his conscience, and conscience is made up of human kindness, justice, decency, and wisdom. These are there and, in the view of Mencius, obviously there. You have only to use them and all will be well. This was not the experience of the Hebrew All-man: he had disobeyed God, and in so doing he realized that he was naked. He realized that he had become a rational animal separate from his kind, and that now he must defend himself by the new faculty he had acquired—reason, which separated him from Nature and estranged him from God, reason, the serpent's gift. He now saw that he had emerged out of the immortal life of the All and that since he was naked and alone he must surely die. This, man's experience of unease and loneliness on his emergence into self-consciousness, we meet with in the Hindu scriptures too:

In the beginning this [universe] was the Self alone—in the likeness of a man. Looking round, he saw nothing other than himself. First of all he said: 'This is I.'

[1] *Katha* Upanishad 4: 1.

Hence the name 'I' came to be. So even now when a man is addressed, he says first, 'This is I', and then speaks out any other name he may have. . . . He was afraid. So [even now] a man who is all alone is afraid.[1]

In the case of the Hebrew All-man he was afraid because he knew that he must die: the image of God within him which cannot but be immortal had become totally submerged, and death then, so far as he could see, must be total. All he could expect was a shadowy and miserable existence in Sheol, unimaginably dreary and obscure. But there are yet two sides to the picture; and though the so-called 'higher criticism' has done well to make us conscious of the different layers of tradition that go to make up the Old Testament as we know it, this does not alter the fact that the two accounts of creation that we find in Genesis admirably complement each other and fit in remarkably well with what the Indian tradition has to tell us. Man has a dual nature. First:

> God created man in the image of himself,
> In the image of God he created him.[2]

Second:

Yahweh God fashioned man of dust from the soil. Then he breathed into his nostrils a breath of life, and thus man became a living being.[3]

The 'image of God' we find in other traditions too, for both the Hindus of the Vaishnavite school and the neo-Confucians know it.[4] For them it is the reflection in man of the changeless glory of God—a glory of which man is not normally conscious but which he can recover by reflecting on his own true nature. This is what constitutes the greatness of man in virtue of which he is 'little less than a god'[5] and God's viceroy on earth;[6] but this is a glory of which the Old Testament knows nothing, for by virtue of the fact that man was also 'fashioned of the dust from the soil', he is no better than the beasts, and once his eyes are opened this is what he learns. Even so he is not totally corrupt since, thanks to the good offices of the serpent, he has become a responsible and free creature, 'knowing good and evil'. Hence it is still possible for him to accept God's decrees and to co-operate with his grace. But in the Hebrew tradition, unlike the Indian, he is totally corrupt in the sense that the image of God within him has become totally obscured: no longer can he restore the divine image within himself, no longer can he recapture his timeless essence, for he has received the serpent's gift of discursive reason, and this is always the enemy of contemplation—more even than the flesh.

---

[1] *Brihadāranyaka* Upanishad 1: 4: 1–2.   [2] Genesis 1: 27.   [3] Ibid. 2: 7.
[4] Above, pp. 274 ff., p. 309.   [5] Psalm 8: 5.   [6] Koran 2: 28.

In his early writings Rousseau attributes all man's ills to the acquisition of knowledge: the arts and civilization are of their very nature corrupt because they impede the vision of the totality of being which he considered to be the prerogative of primitive man. This is very Taoist. In the 'Profession de foi du vicaire savoyard', however, he reverts to what had become the orthodox Christian view, the seeds of which are in St. Paul and the unpleasing fruit of which emerges all too clearly in Augustine: man is half angel and half beast, and what is beastly, that is to say, what is material, must be ruthlessly suppressed. From being a Taoist Rousseau has become a Manichee. Thus

> In meditating on the nature of man [he writes] I thought I could distinguish two different principles, one of which raised him to the contemplation of eternal truths, to love of justice and of moral beauty, to the regions of the world of mind, the contemplation of which is the joy of the wise, while the other dragged him down deep into himself, enslaving him to the dominion of the senses and the passions which minister to them, undoing thereby all that the consciousness of the first had inspired in him. Feeling myself carried away and buffeted by these two opposing currents, I said to myself: 'No, man is not one: I will and I do not will; I feel that I am a slave and yet free; I see the good and I love it, yet it is evil that I do. I am active when I listen to reason, passive when I am carried away by my passions; and the worst torment I suffer when I succumb is that I feel that I could have resisted.'[1]

By 'reason' Rousseau here means the contemplative intellect: he most emphatically does not mean the 'reason' employed by the philosophers, for this he considered to be a deliberate human misuse of a divinely implanted faculty. 'Ideas general and abstract are the source of man's greatest errors', he says. 'Never has the jargon of metaphysics led to the discovery of a single truth; rather it has filled philosophy with absurdities one can only be ashamed of once one has stripped them of their high-sounding words.'[2]

This is the *abuse* of our faculties which makes us unhappy and evil.[3] And here Rousseau aligns himself with Catholic tradition: the tree of knowledge is not in itself evil, it is man's use of it that has led him astray. For the highest form of knowledge is contemplation, the contemplation of self first, as in Richard of St. Victor and the Bhagavad-Gītā, and then the contemplation of God. Man goes wrong when he passes beyond *l'amour de soi*, love of the self as it is in its essence, and instead of raising himself to God, descends to *amour-propre*, love of self for what it can get out of others and out of God. This is the meaning of the Fall; and for Rousseau, as for

---

[1] *Émile*, p. 362.   [2] Ibid., p. 356.   [3] Ibid., p. 366.

La Rochefoucauld and the Buddha, *amour-propre* is the root-sin of mankind.

Rousseau's 'self' or soul, however, is never a totally detached entity as it so often is with the Hindus. 'I *feel* my soul,' he says, 'and I know it by feeling and by thinking: I know it exists without knowing its essence.'[1] And yet this self or soul cannot but be affected by the life it leads on earth: it can never shake itself free of *karma*, for it is bound to *karma* by memory. The soul is the image of God, but the image is an individual image, and the picture reflected may be beautiful or vile depending on the quality of one's life on earth. Here Rousseau, and indeed the whole Christian tradition from which he derives, parts company with the Hindu. The Hindu aims at restoring the image in all its purity, a changelessness devoid of all impressions derived from life, whereas for Rousseau the image may emerge from bodily life, either embellished by the memory of works well done or distorted by an evil life. As for Teilhard de Chardin, so for Rousseau, good is simply another word for concord, evil for discord: good unites, evil divides. Hence in German the word for sin, *Sünde*, comes from the same root as separation, *Sonderung*—separation of man from God, of man from man, and of the 'image of God' in man from its material envelope, and most important of all the separation of the individual from the ties that bind him to all things through the centre of all things which is God. 'The difference [between good and evil] is that the good is ordered in relationship to the All while evil orders the All in relationship to itself. It makes itself the centre of all things, while the other takes due account of its radius and remains on the circumference. And so he is himself ordered in relationship to the common centre which is God, and in relationship to all the concentric circles which are creatures.'[2] This is the harmony which 'man's first disobedience' shattered and which must somehow be restored.

Rousseau, in his 'Profession de foi', might have been writing a commentary on the first chapters of Genesis. He was not. But in his thought he remained without knowing it, or knowing it only partially—for his *vicaire savoyard* is based on a real Catholic priest from Savoy whom he had met in his youth—he remained firmly within the Catholic tradition; he did not denounce God, who, for inscrutable reasons, permits evil, as did Marcion and the Gnostics and his contemporary Voltaire, but submitted to him in uncomprehending contemplation. The villain of the piece is not Yahweh, but the flesh and above all the serpent who tempted man out of his original innocence into his baleful experience of good and evil. Despite

[1] *Émile*, p. 368.   [2] Ibid., p. 380.

his sometimes almost rapt adoration of Nature, he did not identify God with Nature as Spinoza and the Taoists did, nor did he identify him with the soul as did the non-dualist Vedāntins among the Hindus. But the point at which Rousseau remains most Catholic is in his fervent championship of the freedom of the human will which he considered, despite man's disastrous misuse of it, to be God's most precious gift to man. And man, whether in a state of original innocence and ignorance or when he has accepted the serpent's gift of knowledge, must always bow down before the transcendent majesty of God:

As I draw near in spirit to the Eternal Light, [he says,] its effulgence blinds me and throws me off my balance and I am forced to abandon all the earthly ideas which helped me to imagine him. . . . The Supreme Intelligence which rules the world is yet not the world, and it is in vain that I lift up my spirit and tire it in trying to conceive of his essence. When I think that it is this Intelligence that gives life and activity to the living and active substance that rules these living bodies; when I hear it said that my soul is spiritual and that God is a spirit, I revolt against this degradation of the divine essence—as if God and my soul were of the same nature, as if God were not the only absolute Being—he alone who is really active, really feels and thinks, really wills through his own power (*par lui-même*) and through whom we are endowed with thought, feeling, activity, will, freedom, and Being.[1]

How strange that Rousseau, the apostle of Nature and man's freedom, should in his old age come down so firmly on the side of the Christian God and his essential distinction from man, his image, and from the whole created order. What did it matter if the world were created out of nothing or not? These are matters outside our ken, and to delve into them as the theologians, his enemies, did was yet another sign of man's intellect being confused and perverted by an unseemly pride. How futile to compare the intelligence of God to the intelligence of man. 'God is intelligent,' certainly, 'but in what way? Man is intelligent when he reasons, but the supreme intelligence has no need to reason: it knows nothing of premises or consequences—nor even of propositions: it is purely intuitive, seeing equally all that is and all that can be. In its eyes all truths are but a single idea, just as all places are but a single point and all times a single moment.'[2]

All this fits perfectly into the grand pattern of the universal mystical tradition, and yet how Christian it is! For Rousseau will not permit man to exalt himself to the level of deity as the Hindus did, nor will he question the goodness and justice of God despite all the evidence to the contrary. To him the goodness of God was 'obvious', since it manifests itself in his

---

[1] Ibid., pp. 370-1. [2] Ibid., p. 371.

'love of order' while human goodness manifests itself in love of one's neighbour. God is just: injustice is of man. 'Moral disorder', he says, 'which bears witness against Providence in the eyes of the philosophers only goes to prove [its goodness] in mine.'[1]

The Hindus are perpetually talking about transcending good and evil. Rousseau, who has much in common with them in other respects, will have none of this, for 'the justice of man is to render to each his due, while the justice of God is to demand an account of each for what has been given him'.[2] How very Christian it all is, and how Christian again his final act of adoration!

In fine [he says] the more I try to contemplate [God's] infinite essence, the less can I conceive of it. The mere fact that it *is* is enough for me. The less I can conceive of him, the more do I adore him. I humble myself and say to him: 'Being of beings, I am because you are. To meditate on you continually means to be raised to the source of my being; and the best use of my reason is to annihilate it before you. This is the rapture of my mind, this the charm of my weakness, that I should feel myself overcome by your greatness.'[3]

How strange it is that Rousseau's religious thought should have been so entirely neglected by Christians! In his disbelief in miracles, his recognition that religious truth is to be found in all religions, in his impatience with the theologians' dissection of scripture, he merely anticipated the modernists of a later day, while in his intensity of belief, in his intuitive apperception of the ineffable concord that refused to be disturbed by the discord for which man is alone responsible, in his affirmation of both God's transcendence and his immanence, even in, or, should we say, most of all in his not desperate but hopeful clinging to God during his last years of persecution mania, how much he has to teach us Christians still! and not least in his interpretation of the Fall of man. There he is squarely at one with the Christian tradition. He does not, like Job, question the ways of omnipotence. Perhaps he was more naïve, but he never doubted the goodness and justice of God. Tried more severely than ever Job was, he came to know God not through a vision of his implacable and inexplicable grandeur, but as the source of all harmony, all-pervading, indwelling, vivifying both the human soul and the universe, yet standing outside them both in inaccessible majesty.

How Christian again (though how un-Augustinian) is his analysis of man's fallen estate as being primarily due to the misuse of the intellect, only secondarily to the concupiscence of the flesh. In Genesis there is God, and there is man, both as the image of God and as the material

---

[1] *Émile*, p. 371.   [2] Ibid., pp. 371–2.   [3] Ibid., p. 372.

creature formed from the dust of the earth, and there is the serpent. For Rousseau the serpent is the intellect misused: and this again is wholly consonant with the Christian tradition. Were it reason as such, then it would be impossible to justify the ways of God to his rational creatures.

In the Koran we are told not only of the fall of Adam but also of the fall of Satan. Both are due to disobedience to a divine command. Of Satan (or Iblīs as he is here called) it is said:

> Thy Lord said to the angels, 'I am setting in the earth a viceroy.' They said, 'What, wilt thou set therein one who will work corruption there, and shed blood, while we proclaim thy praise and call thee holy?' . . . And when We said to the angels, 'Bow yourselves to Adam'; so they bowed themselves, save Iblīs; he refused, and waxed proud, and so he became one of the unbelievers.[1]

Satan then tempts Adam and Eve to eat of the forbidden tree: they do so, and are expelled from paradise as in Genesis. Satan, replacing the biblical serpent, tempts Adam after he had himself fallen. Satan himself was not tempted but fell of his own volition through a direct act of disobedience. The ninth-century mystic Al-Hallāj has an interesting interpretation of this. Satan, he says, was really the most selfless of all God's creatures since he knew that the one really unforgivable sin was to worship what was other than God: hence he refused to worship God's viceroy on earth, man. He disobeyed an individual command but obeyed the *will* of God. Much the same defence might be made of the serpent in Genesis. It was inevitable that man should grow up into full self-consciousness, and this must have been the *will* of God, contrary though it was to his express command. The serpent is, then, the real agent of God's will: he merely accelerates an inevitable process. He is the symbol of evolution, the immanent will of God that man should grow up as a self-conscious and responsible agent, knowing good and evil. The serpent's only crime was that he hastened the process. As Dr. Evans says: 'Only if Adam was in some way immature could his Maker have commanded him to abstain from something which was in essence good. . . . The Fall [then] consisted in eating the fruit too soon and so growing up too quickly.'[2] The serpent merely hastens an inevitable process. In a sense he is God's servant just as Satan is in the Book of Job. His character, like Yahweh's, is thoroughly ambivalent—neither good nor evil—and both are open to attack. Voltaire, needless to say, sprang to the defence of the serpent and put these words into his mouth:

> I have been wronged. I gave [Eve] the best possible advice. She honoured me with her confidence. My opinion was that she and her husband should gorge

---

[1] Koran 2: 28–32.   [2] J. M. Evans, op. cit., p. 80.

themselves on the fruit of the tree of knowledge. I thought that in so doing I would please the Master. It seemed to me that a tree so necessary to the human race could not have been planted to no purpose. Would the Master really have wished to be served by a lot of ignoramuses and idiots? Is not the mind made to achieve enlightenment and perfection? Is it not necessary to know good and evil if one is to do the one and avoid the other? Really I deserved some gratitude.[1]

The serpent *has* been wronged. Being the 'most subtle of all the wild beasts that Yahweh God had made', he knew that it was God's plan that man should become a rational being and he knew the price that man would have to pay. Knowing this he thought that the leap might as well take place sooner rather than later, since it was bound to take place anyway. Thus, like Satan in the Koran, he obeys the unexpressed will of God though he disobeys a command. The Fall, if by that we mean man's emergence into full self-consciousness, *had* to happen. Hence in the liturgy for Holy Saturday the Catholic Church hails it as a *felix culpa*, a 'happy fault', and *certe necessarium Adae peccatum*, the 'absolutely *necessary* sin of Adam'. It had to happen, and it was bound to bring suffering. And so the angels in the Koran were also right, for they too foresaw that man, once he had reached self-consciousness, 'would work corruption and shed blood'. This was the price he had to pay in order to grow up, and it was the serpent who jolted him out of his pre-conscious state of a blissful participation in all things into the tough reality of the world of adult men. Like Yahweh himself the serpent is neither good nor evil: he is the evolutionary drive which is at the disposal of both. He is as ambivalent as matter itself, and he is ambivalent in the Bible too.

Now in Genesis it is said that 'the serpent was the most subtle of all the wild beasts that Yahweh God had made'; and Jesus certainly knew his Bible. Why, then, did Christ, on sending out the Twelve, bid them to be 'as subtle as serpents and gentle as doves'?[2] 'Gentle as doves' seems obvious enough; for the dove is already the symbol of the Holy Spirit, who is also the Spirit of Wisdom and Understanding, the Lord and giver of life. But why the serpent? The serpent too, who is the 'most subtle' of the beasts that God had made, is a spirit of understanding, the author of rationality. He is also, in a later context, a 'giver of life', for Jesus likens himself to the fiery serpent that Moses raised up in the desert so that all who looked on it might live. The serpent, however, is mentioned before the dove, and there seems to be method in this. He appears 'in the beginning', and is neither good nor evil: he is the author of discursive thought,

[1] Voltaire, *Le Taureau blanc*, ed. Pléiade, p. 618.   [2] Matthew 10: 16.
[3] John 3.14-15; cf. Numbers 21: 8-9.

that which sifts and divides the material presented by Nature, and hence the *necessary* break with pre-human collective consciousness and the author of individual self-consciousness. He brings death because he brings the consciousness of death, but he also brings life in that self-conscious man, now conscious of death, must also seek *meaning* in life. He shatters the old concord and brings discord into the world of men: his function is essentially divisive. The dove, like Jesus himself, is 'gentle and mild'; and his function is to unite what had been separated by the serpent, to bring together what reason had put asunder, and to reassemble the whole in a new synthesis, the corner-stone of which was to be Christ. The serpent comes first. Coming first he is the precursor of the dove. But traditionally he is also the precursor of Satan; and that is natural enough, for he contains the seeds of both good and evil. He, like evolution itself, is eternally ambiguous—good if acting in association with the gentleness of the dove, evil if acting in concert with the unremitting malice of Satan.

If the serpent, then, is the spirit of rationality, what then is Yahweh? The Genesis account on the surface represents Yahweh in the role of a *vis inertiae* that would at all costs thwart man's growth into self-consciousness and rationality. He *is* Rousseau's 'eternal wisdom' who would 'preserve [man] from knowledge just as a mother would wrench a dangerous weapon from the hands of her child',[1] and he does 'wish to be served by a lot of ignoramuses and idiots'. This is not a very flattering role. But let us be fashionable and demythologize a little. However inevitable the 'Fall' may have been, Adam and Eve knew that they had done wrong and they were ashamed, and shame is something that only human beings feel: it is a moral feeling, and as such distinguishes man from the beasts just as much as does reason. If, then, the serpent and his gift are reason, Yahweh is conscience, what Rousseau calls the 'voice of the soul'. Reason comes first, and like the serpent, it is neither good nor evil but at the disposal of both. Conscience comes second, and it is of God. Reason, the serpent's gift, is therefore fallible: 'all too often it deceives us and we have every right to challenge it; but conscience never deceives, being man's true guide.'[2] Thus Yahweh in the Genesis account is this accusing 'voice of the soul' which will never be stilled. Put into evolutionary terms it seems to me that we are faced with a miracle more stupendous than anything Christianity has to offer. To me, not being a scientist, the mere fact that life has evolved from inanimate matter, and that consciousness has emerged from life, has always seemed miraculous. Call it a 'qualitative leap' if you like, it remains miraculous all the same. The birth of conscience,

[1] Above, p. 330.   [2] Rousseau, *Émile*, p. 372.

however, seems to be a miracle of an altogether higher order if there is no pre-existent principle of morality, no God, from which it might proceed. That consciousness should emerge from matter is perhaps not altogether surprising, since the Indians centuries before Darwin and Marx always assumed that it did; but that conscience should do so seems to me, as it did to Rousseau, simply incomprehensible.

Yahweh is conscience personified, and as conscience he speaks to Adam in the garden, and as conscience he speaks to Cain, the first murderer and grandsire of that fraternity from which the French and Russian revolutions have taught us to recoil with horror. When Cain killed Abel no law had as yet been delivered: only conscience could have told him that he had sinned, and sure enough Yahweh appears to condemn him and to curse him.

Original sin, the result of which was the emergence of our first ancestors into self-consciousness and their inability to use the splendid gift correctly, was probably inevitable, the 'absolutely necessary sin' that alone could bring redemption. It was a case of 'Father, forgive them, for they know not what they do'. Cain's sin was actual sin, consciously committed; and Yahweh appears again as the avenging conscience from which there is no escape. Moreover, Cain's sin is a purely human sin: it is a sin of the spirit and has nothing to do with his animal heritage, the flesh. It is threefold: it is envy, it is pride, and it is refusal to take responsibility: 'Am I my brother's keeper?' The serpent has now played out his ambiguous role, and man, without knowing it, now finds himself face to face with his real enemy, a pure spirit, a 'murderer from the start' and the 'father of lies',[1] Satan, who, according to a Muslim tradition, courses in the veins of all of us and under whose sun we are condemned to live.

At baptism Christians solemnly renounce the world, the flesh, and the Devil. Of course they do nothing of the kind, for to all who are not Buddhists or Manichees the world and the flesh have their due place in their lives. The Devil is another matter, for he is a pure spirit, and he is pride: he is the power that brought man to say 'I' and 'mine', the source of all egoism which, according to the Buddha, is the root-sin or rather the root-delusion of mankind. This is the mask under which Satan masquerades, impersonating us as if he were our true self, substituting for a legitimate love of self as the image of God love of self as the centre of the universe, substituting *amour-propre* for *amour de soi*. This is the real Fall—the assertion of a spurious self and the desire not merely to be but to have, to be seen to have, and to glory in the having.

[1] John 8: 44.

XVII

THE WORD BECAME FLESH

MODERN psychology is associated with three great names—Freud, Adler, and Jung. Freud still has his vogue among the so-called intellectuals, largely because he is believed to have debunked religion: his influence has been immense. Adler, it seems, is largely out of fashion, and this is understandable, since Adler tried to explain all our neuroses and all our perversities by the will to power. Freud, of course, reduced everything to sex, and he may legitimately be described as the father of what some are pleased to call the 'sexual revolution' which is becoming such a bore to all of us, not least to the 'revolutionaries' themselves. Jung, at least, has this in his favour: he did not reduce all human activities to any single instinct, impulse, or drive. He abuses the serpent's gift less obviously: for like the serpent himself he is more subtle—and more ambivalent—than the other two. For, unlike them, he realized that religion is perhaps the deepest thing in man, and that, in seeking to destroy it, you are only banishing it from the conscious mind into the depths of the unconscious.

We saw last term that Jung rejected Protestant Christianity in his early youth because he thought it had ceased to be relevant to his own inner spiritual development: the salt had lost its savour, and the symbol symbolized nothing. Hence his impassioned interest in the Oriental religions and his highly original presentation of them to the Western world. Like Dr. John A. T. Robinson (and for that matter the whole long trail of Christian mystics) he was not interested in the God 'up there' or the God 'out there', he was interested in the God who, he considered, formed not only part of the human psyche but its very centre and 'self'. As to the God of metaphysics, whether Eastern or Western, he was impatiently indifferent:

> To be specific in this matter [he writes] I can say that my admiration for the great Eastern philosophers is as great and as indubitable as my attitude toward their metaphysics is irreverent. I suspect them of being symbolical psychologists, to whom no greater wrong could be done than to be taken literally. If it were really metaphysics that they mean, it would be useless to try to understand them. But if it is psychology, we can not only understand them, but we can profit greatly by them, for then the so-called 'metaphysical' comes within the range of experience. If I accept the fact that a god is absolute and beyond all human experience,

he leaves me cold. I do not affect him, nor does he affect me. But if I know, on the other hand, that God is a mighty activity in my soul, at once I must concern myself with him; he can then become even unpleasantly important, and in practical ways too, which sounds horribly banal, like everything appearing in the sphere of reality.[1]

Yahweh *is* unpleasantly important, and from time to time he reminds us forcibly of the unpleasant side of his character. Rousseau had faith in a good and just God; hence he attributed evil entirely to man. Hence again, as for Marcion, the God of the Old Testament could not be the true God— for he is 'irascible, jealous, vengeful, partial, hates mankind, is a God of war and battles, always ready to destroy and strike [his enemies] down by lightning. He never stops talking of torments and retribution and boasts that he punishes even the innocent.'[2] Rousseau was not exaggerating; for this *is* the impression that must strike anyone who comes to the Old Testament for the first time from the sacred books of either India or China. And yet whenever the human race runs into serious trouble, it takes refuge in God's mercy against his wrath, as the Muslims so aptly put it. Rousseau knew God as an inner experience in which there was only harmony and peace: he simply could not imagine that the Old Testament God could exist except in the diseased minds of a deluded people. Voltaire had for decades poured scorn on this ferocious figment of the morbid imagination of a small, vindictive, and savage tribe. It took the Lisbon earthquake to make him face up to the insoluble problem of the coexistence of a just God and unmerited suffering. He refused to take the easy way out of the mystics and the mystical optimists among the philosophers of his time who taught, as the Taoists, the Upanishads, and in his own time Rousseau had all taught, that because the All is perfect, the sufferings of the parts cannot matter when seen against the back-cloth of eternity. Voltaire's *Poem on the Lisbon Disaster* is to my mind the best and certainly the most moving thing he ever wrote. Here all his wit, all his light mockery, all his merciless indignation melt into a deep compassion, the more moving because it is groping in the dark and not afraid to admit it. Rousseau knew God and ended up by being totally estranged from his fellow men. Voltaire, despite the now outmoded persiflage, had a real because a fearless compassion for the downtrodden and the wronged, and it is this that brought him in his old age to an obscure understanding of God. His attack on the 'God of the philosophers' is at least as telling as is

---

[1] Richard Wilhelm and C. G. Jung, *The Secret of the Golden Flower*, London, 1938, p. 129.
[2] Rousseau, *Émile*, pp. 390–1.

Pascal's. This God is a chimera, and the men who professed to believe in him (of whom he himself had not been the least) were simply deceiving themselves:

> O rêves des savants! ô chimères profondes!
> Dieu tient en main la chaîne, et n'est point enchaîné;
> Par son choix bienfaisant tout est déterminé:
> Il est libre, il est juste, il n'est point implacable.
> Pourquoi donc souffrons-nous sous un maître équitable?
> Voilà le nœud fatal qu'il fallait délier.
> Guérirez-vous nos maux en osant les nier?[1]

'Will you cure our ills by daring to deny them?' That is the crunch, and that is what the mystics and the metaphysicians ask us to do. But Voltaire will not avert his eyes from the anguish of mankind, nor can he be unaffected by it, for he saw the world very much as the Buddha and Hugh of St. Victor saw it, but, unlike them, he could find no cure for it nor could he escape it. And so, he is not ashamed to admit, he is no better than a university professor:

> Je ne conçois pas plus comment tout serait bien:
> Je suis comme un docteur, hélas! je ne sais rien.[2]

'I am like a Ph.D.: alas, I know nothing.' Like Jesus, Voltaire had no use for the scribes. The world he knew was hell, but he could not believe any more than could Engels in the following century that man—thinking man, the end-product of all Nature's evolutionary travail—could be extinguished forever:

> Le passé n'est pour nous qu'un triste souvenir;
> Le présent est affreux, s'il n'est point d'avenir,
> Si la nuit du tombeau détruit l'être qui pense.
> *Un jour tout sera bien*, voilà notre espérance;
> *Tout est bien aujourd'hui*, voilà l'illusion.
> Les sages me trompaient, et Dieu seul a raison.[3]

'All will be well one day, that is our hope.' And if there is hope, then there must be a God in whom we must believe but whom we can never understand:

> Je respecte mon Dieu, mais j'aime l'univers.[4]

If it is true, as the editors of the Jerusalem Bible would have us believe,[5] that 'the fear of the Lord is approximately what we call the virtue of

---

[1] Voltaire, *Mélanges*, ed. Pléiade, p. 306. [2] Ibid., p. 308.
[3] Ibid., p. 309. [4] Ibid., p. 305. [5] On Proverbs 1: 8.

religion, or devotion to God', then Voltaire was a religious man: he respected God but was stunned at the incomprehensibility of his ways. Yahweh, the God of the Old Testament, had struck once again in Lisbon; and Voltaire had no longer got it in him to mock. Yahweh has been striking us ever since.

So too Jung, despite his remythologizing of the Deity, can write:

> Since the Apocalypse we now know again that God is not only to be loved, but also to be feared. He fills us with evil as well as with good, otherwise he would not need to be feared; and because he wants to become man, the uniting of his antinomy must take place in man. This involves man in a new responsibility. He can no longer wriggle out of it on the plea of his littleness and nothingness, for the dark God has slipped the atom bomb and chemical weapons into his hands and given him the power to empty out the apocalyptic vials of wrath on his fellow creatures. Since he has been granted an almost godlike power, he can no longer remain blind and unconscious. He must know something of God's nature and of metaphysical processes if he is to understand himself and thereby achieve gnosis of the Divine.[1]

This is from *Answer to Job*, and Jung was seventy-six when he wrote it. His view of the Old Testament differs little from that of the Gnostics, Rousseau, and Voltaire. Yahweh, throughout the Old Testament as distinct from the Apocrypha, is not wholly other than man. Far from it: he is, except in power, far inferior to man. In writing this book Jung said: 'I hope to act as a voice for many who feel the same way as I do, and to give expression to the shattering emotion that the unvarnished spectacle of divine savagery and ruthlessness produces in us.'[2] This is scarcely an exaggeration; and I cannot help feeling that the medieval Church showed unusual wisdom in keeping this literally frightful book in the Latin tongue so that it should not unduly distress the untutored. If the Old Testament still has any relevance to Christianity, then it can only be as a *propaideutikon* to the revelation of the New.

It is not my purpose to trace Jung's somewhat peculiar treatment of the development of God's character throughout the Old Testament, although Jung was a psycho-analyst who did not seek, as Freud did, to explode religious myth, but to explain it. He aimed at nothing less than to psycho-analyse God out of savagery ('the paragon of all creation is not a man but a monster'[3]) into sanity. Hence he chooses as his hero Job, 'a sound and honest man who feared God and shunned evil',[4] but who was nevertheless subjected by God to the most fearful testing at the hands of

---

[1] C. G. Jung, *Answer to Job*, London, 1954, pp. 163–4.   [2] Ibid., p. 4.
[3] Ibid., p. 53.   [4] Job 1: 1.

his son, Satan. For Jung God's behaviour is both outrageous and inexcusable, and one is reminded of Draupadī's onslaught on *her* God, Krishna, in India's great Epic, the Mahābhārata. It is true that the wrongs she had suffered pale into insignificance beside the sufferings of Job. But then she belonged to what used to be considered the weaker sex, and in any case resignation formed no part of her character. Her indictment is, then, the more virulent, for, like Job, she is confronted not with God's inscrutable justice but with his apparently senseless cruelty:

> As a man splits log with log, [she says,] stone with stone, iron with iron—things that [of themselves] can neither move nor think—so does the Lord God, the Self-subsistent, the primal Grandsire, hurt one creature by means of another, establishing for himself an alibi. Joining things together only to disjoin them again the Lord acts at his own good pleasure, playing with his creatures as children play with dolls. He does not treat his creatures as a father or a mother would but acts in raging anger; and since he acts so, others follow his example.[1]

This is exactly how Jung sees Yahweh's treatment of Job—except that Yahweh is not playing; he is in deadly earnest, although, according to Jung, he is not fully conscious of what he is doing. It is only through Job's dignified acceptance of the divine injustice that Yahweh begins to doubt his own righteousness and to seek to mend his ways. He becomes conscious of the other side of his nature, the eternal feminine, which must form part of the divine as of any other personality, if the *conjunctio oppositorum*, the union of opposites, is to be achieved. This is the divine Wisdom that first appears in the Book of Proverbs and which continues to play so important a part in the Book of Wisdom and Ecclesiasticus. The emergence of the gentler, creative female principle is, in any case, consistent with a general tendency in all religions. In the Indian tradition we have Śakti, God's creative power represented in mythology as his consort, appearing alongside Śiva, the eternal and unchanging principle, and Rādhā appearing as the consort of Krishna; in Chinese religion there are the male and the female principles, the *yang* and the *yin* which together make up the Tao. In Proverbs and the Apocrypha it is Wisdom that fulfils this role, whereas in the Catholic tradition Wisdom becomes a 'figure' of the Virgin Mary, the dogmatic definition of whose Assumption Jung sees as the most important religious event since the Reformation,[2] for, as he says, 'the motive and content of the popular movement which contributed to the Pope's decision solemnly to declare the new dogma consist not in the birth of a new god, but in the continuing incarnation of God which began

---

[1] *Mahābhārata* 3: 31: 3–37; see above, p. 177.
[2] *Answer to Job*, p. 169.

with Christ'.[1] This is 'a renewed hope for the fulfilment of that yearning for peace which stirs deep down in the soul, and for a resolution of the threatening tension between the opposites'.[2] There seems to me to be much truth in this, though nothing particularly new since the Assumption has been a holy day of obligation in the Catholic Church for nearly a thousand years, and this has in fact meant the exaltation of the eternal feminine right up into the heart of the masculine Trinity itself, which has always been a stumbling-block to Protestants. This is, no doubt, primarily a matter of theology, and as theology I am content to leave it to the theologians; they will no doubt continue to chew over it in a fraternal ecumenical spirit, let us hope, while the rest of us pass by on the other side in the mistaken belief, perhaps, that there are more important things to do. Yet, this at least I would say as a still largely pre-conciliar Roman Catholic: to me the near divinization of the Bible (minus the Apocrypha) seems at least as questionable as the exaltation of the Virgin Mary to a rank that is nearly divine—questionable and surely much more absurd. For if we must have a 'biblical' religion, if we must have a deified book, then surely the claims of the Koran which, Muslims maintain, was revealed all of one piece in the lifetime of the Prophet Muhammad and which received its definitive form thirty years after his death, must take precedence over that very composite affair we call the Bible, the claims of which, either to historical accuracy or to the authenticity of the authors who are alleged to have composed its heterogeneous books, have been all but demolished by the extravagances of Protestantism itself. With the near deification of Mary, on the other hand, we are on very different ground. First, the Catholic Church (which, after all, drew up the Canon of the Bible centuries before Luther and Calvin were heard of) has always maintained the validity of the tradition of the universal Church, and secondly Mary was and is a powerful symbol of the eternal feminine within the soul of man himself. We may accept or reject the non-biblical mythology and imagery associated with her, but what she symbolizes we reject at our peril. In this at least I venture to think that Jung is right. Some of us are getting a little tired of 'the Lord God of armies' who plagued the Jews in olden times and is plaguing us still in our deeply divided world. In the Wisdom literature certainly he becomes a little more civilized, and in Jesus Christ he revealed an altogether different aspect of himself; but once again in the Book of Revelation, attributed to the apostle of love himself and for long regarded with deep suspicion by the Church, he shows his latent savagery, as Jung again has pointed out. He is, after all, that God 'in whose image

[1] *Answer to Job*, p. 167.   [2] Ibid., p. 171.

we are made', and it would indeed be surprising if our own unreasoning violence were not a reflection of his.

Jung did well to psycho-analyse the Hebrew God and to point out that his terrible side is real because it is a reality within ourselves; but is this the whole story?

For Jung Job was the symbol of righteous man unjustly tormented by a savage God. Yet did he not miss at last half the point? Let us accept for the moment his thesis that Yahweh is an irrational savage who, though ceaselessly talking of justice, is not just himself. This may be true, but he is also a teacher of men and he insists that *man* shall be just. His fury with the chosen people may seem excessive, but what is it that makes him furious? Always their obstinacy, self-will, pride, and self-centredness. The mythology is often crude, but the sin is always the same, putting self—which may be either tribal or individual (it scarcely matters which)—before God: *amour-propre*, the basic sin of mankind—a concept for which the British have no unambiguous word—a fact that should give us food for thought.

Yahweh had, after all, chosen the Jewish people from all the peoples of the earth; he was to be their God and they were to be his people, and this implied a relationship of master and servant, later to be converted into one of husband and wife. Both relationships imply submission on the part of Israel and on the part of the individual Jew. This should have been the attitude of Job too. It is true that he was 'a sound and honest man who feared God and shunned evil'. So were the scribes and Pharisees, the 'hypocrites' whom Christ so scathingly denounced. So are many of our prelates and pastors of this and former times: but this is clearly not enough. For we learn more about Job than this. 'This man was indeed a man of mark among all the people of the East.' And we are then told in just what way he was remarkable:

> It was the custom of his sons to hold banquets in each other's houses, one after the other, and to send and invite their three sisters to eat and drink with them. Once each series of banquets was over, Job would send for them to come and be purified, and at dawn on the following day he would offer a holocaust for each of them. 'Perhaps' Job would say 'my sons have sinned and in their hearts affronted God.' So that was what he used to do after each series.[1]

This is a picture of a conventionally religious man, a pillar of the Church, self-righteous and prudent, a fair-weather Jew (or Christian) who is satisfied that he has omitted nothing in the prompt performance of his

---

[1] Job 1: 4–5.

religious duties. He is the exact obverse of the wretched publican who would not so much as raise his eyes to heaven but 'only beat his breast and said, "God, be merciful to me, a sinner" '.[1] Job was rather the prototype of the Pharisee who 'said this prayer to himself, "I thank you, God, that I am not grasping, unjust, adulterous like the rest of mankind. . . . I fast twice a week; I pay tithes of all I get" '. Can one be surprised that God allowed Satan to do his worst to this bourgeois 'saint'?

Yahweh, in the Book of Job at least, is very much more 'conscious' than Jung would have us believe. It is true that he does not bother to argue with Job, and that he overawes him with a demonstration of overwhelming power which Job, after his sufferings, scarcely needed, and that he vindicates Job in the end and restores to him his worldly goods. But the point of the story is surely that Job could not be acceptable to Yahweh until his pride was completely shattered and he had proved that there was more to him than a pious landowner, rich, respectable, and self-assured.

Satan, in the Book of Job, stands half-way between the ambivalent serpent of Genesis and the dark Prince of this world we encounter in the New Testament. He is the astute advocate who demands of God that a 'good' man should prove his goodness and not only his respectibility. This comes out clearly in the prologue, where Satan is seen, not as a tempter in the ordinarily accepted sense of that word, but as one permitted to put to the test the sincerity of a very rich man who likes to be known as a 'sound and honest man who fears God and shuns evil'. Satan's scepticism is as relevant today as it was then:

'Yes,' Satan said, 'but Job is not God-fearing for nothing, is he? Have you not put a wall round him and his house and all his domain? You have blessed all he undertakes, and his flocks throng the countryside. But stretch out your hand and lay a finger on his possessions: I warrant you, he will curse you to your face.' 'Very well,' Yahweh said to Satan, 'all he has is in your power. But keep your hands off his person.' So Satan left the presence of Yahweh.[2]

The rest of the story is well known. Yahweh allows Satan to attack Job's person too, he is 'struck down with malignant ulcers from the sole of his foot to the top of his head'. His wife bids him curse God and die rather than 'persist in his blamelessness'. He refuses in the prologue but comes perilously near to doing so in the main body of the book. Despite his reputation Job is neither a patient nor a humble man, for, until the final theophany of naked power, he cannot and will not admit that his righteousness is self-righteousness rebelling against a power he had

[1] Luke 18:13.   [2] Job 1: 9–12.

presumed to understand because, in his vanity, he had seen himself as 'a man of mark among all the people of the East'—a man of status, as we would say today. The picture of Yahweh with which the Old Testament presents us is not a pleasant one, but Job makes it needlessly unpleasant. He keeps prating about being a mere man, which God is not, proclaiming his own spotless innocence the while:

> Yes, I am man, and he is not; and so no argument,
>   no suit between the two of us is possible.
> There is no arbiter between us,
>   to lay his hand on both,
> to stay his rod from me,
>   or keep away his daunting terrors.
> Nonetheless, I shall speak, not fearing him:
>   I do not see myself like that at all.[1]

No one can accuse Jung of being unfair to Job, and yet it is the Book of Proverbs, revealing for the first time, according to him, the 'feminine' aspect of the Deity, that declares that 'the fear of Yahweh is the beginning of knowledge'.[2] Job *will* not fear God; and this is presumption and arrogance—*amour-propre* at its most malignant. Not for a moment does this 'respectable' man doubt his innocence:

> You, who inquire into my faults
>   and investigate my sins,
> you know very well that I am innocent,
>   and that no one can rescue me from your hand.[3]

The man's blindness to his own defects is astonishing:

> A man becomes a laughing-stock to his friends
>   if he cries to God and expects an answer.
> The blameless innocent incurs only mockery.
> 'Add insult to injury,' think the prosperous,
>   'strike the man now that he is staggering!'
> And yet, the tents of brigands are left in peace,
>   and those who challenge God live in safety,
>   and make a god of their two fists![4]

Who, one might ask, is doing the challenging now? A 'sound and honest man', no doubt, who no longer fears God but cannot escape the evil that has befallen him. So this is the 'patience of Job'. Satan, after all, was not far out: 'I warrant you,' he had said, 'he will curse you to your face.' This is precisely what Job does: his motto is the motto later

---

[1] Ibid., 9: 32–5.   [2] Proverbs 1: 7; cf. Job 28: 28.
[3] Job 10: 6–7.   [4] Ibid. 12: 4–6.

attributed to Satan himself—*Non serviam*, 'I will not serve'. It is, after all, his loss of status much more than his sores or even the loss of his sons and daughters that really hurts Job. Even the young laugh at him—and the lower-class young at that:

> And now I am the laughing-stock
> of my juniors, the young people,
> whose fathers I did not consider fit
> to put with the dogs that looked after my flock.[1]

And still, in his wonderful self-righteousness, he still protests his innocence—and his contempt for the poor. It seems fitting that Yahweh should not deign to justify his ways to one as blinded by self-righteousness as was Job. This he leaves to the young man Elihu who speaks—and Jung seems not to have noticed this—in the name of Wisdom, Yahweh's feminine counterpart.

Elihu represents something new in the dialogue. He makes his appearance totally unannounced, and after he has spoken he is not referred to again. Hence, the higher criticism tells us, the whole episode must be an interpolation. This may well be so, but the interpolation is highly relevant; and I sometimes wonder why it is that what the 'higher' critics dismiss as interpolation usually contains what is humanly most vital in the work they criticize. But then they are principally interested in the text, not in what the text says and why. We have seen them at work on the Bible, and we have seen them pawing away at the Bhagavad-Gītā: in neither case have they added to our understanding of the sacred text. As Nietzsche said in another context, 'Sie haben keine Finger für uns, sie haben überhaupt keine Finger, sie haben bloß Tatzen.' 'They have no fingers for us: in fact they have no fingers at all: they have only got paws.' This was Nietzsche's verdict on his fellow-countrymen, but it is equally applicable to much that calls itself modern scholarship on which our youth is crucified: and in this case it is applicable to Jung too, for the intervention of Elihu is in fact the intervention of Wisdom speaking out clearly in defence of Yahweh and in stern condemnation of the pride of man. In his prosperity it had never occurred to Job to criticize God's ways with man. Since he was 'a man of mark among all the people of the East', since he then 'feared God and shunned evil', he could afford to despise and mock at those less fortunate than himself:

> . . . I did not consider fit
> to put [them] with the dogs that looked after my flock.

[1] Job 30: 1.

The strength of their hands would have been *useless to me*,
    enfeebled as they were,
    worn out by want and hunger . . .
Their children are as worthless a brood as they were,
    nameless people, outcasts of society.[1]

So this is the 'sound and honest man who feared God and shunned evil'. No wonder that Satan was allowed to strip him of all he had, for he, the rich man, despised the poor, first simply because they were poor, and secondly because, being poor, they were too weak to be of any use to him. People you cannot use as things, he says, are simply not worth a thought. Job is the prototype of the wicked bourgeoisie of Marxist folklore and the arch-enemy of all the Buddha stood for, the man who thinks only in terms of 'I' and 'mine', the champion of that accursed *amour-propre* that led man into sin and through sin into needless and sterile sufferings. *Pace* Jung he cannot even talk sense once he has been deprived of property and status: he can only accuse God of doing to him what he had himself done to others. Into all this undisciplined fury and into the dreary sermonizing of his three eminently respectable friends Elihu breaks in like a breath of fresh air, for he represents Wisdom and talks sense:

Now, Job, be kind enough to listen to my words, [he says with admirable
    self-restraint,]
    and attend to all I have to say.
Now as I open my mouth,
    and my tongue shapes words against my palate,
my heart shall utter *sayings full of wisdom*,
    and my lips speak the honest truth.[2]

He speaks as a fellow man, not as a god; and since no man can understand God, he will, like Voltaire, at least respect him, he will not rail against what is in any case entirely beyond his control. And so, unlike the three imbecile friends who had preceded him, he hits Job where he deserves to be hit—in his self-righteousness and *amour-propre*:

How could you say in my hearing—
    for the sound of your words did not escape me—
I am clean, and sinless,
    I am pure, free of all fault.
Yet he is inventing grievances against me,
    and imagining me his enemy . . .
In saying so, I tell you, you are wrong:
    God does not fit man's measure.[3]

---

[1] Ibid. 30: 1–8.   [2] Ibid. 33: 1–3.   [3] Ibid. 33: 8–12.

Job is not only sinful in his presumption, he is also a fool and a snob. Elihu does not pull his punches:

> If you have any intelligence, listen to this,
>   and lend your ear to what I have to say.
> Could an enemy of justice ever govern?
>   Would you dare condemn the Just One, the Almighty,
> who can tell kings that they are good for nothing,
>   and treat noblemen like criminals,
> who shows no partiality to princes
>   and makes no distinction between the rich and the poor,
> all alike being made by his own hands?[1]

Job is both sinful and rebellious; he has lost faith, the one virtue that could possibly sustain him in a religion that gave no hope of an after-life. Suffering has not chastened him; it had only deprived him of all sense:

> There is no wisdom in Job's speech,
>   his words lack sense.
> Put him unsparingly to the proof
>   since his retorts are the same as those that the wicked make.
> For to sin he adds rebellion,
>   calling justice into question in our midst
>   and heaping abuse on God.[2]

Thus it is Elihu who justifies the ways of God in the name of Wisdom and common prudence. Yahweh himself disdains to argue but is content to exhibit his naked power. Job at last submits, his pride finally broken:

> I am the man who obscured your designs
>   with my empty-headed words.
> I have been holding forth on matters I cannot understand,
>   on marvels beyond me and my knowledge . . .
> I retract all I have said,
>   and in dust and ashes I repent.[3]

No, Jung is entirely wrong. The moral victor in the story is not Job, nor does Yahweh emerge from the episode with a guilty conscience. Job is convicted of self-sufficiency, rebelliousness, and pride, and in this respect, so far from being a 'figure' of Christ, he is a figure of the Antichrist since, until humbled to the dust, he will not serve. Job is the man who will not accept suffering: Christ is the God who did. And Christ is the only true answer to Job, as he is the answer to the Buddha, to Krishna, and above all to the saintly Yudhishthira.

Those of you who attended these lectures last year may remember that

[1] Job 34: 16–19.   [2] Ibid. 34: 35–7.   [3] Ibid. 42: 3–6.

for the duration of one lecture you were granted respite from mysticism. The lecture was entitled 'The Greatness of Man and the Wretchedness of God', its hero was Yudhishthira, the King of Righteousness who, like Job, found himself faced with the unrighteousness of God. Unlike Job, however, the reason for his ultimate revolt was not the personal suffering that God had inflicted on himself, but the misery that God had caused him against his will to inflict on others. Job railed against God because God had deprived him of status: Yudhishthira did not rail against God at all, he cursed a social system which glorified war without for that reason openly condemning the God who had founded that system. Job is the figure of wounded pride: Yudhishthira the figure of outraged compassion. Job is the man who will not serve: Yudhishthira the servant of the servants of God. Job has the assertiveness of the Satan of a later age: Yudhishthira has the meekness of Christ. Job is finally rewarded with riches and status, the only kind of reward he understands: Yudhishthira loses all that is dear to him because he was ready to lay down his life for his friends. Yudhishthira, not Krishna, is the figure of Christ among the Hindus. But Yudhishthira was not God.

Christ became man that he might show forth the true nature of God. And this was in every sense a revelation, for how else could one have conceived of the creator of heaven and earth as humble and meek, 'cursed for our sake',[1] 'despised and rejected by men'?[2] In the Indian tradition both Rāma and Krishna were earthly kings, and both in their way prefigure Christ; Krishna because it is he who speaks the Bhagavad-Gītā and reveals the love of God for man, Rāma because he is prepared to divest himself of his royalty and lead a beggar's life. And yet neither is quite satisfactory as an incarnation of God, for they lack all ultimate seriousness. Rāma gives up a kingdom to satisfy the spiteful whim of a spoilt queen: Krishna, outside the Gītā, is a trickster and the author of foul play. Rāma tends to stiffness and his respectibility is a bore: Krishna, in the later cult, becomes a wanton lover too frivolous to be taken seriously outside India. Christ detested respectibility and must be taken seriously unless, of course, he is simply ignored or made the subject of academic study.

In the Gītā Krishna starts from the Buddhist assumption that this world must be renounced: Christ takes upon himself the sufferings of this world and makes them his own. And in this he remains firmly within his Hebrew background: life in this world is a serious affair, it is not the sport of an irresponsible God, nor is it a meaningless flux as it is for the Buddha. This is the unbridgeable gulf that separates traditional

[1] Galatians 3: 13.   [2] Isaiah 53: 3.

Christianity from traditional Buddhism. Christ becomes man so that he may make all mankind his own, and beyond mankind all the world of matter. Matter indeed, was already sanctified, for in the beginning God's spirit had hovered over the waters: spirit had penetrated and sanctified matter. God breathed into man the breath of life and man became a living being; for the spirit is life as it is in the Upanishads, and life is thereby holy and good. But man fell, misused his consciousness and his conscience, and made God's earth a living hell. Man had been made in the image of God: he dropped the mirror and smashed the image. His links with Nature were broken, and he found himself naked and alone, at war with himself and with his fellow men.

Job was not alone to see that life on earth makes no sense. The Buddha was at one with him in this. But how different were their reactions! Job cursed the day on which he was born:

> Why give light to a man of grief?
> Why give life to those bitter of heart,
> who long for a death that never comes,
> and hunt for it more than for a buried treasure?[1]

This too was the Buddha's anguished cry, but he, or so he claimed, had found the answer. Yahweh had not taught the Hebrews the secret of timeless existence, he had not revealed to them that beyond this vale of tears where all is flux there is that which is never born, never becomes, is not made, and is not compounded, and that this state which is neither being nor not-being can be obtained by all men if their disposition is right. For there are two ways for fallen men. The image of God in Adam, the All-man, is broken: this is the fact. It can, however, be partially restored in the individual: this is the Buddhist way. The second way is to attempt to restore it in the religious group, the nation, or the state: this is the way of Confucius, of Israel, and of Islam. Neither is complete in itself as Job discovered; for the Book of Job is the only book in the Old Testament that dwells on the sufferings and sins of an individual man separated from his kind. The Buddha's way does indeed claim to be self-sufficient, but it breaks man at his very roots, it separates him from the soil out of which he had grown. It is literally a counsel of despair, for despair, not hope, is a Buddhist virtue. And the taunt that Henriette addresses to her sister, Armande, in Molière's *Femmes savantes* might with justice have been addressed to the Buddha:

> Mais vous ne seriez pas ce dont vous vous vantez,
> Si ma mère n'eût eu que de ces beaux côtés;

[1] Job 3: 20-1.

Et bien vous prend, ma sœur, que son noble génie
N'ait pas vaqué toujours à la philosophie.
De grâce, souffrez-moi, par un peu de bonté,
Des bassesses à qui vous devez la clarté;
Et ne supprimez point, voulant qu'on vous seconde,
Quelque petit savant qui veut venir au monde.[1]

Mutatis mutandis this could be translated as follows:

But you could never have been what you boast you are if my mother had
had only a spiritual side. You may take it, dear sister, that her noble mind was
not always occupied with philosophy. So, allow me, please, if you will be so good,
my share in those base acts to which *you* owe your enlightenment. And, simply
to indulge your ideals, do not prevent a little Buddha from coming into the
world.

This is a fair enough comment on the ascetic life, and ascetics neglect
it at their peril. Asceticism, no doubt, has its due place in all religions, but
to seek to eliminate matter altogether from our lives is as unbalanced as
the orthodox Marxian elimination of the spirit; and it has been the notable
achievement of Pierre Teilhard de Chardin in our own times that he
sought to give matter its due place even in the mystical life. The message
of Christianity has too long been perverted. The Christ is not the Buddha,
for by his Incarnation he sanctifies matter and promises us not Nirvāna,
but eternal *life*: 'I have come so that they may have life and have it to the
full.'[2] And without matter of some sort I do not understand how there can
be life.

The Buddha came into this world of un-ease and suffering and flux to
save us *from* the world. Christ came into the world in order to be with the
world, to *be* the world, and to suffer with the world:

Jesus did not come to dominate the world. He came to save the world. . . . He
did not come to separate himself or withdrawn from the world. He came to save
the world—quite a different method. Don't you understand, if he had wanted to
withdraw, be withdrawn from the world, all he had to do was nott o come into
the world. It was as simple as that. . . . If he had wanted to withdraw from the
world, if *that* was his object, it was so simple: all he had got to do was not to
come into the world. The centuries had not yet unfolded, the door of salvation
was not yet open, the great story had not yet begun.[3]

This is Charles Péguy speaking, who after centuries of other-worldliness
pulled back Christianity to where it belonged, belongs, and, if it is to last,

---

[1] Molière, *Les Femmes savantes*, Act I, sc. i.   [2] John 10: 10.
[3] Charles Péguy, *Dialogue de l'histoire et de l'âme charnelle*, ed. Pléiade, *Œuvres en prose 1909–1914*, p. 372.

always will belong—to this world of flux and pain. 'As God he became man,'
Péguy continues, 'which, you will admit, is not exactly a way of withdrawing from the world', the Infinite did not despise the finite, 'did not
abhor the Virgin's womb', but assumed the finite into itself. The finite is
you and I, made in the image of God, yet drawn from the dust of the earth.
The Buddhist way may seem heroic in its total self-abnegation, but it is
surely the easy way out, for it is to deny our humanity and our specific
status in the order of creation as *men*, existing here and now in time.

The Incarnation means, among other things, the irruption of the
eternal into the temporal, the marriage of Spirit with Matter—concretely
of the Holy Spirit with the Blessed Virgin Mary—thereby producing the
God-man Jesus in whom Spirit and Matter are indissolubly linked. The
tendency to undo this union effected by the Incarnation has been with
the Church ever since St. Paul, and St. Paul himself is torn between his
own Hebraic heritage on the one hand, in which the survival of the spirit
apart from a spiritual substrate is only with difficulty conceived of, and the
Greek world-view dominant in his time on the other, for which the body
was, as for the Indians, the dark prison of the luminous soul. With part of
his being he cried out that he might be 'rescued from this body doomed to
death':[1] with the other part of his being he sees in the resurrection of
Jesus the sanctification of the body itself, its transformation from a merely
physical body into what he is bold enough to call a 'spiritual body'. The
first is contemptible, the second is glorious:

> The thing that is sown is contemptible but what is raised is glorious; the
> thing that is sown is weak but what is raised is powerful; it is sown a physical
> body, it is raised a spiritual body. . . .[2] We who have been modelled on the earthly
> man, will be modelled on the heavenly man. Or else, . . . put it this way: flesh
> and blood cannot inherit the kingdom of God; and the perishable cannot in-
> herit what lasts for ever'.[3]

Of course, St. Paul is telling us, the purely physical body cannot survive,
nor is there rebirth in a new physical body, as with the Indians, for this
would merely be a return to where we started. The spirit is what the Hindus call the self—the self which is 'exempt from evil, untouched by age or
death or sorrow, untouched by hunger and thirst: its desire is the real, its
idea is the real. This is what you must seek, this is what you want to understand. Whoso has found this self and understands it wins all states of being
and all objects of desire.'[4] But this self which is 'in the image of God'
must first be sown in a physical body, in order to arise enriched in a

---

[1] Romans 7: 24.   [2] 1 Corinthians 15: 43–4.
[3] Ibid. 15: 49–50.   [4] *Chāndogya* Upanishad 8: 7: 1.

'spiritual body' where it will be glorified by all the good it has done on earth, and purified by all the suffering it has voluntarily endured either here or in what Catholics call Purgatory.

Both matter and spirit are morally neutral; and just as the body is condemned to corruption by its own inherent instability, so can the image of God be turned into the image of Satan, for man is a free agent, and, as both the Indians and the Marxists would have us believe, free will, in so far as it exists at all, derives from matter, not from spirit. If our matter is 'turbid', as the neo-Confucianists would say, then it can deface the image of God within us: if it is 'clear', it will be assumed into spirit, into that 'particle of God'[1] which is our true self. Life, as both the Buddha and Marx showed, depends on matter: what is not materially based is dead, for life is movement, and 'movement is the most important of the inherent qualities of matter'.[2] Nirvāna is the extinction of life and therefore of all the variety that is inseparable from life: it is 'something with which there is no commerce, impalpable, devoid of distinguishing mark, unthinkable, indescribable, its essence the firm conviction of the oneness of itself, bringing all development to an end, tranquil and mild, devoid of duality',[3] the sterilized purity that is death. This is the very opposite of eternal life. And it is eternal *life* which is the good news of the Incarnation and the Resurrection. This is, if you like, the fertilization of Nirvāna and the sanctification of matter itself. Of course, the seed must die if the plant is ever to be born, and the Buddhist doctrine of selflessness is the precondition of any real Christian rebirth. And so the Christ himself tells us:

> I tell you, most solemnly,
> unless a wheat grain falls on the ground and dies,
> it remains only a single grain;
> but if it dies,
> it yields a rich harvest.
> Anyone who loves his life loses it;
> anyone who hates his life in this world
> will keep it for the eternal life.[4]

What then, is Christ telling us? He is telling us that unless and until we can accept the Buddha's message of selflessness and all the agonies of self-denial that that entails, we cannot share in his own resurrected life. This is bound to be bitter medicine. For:

[That pleasure] which a man enjoys after much effort [spent] making an end thereby of suffering, which at first seems like poison but in time transmutes

---

[1] Bhagavad-Gītā 15: 7.   [2] Above, p. 59.
[3] *Māndūkya* Upanishad 7.   [4] John 12: 24–5.

itself into what seems to be ambrosia, is called the pleasure of purity, for it springs from that serenity which comes from apperception of the self.[1]

How should you see God until you have seen the image of God which, as Richard of St. Victor saw, is your own true self? For only so can you clean away the 'turbid' matter you have received from life, and become 'pure of heart' and fit to see God.

'The Word became flesh.' God became man. Spirit became matter. In China they had never been separated; but in India and in the West among the Platonists Spirit had ever more imperiously demanded to be separated from his impure sister. So too in Christianity it would have been so easy for the Son of God to remain forever seated in glory at the right hand of the Father and to 'abhor the Virgin's womb'. This, however, was not God's way: God must become man if man were ever to participate in God's own nature. The eternal must enter the temporal, must fully share in the temporal process, in what we call history, if man, fashioned from the dust of the ground, were to regain his lost self and be restored to his Father. It is easy to deny the eternal and, apparently at least, more noble to deny the temporal. It is easy to be a Marxist, more noble no doubt to be a Buddhist; but to be a Christian you must be both a Marxist and a Buddhist, both Confucian and Taoist, for in Christ all that has abiding value meets. There are the materialists and there are the spiritualists, and there are both materialists and spiritualists who claim to be Christians—but they are not really Christians. Péguy calls the two parties the *laïques* and the *ecclésiastiques*, the 'seculars' and the 'religious', if you like. The first, he says, 'deny the eternal in the temporal, . . . from within the temporal', while the second 'deny the temporal in the eternal, want to undo and disentangle the temporal from the eternal, from within the eternal. And so neither the one nor the other is Christian, for the very technique of Christianity, the technique and mechanics of its mysticism, of Christian mysticism, is just that; it is the fitting together of one piece, mechanically, into another; it is this interlocking of these two pieces, this singular fitting together—mutual, unique, reciprocal, not to be undone, not to be disentangled—the one in the other and the other in the one; of the temporal in the eternal and (but above all, for it is this that is most often denied) (and it is this that is really the most wonderful) of the eternal in the temporal.'[2] Through the Incarnation the temporal is raised to the status of the eternal, and the eternal in turn is enmeshed and suffused in the temporal. To deny this marriage of spirit and matter is to be less than a Christian; and to concentrate on the one rather than the other has its dangers. For

---

[1] Bhagavad-Gītā 18: 36–7.   [2] Péguy, op. cit., p. 386.

there is a mysticism of matter—the mysticism of Whitman and the nature mystics; and there is a mysticism of pure spirit—the mysticism of the Buddha and the non-dualist Vedānta. Of the two it is the latter that is the most dangerous. 'Materialism has its own mysticism. Indeed of all the philosophical systems, it is the one perhaps which has the most, certainly the one which needs it most, which *lacks* it most. In a certain sense. But it is a mysticism of a peculiar kind which is not (very) dangerous. It cannot reach, it has no prestige for tender and unquiet souls (soft souls), profound souls, it has no attraction for souls specifically mystical, for souls specifically (pre) destined for Christianity, for souls Christian before the event, ante-Christian. It is inoffensive, does not offend because of its opaqueness (*grosseur*), its very grossness. Relatively, then, it is not very dangerous.'[1]

Much more dangerous is the mysticism of pure spirit, for it makes nonsense of the Incarnation. 'To deny the temporal, matter, to be precise, to deny what is gross and impure, to deny me [for it is History who is speaking], to deny me, the temporal, that is indeed the distilled essence (*le fin du fin*), the pure, purity, the sublimely pure. That is the most grave, the supremely grave and the temptation of great souls.'[2] It is this, not materialism, that is most profoundly un-Christian; it is this that is 'the most odious, insufferable, unpleasant, and hateful'.[3] To equate Indian with Christian mysticism, as many neo-Vedāntins and neo-Buddhists so often do, is to deny the central theme of Christianity itself, God's concern with matter, with the world, and with men. After all 'the good God had only to keep quiet in heaven before creation; he was nice and quiet; in his heaven; before creation; he was nice and quiet. He didn't need us. And Jesus too had only to keep (nice and) quiet, . . . before the Incarnation, before the redemption—his Incarnation, his redemption. He was so quiet in heaven, and he had no need of us. Why did he come, why did the world come? We must believe, my friend, that I [again it is History who speaks] have a certain importance, I a wretched woman not worth a penny. . . . We must believe that man and the creation of man, the destiny of man and the vocation of man, man's sin and man's freedom and man's salvation were really quite important: [herein] lies the mystery of man, all the mysteries of man.'[4]

In the Christian mechanism there are two halves which seem quite disproportionate:

One of the halves is the infinite, both in itself and as the eternal. The second of the two halves is the infinitesimal, both in itself and as temporal. And the

[1] Ibid., pp. 386-7.   [2] Ibid., p. 389.
[3] Ibid.   [4] Ibid., pp. 392-3.

most outrageous thing of all is that by a new miracle the infinitesimal part is no less necessary, no less indispensable to the whole, to the 'play' of the whole, than the infinite part, for . . . by a kind of inversion, it is itself necessary, indispensable to that infinite part, to the play of that infinite part. So to deny either part is to deny the whole, to take to pieces the wonderful machine. A God man. A man God. But to deny heaven is almost certainly not dangerous. It is a heresy without any future. It's so obviously gross. But to deny the earth is tempting. First of all it is distinguished. And that's bad—very bad. That's why it is the dangerous heresy, a heresy with a future. [For] *a learned fool is a worse fool than an ignorant one.*[1]

The angel in man is sometimes more dangerous than the beast; for angels can always fall and the cause of their fall is pride. Hence God decided to enter the world as a man. But his appearance was not at all what the Jews expected: he did not come as the expected national hero, the Messiah, but as a carpenter's son without status or obvious credentials. He came as the Taoists would have expected him to come—the weakest of the weak in appearance, but in reality the strongest of the strong. He was born unnoticed among the humble and became the scourge of the hypocrites and the scribes. The power of the Christ, like the power of the Tao, can be likened to the power of water (and water, after all, is the 'matter' of the sacrament of Baptism); for its power lies in its very weakness, and this is the power of the true sage:

> How did the great rivers and seas get their kingship over the hundred lesser streams?
> Through the merit of being lower than they; that is how they got their kingship.
> Therefore the Sage
> In order to be above the people
> Must speak as if he were lower than the people.
> In order to guide them
> He must put himself behind them.
> Only thus can the Sage be on top and the people not be crushed by his weight.
> Only thus can he guide, and the people not be led into harm.[2]

This was the way of Jesus, but to this he added the role of the 'suffering servant' of Yahweh, thereby taking up into his own body and his own human soul all the sufferings and sins of mankind. The Incarnation has not noticeably been a turning-point in the history of mankind, but it is a turning-point in the history of God. In the beginning 'God's spirit hovered over the water' and matter was slowly raised from mere movement into life and from life into self-consciousness: individual men appeared.

---

[1] Péguy, op. cit., p. 394. [2] *Tao Tê Ching*, 66.

Free—free to sin and prone to sin—the All-man sinned. Human concord gave way to human discord. How was the original harmony to be restored? By God, the principle of unity, becoming man, who since the Fall had made himself the very incarnation of disunity and pride, and by God manifesting himself not as he had manifested himself to Job, but as one who was 'humble and meek' like the Chinese Tao, and of whom it was said, as it might have been said of Yudhishthira, the King of Righteousness in the Hindu legend:

> Faithfully he brings true justice;
> he will neither waver, nor be crushed
> until true justice is established on earth,
> for the islands are awaiting his law.[1]

But though his coming may have been adumbrated in China and India as well as in Israel, no one could have foreseen the form it took—the total abdication, or so it seemed, of Yahweh God to man:

> As the crowds were appalled on seeing him
> —so disfigured did he look
> that he seemed no longer human—
> so will the crowds be astonished at him,
> and kings stand speechless before him;
> for they shall see something never told
> and witness something never heard before.[2]

> Without beauty, without majesty (we saw him),
> no looks to attract our eyes;
> a thing despised and rejected by men,
> a man of sorrows and familiar with suffering,
> a man to make people screen their faces;
> he was despised and we took no account of him.

> And yet ours were the sufferings he bore,
> ours the sorrows he carried . . .
> He was pierced through for our faults,
> crushed for our sins.
> On him lies a punishment that brings us peace,
> and through his wounds we are healed.[3]

He is not only the true Tao, and the fulfilment of the hope of Yudhish-thira, the righteous: he is also, in his serene acceptance of suffering, the true answer to Job:

> Harshly dealt with, he bore it humbly,
> he never opened his mouth,

[1] Isaiah 42: 4.   [2] Ibid. 52: 14-15.   [3] Ibid. 53: 2-5.

like a lamb that is led to the slaughter-house,
like a sheep that is dumb before its shearers
never opening its mouth.[1]

Where else in the history of religion have we met a God like this? There stand the Buddha and the Christ. The one conquers suffering and sin by rising high above them as one standing on a peak, sublime, aloof: the other accepts the ultimate disgrace of a felon's death, taking upon himself, absorbing into himself all the wickedness and misery of man.

[1] Isaiah 53: 7.

XVIII

HOSEA'S WIFE

When Yahweh first spoke through Hosea, Yahweh said this to him, 'Go, marry a whore, and get children with a whore, for the country itself has become nothing but a whore by abandoning Yahweh.'[1]

YAHWEH too had taken to himself a wife, and she too had turned whore. Her name was Israel; and the punishment for her adulteries was and continues to be terrible.

Yahweh had a son in eternity, 'God from God, Light from Light, True God from True God'. Yahweh willed that his son should become man, and so he was born of the Virgin Mary through the power of the Holy Spirit. The mission of this son of Mary and the Holy Spirit was to deliver the world from the bondage of sin by assuming into himself all the suffering and sin of mankind. He was to know the agony of despair in the garden of Gethsemane, abandonment by all his friends and followers, and a felon's death upon a cross. This is the dark side of the picture, the obverse of the mystic's union with God. The mystic's union is a union of pure joy, and it is necessarily a purely personal affair. Israel's *hieros gamos*, her sacred nuptials, with Yahweh, however, was of quite another kind; for Israel was unfaithful, and Yahweh is a jealous God, demanding exclusive obedience, worship, and love. Israel's marriage was a tempestuous affair, and Yahweh's love was never separate from his fury. Jesus, the Son of God, was not like this. He was humble and gentle, and promised nothing but persecution to his Church. He promised nothing but what he had himself endured—a cruel death at the hands of unjust men. But he had risen from the dead, and so, after the humiliation and the agony, he had promised a resurrection in joy.

Of all the great founders of religions Jesus alone was celibate. But this applied to his earthly life only, for just as his Father, Yahweh, had taken Israel to wife and she had proved unfaithful, so when he sent his Son to her and she rejected him, the vineyard was given to others—the new Israel which is the Church. What more natural, then, than that the Son, having risen from the dead in glory, should in his turn take the Church to himself as his bride?

[1] Hosea 1 : 2.

It has often been said that the strongest argument against the Christian religion is the Christians themselves. This is true, but scarcely surprising, not only because, in the natural order of things, the original impetus given to any religion by a 'charismatic' founder is bound to peter out, is bound to be appropriated by lesser men and institutionalized, but also it is only natural to suppose that the pattern of Yahweh's marital relationships would be repeated in the nuptial union of his Son with the Church. Why be surprised and indignant that the Bride of Christ should so soon become unrecognizable and appear in the tainted finery of the Whore of Babylon? Hosea's wife, though a whore, remained his wife none the less, as did Israel, despite her constant infidelity, remain the bride of Yahweh. Is there really any reason why one should ever expect the new Israel to behave any better than the old? The mere assumption of the name would indicate that the Church, the new Israel plighted to the Son of God, would repeat the backslidings of the old, but this time on a world-wide scale. The marital relationships between Israel and Yahweh were of little concern to the Gentiles. But the new alliance between the Son and the new Israel was bound to become the concern of the whole human race, because the first apostles had been bidden by the risen Lord to 'make disciples of all nations'. And the nations that came flocking into the Church were an un-ruly lot, as they were bound to be: they were 'bad and good alike',[1] 'the poor, the crippled, the blind and the lame',[2] people 'forced to come in from the open roads and hedgerows'[3]—a motley enough crowd, you might have thought, and not one respectable citizen among them. And what would you expect a crowd like that to do, once it had tasted of the joys of the wedding-feast, and once it had put on the wedding-garment the likes of which it had never seen before? Well, of course it would like things to go on that way for ever because, as we have now come to realize, the highest aspiration of the proletarian is to become a respectable bourgeois; and even Christ could not conquer man's ineradicable longing to appear other and more than he really is—his *amour-propre*.

We tend to forget that it was the Prince of Peace himself who said: 'Do not suppose that I have come to bring peace to the earth: it is not peace I have come to bring, but a sword. For I have come to set a man against his father, a daughter against her mother, a daughter-in-law against her mother-in-law. A man's enemies will be those of his own household.'[4]

Mary was elected to be the mother of Jesus because of her unques-tioning humility and ready acceptance of God's will; and she praises God

---

[1] Matthew 22: 10.   [2] Luke 14: 21.
[3] Ibid. 14: 23.   [4] Matthew 11: 34–6.

because 'he had pulled down princes from their thrones and exalted the lowly', because 'he had filled the hungry with good things and sent the rich empty away';[1] yet even she could not escape the sharp sword of discord her son had brought into the world:

You see this child: [old Simeon prophesies,] he is destined for the fall and for the rising of many in Israel, destined to be a sign that is rejected—and a sword will pierce your own soul too—so that the secret thoughts of many may be laid bare.[2]

The Incarnation is a milestone in the history of God: it can scarcely be said to be a milestone in the history of man. 'After so many mysteries,' Péguy exclaims, 'the world, alas, the world, as you can very well see, has not noticeably changed: . . . since this unique story, the face of the world has not been noticeably modified, the history of the world has not been noticeably changed.'[3] If God is the Lord of history, then it is very difficult to see what difference his Incarnation has made in history—except to produce more, and more bitter, because ideological, strife. If change there has been, it has taken place in secret, in the deep places of the heart to which few can penetrate. On the surface, after the Incarnation, nothing has changed: there have been wars and pestilence, 'terrifying hatreds and shocking displays of impurity; and man has hated man with an appalling hatred, and man has massacred man'.[4] And so, Péguy continues, 'the spectacle of mankind, seen as spectacle, given and presented as historic spectacle, the spectacle of mankind, considered in its gross aspect, its temporal aspect, its historical aspect, with the eye of the historian, the spectacle of mankind is even worse than it was before; and unfortunately, much worse than it was before, sadder, uglier'.[5] But why should anyone be surprised? Is it not just this that Christ had foretold? And seeing history, as we now must, in terms of hundreds of thousands of years, can we expect anything else? We already knew that 'with the Lord a day can mean a thousand years and a thousand years is like a day'.[6] That would make the Church exactly two days old, and it would then seem miraculous that she has produced any fruits at all. Mankind has still not learnt how to use the serpent's gift, and the coming of Christ seems to have changed nothing.

'To create is to unite,' Teilhard is continually telling us. He may or may not be right; but out of an original unity there can only come diversification, and, man being what he is, diversification must degenerate into disunity and discord. But together with disunity there is also clarification,

---

[1] Luke 1: 52–3.　　　　　　　　　　[2] Ibid. 2: 34–5.
[3] Péguy, Œuvres en prose 1909–1914, p. 484.　　[4] Ibid.
[5] Ibid., p. 491.　　　　　　　　　　[6] 2 Peter 3: 8.

for the essential opposites have first to appear in their apparent irreconcilability if ever they are to be harmonized at a higher and more self-conscious level. In the Book of Job God and Satan are not yet separated, and in Genesis the serpent seems to share in the wisdom of the Holy Spirit, and we meet with the same strange companionship again in the temptation of Jesus in the wilderness:

> Then Jesus was led by *the Spirit* out into the wilderness to be tempted by *the Devil*. . . . Next, taking him to a very high mountain, the Devil showed him all the kingdoms of the world and their splendour. 'I will give you all these,' he said, 'if you fall at my feet and worship me.' Then Jesus replied, 'Be off, Satan! For scripture says:
>
> > You must worship the Lord your God,
> > and serve him alone.'[1]

So saying Jesus showed to the Adversary of God and man that his kingdom was not of this world: that is to say, although his mission was directed to the world, 'to all the nations', his kingdom was not and was never intended to be a temporal kingdom. What the Bridegroom had contemptuously refused from Satan the Bride was joyfully to accept. She saw herself as ruling the nations: she ruled the nations and was miserably overthrown.

From the beginning too she was a casuist; and for this at least she cannot be blamed, for the sayings of Jesus are themselves quite often not consistent. 'Ye cannot serve God and Mammon', 'You cannot be the slave both of God and of money',[2] Jesus had said. This, however, she has successfully done throughout her chequered career, and in this she could have claimed the authority of the Lord himself, for it was he, not she, who commended the unjust steward. You will all remember this most puzzling of all the parables—the incompetent steward who was dismissed for extravagance and who then proceeded to cook the accounts of his master's debtors. But 'the lord commended the unjust steward, because he had done wisely: for the children of this world are in their generation wiser than the children of light. And I say unto you, Make to yourselves friends of the mammon of unrighteousness; that, when ye fail, they may receive you into everlasting habitations.'[3] Or, in a more modern version:

'The master praised the dishonest steward for his astuteness. For the children of this world are more astute in dealing with their own kind than are the children of light. And so I tell you this: use money, tainted as it is, to win you friends, and thus make sure that when it fails you, they will welcome you into the tents of eternity.'

---

[1] Matthew 4: 1–10.　　　　[2] Ibid. 6: 24.　　　　[3] Luke 16: 8–9 (A.V.).

In these two things, then, at least the Church has been faithful: she has wielded the sword and she has never hesitated to 'make friends of the mammon of unrighteousness'. In neither case was she totally disloyal to her master: rather it was in her failure to resist Satan's temptation to 'accept the kingdoms of the world and their splendour' that she and her daughters betrayed the heavenly Bridegroom.

In the eyes of the world Christ was a failure, and the early Church was a failure. But this was in the nature of the case, for Christ's mission was to turn worldly values upside-down. The growth of the Church was to have been slow but organic: she was to be the leaven which in the course of time was to raise the whole lump. St. Paul saw her as a living organism; she was to be both the Bride and the Body of Christ in which each member was to play his allotted part. If she were an organism, then this implied organization, for Christianity is not simply a religion of individual salvation. Like Israel, the root from which she springs, and like Confucianism in far-off China, the Christian Church is primarily a community affair in which the individual must take second place. Of course, the salvation of the individual soul is important, but the growth of the community towards a fulfilment that seems to recede ever further and further away is the eschatological hope to which all must look forward. But, as the history of the Church has shown, for every step we take forward we seem to slip back two.

The conversion of Constantine was the fatal step; for the Church willy-nilly became associated with the supreme secular power. It is true that in the Roman Pontiff she found an ecclesiastical centre, traditionally the successor of St. Peter, the head of the apostles, who was to provide a counterweight to the Imperial power of Constantinople; but Rome itself was very soon drawn into secular politics by the now notorious forgery known as the Donation of Constantine. Israel had flirted with the Baalim, but prophets had been sent to warn her of the terrible wrath to come. With the coming of Christ, the Son of God, prophecy, it was thought, had come to an end, and there was as yet no one to warn either Rome or Constantinople of the vengeance to come. When it came it fell most heavily on Constantinople, the Imperial city that had sought to make the Church a department of state; for, out of the Arabian desert, literally out of the blue, a new prophet arose, who was to be the scourge of Christendom. He came in the name of the One God, and his mission was to spread the pure religion of Yahweh among the Gentiles.

The contrast between the rise of Christianity and that of Islam could scarcely be greater. As far as the world was concerned Jesus had died on

the Cross and that was the end of the story. The scribes and Pharisees had
asked for a sign, and he had refused to give one:

It is an evil and unfaithful generation that asks for a sign! The only sign it will
be given is the sign of the prophet Jonah. For as Jonah was in the belly of the
sea-monster for three days and three nights, so will the Son of Man be in the
heart of the earth for three days and nights.[1]

Here he was clearly prophesying his own resurrection from the dead;
and yet when he did rise from the dead he did not deign to show himself
to the scribes and Pharisees, his sworn enemies, but only to his intimate
friends. So momentous an event could scarcely have been kept more
secret: nothing appeared in the full light of day. This may have been
because the hardened rationalist as much as the hide-bound traditionalist
cannot be shaken out of their various complacencies: 'If they will not
listen either to Moses or to the prophets, they will not be convinced
even if someone should rise from the dead.'[2] The revelation of Jesus in
his resurrected body (and I am old-fashioned enough to believe that there
was a resurrected body like ours in that it could be seen, touched, and
heard, but unlike ours in that it had, as the *Chāndogya* Upanishad puts it,
'freedom of movement in all states of being'[3]), the resurrected body of
Jesus which was in fact what turned a frightened and demoralized group of
men into a dedicated and selfless band of enthusiasts who positively
thirsted for martyrdom, was manifested only to a chosen few. For the
world at large it could only remain an unsubstantiated fable. The Church,
like the mustard-seed, was to grow into a mighty tree, but only gradually
and, as it were, naturally under the benign influence of the Holy Spirit, the
Breath of Life. The conversion of an Emperor changed all that, and
Christianity became a world religion—a triumphant because established
cult. This was the exact opposite of what Christ had promised: all he had
offered was persecution as the acid test of faith:

Blessed are they which are persecuted for righteousness' sake: for theirs is the
kingdom of heaven. Blessed are ye, when men shall revile you, and persecute you,
and shall say all manner of evil against you falsely, for my sake. Rejoice, and be
exceeding glad: for great is your reward in heaven: for so persecuted they the
prophets which were before you.[4]

Blessed are the persecuted: to submit to persecution is, then, the
natural state of the Christian. In becoming the state religion of the Empire
and, worse still, in becoming a secular power herself the Bride of Christ
bowed the knee to Satan and to Mammon. Those who remembered or

---

[1] Matthew 12: 39–40.   [2] Luke 16: 31.
[3] *Chāndogya* Upanishad 7: 25: 2.   [4] Matthew 5: 10–12 (A.V.).

thought they remembered better times reviled her as the Whore of Babylon, but this did not undo her marriage-tie with Christ any more than Hosea was released from his wife. But in becoming a secular power she was false to her origins, betraying the trust of her founder.

With Islam things were quite different. From the beginning it was a militant religion. Christ had firmly rejected the current interpretation of the role of the Messiah as a national liberator of the Jews from foreign domination: he did not see himself as a second Judas Maccabaeus. Muhammad from the beginning saw himself as the apostle of the One God whose duty it was to stamp out polytheism in the Arabian peninsula. Prestige was much to his liking, and when the people of Medina invited him to become their leader on the understanding that he would lead them to war against his native Mecca, still predominantly polytheist, he accepted with alacrity. Hence the Muslim era starts not with the birth of the Prophet nor with his call to proclaim the new religion, but with his emigration from Mecca, where he had as yet few followers, to Medina where he was to enjoy secular power. From the very beginning Islam was a militant, aggressive, potentially a persecuting religion. If Christ came to bring the sword, it can be said that Muhammad was the sword he brought—a sword directed at the fattened heart of a squabbling Christendom. Islam alone among the world religions started as a militant and at least potentially an intolerant political and social force. Its initial conquests were sensational: the Persian Empire and with it the Zoroastrian religion were destroyed, vast tracts of the Christian Roman Empire, including Augustine's see of Hippo and the ancient patriarchates of Jerusalem, Caesarea, Chalcedon, and Alexandria were overrun in the name of the One God, Allah—the God who claimed to be identical with the Jewish Yahweh. Indeed the identity is obvious as both the Jews and the Muslims agree— in their somewhat differing ways. For the Jews it was obvious that the Koran contained much authentic Jewish material, but Muhammad was not a lettered man, and he had frequently got points of detail hopelessly mixed up. For the Muslims—since they believed the Koran to be a direct revelation from God which they had witnessed within their own lifetime and which therefore superseded all previous revelations—it was the Jews who were at fault: knowingly or unknowingly they had falsified God's revelation. But whichever view you took, the core of the revelation was the same—God is One, and he is absolutely transcendent: he is not an attributeless Absolute, but has an almost oppressive concern with the world. For the Jews:

Hear, O Israel: the Lord our God is one Lord.[1]

[1] Deuteronomy 6: 4.

For the Muslims:

> Say, He, God, is the One, God the eternal;
> He does not beget nor is he begotten;
> And like unto him there is no one.[1]

The Koran was revealed partly in Mecca and partly in Medina. The Meccan *sūra*s ('chapters') are more obviously 'prophetic', the Medinan more concerned with law. Islam, then, like Judaism is both a prophetic religion and a religion of law: it is Judaism directed to and modified for the Gentiles. Christianity, on the other hand, was from the beginning a mystery religion—transmitted, as any other religion is, by what we call the ministry of the Word, but much more essentially by the sacraments, and particularly the sacrament of the Eucharist, the point of communion and union between man and God.

The association of the Christian Church with temporal power was the beginning of its undoing and the source of all its ills. There is no affinity between Christ and Caesar. For Islam, on the other hand, there is no distinction between the Prophet and Caesar, between the religious and the secular; for the Prophet is God's viceroy on earth, and so long as he was alive his sole authority was undisputed. For the Sunnīs this ideal state of affairs lasted until the violent death of the fourth 'orthodox' caliph. Thereafter things went wrong: the Caliph, the Prophet's 'successor', was no longer regarded as the infallible guide and leader of the *religious* community, purely religious affairs being now left to the lawyers and the *'ulamā*, the doctors—the scribes and Pharisees in Muslim dress. The ideal of the unity of religion and state was, however, never lost sight of. For Islam this is normative: for Christianity it is an aberration and the temptation of Satan.

So too in the matter of persecution. For the Christians the blood of the martyrs is the seed of the Church; and each renewal of Christianity has in fact been brought about by persecution. For Islam the role of persecutor comes naturally; and this is because, for Islam as for Israel, idolatry is the supreme evil and must be mercilessly extirpated. This was not so at the very beginning because Muhammad had not yet the power to persecute: *then* he was perfectly prepared to leave the unbelievers to their own devices:

> Say: 'O ye unbelievers,
> I serve not what ye serve,
> And ye are not servers of what I serve . . .
> Ye have your religion, and I have mine.[2]

---

[1] Koran 112.   [2] Ibid. 109.

Later, however, even the 'people of the book', the Jews and Christians, were to be faced with the alternative of conversion or total submission:

Fight against those who do not believe in Allah nor in the Last Day, and do not make forbidden what Allah and his Messenger have made forbidden, and do not practise the religion of truth, of those who have been given the Book, until they pay the tribute off-hand, being subdued.[1]

The ideal has now become that all should submit (Islam, after all, means 'submission') to the new religion which in Muhammad's later days was alone considered to be absolutely true: 'Fight them until there is no dissension and the religion is entirely Allah's.'[2]

These examples of the legitimacy, or rather the sanctity, of warfare are typical of the whole Koranic outlook. As in the Old Testament, so in Islam, fighting is God's favourite way of achieving his ends. Whatever Islamic modernists may say, war is the normal state of affairs between the Muslim community and the surrounding infidels: it is the Muslim's duty in the long run to subdue the whole world to Allah. In so doing he is serving, not betraying, his God; for Muhammad is at once the Jesus and the Constantine of Islam. The case is quite otherwise with Christianity.

Once the Bride of Christ had fallen to the temptation of Satan and accepted 'all the kingdoms of the world and their splendour', she never looked back. From persecuted she became persecutor, and it was left to Augustine of Hippo with all his immense authority to saddle her with this unforseen duty. Let us not blame him too much, however, for, though she had moments of compassion, she on the whole found 'this yoke easy and this burden light'. And yet a heavy burden still remains with Augustine, for he has set his sombre stamp on the Western Church right up to the present day. He never fully recovered from his Manichaean past, from the dualism that conceived of salvation as the final separation of spirit from matter. True, asceticism had already taken firm root in Christianity in its most extreme and revolting form, but it is Augustine above all others who came very near to equating the flesh with the Devil and condemned sexuality as such as being intrinsically evil. We are paying for this attitude to this day. In his attitude to sexuality Augustine is the father of Puritanism, and Puritanism is the mother of the 'sexual revolution' of today. Both are deviations from a golden mean which is or should be the position of the Catholic Church, the mean between an exaggerated respect for chastity (this deriving again at least in part from the Manichees and, through the Manichees, from the Buddhists) and simple promiscuity.

[1] Ibid. 9: 29.   [2] Ibid. 8: 40.

These two extremes seem to succeed each other with the monotony of the swing of a pendulum, and perhaps the true point of equilibrium will never be found. In modern times the Roman Catholic Church has not been notably successful in finding it.

Augustine too we have to thank for the sombre view of predestination, thereby anticipating what Pascal (himself an Augustinian) was to call *l'opinion épouvantable*—'the ghastly doctrine of the [Calvinist] heretics at once insulting to God and unbearable to man'.[1] And yet Pascal himself accepts his ferocious master's doctrine that God takes pleasure in the torments of the damned:

> So far from its being impious to laugh at [Adam's Fall], [he writes,] it is rather an effect of the divine wisdom, as St. Augustine says: the wise laugh at fools because they are wise—not by their own wisdom, but by that divine wisdom which will laugh at the death of the wicked.[2]

These are savage doctrines which, thank God and the Enlightenment, are seldom seriously defended today and which, thank God and the Society of Jesus, have been almost totally abandoned by the Roman Church. The free-will-versus-predestination controversy, however, is a philosophical and theological issue with little relevance to practical life, since everyone behaves as if his will were free. The matter of persecution, however, is something that affects us all, and it is here that Augustine has no defence.

Let me now repeat what I have already said in earlier lectures. The Catholic ideal (and I am using the word 'Catholic' in its broadest connotation) is first and foremost unity, both on the individual level and in the community—unity through the Holy Spirit in Christ for the Father. In the individual it means the gathering up of all the functions into their immortal centre, what the Hindus call the 'self'; and this is surely what St. Paul referred to when he said, 'I live now not with my own life but with the life of Christ who lives in me.'[3] In the community it is the Church, seen now not as the Bride but as the Body of Christ, in which each Christian has his individual part to play in harmony with the whole, and which lives by the breath of the Holy Spirit and the blood of Christ which, through the sacrament of the Eucharist, feeds the individual cells and nourishes the whole. This is the ideal. The Church is not just an organization; it is a living organism in which the part cannot live in separation from the whole. This, you will rightly say, is nonsense—a form of collective mysticism which has never existed and perhaps never will exist. Perhaps: but it is nevertheless what we mean by the Communion of Saints, and it is

---

[1] Pascal, *Œuvres complètes*, ed. Pléiade, p. 951.
[2] Ibid., p. 781.   [3] Galatians 2: 20.

the hidden aspiration of all mankind. For the mystic, union and unity are lived realities: for the rest of us they can only be a matter of faith; and faith is make-believe, but a make-believe that, contrary to all the evidence, makes you believe.

Unity of the self, and unity of the Church. Augustine knew all about this. He was a Catholic; and for him the outward and visible sign that the Church was Catholic was that it was one—one in doctrine, one in its sacraments, and one in its ecclesiastical magisterium; and not only must it be one, it must be seen to be one. Woe, then, to those stubborn Donatists and Pelagians who would not submit to the decree of unity. Augustine knew well enough that conversions such as these merely furthered the paganization of the Church which the conversion of Constantine had inaugurated. This no doubt worried him, but Christianity must at all costs be seen to be one. He is, then, not only the father of Puritanism and of Predestinarianism in its most unattractive form; he is also the first Inquisitor, the father of intolerance which has been the ineffaceable blot on the unlovely face of the Catholic Church.

I do not need to repeat the wearisome history of the crimes and follies of the Catholic Church: in Scotland it should not be necessary. On the credit side it can at least be said that through the Dark and Middle Ages she preserved and revived European culture, not disdaining to borrow from Islam what she had herself lost through the shock of the barbarian invasions. The debit side is all too well known—the attempt of the Papacy to establish itself, not only as the arbiter of nations and the head of Christendom (which is legitimate enough), but also to set up in its own right as a secular power. This was not only to bow the knee to Satan but also to bring about the ruin of itself. We know it all so well: the quite unnecessary struggle between Papacy and Empire, the schism with the East, the Babylonish captivity, the great internal schism, the burning of Hus and the anti-Hussite wars, the open simony and corruption of the popes and the higher clergy, the wanton luxury of the papal court. In very truth the Bride of Christ had become the Whore of Babylon. There she was, just as St. John the Divine had prophesied in the Book of Revelation:

Come hither; I will show unto thee the judgement of the great whore who sitteth upon many waters: with whom the kings of the earth have committed fornication, and the inhabitants of the earth have been made drunk with the wine of her fornication. So he carried me away in the spirit into the wilderness; and I saw a woman sit upon a scarlet-coloured beast, full of names of blasphemy, having seven heads and ten horns. And the woman was arrayed in purple and scarlet colour, and decked with gold and precious stones and pearls, having a golden cup in her hand full of abominations and filthiness of her fornication: and upon her forehead was a name written, Mystery, Babylon the Great, the mother of harlots and abominations of the earth. And I saw the woman drunken with the blood of the saints and with the blood of the martyrs of Jesus: and when I saw her, I wondered with great admiration.[1]

This is how the precursors of the Reformation and the Reformers themselves saw the Church of Rome; and the picture fitted the case. There was she who had deserted Christ and flirted with the European kings against the Emperor, 'full of the names of blasphemy'—the Renaissance popes trafficking in holy things; 'arrayed in purple and scarlet'—the cardinals and bishops of Holy Church; 'decked with gold and precious stones'—with all the treasures of Renaissance art of which she had herself been the chief patron (and all honour to her for that); 'drunk with the blood of the saints and with the blood of the martyrs of Jesus'—with the blood of Hus and Savonarola and countless others both remembered and forgotten. Is it surprising that they 'wondered with great admiration' that the Bride of Christ should have transformed herself into the image of the world and the flesh?

The Reformation came, that happy release, or so we were taught in my youth. But let us return to Hosea's wife, for we have not finished with her yet. She bore him two sons and a daughter, Jezreel, Lo-Ruhamah, and Lo-Ammi. Of Jezreel it is said that he was 'to put an end to the sovereignty of the House of Israel'. The sovereignty of Israel was indeed terminated by the Babylonian captivity, but she survived and was once again restored. So too the sovereignty of the Church of Rome was smashed by Luther and the German princes, but restored by the penitence of Pius V and the steely devotion of the Society of Jesus which did its best to drag the Church out of the Middle Ages into the post-Renaissance world. The name of the second child was Lo-Ruhamah, 'Unloved'—surely the second of the great Reformers, Calvin, of all the great figures of the Reformation the most unloved in that he was prepared to view with elation the preordained condemnation of the great majority of the human race to everlasting torment, secure in the belief that he and his own elect were predestined to eternal bliss. And then there was the third child, Lo-Ammi, 'No-people-of-mine', the third great Protestant community, the Church of England, which presumed to set one people, the English, apart from the Universal Church.

These were the children of the new Israel, the Bride of Christ and the Whore of Babylon, and she has little reason to be proud of them. The

[1] Revelation 17: 1–7 (A.V.).

Roman Church, it is true, had committed fornication with the kings of the earth; and this was inexcusable, for she did this to preserve her own temporal domains which she had no business to possess. Two of her children went further than this: they no longer committed fornication with the kings of the earth but entered into formal wedlock with them. Only 'Unloved' preserved a qualified chastity, but this made her unbearably self-righteous.

Christianity is supposed to be a religion of love. This was never true except at the very beginning: after the Reformation neither side bothered to conceal its ferocious hatred of the other. The justification of persecution by the great Augustine and the fratricidal wars of the Reformation period gave the lie to the Christian claim that the Christian religion was based on love:

Do not suppose that I have come to bring peace on the earth: it is not peace I have come to bring but the sword.

How tragically true this terrible prophecy has turned out to be! But Christ is also the Prince of Peace, and he had said:

Peace I bequeath to you,
my own peace I give you,
a peace the world cannot give, this is my gift to you.[1]

I have told you all this
so that you may find peace in me.
In the world you will have trouble,
but be brave:
I have conquered the world.[2]

Two thousand years of Christendom has only proved that to the naked eye it is rather the world that has conquered Christ or at least the Bride of Christ and her three children. If there is peace, then it can only be an inner peace, the peace of Nirvāna which the Buddha had preached long ago, but which, so far from conquering the world, merely withdraws the soul from all the struggle and suffering that bedevil existence in the world. Again we must bear in mind that 'with the Lord a day can mean a thousand years and a thousand years a day'. We still live under the sign of the sword. Individual peace can be found by many, but the promised peace when Christ will conquer the world is still no more than a hope.

'And now abideth faith, hope, charity, these three; but the greatest of these is charity.'[3] Faith, the great virtue of the Old Testament that sustained Israel throughout its trials: charity—love—supposedly the Christian

[1] John 14: 27.   [2] Ibid. 16: 33.   [3] 1 Corinthians 13: 13 (A.V.).

virtue *par excellence*, but, as we can all see with appalling clarity, the reign of charity is only a far-off dream. What then of hope, the humble virtue, which nobody except Péguy talks much about? This is the real Christian virtue (in Hinduism and Buddhism it is a vice), hope in the perfectibility of the world, hope that one day we will emerge from beneath the sun of Satan under whose sweltering malevolence we have so long revelled in our existential *Angst*, hope that God's creation will one day converge upon the cosmic Christ of whom Teilhard de Chardin speaks, hope that all the senseless suffering we see around us may be turned to joy. *La petite espérance*, as Péguy calls her, the little school-girl whom nobody notices as she marches along between her two strapping grown-up sisters— nobody bothers about *her*. Yet it is she who keeps us alive and saves us from that despair of this world, from which, the Indian religions would have us believe, salvation will ultimately come:

> Faith sees what is
> In time and in eternity.
> Hope sees what is yet to be
> In time and for evermore. . . .

> Charity loves what is
> In time and in eternity,
> God and one's neighbour;
> Just as faith sees
> God and his creation.
> But hope loves what is yet to be
> In time and for evermore.[1]

But in recent times it has not been the Christians who have put their trust in *la petite espérance*. Stripped of her dependence on God she was adopted by the Enlightenment and refurbished as the belief in the triumphant progress and ultimate perfectibility of man.

The French Revolution came—the savage shock that at last made Catholics and Protestants see that they had more in common than what divided them. And it was the French Church, the Church which had persecuted the Huguenots whenever and wherever it could and had acquiesced in the iniquitous and senseless Revocation of the Edict of Nantes, that in its turn became the victim of savage persecution. And the Whore of Babylon was finally humiliated to the dust by the abduction of two popes in succession, one by the Directoire, the other by Bonaparte. Yet it was persecution that revitalized the Church, and it is no accident

[1] Péguy, *Œuvres poétiques*, ed. Pléiade, pp. 539–40.

that the French Church, though not particularly strong in numbers, is yet full of vigour today.

Shortly after the July Revolution in 1830 which brought to power the bourgeois monarchy of Louis-Philippe, Balzac had a vision of the Whore of Babylon humiliated at last, and divested of all her splendour. The vision is described in what must be one of the greatest short stories of the world, *Jesus Christ in Flanders*.

The hero strays into a cathedral in Flanders where he falls into an ecstasy so sweet that he would have given his life could it have lasted longer: he had passed clean outside this world. But suddenly he is brought down to earth by a harsh cry: 'Wake up, and follow me.' Whom is he asked to follow? A little dried up old woman so thin that you could hear her bones crack as she walked, looking as if she had just risen from the grave. She had only two things to say, and they seemed to contradict each other: 'il faut souffrir', 'you must suffer'; and 'I want to make you happy for ever, [for] you are my son'. Why had he been dragged out of an ecstasy for *this*? He looked at the old woman again; and then he saw in a flash that once she had been 'young and beautiful, blessed with all the graces of simplicity, pure and immaculate as a Greek statue'. He recognized her: for it was she, the Bride of Christ who had played the whore with the children of men. His indictment is terrible, far more terrible than Dostoievsky's indictment of the Catholic Church in the *Brothers Karamazov*, for Balzac was a Catholic and saw the full horror from inside:

O wretched, wretched woman, [he cries out in despair,] why did you prostitute yourself to men? At an age when the passions are aroused, you became rich, you forgot the purity and meekness of your youth, your devotion, your innocence, your fruitful faith, and you abdicated from the power that was originally yours, your purely spiritual supremacy, for the powers of the flesh. . . . You became brazen and proud, wanting everything, getting everything, upsetting everything as you pleased, like a fashionable prostitute in search of pleasure; you became bloodthirsty like a queen stunned by her own self-will. Can't you remember how stupid you were from time to time? And then, suddenly, how wonderfully intelligent you became. . . . Poet, painter, singer, you loved your splendid ceremonies, or was it merely a whim which made you patron of the arts? . . . And then, there you were, fantastic and brazen, you who were to have been chaste and modest. What did you do? You subjected everything to your slipper, and then you hurled it at the heads of kings who here on earth had the power, the money, and the talent. Insulting the human race, how pleased you were to see just how far human stupidity could go; and then you would tell your lovers to walk on all fours, to give you their property, their treasures, even their wives if they were worth it. Without any motive you swallowed up millions of men, hurling them like clouds of sand from the west to the east. You abandoned the high places of thought to seat yourself among kings. Woman, instead of consoling men, you tormented and persecuted them. Knowing that you would get it, you clamoured for blood. . . . Original in everything, you forbade your exhausted lovers to eat, and they didn't. Why were you so mad as to demand the impossible? Why did you—like a harlot spoilt by her admirers—why did you go mad on trivialities, why did you not undeceive the men who tried to explain away and justify all your mistakes? And then you had your final fling. Like a woman of forty, terrible, you bellowed aloud! You wanted to embrace the whole world in one last hug, and the universe which belonged to you by right escaped your grasp. And then, after the young men, the old came and prostrated themselves at your feet—impotent old men who made you hideous. And yet there were some with the eyes of an eagle who told you: You will perish in infamy because you have deceived, because you have broken your maiden's vows. You who should have been an angel with peace inscribed on your brow, you who should have sown light and happiness wherever you went, you became a Messalina, loving circuses and debauchery, and abusing your power. Never can you recover your virginity. What you need is a master. Your time is up. You already smell of death. Your heirs think you are rich; they will kill you and get nothing. . . . You have committed suicide! Well, isn't that a fair account of your history? . . . You are old, decrepit, toothless, cold, forgotten now—who will look at you as you pass on? . . . Where is your fortune now? Why did you squander it? Where are your treasures? What good have you ever done?

Thus, in shocked incomprehension, does Balzac attack the Church, the Bride of Christ turned whore. Like Job he demands an explanation, and like Job he gets none—only a sign. And the sign is that it is only when the Church has been humiliated almost to annihilation that she rises again renewed. And so the little old woman sheds her rags and emerges like a butterfly in all the splendour of her youth. And then he sees the other side of the picture—millions of cathedrals scattered over the face of the earth, monks copying manuscripts in the Dark Ages, selfless service of the poor. 'See and believe,' the Church admonishes him. But first you have to *see* through the pomp and legalistic trappings before you can believe in the truth hidden beneath them. Balzac's eyes are opened, He sees and believes. 'Believe,' he says, yes, 'to believe is to live', hence he has no alternative but to defend the Church. And the Church's reply to his rallying to her defence was to put his *omnes fabulae amatoriae* on the Index. 'How pleased you were to see just how far human stupidity could go,' Balzac had said to the Church; but purely human stupidity is as nothing to the learned folly of the Roman clerks. And yet—as Galileo said in another context—*eppur, si muove*, 'and yet it goes on'.

Jesus Christ in Flanders was written in 1831 when it was confidently expected that the Roman Church would quietly disappear or remain only as an object of antiquarian interest like the Parsees: it already smelt of death. This too was the view of Engels who rightly thought that persecution alone could save the Christian churches. 'This much is sure,' he added, 'the only service that can be rendered to God today is to declare atheism a compulsory article of faith.'[1] His followers have not had the courage to take his advice.

With such a record, then, how has the Catholic Church survived? What accounts for its strength and renewed vigour today? For now of all times is the testing-time of all religions. Secularism has come to stay: we may deplore or or we may welcome it. It does not matter, it is a fact. And by secularism I mean a state of society in which religion has ceased to play a leading part. Formerly religion formed the basis of all the great civilizations—with the single exception of our own, for our *civilization* comes from Greece and Rome, for neither of which was religion more than a sideline. Thus it is possible to study the Greek and Roman classics without even being aware that they had a religion, certainly not one that they took seriously. In no other great literature until recent times would that have been possible. We are the heirs of Greece and Rome. We always knew this, even in the Dark Ages, but we became acutely conscious of it during the Renaissance. In all but name the Renaissance popes were pagans, and it was against the paganization of Christianity that the Reformers revolted. Their revolt, however, recoiled on their own heads, for they had sold themselves to the State: religion became a Department of State and ceased to have an independent voice in the councils of the new nations which had arisen out of the ruins of the Catholic Church built on the foundations laid by Augustine. *Cujus regio ejus religio* was the accepted formula for religious peace—a formula accepted by Voltaire himself and more strongly still by Rousseau who, though he had been born a Calvinist, was converted to Catholicism only to abjure it, and yet he could maintain that in the interest of the State, if for no other reason, one should remain in the religion into which one is born. 'If', he said, 'the son of a Christian does well to follow the religion of his fathers without examining it in depth and with impartiality, why should the son of a Turk do ill in following the religion of his?'[2] Note the words 'son of a Turk'; for in the eighteenth century, as in Greece today, 'Turk' is a synonym for 'Muslim'. *Cujus regio ejus religio*. In Europe and particularly in Protestant Europe this has long ceased to be true. Religion has become a private matter which may be respected but which has nothing to do with the community. 'Il n'y a

---

[1] F. Engels, in K. Marx and F. Engels, *On Religion*, Moscow, 1957, p. 142.

[2] Rousseau, *Émile*, p. 400.

plus de paroisse,'[1] 'the parish no longer exists,' the parish priest cries out in despair in Bernanos's masterpiece, *Monsieur Ouine*. I, too, in the first of these Gifford Lectures, had the temerity to say that the world was my parish; and now that I am nearing the end I can only conclude 'il n'y a plus de paroisse! il n'y a plus de paroisse', for, to quote Bernanos again, we are living 'sous le soleil de Satan', 'beneath the sun of Satan', and it looks as if the world will soon be only 'rottenness and gangrene'[2] without even the Devil to give it the semblance of life.

There is no parish: the old certainties have gone, and so departments of religion are springing up like toadstools throughout our demented Anglo-Saxon world. The less we believe, the more we talk about what other people believed. Are we really interested, or are we just kidding ourselves? Faith is a gift freely given and freely withheld, as Michelet quite correctly pointed out.[3] But there remains hope and there remains charity. The modern world can neither hope nor love. It has too long put its faith in its prelates and pastors: too often it has been given not bread but a stone, not a fish but the serpent of doubt and undigested knowledge. Hence the stampede towards the cults of the East and LSD, as if they had anything in common. None of this will work, for you do not and cannot win enlightenment overnight: it needs strong nerves and an iron will. The modern world has neither.

The younger generation has turned against us. Why? Try reading the twenty-third chapter of the Gospel according to St. Matthew, for it is an indictment of everyone of us who has grown fat and smug in our nice snug bourgeois world: it is the final condemnation of *amour-propre*:

Woe unto you, scribes and Pharisees, hypocrites! for ye shut up the kingdom of heaven against men: for ye neither go in yourselves, neither suffer ye them that are entering to go in.[4]

Christians believe that Christ is God. If that is so, his indictment of the scribes and Pharisees is not simply an indictment of the religious establishment of his time: it is a permanent indictment of all religious establishments as such. It is an indictment not only of the Catholic hierarchy but much more of organized Protestantism which has always seemed to me to be the religion of the scribes *par excellence*. For, whether the Reformers willed it or not, historically Protestantism has in fact substituted what it is pleased to call the ministry of the Word for the regular administration of the sacraments: it has offered us sermons (no doubt very good and learned sermons, as one would expect from the

---

[1] Bernanos, *Œuvres romanesques*, ed. Pléiade, p. 1484.   [2] Ibid., p. 1492.
[3] Above, p. 32.   [4] Matthew 23: 13 (A.V.).

scribes) as a substitute for the bread of life, the Body of Christ available to all in the Eucharist. The Reformers prided themselves on having rid Christianity of the priesthood; but it is not the priesthood that Christ attacks in Matthew 23 but the scribes—and that means precisely the ministers of the pen and the ministers of the word, the confraternity to which I too shamefully belong.

It cannot be sufficiently emphasized that Christianity is the religion of the Word made flesh. The Word's name is not only Jesus but Emmanuel, 'God with us', not only in Palestine nearly two thousand years ago but here and now in the sacrament of the Eucharist. This is the essential difference between Christians and Muslims. For the Christians God becomes flesh and blood, and he leaves as a token of his abiding presence with us the sacrament not of his soul or of his godhead but of his flesh and blood: for the Muslims the Word is made Book, *Biblos*, Bible. Hence Islam is the only truly *biblical* religion, and biblical Christianity can therefore never be much more than an inadequate substitute for Islam, the religion of the Book, the religion of the scribes. In these ecumenical days it is unfashionable to emphasize the differences between religions. Nevertheless there is a gulf fixed between biblical Protestantism and sacramental Catholicism; and Péguy has put his finger on the point of difference more effectively than I can hope to do:

The Catholic [he says] is a man who knows very well that he is on the right spiritual road but nevertheless feels that he needs to consult the signposts.

Or rather, who experiences joy, deep, deep joy in consulting the signposts.

If some of one's best friends are Protestants and Jews, as mine are, one very soon realizes, one knows that they cannot even imagine what it is to be a Catholic. And the Protestants are further away from us, more incapable of imagining it, than the Jews. They think they know, they think they understand it, oppose it, and fight it. In actual fact not only do they not know it, but they don't understand it, they don't see it, cannot even imagine what it is. That sort of gratuitousness that indwells the Catholic. And here we touch on one of those points of difference, one of those points that count, one of those points at which the Protestant cannot imagine what it is to be a Catholic. The Protestants are people who make their own signposts. Each one of them has his own signpost. And not only do they make them, they never stop justifying them.

The Catholic on the other hand . . . is the lad who follows the highway and is quite happy with the signpost that is there for everybody. And not only that, those signposts which are there for everybody, he doesn't even consult them to know which way he should go. He *knows* his way, recognizes it, sees it: he does what everybody else does, he follows it like everybody else. . . . He consults the signposts so as to feel a kind of joy which is the ritual joy of the highway, so as to perform a kind of rite which is the rite of the highway.

A ritual joy of his own which cannot be communicated or known by anyone who is not a Catholic, a ritual joy, a communal joy, a parish joy . . .

A useless, gratuitous, superfluous joy.

The only joy.[1]

Useless, gratuitous, superfluous. In other words grace gratuitously given and gratefully received. And grace, for the Catholic, is really received not through sermons, however learned, however inspired, but through the sacraments which operate in silence. And so it does not matter one bit how wicked the Bride of Christ has been, is, or will be. Let the theologians have their theology, let them even be Thomists if that is what they want, it really doesn't matter very much. Of course it is nicer for everybody if the Pope is a good and saintly man like John, and it is a little awkward if he is not really nice at all like Alexander VI; it is nicer if the Bride of Christ is behaving herself and not playing the harlot with Satan or Mammon or both, but it doesn't really matter because, however she behaves, she has the sacraments with which she feeds the souls and bodies of her children so that in the course of time they may all grow together with all their virtues and all their sins into the one Body of Christ which is the Church. This is why the Eucharist, the mass, means everything to the Catholic, the ministry of Word nothing. But before the Eucharist there is the sacrament of Penance, the certainty that sin is forgiven and that there is now nothing that separates you from God, and the joy that Christ did not come to call the righteous, but sinners to repentance.[2] So why should we be scandalized at the sins and follies of the Church? Hosea did not leave his wife because she was a whore, nor did Yahweh turn his back on Israel. Why, then, should Christ, the Son of God, desert his Bride, the Church, simply because she is and probably always will be a sinner and a harlot? After all, 'there is more joy in heaven over one sinner who repents than over ninety-nine righteous men who have no need to repent'.[3] And because there is joy in heaven because there are sinners to repent, therefore on earth our holy days are holidays.

[1] Péguy, *Ouvres en prose 1909–1914*, pp. 1551–2. [2] Matthew 9: 13.
[3] Luke 15: 7.

XIX

BENEATH THE SUN OF SATAN

Why callest thou me good? there is none good but one, that is, God.[1]

IN his *Answer to Job* Jung took it upon himself to psycho-analyse Yahweh, the Old Testament God. By the time he wrote this provocative book, he had evolved his own psychological system which is surely as dogmatic as anything Christianity has to offer. This is largely based on Nicolas of Cusa's *conjunctio oppositorum*, the union of opposites, which is itself the Chinese *yin–yang* theory in European dress. The world in which we live is characterized by the confrontation of seemingly irreducible opposites, the most fundamental of which is that of sex; all the other opposites such as light and darkness, good and evil, spirit and matter, hard and soft, and so on, merely reflect the fundamental pair of opposites on which the very structure of the universe is based—male and female. Of these two it is always the female which is the junior partner: she is matter which must await the fertilization of spirit, the moon which has no light of its own but receives it from the sun, she is evil which must be transformed into good. This *conjunctio oppositorum*, it seems to me, is basic to what Lord Gifford considered to be natural religion. In both China and India it stared you in the face, and it is basic to the whole alchemical tradition which Jung found to be so fruitful a breeding-ground for his own psychology. It is the basis of natural religion as it is the basis of natural law. Because it is, so to speak, genetically present in human thought, it turns up time and time again from its earliest manifestations in China and India up to its more recent efflorescence in Hegel and Marx.

Marx, as we all know, turned Hegel upside-down, or rather stood him on his feet again since the old fuddy-duddy was in fact standing on his head. It was matter, not spirit, which played the leading role in human evolution; it was matter that was the mother of spirit, not the other way round. Similarly it was Mary who gave birth to Jesus, thus setting in motion the whole process of the spiritualization of man.

But here we must pause for a moment and consider once again the nature of these opposites. In both India and China spirit is the male

---

[1] Matthew 19: 17; Luke 18: 19.

matter the female; and spirit is the eternally changeless, matter the ever-changing flux of life, eternally fecund and eternally destructive, destroying what she has herself brought into existence and then again recreating new life from what she had herself destroyed. In the early Hindu period and in Chinese religion in all its stages the sacred marriage of the two means reconciliation and peace: 'What God hath joined together let no man put asunder.'[1] Men have, however, never stopped doing so, and with disastrous results.

There is the carnal man and there is the spiritual man, St. Paul tells us, the angel and the beast of the Jansenist Pascal. Spiritual man has never of his own accord been content to live with his dark sister: the 'image of God' will have nothing to do with the 'dust of the earth' in which, through 'the breath of life', he had become a 'living soul'. Of all spiritual men the Buddha is the most perfect example: among carnal men it was the Jews who were the object of God's election. The very idea of Nirvāna was foreign to them; they were not promised eternal life, only life in this world—a life of toil and duty in which the only immortality consists in solidarity with the race in its gradual progress towards God. Only the Jews accept our fallen condition without demur; and hence only among them could God conceivably become flesh.

The Buddha 'walks like the horn of a rhinoceros alone',[2] and he is indeed the ideal of all ascetics as he is probably the source of them all. He is the 'spiritual man' *par excellence*, sublime in his wisdom and frosty compassion, aloof, and standing on a peak. He is the antithesis of the flesh and, as far as the flesh is concerned, he is *der Geist, der stets verneint*, the spirit that always says no—the divine counterpart of Goethe's Mephistopheles. He did not, it is true, identify matter with evil as such; this was left to the Parthian prophet, Mānī, for whom matter and evil were interchangeable terms. Through him the ascetic ideal seeped into Christendom, making nonsense of the 'Word made flesh'.

It has always been Catholic dogma that grace perfects Nature. How, then, has this anti-natural thing defaced the Christian image for so long? After all, unlike John, Christ 'came eating and drinking, and they say, Behold a man gluttonous, and a winebibber, a friend of publicans and sinners',[3] or in the more comprehensible version of the Jerusalem Bible, he 'came eating and drinking, and they say, "Look, a glutton and a drunkard, a friend of tax collectors and sinners"'. Well, perhaps it needed a God to be the friend of tax-collectors. But this is not the point: the point is that if the Incarnation means anything, it means the sanctification

---

[1] Matthew 19: 6. (A.V.)   [2] *Suttanipāta* 35 ff.   [3] Matthew 11: 19.

of ordinary life and it also means the sanctification of marriage and of the reproductive instinct on which marriage is based. Why else should Christ's first miracle have been the blessing of marriage itself and of the indecorous winebibbing that is its normal concomitant? The Protestant tradition of stern duty is all very well, but not very original, not very compassionate, and not, to my mind, very Christian. For too long have we been obsessed with theology, too intent on demythologizing the faith and obfuscating the very clear image of God made man that emerges from the synoptic gospels, with all his detestation of cant and of the scribes, the authors of cant and pillars of respectability. Jesus may have been, and was, many things, but he was not respectable and he detested respectability. He constitutes and always will constitute what Bernanos called *la grande peur des bien-pensants*, the great fear of all right-thinking people. Why has his teaching been so grossly misrepresented? The answer is not far to seek: like the Manichees, we have identified the flesh with the Devil.

Jung tried to psycho-analyse God; and he saw that in the Old Testament God and the Devil are one: they coexist in apparent concord. God is not good, nor is Satan particularly evil; and it needed the coming of the Son of God among us, it needed Emmanuel, to tell us that God alone is good, not because he was a pure spirit (if so, what sense could the Incarnation have?), but because he was Love and therefore committed to his creature, man. Again, it is with the coming of Christ that another pure spirit, Satan, first shows himself to be what he is, the tempter and the enemy of God and man, who may or may not make use of the flesh (for this is no direct concern of his) but who seeks—and O how subtly—to pervert and corrupt the spirit and to tear it away from its moorings in God. Israel knew nothing of the unwearying malice of this impurely pure spirit, and we too have forgotten about him, but he is still the Prince of this world, and we live, as Bernanos puts it, beneath the sun of Satan: and he rules us with a greater ease because we no longer know that he is there.

Israel knew nothing of him: she learnt about him from the Zoroastrians, from a prophet outside Israel, but a prophet none the less. There, for the first time, we see the confrontation of two antagonistic spiritual powers in all its stark reality. And this is the necessary antidote to all the talk you have heard in the last two years about the ultimate reconciliation of good and evil and of the transcendence of good and evil. All this talk, you may be very sure, is most pleasing to Satan, our master, the Prince of this world. Listen to what the Prophet says:

I will speak out concerning the two Spirits of whom, at the beginning of existence, the Holier thus spoke to him who is evil: 'Neither our thoughts, nor our teachings, nor our wills, nor our choices, nor our words, nor our deeds, nor our consciences, nor yet our souls agree.'[1]

Between good and evil there is an unbridgeable gulf fixed; and between them all rational creatures must choose. Man is a responsible being; and if he is evil, then he is evil by his own choice:

Hear with your ears, behold with mind all clear, the two choices between which you must decide, each man [deciding] for his own self, [each man] knowing how it will appear (?) to us at the [time of] the great crisis.[2]

And then comes the account of how God and the Devil had to make *their* choice at the beginning of time:

In the beginning those two Spirits who are the well-endowed (?) twins were known as the one good and the other evil, in thought, word, and deed. Between them the wise chose rightly, not so the fools. And when these Spirits met they established in the beginning life and death that in the end the followers of the Lie should meet with the worst existence, but the followers of Truth with the Best Mind. Of these two Spirits he who was of the Lie chose to do the worst things; but the Most Holy Spirit, clothed in rugged heaven, [chose] Truth as did [all] who sought with zeal to do the pleasure of the Wise Lord by [doing] good works. Between the two the false gods did not choose rightly; for, as they deliberated, delusion overcame them, so that they chose the most Evil Mind. Then did they, with one accord, rush headlong unto Fury that they might thereby extinguish (?) the existence of mortal men.[3]

Here the doctrine of an irreconcilable hostility between two separate and eternally antagonistic principles is not yet fully developed. The Spirits are twins, and they each have to make their own individual choice. If, however, they are twins, this must imply that they have a common father. In the context of the *Gāthās*, the 'hymns' which in all probability go back to Zoroaster himself, this can only be the supreme God whom he called the Wise Lord. In the later literature this God, this Wise Lord, became identified with the Holy Spirit, and this led to complications. But the situation just quoted corresponds very closely to the rather composite theology which Jung put together from various Jewish and Christian sources. According to him Yahweh has two Sons, Satan and Christ; and Satan is the first-born. Satan, in the Christian tradition, is of course Lucifer; and Lucifer is the bright spirit who sins by pride and refuses to serve. This is exactly the situation as you find it in the passage I have just quoted. The Zoroastrians, however, took the further step and exalted Satan to the rank of a separate eternal principle. Christian monotheism

[1] *Yasna* 45: 2.　　[2] Ibid. 30: 2.　　[3] Ibid. 30: 3–6.

could never go as far as this: the dualism remains, but Satan is forever subordinate to God. In Jung's account of the matter God in the beginning is not fully conscious; and self-consciousness invariably reveals the opposites, brings 'knowledge of good and evil'. Later Zoroastrianism, like its founder, was acutely conscious not only of the problem but of the reality of evil. The Prophet himself had not pronounced unambiguously; so there was always room for theology to step in. Evil is a fact, but then so is God; and God is One. Should one then sacrifice the unity of the God-head so as to absolve it from all responsibility for evil, or should one attempt to keep the unity of the Godhead, thereby making it responsible for evil, however indirectly? Both theories had their partisans, some postulating a neutral first principle, Infinite Time, from which the holy and devilish twins proceeded, while others, cutting the Gordian knot, proclaimed that evil was a separate principle eternally antagonistic to God. There was also an intermediate position which is very Jungian indeed: by becoming self-conscious God becomes aware of the potentiality of evil within himself. He has eaten of the tree of knowledge: and the tragedy of the Fall is transferred from man to God himself. God, however, having received the serpent's gift, does not fall: he recognizes evil for what it is and expels it from his system. This particular solution of the problem of evil is, so far as I know, unique in Zoroastrianism, and it is one that I personally find most attractive:

Of knowledge (that is, of the condition of coming to self-consciousness) thus is it taught.

By the Creator's marvellous power—in infinite Time and by its power—knowledge became self-conscious. . . . From this [act of knowing] resulted the rising up of the Aggressor [Ahriman, Satan], unwilled [by Ohrmazd God], to destroy the essence [of Ohrmazd, that is, his changeless being] and his attributes by means of lying speech. The immediate result of this was that [Ohrmazd]'s essence and attributes turned back [into themselves] in order to [come to] know their own ground. So much knowing was necessary for the Creator [himself] to rise up for the creative act. The first effect of this rising up was the Endless Light. From the Endless Light is the Spirit of Truth which derives from Wisdom because it has the potentiality of growing into the knowledge of all things. By knowing all things he has the power to do all he wills. Thence creation and Satan's defeat thereby, the return of creation to its proper sphere of action, and the eternal rule of Ohrmazd in perfect joy; for it is he who is the origin of good things, the source of good, the seed and potentiality of all that is good. All good creatures are from him as a first effect by creation or by emanation, as sheen is from shining, shining from brilliance, brilliance from light.[1]

[1] See R. C. Zaehner, *The Dawn and Twilight of Zoroastrianism*, London, 1961, p. 220.

In becoming self-conscious God suddenly becomes aware of something within his own nature which is not only at variance with it but self-destructive: it must be expelled if God himself is not to be destroyed. Even by expelling it, by objectivizing it as the dark side of his personality, he is not safe from it, for 'its will is to smite' and 'its substance is envy'.[1] Only after his realization of the dark side of his own being does God become omniscient, knowing good and evil. Omniscience implies omnipotence, but since God is now limited by what has become an external power and an implacable enemy, his omniscience must needs take account of the new situation. God is now wholly good, and goodness implies peace and is therefore singularly ill-equipped to defend itself against what is by nature aggressive. Hence God, in self-defence, is more or less compelled to create and, as in the first chapter of Genesis, what he creates is 'very good'. He creates both a spiritual world, a world of 'ideas' very much as in Plato, and a material world which too is 'very good', since it is to be the first bulwark against Satan's attack when it comes.

Good and evil, then, in all phases of Zoroastrianism are *spiritual* opposites: matter is not, as it was for Teilhard de Chardin, a neutral force which can turn out to be either a blessing or a curse; in itself it is good because it is productive. And the two concepts, 'productive, bounteous, giving increase' and 'good and holy', are interchangeable in Zoroastrianism since they are both contained in the same word *spenta* etymologically connected with the Slavonic *svaty*, 'holy', but translated by the Middle Persian scribes as *afzōnīk*, 'productive, bounteous, bringing increase'. Matter is holy; production is holy, and reproduction is holy. Hence there are still traces in the later Zoroastrian texts of a sacred marriage between the sky-God Ohrmazd and the good earth.

There is nothing evil in matter itself. In Zoroastrianism to assert that matter is evil would amount to blasphemy, for it is God, not Satan, who created this fruitful world. Evil is of the spirit, not of matter. The classical pairs of opposites of natural religion do not fit: male and female may be comparable in the dream-world of Jungian psychology to spirit and matter, heaven and earth, sun and moon, and so on, but even here, I suspect, we are being played a not very clever trick since the sun is not only feminine in gender in German but also female in sex, and Wagner at least speaks of it as *Frau* Sonne. However, even if we admit that the 'opposites' broadly correspond to male and female, of the most disquieting one, that is, the opposition between good and evil, this is most emphatically not so. It is both ridiculous and wicked to equate the male with good and the female

[1] See R. C. Zaehner, *Zurvan, a Zoroastrian Dilemma*, Oxford, 1955, p. 313.

with evil. This is alchemy, not sense. Christianity, of all religions, should have put this right, for Christ's friendship with and compassion for the so-called weaker sex is paralleled in no other religion, and the bestowal on the Virgin Mary of the wonderful title 'Mother of God' goes a long way to exalt womanhood as an ideal as great and as noble as any that man can arrogate to himself. The ascetic horror of woman as the incorrigible temptress of man is both a gross perversion of what seems to have been the earliest teaching of the Church and a proof of the inner unsureness of these celibate ascetics themselves.

There are the sins of the flesh and the sins of the spirit; but the source of evil is a pure spirit who, according to the Zoroastrians, can create other spirits as wicked as himself, but who cannot create matter. The 'opposites' are here not male and female, not spirit and matter, but two spirits, two males: 'Neither our thoughts, nor our teachings, nor our wills, nor our choices, nor our words, nor our deeds, nor our consciences, nor yet our souls agree.' There can be no doubt about it: here speaks the voice of the dogmatic male. No woman, I hope, ever talked like that. The war of the spirit is, like all wars, a war of men.

Let us consider very briefly how this war was conducted in Zoroastrian myth.

God created the material world as a bastion against his eternal enemy: this he had to do, first in order to prevent him from attacking him on his home ground, and secondly in order to ensnare him within the vault of the sky which is made of hardest steel and from which it would be impossible for him to escape until he had destroyed himself. Before the fiend attacked, however, God had created man in his own image and likeness—not only Adam, the collective man, but the souls of all men who were ever to come to be in time; and these he created free. Man was not to be forced on to the battlefield to fight and to suffer in the service of God against a pitiless foe, he was to go of his own free will to gain experience and ultimately to return to the bosom of the Father. And so God

took counsel with the consciousness and the pre-existent souls of men and infused omniscient wisdom into them, saying: 'Which seems more profitable to you, whether that I should fashion you forth in material form and that you should strive incarnate with the Lie and destroy it, and that we should resurrect you in the end, whole and immortal, and recreate you in material form, and that you should eternally be immortal, unageing, and without enemies; or that you should forever be preserved from the Aggressor?' And the pre-existent souls of men saw by that omniscient wisdom that they would suffer evil from the Lie and Ahriman in the world, but because, at the end, at the Final Body, they would be resurrected free from the enmity of the Adversary, whole and immortal for ever and ever, they agreed to go down to the material world.[1]

In Hinduism and in Buddhism the soul or self is willy-nilly enmeshed in matter, in its blood, its sweat, and its tears. It is there much against its will and it can see salvation in no other terms than escape. The Zoroastrian and, following him, the Christian see that matter itself is involved in the redemptive process and that until the trend of the Incarnation is reversed and the flesh in its turn becomes Word, as Balzac puts it, we cannot see the whole significance of the Incarnation, matter transformed into spirit in what the Zoroastrians call the Final Body, the mystical body of Christ which is the Church brought to fruition in the all-embracing cosmic Christ which Teilhard de Chardin saw as the consummation of the world. And so we can say with St. Paul:

I think that what we suffer in this life can never be compared to the glory, as yet unrevealed, which is waiting for us. The whole creation is eagerly waiting for God to reveal his sons. It was not for any fault on the part of creation that it was made unable to attain its purpose, it was made so by God; but creation still retains the hope of being freed, like us, from its slavery to decadence, to enjoy the same freedom and glory as the children of God. From the beginning till now the entire creation, as we know, has been groaning in one great act of giving birth; and not only creation, but all of us who possess the first-fruits of the Spirit, we too groan inwardly as we wait for our bodies to be set free. For we must be content to hope that we shall be saved—our salvation is not in sight, we should not have to be hoping for it if it were—but, as I say, we must hope to be saved since we are not saved yet—it is something we must wait for with patience.[2]

In the *Chāndogya* Upanishad[3] the liberated soul was promised 'freedom of movement in every state of being'; but this can be the privilege of only the individual few. Meanwhile the human race as a whole is 'groaning in one great act of giving birth'. The Son of God has indeed entered the world and has brought us hope—a very little hope, Péguy's *petite espérance*, so insignificant between her great sisters, faith and charity—a very little hope because Satan is still Prince of this world and Satan's yoke is heavy and difficult to bear. We still live beneath the sun of Satan, and he still exults in the victory which, according to the Zoroastrians, he won when he first attacked the material world.

He is Prince of this world but he is also a prisoner in this world; for the good God, Ohrmazd, has ensnared him in the world as a gardener ensnares a wild beast in his garden. Throughout the garden the traps are

[1] See R. C. Zaehner, *The Dawn and Twilight of Zoroastrianism*, p. 261.
[2] Romans 8: 18–25.   [3] 7: 25: 2.

set, and into the biggest trap of all the wild beast falls, greedily gnawing at the bait. But God, who is likened to the owner of the garden 'and who devised the trap knows full well just how great the beast's strength is and how long [it can hold out]. All the strength of the beast's body is used up in its struggles, and by trampling on the snare and rending it, by worrying it and fighting with it, it [only succeeds in] exhausting itself. Since its strength is [now] insufficient, its fighting-spirit collapses and it is reduced to powerlessness.'[1] But Satan, as he developed out of his Zoroastrian origins, is more powerful and more subtle than his Zoroastrian prototype. Yet in the Zoroastrian confession of faith his essential character is already clearly etched: he is not only an aggressor but also a liar and deceiver:

I must firmly believe, [the Zoroastrian neophyte confesses,] that there are two principles, one the Creator, and the other the Destroyer. It is the Creator, Ohrmazd, who is all goodness and all light, and the accursed Destroyer, Ahriman, who is all evil, full of death, a liar and a deceiver.[2]

This is the Devil that Zoroastrianism has passed on to Christianity, for it is only in the New Testament that Satan reveals himself in his full and formidable stature. No longer is he associated with God, for we are now told that 'there is none good but one, that is, God'.

In the Old Testament Satan is one of the 'sons' of God whose function, as in Job, is to test the faith and humble the pride of man, while in the matter of David's census Satan, in 1 Chronicles, plays the very part that God himself performs in 2 Samuel: Yahweh and Satan are one and the same. Only in the New Testament is God declared by his other Son, Jesus, to be good; and Satan is shown up in his true colours—and these are Zoroastrian: he is 'all evil, full of death, a liar and a deceiver':

> He was a murderer from the start;
> he was never grounded in the truth;
> there is no truth in him at all:
> when he lies
> he is drawing on his own store,
> because he is a liar, and the father of lies.[3]

He 'was a sinner from the beginning', and 'it was to undo all that the devil has done that the Son of God appeared'.[4] But he is and remains the 'Prince of this world', and though he may have no power over the Christ, it is only with the coming of Christ that his unwearying malice becomes plain for all to see. St. Paul himself, though he was as conscious as anyone

---

[1] R. C. Zaehner, *The Teachings of the Magi*, London, 1956, p. 50.
[2] Ibid., pp. 22–3.   [3] John 8: 44.   [4] 1 John 3: 8.

of the struggle between spirit and the flesh which is natural to our fallen
nature, knew full well that this was not the real battle in our struggle
against evil. The decisive battle was purely spiritual, 'for we wrestle not
against flesh and blood, but against principalities, against powers, against
the rulers of the darkness of this world, against *spiritual* wickedness in high
places'.[1]

In the Zoroastrian myth Ohrmazd and Ahriman are twins. In the
Bible both Christ and Satan are 'sons' of God. One of the results of the
Fall, of man's rise to self-consciousness and his terror at finding himself
alone and separated from his fellow men through having lost the sense of
what the Chinese call the Tao, was that Satan entered into him. Hence the
first actual sin is murder, Cain's murder of his brother, Abel. What could
be more natural?—for Satan was 'a murderer from the start'. But he is
also a 'liar and a deceiver' and 'the father of lies'. His will is to smite and to
corrupt. We have heard much about evil being transmuted into good:
Satan transmutes good into evil, and therein lies his deepest satisfaction.
Satan became incarnate in Adam—in the whole human race: God the
Son became incarnate in Jesus Christ and through Christ in the Church.
Over Christ himself Satan had no power, but at the coming of Christ he
'fell like lightning from heaven'[2] on to the earth. This is his second
incarnation, the beginning of his second mission, the corruption and
destruction of the Church. His coming was yet more quiet than Christ's:
he took no single human form but infiltrated the whole Church, for of all
his weapons the most to be feared is his dreadful power to counterfeit all
that is holy. His temptation of Christ was open: his temptation of the
Church passed unperceived. There is nothing he likes more than to be
demythologized, for then he can do his patient work without anyone
noticing.

In tempting Christ in the wilderness he for once gave us fair warning—
against materialism, against presumption on the divine mercy, and against
the lust for power:

Then Jesus was led up of the spirit into the wilderness to be tempted of the
devil. . . . And when the tempter came to him, he said, If thou be the Son of God,
command that these stones be made bread. But he answered and said, It is
written, Man shall not live by bread alone, but by every word that proceedeth
out of the mouth of God.

This is the temptation to which the modern world has succumbed and
to which, unless the tide turns, it will increasingly succumb. True, we do

[1] Ephesians 6: 12 (A.V.).   [2] Luke 10: 18.

not live by bread alone, but for 'every word that proceedeth out of the mouth of God' we have substituted a vast array of material superfluities which have already become necessities. Instead of the 'words of God' we have the motor car, television, and washing-machines. We have lost all spiritual direction as we bask beneath the sun of Satan as we have never done before:

> Again, the devil taketh him up into an exceeding high mountain, and sheweth him all the kingdoms of the world, and the glory of them; and saith unto him, All these things will I give thee, if thou wilt fall down and worship me.
> Then saith Jesus unto him, Get thee hence, Satan: for it is written, Thou shalt worship the Lord thy God, and him only shalt thou serve.[1]

Worship of the Prince of this world, worship of temporal power: how appallingly has God's Church, the Bride of Christ, fallen into *this* temptation, and following her, all that has sprung from her impure womb— the national Orthodox and Protestant churches, the heirs of the French Revolution, the totalitarian states of the first half of this century, and finally the world Communist movement. How well he has been served, but how many of us have ears to hear what Bernanos calls 'the laugh, the incomprehensible joy of Satan'?[2]

Let us enumerate his victories. The conversion of Constantine which subjected the Eastern Church to the imperial power; the spurious Donation of Constantine which made the Papacy itself a temporal power; the legitimation of persecution, the raising of the flesh to the rank of the Devil himself as the enemy of man, and the inhuman doctrine of predestination which the great Augustine bequeathed to the Western Church; the great schism between East and West; the dissensions and corruption of medieval Christendom; the religious wars of the sixteenth and seventeenth centuries; the rejection of Christianity by the French Revolution and the instant corruption of the ideals of the revolutionaries themselves; the tyranny of Bonaparte and his insane wars, prefiguring the far worse tyrannies and bloodbaths of this century; the perversion of Communism almost at its birth; and last but not least the conversion of the American ideal of liberty into the most crassly materialist, soulless civilization the world has ever seen. It is not the Galilean who has conquered but Satan, under whose noonday sun 'we live, and move, and have our being'.

That he should corrupt the Christian Church and all its offshoots is only natural, for it is Christ who is his enemy. But his malice does not stop here, for every new ideal that has appeared since he crippled the Catholic

---

[1] Matthew 4: 8–10. (A.V.)   [2] Bernanos, *Œuvres romanesques*, ed. Pléiade, p. 255.

Church he has immediately distorted, perverted, and made his own. The French Revolution was supposed to have inaugurated a new era of liberty, equality, and fraternity: it did nothing of the kind, it merely heralded the Terror of Robespierre, tyranny practised in the name of an ideal, the scourge of the modern age. To corrupt what is itself good, this is his favourite weapon, for he is not only a murderer but a liar and a deceiver. In the last two hundred years he has had it all his own way: he has murdered and lied with complete impunity. His element, of course, is war, since war is simply murder and lying exalted as the highest national virtue.

And even now, as if two world wars were not enough, he has the whip-hand yet, for the two super-powers of today are his willing or unwilling slaves: the U.S.A. worshipping Mammon in the name of God, and the U.S.S.R., like the Whore of Babylon, 'drunken with the blood of the saints', persecuting still with unparalleled cynicism in the name of a society of which Marx had prophesied that it would be 'an association in which the free development of each would be the condition for the free development of all'.

Europe has been convulsed for two hundred years, and ideologically Europe has conquered the world. It has destroyed the ancient tyrannies and put new ones in their place. It had hoped to spread democracy in countries which had no conception of what the word might mean, and has only succeeded in making confusion worse confounded. It is ridiculous to suppose that we are in control of our own affairs: collectively as well as individually we are up against 'not flesh and blood', but 'against princi-palities, against powers, against the rulers of the darkness of this world, against spiritual wickedness in high places'.

Of course, this sounds hopelessly old-fashioned, for who believes in Satan today? That is his triumph, for when no one believes in him he has it all his own way. Of modern writers only two have been seriously inter-ested in him, and these, you will scarcely be surprised to hear, were novelists, not theologians—Dostoievsky and Bernanos. Dostoievsky is still read; but very few people seem to have read any Bernanos except the *Diary of a Country Priest*, perhaps the weakest of his major works. Both have represented Satan in human form, and in both of them he appears so ordinary, so unassuming, so apparently benevolent. You may remember that to Ivan Karamazov he appears in the form of an unassuming poor relation whose 'countenance was not so much good-natured as accom-modating and ready to assume any amiable expression as occasion might arise'.[1] But as he rambles humbly on he opens up a vista of the world to

---

[1] Dostoievsky, *The Brothers Karamazov*, bk. 11, ch. ix, Heinemann, p. 674.

come, his world, 'all the kingdoms of this world' which he had offered to Jesus if only he would fall down and worship him. It is an attractive world from which God (and of course Satan himself) will be forever banished. In this world:

Man will be lifted up in a spirit of divine Titanic pride and the man-god will appear. From hour to hour extending his conquest of nature infinitely by his will and his science [the serpent's gift], man will feel such lofty joy from hour to hour in doing it that it will make up for all his old dreams of the joys of heaven. Everyone will know that he is mortal and will accept death proudly and serenely like a god. His pride will teach him that it's useless for him to repine at life's being a moment, and he will love his brother without need of a reward. Love will be sufficient only for a moment of life, but the very consciousness of its momentariness will intensify its fire, which now is dissipated in dreams of eternal love beyond the grave.

But, the tempter continues,

the question now is, . . . is it possible that such a period will ever come? If it does, everything is determined and humanity is settled for ever. But as, owing to man's inveterate stupidity, this cannot come about for at least a thousand years, everyone who recognizes the truth even now may legitimately order his life as he pleases, on the new principles. In that sense, 'all things are lawful' for him. What's more, even if this period never comes to pass, since anyway there is no God and no immortality, the new man may well become the man-god, even if he is the only one in the whole world, and promoted to his new position, he may light-heartedly overstep all the barriers of the old morality of the old slave-man, if necessary. There is no law for God. Where God stands, the place is holy. Where I stand will be at once the foremost place . . . 'all things are lawful' and that's the end of it! That's all very charming; but if you want to swindle, why do you want a moral sanction for doing it?

'All things are lawful': there in a nutshell you have our permissive society. One thing shades into another—from fornication to contraception, from contraception to abortion, from abortion to infanticide, from infanticide to euthanasia, from infanticide and euthanasia to legal murder on political and ideological grounds, from the legal murder of individuals to mass murder. This is just the new way of setting about Satan's business. We all know about the Inquisition and St. Bartholomew's day; but those were crude times, and Satan has had time to perfect his techniques. He has shown that from fornication to mass murder there is a straight and logical line, but he leaves us in doubt about where to stop. Who can tell us except the man-God who is yet to come, but the lineaments of whose countenance we have already seen in Hitler and Stalin, the logical culmination of our rejection of the God who is love?

'Beneath the sun of Satan'—this is the title of one of Bernanos's novels. In speaking of prayer St. François de Sales asked: 'What do we talk about in prayer? What is our topic of conversation? God—nothing else.' Were you to ask, 'What does Bernanos talk about in his novels? What is his topic of conversation?' we would reply, 'Satan—nothing else.'

As in the *Brothers Karamazov*, so in *Sous le soleil de Satan* Satan appears in human form. This time he is a horse-dealer, 'a jolly lad whose voice has a certain secret gaiety, absolutely irresistible'. He has come to comfort a poor parish priest who, friendless, is plodding through the night in that not wholly attractive part of France, the Pas de Calais. He is a good priest, humble to an almost absurd degree but, like the Curé d'Ars on whom he is modelled, relentlessly pursued by the grace of God which he cannot resist. He is awkward, uncouth, and much frowned on by his prudent, respectable superiors. He needs a friend and, miraculously, the friend turns up—jolly, kind, irresistibly gay. The priest is utterly exhausted, so his good Samaritan spreads his cloak on the damp earth and makes the priest lie on it. 'How attentive, delicate, and brotherly was this gesture of the rough Samaritan! How could he altogether resist this tenderness he had never known before? How could he refuse his confidence to those friendly eyes which seemed to long for it?'[1]

Jung claimed to have psycho-analysed God. Bernanos did not psycho-analyse Satan: he simply got to know him in all his manifold disguises as no one has known and described him before. 'Love will be sufficient only for a moment of life.' Dostoievsky's relatively harmless Devil had said, 'but the very consciousness of its momentariness will intensify its fire.' So too in *Sous le soleil de Satan* Satan shows an extraordinary tenderness with which he hopes to break the almost desperate faith of the friendless priest:

An arm encircled his waist in a slow, sweet, irresistible embrace. He let his head drop right down until it came to rest between his shoulder and neck— closely—so closely that he felt the warmth of his breath on his forehead and cheeks. 'Sleep on me, child of my heart', the voice continued on the same tone. 'Hold on to me closely, you stupid ass, dear little priest, my comrade, friend. Rest. How long have I sought you out, how long have I hunted you. There you are. How much you love me! But you are going to love me much more because I am not going to leave you alone, my cherub, my tonsured little tramp, my companion for evermore.'[2]

'I will make all creatures hate you and love me', Satan says to God in one of the Zoroastrian books. So too in *Sous le soleil de Satan* does he start by comforting the priest with almost maternal tenderness, only to

[1] Bernanos, *Œuvres romanesques*, p. 171.   [2] Ibid., p. 173.

mock him to his face. But the change has been too sudden, and the priest realizes for the first time that he is face to face with his life-long comrade, our life-long comrade, Satan, the sickly-sweet corrupter of the soul:

It was the first time that the saint of Lumbres heard, saw, and touched him who was the vile, ignoble associate of his life of suffering. . . . And how many times was he to hear him again until his final liberation![1]

'The new man may well become the man-god', Dostoievsky's Devil had said. In his own way Bernanos's miserable little priest is a man-god too, and these are the ones whom Satan longs to ensnare with his abominable tenderness:

'You have received the kiss of a friend', the horse-dealer said quietly, pressing his lips on to the back of his hand. 'It is my turn now, and I have filled you with myself, dear tabernacle of Jesus Christ, my poor silly boy. Don't be afraid; it isn't anything really. . . . Shall I tell you? I kiss you all whether you are awake or asleep, dead or alive. That's the plain truth. How I love to be with you, little man-gods—strange, strange, such strange creatures. Frankly, I scarcely ever leave you. You carry me in your dark and heavy flesh—me whose essence was once the light, . . . me, Lucifer. I count you all. Not one of you escapes me. Why, I'd recognize every animal of my little flock by their smell alone.'[2]

But the priest is obstinate; though half-dead with fatigue he realizes that his life is at stake, not his mortal life on earth but his life in eternity when, standing on a peak, he is forever fixed in a timeless joy or a timeless despair. Satan is nonplussed; for he is rarely baulked of his prey. Then, suddenly it is cold:

'I scarcely feel the cold,' said the horse-dealer, 'I am *wonderfully* resistant to cold and heat. But I am really surprised to see you still there, sitting stock-still in the icy mud. You should be dead, my word, you should. . . . As for me, I'm cold, I admit it. . . . I'm always cold. . . . These are things that you won't get me to say easily. . . . They're true though. I am the Cold itself. The essence of my light is an unbearable cold.'[3]

It is cold too on the mountain peak—cold under the sun, whether it be God's sun or the sun of Satan. And Satan, not God, is the only Absolute— absolute zero, absolute cold, the absolute cold of Lucifer, the bringer of light. No wonder that St. François de Sales could say:

When a man enraptured has more clarity in his understanding with which to wonder at God than he has warmth in his will with which to love him, then he had better be on his guard; for there is a danger that this ecstasy may be false,

[1] Ibid. [2] Ibid., p. 174. [3] Ibid., p. 175.

inflating rather than edifying the spirit, ranking him indeed among the prophets like Saul, Balaam, and Caiaphas, but leaving him none the less among the outcast.[1]

Nirvāna too is cold—indeed it has been translated as 'the cool'. The Buddha knew nothing of either God or Satan, hence the maddening ambiguity of Buddhists of all schools. They themselves leave the question open, as well they might, for it seems that there is a true Nirvāna which is of God, as the Bhagavad-Gītā affirms, and there is another Nirvāna, another Void, another Emptiness which is the absolute cold of Satan.

But to return to Bernanos. For the time being the little priest has won and Satan must go *empty* away: but he promises that they will be seeing each other again. And then 'for the first time the Abbé Donissan saw his eyes and groaned':

> Imagine a man, with both his hands tied to the top of the mast—imagine him losing his balance. Suddenly he sees, yawning and swelling out beneath him, no longer the sea but the whole starry abyss and the foam of all the galaxies in the process of formation seething trillions and trillions of miles away across the void which nothing can measure and which he must cross in his eternal fall. Such a man would not feel a more absolute giddiness in the pit of his stomach [than the Abbé felt in looking into those fearful eyes]. His heart beat twice as furiously against his ribs, and stopped. His guts were turned upside-down with nausea. His fingers, clutching desperately, the only thing left alive in a body petrified with horror, scratched at the soil like claws. . . . This dauntless man, bent double and wrenched from the earth by the immeasurable attraction of nothingness, this time saw himself lost beyond recall.[2]

And yet at the same moment his last thought was an obscure defiance.

Un obscur défi: an obscure defiance. Satan had not won—not yet. Defiance: but defiance is a form of pride, and pride is the deadliest of the deadly sins, the sin by which Satan had himself fallen. Satan knew it, and Satan took his chance. As time went on the Abbé Donissan learnt to read in the souls of others, and this earned him a vast reputation that spread far and wide beyond the confines of his own parish of Lumbres. People flock to him to hear their confessions. He is hailed as a saint. This is the chink in his armour, for it leaves him wide open to the sin of pride. Satan sees the chink, and how gently he creeps in. The poor priest thinks he has found the 'holy indifference' of Nirvāna: 'he tingles with an exultation without joy. He no longer suffers, or scarcely at all, he is forever fixed.' In the 'fixed, still state of Brahman' he stands on his mountain-peak. 'He

[1] St. François de Sales, *Traité de l'amour de Dieu*, 7. 6.
[2] Bernanos, op. cit., p. 177.

desires nothing: he is conquered. By the open breach pride comes flooding into his heart.'¹

Very soon temptation comes. There is a child in a neighbouring parish who is desperately ill, and his parents send for the saint to cure him. When he arrives, the child is dead. The whole family and even the vicar of the parish in which they live, usually a sensible man, believe fervently that he can raise the child from the dead if he only will. The priest falls into the trap so delicately set for him. He enters the room where the dead boy lies; he leans over the bed, willing the child to live. Sure enough the child's eyes slowly open. Then, suddenly, they are wide open and staring at him, but there is nothing human about them. Then in a flash he recognizes them, for he has seen those eyes before, the eyes of Satan. Face to face with the enemy of God and man he is determined to overcome him if only to save the honour of God:

'Is it then true, [he says to himself], is it then true that before he is swallowed up in the night in his turn, this hangman who never gives in will forever play with men as with his prey, ensnare them with his marvels, entice them, lead them astray, order them about, caress them, give them hope only to take it away again, assuming every kind of voice, angel or demon, innumerable, efficient, powerful as a God. Like a God! Ah, who cares about hell and its flames provided that once, if only once, this monstrous malice can be crushed. Can it be possible, can it be God's will that the servant who has followed him should find—not God, but only the laughable king of the flies, the Beast seven times crowned? Is this all he will give to the mouth that seeks the Cross, to the arms that press it to the breast— this, only this? . . . Is it possible?' the saint of Lumbres repeats in a low voice.

And then, he cries aloud to God, 'You have deceived me!' He has blasphemed, but nothing will stop him now:

He raises the little boy up like a host. Fierce and defiant he looks up to heaven. How can I hope to describe the cry of distress, the hero's curse that demands neither pity nor pardon but justice. No, no! he does not beg for a miracle, he demands one. God owes it to him, God will give it to him, or else everything is only a dream. 'Speak up,' [he cries,] 'which one of you is the master, he or you? . . . Show yourself before you abandon me for ever.' Oh, the wretched old priest, ready to cast to the winds everything he has in order to obtain a sign from heaven. And the sign will not be denied him, for the faith that moves mountains can surely raise the dead. . . . But God only gives himself to love.²

The Abbé Donissan has committed the sin of Job, and Satan has triumphed. But his victory is too complete, for this paroxysm of heroic pride has broken the indomitable spirit of the saint of Lumbres: and God, not Satan, dwells in a broken and contrite heart.

¹ Ibid., p. 236. ² Ibid., pp. 267–8.

Bernanos is not an author to everyone's taste: what he writes is too profoundly, too frighteningly true. Also practically all his heroes and anti-heroes are priests, and practically all his anti-heroes are men of learning, respected, unloving and unloved. They are sometimes frighteningly like this year's Gifford Lecturer, for the Abbé Cénabre, whose monstrous pride not even the innocent joy of a martyred young saint can break, dabbles in mysticism and is widely read and respected; and Monsieur Ouine, whose sinister despair masquerades under the mask of a jaundiced saint, is a *professeur de langues étrangères*—Monsieur Ouine, the eternal enigma, the eternally ambiguous *oui–non*, the incarnation of the void and the cold, the man who has found an abominable peace, the man who loves only to destroy and to make his victim as corrupt as himself, Monsieur Ouine, who can bring the worm that never dies into Nirvāna itself, Monsieur Ouine, *professeur de langues étrangères*.

He lives in a dilapidated house with a dying baron and his crazy wife; but the châtelaine has the insight of the mad, and she warns the young hero who is under his spell that it is impossible to love Monsieur Ouine since everything he says and does is false, and you cannot love a lie:

'God! Love him!' she exclaims, 'Why, my angel, you have only to get near him, and you don't even *want* to love—what peace, what silence! Love him? Let me tell you, dear heart. Just as some people radiate light and warmth, so does our friend absorb all light and all warmth. You see, the genius of Monsieur Ouine is the cold. In the cold the soul finds rest.'[1]

The clear light of the Void of the Tibetan *Book of the Dead* is also cold, it seems; and reading Bernanos one cannot help being struck by the uncanny resemblance between the 'abominable peace' which is the cessation of life and the Buddhist idea of Nirvāna, the 'snuffing out' of life as we know it, of *nirodha*, the 'bringing to an end' of all human passion, all love as well as all hatred. Indeed Theravāda Buddhism, generally considered to be the nearest to the teaching of the Buddha himself, is the great stumbling-block to any student of mysticism; for whereas in Christianity, in Islam, and in Hinduism as it developed after the Bhagavad-Gītā, the symbolism is always of fire, in Buddhism fire is the symbol of the passions, and the goal is not to extinguish self in the fire of love but to extinguish the fire itself, for there is no self in any recognizable form which can be extinguished. True, the extinction of self, that is, the extinction of *amour-propre*, is an essential stage in the process of 'deification' of the human soul; but, as Rousseau saw, *amour-propre* is not the same as

---

[1] Bernanos, op. cit., p. 1423.

amour de soi, but a distortion of it. *Amour de soi* is to accept oneself as a human being—and the mystic is still human, not an angel—and hence, as the *Cloud of Unknowing* says, he 'desireth not to un-be; for that were devil's madness and despite unto God';[1] and this is so because 'the devil hath his contemplatives as well as God'.[2] *Amour-propre*, on the other hand, is the desire to *have*, and that, for Rousseau, as for all sane religion, is the beginning of all evil. The Buddhist insistence on the absolute necessity of getting rid of all idea of 'I' as well as 'mine' is right and good, but Satan is ever watchful and, as most of the great Christian mystics have seen, he is forever seeking to replace the peace that is of God with his own abominable peace 'which passeth all understanding'.

No one believes in the Devil nowadays: certainly no one takes him seriously. Only Bernanos has disclosed his hateful countenance and revealed his uncanny power to imitate the ways of God:

> He is in the prayer of the hermit, in his fasts and penances, at the heart of the deepest ecstasy, and in the silence of the heart. He poisons holy water, burns in the consecrated wax, breathes in the breath of virgins. . . . corrupts all life. He lies on the lips half opened to spread the Word of truth: in the midst of the thunder and lightning of the most beatific rapture he pursues the just right into the arms of God. . . . What need has he to struggle for the souls of so many men on this earth where they crawl about like beasts since they will return to the earth tomorrow? The dark and medley flock meets its destiny of its own accord. . . . His hatred is reserved for the saints.[3]

After Bernanos we cannot say that we have not been warned; but one thing Satan cannot simulate, and that is joy—joy without which all sanctity is void:

> He comes suddenly, in a flash, without warning, horribly peaceful and assured. But however far he may stress this likeness to God, no joy can ever come from him, but, far higher than the pleasures that only stir your entrails, his masterpiece is a silent peace, solitary, icy, comparable only to the enjoyment of nothingness. When this gift is offered and accepted, our guardian angel turns his face away, amazed.[4]

The Buddhists rarely speak of joy. Are they too living beneath the sun of Satan? Of course they are, for he is still the Prince of this world. Christ may have brought us hope and joy: *he* brings us *Angst* and despair. He is the great existentialist, playing his sordid game with the existentialist ideal as he does with all ideals. Must his peace abide with us always?

---

[1] *The Cloud of Unknowing*, E.T., Justin McCann, revised ed., London, 1952, p. 61.
[2] Ibid., p. 63.　　　[3] Bernanos, op. cit., p. 154.　　　[4] Ibid., p. 213.

XX

THE FLESH WILL BECOME WORD

> The old house has collapsed behind our backs and when we came to take our place in the homes of the young, they hadn't yet found out how to build their own, and we found ourselves in an indeterminate sphere, among the stones and the rafters, in the rain. . . .[1]

THE quotation is from one of the less-known novels of Bernanos, *Un mauvais rêve*, 'A Bad Dream': and his analysis of our present predicament is even more valid now than when it was penned in 1935. Our house has collapsed—that is clear enough; and the young have not yet built theirs. We and they wander helplessly beneath the sun of Satan, and neither, it seems, can help the other—on the one hand blind guides, on the other dead souls struggling for life. The serpent's gift has yielded its deadly fruit. 'Man is born free,' Rousseau had said, 'yet everywhere he is in chains. He believes himself to be the master of others, but is really more enslaved than they.'[2] Long, long ago man mastered the beasts: now he has created beasts of his own, the work of his own hands; and the old story repeats itself. Just as man rebelled against God, refusing to follow the course assigned to him, so too has man's creation, the machine, rebelled against man and enslaved him—or rather not the machine but what Mr. Arthur Koestler has called the 'ghost in the machine'; and the ghost in the machine is Satan.

Initially we are indebted to the Zoroastrians for having dealt a salutary blow to the mystic's vision of the coincidence of opposites; for however true this 'coincidence' may be in Nature or even *sub specie aeternitatis*, it is a useless truth, if truth it be, and a callous mockery of human suffering. Of modern writers it is Bernanos who has unmasked the hideous face of Satan as a purely spiritual power having no essential connection with the flesh. The flesh is of matter, and matter is neither good nor evil. Like God, it can attract or repel. Sometimes it 'smiles with poetical sensuous brightness', sometimes 'it becomes hostile to humanity'.[3] Marx denied any reality to spirit except as an outcrop of matter, but by matter he understood not the soulless matter of the mechanistic materialists but something

---

[1] Bernanos, op. cit., p. 918. [2] Rousseau, *Du contrat social*, i. i.
[3] Marx and Engels, *The Holy Family*, Moscow, 1956, pp. 172–3.

that has the potentiality of transforming itself into thought and spirit. Hence he says:

The first and most important of the inherent qualities of *matter* is *motion*, not only *mechanical* and *mathematical* movement, but still more *impulse, vital life-spirit*, or, to use Jacob Boehme's expression, the *throes [Qual]* of matter. The primary forms of matter are the living, individualizing *forces of being* inherent in it and producing the distinction between the species.[1]

For centuries Christians have been terrified of matter, terrified of the flesh, terrified, one might almost say, of life itself which must in some way be rooted in matter. It is in truth the opposite of spirit if by 'spirit' we mean the utterly changeless, the 'fixed, still state of Brahman', Nirvāna, the 'God of the philosophers' who was not the God of Pascal's mystical experience, the 'true simplicity and everlasting changelessness' of Hugh of St. Victor, which seems to be indistinguishable at times from the gaping void into which, as Bernanos says, Satan longs to draw us. Too long has Christianity turned its back on matter; too long has it frowned on sexuality, the very source of life, and shown indifference to the astonishing achievements of the natural sciences as being irrelevant to the salvation of man's soul. Matter has taken her revenge, for we have left her to Satan, and the result is what you see.

If Bernanos is the prophet of Satan, then Teilhard de Chardin is the mystic of matter. From the very beginning of his career he saw the potential holiness of matter: it is not she but we who are bad; she, on the other hand, is 'the combined essence of all evil and all good';[2] and she demands to be sanctified:

The man was walking in the desert, followed by his companion, when the Thing swooped down on him.

From afar it had appeared to him, quite small, gliding over the sand, no bigger than the palm of a child's hand—as a pale, fleeting shadow like a wavering flight of quail over the blue sea before sunrise or a cloud of gnats dancing in the sun at evening or a whirlwind of dust at midday sweeping over the plain. . . .

And then the man perceived that the little pale cloud of vapour was but the centre of an infinitely greater reality moving towards him, uncircumscribed, without form or limit. The Thing as it approached him spread out with incredible speed as far as the eye could see, filling the whole of space. . . . And all about it the ether had become alive. . . .

What was advancing towards them was the moving heart of an immeasurable pervasive subtlety.

The man fell prostrate to the ground; and hiding his face in his hands he waited.

[1] Ibid., p. 172.
[2] Pierre Teilhard de Chardin, *Écrits du temps de la guerre*, Paris, 1965, p. 438.

THE FLESH WILL BECOME WORD

A great silence fell around him. . . .

The man felt that he was ceasing to be merely himself; an irresistible rapture took possession of him as if all the sap of all living things, flowing at one and the same moment into the too narrow confines of his heart, was mightily refashioning the enfeebled fibres of his being. And at the same time he was oppressed by the anguish of a peril more than human, a confused feeling that the force which had swept down upon him was ambiguous, unquiet, the combined essence of all evil and all good.[1]

At the very beginning of these lectures I contrasted the mysticism of Whitman with the mysticism of the Buddha—the mysticism of matter in all its uncontrolled turbulence with the still, frozen changelessness of Nirvāna. So too here, two men are walking in the desert—the desert of total spiritual denudation of which Meister Eckhart speaks, the desert of uncontaminated purity 'standing on a peak'—far from life and all its vicissitudes, its joys as well as its pain. Elsewhere Teilhard had himself said: 'Hitherto [the mystic] had hardly been able to distinguish, in the cosmic Godhead, anything more than a sort of *unchanging Entity*, and what mattered was to make as close a contact as possible with it'[2]—what the Gītā calls 'Brahman's saving touch'.[3] This is the mysticism of pure spirit, the denial of matter, 'the pure, purity, the sublimely pure', 'the temptation of great souls', the 'distinguished heresy', the 'heresy of the future', as Péguy had said.[4] It is to destroy this altogether too immaculate detachment that the Thing swoops down upon the traveller and presents itself to him in all its stormy reality—not 'beyond good and evil' but the essence of all evil and all good. This is the challenge: use matter, transform it, if you will; but do this only with your eyes firmly fixed on what is beyond matter and beyond yourself, on what gives coherence to all things and draws them on to itself, on the point of convergence to which the world of multiplicity, despite the divisive and reactionary power that is Satan's, seems to be directed. If you will not do this, you will be overwhelmed, and since Satan is still the Prince of this world, the odds are heavily against you. It is so easy to 'drop out', so easy to take refuge in the 'artificial paradises' of which Beaudelaire spoke, but your material nature must assert itself in the end. Without matter there can be no growth, and it was surely not to sanctify the capitalist system that Christ gave us the parable of the talents; it was in order to tell us that we must develop ourselves to the limit, to kill the seed of *amour-propre* so that we may grow

---

[1] Teilhard de Chardin, op. cit., pp. 437–8: E.T., in *Hymn of the Universe*, London, 1965, pp. 59–60.

[2] *Écrits du temps de la guerre*, p. 155: E.T., *Writings in Time of War*, London, 1968, p. 136.

[3] Gītā 6: 28.   [4] Above, p. 361.

from earthly life into eternal life, into the very life of God. Hence, in Teilhard's parable, the Thing—matter—goes on to say:

'You needed me in order to grow; and I was waiting for you so that you might sanctify me.

Always, you have desired me though you did not know it, and I have been drawing you on.

And now I am on you, for life or for death. You cannot go back; you cannot return to your everyday comforts and your untroubled worship. Once you have seen me, you can never forget me: you must either be damned with me, or I shall be saved with you.' . . .

'O you who are godlike and mighty, what is your name?' (The traveller asks.)

'I am the fire that consumes and the water that overthrows; I am the love that initiates and the truth that passes away. All that compels acceptance and all that brings renewal, all that breaks apart and all that unites—power, experience, progress—matter: all this am I.

Because of my violence I often kill my lovers; because he who touches me never knows what power he is unleashing, the wise fear me and curse me. They speak of me with scorn, calling me beggar-woman or witch or harlot. But their words are at variance with life, and the Pharisees who condemn me waste away in the spirit to which they restrict themselves. They die of inanition, and their disciples desert them because I am the essence of all that is tangible, and men cannot do without me.

You who have grasped that the world—the world beloved of God—has, even more than individuals, a soul to be redeemed, lay your whole being wide open to my inspiration, and receive the spirit of the earth which must be saved.

The last word of the enigma, the dazzling utterance which is inscribed on my brow and which will henceforth burn into your eyes even if you close them is this: *Nothing is precious save what is yourself in others and others in yourself. In heaven all is but one. In heaven all is but one.*'

If Christ is the answer to Job, then Teilhard de Chardin is the answer to Augustine, the enemy of matter and the flesh. His mysticism is a fusion of the mysticism of the Buddha and that of Walt Whitman: he confirms and completes the mysticism of the Upanishads and the Bhagavad-Gītā as well as that of the neo-Confucians in China; and he gives a new dimension to Christianity itself. Nature—Matter—is not God, nor is God Nature. The Christian mystics tell us that the soul is the bride of Christ, and St. Paul tells us that the Church is the Bride of Christ; for Teilhard both are equally true, for the part cannot really be saved, cannot be wholly united to the heavenly Bridegroom except in and through the stuff of the whole. According to Rousseau,[1] with the birth of self-consciousness men lost their sense of solidarity, their ability to 'interpenetrate'

---

[1] Above, p. 330.

one another in a shared consciousness of the whole: the soul of the All becomes atomized and this atomization is made permanent by the persistence and growth of *amour-propre*. To regain this sense of solidarity and interpenetration in a common effort towards God, the point of cohesion of all things, is how Teilhard sees the destiny of mankind. From the early works written during the First World War until his last testament written three days before his death, Teilhard's theme remains consistently the same: man evolves from the 'dust of the earth' into the perfected 'image of God'. To create is to unite; and 'being' is even more process than the eternal and static Being of the philosophers. It is a surging forward and upwards, a soldering of multiplicity into unity, an aspiration of matter towards spirit, of individuality towards totality, of all individual souls, each in its way a bride of Christ, towards the universal Bride of Christ, the soul of the Church—the Church as it may one day be, the universal and Catholic Church of all mankind. Then the Body and Bride will coalesce into a 'spiritual body', purified and fit for the final consummation of the sacred marriage with the Son of God.

Teilhard's theme is solidarity and convergence. This sense of solidarity is ever with him, but it is a shared solidarity of shared worship, shared endeavour towards a common goal which is the goal of evolution itself— call it Omega if you like, as Teilhard himself did in his later work. No matter, it is the point of convergence which is the aspiration of each as it is the aspiration of all. In his 'pantheism' Teilhard is in the line that runs from Rousseau to Péguy through Balzac in his *roman mystique* and Rimbaud, and in his forward-looking and collective dynamism he brings together Marx and Bergson. To the core of his being he is a mystic—the mystic of matter as well as of spirit, of the 'All-man' as well as the individual: he is the mystic of evolution as Marx is the prophet of evolution.

Nothing is precious save what is yourself in others and others in yourself.

This is what Matter had told the astonished traveller who now lay prostrate on the ground. But he could not accept a permanent passivity: he could not accept the quietism so often associated with the East:

He leapt to his feet and stood erect, facing the storm.

It was the soul of the entire race that shuddered within him: an obscure memory of its first awakening in the midst of beasts stronger and better armed than he—a painful echo of its long struggle to tame the corn and master the fire—a rancorous dread of the maleficent forces [of Nature]—a lust for knowledge and possession. . . .

A moment ago, in the sweetness of the first contact, he had, instinctively, longed to lose himself in the warm breath which enfolded him.

Now, this wave of bliss in which he had all but melted away was turned into a harsh determination towards increased being.

For matter is pregnant of good and evil; you may sink back and melt into the All, or you may seek to come to terms with her, to master her, and to seek both her proper place and yours in the universal order. Matter may appear as an enemy, or she may 'smile at man with poetical sensuous brightness'. And so the traveller

in a reciprocal awakening of their opposed powers stirred up his utmost strength to master her, while she revealed her treasures in order to surrender them to him.

In Indian religion there is a gulf fixed between *karma* and *jñāna*, action and 'wisdom', and the best that can be said of action is that one day it may be absorbed into wisdom, 'reduced to ashes'[1] in it. For Péguy this was the temptation of refined minds: for Teilhard it was rather an invitation to suicide; for it is matter that diversifies, spirit, like Brahman in India, that is the same in all. And so Matter goes on, admonishing the traveller:

Son of the earth, steep yourself in matter, bathe in its fiery waves, for it is the source and the [eternal] youthfulness of your life.

You thought that you could do without her because the power of thought had been kindled in you! You hoped that the more carefully you rejected what can be touched, the closer you would be to spirit; that you would be more divine, if you lived in the world of pure ideas, or at least more angelic, if you fled the body. . . .

Never say, as some say: 'Matter is worn out, matter is dead': till the very end of time matter will always remain young, exuberant, sparkling, and new for those who are willing.

Never say, 'Matter is accursed, matter is evil, for one has come who has said, . . . uttering the final promise of my liberation, "This is my body." ' . . .

No, purity does not mean separation from the universe but an ever deeper penetration into it. It means the love of the unique Essence, which knows neither bounds nor fetters and which penetrates all things from within—beyond the mortal zone in which persons and numbers struggle and fret. *Purity is a chaste contact with that which is the same in all.*

Yes, and this is one of the themes of the Bhagavad-Gītā too; for there too we read:

While yet in this world they have overcome [the process of] emanation [and decay], for their minds are stilled in that which is *ever the same*; for devoid of imperfection and ever the same is Brahman: therefore in Brahman [stilled] they stand.[2]

[1] Bhagavad-Gītā 4: 37.   [2] Ibid. 5: 19.

But though you may have overcome the world, you must still bring with you the riches she has conferred on you and lay them at the feet of the Father. 'How beautiful he is—how beautiful is spirit as he arises aloft adorned with the riches of all the earth. Son of man, bathe yourself in matter, dive into her where she is at her deepest and most violent! Struggle in her current and drink of her waters! For it is she who cradled you of old while yet you were unconscious; and it is she who will carry you right up to God!'[1]

Apart from such fringe Catholics as Bergson and Péguy, this strikes an entirely new note in modern Christianity. It is, however, prefigured in Balzac's extraordinary novel *Séraphîta*, and indeed here Balzac anticipates Teilhard both in his mysticism of total coherence and in his view of human society as a prolongation of the evolutionary process on the plane of self-consciousness.

The dynamic mysticism of Teilhard which embraces and sanctifies science, the serpent's gift, and the hermaphroditic mysticism of Jung which sees the 'sacred marriage' as taking place in the individual soul, both find their place in *Séraphîta*.

Séraphîta is also Séraphîtus, both female and male: he or she is not of this world but sent to this world to reveal the inner structure of the universe and the manner of its ascent to God. The last chapter is, then, appropriately called the 'Assumption'—the assumption of a perfected soul into heaven. As she approaches the throne of God:

The true light appeared, lighting up the creations which had hitherto seemed arid to them; and then they saw the source from which all the worlds—terrestrial, spiritual, and divine—derive their impulse.

Each world had a centre towards which all the points of its own sphere inclined. And these worlds themselves were points which inclined towards the centre of their species. Each species had its centre turned towards the vast celestial regions which themselves communicated with the inexhaustible, radiant mover of all that is.

And so, from the greatest to the least of the worlds, and from the least of the worlds to the smallest particle of the beings that compose it, all was individual, and yet all was one.

What was the design of that Being, fixed and still both in his essence and in his faculties which he transmitted without losing them, which he manifested outside himself without allowing them to be separated from him, who made all his creatures outside himself fixed and still in their essence but mutable in their forms? The two guests invited to this feast could not help seeing the order and disposition of all beings and marvel at their immediate purpose. Only the angels penetrated deeper, learnt to know the means and understood the end.

---

[1] Teilhard de Chardin, *Écrits du temps de la guerre*, pp. 441–2: E.T., p. 65.

But what these two chosen ones could contemplate, that to which they bore a witness which illumined their souls for ever, was for them a clear demonstration of the mode of operation of worlds and beings, and the consciousness of the struggle through which they tend towards their appointed end.

They heard the different parts of the Infinite combine in a living melody; and whenever the concord made itself heard like a mighty breath, the worlds, drawn on by this unanimous movement, bowed down before this immeasurable Being who animated all things from his impenetrable centre and restored them all in himself.

This never-ceasing alternation of voice and silence seemed to be the very tempo of the sacred hymn which echoed and re-echoed in the never-ending continuum for ever and ever.

Then Wilfrid and Minna understood some of the mysterious words which he had spoken to them on earth, . . . and they saw that there, in heaven, all things are homogeneous.

Light engendered melody, melody engendered light, the colours were light combined with melody, and movement was Number endowed with the Word. There all was simultaneously resonant, translucent, mobile, so that each thing penetrated and was penetrated by all others, and space, presenting no obstacle, could be traversed in a moment by the angels in the depths of the infinite.

Up and up soars the blessed spirit:

He rose aloft like a radiant sun emerging from the bosom of the waves; but, more majestic than the sun and promised a destiny yet more fair, he was not, like the lower creations, to be fettered to a life in cyclic time: he followed the straight line of the infinite, aiming unswervingly at the unique centre, ready to plunge into it and into his own eternal life, there to receive, in his faculties and in his essence, the power to enjoy through love, and the gift of understanding through wisdom. . . .

How humble and yet how sublime are these two points—strength and love— which the Seraphim, in the first flush of his desire, fixed in their place like two rings which would unite the immeasurable spaces of the lower worlds to the vastness of the higher.

They understood the invisible links by which the material worlds adhere to the spiritual ones. . . .

Then myriads of angels flocked together, flying with an equal flight, without confusion, all alike, all different, simple like a wild rose, immeasurable like all the worlds. . . .

And the Seraphim appeared again, shining with a blazing light and crying aloud, ETERNAL! ETERNAL! ETERNAL!

All the universes heard it and recognized it. And he penetrated them as God penetrates them and entered into possession of the infinite.[1]

---

[1] Balzac, *Séraphîta* in *La Comédie humaine*, ed. Pléiade, vol. x, pp. 583–7.

Everything you have heard in these lectures is here—except Satan. And now at the end we are back to where we started: we are back again to St. François de Sales:

Introduce unity into diversity, and you create order; order yields harmony, proportion; harmony, where you have perfect integrity, begets beauty. There is beauty in an army when it has order in the ranks, when all the divisions combine to form a single armed force. There is beauty in music when voices, which are true, clear, distinct, blend to produce perfect consonance, perfect harmony, to achieve unity in diversity or diversity in unity—a good description might be discordant concord; better still, concordant discord.[1]

Being is not unfractionably one. Only of the divine can it be said that both its essence and its function are fixed and still, and this only because in God time and space are abolished. Man, both as an individual and as a phylum, is a pilgrim born in the natural world, earthy because formed from the dust of the earth, taken up into the spiritual world, and destined for the divine world. In the natural world nothing is fixed either in its essence or in its faculties: as Teilhard would say it is pure multiplicity. The spiritual world is fixed in its essence but mutable in its faculties—the world of man, more specifically the world of the Hindus and Buddhists, where the essence can only be realized by separating it from the faculties.[2] Only in the divine world is everything fixed both in its essence and in its faculties, though not simply frozen as on a mountain-peak, as in early Buddhism and Hugh of St. Victor, but in a vast movement that is yet rest, a perfect symphony in which each instrument and each note has its allotted, indispensable part.

As in Rousseau each man's essence is the centre of his faculties, and each individual essence is as it were a 'faculty' to the essence of the species, while the essence of the species humanity, the All-man or World Soul as Teilhard calls it, is itself centred on God, the centre of all centres. Everything penetrates everything else, and each is appointed to its individual end in accordance with the pattern of the whole. Cyclic time, which is the curse of the Orient and which conditions their religion, is broken, and the soul of man, and in the course of time the soul of the All-man, 'the Soul of the world', is destined to follow the straight line of the infinite, aiming unswervingly at the unique centre, ready to plunge into it and into its own eternal life, there to receive, in its faculties and its essence, the power to enjoy through love and the gift of understanding through wisdom.

In the still centre spirit and matter, male and female, strength and love, are reconciled; for no more than Teilhard did Balzac fall into the

[1] Above, p. 1.   [2] Balzac, *Louis Lambert*, ed. Pléiade, vol. x, p. 452.

Manichaean blasphemy which identified matter with evil. Rather the essence of matter is not only movement, as Marx insisted, but a convergent movement, a hot embrace in the 'throes' of matter, to quote the Marxian phrase again. And as love reaches ever higher degrees of expression, it not only unites ever more closely but it also differentiates ever more sharply. This is a truth that every lover knows: with the Trinity, we may assume, it is absolutely true. In heaven they 'flock together, flying with an equal flight, without confusion, all alike, all different, simple like a wild rose, immeasurable like all the worlds'.

Creation bears the impress of the Trinity, for if it is true that two is the number that implies opposition and discord, three is the number of reconciliation and concord. The third is the Holy Spirit, the bond of union between the Father and the Son, without whose eternal and indefectible presence the Godhead, like its creation, might well be riven asunder. 'God is Love', St. John had said,[1] and this, as we saw last year, is echoed in India in the Śaiva Siddhānta.[2] Throughout the *Comédie humaine* the same message comes through, for the great theme of Balzac's immense corpus is that although human love is a reflection of divine love, this reflection must always remain imperfect and distorted since we are human and always subject to *amour-propre*. If man is made in the image of God, then human love is made in the image of the Holy Spirit. In each case the image is bound to be distorted and sometimes made unrecognizable by the accumulation of the rust and grime of selfishness and sin, but it is better to have loved wrongly than not to have loved at all. This is the whole message of the *Comédie humaine*.

Basically Balzac was an optimist: he believed in the slow perfectibility of human society because, like Darwin, Marx, and Teilhard de Chardin, he believed that this was the long-term trend of evolution itself. The development of human society was simply the development on the self-conscious level of biological and zoological evolution—the slow birth-pangs of a better world to come. As St. Paul says: 'From the beginning till now the entire creation . . . has been groaning in one great act of giving birth.'[3] Creation proceeds in an upward spiral from purely instinctual life through 'abstraction' to what he calls 'speciality'. By abstraction he means the power to discriminate one thing from another, to abstract general laws from particular incidences, the source from which science and the arts, law and social ideals proceed. This is not a regress, as Rousseau had supposed, but a necessary progress in man's journey towards God. The 'specialist' is the highest type of man, and by speciality Balzac

---

[1] 1 John 4: 8.   [2] Above, p. 165.   [3] Romans 8: 22.

understands '*species*, vision, speculating, seeing all things in one flash; *speculum*, the mirror or means of assessing a thing by seeing it in its entirety'. 'Speciality' in this sense is the most perfect expression of man, and the specialist is 'the ring that links the visible world with the higher worlds' because he is the man who, since he sees his own destiny clearly before him and sees it in its relation to the infinite, can show the way to others.[1]

You die alone, but it is doubtful whether you can be saved alone. The crime of post-revolutionary France was that it substituted *amour-propre* for service to the collectivity. The medieval collective ideal had been lost, but it was useless to try to restore it. The revolutionary idea could not survive because it lacked a religious background. And so, according to Balzac, 'the only societies that still count are the religious institutions against which savage war is being waged at the moment, for the natural tendency of the sick is to attack the remedies offered them and often the doctors who administer them. . . . And so, there can be no life in any association except through religious feeling, for it alone can tame the revolt of the spirit, the cold self-interest of ambition and every kind of cupidity. Those who seek to win a world of their own do not know what worlds association has to offer.'[2]

The bulk of Balzac's work is not concerned directly with religion, hence one of the few novels devoted to practical religion is entitled *L'Envers de l'histoire contemporaine*, 'The Obverse of Contemporary History'; for even in his day religion was very much the obverse, the hidden side, of contemporary society, the ruling god of which was Mammon. True religion, true charity works in secret, is never seen and rarely heard. It is the obverse again of official religion, of the visible religiosity of the conformist devout. It is the real leaven of society because, since it hides itself, it can never be fashionable. Hence it rarely supplies the main theme of the novels that go to make up the *Comédie humaine* which purports to be a portrait of society as it was seen to exist in Balzac's day. Only in *L'Envers de l'histoire contemporaine* do we catch a glimpse of Balzac's idea of a religious *association* which transcends and absorbs the individuality of the participating member. This is a source of immense strength, and so we read of the young hero recently initiated into a Catholic society which works in secret:

As he walked in the streets Godefroid felt himself a new man. Had anyone been able to get inside him, he would have been able to observe the strange

[1] Balzac, *Louis Lambert*, ed. Pléiade, vol. x, pp. 451–2.
[2] Balzac, *La Comédie humaine* (*L'Envers de l'histoire contemporaine*), ed. Pléiade, vol. vii, p. 341.

phenomenon of collective power and how it can communicate itself to the individual. He was no longer just one man but a being raised to a higher power,
knowing himself to be the representative of five people whose united strength
supported all he did and who walked beside him. With this strength in his
heart he experienced a plenitude of life and altruistic power which elated him.
It was . . . one of the most beautiful moments of his life, for he had a quite new
feeling; it seemed he was omnipotent, but with an omnipotence more sure than
that of any despot. For moral force, like thought, knows no limits.

To live for others, he said to himself, to act in common like one single man,
and to act on one's own as if all were acting together! To have as one's chief
Charity, the most beautiful, the most living of all ideal figures that have been
created from the Catholic virtues, this is to live.[1]

Balzac writes about individuals (and how recklessly individualistic they
are!), but he sees that individualism, the besetting vice of the French,
leads inevitably to a fragmentation of society. He sees, as Marx was to see
later, that 'in the place of the old bourgeois society, with its classes and
class antagonisms, [one must seek to create] an association in which the
free development of each is the condition for the free development of all'.[2]

Balzac was Marx's favourite novelist. This is scarcely surprising since
the bulk of the *Comédie humaine* is both a description and an indictment of
bourgeois capitalism as it had developed in France under Louis-Philippe.
It might be an indictment of modern America, for there too money,
Mammon, is the god who dictates everything, 'laws, politics, and morals,
institutions, books, men, and doctrines'.[3] In such a society 'capital is
independent and has individuality, while the living person is dependent
and has no individuality'.[4] 'No longer are you asked, "What do you think?"
but "What do you pay?" '[5]

Both Marx and Teilhard de Chardin looked forward to a socialist
society in which the human person, freed at last from the tyranny of
Mammon, would be able to develop to the utmost in association with his
fellows. Such a development was, for Balzac, ultimately only possible
within the framework of the Catholic Church by which he meant, emphatically, the Roman Catholic Church; for Protestantism, he maintained, by
banishing the Blessed Virgin from heaven, had in so doing banished the
treasures of mercy and compassion traditionally associated with her from
the earth.[6]

[1] Ibid., pp. 341–2.
[2] Marx and Engels, *The Communist Manifesto*, II, end.
[3] Balzac, *La Comédie humaine* (*Eugénie Grandet*), vol. iii, p. 553.
[4] Marx and Engels, op. cit., ed. Laski, London, 1958, p. 138.
[5] Balzac, op. cit., p. 554.   [6] Id., *Avant-propos*, vol. i, p. 11.

In an earlier book, *The Convergent Spirit*, I wrote that if the world was really to converge upon itself, as Teilhard had prophesied, this convergence could only take place within the framework of the Catholic Church or the Communist party. Seven years have now passed since that book was written; and much has happened since. On the one side we have had the amazing pontificate of good Pope John and the second Vatican Council which has completely changed the face of the Roman Church. On the debit side we have that little matter of birth control, but that will no doubt be dealt with one day with as much regard for precedent as was Friday abstinence. In the Communist camp the split between the two giants, the U.S.S.R. and China, now seems to be unbridgeable, while the U.S.S.R. itself, this time under the leadership of a Directoire of gloomy mediocrity, has relapsed into its own miserable form of Stalinism and has, in the name of Marx, extinguished the first experiment in Marxian freedom by brute force alone. And so we are left with only Péguy's *petite espérance*— a little hope that the spirit of Czechoslovakia may yet one day prevail.

It is depressing but true that in the last fifty years Communism has faithfully reproduced all the mistakes and crimes committed by Christendom in nearly two thousand years. Like Christianity its beginnings were obscure, and Marx himself dissolved the First International. All this changed with the accession to power of the Bolshevik party in Russia. Marx, like the Buddha, had seen very early that the basic evil with man is his *amour-propre*, his assertion of the ego as an entity and a centre distinct and separate from all other entities and centres and the ego's assertion of its right to *have*. His premises, however, were very different. True, he accepted the phenomenal world as being a flux, but, as in Buddhism, it was a flux ruled by causation—ruled indeed by unchangeable law which it was the duty of science to discover. This law was thought to be based on the age-old principle of the *coincidentia oppositorum*, the Chinese *yin* and *yang*, which had been miraculously resuscitated in the Hegelian dialectic. But whereas the Buddha could see no salvation in this world and pointed to Nirvāna, a state of perfect peace outside the world, Marx substituted for Nirvāna a final reconciliation of all the opposites, the final synthesis of all antitheses here on earth in the not very distant future. The attitudes of the two men were largely conditioned by their view of time. Marx, like the whole tradition out of which he sprang, sees time as a straight line which leads to an end-point, for him the establishment of the classless society: hence there is hope in this world. For the Buddha, as for all Indians, time was cyclic: it evolves from a given point on the circumference of the circle—creation—and returns to the same point—dissolution—and then the whole process starts all over again. Man is trapped in this infernal machine; like Sisyphus he rolls his stone up the hill only to see it fall down again. There is no hope in this world, and despair of the world is therefore a Buddhist virtue.

At the present time perhaps the only Christian virtue we have left to us is hope—*la petite espérance*—not charity, not love, for that would be setting our sights altogether too high. Christ's resurrection is only the promise of redemption: it is not actual redemption as any sensible person who bothers to look round at the modern world can see. Christ promised the sword first, only in the second instance did he promise peace. He has kept his promise, and the sword has come with Muhammad, with Luther and Calvin and Cromwell, with Robespierre and Napoleon, with Marx, Lenin, and Stalin. Through all these trials, however, he has kept his unfaithful and wayward Bride alive with hope; 'for we must be content to hope that we shall be saved—our salvation is not in sight, we should not have to be hoping for it if it were— . . . it is something we must wait for with patience'.[1] Hope is the virtue that first the Enlightenment and then the Marxists took over from the Christians, and what they had hoped for has not come to pass. It is, then, not so much the loss of faith that constitutes the malaise of the modern world as the loss of hope. It cannot even see its way to accepting Voltaire's long-term optimism: it can no longer say:

> *Un jour tout sera bien*, voilà notre espérance;
> *Tout est bien aujourd'hui*, voilà l'illusion.[2]

'One day all will be well, that is our hope; all is well today, that is the illusion.'

Marx brought renewed hope; and he was clear-sighted enough to see that this too is what the Christian Church had offered. He thought, however, that the Christian hope was illusory, and who shall say that he was wrong?

> *Religious* distress [he wrote] is at the same time the *expression* of real distress. Religion is the sigh of the oppressed creature, the heart of a heartless world, just as it is the spirit of a spiritless situation. It is the *opium* of the people.
> The abolition of religion as the *illusory* happiness of the people is required for their *real* happiness. The demand to give up the illusions about its condition is the *demand to give up a condition which needs illusions*. The criticism of religion is therefore *in embryo the criticism of the vale of woe*, the *halo* of which is religion.[3]

'Religion is the sigh of the oppressed creature, the heart of a heartless world, just as it is the spirit of a spiritless situation. It is the *opium* of the

---

[1] Romans 8: 24–25.   [2] Above, p. 345.
[3] K. Marx, *Contribution to the Critique of Hegel's Philosophy of Right*, introduction.

people.' All this is true enough, and it is a pity that it is only the last sentence that is ever quoted. But what happens when the creature ceases to be oppressed, when there is no need of the blood of martyrs to fertilize the Church? This is the problem of the affluent society, the effects of which Marx had not foreseen. His maxim has been reversed, and opium in the shape of psychedelic drugs may well become the religion of the people. The religious instinct in man is not so easily suppressed.

The strength of Marxism itself is that it is a revolutionary creed which offers an earthly paradise here and now, which claims to be scientific, and which would have us believe that the classless society is the *inevitable* result of the evolutionary process, the final resolution of all antitheses into one final synthesis, of all discords into an ultimate concord. It is the logical antithesis of the individualism of the French Revolution with its vindication of private property and private enterprise. It is the rejection of *amour-propre*, not as being of the Devil but as being condemned at the bar of history and evolution. Private property, according to Marx, needs wage-slaves; it needs the proletariat to maintain itself in existence. Private property and the proletariat are the two poles of the antithesis, neither of which can exist without the other. The exploited needs the exploiter just as much as the exploiter needs the exploited: this is the axiom on which bourgeois society is built. Hence Marx says:

> Private property as private property, as wealth, is compelled to maintain *itself*, and thereby its opposite, the proletariat, in *existence*. This is the *positive* side of the contradiction, self-satisfied private property.
>
> The proletariat, on the other hand, is compelled as proletariat to abolish itself and thereby its opposite, the condition for its existence, what makes it the proletariat, i.e. private property. That is the *negative* side of the contradiction, its restlessness within its very self, dissolved and self-dissolving private property. . . .
>
> The proletariat executes the sentence that private property pronounced on itself by begetting the proletariat. . . . When the proletariat is victorious, it by no means becomes the absolute side of society, for it is victorious only by abolishing itself and its opposite. Then the proletariat disappears as well as the opposite which determines it, private property.[1]

With the abolition of private property or, more strictly speaking, of the private ownership of the means of production, all would be well, for 'the theory of the Communists may be summed up in the single sentence: Abolition of private property'.[2] Once that is done utopia is achieved.

[1] Marx and Engels, *The Holy Family*, Moscow, 1956, pp. 51–2.
[2] Id., *The Communist Manifesto*, ed. Laski, p. 136.

Marx and Engels's conception of the new society is vastly naïve, starry-eyed, and idealistic; and it has been belied by history of which they claimed to be the sole interpreters. This is what the Communist Manifesto actually says:

When, in the course of development, class distinctions have disappeared, and all production has been concentrated in the hands of a vast association of the whole nation, the public power will lose its political character. Political power, properly so called, is merely the organized power of one class for oppressing another. If the proletariat during its contest with the bourgeoisie is compelled, by force of circumstances, to organize itself as a class; if, by means of a revolution, it makes itself the ruling class, and, as such, sweeps away by force the old conditions of production, then it will, along with these conditions, have swept away the conditions for the existence of class antagonisms and of classes generally, and will thereby have abolished its own supremacy as a class.

In place of the old society, with its classes and class antagonisms, we shall have an association in which the free development of each is the condition for the free development of all.[1]

Or again:

The possibility of securing for every member of society, by means of socialized production, an existence not only fully sufficient materially, and becoming day by day more full, but an existence guaranteeing to all the free development and exercise of their physical and spiritual faculties—this possibility is now for the first time here, but *it is here*.[2]

Then, when the revolution has become a fact, 'the development of [socialized] production makes the existence of different classes of society an anachronism. In proportion as anarchy in social production vanishes, the political authority of the State withers away. Man, at last the master of his own form of social organization, becomes at the same time the lord over Nature, his own master—free.[3]

Marx and Engels's vision of the future socialist society is inspiring, but it has not come true. As a prophet Dostoievsky's Devil seems to have the clearer vision:

Man will be lifted up in a spirit of divine Titanic pride and the man-god will appear. From hour to hour extending his conquest of nature infinitely by his will and his science, man will feel such lofty joy from hour to hour in doing it that it will make up for all his old dreams of the joys of heaven.

But the new man who becomes the man-god may be one man only— 'the only one in the whole world, and promoted to his new position, he

[1] Op. cit., II, end.
[2] F. Engels, *Socialism Utopian and Scientific*, London, Allen & Unwin, 1950, pp. 80–1.
[3] Ibid., p. 86.

may light-heartedly overstep all the barriers of the old morality of the old slave-man, if necessary.... "All things are lawful" and that's the end of it.'[1]

The Communist Manifesto was first published in 1848. Satan has worked fast and well; for he has turned the Marxian dream of 'an association in which the free development of each is the condition for the free development of all' into a bureaucratic tyranny. As Marx might have foreseen, new contradictions have appeared, and these too will have to be resolved. Once Marx had accepted the dictatorship of the proletariat as the necessary first step to the establishment of a truly free society, he should have foreseen the inevitable result. For Marxian society is also a permissive society where relativism rules supreme. I have already said that there is a logical chain that links contraception with genocide. This may be far-fetched. The chain that links the dictatorship of the proletariat with personal tyranny, however, is not far-fetched, and in both Russia and China this development came to pass with frightening suddenness, and under Stalin the original Marxian ideal completely disappeared. The Marxist dogma of the unity of theory and practice was made to operate at its simplest level: one man interpreted theory to match his own day-to-day practice and then justified the practice by the theory. Man proposes, God disposes. This may or may not be true. But once the man-God had appeared on earth, the problem no longer arose: he both proposed and disposed. The price that was paid by the 'people' we all know. And the 'dictatorship of the proletariat' was never more than a phrase, no more than make-believe anyhow: for how can the majority in any country dictate anything? This fatal phrase was pregnant with tyranny from the beginning. And the tyranny, when it came, was to extend over every sphere of life—art, science, the family, religion. The Soviets made the same mistake as Augustine: you cannot create a collective organism by force.

The strength of Marxism as originally propounded was its dynamism and its adaptability: it was a revolutionary creed. No one had given a thought to what would happen after the revolution: it was simply and naïvely assumed that the State would wither away. The problem remains, and the problem was set by Marx himself. 'Religion is the sigh of the oppressed creature, the heart of a heartless world.' But, according to Marx, the heart is in the wrong place, for the happiness that religion allegedly provides is an illusory happiness; and this must be abolished if man is to achieve real happiness. '*The task of history*', he grandly says, 'therefore, once *the world beyond truth* has disappeared, is to establish *the*

[1] Above, p. 397.

truth of the world.' But the truth of the world is a bitter truth—the truth of Stalin and his epigones, not the truth of Marx. In Russia all creative Marxist thought had been suppressed; and when it appeared for one brief, bright moment of hope in Czechoslovakia, the tanks moved in. Communism has failed to replace the Christian heart of the West with any heart of its own making. The heart-transplant has failed.

Somewhere, I believe, Péguy contrasts the legalistic and the mystical type of mind—the men of the letter, the scribes, and the men of the Spirit. Teilhard de Chardin too has said that he had reached the conclusion that there are among men two categories of mind which can never see eye to eye—'the physicists (that is, the "mystics") and the lawyers'.[1] The lawyers are the men who try to categorize and pigeon-hole everything, the men who for centuries have told the Catholic faithful that it is mortal sin to eat flesh-meat on Friday and who then blithely turn round and say that it is no sin at all. Not only do they strain at a gnat and swallow a camel; they would have us believe that the camel has turned into a gnat! The lawyers, the bureaucrats, what Balzac so aptly and prophetically called the 'medio-cracy', no doubt will always be with us in both capitalist and communist societies; and in the world of giant industry in which we live and move and stifle this is inevitable, since they have not only made themselves indis-pensable but are so. But just as Marx never made the mistake of identifying the individual bourgeois with the *vere necessarium peccatum*, the 'absolutely necessary sin' that history forced the bourgeoisie to commit, so must we not condemn the individual bureaucrat or indeed the bureaucracy in general since we have as yet found nothing to put in their place. But at least we can echo the words of the Master which condemn for all time the legalistic and bureaucratic spirit now more rampant in Moscow than ever it was in the capitalist world and still kicking but, let us hope, dying in the ancient imperial city of Rome: 'Woe unto you also, ye lawyers! for ye lade men with burdens grievous to be borne, and ye yourselves touch not the burdens with one of your fingers.'[2]

The 'physicist' whom Teilhard oddly identifies with the 'mystic', since, according to him, science itself has become 'tinged with mysticism and charged with faith',[3] can never understand the juridical mind, nor can the lawyer ever understand the mystic. And let us be quite clear what Teilhard understands by a 'mystic': it is not the classical mysticism with which I have bored you for so long and which nearly always implies a flight from the world: it is a mysticism of process, not of stagnation, of the

---

[1] Teilhard de Chardin, *Œuvres*, ix, p. 83.   [2] Luke 11: 46 (A.V.).
[3] Teilhard de Chardin, *The Phenomenon of Man*, E.T., London, 1959, p. 284.

fulfilment of one's own being in the context of the All, of fruitfulness, shared adoration, solidarity, convergence, and joy. This does not mean that the classic paradoxes of mysticism are resolved, for self-denial, the extrusion of *amour-propre*, will always be necessary if only to give birth to that charity that has yet to be born. But to deny self is not enough: there must also be self-giving under God and in the context of all, each giving according to his kind. The mysticism of Teilhard is grounded in matter but refuses the temptation to return to the inert state of primal matter which seems to be characteristic of Taoism: it is the aspiration of matter towards spirit, of multiplicity towards unity, directed not to the past but in Messianic hope to the future—a Marxist mysticism for which perhaps the world may be becoming ripe. The cult of Zen and Oriental mysticism in the West is not serious; like all religion and pseudo-religion it is make-believe. It is ceasing to be relevant in the East itself: how should it be relevant in the West? 'The hour has come', Teilhard proclaims, 'when, at the opposite pole of a dated orientalism, a new mysticism can and must arise which is both fully human and fully Christian: the highway of the West—the highway of the world of to-morrow.'[1]

The highway of the West: since the seventeenth century the Church of Rome and the other churches have been following country lanes far removed from the main highway of Western civilization. In the past it was the great service of the Catholic Church that she absorbed and transformed into herself the thought and outlook of Greece and Rome: she has not succeeded in doing this with the thought and outlook of modern Europe. She has not baptized the Enlightenment or the industrial revolution or the more just society that was Marx's vision, however it may have been distorted by our latter-day Marxists. Did we really have to wait for Teilhard to tell us that 'in the religion of science as it was originally formulated, whether in the philosophic dissertations of the Great Encyclopedia or in the positivist conclusions of Auguste Comte and Marx, or in the Christian or semi-Christian aspirations of Lamennais and Renan, it is only fair to see and to accept a real upward surge that is in itself most noble and boundlessly sincere'.[2] It is, then, no accident that in these last five lectures which were supposed to be concerned with Christianity I have seen my Christianity, not through the eyes of the orthodox scribes and lawyers who have still by no means abdicated in the city of Rome, but through the eyes of Rousseau, Voltaire, Péguy, Bernanos, Balzac, Marx, and Teilhard de Chardin, the first Christian Marxist.

[1] Teilhard de Chardin, *Œuvres*, vii, p. 236.
[2] Ibid., vi, p. 213.

Teilhard is a Marxist in the sense that he takes the socialization of man for granted, and by socialization he meant what Engels meant—'the possibility of securing for every member of society, by means of socialized production, an existence not only fully sufficient materially, and becoming day by day more full, but an existence guaranteeing to all the free development and exercise of their physical and spiritual faculties'. But, as a Christian, Teilhard had to go further because 'man liveth not by bread alone but by every word that proceedeth out of the mouth of God': he had to reinfuse the spirit into a spiritless situation, and find a new heart for a heartless world.

The Word was made flesh: this is his starting-point, for it is here that the sanctification of matter begins. Sanctification, like creation, means to unite, to draw all that is disparate into a coherent whole; and this is the force that operates in the evolutionary process itself and which continues to operate in human history, for there is no discontinuity between the two. Call it, with Bergson, *élan vital*, call it 'vital life-spirit' with Marx, call it what you like; for Christians it is the Holy Spirit, 'the Lord and giver of life', for 'it is the Spirit which saves and ennobles matter, carrying it forward and sustaining it constantly in its ascent towards consciousness, while matter in return allows Spirit to subsist in it, supplying it with a field of action and something on which to live'.[1] Of itself matter is indeterminate and in a perpetual state of flux, but the flux is directed onwards and upwards 'towards some kind of *collective* reflection and sympathy in which everyone can share by participation, . . . and [in which] each human being would find his intellectual and affective fulfilment by forming one body with the whole'.[2] This, Teilhard rightly says, is the Marxist solution. But the Marxist vision lacks two things—it lacks a true centre of convergence which will make physical death irrelevant, and it turns its back on love: it lacks the Word made flesh and rejects the Holy Spirit.

'Religion is the sigh of the oppressed creature, the heart of a heartless world', Marx had said, and the orthodox Marxists have done their best to tear the heart out of European civilization. Perhaps Teilhard is the answer to Marx, and the only form of Christianity that may prove acceptable to modern man is perhaps the gospel according to Teilhard. The attraction that he exercises on modern man is the same as that of Marx: he claims to be scientific. Both make this claim as firm believers in evolution, and both are broadly rejected by the scientists. And rightly so; for it is not as yet generally accepted that entropy is cancelled out by what Teilhard calls the law of increased complexity-consciousness which is basic to his whole

[1] Ibid., ix, p. 78.   [2] Ibid., v, p. 373.

vision; and to treat him as other than a visionary would be to do him an injustice. His vision is forward-looking to a new mode of existence already adumbrated in neo-Confucianism, in Rousseau, Balzac, and Marx, in which individual men will become conscious of their own solidarity and 'sameness' in what he had once called the 'Soul of the world'. Man as an individual, he thinks, has perhaps developed as far as he can; but just as evolution has advanced in what Engels called 'qualitative leaps'—from lifelessness to life, and from life to consciousness—so we may even now be on the verge of yet another qualitative leap from individual consciousness into what has been called 'cosmic consciousness'—not indeed the cosmic consciousness of R. M. Bucke which can only be an individual experience, but a new form of consciousness common to all mankind, a 'synthesis of the (Christian) God "above", with the (Marxist) God "ahead" '.[1] This implies the spiritualization of matter when evolution will develop 'in a richer and more complex domain, to construct, by means of all spirits joined together, Spirit itself'.[2] This collective Spirit, which the Communists seek to impose by force, Teilhard conceives of partly as the result of a whole new world opened up to us by science and partly as a mystical apprehension of the unity of all things. Naïvely perhaps, he writes:

Through the discovery yesterday of the railway, the motor car and the aeroplane, the physical influence of each man, formerly restricted to a few miles, now extends to hundreds of leagues or more. Better still: thanks to the prodigious biological event represented by the discovery of electro-magnetic waves, each individual finds himself henceforth (actively and passively) simultaneously present, over land and sea, in every corner of the earth.[3]

There is no essential conflict between religion and science any more than there is between spirit and matter; for these have been artificially separated even after they had been soldered together in the Man-God Christ whose body is the Church. This is an unnatural, un-Christian, Augustinian state of affairs, and

inasmuch as the tension is prolonged, the conflict visibly seems to need to be resolved ... —not in elimination, nor duality, but in synthesis. ... In the mutual reinforcement of these two still opposed powers, in the conjunction of reason and mysticism, the human spirit is destined, by the very nature of its development, to find the uttermost degree of its penetration with the maximum of its vital force.[4]

---

[1] Quoted in Claude Cuénot, *Teilhard de Chardin*, E.T., London, 1965, p. 369.
[2] Teilhard de Chardin, *The Phenomenon of Man*, E.T., p. 278: French original, *Œuvres*, i, p. 309. I have rendered 'esprit' by 'spirit' rather than E.T. 'mind'.
[3] Ibid., p. 240.   [4] Ibid., pp. 284-5.

This is Marxian, 'dialectic' thinking. There are two focal points out of which the new synthesis will arise—the collective Christ, the 'mystical body' of the Church so vividly described by St. Paul in 1 Corinthians, and the goal of evolution as seen by Teilhard, the convergence of matter upon itself and its transmutation into spirit. This he calls 'the coincidence of Christ with the Centre . . . of a global co-reflection':

Its probable effect will be very shortly to weld together science and mysticism in a flux of liberated evolutive power—with, as a centre, a Christ who two thousand years after Peter's acknowledgement will have been identified at last, after centuries of toil, as the final summit (i.e. as the only possible God) of an evolution now definitively recognized as a movement of convergence.[1]

A magnificent dream, you will say. And we can only hope that there is substance in it; but the time is not yet, for we still live beneath the menacing sun of Satan and the anguished cry of the Abbé Donissan still rings in our ears:

Is it then true that before he is swallowed up in the night in his turn, this hangman who never gives in will forever play with men as with his prey, ensnare them with his marvels, entice them, lead them astray, order them about, caress them, give them hope only to take it away again, assuming every kind of voice, angel or demon, innumerable, efficient, powerful as a God. Like a God! . . . Which one of you is the master, he or you?[2]

Even Teilhard, so often written off as an incurable optimist, could not be sure, neither in the case of the individual man, nor in the case of the All-man, the Soul of the world, or, to use his own dreadful neologism, the 'noosphere'.

In the case of the mystics it had been their proud boast that they had overcome death. They had laid aside matter and realized themselves as pure spirit. For Teilhard, however, death is a transformation of the most subtle kind of matter into something higher and greater, just as in our mortal life the bread we eat is transformed into our flesh. The gross body is left behind, and a 'spiritual body'—what the Hindus call a 'subtle' body —takes its place. So, too, according to Teilhard, the final Parousia will entail the spiritualization of all of matter that can be transmuted and saved:

The end of the world: the wholesale internal introversion upon itself of the noosphere, which has simultaneously reached the uttermost limit of its complexity and its centrality.

The end of the world: the overthrow of equilibrium, detaching the spirit, fulfilled at last, from its material matrix, so that it will henceforth rest with all its weight on God-Omega.

[1] Cuénot, op. cit., p. 370.　　　　[2] Above, p. 401.

The end of the world: the critical point at one and the same time of emergence and emersion, of ripening and release (*évasion*).

We can entertain two almost contradictory suppositions about the physical and psychical state our planet will be in as it ripens and draws near to its fulfilment.

According to the first hypothesis which expresses the hopes towards which we ought in any case to turn our efforts as to an ideal, evil on the earth at its final stage will be reduced to a minimum. Disease and hunger will be conquered by science and we will no longer need to fear them in any acute form. And, conquered by the sense of the earth and human sense, hatred and internecine struggles will have disappeared in the ever-warmer radiance of Omega (God-as-end). Some sort of unanimity will reign over the entire mass of the noosphere. The final convergence will take place *in peace*. Such an outcome would of course conform most harmoniously with our theory.

But there is another (and a darker[1]) possibility. Obeying a law from which nothing in the past has ever been exempt, evil may go on growing alongside good, and it too may attain its paroxysm at the end in some specifically new form.

There are no summits without abysses.

Enormous powers will be liberated in mankind by the inner play of its cohesion, though it may be that this energy will still operate discordantly tomorrow, as it does today and did in the past. Are we to foresee a mechanizing synergy under brute force (the Stalinist way[1]), or a synergy of sympathy (the Christian way[1])? Are we to foresee man seeking to fulfil himself collectively upon himself, or personally on a greater than himself? Refusal or acceptance of Omega (God-as-end)? A conflict may supervene. In that case the noosphere, in the course of and by virtue of the process that draws it together, will, when it has reached its point of unification, split into two zones each attracted to an opposite pole of adoration. Thought has never been completely united upon itself here below. Universal love would then, in the last instance, only vivify and liberate a fraction of the noosphere and thereby bring it to its consummation—the part which decided to 'cross the threshold', to get outside itself into the Other. . . .

[This will mean] the death of the materially exhausted planet; the split of the noosphere, divided on the form to be given to its unity; and simultaneously . . . the liberation of that percentage of the universe which, across time, space, and evil, will have succeeded in laboriously synthetizing itself to the very end.[2]

If I understand this passage aright, it can only mean that the 'Soul of the world', that is, everything that has made its millennial journey from an original diffusion of 'dead' matter to an ultimate union of Spirit, will be drawn irresistibly up to partake, individually and collectively, in the spiritual marriage with what Teilhard calls Omega—God-as-end; while the rest, enfeebled by lack of will and spiritual power, will be dragged back

---

[1] Author's addition.
[2] Teilhard de Chardin, *The Phenomenon of Man*, E.T. (slightly modified), pp. 288-9.

by the *vis inertiae* which is entropy into its original amorphous and unconscious state. The All-man, created from the dust of the earth, will realize himself as the image of God; but his waste products, 'the inert and uninteresting mass of those who believe in nothing',[1] will sink back into the dust of Sheol from which they were originally drawn; and they will do this because to the end they will cling to self, to *amour-propre*, refusing to take their allotted place in the one body of Christ, the 'Soul of the world', apart from which there is no true life. This is the meaning of heaven and hell, of salvation and damnation.

Ecstasy there will be—in concord, the knitting together of all spirits in one Spirit and through the Spirit into God: or in discord,[2] the dissolution of the personality into its material fragments. On the one hand, 'the inert mass of those who believe in nothing': 'Dust you are and to dust you shall return.' On the other, 'the last word of the enigma, the dazzling utterance which is inscribed on the brow' of matter redeemed:

The obverse of *Et verbum caro factum est* will become the new Gospel which will be summed up in the words: 'And the flesh will become Word: it will become the living Word of God.'[3]

---

[1] Id., *Œuvres*, v, p. 101.   [2] Cf. ibid., p. 289.

[3] Balzac, ed. Pléiade, vol. x (*Louis Lambert*), p. 452.

APPENDIX

FOOLISHNESS TO THE GREEKS

An Inaugural Lecture
delivered before the University of Oxford
on 2 November 1953

ACCORDING to the Persian poet Firdausī, a notoriously bad authority, it was the custom of the Sassanian kings, on first mounting their ivory throne, to pronounce an inaugural lecture for the edification of their obedient subjects. In the course of this lecture it was customary to say something in praise of the deceased monarch, and reference might be made to the founder of the dynasty. In taking up my duties as Spalding Professor of Eastern Religions and Ethics I shall not attempt to depart from this respectable precedent. In the present case the foundation of the dynasty is of such recent occurrence that I feel it my duty to outline the late Mr. Spalding's intentions in founding the Chair and to offer some suggestions for the further implementation of those intentions.

The endowment of a Chair in Eastern Religions and Ethics was an act of faith. It was an expression not only of Mr. and Mrs. Spalding's faith in an ultimate unity underlying all the great world religions, but of their faith in the University of Oxford as a suitable channel through which to make these outlandish systems more widely known. It was, however, more than an act of faith: it was an act of statesmanship. For it showed a keen realization on the part of Mr. and Mrs. Spalding that any view of world history which was based exclusively on the European contribution must be, to some extent, lop-sided. For they realized, earlier than most of us, that Asia, so long the unwilling ward of Europe, could not for ever be subjected to an alien way of life and an alien way of thought. They understood that it is not possible for one culture permanently to be imposed on another, and that sooner or later the cultures of Europe and Asia would have to meet on equal terms. They understood equally well that though Europe has made spectacular efforts to break away from her Christian past, and though it is tolerably certain that Asia, having absorbed the accidents of European civilization without comprehension of the substance, will play fast and loose with her own cultural heritage with that reckless abandon already displayed by the Chinese, the time may come when the old values will reassert themselves: and these values, in Asia even more than in

Europe, are religious values. The endowment of a Chair in Eastern Religions and Ethics was, then, not only an act of faith but an act of practical good sense: for it is not easy to see how we are to establish mutually satisfactory relations with the newly independent nations of Asia unless we have a thorough understanding not only of their beliefs but of the way of life and above all the way of thought engendered by those beliefs. This seems to have been at the back of Mr. Spalding's mind when he defined the functions of the Professorship in the following terms:

> The purpose of the Professorship shall be to build up in the University of Oxford a permanent interest in the great religions and ethical systems (alike in their individual, social, and political aspects) of the East, whether expressed in philosophic, poetic, devotional, or other literature, in art, in history, and in social life and structure, to set forth their development and spiritual meaning, and to interpret them by comparison and contrast with each other and with the religions and ethics of the West and in any other appropriate way, with the aim of bringing together the world's great religions in closer understanding, harmony, and friendship; as well as to promote co-operation with other Universities, bodies, and persons in East and West which pursue the like ends.

These, then, are the objectives that Mr. Spalding had in mind when he endowed the Chair: and it is the plain duty of the occupant to consider how his intentions can best be put into effect. The Professorship would seem to have three main functions:

(i) to build up in this University a permanent interest in the great religious systems of the world, by which are commonly understood Confucianism, Taoism, Hinduism, Buddhism, Zoroastrianism, Judaism, Islam, and Christianity;
(ii) to interpret, compare, and contrast these systems;
(iii) to bring them together in closer understanding, harmony, and friendship.

Of these functions only the first and second would normally fall within the scope of an academic discipline. The third—the promotion of understanding between the great religions—can hardly be pursued in a British university where the non-Christian religions can scarcely be said to be represented at all. Nor do I think that it can be a legitimate function of a university professor to attempt to induce harmony among elements as disparate as the great religions of mankind appear to be, if, as seems inevitable, the resultant harmony is only to be apparent, verbal, and therefore fictitious. Such a procedure may well be commendable in a statesman. In a profession that concerns itself with the pursuit of truth it is damnable.

Yet even if we are prepared to set aside this third function as not being proper to the academic profession, the two remaining tasks remain formidable enough: for each of the great world religions, treated as a historical study alone, would fully occupy the lifetime of any one man, however long-lived. I am therefore fortunate in having Sir Sarvepalli Radhakrishnan as my predecessor, not only because he has so greatly distinguished himself in so many and various fields, but also because he has shown by his example how best to approach the apparently Herculean tasks facing the Spalding Professor. Sir Sarvepalli realized that it was scarcely possible for any one man, however gifted, even to attempt to cover the whole field of Eastern religion, and that in practice the field would have to be narrowed and the Professor would perforce have to concentrate on those Eastern religions with which he was most familiar. It was, then, right and fitting that the first occupant of this Chair should—at a time when India had not yet achieved her independence—have been a Hindu of the Hindus and thereby a representative of the majority religion within the British Commonwealth. It was right that the religions of India—so long the object alternately of the patronizing incomprehension and of the foolish adulation of the West—should have their own representative and spokesman at Oxford whose voice could be heard from a new Chair founded by an Englishman whose admiration for the Indian contribution to religious thought was whole-hearted and sincere.

Sir Sarvepalli succeeded in establishing the new Chair on a firm basis and gave the comparative study of religions the initial impulse that it needed if it was to make its impact on the University. It would be untrue to say that, in the past, there had been little interest in Oriental religions in this country, but it is unfortunately true that much of it was, and is, displayed by 'cranks', ζητοῦντες ἄλλο τι and not caring much what, provided it was incomprehensible enough to appear profound. This will happen in any age when the traditional faith seems to be crumbling and when the credulous are all too anxious to believe in something, no matter what, so long as it provides present comfort and offers escape from present ills. The Oriental religions were thus called upon to supply a need furnished in an earlier age by Attis, Cybele, Isis, Mithras, and the grotesque speculations of the Gnostic sects. Sir Sarvepalli at least rescued his religion from this morbid and unwelcome interest, and confined himself to explaining Hinduism as he saw it to a Christian and agnostic audience. He rightly saw that this is what he was in a unique position to do, and he therefore did it. Theoretically the Spalding Professor should be equally capable of talking authoritative sense on all the great religions of the world from the time of their foundation to the present day: he should be equally at home in the writings of the Confucians and the Taoists; the Hīnayāna and Mahāyāna Buddhists with their myriad subsections in Burma, Malaya, China, and Japan; the Zoroastrians and the Manichees; Christians both orthodox and heretical; Moslems, both Sunnī and Shī'a; and the six schools of philosophy among the Hindus as well as the hundreds of sects that, to a greater or lesser extent, derive from them. This considerable task Sir Sarvepalli, quite rightly, did not attempt to shoulder in its entirety. He concentrated on the religions native to India; and that is fully as much as could be expected from any one man.

To create an abiding interest in Eastern religions in a modern university is not an easy task. The Faculty of Theology is traditionally concerned with the teaching of Christian doctrine and the history of the Christian Church: it has never bothered itself overmuch with its traditional rival, Islam, nor can it be expected to burden the minds of its students with the theories and practices of the far remoter Hindus, Buddhists, and Confucians. Historically it could, perhaps, have paid a little more attention to the Zoroastrians, many of whose dogmas seem so strikingly to prefigure ideas that we have come to regard as specifically Christian—the freedom of the human will, the reality of heaven and hell, the individual judgement of the soul at death, and a universal judgement on the last day, to mention only the most important. This, however, has not been done; for the Theological Faculty is after all concerned not with the comparative study of religions but with Christianity itself. Nor does 'Comparative Religion' figure even as an optional special subject in the Oriental Faculty; for the various courses in Oriental studies are necessarily grouped around a specific language, the acquisition of which is liable to keep those wayward enough to embark on these exotic seas fully occupied for the duration of their course. At present, then, the Spalding Chair, concerned as it is with the comparative study of religions, is an anomaly, since these studies cannot be seriously pursued by junior members of the University except as a hobby. And this too is an anomaly: for Great Britain has been associated with Asia far more intimately than has any other European Power; and the civilizations of Asia are far more firmly rooted in the various Oriental religions than is Europe in its own Judaic faith. Moreover, in the Commonwealth today only a minority is Christian, for the majority of the peoples associated with the British Crown still remain Hindu and Moslem. The mere fact that the Empire has been transformed into a Commonwealth, the whole theory of which rests on voluntary association for which a modicum of mutual comprehension might be considered desirable, should be reason enough for encouraging the comparative study of religions in Great Britain's senior university. We pride ourselves on our eccentricity: sometimes we would do better to bewail it. So it is that in the academic capital of a multi-religious Commonwealth it is not possible to qualify for the degree of Bachelor of Arts in the subject of 'Comparative Religion'; and it was left to the enterprise of a more than usually enlightened private individual to endow a Chair in this not inconsiderable subject.

There are, perhaps, three main reasons which may account for this lack of interest in the non-Christian religions. The first is the progressive secularization of the University. The second is the attitude of the Christian minority, which seems to take it for granted that God has revealed Himself once and for all through Jesus Christ, and which therefore tends to ignore the other world religions completely or to treat them with a tolerant contempt. The third is the spread of secularist ideas throughout the educated classes of the Orient and the progressive undermining of societies hitherto firmly based on a given religion, and the fear of the more conservative-minded that the comparative study of religions can only lead to a further loss of faith in the traditional creeds, since these creeds are so manifestly at loggerheads with one another.

These, then, would appear to be the principal reasons militating against these studies. Let us examine them in turn.

The secularization of the University has come to stay. It was inevitable, since the secularization of the University merely endorsed a nation-wide fact, the dechristianization of the United Kingdom. Yet it is not for Christians of any denomination to bewail this development, for they have largely brought it upon themselves. 'Because thou art lukewarm and neither cold nor hot, therefore will I spue thee out of my mouth.' Such was the verdict on the Church of Laodicea, and such is the verdict on the churches in England today.

Yet though we may not be disposed to lament overmuch the decline of religion in this country, there is a very real danger that an exclusively rationalist outlook will put a further barrier between ourselves and the Eastern countries still associated with us. Religion still plays an enormously important part throughout the non-Communist East; and religion is only secondarily concerned with reason. To seek to apply rational processes to what is beyond reason is simply to waste time. Yet the non-rational exists and refuses to be suppressed, and we ignore it at our peril. Christianity has been rejected by the majority of the British people precisely because foolish men have either sought to defend its dogmas on purely rational grounds or have undermined their own position by abandoning those dogmas. They find themselves in the ridiculous situation of having nothing left to defend. Too often have they sought to explain rationally what cannot be explained at all; and rather than be thought unfashionable or even 'reactionary'—titles of which they might well have been proud—they have progressively abandoned the mysteries of their faith and reduced their religion to a meaningless benevolence. They have allowed themselves to forget τὸ μωρὸν τοῦ Θεοῦ, 'the foolishness of God', that so often and so disconcertingly confounds the wisdom of men.

It was the weakness of the Christian defence against the secular attack that emboldened the 'laïques' to underestimate the religious and irrational in man everywhere. It had been the strength of the Christian Church that it brought reason into the service of faith and thereby restrained mankind from following all and every supposedly religious impulse that might come its way. It was left to Hitler's great precursor to dub reason a whore, thereby destroying the precarious equilibrium between faith and reason that centuries of experience had built up. The rationalists reacted by seeking to eradicate the non-rational or religious element in man altogether. Their efforts failed, as they were bound to do, because this element is a hard fact, and if suppressed, will only break out the more violently, as the history of this lamentable century all too plainly shows. Had reason not presumed to pry into matters outside her ken, had she not been so foolish as to tempt the foolishness of God, had she not baited the non-rational but humbly sought to appreciate it as it is and to live in harmony with it, we might, perhaps, have been spared at least the worst excesses of twentieth-century barbarism: we might have been spared the sanguinary claptrap of blood and soil which for a moment became the religion of a great nation: we might even have been spared the moronic cult of lunacy preached and practised by the Surrealists. If the twentieth century has taught us nothing else, it should have taught us that there is an element in man other than reason, and that if this element is neglected, it is liable to fester and to erupt into something monstrously evil. This element is usually called the religious impulse; and it is this impulse and its manifestations which are the proper sphere of the comparative study of religions.

Religions are based on dogmas. They are based on certain fundamental assumptions which, of their nature, do not admit of logical proof. These form the ideological content—to use a horrible phrase—of a given religion; and each religion provides the basis of the society within which it is dominant. The continued existence of the caste system in India is perhaps the most palpable example of this truth.

It is, then, both dangerous and stupid to disregard the religious foundation on which any given civilization is built. Even the most rationalistic of us frequently prefer to ignore how many of the institutions that we take for granted are essentially Christian in origin. Few Englishmen, probably, feel any desire to have more than one wife: and this seems strange, for the practice of polygamy is hallowed by antiquity and enjoys the sanction of both the Moslem and the Hindu faiths. Again, few Europeans would nowadays advocate the seclusion of women; yet this is a practice for which Koranic sanction is most justly claimed. Or again, how many would wish to legalize what are usually called incestuous marriages: yet precisely such marriages were prescribed by the ancient Zoroastrians as the surest way to heaven. Yet had Europe fallen to the Moslem conqueror, both polygamy and the seclusion of women would be part of our Moslem heritage.

If then we, despite our lapse into paganism, have retained so much of the Christian ethic; and if our customs appear incomprehensible to polygamists and the partisans of purdah, except when seen in the context of a civilization whose roots are still Christian, how much more necessary is it for us to study the beliefs of Eastern peoples who still live in and by their religions, yet whose customs may appear to us eccentric or even reprehensible? For any code of morals springs from a faith, or if you prefer it, an ideology of which the code is the practical expression. Beneath the faiths are the non-rational dogmas or first assumptions on which all else depends. In each of the great religions these basic assumptions differ; and the alarming extent of these differences constitutes part of the fascination of this study.

The second reason for the apparent lack of interest in the non-Christian religions is the indifference generally shown by the Christian minority. Christians can be conveniently divided into two categories. First there are those who have been brought up in a traditionally Christian atmosphere, who accept their religion as something given and something good, and who have never seriously bothered themselves about why they believe or indeed what they believe. For these my distinguished predecessor had nothing but praise; for, said he, 'As a means of creative religion the native cult has an absolute advantage over any imported religion, for a convert to a new religion feels an utter stranger to himself. He feels like an illegitimate child with no heritage, no link with the men who preceded him. What in other people is a habit or an instinct seems to be with him a pose or an affectation. There is no inner development or natural progress to the new religion. It does not arise out of the old, but falls from one knows not where.' If I understand these words aright, I can only register an astonished protest. For if it is true that only those whose religion is 'a habit or an instinct' are the authentic representatives of their respective religions, this Chair was founded in vain; for on these premises must it not be a great wickedness to advertise Hindu or Moslem or Buddhist alternatives to the Anglican 'habit and instinct' in this its home? And if our motto is to be *cujus regio, ejus religio*, can there be any justification for unsettling the minds of the young in the very heart of the *regio anglicana*?

There remains, however, the minority of 'illegitimate children', the unfortunates who are 'utter strangers to themselves', whose misfortune it seems to be that they found their inherited religion inadequate and, like Mr. Aldous Huxley, set out in search of another. These might be expected to take an interest in the non-Christian religions rather than the followers of the 'native cult' which in this context can only mean the Church of England; and it was presumably such persons that Mr. Spalding had chiefly in mind when he so generously founded this Chair. For it is these 'illegitimates' who have the intelligence to question the faith in which they have been brought up and who are therefore likely to approach the Oriental religions, if not with sympathy, at least with an open mind.

Yet even those Christians who have never given a thought to the other great religions, some of which are far more ancient than Christianity, yet still retain their vigour, should at least be acquainted with what they teach and what they claim. Were they so greatly inferior to Christianity, how can we account for the hold that these religions still have on millions of souls? and why has Christian missionary activity met with so little success in the countries where these ancient cults are entrenched? Was it, perhaps, a lack of comprehension and sympathy in the missionaries themselves, or is it after all true that the 'native cult' is necessarily the best despite the evidence of history and the astonishing fact that close on a quarter of the world's population has been induced to worship God in the likeness of a Jew?

Yet it is not so much the follies and crimes committed in the name of the various religions that lead humane persons to conclude that none of them can be either good or true—though the history of crimes committed in the name of religion and the reasons why these crimes were committed is a fascinating subject in itself—nor is the fact that all religions, to a greater or lesser extent, affront the reason, but rather the fact that the paradoxes from which they severally start are so distressingly at variance with one another. Thus, it scarcely occurs to the devout Christian that, seen from a purely rational point of view, his religion is wildly absurd. St. Paul, whose religious experiences were more intense than most, was almost guilty of meiosis when he described the Cross as 'folly to the Greeks and a scandal to the Jews'. Folly and scandal it is. Yet is not the Vedānta at least as foolish and as scandalous? For though the Hindu is perfectly entitled to be scandalized at the folly of the Cross, we in our turn may justifiably gasp at the Hindu's wild assertion, 'I am Brahman', and 'What I am, that art thou': for this means nothing less than that I am the sole truly existing reality, that you are the same, and that therefore I am you. Folly to the Greeks; not so to the Hindus: for as their sacred books assert, *parokṣapriyā devāḥ pratyakṣadviṣaḥ*—'The gods love the obscure and hate the obvious.'

'The gods love the obscure and hate the obvious.' This observation, which appears again and again in the Brāhmanas and Upanishads, seems unusually apposite today. For, if we bother about these things at all, it is no longer possible to argue in a vacuum about the validity of the Christian religion alone. We must take into consideration the rival and conflicting claims of the Moslems, Hindus, and Buddhists at least. Just how conflicting these claims are is sufficiently and cruelly demonstrated by the separate existence of the Dominions of India and Pakistan. If any religion were obviously true, such deep cleavages could not exist. The variety of religions is a scandal in the literal sense: it is a stumbling-block. And the tendency today is to give up the whole business as a bad job, for the great religions do not even start from the same premisses. The only common factor between them is the observed fact of human unhappiness; for man, as the Buddha never tired of pointing out, is subject to birth, old age, and death—and life, when reduced to these bare essentials, is meaningless, or, as the Buddha put it, it is 'pain'—simply that and nothing else. No doubt the Buddha was perfectly right, and for once Christians, *gementes et flentes in hac lacrimarum valle*, can heartily agree. But there is no greater mistake than to suppose that this depressing fact on which the great religions do substantially agree is at all evident to modern humanity at large. It is no good telling people that life is 'pain' if they persist in regarding it as 'fun', just as it is no good asking them if they are saved if they have not the slightest idea of what on earth they are supposed to be saved from, and would not in any case want to be saved from 'it' even if they knew what 'it' was supposed to be. And it is precisely on the subject of 'it'—namely that from which release is sought—that the world religions so profoundly disagree.

Both the Hindus and the Buddhists regard the 'desire for release' as being a self-evident component of human nature, just as Europeans once believed in the validity of conscience and the reality of sin. Yet it would come as a shock to most of us who have been brought up to believe that the Christian's reward is eternal life, to be told that what makes man's lot unendurable is precisely his inability to die: and this is part and parcel of the creed of Hindus and Buddhists alike. The transmigration of souls is accepted not merely as a dogma but as a self-evident fact: and salvation, for them, means final release from the world of *saṁsāra*, the unending round of births and deaths from which there appears to be no escape. It is very difficult indeed for a European even to imagine himself into such a position. To us it seems preposterous that the whole conduct of one's life, and even one's social system, should be based on an unprovable hypothesis. Yet when a Hindu or Buddhist speaks of *moksha*, 'release' or 'salvation', he is not thinking of sin, a concept that is foreign to his religion, he is thinking of release from transmigration; and the achievement of this is the aim and purpose of his religion. For the Buddha it was the sole purpose. Thus to maintain that all religions are paths leading to the same goal, as is so frequently done today, is to maintain something that is not true. 'With numerous, coherent symbols the same knowledge is revered. All people, whatever their cult, station, or way of life, who are inwardly at peace attain to the same truth, as rivers (flowing into) the sea.' So says the *Anugītā*. And this is what the Hindus, in their large tolerance, genuinely believe and what all men of goodwill would like to believe; for the diversity of religions is a very real stumbling-block for all who are interested in finding one that is true. Were this diversity merely one of emphasis, it would matter little. Unfortunately it is not; it is one of principle. For even if it is quite fair to argue that Buddhism, in its original form, failed because it recognized no power higher than man, and only survived as a world religion because it became frankly theistic and when, with the development of the Mahāyāna, its founder, who acknowledged neither God nor Absolute, was himself endowed with all the attributes of both, it is nevertheless true that basically Buddhism is, as much as Marxism, an atheistic creed, and that salvation for the Buddha meant final release from transmigration and nothing else. The fact that Buddhism developed a morality of unselfishness, sometimes compared with that of Christ, is incidental; for the practice of unselfishness is, for the Buddhist, simply part of the over-all technique of divesting oneself of the illusion of self. Compassion is recommended not as being intrinsically good but as being empirically efficient in ridding the mind of the erroneous idea of individual personality. It is part of what the Buddha called 'right mindfulness', which is one of the stages on his Noble Eightfold Path.

So, too, with the mysticism of the Hindus. Because the great majority of us have only the vaguest idea of what constitutes a mystical experience, we are inclined to think that all mystical experiences must be identical, and that mysticism must therefore be a *philosophia perennis* transcending all so-called revealed creeds. This is the view now advocated by Mr. Aldous Huxley. It would be difficult to fall into more manifest error.

By mysticism Christians normally understand a direct apprehension of the godhead. Mysticism is a personal relationship between God and man: it is a love-affair. Such an experience is plainly only possible if God exists, and exists as a Person distinct from man. Certainly the final state of the mystical experience is referred to as the unitive state in which the soul is purged of all that will not surrender absolutely to God: but this does not mean that there never was any diversity; it simply means that one party in the love-duet has totally surrendered to the other: the soprano no longer sings her independent part, but 'conforms' herself in unison with the *Heldentenor* who is God. This is not to deny the reality of either God or the human soul.

Hindu mysticism, on the other hand, as expounded by Śankara, who is still regarded as the most orthodox exponent of the Vedānta, is utterly unlike this: for the Vedānta system is based on the *mahāvākyam* or 'great utterance' of the *Chāndogya* Upanishad, *tat tvam asi*, 'Thou art that', meaning that the individual soul is really and substantially identical with Brahman who is the unqualifiable Absolute. In such a system there can be no union: there is only a Parmenidean One; and if nothing *is* except the One, then plainly to speak of union is nonsense since Brahman is by definition *advitīyam*, 'without a second', and union implies something other than itself with which the One can be united. Thus not only on the dogmatic, but on the mystical plane too, there is no agreement: for 'the gods love the obscure and hate the obvious'.

We have seen that the doctrine of transmigration is accepted as a self-evident fact by the religions of Indian origin. Though both the Pythagoreans and Plato accepted the doctrine and it was adopted into the Manichaean system, it has never made serious progress in those parts of the world that derive their religion, directly or indirectly, from the Jews. And just as we see no reason at all for believing in such a doctrine—let alone for regulating our lives in accordance with it—so does the basic Semitic dogma of the reality of sin seem quite unreal to the Hindu, particularly if by sin we mean an offence against God, as Christians normally do. So insidious does the spread of Christian moral ideas appear to have been that Hindu apologists tend to insist that their sacred books are, in fact, seriously concerned with the problem of evil. This cannot be true, since evil only becomes a problem if God is both all-powerful and all-good. For the Upanishads Brahman is beyond good and evil and can be touched by neither, 'he does not become greater by good action or less by bad action'. Good and evil, being a *dvandva* or pair of opposites which can have no place in the One, can therefore have no real significance, no more than can truth and falsehood. In one of the Upanishads the word *satyam*, meaning 'truth' or 'what is real', is analysed as follows: 'The first and last syllables are truth. In the middle is falsehood. This falsehood is surrounded on both sides by truth: it partakes of the nature of truth itself.' It is doubtful whether Pilate would have been satisfied with such an answer to his question, 'What is Truth?' Moreover, if we believe, with the orthodox Hindus, that the world of *saṁsāra*, that is our empirical world, is ultimately illusory, it follows that good and evil are themselves illusory and therefore meaningless: they can only be conventional terms denoting what promotes release from illusion and what prevents it, just as to the Communist they can only denote what promotes the interests of the party and what opposes them. That this is the authentic Hindu view seems sufficiently proved by the following verse from the *Katha* Upanishad repeated in the Bhagavad-Gītā, books rightly considered to contain the essence of the Hindu way of thought:

> If the slayer thinks he slays
> Or the slain thinks himself slain,
> Both these do not understand;
> For there is neither slayer nor slain.

It is then only too true that the basic principles of Eastern and Western, which in practice means Indian and Semitic, thought are, I will not say irreconcilably opposed; they are simply not starting from the same premises. The only common ground is that the function of religion is to provide release: there is no agreement at all as to what it is that man must be released from. The great religions are talking at cross purposes.

It is therefore foolish to discuss either Hinduism or Buddhism in Christian terms; and it is at least as foolish to try to bring the New Testament into harmony with the Vedānta. They do not deal with the same subject-matter. Even Indian theism is not comparable to Christianity in a way that, for example, Zoroastrianism and Islam are: nor are the various *avatār*s of Vishnu really comparable to the Christian doctrine of the Incarnation. Nobody would seriously maintain that Rāma and Krishna were historical characters; but the fact that they belong to the world of fantasy rather than to that of fact is not likely to make the slightest impression on the Hindu, who makes no clear distinction between the two.

For him the phenomenal world is simply the *līlā* or sport of the deity and has no real existence in itself. The incarnations of Vishnu too, occurring as they do in the phenomenal world, are equally illusory: they are part of a conjuring act put on by the Supreme Being for his own entertainment. This is almost the *reductio ad absurdum* of idealism: it is the Red King's dream, for by denying the empirical world one reaches the position where one denies the reality of the empirical self, the poor old Brother Ass of St. Francis who blunders into the objective world whichever way he turns.

'He's dreaming now,' said Tweedledee: 'and what do you think he's dreaming about?'

Alice said 'Nobody can guess that.'

'Why, about *you*!' Tweedledee exclaimed, clapping his hands triumphantly. 'And if he left off dreaming about you, where do you suppose you'd be?'

'Where I am now, of course,' said Alice.

'Not you!' Tweedledee retorted contemptuously. 'You'd be nowhere. Why, you're only a sort of thing in his dream!'

'If that there king was to wake,' added Tweedledum, 'you'd go out—bang!— just like a candle!'

'I shouldn't!' Alice exclaimed indignantly. 'Besides, if *I'm* only a sort of thing in his dream, what are *you*, I should like to know?'

'Ditto,' said Tweedledum.

'Ditto, ditto!' cried Tweedledee.

Folly to the Greeks; but, believe me, wisdom to the Hindus.

I do not wish to conclude this lecture on so depressing a note; nor do I wish to exaggerate the differences that separate the great religions, though these are real enough.

For, though it may be true that between orthodoxies there is no agreement, historically resemblances do appear as the various religions develop and, in the course of development, come to deny or ignore doctrines which were fundamental to their sacred books. The Christian doctrines of the Holy Trinity and the Incarnation are often held to be what marks Christianity most sharply off from the other great religions: and so they do. Both doctrines are wholly beyond the comprehension of reason. Yet, though the whole idea of divine incarnation is anathema to the Moslems as impairing the absolute unity of the godhead, we find that even in this most rigid of all monotheistic creeds, as early as the third century of the Muhammadan era, the person of the Prophet is endowed with all the attributes of the Christian Logos. Muhammad, or rather the 'truth' (*ḥaqīqa*) or 'light' of Muhammad, has ceased to be merely the Prophet of Arabia who claimed neither divinity nor supernatural powers, who performed no single miracle, and whose life was marred by numerous imperfections: he has become the pre-existent 'centre and animating principle of the whole created universe, the spirit and life of all things, and secondly . . . the Mediator of Divine grace, the channel through which God imparts knowledge of Himself to his worshippers and endows them with every spiritual gift'. Muhammad has, in fact, ceased to be merely a prophet—and this was the only claim he consistently made—he has become something very like the incarnate Wisdom of God. This he became not in accordance with any doctrine naturally deducible from the Koran, but in the teeth of the plain sense of that sacred text.

Much the same appears to have happened in Hinduism and Buddhism. It is arguable that we ourselves and the whole phenomenal world have about as much claim to existence as have Tweedledum and Tweedledee in the Red King's dream (or was it Alice's?), but as a basis for living in this world such a hypothesis seems unhelpful. Here again we find that Hindus rebelled again and again against this Upanishadic dogma, and transferred their allegiance to Vishnu and Śiva, personal gods with recognizable attributes. For lack of a historical Person *vere natus vere passus*, they filled out the dreary frame of fact with the creations of a lively fancy. Rāma and Krishna may well never have existed. No matter: they ought to have existed, and because the Hindu feels this passionately, for him they do exist. It is true that the *Vishnu* and *Bhāgavata Purāṇa*s which rank as the sacred books of the Krishna cult emphasize the illusory nature of the whole phenomenal world as a 'game' played by the Deity for its own delectation, yet for the actual worshipper this is so much nonsense: he is not to be put off by the Brahmanical Tweedledums and Tweedledees; he will not, with Alice, burst into tears, because for him at least his God is *vere natus*, and that is what appears to matter.

Much the same happened in the case of the Buddha. He, too, had no pretensions to divinity since that term meant nothing to him at all. It fell wholly outside the proper sphere of religion which, according to him, was confined to the business of putting an end to pain as manifested in human life and human reincarnation. He refused to commit himself about God or the Absolute because, he maintained, metaphysics was irrelevant to the religious life:

And why, monks, have I not declared it? Because it is not profitable, does not belong to the beginning of the religious life, and does not tend to revulsion, absence of passion, cessation, calm, higher knowledge, enlightenment, Nirvāna. Therefore have I not declared it.

And what, monks, have I declared? This is pain, I have declared; this is the cause of pain, I have declared; this is the cessation of pain, I have declared; this is the way leading to the cessation of pain, I have declared. And why, monks, have I declared it? Because it is profitable, it belongs to the beginning of the religious life, and tends to revulsion, absence of passion, cessation, calm, higher knowledge, enlightenment, Nirvāna. Therefore have I declared it.

The Buddha himself made no claim except to have achieved enlightenment and final release from pain, and to have won Nirvāna, which is the complete extinction of desire in all its forms. He was no more than a Buddha, 'an enlightened one', and a Tathāgata, 'one who has gone thus'. Yet he too could not escape deification, and in the later Mahāyāna schools the human Buddha is almost forgotten, and he appears as the Supreme Deity in trinity, manifested in the Body of the Law, the Body of Bliss, and the Magic or Transformation Body, the last of which enabled the triune God to adopt the form of Śākyamuni, the human Buddha, born on earth in the sixth century B.C. in the town of Kapilavastu. That such doctrines are totally at variance with the Buddha's own teaching as it appears in the Pāli canon is obvious.

And this seems to me to constitute one fundamental difference between Christianity and the Eastern non-Christian religions. Christianity bases itself firmly on the doctrine of Incarnation, the doctrine that God became Man to deliver mankind from sin and to reconcile him with Himself. There is nothing comparable to this in the sacred books of the Hindus, the Buddhists, or the Moslems—or, for that matter, of the Confucians and Taoists. Yet the later developments of the first three of these religions show that each has evolved, independently it would appear, a theory of Divine incarnation and of a Divine Mediator between God and man. This is a genuine parallelism; but in all religions except Christianity it develops in logical opposition to the dominant view of each of the sacred books. There is nothing in the Koran to justify the quasi-deification of Muhammad; even less justification is there for the deification of the Buddha. Again, according to orthodox Brahmanical teaching, no divine incarnation can in any sense be real since the whole phenomenal world of which the incarnate God must necessarily form a part is illusory. In each case the need for an incarnate God seems to have been so strongly felt that the doctrine of incarnation made its appearance in surroundings where it had no rightful place.

In this lecture I have only had time to touch on two points in the study of religion which seem to me fundamental. First, the great religions as represented by their sacred books are not even talking about the same thing. Each religion is based on a sacred book, and so long as it remains faithful to it, its essential distinction from all others cannot be blinked or overcome. This is as true of the mystics as it is of the theologians; for in a religion that asserts the identity of the human soul with the Absolute, to speak of a *unio mystica* is meaningless. There can only be a *unitas mystica*, whatever Mr. Aldous Huxley and his *pusilla grex* may say or think. Secondly, I have alluded to the development of theism from an originally atheist creed and the growth of the idea of a Divine incarnation and a Divine Mediator in all the great religions; and I have indicated that this idea arises not in accordance with, but in opposition to, the whole sense and tenor of all the non-Christian sacred books. Similarity, then, there is: but the similarity is between Christian orthodoxy and non-Christian heterodoxy. What similarity there is proves not that there is an inner unity underlying all the great world religions, but that there is in man a craving for an incarnate God strong enough to force its way into the most unpromising religious systems. This idea is the corner-stone of Christian belief: essentially it is at variance with all the non-Christian orthodoxies. Its constant reappearance demonstrates the truth of Tertullian's great saying, *O testimonium animae naturaliter Christianae.* The difference is that whereas Muhammad and the Buddha achieved deification in flat contradiction to what they claimed and wished, and whereas the incarnations of Vishnu have no basis in fact, Jesus Christ both lived and died and claimed to be the Son of God: Σὺ εἶ ὁ Χριστός, ὁ υἱὸς τοῦ εὐλογητοῦ; ὁ δὲ Ἰησοῦς εἶπεν, Ἐγώ εἰμι.

These then are some of the topics that fall within the province of the comparative study of religions. I hope that I may have convinced some of you that they are not wholly without interest; and I think that the University owes a great debt to the late Mr. Spalding for endowing this Chair with a view to stimulating interest in what is, by any standard, an important subject. In accepting his gift the University demonstrated that they shared this view. Let us hope that theory will soon be translated into practice, and that the comparative study of religions will, within measurable time, be included in the syllabus of the School of Oriental Studies. I am greatly sensible of the honour conferred on me by the board of electors; but I ask leave to point out that whereas *kaivalyam* or 'isolation' is undoubtedly the aim and goal of the orthodox Yoga as laid down by Patañjali, and though the Buddha himself recommends his disciples to live 'as lives the rhinoceros—alone', the Spalding Professor, in the present case at least, is neither Yogi nor rhinoceros: and if it is true that 'even a joke should have a meaning', so should even a professor have someone to teach.

INDEX

creation, 27, 158, 334, 392, 413; in Rig-Veda, **68–73**; in Teilhard de Chardin, 54, 367, 408; in Upanishads, **74–7**.
'crisis theology', 11.
Cromwell, 417.
Cross, 14, 207, 370, 401, 436.
Crusades, 1.
cujus regio ejus religio, 381, 435.
Curé d'Ars, 398.
Cybele, 430.
Cyrus the Great, 26–7.
Czechoslovakia, 416, 421.

daivas, 25.
damnation, 427.
dance, 159, 160, 249.
Dante, 47, 48.
Darius the Great, 26.
'dark night of the senses', 312, 320.
'dark night of the soul', 312, 320.
Darwin, 74, 342, 413.
David, his census, 393.
death, 64–6; 215, 222, 291, 330; according to Teilhard de Chardin, 425, and baptism, 139; and dreamless sleep, 90; and love, 57–8; and sex, 55, 58; as absorption into Logos, 277; as first principle, 75; as new form of life, 57–8, 270; as oneness, 94; consciousness of, 46, 218, 226, 341; delight in, 227; 'immortality' of, 270; in Christianity and Buddhism, **207**; in Zoroastrianism, 27–8; is 'this is mine', 189; Mesopotamian, Greek, and Jewish views on, 64–5; of self, 208; problem of, 74; total, 334; transcending —, 151; unawareness of, 224, 226; Vedic ideas on, 63–4.
death of God theology, 208, 287.
deification, 168, 171, 402; of Buddha, 442; of Muhammad, 442.
democracy, 396.
demythologization, 116, 156, 341, 387, 394; in Bhagavad-Gītā, 153, 155; in Upanishads, 117.
depersonalization, 85, 96, 163.
Descartes, 178.
desire, 146–7, 149, 182, 216, 229, 249, 263, 266, 291, 306; and possession, 87; canalized by ritual, 250; for God, 317–18; freedom from, 228; in God, 190; in praise of, 190; incitement of (Hindu), 158; infinite, 87; suppression of, 107, 121, 125, 152, 173.
despair (of the world), 365, 399, 403; a Buddhist virtue, 207, 356, 378, 417.
destiny, 253, 259, 296.
detachment, 60, 100, 107, 121, 122, 130, 133, 134, 136, 139, 142, 148, 152, 168,

172, 199, 289, **290**, 302, 303; and love, 156; from creatures, 156; from Nirvāna, 290; recommended in all mystical traditions, 128.
Devil, the (*see* Satan), 211, **342**, 373, 388, 418, 419; and the flesh, 387; his peace, 301.
dhammabhūto, 172.
Dhammapada, 206.
Dharma (god), 119, 176, 189, 191, 192.
dharma (Buddhist), 172, 175, 214–15, 286, 288.
dharma (Hindu), **37, 177–82, 185–91**, 197; and conscience, 180, 184, 185, 196; and 'liberation', 188, 190; and Nirvāna, 172, 178, 198; is desire, 190.
Dhavamony, Fr. M., 164, 168.
Dhritarāshtra, 176, 181, 182, 183.
'dialogue', 2.
Directoire, 16, 33, 34, 378.
discord, 42, 213, 224, 225, 236, 265, 319, 324, 329, 332, 336, 338, 341, 367, 413, 418, 427; in man, 266; vanquished by ritual, 249.
'divine darkness', 3.
dogma, 7, 13, 21, 28, 433, 434.
Donatists, 35, 375.
Dostoievsky, 379, 396, 398, 399, 419.
dove, 340–1.
Draupadī, 177–9, 183, 186, 192, 193; her denunciation of God, 177, 347.
dream, 89–90, 91, 94, 95.
dreamless sleep, 89–90, 91, 94, 95, 104, 218; beyond —, 130, 314; is Lord of all, 94.
Drona, 154, 181, 182, 189.
drugs, 30, 41, 159, 323; and cosmic consciousness, 47; psychedelic —, 42, 209, 418.
dualism, 272, 275, 373; in Buddhism, 238, 269; Sānkhya, 98, 108, 142, 151; Zoroastrian, 389 ff.
duality, 168–9, 185, 270, 291; not real, 77, 268; of male and female (q.v.), 271.
Dumézil, Georges, 196.
Duryodhana, 119, 154–5, 179, 180; his death, 181–2.
duty, 178, 229, 255, 262, 263, 265, 321, 387.
Dyāvā-prithivi, 61.

earth, 226–7, 252, 264, 362.
Ecclesiastes, 1, 305.
Ecclesiasticus, 347.
Eckhart, Meister, 38, 96, 168, 201, 213, 294, 299–300, 305, 321, 406.
ecstasy, 158, 159, 160, 162, 190, 210, 211, 313, 318, 321, 324, 331, 379, 399, 403, 427; sexual, 162.

INDEX

INDEX

Iblīs (*see also* Satan), 339.
Ibn Tufayl, 169.
idea of the Good, 273.
identification, 92, 331; in *Brāhmanas* and Upanishads, 67–8; mysticism of, 152, 153, 212; of self and other, 275, 277; of spirit and matter, 199; with Heaven, 232; with the universe, 93, 96, 271, 277.
identity, 51, 80, 85, 291; in difference, 169; of Absolute and individual self, 88, **106,** 129, 166, 203; of being, 145; with God, 205; with human beings, 57; with the All, 52, 58, 87.
idolatry, 147, 197, 372.
'ignorance' (cosmic), 63, 64, **110,** 173, 185, 290; is the compounded, 131.
I-hsüan, 285.
illumination, 40–1, 44.
image of God, 79, 126, 203, 289, 295, 308–14, 316, 325, 328, 330, 334, 336, 337, 338, 342, 358, 359, 360, 386, 391, 408, 427; and God, 276, 318; in China, 333, 334; in Christianity, Islam, and theistic Vedānta, 209; in India, 333, 334, 336; obscuring of, 333–4; restoration of, 333; shattering of, 318, 320, 356.
imago mundi, 79.
immanentism, 150.
immortality, 67; and sex, 55; Buddhist and Christian, 102–3; experience of, 110; quest for, 74; within, 89.
'Imperishable', the, 89, 105–6, 108, 109, 110, 115, 138, 144; depends on God, 112, 137.
inactivity, acting by, 219, 231, 236, 241–2, 265, 266.
Incarnation, the, 21, 347, 355, **357–64,** 386, 392, 394, 439, 440, 442, 443; changed nothing, 367; sanctifies matter, 357.
India(n), 2, 8, 24, 27, 30, 44, 209, 252, 280, 363, 385, 430, 431, 433, 436; philosophy, 12; religion, 19, 21, 36–8, **61–213**; concerned with individual, 237.
indifference, 99, 122, 130, **137,** 139, 177, 193, 196, 231, 232, 400.
indifferentism, 34.
Indra, 61, 62, 166, 188, 291; and Yuddhishthira, 191–3; his dialogue with Prajāpati, 90–1.
infinite and infinitesimal, 78, 83, 233, 361–2; identity of, 85.
Infinite Being, 2, 3, 6, 9, 21, 269.
Infinite Time, 389.
Inner Controller, 86, 104; as dreamless sleep, 94.
Inquisition, 397.
institutional religion, 58–9.

integration of personality, 116, 122, 123, 125, 126, 129, 130, 135, 162, 168, 204, 212, 301, 310, 316, 318; and *bhakti*, 156; in Brahman, 125, 130; in cosmic harmony, 250; in Tao, 233; —, liberation, and contact with God, 138, 205.
interconnectedness, 129, 131, 132, 231, 232, 259, 263.
interdependence, 263, 294.
interpenetration, 151, 170, 264, 294, 316, 330, 407–8, 411, 412.
interpretation, of mystical experience, 43–4, 49, 60, 79, 129–30, 138, 205, 290, 292, 298–9, 305, 308; of monist experience, 100, 104, 129, 166–7, 203.
intuition, 42, 83, 108, 131, 132, 261, 285; of eternal Being, 210; of oneness, 204.
Iran, 25.
Irkalla, 65.
Iśā Upanishad, on 'Knowledge', 131; theology of, **108–10.**
Ishmaelites, 325.
Isis, 430.
Islam (*see also* Muslim), 1–2, 6, 8, 12, 14, 19, 24, 27, 28–9, 30, 38, 215, 268, 286, 356, 369, 373, 375, 429, 431, 439; and Christianity, 14–15, 28, 32, **371–3,** 383; and idolatry, 372; and persecution, 372–3; religion of law, 372; true biblical religion, 383.
isolation, of spirit from matter, 59, 97, 98, 99–100, 104, 114, 115, 317, 443; of the One, 138.
Israel (*see also* Hebrew, Judaism, Jew(ry)), 25, 26, 74, 349, 356, 369, 371, 376; and the Baalim, 369; and idolatry, 372; Yahweh's wife, 365–6.
Iśvarakrishna, 97.

Jainism, 61, 64, 151.
James, William, 41–2, 47, 199, 323.
Japan(ese), 38, 172, 201, 287; and love, 294, 299.
Jarā ('old age'), 191.
Jayadeva, 160.
Jefferies, Richard, 201, 210.
jên ('human kindness' (q.v.)), 216, 226, 241, 243, 244, 248, 254, 259, 262; Arthur Waley on, 239; essence of, 242; identified with Great Ultimate, 276, and with 'principle', 275.
Jeremiah, 23.
Jerusalem, 371.
Jerusalem Bible, 23, 25, 206, 345, 386.
Jesuits, 374, 376; missions, 2, 11, 35.
Jesus (*see also* Christ), 13, 14, 15, 21, 24, 31, 47, 48, 136, 150, 166, 179, 256, 280, 340–1,

self-righteousness, 230, 350, 352, 353, 377.

self-transcendence, 163.

self-will, 137.

Semites, 8, 25, 26, 29, 150.

sensus communis, 97.

Sermon on the Mount, 205.

serpent, the, 224, 329, 331, 333, 334, 336, 337, 339–42, 350, 367, 404, 410; agent of God's will, 339; ambivalence of, 340–1; and Holy Spirit, 340, 368; and Satan, 328, 339, 341; giver of life, 340; is intellect misused, 339; represents evolution, 327, 328, 339, 340; spirit of rationality, 328, 334, 340, 341; Voltaire on, 339–40.

sex, 171, 373, 385, 405; and death, 55; and immortality, 55; and mysticism, 86–7, 92, 107, **160–3**, 168; in Buddhism, 60; in Whitman, **52–8**, 199.

'sexual revolution', 293, 343, 373.

Shakespeare, 47, 49.

Shang Ti, 252.

Shelley, 40.

Shen-hsiu, 309.

Sheol, 65, 334, 427.

Shī'a, 431.

shih ('wisdom' (q.v.)), 249.

Shun, 241, **242**, 243, 255, 264, 273.

Simeon, 367.

simple consciousness, 42, 45, 46, 57, 103, 128, 230, 327.

sin, 23, 27, 32, 45–7, 52, 169, 245, 289, 324, 327, 349, 353, 361, 363, 365, 413, 421, 436, 437, 438, 442; actual, 342, 394; disobedience, 333; of flesh, 391; of spirit, 342, 391; separation from God, 260, 336.

Sisyphus, 417.

Śiva, 54, 62, 110, **116**, 117, 156, **163–71**, 182, 197, 318, 441; and Brahman, 116; and Śakti, 52, 165, 316, 347; as highest Brahman, 157, and Yogin, 111, 117, 164; beyond attributes, 112, 113; chaste, 164, 165; his attributes, 112; in mythology, 170; in Śaiva Siddhānta, **164–71**; in *Śvetāśvatara* Upanishad, **110–16**; is love, 165; ithyphallic, 111, 117, 164; Lord of *māyā*, 113; sustains spirit and matter, 111; trinity, 164–5; unites male and female principles, 117–18, 165.

social contract, 265.

social service, 133.

socialism 413, 419.

solidarity, 212, 213, 386, 407–8, 422, 424.

solitude, 212, 213, 313.

Son of God, 13, 14, 15, 30, 150, 360, 365, 369, 384, 387, 393, 408, 443.

Son of Man, 370.

song, 159, 160.

Song of songs, 156, 320.

soul, 306–21; as bride, 210, 407, 408; between God and the world, 306; in Rousseau, 336; in Whitman, 51–3, 80; indestructibility of, 189; unity of — and body, 92.

soul of the All, 408.

soul of the Church, 408.

soul of the world, 412, 424, 425, 426, 427.

Soviets, 420.

space, transcendence of, 200, 201–2, 204, 315.

Spalding, H. N., 1, 2, 5–7, 8, 13, 428–9, 435, 443.

'speciality', 413.

Spinoza, 35, 226, 237, 254, 298, 330, 337.

spirit, 27, 44 and *passim*; and God, 94; and matter, 70 72, 74, 75, 83, 94, 96, 267, 268, 272, 358, 360, 373, 385, 390, 408, 411, in Chinese religion, 245, 360; becomes Lord of all things, 74; considered male, 74, 385; construction of, 424; effect of matter, 277; in Sānkhya (*purusha* (q.v.)), **97–101**; infinite, 79; is changeless, 73, 74, 75; marriage of — and matter, 358, 360; morally neutral, 359; of the earth, 407; sins of, 342; wasting away in, 407.

spiritual body, 92, 358, 359, 408, 425.

spiritual marriage, 160, 168, 170, 299, 312, 315, 320, 426; of Christ and the Church, 159; of Christ and the soul, 159.

spiritual monads (*see also purusha*), 98, 115, 120, 124, 139, 142, 158, 204; oneness of, 129, 203.

spiritual pride, 311, 314, 322.

spiritual senses, 159.

spontaneity, 220, 223, 224, 229, 230, 231, 276, 285, 288, 329.

Squire, Aelred, 308.

śruti, 118.

Stace, W. T., 199–200.

Stalin, 397, 417, 420, 421.

Stalinism, 416.

status, 147, 351, 352, 353, 355, 362.

Stoicism, 280.

Śūdras, 180, 196, 197.

Sūfi(sm), 38, 159, 194; Persian —, 53.

Sunnīs, 372, 431.

śūnyatā (*see* emptiness, Vacancy, Void), 210, 233, 285.

Surrealism, 433.

Śvetāśvatara Upanishad, 70, 117, 121, 137, 138, 157, 164, 202, 235, 252, 309; bisexuality in, 141; theology of, **110–16**.

sympathetic magic, 79.